LIVIA

LIVIA

FIRST LADY OF

IMPERIAL ROME

ANTHONY A. BARRETT

Yale University Press
New Haven & London

Set in Janson Oldstyle type by Keystone Typesetting, Inc., Orwigsburg, Pennsylvania.
Printed in the United States of America.

The Library of Congress has cataloged the hardcover edition as follows:
Barrett, Anthony, 1941–
Livia: first lady of Imperial Rome / Anthony A. Barrett.
p. cm.
Includes bibliographical references and index.
ISBN 0-300-09196-6 (cloth : alk. paper)
1. Livia, Empress, consort of Augustus, Emperor of Rome, ca. 58 B.C.–A.D. 29.
2. Empresses — Rome — Biography.
3. Rome — History — Augustus, 30 B.C.–A.D. 14. I. Title.
DG291.7.L5 B37 2002
937′ .07′092 — dc21   2002003073

ISBN 0-300-10298-4 (pbk. : alk. paper)

A catalogue record for this book is available from the British Library.

The paper in this book meets the guidelines for permanence and durability of the Committee on Production Guidelines for Book Longevity of the Council on Library Resources.

10 9 8 7 6 5 4 3 2

CONTENTS

ILLUSTRATIONS

FIGURES

PLANS

STEMMATA

PREFACE

If the general public has any impression of Livia, the wife of the first Roman emperor, Augustus, it is of the character created by the Welsh actress Siân Phillips in the highly acclaimed BBC-TV production of *I, Claudius*, first broadcast in 1976. This popular confusion between the historical and the fictional is hardly surprising, given Phillips' riveting performance. Cunning and sinister, her Livia devotes every waking hour to her consuming interests: plotting, scheming, conniving, and the cheerful eradication of an assorted variety of fellow citizens, be they strangers, friends, or even close family.

One of the burdens shouldered by the modern historian is that of correcting false impressions created by the popular media, particularly dangerous when a production is distinguished and the performances brilliant. This process usually involves the thankless task of demonstrating pedantically that, contrary to popular belief, truth is rarely stranger than fiction, and is usually far less exciting. For the historian of the ancient world the undertaking is difficult enough at the best of times, because the truth about any individual who lived some two thousand years ago must, by its very nature, be an elusive entity. But Livia poses a particular challenge. Robert Graves, whose two novels about the imperial family were the basis for the television series, might well have defended the integrity of his portrait by pleading that it rests on impeccable historical foundations, and that he took his lead from Rome's premier historian, Tacitus. But that argument has surprisingly little merit in this specific

case. Livia achieves the near-impossible, for she forces us to shift our traditional allegiance and accept the authority not of the normally magisterial
Tacitus but of ancient writers whose historical reliability is by and large seriously suspect: Dio, often naive and uncritical; Suetonius, incapable of resist-
ing spicy anecdotes; and Seneca, invariably sycophantic or denigratory, whichever profited him most. On this one topic it is generally recognised that
Tacitus was the weak brother, his portrait of Livia vitiated both by his deep-
seated contempt for the Julio-Claudian family and by his unshakable conviction that the ambitious woman was evil incarnate.

The historical Livia was a much more complex individual than the cold-
blooded schemer that Graves created for *I, Claudius* or that Tacitus created
for his *Annals*. The simple fact that she survived intact and unscathed for
more than sixty years at the very heart of Roman power — and, perhaps more
remarkably, was revered and admired for many generations more after her
death — is a testament to her adroit ability to win the support, sympathy and
even affection of her contemporaries. Livia could thus be called Rome's first
lady in the broad sense, in that no Roman woman before or after her succeeded in evoking a deeper or more long-lasting respect and devotion. She
managed to live through a dramatic shift in the Roman constitutional system
without creating clearly identifiable enemies — apart, of course, from Tacitus.
Perhaps most impressively, she achieved this even though her status and position were never properly defined. Livia is the link between the two reigns that
established the basic pattern of government for the Roman empire for the next
four centuries. As the wife of Augustus, she was expected to embody the
dignity and majesty of the newly created principate, yet at the same time
remain a self-effacing and decorous symbol of domestic virtues. In this respect
her role was very much that of a first lady in the more narrow American sense,
that of someone who plays a public role but does not hold a public position,
and indeed is liable to severe criticism should she presume to encroach into the
sphere of a public position, and of someone whose domain is a private home
but is traditionally expected to represent the domestic values and mores of the
whole citizenry. Her position during the reign of the second emperor, her son
Tiberius, was even more extraordinary, and presents the scholar with serious
challenges. Women, with the possible exception of the Vestal Virgins, could
not play a public role in the Roman state, no matter how much power and
influence they might exercise informally behind the scenes. By her late husband's will, however, Livia was elevated to a status that brought her very close
to an institutional position. Exactly what role he envisaged was not defined,

and perhaps was incapable of precise definition — Augustus certainly never attempted it during his lifetime — because it would have been unaccompanied by the traditional powers of official magistrates. In any case, the question was moot, because it was a role, no matter how loosely defined, that Tiberius was unwilling to countenance for his mother. I shall argue that it was this ambiguity in Livia's position, a problem largely created by Augustus, that led to the well-documented tension between mother and son. Their inability to reach a mutually acceptable *modus vivendi* at the very least contributed to Tiberius' eventual decision to leave Rome and all its problems, and to spend much of the last decade of his reign in the less stressful surroundings of Capri.

Outside the field of portraiture and sculpture, Livia has been surprisingly neglected in the English-speaking world. The first biography was Joseph von Aschbach's *Livia: Gemahlin des Kaisers Augustus*, published in Vienna in 1864, and there have been two further German treatments since then. There have been no general studies in English, however, and relatively few articles devoted to her career, the notable exception being the work of Marleen Flory, who before her untimely death published a number of valuable pieces on Livia, especially on the symbolic aspects of her role within the principate. This book is the first biographical study of Livia in English, and it comes with all the usual limitations that afflict biographies, in that by its very nature it offers a lopsided and limited view of a historical period. That conceded, I take the position that noteworthy individuals do affect the course of history and that their influence can be felt for many generations. That is what makes them worth studying, apart from the perfectly legitimate consideration that they are inherently interesting.

I repeat a warning issued in other books in this series. Rumours abounded in antiquity — as they did about other women of the imperial family — that Livia was given to eliminating her opponents by poison. Much ink has been spilt in trying to establish the truth about such ancient poisoning cases, and, regrettably, it has been ink largely wasted. Even in a modern murder investigation, conducted by a professional police force, aided by forensic science and chemical analyses, and tried by a systematic court procedure, it is often impossible to reach a secure verdict where poisoning is suspected. To try to determine the truth in an age when the failure of a heart to burn on the funeral pyre was considered proof of poisoning is clearly futile. Poison was certainly widely used in antiquity, but common sense dictates that in any specific case the only prudent course is to settle for the Scottish verdict of Not Proven, and to rest content with that.

The format of this book is dictated by the nature of the material. The first part follows Livia's life and career and sets it out diachronically within its historical context. The second adopts a more thematic and analytical approach. The sources, both literary and material, are dealt with in an appendix, as are other topics whose analysis would interrupt the flow of the text. The material in the first part of the book will be familiar to those with specialist knowledge of the early period of Roman imperial history. For such individuals, the second part and the appendices are likely to be of more interest. The division into separate parts is not an ideal arrangement, but it offers the only workable solution to a problem imposed by the nature of the evidence. Information about Livia tends to come in spurts. It comes consistently enough to enable us to reconstruct a fairly coherent picture of her life and career, but there is an obvious and unavoidable imbalance in the degree of factual information available for any given period. Certain events, especially those associated with the death of Augustus and the accession of Tiberius, are recorded in a depth of detail not usually available in Roman history. At other times, in particular during the first part of her life, Livia can evade serious notice for years at a time. As a consequence, while we can gain a reasonable sense of her legal and constitutional status within broad chronological frameworks, the evolution of that status is far from clear, and any attempt to interlace it with specific events of her life is bound to fail. Hence the decision to separate the broader thematic discussions from the historical narrative.

A number of concessions have been made for the nonspecialist. Some of the more arcane historical problems are dealt with in the appendices, rather than in the text. Roman *praenomina* (given names) are provided in their full, rather than conventionally abbreviated, forms in the text, though not in the notes or appendices. Translation of Latin and Greek words or phrases that are not self-evident is regularly provided in the text, but, again, not necessarily in the appendices. Identifying markers, such as family relationships, are frequently repeated. Specialists will not need to be constantly reminded, for instance, that Octavia is Augustus' sister or that Drusus is Tiberius' son, but general readers may feel that they benefit from having their memories jogged.

Monetary values are expressed in sesterces. Monetary equivalence is a tricky issue, but, as a rough guide, in the early empire the annual pay for a legionary soldier in the ranks was 900 sesterces.

I have been fortunate in enjoying the help and support of a number of individuals and institutions. Duncan Fishwick guided me on some of the epigraphic problems and kindly made available to me material from his files. Susan Wood provided valuable assistance in the acquisition of plates, and Luigi Pedroni helped with the numismatic material. I am once again indebted to Tony Birley for permission to use his map of the Roman world, with minor adaptations. Michael Griffin aided me with computer problems and with reformatting my text. My friend Karl Sandor read through the finished manuscript and made several observations, invariably to the point and invaluable. Shirley Sullivan and Richard Talbert offered useful thoughts on the book's subtitle. I was assisted by the helpfulness of the staff at a number of institutions, particularly in the libraries of the University of British Columbia and of the Ashmolean Museum, Oxford (now the Sackler Library). I was aided in my work by a research grant from the Social Science and Humanities Research Council of Canada, to which I am pleased to express my gratitude. A special debt is owed the anonymous reader for Yale University Press, who offered sage guidance on the format and organization of the book. Any remaining faults are my own, but they are certainly fewer as a result of that advice. Also, I have benefitted from the industry and keen eye of Dan Heaton, my manuscript editor at the Press, who imposed order and consistency where both tended to be lacking. Finally, my family have once again not only endured the domestic clutter and distraction that such an undertaking invariably brings but have also taken on the task of proofreading with a brave show of cheerfulness.

The Roman World at the Time of the Death of Livia

Danube

MOESIA

ACIA

Phasis

HIBERI

Artaxata

PONTUS et
BITHYNIA

ARMENIA

GALATIA

CAPPADOCIA

Tigris

ASIA

P A R T H I A

Ephesus

LYCIA

CICILIA

Euphrates

Ctesiphon

Antioch

Seleucia

SYRIA

CYPRUS

JUDAEA

Alexandria

ARABIA

AEGYPTUS

Nile

SIGNIFICANT EVENTS

63 BC
September 23   Birth of Augustus

59/58 BC
January 30   Birth of Livia

44 BC
March 15   Assassination of Caesar

43 BC?   First marriage of Livia

42 BC
Autumn   Death of Livia's father at Philippi
November 16   Birth of Tiberius

40 BC   Flight from Italy to Sicily, then Greece

39 BC
Late summer?   Return to Rome
Autumn   Betrothal to Octavian (Augustus)

38 BC
January 14   Birth of Drusus
January 17   Marriage to Octavian

36 BC
September   Livia celebrates the battle of Naulochus

35 BC   Livia and Octavia granted special honours

33/32 BC   Death of Livia's first husband

31 BC
  September   Battle of Actium
                         Cleopatra's supposed hope for Livia's intercession

27 BC
  January   The Augustan Settlement
27–24 BC   Livia possibly in Gaul and Spain
22–19 BC   Livia probably in the East

12 BC
  March   Death of Marcus Agrippa

11 BC   Death of Octavia

9 BC
  January 30   Dedication of Ara Pacis
  September   Death of Drusus
  Autumn?   Livia honoured by special privileges
                         Banquet sponsored by Livia for Tiberius

7 BC
  January?   Dedication of Porticus Liviae

6 BC   Retirement of Tiberius to Rhodes

AD 2   Return of Tiberius to Rome
  August 20   Death of Lucius Caesar

AD 4
  February 21   Death of Gaius Caesar
  June 26   Adoption of Tiberius by Augustus

AD 7   Banishment of Postumus to Planasia

AD 14
  August 19   Death of Augustus
  August 20?   Execution of Postumus ordered
  September   Adoption of Livia into Julian *gens*
                         Assumption of name Julia Augusta

AD 16   Participation of Livia in fighting fires

THE LIFE
OF LIVIA

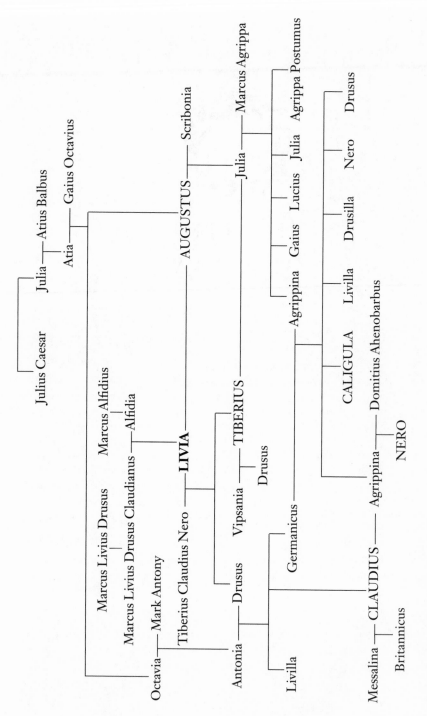

Stemma 1. Livia's significant family connections

FAMILY BACKGROUND

The expulsion of the last hated king from Rome, an event dated traditionally to 510 BC, ushered in a republican form of government that was to endure for more than four centuries and which was regarded by later Romans, especially those from the elite levels of society, with pride and an often naive nostalgia. At the outset, Roman society was characterised by a fundamental division between the patricians, who held a virtual monopoly over the organs of power, and the plebeians, who were essentially excluded from the process. Although the power and privileges of the patricians were eroded during the first two centuries of the republic, it is a mistake to think that the system became open and democratic in the modern sense. The removal of the barriers facing ambitious plebeians resulted in a modification of the aristocracy, not its abolition. The chief magistracies became the almost exclusive reserve of a small number of families, whether plebeian or patrician, and the historical record is dominated by a handful of prestigious families, such as the Cornelii or the Julii, who succeeded in keeping a tight grip on the key offices (the system is summarised in appendix 2). Anyone who broke into the closed system and reached the highest office, the consulship, despite lacking a consular ancestor was such a novelty that he was known as a "new man" *(novus homo)*. The popular assemblies, through which legislation had to be enacted and which might seem on the surface to have offered the masses scope to exercise an influence, in fact did little to upset the balance, because a complex voting procedure gave a distinct advantage to the wealthy.

The importance of family background as a virtual prerequisite to success in Roman society can not be overstated, and, as Tacitus acknowledges, few could have rivalled Livia's claim to family distinction.[1] On her father's side, she was descended by blood from one of the proudest and highest-flying of all the great Roman families, the Claudian. According to legend, the family's founder was Clausus, who supposedly helped Aeneas when the Trojan hero sought to establish himself in Italy.[2] In the historical record, the Claudii were in reality immigrants who did well, and their association with the city might be said to begin with the migration to Rome of the Sabine Attus Clausus and all his dependants in 503 BC. Co-opted into the patricians, Attus claimed the first Claudian consulship in 495. Subsequently his descendants would expect, almost as an entitlement, a consulship each generation. Suetonius records that they eventually boasted twenty-eight consulships, five dictatorships, seven censorships, six triumphs, and two ovations.[3] Their family history is a veritable parade of some of the giants of Rome's past. In 451, as a member of the Decemvirate (Commission of Ten Men), Appius Claudius was instrumental in giving Rome its first written legal code. One of his descendants was among the most distinguished and venerated figures of the old republic, and probably the first figure of Roman history to emerge as a clear and distinct personality — Appius Claudius Caecus, consul in 307 and 296. Even when aged and blind he was still consulted as an elder statesman, as on the celebrated occasion when in about 280 BC he addressed the Roman Senate, the senior deliberative and legislative body, made up of men who had held the important magistracies. In a speech passed down through the generations and still used as a school text when Livia came into the world, he persuaded his fellow senators to reject as dishonourable the peace terms offered by King Pyrrhus. Claudius Caudex led the Roman forces into Sicily at the outbreak of the First Punic War against Carthage in 264, and during the Second War, Gaius Claudius Nero defeated Hasdrubal in 207 as he made his way to join his brother Hannibal. This pattern of high office continued to the end of the republic.[4]

Like their modern counterparts, the important Roman families were often made up of more than one branch. Appius' two sons, Tiberius Claudius Nero and Publius Claudius Pulcher, were the founders of the two main subdivisions of the patrician Claudians, the Claudii Nerones and the Claudii Pulchri. Livia could claim descent from one and would marry into the other.[5] The Nerones apparently soon faded from view. Tiberius Claudius Nero was the last Neronian consul, in 202, until Livia's son, the future emperor Tiberius, was elected to the office in 13 BC. The Pulchri, on the other hand, went from strength to strength, and carved out a preeminent role in Roman political life.[6]

Amidst the paragons of public service and duty, however, tradition also ascribed to the patrician Claudii a motley collection of rogues and eccentrics, linked to the white sheep of the family by common possession of the notorious Claudian pride. Tacitus could speak of one of their descendants as marked *vetere ac insita Claudiae familiae superbia* (by the old inborn arrogance of the Claudian family); Livy speaks of a family that is *superbissima* and *crudelissima* (excessively haughty and excessively cruel) towards the plebeians, a sentiment echoed by Suetonius' description of them as *violentos ac contumaces* (violent and arrogant). Whether this reputation was deserved, or resulted from a hostile historical tradition, is perhaps not particularly relevant in the present context, because it was the *reputation* that would be bequeathed to Livia and the line of emperors that followed her.[7] Tradition has grafted onto the worthy if dull achievements of Appius Claudius, the decemvir and lawgiver, a luridly sinister role of would-be tyrant and insatiable defiler of women, the most noteworthy being Verginia, slain by her own father to save her from Appius' lust — and, of course, to save her father loss of face. Publius Claudius Pulcher, consul in 249, had contempt not only for man but also for the gods. He suffered a major defeat in a naval battle against the Carthaginians at Drepana, losing 93 of his 123 ships. His defeat was blamed by some writers on his outrageous behaviour when the auspices hinted strongly that his enterprise was headed for disaster. The sacred chickens refused to eat. He ignored the sign and, according to some, in a fit of pique dumped them into the sea, announcing, "If they won't eat, let them drink."[8] The stories seem endless. Appius Claudius Pulcher, father-in-law of Tiberius Gracchus, provoked the Salassi of Gaul into a costly war during his consulship in 143 and suffered a defeat and the loss of five thousand men. In a later engagement he redressed the balance by killing five thousand of the enemy. He assumed arrogantly that he was entitled to a triumph, the grand procession through Rome granted victorious generals who fulfilled a specific set of conditions, and he requested the necessary funds from the Senate. When his request was refused, he simply went ahead and staged the triumph at his own expense.[9] Suetonius tells a story, otherwise unknown and whose historicity cannot be determined, of a Claudius Drusus who set up his own crowned statue at Forum Appi and tried to use his clients to take over Italy.[10]

Tradition was even-handed in one respect, for the Claudian women were painted as no less arrogant than the males. Claudia, for instance, was the daughter of the distinguished statesman Appius Claudius Caecus and the sister of the Claudius Pulcher who lost his ships to the Carthaginians. When Claudia's carriage was blocked by a crowd of pedestrians, she lost her temper and prayed, loudly of course, for her brother to come back to life to lose another fleet of Romans. She was fined for her outburst. Another Claudia, the daughter of the pseudotriumphator Appius, joined him in his chariot during the triumphal parade. There was a danger that he would be hauled out, but she, as a Vestal Virgin with sacrosanctity, would be able to protect him from the intervention of the tribune. Arguably the most notorious Claudian woman of all time was still alive during Livia's youth. Clodia Metelli was famed for her profligacy and political power. Her numerous lovers almost certainly included the poet Catullus (he gave her the pseudonym Lesbia) and her brother, the demagogue Publius Clodius. She was berated by the orator Cicero for bringing shame on her distinguished Claudian ancestors.[11]

One of the descendants of this celebrated if eccentric family was Livia's father, Marcus Livius Drusus Claudianus. We have no knowledge of Marcus' biological parents, though he is described as a Claudius Pulcher by Suetonius (the only one actually to claim this), and his family seems to have had a connection with Pisaurum. This old colony, at the mouth of the Pisaurus in Umbria, was apparently a depressing place. Catullus, writing in the 50s, calls it *moribunda*, and Cicero describes it as a hotbed of discontent. Thus when Cicero at one point mockingly calls Marcus a Pisaurensis, it was clearly intended as a slur.[12] But Pisauran or not, Marcus was still a Claudian. Livia's mother Alfidia came from far less distinguished stock. She was the daughter of a Marcus Alfidius, a man of municipal rather than senatorial origins, and she may have attracted an eligible aristocrat like Marcus Livius Drusus through her family wealth.[13] She seems to have come from Fundi, a pleasant town on the Appian Way, in the coastal area of Latium near the Campanian border. Fundi was noted for its fine wine but was generally been viewed as a place for escape — many Romans had country villas in the vicinity. Suetonius twice alludes to Livia's connection to the town. He reports that some (wrongly) believed that Livia's son, the emperor Tiberius, had been born at Fundi because it was his grandmother's hometown. In another context, to illustrate one of the many vagaries of her great-grandson Caligula, Suetonius cites a letter to the Senate in which the emperor alleged that Livia had been of low birth because her maternal grandfather had been merely a decurion (town official) of Fundi. Caligula, of course, was much given to wicked jokes at his family's expense, and his charge should perhaps not be taken too seriously (see appendix 3).[14]

Livia's descent on her father's side from one of Rome's oldest and most prestigious families would have conferred enormous status on her. That status would have been enhanced by another link, no less important politically and originating in this case through adoption. An admirer of Livia's, the contemporary historian Valerius Maximus, describing the feud of Claudius Nero and Livius Salinator, censors of 204 BC, remarks that if they had realised that Livia's son would be descended from their blood, they would have ceased to be rivals. With this eloquent display of sycophancy Valerius testifies to the "dual line" of Livia. Her name, Livia Drusilla (see appendix 4), in itself gives no hint of a Claudian connection. Rather it reflects her family connection with a man who earned a secure if controversial place in Roman history. The Livii seem to have been an eminent Latin clan who received Roman citizenship in 338 following the Latin revolt.[15] Their most famous member emerged in the aftermath of the disintegration of the social order that followed the adoption by the Senate of violent emergency measures to counter the land resettlement schemes proposed in 133 BC by Tiberius Gracchus and subsequently by his brother Gaius. The republic was not to recover from the severe blows it suffered during this crisis, which brought martyrs' deaths to the Gracchi. The crisis also brought to the fore a distinction between the *optimates*, who represented the old senatorial class, with its traditional claim over the higher magistracies, and the *populares*, who sought to promote the initiative of the tribunes and the consuls to introduce legislation free of the heavy hand of the Senate.

Gaius Gracchus had included among his proposals a measure to extend the franchise to Rome's Latin allies, and a limited franchise to the Italians. In 91 BC the issue of the Italian franchise returned with a vengeance, and it was during this critical phase that Marcus Livius Drusus came into prominence, when as tribune of the plebeians he took up a number of causes, including agrarian reform and, most notably, a move to enfranchise all Italians living south of the river Po. He somehow succeeded in firing the imagination of the Italian communities to see him as the man to champion their rights. At the same time, however, he encountered considerable opposition in Rome. There were outbreaks of disorder, and Drusus was murdered by an unknown assailant. His death fomented widespread resentment and was the decisive element leading to the outbreak of armed revolt in the Social War. What he had sought through political action eventually came about through conflict, and by 89 the allies had been absorbed into the Roman state. Livia's family connection with the champion of the rights of the Italians must be seen as a major asset, especially in the later stages of the civil war that would end the republic, when warring factions competed for broad support.

As Drusus breathed his last he reputedly declared to his weeping entourage, *ecquandone similem mei civem habebit res public?* — when will the state have another citizen like me?[16] What precise qualities he had in mind in his final moments are not known, but his family, through adoption rather than bloodline, was to produce in Livia someone whose fame would far eclipse the tribune's. Livia's father, Marcus Livius Drusus Claudianus, was born a Claudius, as his name indicates, but was adopted into the Livian family. In the Roman fashion he assumed the *nomen* of the adopting *gens*, the Livii, and appended an adjectival form of his original gens, the Claudii.[17] With adoption he would have been expected to assume the *praenomen* of his adoptive father; the fact that he was a Marcus, combined with the absence of any prominent Livian other than the famous tribune with the *cognomen* Drusus, strongly suggests that this Drusus was the adoptive father.[18] From her link with the tribune Livia acquired her cognomen, Drusilla. It also gave her family the name Drusus, which some of her descendants opted to bear as a praenomen.

If Marcus was the adopted son of the tribune, he would have found himself in an advantageous position. On the death of his new father he could have inherited all or part of his estate. Diodorus Siculus called the tribune Marcus Livius Drusus the richest man in Rome, and his observation seems to be supported by other sources.[19] This wealth would have given an important boost to his son's career. Moreover, as we have seen, Marcus' inherited wealth might have been amplified by money from his wife's family. The Alfidii would have considered a lavish dowry a small price to pay for a connection with such a socially prominent Roman, a man described by Velleius Paterculus as *nobilissimus.* [20]

Livia's father steps onto the stage of Roman history in 59 BC, during a period of great political tension. The end of the struggle over the franchise in Italy did not mean an end to overseas conflicts. In 83 the general Sulla, flushed with his victories over king Mithridates, who ruled in the Black Sea area, returned to Italy at the head of his troops and after a period of turmoil and conflict was appointed dictator with special powers. He made it his mission to restore the supremacy of the Senate, retiring in 79. The Senate squandered their advantage. They offended the military commander Pompey, who, having undertaken a successful campaign in the East, on his return found the senators unwilling to ratify the measures he had undertaken. The Senate also offended the wealthy financier Crassus by restricting his financial dealings in Asia. The same body further alienated a new rising star, Julius Caesar, denying him the prospect of the consulship on his return from Spain in 60. In that year Caesar, Pompey, and Crassus found common cause and formed an compact often referred to casually by modern scholars (although not by the ancients) as the First Triumvirate, although the loose alliance did not have the formal status that the term might imply. Pompey married Caesar's daughter Julia to seal the agreement.

It is at this point that we find the first reference in the sources to Livia's father, Marcus. He was evidently an energetic opportunist, for he hitched his wagon to the triumvirate and was sent—or at least had reasonable expectations of being sent—on a mission to Alexandria in 59 BC to raise funds.[21] Marcus had perhaps just shortly before married Alfidia, and on January 30 of either 59 or 58 he became a father, with the birth of his daughter, Livia. The month and day of Livia's birth are established by inscriptions of the post-Julian period as *a.d.III Kal. Febr.*, the third day before the first of February, reckoned inclusively. This date is by convention given as January 30 in the modern calendar system, although there is in reality no truly satisfactory way of expressing it, because in the pre-Julian calendar January had only twenty-nine days.[22] The year is more problematic (see appendix 5). The place of birth is even more obscure; we have no direct hint of where it might have been. The absence of any boast in extant inscriptions from a town proudly claiming distinction as her birthplace, and the lack of speculation in the literary sources, suggest that she might have been born in Rome.

Livia's father is next heard of in 54, when he was prosecuted for improper legal practices *(de praevaricatione)* but acquitted through the efforts of Cicero—the kind of case, as Tacitus notes, that does not later arouse much interest.[23] In any event, the publicity does not seem to have impeded his career. By 50 he was praetor, or *iudex quaestionis* (president of a court), presiding over a case being tried under the Scantinian law, which covered prohibited sexual activity. Although there are grounds for suspecting that he might have been wealthy, through his adoptive father or his wife, he seems to have fallen into some financial difficulties at about this time, and we later find him trying to sell his gardens to Cicero. Marcus was a hard bargainer, but he met his match in the famous orator, who was determined to come out best in the deal.[24]

Meanwhile, the loose alliance of the powerful leaders had broken down. Crassus was killed by the Parthians at the Battle of Carrhae in 53. Pompey, a man of considerable integrity but little moral courage, was persuaded to lead the opposition to Caesar, and paid for the decision with his life, when he was assassinated as he disembarked in Egypt in September 48. Caesar was now preeminent. He was appointed dictator for two terms and, in 44, for life. He proved a vigorous and effective legislator, settling veterans, founding settlements (colonies), extending the franchise, reorganizing the corn dole, regulating traffic within the city of Rome, and, his most enduring measure, reforming the chaotic Roman calendar. But Caesar offended many in Rome by what was perceived to be his excessive ambition, rousing fears that he planned to make himself monarch. Although his person had apparently been declared sacrosanct, which made it a crime to harm him, in the end the privilege did him little good. A conspiracy was formed, led by Marcus Brutus and Gaius Cassius, and on the Ides of March, 44 BC, Caesar was assassinated.

It was probably not long after this pivotal moment in Roman history that a pivotal event took place in Livia's life also, her first marriage. Indeed, because nothing at all is known of Livia's early life apart from her birth, this is the first incident that the historian can infer. Her husband, Tiberius Claudius Nero, belonged to the less distinguished branch of the patrician Claudians. As we have seen, the last consulship the family could claim was in 202 BC. Very little has been passed down about Tiberius Nero's immediate forebears, although we know from a very fragmentary inscription that his father was also a Tiberius. The older Tiberius Nero served in 67 BC as legate of Pompey against the pirates, with command at the Straits of Gibraltar, and in 63 made a speech against the summary execution without trial of the associates of Catiline, who had been exposed by Cicero in a major conspiracy.[25] Their family names leave little doubt that Livia and her husband must have been related. How closely is far from clear, although some scholars assert with confidence that they were cousins.[26]

Tiberius Nero might have seemed a good marriage prospect. Cicero speaks of him having the qualities of an *adulescentis nobilis, ingeniosi, abstinentis* (a young man of noble family, of native talent, and moderation) and remarks that there was no one among the noble families he regarded more highly. (Of course, these warm testimonials appear in a letter of recommendation, a common repository of inflated praise.)[27] Tiberius Nero makes his own entry into history in 54 BC. In that year a Pompeian supporter, Aulus Gabinius, returned from Syria after a governorship that seems to have been marked by administrative incompetence and large-scale bribery, a common enough situation in many of the provinces of the late republic. Gabinius became the celebrity of the year, denounced by Cicero and hounded in a series of showy trials. Before his trial for extortion *(de repetundis)* there was a scramble for the high-profile role of prosecutor, and Tiberius Nero competed against Gaius Memmius and Mark Antony. The contest was keen and Cicero comments on Tiberius Nero's fine effort and the quality of his supporters. But Cicero anticipated that Memmius would win out, and was proved right. The outcome marked Tiberius Nero down in this first highly public incident as a worthy failure, a characterization that could probably be applied to his whole career.[28] In late 51 or early 50 he visited Asia, where he had a number of clients, and he called on Cicero during the latter's governorship of Cilicia. At this time the tortuous negotiations for the third marriage of Cicero's daughter Tullia were under way.

Tiberius Nero seems to have made a strong impression on his host, to judge from the warm letter of recommendation that Cicero wrote for him to Gaius Silius, propraetor of Bithynia and Pontus.[29] The young man declared an interest in Tullia and obtained her father's consent for the match. Messengers were despatched to Rome to give mother and daughter the happy news. Unfortunately, Tiberius' hostile *daemon* intervened — it seems that before he left, Cicero had told Tullia and her mother to arrange the negotiations in Rome themselves, and because he was going to be away for so long in his province, not to feel obliged to refer the issue to him. The messengers arrived in Rome just in time to miss Tullia's engagement party. Tiberius Nero would probably have been a better choice than his successful rival, the seedy Dolabella, a ruthless adherent of Caesar's and a man whose career was enlivened by dissipation and debts.[30]

Cicero had approved of Tiberius Nero as a potential prosecutor in the Gabinius case because of his stand against the power block represented by Caesar and Pompey (and Crassus). By 48 BC he was doubtless dismayed when his young champion displayed the often crass opportunism typical of the period. Putting his support behind Julius Caesar, Tiberius Nero signed up as his quaestor and commanded the fleet at Alexandria.[31] As a reward for his services he received a senior priesthood and in 46 was given responsibility for founding colonies at Caesar's behest in Narbonese Gaul, including Narbo and Arelate.[32] He might have seemed to the outside world to be on an upward trajectory, but cruel fate intervened. The Ides of March in 44 and the assassination of Caesar changed the destiny of many besides Caesar himself. Tiberius Nero had to make a career choice, and characteristically made the wrong one. Perhaps under the influence of Livia's father, he followed the course of many Caesarian supporters and jumped sides, hitching his wagon to the assassins' team, even proposing special honours for the killers.[33]

We do not know for certain when Tiberius Nero and Livia were married. The normal age of marriage for women at this period seems generally to have been in the late teens, but in upper-class families marriage at fifteen was probably the norm, and even earlier marriages were common in aristocratic circles, when there was a political advantage to the match. By this reckoning Livia, depending on her date of birth, might have reached a marriageable age in 46 or 45. But this earlier date may not have been possible if Tiberius Nero was serving in Gaul at that time. The birth of their first son in November 42 gives us a limit, and places the marriage probably in 43, when Livia was fifteen or sixteen. Her husband would likely have been in his late thirties.[34]

The marriage took place during the dramatic aftermath of Caesar's assassination. Two men competed to fill the vacuum left by his death. One was Caesar's lieutenant Mark Antony. The other was his great-nephew, Octavian, named his heir and adopted son in his will, the man destined to transform the character of the Roman state and to become Livia's second husband (fig. 26). He was born Gaius Octavius, on September 23, 63 BC, in Rome. Although malicious gossip claimed that his great-grandfather was a freedman and rope maker, the family, though not distinguished, was well-to-do. The Octavii originated from the Volscian town of Velitrae, two days' journey south of Rome. His father, also Gaius Octavius, was a prosperous banker, a member of the entrepreneurial middle class that largely constituted what is known as the equestrian order. By reaching the praetorship in 61 BC, he became the first of his family to move from that class into a senatorial career. The younger Octavius and his sister Octavia were the children of their father's second wife, Atia (another Octavia had been born to a first wife, Ancharia). Atia was the daughter of Atius Balbus, the son of Julius Caesar's sister, Julia, a family connection that proved useful indeed to her ambitious son. From 61 to late 59 Octavius' father was away from Italy, in Macedonia, where he served a term as governor. Not long after his return, when he might reasonably have been planning for a consulship, he died, leaving his son and two daughters to be brought up by Atia. She remarried some two or three years later.[35]

Through his link with Caesar, Octavius obtained some minor civil positions; then, because a career in Roman politics was difficult without some military background, he was chosen to join Caesar in an expedition to Africa in late 47 to deal with the remnants of Pompey's forces. But the young man was not in good health, and at his mother's insistence the plan was shelved. Ill health continued to dog him throughout his life. He seems to have been prone to nervous exhaustion and was particularly liable to sunstroke — he made it his lifetime practice to wear a hat when outdoors. Caesar returned from Thapsus in April 46, and for the remainder of the year he was active in promoting Octavius' prospects in Rome, even to the extent of allowing him to ride behind his own chariot in the triumph for the African war, which Octavius had missed. At the end of the year Caesar was off to Spain, where Pompey's elder son had gathered a large army. Once again Octavius was unable to leave with him. He fell dangerously ill, so ill that his life was feared for.[36] He recovered and followed Caesar, although he seems to have arrived in Spain too late to take part in the final battle of Munda, were the remnants of Pompey's supporters were finally crushed.[37]

In September 45, before he reentered Rome, Caesar stopped at one of his estates at Labici and wrote his will. His decision was a momentous one. He had been married several times and had a reputation among his soldiers as a sexual dynamo. But despite these promising attributes, he had produced only one child, a daughter Julia (Pompey's wife), to whom he was deeply attached. She died, leaving no surviving offspring. He now named Octavius as his chief heir and in a clause appended to the will adopted him. The will was deposited in the Temple of the Vestals, and its contents seem not to have been made known to the main beneficiary. Before the end of the year Caesar sent his heir to Apollonia on the coast of Macedonia to complete his education. Apollonia was not a great educational centre, and it was possibly hoped that Octavius would develop a closer familiarity with military matters from contact with the five legions stationed in the province.

Octavius had been in Apollonia for a few months only when a messenger arrived from his mother with the dramatic news that Caesar had been murdered. He decided to return to Italy at once with a few friends, including Marcus Agrippa. In Brundisium he learned from letters sent by his mother and stepfather that he had inherited most of Caesar's estate and, more significantly, had been adopted as his son. His family advised him to decline the adoption, perceptively anticipating the political firestorm that it would create. He did not follow their advice and proceeded to Rome. He now began to style himself Gaius Julius Caesar Octavianus, following the Roman custom of assuming the name of the adoptive parent with a form of the original gens appended.

The adoption fuelled Octavian's ambitions, and its importance to him is demonstrated by his desperate efforts to have it confirmed. The adoption of relatives or even of nonrelatives was a well-established tradition in Rome, and adopted sons and daughters naturally styled themselves henceforth as children of the adoptive, not the natural father. But testamentary adoption, which later played a significant part in Livia's own career, seems to have been in a dubious category of its own. The ancient evidence is not explicit, and the ancient jurists are silent on the matter, but it seems that adoption stipulated in a will was almost certainly not an adoption in the full sense of the word, but mainly a device to allow for the inheritance of property on condition that the adopted child assume the name of the legator (see chapter 8). This ambiguity explains why Octavian was determined at all costs to have the status of the adoption legally ratified. He attempted to do this soon after his arrival in Rome and took on as an ally in his campaign Antony, who pretended to be making every effort to have the appropriate law passed but was in fact doing everything he could to block it. When Octavian became consul, in May 43, one of his first measures was to have the proposed law presented to the popular assembly.[38] The symbolic importance of the adoption cannot be stressed enough. In practice he ignored the final element of his name, Octavianus, and preferred to use only Gaius Julius Caesar.[39] Although clearly an unfriendly source, Antony was not far off the mark when he said of him *et te, o puer, qui omnia nomini debes* (and you, lad, who owe everything to a name).[40] And more was to come. There is evidence that Caesar might have received divine honours even before his death. At all events, in 42 posthumous divine honours were granted him. Henceforth, Octavian could style himself not only as the son of Julius Caesar but as the son of *Divus* (the deified) Julius.[41]

The following years did in a sense vindicate his parents' reservations, for conflict arose between Octavian and Antony in their zeal to assume Caesar's mantle, a struggle that was punctuated by a series of pacts but was not resolved finally until the suicide of Antony in 30 BC following the decisive battle of Actium. Their first temporary rapprochement was reached in November 43, when the two joined a supporter of Antony's, Marcus Lepidus, to create the "Second" Triumvirate. This was a more formal arrangement than its predecessor and gave the trio almost absolute power for five years. It enabled them to eliminate their opponents, including Cicero, and to prosecute a campaign against the tyrannicides Brutus and Cassius, who were eventually defeated and induced to suicide at Philippi in Thrace in the autumn of 42.

The struggle between powerful and ambitious Roman political and military leaders in the last century of the republic inevitably embroiled the rest of the population, especially Romans of prominence, who, as is usually the case in a civil war, found it impossible to stand on the sidelines of the conflict. It also brought tragedy into Livia's life. Nothing explicit is known about her father Marcus' stand during the clashes between Caesar and Pompey or during the ascendancy of Caesar. Shackleton-Bailey has tentatively suggested that Marcus was a Caesarian, but whatever loyalty he might have felt certainly did not survive the dictator's death, when he emerges as a champion of the tyrannicides. In 43 we find him one of the sponsors of a senatorial decree to give command of two legions to the assassin Decimus Brutus. By the end of that year he had been proscribed by the triumvirs. He fled east to join Brutus and Cassius and shared with them their final defeat at Philippi. He personally survived, but afterwards reputedly died a courageous death. Refusing to ask for mercy, he committed suicide in his tent.[42]

We do not know what happened to Marcus Livius' property. Livia may have been his only natural child, but there are strong grounds for believing that in the absence of a natural son, Marcus before his death arranged in his will for the adoption of Marcus Livius Drusus Libo (consul in 15 BC). Libo's natural father, Lucius Scribonius Libo, later demonstrated powerful political connections.

. . . . Denotes adoption

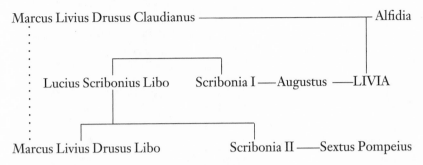

Stemma 2. Possible connections of Livia and Scribonia

Destined for a consulship in 34, Lucius was the brother of Scribonia, first wife of Octavian (see chapter 2), and father of a second Scribonia, who became the wife of Sextus Pompeius, the renegade son of Pompey. If the adoption of Marcus Libo did take place, it, like Octavian's, and like Livia's more than half a century later, would have been testamentary and would in time have resulted in the irony that Livia's stepbrother was the nephew of her husband Octavian's first wife (stemma 2). Marcus Libo would have inherited the bulk of his adoptive father's wealth. As a woman, Livia would have been limited by law (the Lex Voconia) to just less than half. But because the father was proscribed, there would in fact have been very little to collect.[43]

In the meantime, the conduct of Livia's husband, Tiberius Nero, highlighted the two dominant traits in his makeup: an inordinate opportunism and a penchant for guaranteeing that whatever opportunity he seized, it would be an injudicious choice. He did not follow Marcus in sticking to his principles to the bitter end. Once he recognised that the plight of the assassins was hopeless, he broke away from his father-in-law's position. The struggle for supremacy now clearly lay between Octavian and Marc Antony, and Tiberius Nero opted to back Antony. He was elected to the praetorship in 42, but following a dispute that arose among the triumvirs, he refused at the end of his term to leave office and stayed in place beyond his legally defined period.

Early in the same year, Livia became pregnant. It is said that she was very keen to bear a boy and used a method of determining the sex common among young women of the time: she took an egg from under a brooding hen and kept it warm against her breast. Whenever she had to yield it up, she passed it to her nurse under the folds of their dresses so as not to interrupt the warmth. A cock with a fine crest was hatched, a portent of a vigorous son.[44] Later in the year we have the first specific recorded evidence of her whereabouts. On November 16, 42, the first of her two sons, Tiberius (fig. 27), was born on the Palatine in Rome. Suetonius records both the date and the year, as well as the location in Rome, where it must be assumed that Tiberius Claudius Nero owned property on the highly fashionable Palatine Hill. Later a story arose that Livia, now aged sixteen or seventeen, was in Fundi at her mother's family home at the time of Tiberius' birth. Suetonius argues against this and also against those who place the birth in the following or preceding year. He notes that the correct date appears in both the *fasti* (the official calendars) and the *acta publica* (public gazette), and it is in fact vindicated in surviving inscriptions.[45]

After the successful campaign against Caesar's assassins at Philippi, the triumvirs had agreed on areas of command. Marcus Lepidus was restricted to Africa. Antony took the East, where he launched a campaign against the Parthians. Octavian commanded in the West. His task was to restore order in Italy and keep a check on Sextus Pompeius, the younger son of Pompey, who had set himself up with a large fleet in Sicily and had established a haven for fugitives from the triumvirs. Octavian also undertook the grim task of confiscating territory in Italy for the retiring veterans. Antony's brother Lucius Antonius, and Antony's wife, Fulvia, became the champions of the dispossessed Italians and sought to instigate an uprising against Octavian; Tiberius Nero joined the effort, and Livia and her son followed him to Perusia, the main centre of opposition. When Perusia fell in early 40, Tiberius Nero escaped with his family first to Praeneste and then to Naples, where he sought to instigate a slave uprising, helped by Gaius Velleius, the grandfather of the historian. That effort collapsed and the family had a hair-raising escape. As Octavian's forces broke into the city, the family decided to make a break for it. Velleius, by now old and infirm, was too weary and ran himself through with his own sword. Tiberius Nero and his family set out to make their way stealthily to a ship, avoiding the regular routes and going off into the wilds of the countryside. On the journey little Tiberius started to cry. There was panic that he might give them away. Livia snatched him from the nurse, and when he still did not settle down, one of her followers seized him from her and apparently saved the day. The ancient authors were quick to spot the irony of Livia fleeing the man she would eventually marry, with a son who would eventually succeed him.[46]

The family did in the end make their escape and went to Sicily. They perhaps hoped that family connections, through Marcus Libo, the brother-in-law of Sextus Pompeius, would stand them in good stead. But if this connection did exist, it did the couple little good, and their reception in Sicily must have been a considerable disappointment. Sextus Pompeius found Tiberius Nero something of an embarrassment and was reluctant even to grant him an audience. Also, perhaps to avoid unnecessary provocation, he ordered Tiberius Nero not to display the *fasces*, the rods of the office of praetorship, which he had illegally retained in his possession. Sextus' sister, perhaps motivated by personal rather than political concerns, was more welcoming, and even gave the little Tiberius a cloak with a clasp and some gold studs. These survived as celebrity items and were exhibited for tourists in the resort town of Baiae until Suetonius' day. But Tiberius Nero now fell foul of the complex and shifting tide of Roman politics. Octavian, faced with the prospect of a confrontation with Antony, sought to move closer to Sextus Pompeius. Tiberius Nero was obliged to pack his bags once again and go with his wife and infant son to join Antony in the East, where the Claudii Nerones seem to have acquired a large number of clients.[47] It might have been at this time that Tiberius Nero was proscribed. We certainly know that it happened at some point — Tacitus states so unequivocally, although without providing a date.[48] We cannot be sure why Livia followed her husband into exile, unless for the uncomplicated reason of personal affection. It was certainly expected that wives would either accompany proscribed husbands or stay at home and work on their behalf.[49] But they could not be compelled. By now it must have been apparent to Livia that her husband was not destined for greatness, and it perhaps says something for her strength of character that as a young mother of eighteen or so she seems to have put duty before personal convenience. The couple were able to get safe passage by joining a distant kin of Livia's, Lucius Scribonius Libo, who left Sicily to accompany Antony's mother, Julia, to Athens and allowed Tiberius Nero and his family to sail with him.[50] Antony was perhaps no more eager than Sextus to be lumbered with someone so tainted by failure, and he quickly despatched Tiberius Nero to Sparta, where the Claudii had long enjoyed patronage.

Sparta, perhaps because of its ties to the Claudians, offered the couple an extremely cordial welcome, in contrast to their earlier experiences. Livia was later able to acknowledge their support by rewarding the community for the loyalty it had shown her in times of trouble.[51] But Tiberius Nero was unable to break the habit of a lifetime. Once again they had to flee — the reasons are not known. This time it was by night, through a forest where a fire broke out. The family barely escaped. The event would have been especially memorable to Livia, who ended up with burning hair and a charred dress.[52]

In AD 40 Antony and Octavian settled their differences at the Peace of Brundisium, and the compact was sealed by the marriage of Antony and Octavian's sister, Octavia. A further, even shorter-lived compact, the Treaty of Misenum, was reached by the triumvirs and Sextus Pompeius in mid-39 BC. It promised an amnesty to those who had sided with Sextus. Livia and her husband were thus able to return to Rome at the same time as Mark Antony.[53] Livia's mood is not recorded, but it must have been sombre enough. Her father was dead, and she must by now have recognised that her husband's star had started to set even before it had properly risen.

MARRIAGE

In 39 Livia's harrowing experiences of restless exile came to an end when she returned with her husband to Rome. Her return would have far-reaching consequences not only for herself but for the entire Roman world, for it led to her lifelong association with a man who was to determine the shape of Rome's history for centuries to come. If there is such as a thing as the aphrodisiac of power, then Octavian might be said to have exercised an unmatched sexual attraction in the Rome of the time. He was still only in his early twenties, but an individual of remarkable achievement and obvious promise. Like Livia, he was married when they met, in a union that illustrated perfectly the all-important political dimension of marriage in the upper echelons of Roman society. Octavian's wife at the time was Scribonia. In 40 BC, in the complex play of Roman politics, it had been in his interest to move closer to Pompey's son Sextus Pompeius, whose fleets controlled the seas around Italy. (Octavian was particularly concerned about his own weakness in sea power.) One of Sextus' chief allies was Lucius Scribonius Libo, who was to attain the consulship in 34 BC, the first member of his family to reach the office. A consistent supporter of the Pompeian cause, Libo was an ambitious and able man, whose aspirations are marked by the marriages contracted by his female relatives. Sextus Pompeius married Libo's daughter, and, after negotiations conducted through Maecenas, Octavian married Libo's sister, Scribonia.[1] In the following year the alliance was cemented by the betrothal of Marcellus, Octavian's three-year-old nephew, to Pompeia, daughter of Sextus Pompeius, and thus Scribonia's niece.

Scribonia came from a powerful republican family, familiar to the inhabitants of Rome through a striking visible reminder. As people entered the Forum along the Via Sacra, they passed the monument set up by Scribonius Libo, the *Puteal Libonis* (also known as the *Puteal Scribonianum*), a large and handsome stone wellhead, alluded to in the literature and often depicted on coins. According to Suetonius, before Octavian came onto the scene, Scribonia had already been twice married, to two ex-consuls (see appendix 6). Her son by the second, Publius Cornelius Scipio, reached the consulship in 16 BC. For Scribonia to have produced this son (by a second marriage) early enough for him to become consul in 16, she would have needed to be some ten years older than Octavian, born in 63.

The marriage to Scribonia lasted only a year. She does not seem to have been endowed with what Tacitus calls Livia's "affability" *(comitas)*. Seneca describes her as a *gravis femina; gravis* applied to a man would mean something akin to "dignified," but in a woman could probably convey a quality closer to "severe." The only specific reference we have to shrewish behaviour is Mark Antony's claim that Octavian divorced Scribonia because she expressed her feelings very volubly over the influence of his mistress (possibly Livia). Octavian wrote that he was driven to distraction by her bitchy ways, a sentiment that has won over some modern scholars — Syme for instance calls her "morose," "tiresome," and "disagreeable." Perhaps, but she showed considerable character when her daughter by Octavian, Julia, was banished, and Scribonia quit Rome to share her exile (see chapter 4). Both Dio and Velleius agree that her gesture was voluntary and their testimony should probably be taken at face value, despite the modern theories that she might have been personally involved in the scandal that had brought Julia down. Moreover, she had the composure when in her eighties to try to talk her nephew Drusus Libo out of suicide when he was faced with the certain prospect of condemnation for treason early in Tiberius' reign. The image of Scribonia the shrew was almost certainly the end product of a propaganda effort designed to divert attention from the potentially scandalous circumstances of her divorce from Octavian. In the end, she could be said to have had the last laugh. She survived her younger last ex-husband, who died in AD 14, by two years at the least. (Seneca refers to her as alive in AD 16.)

The divorce took place in the latter part of 39, immediately after the birth of their daughter, Julia.[2] In reality, irrespective of Scribonia's charms, or lack of them, Octavian had decided on a new wife. The precise series of events by which this came about is difficult to disentangle. There is the usual problem of dealing with sources that may be incomplete, careless, or hostile. But we have the additional difficulty that these sources might have drawn much of their information on the marriage from material that was essentially fuel in a propaganda war, and thus already distorted at birth. The details have been much debated, and the basis for some of the assumptions in the following narrative are set out in appendix 7.

Livia cannot have reached Rome before late summer 39. She and her husband, Tiberius Nero, would probably have returned to their residence on the Palatine if it was still available to them. It may not have been. The Treaty of Misenum stipulated that those who had left Italy in fear for their safety would get their property back; those who, like Tiberius Nero, had been proscribed would recover only a quarter.[3] Livia might thus have found herself in considerably reduced circumstances. Where and when she and Octavian met we have no idea, and we cannot exclude the possible irony that she might have been introduced to him through her aunt by adoption, his then-wife, Scribonia. Dio is the only source to report on how the affair began. Octavian in 39 BC organised a lavish entertainment to celebrate the shaving of his beard (the event may have been his birthday, on September 23). Dio tells us that Octavian kept his chin smooth afterwards (although coins continue to show him bearded as late as 36). He clearly wanted to look his best because he "was *already (hede)* beginning to love Livia."[4]

For Livia, Octavian certainly represented a good catch. There are hints that in the eyes of contemporaries she quickly recognised his interest in her and turned it to her advantage. There is evidence that Octavian was already turning to Livia for help and advice well before they were married. Scribonia complained about her husband's mistress — almost certainly Livia — upset not by his infatuation, a situation that Roman wives generally learned to handle, but rather by her rival's *nimiam potentiam* (excessive power). *Potentia* is a term generally used of political rather than erotic power. Tacitus seems also to suggest that Livia may well have been active in encouraging Octavian's attentions, when he says that Octavian took her away from her husband *incertum an invitam* (it is not certain that she was reluctant).[5] But what did she have to offer him? We can certainly not dismiss the element of pure sexual attraction. Both Tacitus and Velleius speak of Livia's beauty, *forma*, although such descriptions of aristocratic Roman women tend to be formulaic, and beauty in a bride may have been as much a commonplace in ancient Rome as it is today (chapter 6). Tacitus asserted that Octavian was driven essentially by lust, *cupidine formae*, and a tradition that saw his interest as pure infatuation *(amore)* persisted down to the fourth century.[6]

But Livia had much more than sexual charms to offer. Certainly in his previous matches Octavian had always looked upon marriage as a means of furthering his career. He was betrothed first to Servilia, the daughter of Publius Servilius Isauricus, related by marriage to Brutus, Cassius, and Lepidus, in an engagement that was the product of a political alignment engineered by Cicero early in 43 BC. This first arrangement fell victim to the shifting political tides. When he became reconciled with Antony, to strengthen the new alliance he became engaged to Antony's stepdaughter Claudia, the child of Fulvia (see chapter 7) and her previous husband, Publius Clodius. The marriage was postponed because of his fiancée's youth, and the clash with Fulvia ended the arrangement. The marriage to Scribonia followed in 40 BC.[7] Octavian's ties to Scribonia would similarly have been weakened when the old problems between himself and Sextus Pompeius reasserted themselves. Velleius, in fact, explicitly places the divorce from Scribonia and the fresh outbreak of hostilities with Sextus in close sequence.

In fact, Livia would have seemed an ideal partner. Quite apart from any feelings of affection, she brought significant political benefits to the marriage. Octavian had considerable power. His desperate need now was for status. Although Antony's taunt of *ignobilitas* might have been overstated (Octavian's father had reached the praetorship, which would have given him a technical entrée into the *nobilitas*), Octavian was seen by the old nobility as something of a revolutionary parvenu, and this formidable obstacle had not yet been overcome even more than a quarter-century later, when, in 12 BC, some of the nobility declined to attend the funeral of his old friend and son-in-law Marcus Agrippa. Ancestry was a powerful element in making a marriage advantageous. As Tacitus observed in Livia's obituary notice, she could boast a lofty lineage (*nobilitatis . . . clarissimae*), and Velleius describes her father as *nobilissimus*. Thus she would have helped Octavian to strengthen his ties with the old distinguished families. In fact, the union would have a double advantage. It would link Octavian with the powerful and prestigious Claudii. But beyond this the connection with Livius Drusus would resonate throughout Italy and help to strengthen Octavian's power base. It is worth noting that the names Drusus and Drusilla, both from the Livian side of the lineage, continued to be used by later generations of the family.[8]

If Livia has been correctly identified as the mistress who was the target of Scribonia's complaints, Octavian and Livia began an affair while he was still married to Scribonia. He waited for the birth of his daughter Julia, then immediately arranged a divorce.[9] Livia for her part secured a divorce from Tiberius Nero in turn, and it is likely that in late September or early October, 39 BC, Octavian and Livia became betrothed. They do not seem to have proceeded immediately to the marriage, probably because by early October, Livia was six months pregnant. Tacitus and Dio say that Octavian sought the guidance of the pontiffs on the problem that the pregnancy raised for her remarriage. Both historians present this consultation in sarcastic terms, perhaps reflecting Antony's propaganda. Tacitus says that the question was put, *per ludibrium* (in a farce), whether Livia, with a child conceived but not yet born, could legally wed. Dio provides the same question, and also records their answer: that if there was any doubt about the conception the marriage should be postponed, but if conception was confirmed, then the marriage could take place. Dio is sceptical about their finding this decision in the rules, but says that it was a moot point because they would have given the answer Octavian needed anyhow.[10]

Why go to the priests in the first place? This does not seem to be an issue on which sacred law would have had any say. It is noteworthy that when the emperor Claudius made known his intention to marry Agrippina, his niece, in a relationship considered incestuous, the pontiffs were not asked for a ruling; instead, dispensation was sought from the Senate. The German scholar Suerbaum has argued that the issue here was a simple one. If a woman at the time of divorce was not known to be pregnant, clearly a delay was essential before remarriage, in order to establish the absence of pregnancy, otherwise the paternity and consequent *potestas* over the child would be uncertain *(perturbatio partus)*. Tacitus seems to have got the approach to the pontiffs slightly wrong in stating that the issue was whether a pregnant woman could remarry. Dio had a better grasp of the problem, that it had to be determined whether a woman was pregnant after her divorce. There seems to be no explicit statement in Roman law about the period that should elapse after divorce and before remarriage, and it is not clear what the rule was. In the ancient Law of the Twelve Tables a child born eleven months after the *death* of the husband is deemed not to be his. In the republican period a widow was required to mourn her husband for ten months, and according to the third-century AD jurist Ulpian, a child born more than ten months after the husband's death could not be an heir. Later imperial legislation increased the period to one year. As for the consequences of divorce, the earliest rule belongs to AD 449, when the period is set at one year. When Augustus later passed his laws restricting the rights of inheritance, the widower had to remarry at once to escape their penalties. But because of her duty for mourning and to avoid perturbatio partus, the widow had to be exempted from the immediate application of this new legislation. Initially the Lex Julia allowed women to remain single for one year after the death of their husbands and six months after divorce. (Curiously, under the Lex Julia a perturbatio partus does not seem to be an issue after divorce.) The later Lex Papia Poppaea extended these periods to two years and eighteen months, respectively (on the laws, see chapter 7).[11]

The pontiffs' ruling removed the final obstacle, and Octavian could proceed to the betrothal.[12] But there was another bizarre twist to the event. In two places Tacitus retains a tradition that Livia was forcibly removed from Tiberius Nero, that she was *abducta Neroni uxor* (a wife abducted from Nero) and that Octavian *aufert marito* (carries off [Livia] from her husband). The cruel characterization of Octavian's conduct may, again, have originated in Mark Antony's propaganda. Tacitus and Suetonius refer to letters of Antony's which apparently survived the triumvir's disgrace and death. They are brimming with bitter invective against Octavian. The seeds of the story of Livia's abduction may have been sown by a claim made by Antony that Octavian carried off *(abductam)* the wife of an ex-consul (unnamed) from her husband's dining room before his very eyes and took her into the bedchamber, from where she returned with her hair in disorder and her ears glowing *(rubentibus auriculis)*. Was she Livia? Suetonius seems to relate the hasty marriage and the case of the unidentified consular wife as two separate events. Also, Livia's husband was not of consular rank. Some exaggeration may, of course, be expected in abusive attacks. It is also possible that this relatively minor error arose in the transmission of the anecdote. But Suetonius took the material directly from Antony's letters — it is hard to see why Antony would have given this misinformation, unless, as Flory argues, he obscured Livia's identity intentionally. The idea of the forced abduction was still in vogue during the reigns of Caligula and Claudius. When Caligula chose as his second bride Livia Orestilla, who at the time was betrothed to Gaius Calpurnius Piso, he made the witty comment that he was following the precedent of Romulus (the legendary founder of Rome) and Augustus, who both snatched their new brides away from their husbands. (Hersilia was married [to Hersilius] before she married Romulus.) Caligula got it only partly right. He tired of his new bride very soon — the most conservative figure is two months — in contrast to Octavian, who remained devoted to Livia for forty-one years. In the next reign the senator Vitellius contrasted Claudius, who wished to marry his niece Agrippina the Younger, with the earlier Caesars who had carried off their wives on a whim.[13] In fact, Tiberius Nero had always been prepared to bend in the political wind, even if he failed to benefit much from his compliance. Pliny describes him as Octavian's enemy *(hostis)*, and although this would not, strictly speaking, have been true after the amnesty, there would still have been an inevitable tension between the two men, whose mutual animosity went back to the time of Perusia. The marriage would have offered Tiberius Nero an ideal opportunity to bury his differences with the rising star of the state. Cicero described him as the kind of man who was excessively eager to show gratitude in return for a favour, and most of the ancient sources speak of him as the perfect model of the *mari complaisant*. This motive may well have been sweetened by another consideration. Octavian's divorce from Scribonia and marriage to Livia would cause a rift with Sextus Pompeius; this would be to the advantage of Antony, to whom Tiberius Nero might have had a residual loyalty. And we must also remember that he had received a personal snub from Sextus.

Suetonius says that Tiberius Nero *petenti Augusto concessit* (gave her up to Augustus at his request). In fact, both Dio and Velleius allude to what seems to have been an active, even eager, role for Tiberius Nero in the union, Velleius repeating the same information in two different sections, that he was the one who pledged Livia. Dio says that he officiated at the ceremony, giving away his wife as a father would give up his daughter.[14] It is possible that Antony's propaganda might have exaggerated his willingness to comply. But there were historical parallels for such behaviour. When the great orator Hortensius persuaded Cato Uticensis, a man known for his upright attachment to principle, to divorce his wife Marcia so that he could marry her, Phillipus, her father, refused to betroth her to her new partner unless Cato joined with him in the formal ceremony. They betrothed her jointly. Much later, Caligula compelled Memmius Regulus to betroth his ex-wife Lollia Paulina to him.[15]

Tiberius Nero's eagerness to please did cause one embarrassing moment, when he chose to attend the feast following the betrothal. Present at the event was one of the pretty slave boys, the *delicia*, who were trained in clever and naughty comments and appeared naked as a regular feature at social events of the fashionable. These slaves were selected for their talkativeness, and were particularly appealing if they were impudent and adept at risqué language. Seneca notes that they were trained by special tutors in the art of abuse and observes wryly that because their vulgarity was a matter of professional expertise, what they said was considered not offensive but smart *(nec has contumelias vocamus, sed argutias)*. The slave attending the betrothal feast seems to have lived up to expectations. When he saw Livia reclining next to Octavian, he told her that she was in the wrong place since her husband — as he pointed to Tiberius Nero — was in another part of the room. This would not have been a simple social gaffe, but a deliberately outrageous joke. The story may, of course, be apocryphal, but it does at the very least suggest that relations between Tiberius Nero and Octavian were cordial enough for the discarded husband to have attended the celebratory feast.[16] Some scholars associate this banquet with a notorious event from Octavian's past, the *cena dodekatheos* (Feast of the Twelve Gods), recorded only by Suetonius. At this infamous festivity Octavian and his guests appeared in the guise of gods and goddesses (he took the part of Apollo). Suetonius reports that Antony attacked the escapade in his letters, naming the guests (the list is not provided), and there was also an anonymous and ribald lampoon which suggests that Octavian produced a burlesque about "novel debaucheries of the gods" *(nova divorum . . . adulteria)* ending with Jupiter falling from his throne. According to Suetonius, the scandal became the subject of common gossip, which was all the more avid because there was a severe famine in the city, leading to the jocular comment that the gods had eaten all the grain. In 40 BC Sextus Pompeius had cut off the corn supply and there were popular disturbances; Octavian was even stoned. The Treaty of Misenum would have removed the root cause of these supply difficulties, but it would have taken a while for the problem to be totally alleviated, and there are reports of famine in the years 39, 38, and 36, any one of which might in fact have been the year of the banquet. Whatever the date, Livia would almost certainly have been one of the guests at this celebration.[17]

Following the betrothal it seems that Livia joined Octavian at his home on the Palatine. It is probably safe to assume that at this stage they were not yet married. There is, however, some confusion in the sources about the relationship of their wedding to the birth of Livia's second son, Drusus. The information in Suetonius and Dio that Drusus came into the world after the marriage may have resulted from a confusion between the betrothal and the wedding (see appendix 7). Antony seems to have been the source of this confusion, for he maliciously charged that the "wedding" was hasty *(festinatas Liviae nuptias)*, probably in allusion to a hasty *betrothal* in early October following their initial meeting in September.[18]

Early in 38 Drusus was born in Octavian's Palatine home *(intra Caesaris penates)*. The actual day can be deduced as January 14 (see appendix 7).[19] The marriage took place very soon afterwards, in a year that began with a number of compelling omens. The hut of Romulus was burnt down on the Palatine during a religious ritual. The statue of Virtus fell on its face. A rumour spread that the Magna Mater was angry with the Romans, causing panic. Purification rites were carried out, and people were reassured when four palm trees sprang up near her temple on the Palatine and in the Forum. Dio reports that in the midst of these dramatic occurrences Octavian and Livia married.[20] The *Fasti Verulani* record the date as January 17 (38 BC).[21] It seems that Octavian had simply waited a brief while for Livia to recover from delivering Drusus, then proceeded straight to the wedding.

Inevitably, these events led to considerable gossip about the true paternity of Drusus, and humorists coined a line in Greek, preserved in Suetonius and paraphrased by Dio, about some being lucky in having *trimena paidia* (children in three months). This became a proverbial saying, and seems to have been parodied by Caligula, who married his last wife, Caesonia, when she was close to the end of her term so that he could beget a *paidion triakonthemeron* (a thirty-day child). There was also a rumour that Octavian was Drusus' real father, a belief no doubt encouraged by his deep sorrow on the young man's death in 9 BC. This last particular ghost can surely be laid to rest. Livia must have conceived in late March or early April 39, before the Treaty of Misenum and the amnesty that brought her and her first husband back to Rome and into the company of Octavian.[22] It may have been to discourage such gossip that after the birth Octavian sent the infant Drusus to his father and made an entry in the record (*hypomnemata*) of the fact that it was Tiberius Nero who was the father. But it should be noted that it was normal for a man marrying a pregnant woman to send the child to the natural father.[23]

In the event Tiberius Nero does not seem to have made much, if any, political capital out of his compliance. When he died, some six years after the wedding, in 32 BC or the end of 33, he named Octavian in his will as guardian (*tutor*) to both his sons. In accordance with Roman tradition, his first son, Tiberius, now nine years old, delivered the funeral elegy. Tiberius Nero, Livia's first husband, thus quitted the scene, a tired failure, the brilliant hopes of his youth unrealised.[24]

The scandal provoked by the unusual marriage continued to haunt Octavian. A decade later (29–28 BC), while he was exercising the power of censor, someone brought before him a young man who had committed adultery with a married woman but then had afterwards married the woman in question. Octavian was in a major quandary, but he dealt with it prudently. He suggested that they forget the quarrels of the past and look to the future.[25]

IN THE SHADOWS

We hear relatively little about Livia in the first thirty years or so after her marriage to Octavian, a considerable period in any relationship, and one in which she and her husband passed from youth to middle age. There are a number of reasons for this general silence. To the extent that there was a "first lady" in Rome during these years, this role belonged not to Livia but to Octavian's sister, Octavia, who garnered the lion's share of the attention, almost all of it favourable. A second reason was Livia's own good political sense. She no doubt anticipated that during this formative period of the principate a powerful imperial woman who meddled where she had no business would attract attention to her misdeeds, actual and imagined. When after the death of Octavia she began to play a more prominent and public part in affairs, she had learned to handle her role with considerable skill. The publicity over her marriage to Octavian would have impressed on her the need to maintain a low profile, to project the image to the Romans of the wife as obedient helpmate who stays very much in the shadow of her husband. It is telling that the criticism voiced over the unusual circumstances of the marriage focussed not on her behaviour but on Octavian's. Her dignified demeanour seems to have made her immune to Antony's attacks.

In the period after her marriage Livia would presumably have lived for most of the time in Octavian's residence on the Palatine. But the first recorded event occurred outside Rome. She appears to have possessed a family estate not far from Veii at Primaporta, near the ninth milestone of the Via Flaminia, de-

scribed by Suetonius as "hers," *Veientanum suum* (see chapter 9). How she
came to own this property is not clear. We do not know how much of her
father's assets she would have acquired after his death, given that he was
proscribed. Her first husband, Tiberius Nero, would of course have returned
her dowry on their divorce. At any rate this one estate seems to have remained
in her family's hands. Here, about the time of her marriage, she was singled out
for a dramatic and famous omen.[1] A tradition took hold that as Livia was
returning to the villa, an eagle dropped a white chick with a laurel branch in its
mouth into her lap. She rescued the small bird and raised it, and planted the
sprig. (Pliny says that she did so on the instructions of the augurs [*haruspices*],
as a religious obligation.) A great brood of white chicks was born, which in
itself would have been considered remarkable, because there was a belief that
white hens were sterile. From this event the villa was called *ad Gallinas*, and a
grove of laurels sprang up, from which the *triumphatores* subsequently collected the sprigs that they carried in their hands and which made up their
crowns during the celebration. It also became the tradition, probably begun by
Augustus in 29 BC in his Actian triumph and continued by later Julio-Claudian
emperors, for the celebrant to plant the cutting afterwards. Pliny testifies
to seeing trees with labels identifying the individual triumphator who had
planted them, and it was said that just before the death of one of these victorious generals, the shrub that he had planted would wither and die. The
laurels and the brood of chicks survived for more than a century at least.
According to Dio, the extinction of the Julio-Claudian line was foretold in
Nero's last year, when the whole grove withered from the root up and all the
hens died (Pliny mentions none of this). Julius Caesar had taken the laurel as
his personal symbol, and a senatorial decree of 45 BC gave him the right to
wear a laurel wreath in perpetuity. Octavian continued this association after
the ad gallinas incident by taking a cutting from the grove for his triumph and
replanting it, and at the time of the settlement in 27, laurel bushes were set by
the doors of his house on the Palatine, after which they became important
symbols on coins, altars, and other art.[2]

The story of the omen at Primaporta might well have been invented, or at
least embellished, by Octavian, and it illustrates how from the beginning Livia
was intended to play an important symbolic role in her new husband's career.
Its appeal might be found at a number of levels. It would have reminded
Romans of the sign that prophesied Caesar's ultimate victory over Pompey,
when a kite dropped a sprig of laurel on one of the soldiers on the eve of
their departure for the final campaign (49 BC). The portent clearly foretold
the imminence of triumphant generals, and in Livia's case would have been

appropriate at the time, because there would have been confidence that she and Octavian would have children. It would have been a perfect antidote to the mud thrown at them over their divorce and marriage, and would have told the world that their union met with the approval of the gods. In the event, they did not have living children, and Dio alone preserves an alternative interpretation: that Livia was to hold the emperor's power in her lap and dominate him in everything, a reading that reputedly pleased Livia but alarmed others.[3]

Apart from this striking airborne phenomenon, Livia tends to remain in the background in the thirties, eclipsed by her sister-in-law Octavia, to whom Octavian remained completely devoted throughout her life.[4] She had married Gaius Claudius Marcellus (consul in 50) some time before 54 and produced a son (Marcus Claudius Marcellus) and two daughters (Claudia Marcella Minor and Maior) from the marriage. Her husband Marcellus died in 40. A period of ten months of mourning should have followed, but protocol fell victim to pressing state needs. She was now called upon to render an important service to her brother. Fulvia, the wife of Antony, had also just died (see chapter 7). Antony could hardly be called inconsolable, for in the previous year he had met Cleopatra and begun his torrid love affair. But he did not have a wife. A special measure of the Senate was passed to allow Octavia to bypass the statutory period of mourning and to marry Antony later that year.[5] This was an important political marriage, intended to bring closer together Rome's two most prominent public figures. There was a general feeling that Octavia would be a powerful force for harmony, and their first months together augured well. The couple spent the winter of 39–38 in Athens along with their newborn daughter, Antonia Maior. Their second daughter, the famous Antonia Minor, followed soon after.[6] To all appearances the marriage was initially a happy one.

For all his diplomatic talents, Octavian's political difficulties continued to mount, and his rivalry with Antony simply refused to go away. The two men were saved from a direct clash only by the efforts in 37 BC of Octavia, a *chrema thaumaston gunaikos* (wonder of a woman), as she was called on the occasion (the phrase is almost certainly Octavian's). She prevailed on her brother and husband to agree to the Treaty of Tarentum, which extended the triumvirate for five years.[7] A further promising development came when Marcus Agrippa finally broke Sextus Pompeius' power at the Battle of Naulochus in September 36. (Sextus escaped to Asia Minor, where he was put to death by one of Antony's officers.) The news of Naulochus apparently reached Rome by divine agency, when a member of the praetorian guard had a sudden vision and proceeded to lay his sword at the feet of Capitoline Jupiter to signify that he had no further use for it. The public reaction was ecstatic and brought Livia briefly into the record once again, for among the honours voted was the right of Octavian and Livia and their children to hold a banquet in the Capitoline temple on the anniversary of the battle, and to celebrate a day of thanksgiving.[8]

Antony repaid his debt to Octavia with the same sensibility he had shown his previous wife, Fulvia. He returned with her to the East, but on reaching Corcyra despatched her to Italy, on the specious ground that he did not want to expose her to danger when he went on his campaign against the Parthians. The real reason, it was widely believed, was that he wanted her out of the way to clear the field for his affair with Cleopatra. He made no secret of this infatuation, and in 36 he acknowledged paternity of three of their children. In 35 he instructed Octavia (by letter) to return to Rome.[9] She did so but remained a model wife, staying in Antony's house and begging Octavian not to go to war for her sake. She continued to look after Antony's children, and presented herself as his wife until 32, when Antony formally divorced her and sent representatives to Rome to throw her out of his house, after which she chose to live in secluded retirement. Without the steadying influence of Octavia, the propaganda war between Octavian and Antony resumed its full vigour, catching Livia in its net. There were stories of dubious reliability circulating in Rome, always the best kind to besmirch a rival, and Octavian was happy to make use of them—lurid tales of Antony anointing Cleopatra's feet at a banquet, of leaving the platform while a distinguished orator was in midspeech to join Cleopatra at her litter, even of him reading her love letters while adjudicating legal disputes. Antony's defence was attack. One of his retorts, dating to about 33, came in a letter to Octavian, preserved by Suetonius. The text is difficult, and it is paraphrased here to convey Antony's meaning: "What has changed you? That I'm into the queen? Is she my wife? [No, but so what?] And have I just started or haven't I been doing it for nine years? And anyhow, is [Livia] Drusilla the only one you're into?" Antony's attack is not directed against Livia, of course, but by implication it might be seen as a verbal assault on her.[10]

It is against this background of vicious rivalry between Octavian and Antony that we should place a remarkable measure recorded by Dio in 35 BC. In that year, the historian tells us, Octavian returned to Rome from his campaigns in Illyria and was granted a triumph (deferred until 29). In addition he granted Livia and Octavia a form of protection against verbal insult similar to that of the tribunes, along with two other privileges, namely statues erected in their honour and the right to administer their own estates without a guardian. The constitutional significance of these honours is discussed in chapter 7. They are probably best seen in their historical context, as a response to the relentless indignities heaped on Octavia by her husband, rather than as a general measure designed to enhance Livia's status. Plutarch seems to have had a good insight into the workings of Octavian's mind in the period. He says that when Octavia sought permission from Octavian to join Antony in 35, he granted it, to give him a reasonable pretext for war if Antony resumed his old abusive ways. Antony could almost be guaranteed to perform on cue, and when Octavia was sent back from Athens to Rome that year, her public humiliation was palpable. Octavian could now move to denounce his opponent both in the Senate and before the people, contrasting his sister's noble conduct with Antony's scurrilous behaviour. Thus it was almost certainly Octavia rather than Livia who was at the top of Octavian's agenda in 35 when the special privileges were granted — and it is surely significant that in describing them Dio puts her name first.[11] Not that the protection of Livia would be without political value. Octavian knew that he was vulnerable through attacks on his wife — the insolent comments about his marriage were a prime example of this. But the primary reason for the addition of her name may well have been simply to create the fiction that Octavian was keeping the position of the triumvirs' wives equal.

Little specific information on Livia emerges during the next decade. Her first husband died in 33 or 32 without making any further political progress, placing his sons, Tiberius and Drusus, under Octavian's protection on his death.[12] At this early stage Octavian showed a willingness to bring the two lads within the dynastic scheme that he already seems to have been evolving, and he thus inadvertently inaugurated the process that ultimately led to Tiberius' succeeding him as emperor. Some time before March 32, Tiberius, aged ten, was betrothed to Vipsania. She was the barely-one-year-old daughter of Marcus Agrippa, Octavian's closest colleague and his commander at Naulochus, and Pomponia, whose father was Cicero's friend, the equestrian Atticus. Syme, who subscribes heavily to the principle of female intrigue, believes that the match was contrived by Livia, to bind the great general closer to her and to Octavian. Perhaps, but there is simply no evidence. This is not to suggest that Livia was above scheming, but Agrippa in fact probably had more to gain from the union, as Velleius observes. He was a novus homo, and through the link could anticipate grandchildren who would belong to the Claudian gens. If female machinations are to be sought, they might more likely be detected in what could be seen as Octavia's countermeasure, when Agrippa, after divorcing Pomponia, married Octavia's daughter Marcella, in 28 BC. It would not have escaped Octavia's attention that if her brother had started to visualise the principate now, and as part of that vision saw succession from within his own line, then his daughter, Julia, would clearly be called upon to play a key role. The marriage of Marcus Agrippa and Marcella would in a sense remove a potential rival and clear the way for a union between Julia and Octavia's son Marcellus, which Livia might resent but could do little to prevent. Of course, it has to be stressed that all these family arrangements were made before Octavian's first settlement, and we must be alert to the danger of anachronistic thinking in introducing dynastic considerations prematurely.[13]

The rivalry between Octavian and Antony reached its climax in the naval battle at Actium on September 31. The surrender of Antony's fleet to Marcus Agrippa was followed by the suicides of Antony and Cleopatra. If we are to believe Dio's account, Livia played a role, albeit a minor and indirect one, in the immediate wake of the battle. Cleopatra, who had fallen into Octavian's hands, was convinced that he planned to take her back to Rome to be the chief spectacle in his triumph. She begged him to allow her to take her own life rather than face the humiliation. Cleopatra could not budge him and tried another tack. To put him off his guard, she pretended a change of heart and claimed that she was willing to sail to Rome. Her plan seems to have been a highly convoluted one, to create the impression that she was really hoping that he would relent, or that Livia would intercede for her. This expectation does not imply any special power or influence on Livia's part. Even if the anecdote is true in its details (and it does seem to involve a reading of Cleopatra's mind), the Egyptian queen did not actually expect Livia to intervene. The story is given a slightly different and more colourful twist by Plutarch. In his version, Cleopatra hid away some of her jewellery and gave a false accounting to Octavian. The discrepancy was pointed out by one of her stewards, Seleucus. Cleopatra had to be physically restrained from thrashing poor Seleucus and adroitly made a virtue out of necessity, saying that she had put some things aside not for herself but for Octavia and Livia, hoping through them to per-suade Octavian to take a more gentle line. By this ingenious argument she supposedly convinced Octavian that she had given up any thoughts of suicide. Thus Plutarch and Dio seem to be in agreement that any faith that Cleopatra professed in Livia's assistance was nothing but a front, and indeed, she did shortly after take her own life. To the limited extent that this rather dubious anecdote might provide evidence for female power, Plutarch's version shows that in the eyes of the sources the putative influence was shared between Livia and Octavia. Of course, it could be argued that Cleopatra at the very least recognised that the notion of intervention from female members of the imperial family was not unfeasible. But there would be nothing remarkable in that. There were ample precedents for such intercessions in the republic, not least in Octavia's activities on behalf of Antony.[14]

In January, 27 BC, the history of the Roman world was transformed, and it is then that, by convention, the Roman republic is deemed to have ended and the empire to have begun. In that month Octavian handed over to the Senate the extraordinary powers that he had accumulated. They in return granted him a single large "province," embracing at its core Syria, most of Spain, and the Gallic provinces, for a ten-year period, open to renewal. He was granted other powers, nominally from the Senate and the Roman people, and received a new title, Augustus, which would be handed down to his successors. Augustus (as he is now called) had enough faith in his settlement and in the security of his own position to leave Rome later in the year for an extended absence, to settle matters in Gaul and Spain. This marked the beginning of a regimen, maintained for fifteen years, of spending extended periods in the provinces for three years, alternating the visits with two-year stays in Rome. Did Livia accompany him on these journeys? During the republic the traditional role of the governor's wife had been to see her husband off, look to his interests in his absence, and welcome him back on his return. This was not, however, a universal practice, and in the imperial period it became common for wives, along with the children, to go to the provinces when their husbands assumed the role of administrator, even when this meant that they might be in the vicinity of military action. Octavia, who had accompanied Antony to the East, provided an obvious precedent. The practice would be called into question during the next reign, after a number of highly publicised incidents centred around the conduct of governors' wives, which convinced many Romans that the presence of women was dangerous because it allowed them undue interference in matters of state.[15]

Livia on occasion certainly did venture outside Rome with Augustus. This is revealed in a senatorial debate that took place several decades later. When in AD 21 an unsuccessful attempt was made to force the wives of governors to stay at home, Drusus Caesar, son of Tiberius, spoke against the motion and cited Livia as a precedent, noting that she had gone with Augustus as a companion both to the West and to the East (*in occidentem atque orientem*). Drusus, like any good politician, was using his material selectively, for Augustus was actually on record as believing that the legates of the imperial provinces should not spend time with their wives, and that if they did, it should be between campaigning seasons. That said, it is a fair assumption that he could not simply have made up this claim about a public figure with the high profile of Livia, still alive at the time of the speech. There must have been a basic truth in his assertion.[16] The sources record only two specific instances of Livia and Augustus having taken a journey together: when they went to Ticinum to receive the body of Livia's son Drusus in 9 BC, and when they took their last journey together to Campania in AD 14, just before Augustus' death. Neither of these trips took them outside Italy, and neither would qualify as one of the journeys "to the East and to the West." Clearly Livia must have journeyed with her husband on occasions not recorded in the literature. The trip that Augustus made in 27–24 BC to Gaul and Spain would be a good candidate. It is true that when he returned to Rome in 24, Livia and Octavia took part in the sacrificial ritual that celebrated the homecoming, but this would not preclude her having been with him. Certainly while in Spain he fell seriously ill and retired to Tarraco, where he spent some time recuperating. It is hard to believe that Livia would not have been at his side when his life was at serious risk. We face the recurring problem that in this period she seems to have been deliberately self-effacing, and successful in that effort. The silence of the sources about her possible presence in Spain need not be especially significant or surprising.[17]

After the settlement of 27 BC the issue of the succession dominated political thought for the remainder of Augustus' life. The position of the princeps was unprecedented, despite its veneer of republican respectability, and there was no theoretical mechanism by which his authority could be passed to a successor. To ease the process the princeps adopted the practice of associating his intended successors with him as partners in the chief powers of the principate, his proconsular power and the symbolically important tribunician *potestas*, the traditional authority of the plebeian tribunes. But by restoring openly what was in essence a monarchical principle, Augustus was bound to cause general offence, and particular offence to the old once-powerful families. Moreover, Livia bore no surviving children to him, a fact that was to have far-reaching impact on Rome's political history. The designation of an adopted, not natural, son, which probably made the policy somewhat easier for those same old families to accept, would conversely cause tensions within his own family. Only a natural son could be the undisputed successor, and family members excluded in the process of adoption would inevitably bear a grudge. This made the succession such a sensitive political issue, one that called on all of Augustus' tact and political acumen.

As early as in the immediate aftermath of Actium, Augustus seems to have given serious attention to the career of his nephew Marcus Claudius Marcellus, son of his sister Octavia, and by 25 BC he had decided on the betrothal of Marcellus, then seventeen, to his fourteen-year-old daughter, Julia. Marcellus'

career was now promoted. What thoughts Livia had about these developments are not recorded, and in any case it is unlikely that she would have risked
open opposition to Augustus, who was scrupulously careful to advance her son
Tiberius also, although essentially as second string to Marcellus. In the event,
when Augustus fell seriously ill in 23, he passed his authority on not to Marcellus, who probably was felt to lack the necessary judgement and maturity,
but to his old comrade-in-arms Marcus Agrippa.[18]

Augustus was restored by his physician Antonius Musa, relying on a strict
regimen of cold baths, and could look forward to many more years of active
life. Agrippa would have been aware that his promotion at the time of the
illness was no more than a stopgap. In an unhappy mood he departed for the
East, established his headquarters in Lesbos, and from there governed Syria
through legates. The problem resolved itself of its own accord. In the autumn
of 23 Marcellus took ill, probably a victim of the same plague that had threatened Augustus' life. Despite the best efforts of Antonius Musa, he did not
recover, and died in his twentieth year. This was the first major death for the
imperial family and was treated in a style that later became familiar. After a
grand funeral Marcellus was given a place in the mausoleum that Augustus was
still in the process of constructing, where more than half a century later Livia
herself would rest.

At this point Dio introduces a charge that she resorted to murder to clear
the way for her own sons, bringing about the death of Marcellus because
Augustus had openly given him priority. This is the kind of charge that routinely was made against Livia, often in contexts that make the allegation absurd. It is also the kind of charge that is impossible to refute. But it is worth
noting that although Dio raises the issue, he is himself sceptical about the
claim and notes that previous (unnamed) sources also were in disagreement
over it. He also points out that in that year and the following one, Rome was
suffering from plagues which took many lives.[19] In the very unlikely event that
Livia was party to the death of Marcellus, it would have to be said that she
made a serious miscalculation. Her sons garnered no political advantage from
the death. Marcus Agrippa was the one to gain.

In September of the following year, 22 BC, Augustus set out on an extended
tour of the eastern provinces, after summoning Agrippa back to take charge in
Rome.[20] This eastern trip kept him away for three years, and on this occasion
we can feel all but certain that he was accompanied by Livia.[21] We have the
comment of her grandson Drusus about her visit to the East, and this was the
only eastern trip that Augustus took after Actium. Moreover, there is the

evidence of the special privileges granted during the journey both to Sparta and Samos, communities which particularly enjoyed Livia's favour. The couple went first to Sicily, where Augustus gave colonial status to Syracuse and various other cities and waited until the recall of Agrippa to Rome could be arranged. They seem to have spent the winter there. In the spring they proceeded to Greece. Augustus showed his regard for Sparta by awarding the city the island of Cythera, and he attended a banquet to mark the hospitality accorded to Livia some years earlier when she had passed through with her son and first husband.[22] Athens did not fare so well and was perhaps given a hint of the problems to come when the cult statue of Athena on the Acropolis turned 180 degrees and spat blood. The city lost Aegina and Eretria, supposedly, as some believed, because of Athenian support for Antony. It may have been in an attempt to try to win back the imperial favour that the Athenians at some point voted divine honours to Livia and to Julia.[23] It is also very likely that on this trip Livia visited the famous sanctuary at Delphi. While there she made a generous dedication, in the form of the letter epsilon inscribed in gold. (The exact significance of the letter is somewhat obscure.) Visitors to the site were later told that the inscription was the Epsilon of Livia; a less impressive version, in more modest bronze, was known as the Epsilon of the Athenians.[24]

The couple then passed over to Samos, and there they spent the winter of 21–20. Augustus had spent the winters after Actium there.[25] He had another good reason for choosing the island on this later occasion. The Samians had special ties with Livia, and her family had for long been their patrons (see chapter 10). In recognition of their steadfast loyalty, Augustus restored the colossal statues of Athena and Heracles, which Antony had removed to give to Cleopatra, to their rightful places in the famous Temple of Hera on the island.[26]

The following spring the imperial party were in Asia Minor. Apart from the cities attested in the record, there are others, like Pergamum and Ilium, where Augustus at some stage erected monuments and received honours, probably during this trip. He settled affairs in Bithynia, where Cyzicus lost its freedom because of a dispute in which some Romans had been put to death. They then travelled on to Syria, where Tyre and Sidon lost their freedom on the same grounds. It is likely that while Livia was in Syria, Salome and her brother Herod the Great came from Judaea to greet her, to mark the first stage in what would be a long and warm friendship (see chapter 10).[27] All in all, the year was a great success, crowned by two special achievements. Livia's son Tiberius was able to achieve a diplomatic coup by installing a pro-Roman figure on the throne of Armenia. More significantly, Augustus came to an agreement with

Rome's traditional enemy Parthia, and in a gesture heavy with symbolism succeeded in retrieving the standards lost to the Parthians at the disastrous battle of Carrhae in 53 BC.

In the winter of 20–19 the couple returned to spend the second winter in Samos.[28] On this occasion Augustus finally yielded to Livia's pleas to grant freedom to the island, a request he had previously declined. They were visited in Samos by embassies from far and wide, from the queen of Ethiopia and even from India, which sent gifts of tigers (which the Romans had not seen before), as well as a man born without arms (whom Strabo saw personally), huge snakes, a giant tortoise, and a partridge as large as a vulture.[29] Livia and Augustus seem to have remained on the island until as late as July of 19, at which point they began their return trip to Rome. They went first to Athens. A member of the Indian entourage named Zarmarus entertained the royal couple after he had been initiated into the rites of the mystery religion, presumably in nearby Eleusis. His initiation would have guaranteed him a happy afterlife, and he was clearly impatient to enjoy it. Wearing only a loincloth, he hurled himself into the fire. Augustus may well have been involved in the rites himself during this visit, already being an initiate. It has even been suggested that Livia might have used the opportunity to become initiated herself, an otherwise newsworthy event that might have been eclipsed by Zarmarus' fiery exit.[30] The poet Vergil met them in Athens. The celebrated author of the *Aeneid*, the great nationalistic paean to Augustus' achievements, was planning his own grand tour but was persuaded to return to Rome with the imperial party. He did not make it. He fell ill in Megara, and when the company finally reached Italy in September, he died, on the twentieth of the month, in Brundisium.[31] As Augustus and Livia travelled overland to Rome, one of the consuls, as well as leading senators, came out to meet them in Campania. The gesture was no doubt meant kindly but was not to the princeps' liking, and they managed to evade the deputation and eventually to enter Rome by night.[32]

While on his travels Augustus would have continued to be preoccupied with the old issue of what would happen after his death. He had clearly demonstrated at the time of his departure that he could not manage without Marcus Agrippa, married at the time to Marcella, Octavia's daughter. Agrippa now divorced her (her compensation was to be married to Iullus Antonius, the son of Antony and Fulvia), so as to be free in 21 to marry the widowed Julia. Plutarch says that this marriage came about through Octavia's machinations and that she prevailed upon Augustus to accept the idea. It is not clear what her motives would have been. If we are to believe Seneca we might see pure spite. He claimed that Octavia hated Livia after the death of Marcellus because the hopes of the imperial house passed now to Livia's sons. This could well be no more than speculation, and Seneca does not even hint at any specific action by Octavia against her supposed rival. The whole story sounds typically Senecan in its denigration of dead individuals who are easy targets. Once again, we are told nothing about Livia's reaction to the marriage. She might not have been able to object to the earlier marriage between Julia and Augustus' nephew Marcellus, but in 21 the situation was different. Her older son, Tiberius, who was not yet married, had been passed over in favour of an outsider to the family. But whatever his sense of obligation to his wife, Augustus probably felt that he had little choice in the matter. Agrippa's earlier reaction to having to take second place to Marcellus, a blood relative of Augustus, would have provided a good hint to Augustus of how his friend would have taken to playing second string to Tiberius. Agrippa was now a key figure in the governing of Rome. He was not a man to be provoked.[33]

If Livia had been entertaining hopes that this early stage of a preeminent role for either of her sons (and such a suggestion, while reasonable, is totally speculative), such hopes would have faded with the birth of two sons to Julia and Agrippa. Gaius Caesar was born in 20 BC, and, as if to confirm the line, a second son, Lucius Caesar, arrived in 17. Augustus was delighted, and soon after Lucius' birth signalled his ultimate intentions by adopting both boys. He thus might envisage himself as being "succeeded" by Agrippa, who would in turn be succeeded by either Gaius and Lucius, who were, in a sense, sons of both men. In late 16 BC Augustus set out on an extended trip to Gaul and Spain, where he established a number of veteran settlements. Livia may have accompanied him. Dio does report speculation that the emperor went away so as to be able to conduct his affair with Terentia, the wife of his close confidant Maecenas, in a place where it would not attract gossip. Even if the rumours were well founded, the implication need not necessarily follow that he had left Livia behind. Livia had a reputation as a *femme complaisante*, and Augustus may simply have wanted to get away from the prying eyes of the capital. Certainly at one stage Livia intervened with Augustus to argue for the grant of citizenship to a Gaul, and this trip provides the best context. Moreover, Seneca dates a famous incident to this trip, Livia's plea on behalf of the accused Gaius Cornelius Cinna. It could well be that Seneca misdated the Cinna episode, but he at any rate clearly believed that Livia had been in Gaul with her husband at the relevant time.[34] (These issues are treated in greater detail in chapter 7.)

Agrippa lived to see the birth of two other children, his daughters Julia and Agrippina. The first (born about 19 BC) is the namesake of her mother, and, in the historical tradition, cut from the same cloth; the second was to be somewhat eclipsed in the same tradition by her own daughter and namesake, the mother of the last Julio-Claudian emperor, Nero. Agrippa thus became the natural father of four of Augustus' grandchildren during his lifetime (a fifth would be born posthumously), and his stock rose higher with each event. He had served his princeps well, and could now take his final exit. In 13 he campaigned in the Balkans. At the end of the season he returned to Italy, where he fell ill, and in mid-March, 12 BC, he died. His body was brought to Rome, where it was given a magnificent burial, and the remains were deposited in the Mausoleum of Augustus, even though Agrippa had earlier booked himself another site in the Campus Martius.[35]

In the following year Octavia died. She is celebrated by the sources as a paragon of every human virtue, whose only possible failings had been the forgivable ones of excessive loyalty to an undeserving husband and excessive grief over the death of a possibly only marginally more deserving son.[36] As noted earlier, we should be cautious about Seneca's claim that Octavia nursed a hatred for Livia after the death of Marcellus. But there can be no doubt that her death was in a sense advantageous to Livia, for it removed one of the main contenders for the role of the premier woman in the state. Only Augustus' daughter Julia might now lay claim to a precedence of sorts, but she in fact became an agent in furthering Livia's ambitions, rather than an obstacle. Once her formal period of mourning was over, Julia would need another husband. Suetonius says that her father carefully considered several options, even from among the equestrians. Tiberius later claimed that Augustus pondered the idea of marrying her off to a political nonentity, someone noted for leading a retiring life and not involved in a political career. Among others he supposedly considered Gaius Proculeius, a close friend of the emperor and best known for the manner of his death rather than of his life: he committed suicide by what must have been a painful technique — swallowing gypsum. This drastic action was apparently not in response to the prospect of marriage to Julia but in despair over the unbearable pains in his stomach. In 11 BC, the year of Octavia's death, Augustus made his decision. He could hardly pass over one of Livia's sons again. They were the only real choices, given the practical options open to him. Both were married, and Drusus' wife was the daughter of Octavia, someone able already to produce offspring linked, at least indirectly, by blood to the princeps. Divorce in this case would not have been desirable. Augustus had already demonstrated his faith in Livia's other son, Tiberius, by appointing him to replace Agrippa in the Balkans. He was the inevitable candidate for Julia's next husband.

In perhaps 20 or 19 Tiberius had married Agrippa's daughter Vipsania, to whom he had long been betrothed. Their son Drusus was born in perhaps 14.[37] In 11 Vipsania was pregnant for a second time, but Tiberius was obliged to divorce her, although he seems to have been genuinely attached to her. Reputedly when they met after the divorce he followed her with such a forlorn and tearful gaze that precautions were taken that their paths would never cross again. He was now free to marry Julia. This marriage marks a milestone in Tiberius' career and in the ambitions that Livia would naturally have nursed for her son. Augustus was clearly prepared to place him in an advantageous position, and the process could be revoked only with difficulty.[38] It is inevitable that there should be speculation among modern scholars that Livia might have played a role in arranging the marriage. Gardthausen claimed that she brought it off in the teeth of vigorous opposition. Perhaps, but the suggestion belongs totally to the realm of speculation. If Livia did play some part in winning over Augustus, she did it so skilfully and unobtrusively that she has left no traces, and the sources are silent about any specific interference on this occasion. Nor can it be assumed that Augustus would have needed a great deal of persuading. No serious store should be placed in the claims in the sources that he held Tiberius in general contempt and was reduced to turning to him *faut de mieux*. Suetonius quotes passages from Augustus' correspondence that provide concrete evidence that the emperor in fact held his adopted son in high regard. Suetonius chose the extracts to show his appreciation of Tiberius' military and administrative skills, but his words clearly suggest a high degree of affection that seems to go beyond the merely formulaic. He addresses Tiberius as *iucundissime*, probably the equivalent in modern correspondence of "my very dear Tiberius." He reveals that when he has a challenging problem or is feeling particularly annoyed at something, he yearns for his Tiberius *(Tiberium meum desidero)*, and he notes that both he and Livia are tortured by the thought that her son might be overtaxing himself.[39]

Livia's other son, Drusus, although arguably his brother's match in military reputation and ability, seems to have been quite different from him in temperament. Where Tiberius was private, inhibited, uninterested in courting popularity, Drusus was affable, engaging, and well-liked, and there was a popular belief, probably naive, that he was committed to an eventual restoration of the republic. He had found a perfectly compatible wife in Antonia the Younger, a woman who commanded universal esteem and respect to the very end. They produced two sons, both of whom would loom large on the stage of human events: Germanicus, who became the most loved man in the Roman empire and whose early death threatened to erode Livia's popularity, and Claudius, whose physical limitations were an embarrassment to Livia and to other members of the imperial family, but who confounded them all by becoming an emperor of considerable acumen and ability. They also had a daughter, Livilla, who attained disrepute through her affair with the most loathed man in the early Roman empire, the notorious praetorian prefect Sejanus.[40]

Drusus dominated the landscape in 9 BC. The year seemed to start auspiciously for Livia. In 13 BC the Senate had voted to consecrate the Ara Pacis, one of the great monuments of Augustus' regime, as a memorial to his safe return from Spain and the pacification of Gaul. The dedication waited four years and finally took place in 9, on January 30, Livia's birthday, perhaps her fiftieth (figs. 20, 21). The honour was a profound one, but indirect and thus low-key, in keeping with Livia's public persona.[41] Her sons continued to achieve distinction on the battlefield. A decorated sword sheath of provincial workmanship has survived from this period. It represents a frontal Livia with the nodus hairstyle (see chapter 6), and shoulder locks carefully designed so as to flow along her shoulders above the drapery. She appears between two heads, almost certainly her sons, and the piece pictorially symbolises Livia at what must have been one of the most satisfying periods of her life.[42] To cap her sense of well-being, Tiberius, after signal victories over the Dalmatians and Pannonians, returned to Rome to celebrate an ovation. Following the usual practice after a triumph or ovation, a dinner was given for the Senate in the Capitoline temple, and tables were set out for the people in front of private houses. A separate banquet was arranged for the women. Its sponsors were Livia and Julia. Private tensions may already have arisen between Tiberius and Julia, but at least at the public level they were sedulously maintaining an outward image of marital harmony, and Livia was making her own contribution towards promoting that image.[43]

Similar festivities were planned to celebrate Drusus' victories. Presumably in his case Livia would have joined Antonia, Drusus' wife, in preparing the banquet, as she had joined Tiberius' wife on the earlier occasion. While Tiberius had been engaged in operations in Pannonia, Drusus had conducted a highly acclaimed campaign in Germany. By 9 BC he had succeeded in taking Roman arms as far as the river Elbe. So awesome were his achievements that greater powers felt the need to intervene. He was visited by the apparition of a giant barbarian woman, who told him — she conveniently spoke Latin — not to push his successes further. Something was clearly amiss in the divine timing. Suetonius implies that Drusus heeded the warning, but calamity befell him anyhow. In a riding accident Drusus' horse toppled over onto him and broke his thigh. He fell gravely ill. His deteriorating condition caused consternation throughout the Roman world, and it is even claimed that the enemy respected him so much that they declared a truce pending his recovery. (Similar claims were later made about his son Germanicus.) Tiberius had been campaigning in the Balkans at the time but had returned to Italy and was passing through Ticinum after the campaign when he heard that Drusus was sinking fast. Travelling the 290 km in a day and a night, a rate that Pliny thought impressive enough to record, he rushed to be with his brother. He reached him just before he died in September, 9 BC.

Drusus was universally liked, and his death at the age of twenty-nine could not seriously be seen as benefitting anyone. Nevertheless, it still managed to attract gossip and rumours. The death of a young prince of the imperial house would usually drag in the name of Livia as the prime suspect. In this instance such a scenario would have been totally implausible, and Augustus became the target of the innuendo instead. Tacitus reports that the tragedy evoked the same jaundiced reactions as would that of Germanicus, three decades later in the reign of Tiberius, that sons with "democratic" temperaments — *civilia ingenia* — did not please ruling fathers (Germanicus had been adopted by Tiberius). Suetonius has preserved a tradition that Augustus, suspecting Drusus of republicanism, recalled him from his province and, when he declined to obey, had him poisoned. Suetonius thought the suggestion nonsensical, and he is surely correct. Augustus had shown great affection for the young man and in the Senate had named him joint heir with Gaius and Lucius. He also delivered a warm eulogy after his death. Even Tiberius' grief was portrayed as two-faced. To illustrate Tiberius' hatred for the members of his own family, Suetonius claims that he had earlier produced a letter in which his younger brother discussed with him the possibility of compelling Augustus to restore the republic. But events seem to belie completely the notion of any serious fraternal strife. Tiberius' anguish was clearly genuine. His general deportment is of special interest, because of the light that it might throw on his and Livia's conduct later, at the funeral of Germanicus. According to Seneca, the troops were deeply distressed over the death and demanded Drusus' body. Tiberius maintained that discipline had to be observed in grieving as well as fighting, and that the funeral was to be conducted with the dignity demanded by the Roman tradition. He repressed his own tears and was able to dampen the enthusiasm for a vulgar show of public grief.[44]

Tiberius now set out with the body for Rome. Augustus went to Ticinum (Pavia) to meet the cortege, and because Seneca says that Livia accompanied the procession to Rome, it is probably safe to assume that she went with her husband. As she travelled, she was struck by the pyres that burned throughout the country and the crowds that came out to escort the funeral train. The event provides one of the few glimpses of Livia's private emotions. She was crushed by the death and sought comfort from the philosopher Areus (see chapter 6). On his advice, she uncharacteristically opened herself up to others. She put pictures of Drusus in public and private places and encouraged her acquaintances to talk about him. But she maintained a respectable level of grief, which elicited the admiration of Seneca. Tiberius may well have learned from his mother the appropriateness of self-restraint in the face of private anguish. It was an attitude that was later to arouse considerable resentment against both of them.[45]

During the funeral in Rome, Tiberius delivered a eulogy in the Forum and Augustus another in the Circus Maximus, where the emperor expressed the hope that Gaius and Lucius would emulate Drusus. The body was taken to the Campus Martius for cremation by the equestrians, and the funeral bier was surrounded by images of the Julian and the Claudian families. The ashes were deposited in Augustus' mausoleum. The title of Germanicus was post-humously bestowed on Drusus and his descendants, and he was given the further honour of statues, an arch, and a cenotaph on the banks of the Rhine. Augustus composed the verses that appeared on his tomb and also wrote a prose account of his life. No doubt less distinguished Romans, of varied liter-ary talent, would have written their own contributions. The anonymous *Con-solatio ad Liviam* represents itself as just such a composition, intended to offer comfort to Livia on this very occasion, although it was probably composed somewhat later (see appendix 1). Livia was indeed devastated, but as some form of compensation for her terrible private loss, she now, after some thirty years in the shadows, came into greater public prominence. The final chapter of Drusus' life seems to have opened up a new one in his mother's.[46]

THE PUBLIC FIGURE

The generous tribute that Augustus paid to Drusus at his funeral involved more than empty words strung together for the occasion. The emperor was genuinely attached to his stepson and earlier had publicly stated that Drusus was to be his joint heir. The fact that the funeral procession was accompanied by images of both Claudians and Julians was remarkable, for Drusus had never been adopted by Augustus. There are later parallels of a sort for the arrangement. Augustus' own funeral procession was accompanied by effigies of his own ancestors and of prominent Romans since the time of Romulus. Moreover, when the venerable Junia, half-sister of Cato Uticensis and mother of Marcus Brutus, the conspirator, died in AD 22, in her nineties, the effigies of twenty great families preceded her to her tomb.[1] But the very act of limiting the families to two in Drusus' case effectively made the honour both to him and, indirectly, to Livia all the greater, because it gave the Julian connection a special prominence. It might be seen as foreshadowing the even closer link that was to be established when Livia was adopted into the Julian line in Augustus' will.

For Livia the loss of her son would have been more a personal blow than an issue of state. She sought aid and guidance from the philosopher Areus and eventually came to terms with the death (see chapter 6). But while a mother's sense of bereavement is essentially a private matter, Drusus' death was at the same time considered a *public* sacrifice, and it brought her public recognition. To console Livia in her bereavement, the Senate voted statues for her, and she was granted the *ius trium liberorum*, the exemption from legal disabilities imposed on those who had borne fewer than three children (see chapter 7). We have no information about how many statues were commissioned, and it is to be acknowledged that no statue base has survived from the Augustan period recognizing her as the mother of Drusus, information that surely would have accompanied the statues voted in 9 BC. Moreover, the significance of the ius trium liberorum should probably not be given undue weight in her case. One of the main advantages it conferred, the right to handle property without a guardian, had already been granted her in 35. Dio notes that the Senate (and in his own day, the emperor) had the right to bestow this privilege on those whose failure to bear three children was involuntary. That principle would have applied in Livia's case. She had in fact given birth three times, but the child she shared with Augustus was premature and stillborn and thus did not legally qualify.[2] That said, it is noteworthy that both honours came in the same year as the dedication of the Ara Pacis, on her birthday. In addition, it is very possible that the decision to build a portico in her honour was taken in this same year. Up to this point Livia's role had been preeminently that of the dutiful wife. The events of 9 BC, as Flory has noted, mark her emergence into a much more public role.[3]

Now that Drusus was dead, Livia's maternal pride and hopes would have focussed entirely on her surviving son, Tiberius. He did not let her down. In the year following his brother's death, 8 BC, he took Drusus' place in command of the Rhine armies, joined by Augustus and by Gaius Caesar, who was introduced at this time to military service. Tiberius crossed the Rhine (Augustus stayed on the western side) and conducted a number of successful campaigns. He began to enjoy the marks of true recognition: an imperial salutation and a triumph (for the first time a full one), as well as a second consulship, to be held in 7 BC. The victorious Tiberius returned to Rome to assume his office and pledged himself to use the spoils of his campaigns for a worthy project. He would repair the Temple of Concord on the northwest side of the Forum in his own name and in that of his brother Drusus. Tiberius finally dedicated the restored building on January 16, AD 10. Having discharged this solemn responsibility, he went on to celebrate his triumph.[4]

Rome would have had a further reminder of Livia's special role as mother when she was joined by Tiberius in dedicating the great monument that bears her name, the Porticus Liviae (plan 3; see chapter 10). The dedication brought mother and son together in the first collaborative activity mentioned by the sources. Although this association with her son's recent achievements could have brought Livia nothing but pride and pleasure, we should not read too much into their joint role in the dedication. Augustus at this point was yet again in Gaul, and Tiberius had the task of deputizing for him at important events. The exact date is not known for certain, but Dio's narrative suggests very strongly that it took place in January, 7 BC. The seventeenth of the month, the anniversary of the wedding of Livia and Augustus, is a good candidate. After the dedication of the portico she gave a banquet to the women of the city, to match that given by Tiberius for the men. It is to be noted that two years earlier, on a similar occasion, Julia had joined Livia in giving a banquet. She was not involved in the present festivities. This may well be an early symptom of estrangement between Julia and Tiberius, but it could simply reflect the technicality that while Julia's presence on the earlier occasion as the wife of the victorious Tiberius was de rigueur, she had no proper part to play in a ceremony that belonged to Livia. Tiberius' duty was, after all, to represent Augustus in his role of princeps, not of father-in-law.[5] At some later date the portico received another component. Ovid in his *Fasti* records that on June 11 of an unspecified year Livia dedicated the *aedes* (shrine) to Concordia, to honour her husband (see appendix 8 and chapter 10). Flory draws attention to the different but parallel functions of the portico and the aedes that it housed. The Porticus Liviae was Augustus' work, though closely associated with Livia. The demolition of the luxury house whose site it occupied demonstrated his desire to restrain private luxury and promote public welfare in its place. The aedes was Livia's and stressed the idea of marital harmony, in a gesture in support of Augustus' marriage laws and his desire to revive family life, signalling that "the political unity of the state emanated from the domestic harmony of the imperial household." It can hardly be a coincidence that the dedication of the aedes occurs on the same day as the festivals of Matralia and Fortuna, both of which had their focus on the notion of marriage and women's lives.[6]

After his triumph and the dedication of the Temple of Concord and the Porticus Liviae, Tiberius returned to Germany, where he dealt with fresh disturbances with his usual competence and efficiency.[7] But the old problem of the succession now began to reassert itself. In 6 BC Augustus bestowed the tribunicia potestas on Tiberius for five years, but whatever self-confidence Livia's son might have derived from the grant would have been tempered by the situation of the princeps' adopted sons. Gaius was fourteen in 6 BC, Lucius eleven. Although it would almost certainly be an overstatement to say that the two boys were involved in some sort of political movement, their positions of privilege and luxury, not surprisingly, seem to have gone to their heads and turned them into insufferably arrogant youths. To make matters worse, their insolence was encouraged by hangers-on, eager to store up useful political credit. They may well have been egged on also by their mother, Julia, and she in her turn might have been encouraged by her own mother, Scribonia, still bearing a grudge against Livia. The situation grew worse when, in what seems like a fit of collective lunacy, the people elected Gaius to a consulship for the following year, an absurd gesture which would have installed a fourteen-year-old in an office that was steeped in ancient tradition and whose prestige Augustus was determined to maintain. The effort to promote Gaius' cause may well have been linked to demonstrations of popular support for Lucius when he turned up unattended at the theatre.[8] Although he might have been privately annoyed, Augustus certainly gave no overt signal that Gaius had behaved improperly. Gaius was granted a priesthood and the election was not really cancelled; it was merely postponed.[9]

At this stage a momentous event occurred in Tiberius' political career, one that must be classed as a blunder of epic proportions, mortifying both to Livia, who would naturally have been ambitious for her son, and to Augustus, who up to now had clearly seen him as someone who could potentially play a key role after his own death. Tiberius was offered an important commission in the East. He refused it and, astonishingly, sought permission to retire to the island of Rhodes, without his wife and with only a small retinue of close friends. The motives for this bizarre turn in Tiberius' thinking are unclear and are variously explained by the sources — antipathy towards Julia, a desire to leave the field clear for Gaius and Lucius, fear of Gaius and Lucius. The official reason given by Tiberius, according to Suetonius, was that he felt weary and simply needed a leave of absence. The truth behind Tiberius' action can probably not be recovered, and it may have come about through a complex combination of causes, some psychological, some political. Whatever Augustus' official intentions, Tiberius may well have harboured a sense, rightly or wrongly, that the emperor nurtured a deep-seated hope that it would be one of his adopted sons who would eventually succeed him, even though they had achieved little and were, if anything, showing every sign of being temperamentally unsuited for the task.

Tiberius' decision to leave Rome was a pivotal one, marking a turning point in his relations with Augustus and causing a breach that was to be healed only with the greatest difficulty and, apparently, with the repeated interventions of Livia. The emperor made no secret of his sense of betrayal and even declared openly in the Senate that he felt himself forsaken. In a desperate effort to demonstrate his loyalty, Tiberius opened his will and read it out to Livia and her husband. An imperial will could have political implications. Julius Caesar's did, because it contained Augustus' testamentary adoption. So did Tiberius' final will, invalidated after his death because it seemed to give Tiberius' grandson Gemellus a claim on the succession equal to Caligula's. Thus Tiberius might now have wanted to show that he harboured no feelings of resentment against Gaius and Lucius, and had named them as beneficiaries.[10]

The burden of trying to dissuade Tiberius from his foolhardy decision seems to have fallen on his mother. Livia begged him *(suppliciter)* to change his mind, but to no avail. His response was a petulant one — he went on a hunger strike for four days until he got his own way, an embarrassing stunt that can have done him no good in Augustus' eyes.[11] The blackmail worked, at least in the short term, and in this heavy atmosphere Tiberius made his exit. In Campania he was delayed by news that Augustus had fallen ill. The emperor had always been prone to nervous exhaustion, and his current ailment was probably aggravated by stress over recent events. When it was clear that he would survive, Tiberius continued his journey. On the way he sailed to the island of Paros, where he put pressure on the Parians to sell him the statue of Vesta, to be sent to Rome and placed in the Temple of Concord. He might have intended this as a pious gesture to Livia, often associated with Vesta. But he might also have wanted to convey a more overtly political message, a reminder to Livia not to fail her son. Once settled in Rhodes he moved into a quiet residence. He was based there for the next seven years, quietly attending the lectures of philosophers and debating with them, avoiding the attention of official visitors from Rome as much as possible.[12]

It was widely believed that at least a contributory factor in Tiberius' decision to get away from Rome was his antipathy towards his wife. It would be difficult to imagine a couple so ill-suited. Julia was a woman of considerable intelligence, with a good knowledge of literature and a love of well-informed and amusing company. But she was self-willed and held her own idiosyncratic views on what was socially acceptable. She outraged Augustus by her taste in friends and by her modish dress style. Augustus, who revered what were by his day considered old-fashioned traditions of morality and restraint, was out of touch with what proved to be a free-spirited daughter. He could not have helped the situation by persuading her to emulate the behaviour of Livia, and he scolded her about her acquaintances, her brazen language, her dress, even the fact that she was in the habit of removing grey hairs from her head. He tried unsuccessfully to keep her under a tight supervision and told the young men, even the most respectable, who visited her that they were not welcome in the emperor's home. Augustus' efforts to preserve his daughter's innocence were a failure, as they were bound to be. Julia had affairs from at least the time of her marriage to Agrippa — she is said to have advocated the safe interval offered by pregnancies, observing that she only "took on passengers when carrying freight." [?]

Tiberius and Julia seem to have got along harmoniously at first, but their personalities were so different that it was inevitable that they would drift apart. The death of their infant child seems to have broken the last tie, and any fondness turned to contempt.[13] Matters came to a climax in 2 BC, when the revelation of Julia's promiscuous behaviour shattered the serenity of the *domus Augusta*. Seneca provides the fullest account. He reports in lurid terms that Julia, who had a legion of lovers, took to wandering the streets of the city seeking excitement, even prostituting herself with total strangers in the Forum at the statue of Marsyas. As a consequence many of her lovers were exiled (one was executed), and Julia herself was despatched to the small island of Pandateria, off the coast of Campania. A bill of divorce from Tiberius was sent to her in Augustus' name.[14] She did not face destitution, at least at the outset. The island had an imperial villa, and there was even a small operation to grow grapes (infested with field mice). But she was reputedly refused every comfort, even wine, and no visitors were allowed to land without making preliminary and exhaustive arrangements. By her father's will she was excluded from his mausoleum after her death. She had one champion, her mother, Scribonia, who had not remarried after her divorce from Octavian and now declared herself willing to accompany her daughter. Julia never returned to Rome.[15]

The literary sources put much emphasis on the moral facets of Julia's conduct, and Tacitus is struck by the extreme punishment dispensed to her. But there is a widespread scholarly view that the charges of sexual misbehaviour against members of the Julio-Claudian family were little more than diversionary tactics, intended to cover significant political transgressions, and that claims of sexual misconduct could be used to bring down dangerous claimants or their partisans.[16] The question can legitimately be raised whether Livia had any role in the scandal, and there has long been a suspicion among scholars that she was behind Julia's fall. Syme sees her prompting a reluctant Augustus to action by reminding him that Julia's behaviour was running counter to the tone of the moral reforms. He speculates that it was Livia who persuaded Augustus to launch an investigation into his daughter's conduct. Julia's temperament was such that it may have been difficult for Augustus and Livia to teach her by strict precept and example, and the tense situation that inevitably followed could have bred a certain resentment towards her stepmother. Perhaps, but we have no evidence of any serious political rift between the two women. Admittedly, it would not have helped that Livia was in a sense everything that Julia was not. Macrobius relates that Augustus confronted Julia with the wild behaviour of her friends and contrasted it with Livia's decorous conduct in public — but while such reprimands might well have irritated his daughter, they would hardly have provoked deep enmity between her and his wife. Julia's disgrace, following the earlier death of Octavia, did leave Livia in a unique position of power and prestige within the court, because there was now no female member of the imperial family to challenge her preeminent position. But if Livia's motive was to help Tiberius, it is difficult to see how she would have done so by engineering Julia's ruin. It could be argued that it was very much against Tiberius' interests for his wife to be brought down — she was Tiberius' link with the centre of power, as he doubtless realised when he wrote to Augustus from Rhodes and asked him to pardon her. The literary sources provide no information or even speculation on Livia's reaction to Julia's disgrace. This is an argument ex silentio, of course, but given the propensity of Tacitus in particular to tar Livia with every conceivable suspicion of malicious interference, even when the charge was absurd, the absence on this occasion of even a hint of her involvement in the scandal may well be significant.[17]

Inscriptional evidence, in fact, shows that Livia might have helped Julia when she went into exile, or at least at the stage when in AD 4 she was allowed to move from Pandateria to Rhegium, on the mainland. Such assistance would be in character, as Livia helped Julia's daughter, Julia the Younger, some years later when she was similarly sent into exile. The evidence for her support of the elder Julia is in the form of an inscription found in Rhegium that records the family of a Gaius Gelus, a freedman of Julia's. His father, Thiasus, is also identified as a freedman of Julia's, while his mother, also called Julia (after her mistress, of course), is identified as a freedwoman of Augusta's. The nomenclature of the mother shows that she must have been manumitted after AD 14, when Livia received the title Julia Augusta; thus the mother, and perhaps Thiasus, seem to have been seconded as slaves by Livia to Julia during her exile. What scant evidence we have suggests that Livia played her traditional conciliatory role, and Herbert-Brown even suggests that it might have been at this time that she dedicated the aedes to Concordia in her Portico, to advertise the fact that despite the departure of both Julia and Tiberius, there was still cohesion in the ruling family.[18]

The exile of Julia made Tiberius' position precarious, because it broke an important link between himself and Augustus at a time when relations between them had already soured. His sense of vulnerability would have increased in the following year, when his tribunicia potestas expired. At this point he underwent a change of heart and asked to be allowed to return. He no longer had any constitutional powers, and Gaius and Lucius were old enough that Tiberius would be less likely to be seen as a threat to any plans Augustus had formed for them. Tiberius' excuse for wanting to return was the desire to see his *necessitudines*, his close family, by which he presumably meant his mother and his son, Drusus. Augustus was not a forgiving person when wounded by personal slights from within his own family. He refused. Livia may well have supported Tiberius' request, but if she did, she was no more successful than her son. Suetonius claims that she managed to secure one concession from her husband, and only with the greatest difficulty: that as a front to conceal the fact that Tiberius was being kept out of Rome because of the emperor's displeasure, he would receive a form of commission *(legatio)* in the East.[19] If Livia did indeed intervene for her son in this matter, and we cannot be certain that she did, her intervention would have been natural in the circumstances, and we should not read deep political motives into her actions. It would be little more than what she frequently did for prominent Romans unrelated to her family. Tiberius had expressed a perfectly understandable desire to see his family, and Livia would have had a natural maternal instinct to want to protect the welfare of her only surviving son. Also, it is noteworthy that there were limits to what she could achieve. Augustus was prepared to offer no more than a compromise, and even then with some reluctance. Though willing to listen to Livia, he was in the end very much his own man.

In AD 2 Tiberius tried again to persuade Augustus to allow his return to Rome and once again, we are informed, Livia argued strenuously on his behalf *(impensissimis precibus)*. The emperor was still unwilling to give in to his wife's request, but he did indicate that he would be prepared to take directions on the matter from Gaius. Fortunately for Tiberius, Gaius was apparently prepared to be magnanimous and to support the older man's cause. That year, as Dio reports, the soothsayer Thrasyllus, a close confidant of Tiberius' in Rhodes, was looking out over the ocean when he espied an approaching ship. He predicted, accurately, the message it carried from Livia and Augustus: Tiberius could at last return to Rome. In reporting the prediction, Dio links Livia's name with Augustus' in playing a key role in the recall. It seems unlikely that she could claim much of the decision as hers, but her strenuous efforts on behalf of Tiberius in the recent past would explain why she received much of the credit. At last, Tiberius was recalled, but with the humiliating proviso that he drop completely out of public life. On reaching Rome he moved from his conspicuous house on the Carinae, on the southwest of the Esquiline, and relocated himself to the Garden of Maecenas, much farther away from the centre of the city. There he began to lead a life of quiet retirement.[20]

Tiberius had no doubt reconciled himself to retirement, and Livia might well have accepted that he had left the political scene for good had it not been for two major misfortunes that devastated the domus Augusta and necessitated a major rethinking of Augustus' dynastic intentions. Gaius had been given a command in the East in 1 BC, and after a three-year interval Lucius was given command of the armies of the Spanish provinces.[21] Both appointments were to end in tragedy. In the year when Tiberius was recalled, AD 2, Lucius Caesar fell ill at Massilia on his way to Spain and very quickly died, on August 20. Tiberius was allowed to compose a lyric poem, *Conquestio de Morte L. Caesaris*, to mark the occasion, in a gesture of family solidarity. He could not, however, have reasonably expected a serious change in his own status. Lucius, as the younger of the brothers, would have been essentially a junior partner to Gaius.[22] Two years later a further blow fell. Gaius had been sent to the East to deal with a rebellion in a traditional trouble spot, Armenia, the small mountainous country bordering Parthia east of the Euphrates. One of the rebels, Addon, persuaded him to come to the town of Artagira for a parley. The young Roman, with more courage than common sense, foolishly approached the walls of the town. In violation of the cease-fire he was struck by some sort of missile, presumably an arrow. The town was in the end taken and Gaius was honoured by being acclaimed as imperator. But the wound did not heal. Gaius' physical constitution had never been strong. He now grew weaker and started to behave so erratically that people suspected that his mind had been affected. He sought permission from Augustus to relinquish his command, expressing a desire to live quietly in Syria. Augustus prevailed upon him to return to Italy. Gaius set out on the return journey, taking a trading vessel as far as Limyra in Lycia. He stopped off there and got no farther. He died on February 21, AD 4.[23]

The opportune demise of the two princes inevitably aroused suspicions. Pliny speaks of the whispering campaign that followed (*incusatae liberorum mortes*). Dio reports that Livia was suspected of causing both deaths, particularly because they followed Tiberius' return from Rhodes. Tacitus, once again in a blatant appeal to deep-seated prejudices, uses a familiar technique, saying that they died either by the simple working of fate or because the trickery of their stepmother, Livia, carried them off. He does not expand on this last suggestion, and offers no evidence, but succeeds in planting the seeds of suspicion. The idea seems implausible. Although some sort of plot was not logistically impossible, the complications of arranging poisoning at a great distance should arouse more than the usual scepticism about such charges. It would be stretching the record to the length of incredulity to suggest that Livia had been in league with Addon, especially given that Gaius exposed himself recklessly just before he was wounded, and that the effect of the wound was aggravated by his delicate physical condition. Moreover, there is no indication that anyone on the spot in the entourage of either Gaius or Lucius had any reason whatsoever at the time to suspect foul play by Livia. It is likely that the stories that arose later about Livia's secret plan to poison Germanicus at a distance (see chapter 8) have been grafted onto these earlier events. Suetonius at any rate voices no suspicions.[24]

The death of Lucius and then of Gaius would have left Augustus with one surviving male kin. Not long after the death of Marcus Agrippa in 12 BC a son had been born to Julia. In honour of his old friend Augustus arranged for him to be called Agrippa, dropping the Vipsanius, which his father had not used. He is thus called Marcus Agrippa in inscriptions. The familiar cognomen Postumus, found in some of the literary sources and conventionally attached to him, is not attested epigraphically.[25] Postumus was sixteen in AD 4—and, it seems, a highly immature and irresponsible sixteen, hardly ready for serious responsibilities. In the long term, there were women who might continue Augustus' line. One of these was Augustus' granddaughter, Agrippina the Elder, born to Julia in about 14 BC. Agrippina was to play an important role in the later story of Livia, and her personality ensured that the relationship would be prickly. She was a third-generation imperial woman, who had known no world other than one where she was a child of the imperial house. It showed. She was proud, touchy about her status, and intolerant of those who stood between her and what she saw as owed to her by destiny.[26] There was an ideal husband in the wings for Agrippina. Romans had a predilection for attributing to sons the qualities (or vices) of their fathers. Drusus, the son of Livia, had enjoyed immensely popular appeal. He had left two sons. The younger of these, Claudius, was ruled out because of his physical infirmities. The older, Germanicus, was a perfect candidate. Livia's grandson inherited the enormous popularity of his father. He seems to have combined this with perceived qualities of his own, for Suetonius describes him as handsome and courageous, universally admired for his broad compassion and his ability to win the affections of others. Tacitus saw him as the epitome of moral rectitude.[27]

Like his father, Germanicus was to safeguard his reputation with an early death, before he had been put properly to the test.[28] In fact, the early signs, for those willing to look closely, were not encouraging. Although his motives and intentions might have been unassailable, he could still make serious blunders. Tacitus has no choice but to criticise him on individual points of detail—the record would not allow otherwise—whether a mistake in military strategy in his German campaigns or a lack of judgement in giving in to the demands of the mutineers in the Rhine armies following Augustus' death. But these points of detail are not allowed to detract seriously from the overall enthusiastic portrait, one which survived him by several generations. The third-century record of the garrison at Dura Europus, the so-called *Feriale Duranum*, appears to include the celebration of Germanicus' birthday, a remarkable testimony to the durability of his reputation, showing that in the time of Severus Alexander he was still regarded as one of the great military leaders of the empire.[29]

At the time of Gaius' death Augustus had reached his sixty-fifth year and was not in robust health. He needed someone in place ready to share his burdens and to take over at once should it be necessary. Germanicus, probably only seventeen, was still too young to shoulder any major responsibility. Nevertheless, according to Tacitus, Augustus gave serious thought to adopting him, but was dissuaded by Livia, using what the historian in one place describes as *occultis artibus* (secret devices) and in another as her *precibus* (entreaties). Accordingly, he selected Tiberius instead. Suetonius makes an astute observation. He first cites previous authorities who suggest two possible, very unflattering, motives for Tiberius' adoption. Augustus either was worn out by Livia's appeals, or he thought that if Tiberius succeeded him the contrast with his own reign would be so marked that it would do great things for his own reputation. (An identical motive was ascribed later to Tiberius for his choice of Caligula as successor.) Suetonius adds his own observation that such speculation is nonsense, and sensibly refuses to believe that in such an important matter Augustus would not have given the issues the most careful thought. On the one hand Tiberius was distinguished in the field and a man of sober habits. On the other, his brooding personality had driven him to the disastrous gaffe of retiring from Rome in a huff. Balancing the merits and faults, Augustus decided that the former predominated. Suetonius does more than simply counter speculation with his own speculation. He quotes from a number of letters that demonstrate convincingly Augustus' faith in Tiberius' qualities. Thus while Livia may well have put some pressure on her husband, she clearly would not have been the deciding factor.[30]

Tiberius was the only man with sufficient experience and standing able to take on such a responsibility. Having made the decision to adopt him, Augustus knew that there could be no half-measures. He granted him the tribunicia potestas, probably for five years, although the period differs from source to source.[31] On June 26, AD 4, Augustus adopted Tiberius. Livia's son, forty-four years old, now became officially the son of her second husband.[32] Henceforth he is called Tiberius Julius Caesar and is clearly the man designated to succeed the emperor. As he had in the past, Augustus made provision for the possibility that Tiberius might not necessarily survive him. Agrippa Postumus had not given any evidence of being temperamentally suited for high office, but Augustus perhaps hoped that in the general way of things an unruly youth could mature into a responsible adult. Hence the emperor adopted Postumus on the same occasion. Moreover, Tiberius was obliged, before his own adoption, to adopt his nephew Germanicus, who would thereby become Tiberius' son and would legally have the same relationship to Tiberius as his natural son, Drusus. The marriage of Germanicus and Agrippina followed soon after, probably in the next year. There is no reason why the unconcealed manoeuvring on behalf of Germanicus should have upset Livia unnecessarily, despite the clear implications of Tacitus that it did. Germanicus, after all, was her grandson as much as was Drusus Caesar. The arrangement reinforced rather than weakened the likelihood of succession from her own line, as was to be demonstrated by events. The marriage would prove extremely fruitful. In time Agrippina bore Germanicus nine children, six of whom survived infancy. The first three were sons, great-grandsons of Livia: Nero, the eldest (not to be confused with his nephew Nero, the future emperor); Drusus (to be distinguished from the two more famous men of the same name: Drusus, son of Livia, and Drusus Caesar, son of Tiberius); and Gaius (destined to become emperor, and known more familiarly as Caligula). She also bore three surviving daughters, Drusilla and Livilla, and, most important, the younger Agrippina, mother of Livia's great-great-grandson, the emperor Nero.

The adoption of Tiberius in AD 4 would have been an occasion of joy and satisfaction for Livia, and would have helped to efface any lingering grief that still afflicted her over Drusus' death. If we are to believe Velleius, not only Livia but the whole Roman world reacted jubilantly to the new turn of events. Needless to say, his account should be treated with due caution. There was, he claims, something for everyone. Parents felt heartened about the future of their children, husbands felt secure about their wives, even property owners anticipated profits from their investments! Everyone looked forward to an era of peace and good order. A colourful exaggeration, of course, but there probably was considerable relief among Romans that the succession issue seemed at long last to be settled.[33]

Any possible role that Augustus might have dreamt of for Germanicus or Agrippa Postumus in some remote and distant future was largely academic. It is important to bear this point in mind when considering the last ten years of his life. Livia assumes a key role in the literary accounts of this period, especially towards the end, but that role remains clouded in obscurity and innuendo, and the claims made by Tacitus in particular about her contribution to the events of the decade have rightly been treated by scholars with considerable scepticism. Tacitus makes the charge that Augustus' public show of support for Tiberius was made at the open urging *(palam hortatu)* of Livia, in contrast to the secret campaign *(obscuris artibus)* she had waged earlier. This claim simply fails to convince. That Livia would have supported the adoption of Tiberius and made her pleasure known when it came about should occasion no surprise, or serious censure. But her efforts cannot have been the deciding factor. During Tiberius' quasi-exile in Rhodes, she had supposedly gone to great lengths on his behalf but had been able to wrest only limited concessions from a husband who clearly was resolved to make up his own mind on such matters. Also, the logic of Tacitus' account leaves much to be desired. Livia had supposedly promoted Tiberius' case by obscuris artibus. But Tiberius, along with his brother Drusus, had served openly, and with distinction, in the Roman armies. It is difficult to see how Livia could have been involved secretly, short of bribing the enemy armies to surrender in the field.[34]

In the immediate aftermath of the adoptions the ancient authors inevitably tend to focus on Tiberius and the campaigns he conducted in Germany and Illyricum, and they virtually ignore Agrippa Postumus, whose name was to be invoked later by sources hostile to Livia. A few details about Postumus emerge. In AD 5 he received the toga of manhood. The occasion was low-key, without any of the special honours granted Gaius and Lucius on the same occasion. It also seems to have been delayed. Postumus would have reached fourteen in AD 3, and under normal circumstances might reasonably have been expected to take the toga in that year. Something seems to be wrong. Augustus had certainly endured his share of problems with the young people in his own family. The pressures facing the younger relatives of any monarch are self-evident, given the sense of importance that precedes achievement, to say nothing of the opportunists attracted to the immature and malleable, and prepared to pander to their self-importance. As Velleius astutely remarks, *magnae fortunae comes adest adulatio* (sycophancy is the comrade of high position). These pressures must have been particularly intense in the period of the Augustan settlement, when no established standards had yet evolved for the royal children and grandchildren. Gaius and Lucius, the focus of Augustus' ambitions and hopes, caused him endless grief by their behaviour in public, clearly egged on by their supporters, and on at least one occasion Augustus felt constrained to clip their wings. Gaius' brave but distinctly foolhardy behaviour during the siege of Artagira is surely symptomatic of the same conceit. There is no reason to assume that Postumus would have been immune from the pressures that turned the heads of his siblings.[35]

Whatever traits of haughtiness Postumus might have displayed in his early youth, they were not serious enough to have entered the record, and the exact nature of his personal and possibly mental problems is far from clear.[36] The ancient sources speak of his brutish and violent behaviour. Some modern scholars have suggested that he might have been mad, but the language used of him seems to denote little more than an unmanageable temperament and antisocial tendencies.[37] For whatever reasons, eventually Augustus decided to remove him from the scene. The details of this expulsion are obscure. Suetonius provides the clearest statement, recording that Augustus removed Postumus (*abdicavit*) because of his wild character and sent him to Surrentum (Sorrento). The historian notes that Postumus grew less and less manageable and so was then sent to Planasia, a low-lying desolate island about sixteen kilometres south of Elba.[38]

Tacitus has no doubt about where the ultimate responsibility for Augustus' actions lay. Postumus had committed no crime. But Livia had so ensnared her elderly husband (*senem Augustum*) that he was induced to banish him to Planasia. Tacitus' technique here is patent. The use of the word *senem* is meant to suggest that Augustus was by now senile, even though the event occurred eight years before his death. Incapable of making his own rational decisions, he would thus be at the mercy of a scheming woman, just as later Agrippina the Younger reputedly "captivated her uncle" Claudius (*pellicit patruum*). No reason is given for Livia's supposed manoeuvre — which as usual, according to Tacitus, was conducted behind the scenes — except the standard charge that her hatred of Postumus was motivated by a stepmother's loathing (*novercalibus odiis*). Yet nothing in the rest of Tacitus' narrative sustains his assertion, and the historian himself admits that the general view of Romans towards the end of Augustus' reign was that Postumus was totally unsuited for the succession, because of both his youth and his generally insolent behaviour. Moreover, Augustus had made the strength of Tiberius' position so patently evident that Livia would hardly have considered Postumus a serious candidate. This seems to be confirmed in a remarkable passage of Tacitus which uncharacteristically reports public reservations about a potential role for Germanicus, supposedly Tiberius' rival. After reporting the popular view that Postumus could be ruled out, Tacitus says that people grumbled that with the accession of Tiberius they would have to put up with Livia's *impotentia*, and would have to obey two *adulescentes* (Germanicus and Drusus) who would oppress, then tear the state apart. Tacitus concedes that even the prospect of the reasonable Germanicus and Drusus being involved in state matters caused consternation. This surely offers some gauge of how far below the horizon Postumus was to be found.[39]

The precise reason for Postumus' removal to Sorrento, if it was not simply his personality, is not clear. The initial expulsion may have been provoked by nothing more serious than personal tension between him and his adoptive father. Whatever the initial reason, it soon became apparent that if Augustus had hoped that sending his adopted son out of Rome would solve the problem, he was mistaken. Dio places Postumus' formal exile to Planasia in AD 7. If, as Suetonius claims, he was sent first to Sorrento, what might have precipitated the change in the location and the more grave status of his banishment? We have some hints in the sources. Dio suggests that one of the reasons for Augustus' giving Germanicus preference over Postumus was that the latter spent most of his time fishing, and acquired the sobriquet of Neptune. Now this could point simply to irresponsibility and indolence, but the picture of Postumus as an ancient Izaak Walton serenely casting his line does not fit well with the very strong tradition of someone wild and reckless. His activities may well have had a political dimension. The choice of the nickname Neptune could allude to the naval victories of his father, Marcus Agrippa. The fishing story might well belong to the period after Postumus' relegation to Sorrento. This could have proved a risky spot to locate Postumus, because it lay just across the bay from the important naval base at Misenum that his father had established in 31 BC. The innocent fishing expeditions might have covered much more sinister activities.[40]

Augustus may well have concluded eventually that Postumus was too dangerous to be left in the benign surroundings of Sorrento. During Postumus' second, more serious phase of exile, on the island of Planasia, he was placed under a military guard, a good indication that he was considered genuinely dangerous rather than just a source of irritation and embarrassment. This final stage of banishment was a formal one, for Augustus confirmed the punishment by a senatorial decree and spoke in the Senate on the occasion about his adopted son's depraved character. Formal banishment enacted by a decree of the Senate would be intended to make a serious political statement and should have buried completely any thoughts that Postumus might have been considered a serious candidate in the succession.[41]

We cannot rule out the possibility that Postumus became involved, perhaps as a pawn, in some serious political intrigue, if not to oust Augustus then at the very least to ensure that he would be followed not by a son of Livia but by someone from the line of Julia. If Postumus was being encouraged to think of a possible role in the succession, it might reasonably be asked who was doing the urging. Although there is no explicit statement on the question in the sources, many scholars have accepted the notion that there existed a "Julian party," responsible for much of the "anti-Claudian" propaganda directed against Livia and Tiberius that is found in Tacitus in particular and possibly derived from the memoirs of Agrippina (appendix 1). The notion of Julian and Claudian factions within the imperial family has been called into serious question, on the grounds that division between the two gentes would have been largely annulled by the extensive network of adoption. But a split between those sympathetic to Augustus' first wife, Scribonia, and her daughter Julia on the one hand, and the supporters of Livia and her son on the other, is certainly a feasible scenario. That said, it is far from proved.[42]

A strong hint that Julia's supporters were involved in some sort of intrigue might be seen in yet another family scandal, this time involving her daughter of the same name, Julia the Younger. As confusing as the affair of Julia the Elder might have been, the details of the crisis that swept up her daughter are even more baffling, a situation aggravated by the loss of much of Dio's text for the period when it broke, in AD 8, the year following Postumus' exile.[43] Julia the Younger had been married to Lucius Aemilius Paullus, consul in AD 1, to whom she bore a daughter, Aemilia Lepida. Nothing much more is known about this Julia, except that she lived in some style in Rome. Tacitus tells us that she was found guilty of adultery (in AD 8) and sent into exile to the island of Trimerus, off the Apulian coast, where she remained for the rest of her days. It does not, however, seem likely that she could have been intriguing against Livia's interests, because she was supported in Trimerus by allowances from Livia for the next twenty years, until her death in 28. Tacitus adopts a cynical view of Livia's philanthropy, claiming that she hypocritically laboured to destroy Augustus' family while they flourished, then made a public display of her charity after they had been brought down. This is another good example of the historian's use of innuendo. He does not say that Livia had anything to do with the younger Julia's actual downfall but distorts her public display of charity into an insidious implication that she was somehow responsible. There is a serious logical gap in his argument. There might have been a political advantage for Livia in putting people off the scent during Augustus' lifetime, if she had indeed been responsible for Julia's ruin. But why keep it up for a further fourteen years after his death? The strength of the case, and of the feelings against Julia, can in fact be gauged from Augustus' personal resentment — he ordered that her residence in Rome should be demolished, and he refused to allow her ashes to be deposited in his mausoleum, just as he had refused her mother the same privilege. He reputedly would not allow a child born to her after the affair was exposed to live, or even to be acknowledged.[44]

There is one piece of evidence that Postumus seemed to hold Livia partly responsible for what had happened to him. Dio says that after Postumus was removed *(apekerychthe)*, his property was assigned to the military treasury, the *aerarium militare*. At some point he wrote to Augustus to complain about his ill-treatment on this precise matter, and Dio tells us that Postumus used to rebuke *(epekallei)* Augustus over being shut out of his inheritance. The Greek verb could mean that he simply reproached Augustus, or even that he brought an action against him, and the imperfect tense suggests that the charge was made on more than one occasion. In this same general context Dio says also that Postumus slandered Livia, and it looks very much as though he lumped her in with the complaints about his property.⁴⁵ Any claim launched by Postumus against Augustus (and Livia, indirectly) would have been a very weak one. If his father, Marcus Agrippa, had been aware before his death that his wife Julia was pregnant, he would certainly have made provision for a *tutor* (guardian) in his will; he probably would have appointed Augustus, adoptive father of Marcus Agrippa's other sons, Gaius and Lucius, and inheritor of the bulk of Marcus Agrippa's estate. If he assigned no guardian in the will, the *tutela* would fall to the nearest male relative, of which there is no record. If the decision fell to the praetor to decide guardianship, he probably would have appointed Augustus. Any property that Postumus inherited from his father would thereby have come under Augustus' administration. In any case, with the adoption of AD 4, Postumus was transferred into the *potestas* of Augustus and thereby lost all his private property, including whatever he might have inherited from his father. Like Tiberius, he would have retained control only over whatever allowance *(peculium)* his adoptive father approved. Postumus' complaint that he never received his inheritance might have been factually correct, but it would have had no strength in law. Thus Livia can hardly have played any kind of active or direct role in Postumus' loss of inheritance. Dio in any case argues that Postumus attacked Livia as stepmother, suggesting that he did not have specific charges to make against her.⁴⁶

Whatever the intrigues in Rome, Livia's son was able to keep himself aloof and to play the role that suited him best, that of soldier. Tiberius conducted a brilliant series of campaigns in Pannonia for which a triumph was voted in AD 9. (This was postponed when Tiberius was despatched to Germany in the aftermath of the disastrous defeat of Quinctilius Varus, in which three legions were lost.) When the Pannonian triumph was voted, Augustus made his intentions crystal clear. Various suggestions were put forward for honorific titles, such as Pannonicus, Invictus, and Pius. The emperor, however, vetoed them all, declaring that Tiberius would have to be satisfied with the title that he would receive when he himself died. That title, of course, was Augustus.⁴⁷ It also appears that a law was later passed to make his imperium equal to that of Augustus throughout the empire, and in early 13 his tribunician power was renewed. His son Drusus Caesar received his first accelerated promotion, designated to proceed directly to the consulship in AD 15, skipping the praetorship that should have preceded this higher office.[48]

The virtual impregnability of Tiberius' position should be borne in mind in any attempt to understand the final months of Augustus' life. In the closing chapter of her husband's principate, Livia reemerges in the record to play a central and, according to one tradition, decidedly sinister role. This is perhaps the most convoluted period of her career, where rumour and reality seem to diverge most widely. To place the events in a comprehensible context, it is necessary to note one later detail out of its chronological sequence. As we shall see, after Augustus' death there was a rumour reported in some of the sources that Livia had murdered her husband. In the best forensic tradition, a motive would have to be unearthed to make the charge plausible, especially since sceptics could hardly have failed to notice that Augustus had never enjoyed robust health and was already in his seventy-sixth year. Death from natural causes could hardly be considered remarkable under such circumstances. The requisite motive would indeed be produced, and the kernel of the intricate thesis that evolved is found in a brief summary of Augustus' career by Pliny the Elder. Among the travails that afflicted the emperor, Pliny lists the *abdicatio* of Postumus after his adoption, Augustus' regret after the relegation, the suspicion that a certain Fabius betrayed his secrets, and the intrigues of Livia and Tiberius. Pliny's summary observations are clearly based on a more detailed source, which suggested that Augustus felt some remorse about Postumus. This simple and not improbable notion is developed by other sources into a far more complex scenario that creates an apparently plausible motive, because it could be claimed that Livia would have wanted to remove her husband before he could act on his change of heart. This reconstruction of the events is clearly reminiscent of the closing days of the reign of Claudius, when the emperor supposedly sought a rapprochement with his son Britannicus, to the disadvantage of his stepson Nero, and thereby inspired his wife Agrippina to despatch him with the poisoned mushroom (see appendix 1). But it is important to bear in mind that as Pliny reports the events he limits himself to the claim that Augustus regretted Postumus' exile, without further elaboration, and although Livia and her son supposedly engaged in intrigues of some unspecified nature, Pliny assigns no criminal action to either of them.

Pliny's "skeleton account" is to some degree validated by Plutarch. In his essay on "Talkativeness," Plutarch, in a very garbled passage, relates that a friend of Augustus named "Fulvius" heard the emperor lamenting the woes that had befallen his house — the deaths of Gaius and Lucius and the exile of "Postumius" on some false charge — which had obliged him to pass on the succession to Tiberius. He now regretted what had happened and intended (*bouleuomenos*) to recall his surviving grandson from exile. According to Plutarch's account, Fulvius passed this information on to his wife, and she in turn passed it on to Livia, who took Augustus to task for his careless talk. The emperor made his displeasure known to Fulvius, and he and his wife in consequence committed suicide. This last detail was perhaps inspired by the famous story of Arria, who achieved immortal fame in AD 42 when she died with her husband Caecina Paetus, who had been implicated in a conspiracy against Claudius. Plutarch's confused version of events does not inspire confidence, and in any case, although he gives Livia a more specific role than does Pliny, he follows Pliny in not attributing to Augustus any action, only supposed intentions.[49]

Dio's account is a much contracted one, but derived from a source that has added a very important wrinkle to the story and has Augustus taking action on his change of heart. Dio says that Livia was suspected of Augustus' death. She was afraid, people say (*hos phasi*), because Augustus had secretly sailed to Planasia to see Postumus and seemed to be on the brink of seeking a reconciliation.[50] This bald and surely implausible story, involving a round trip of some five hundred kilometres, is given its fullest treatment in Tacitus, clearly drawing on the same source as Dio. He says that people thought that Livia had brought about Augustus' final illness, because a rumour entered into circulation that the emperor had gone to Planasia to visit Postumus, accompanied by a small group of intimates, including Paullus Fabius Maximus. Fabius, clearly Plutarch's "Fulvius," was a literary figure of some renown, a close friend of Ovid and Horace. He was also an intimate of Augustus, consul in 11 BC, governor of Asia, and legatus in Spain (3–2 BC). He would thus be a plausible participant in this mysterious expedition. Tacitus reports that the tears and signs of affection were enough to raise the hopes of Postumus that there was a prospect of his being recalled. (It is striking that Tacitus is ambiguous about the meeting's purpose and is too good a historian to bring himself to claim that Augustus had gone there to commit himself to Postumus' rehabilitation.) Fabius Maximus supposedly told the story to his wife, Marcia, and she in turn passed it to Livia. The text of the manuscript is corrupt at this point, but Tacitus seems to say that this indiscretion came to the knowledge of Augustus (reading the text as *gnarum id Caesari*). The subsequent death of Fabius, Tacitus says, may or may not have been suicide (the implication is that Augustus ordered it, as Plutarch suggests). Marcia was heard at the funeral reproaching herself as the cause of her husband's downfall (this presumably is how the story got out). After this detailed account Tacitus undercuts his own case when he goes on to say that Augustus died shortly afterwards, *utcumque se ea res habuit*. The force of this phrase is essentially "whatever the truth of the matter." It hardly inspires conviction.[51]

The story of the adventurous journey to Planasia and the tearful reconciliation has generally been greeted with scepticism by modern scholars. Jameson is an exception. She uses the Arval record to argue that Augustus did take the trip, noting that on May 14 there was a meeting of the brethren for the co-option of Drusus Caesar, the son of Tiberius, into their order. Fabius Maximus and Augustus were absent from the ceremony, and submitted their votes, in favour of the co-option, by absentee ballot. But is there anything remarkable in their absence? Clearly, the election of Tiberius' son was not in reality a particularly important occasion, for Tiberius himself failed to attend. Moreover, Syme notes that no fewer than five other arvals were absent from this meeting, and that there could be a host of explanations for Augustus' absence. Also, if the co-option was seen as an important family event, then it would surely have been the very worst time for Augustus to try to slip away unnoticed. The emperor was by this time in declining health, so weak that he even held audiences in the palace lying on a couch. In AD 12 he was so frail that he stopped his morning receptions for senators and asked their indulgence for his not joining them at public banquets. Yet we are supposed to assume that he made the arduous journey to Planasia, and that he did so without Livia realizing what he was up to. It is also important to observe that both Tacitus and Dio drew on a source claiming that Augustus was on the verge of making amends with Postumus. An actual reconciliation seems to be ruled out by the later sequence of events. Certainly he did nothing whatsoever on his return to strengthen Postumus' position or to weaken that of Tiberius. Finally, one might ask whether Augustus could ever have seriously considered recalling Postumus. He had put him under armed guard. There were plots to rescue him. His supporters published damaging letters about the emperor. It all seems implausible. Syme suggests that the details of the journey might have been added soon after Augustus' death, a "specimen of that corroborative detail which is all too apparent (and useful) in historical fictions." Syme bases his argument in part on aesthetic considerations. The episode as it appears in Tacitus is introduced in an inartistic fashion and appears to have been grafted on as an afterthought, introducing two names, those of Fabius Maximus and his wife, Marcia, that will not be mentioned again in the *Annals*. Moreover, neither Pliny nor Plutarch mentions Planasia. In Plutarch's confused account Fabius' role is merely to overhear Augustus expressing his unhappiness over the fate of Postumus.[52]

Making the situation even murkier, Suetonius alludes to a complicated plot hatched around Postumus. He provides only the briefest of details, but enough to establish that the ringleaders did not come from the top drawer of Roman society. There were two of them, otherwise unknown — Lucius Audasius, who had in his younger days been charged with forgery but was now old and decrepit, and Asinius Epicadus, half-Parthian by origin and presumably a freedman of the Asinian gens. They planned to rescue Postumus and Julia (specifically identified as the Elder) from their island prisons and whisk them away to the armies. We know nothing more of the plot or of the fate of the two unlikely ringleaders except that the whole thing was exposed before any harm could be done. It may well be that the plotters were ultimately responsible for the Planasia story, hoping to lay the foundation for a claim that Augustus intended Postumus as his successor. Julia certainly still had her followers in Rome. By the time of the plot she was no longer on Pandateria but in Rhegium, on the mainland of Italy. There had earlier been much popular agitation for her recall, to which Augustus had responded by asserting that fire would mix with water before he would relent. Nothing daunted, her supporters began to thrown firebrands into the sea. They were not completely successful, but in the end Augustus felt under so much pressure that he did make a modest compromise, and at some point after AD 4 moved her to Rhegium. Demands for her total recall continued. These Augustus resisted, ruefully wishing the same daughters or wives on the petitioners.[53] The plot described by Suetonius might then have been a last desperate effort to rescue her. In any case it seems to have come to nothing.

In addition to the supposed political intrigues in the period immediately before Augustus' death, there was no shortage of signs that the gods, too, were feeling distinctly uneasy, ranging from the usual comets and fires in the sky to more opaque portents, like a madman sitting on the chair dedicated to Julius Caesar and placing a crown on his own head, or an owl hooting on the roof of the Senate house.[54] But Augustus seems to have had no premonition that he had little time left when he set out from Rome in August 14. At that time Tiberius was obliged to leave the city for further service abroad, and he departed for Illyricum with a mandate to reorganise the province. Livia and Augustus joined him for the first part of the journey. This very public gesture is an affirmation of the emperor's faith in Tiberius — a very odd signal to send if only a few months earlier he had become reconciled to Postumus and had changed his mind about who would succeed him. The party went as far as Astura, and from there followed the unusual course of taking a ship by night to catch the favourable breeze. On the sea journey Augustus contracted an illness, which began with diarrhoea. They skirted the coast of Campania, spent four days in Augustus' villa at Capri to allow him to relax and recuperate, then sailed into the Gulf of Puteoli, where they were given an extravagant welcome from the passengers and crew of a ship that had just sailed in from Alexandria. They passed over to Naples, although Augustus was still weak and his diarrhoea was recurring. He managed to muster up the strength to watch a gymnastic performance. Then they continued their journey. At Beneventum the company broke up. Tiberius headed east. As Augustus began the return journey with Livia from Beneventum, his illness took a turn for the worse. Perhaps he had a sense that his end was near, as he made for an old family estate, in nearby Nola, where his father, Octavius, had died.[55]

Augustus was not to leave Nola alive. His condition quickly grew worse, and on August 19, 14, at the ninth hour, in Suetonius' precise report, he died.[56] According to Tacitus, as Augustus grew more sick, some people started to suspect (*suspectabant*) Livia of dirty deeds (*scelus*). Dio is more specific, but is still cautious about the charge. He notes that Augustus used to gather figs from the tree with his own hands. She, *hos phasi* (as they say), cunningly smeared some of them with poison, ate the uncontaminated ones herself and offered the special ones to her husband. As can be seen in his handling of other events, Dio does seem to relish rumours of poisoning. He relates, for instance, that Vespasian died of fever in AD 79, but adds that some said that he was poisoned at a banquet. It was similarly said that Domitian murdered Titus in AD 81, although the written accounts agree that he died of natural causes. In the case of Augustus it may be possible to discern the origins of the rumour. Suetonius confirms that the emperor was fond of green figs from the second harvest (along with hand-made moist cheese, small fish, and coarse bread). Given Livia's interest in the cultivation of figs (she even had one named after her [see chapter 6]), she may well have had an orchard at Nola to which she would have given special attention during her stay. Dio in fact seems to have had little personal faith in the fig rumour, for he goes on to speak of Augustus' death as "from this or from some other cause." By its nature the fig story is unprovable yet impossible to refute. It falls in the grand tradition of such deaths, the best-known being the supposed despatch of Claudius by a poisoned mushroom. If Livia murdered Augustus, then her timing was oddly awry, for she had to go to considerable trouble to recall Tiberius, who was by then en route to Illyricum. Why not do the deed when he was still on the

scene? It is perhaps worth bearing in mind that Livia had an interest in cura-
tive recipes (see chapter 6). It is possible that she would have inflicted one or
more of her own concoctions on her husband. In the unlikely event that he was
poisoned, alternative medicine might be a more plausible culprit than the
murderer's toxin.[57]

From Beneventum, Tiberius headed for the east coast of Italy, where he
took a boat to Illyricum. He had barely crossed over to the Dalmatian coast
when an urgent letter from his mother caught up with him, recalling him to
Nola. There are different versions of what happened next. Tacitus describes
Augustus in his final hours holding a heavy conversation with his entourage
about the qualifications of potential successors. Dio and Suetonius allow him a
lighter agenda. They recount that he first asked for a mirror, combed his hair
and straightened his sagging jaws. Then he invited the friends in. He gave
them his final instructions, ending with his famous line of finding Rome a city
of clay and leaving it a city of marble. In conclusion, he asked how they would
rate his performance in the grand comedy of life. He seems to have taken a
high score for granted, because just like a comic actor, he asked them to give
him applause for a role well played. (The curious coincidence of the comic
actors brought in during Claudius' last hours should be noted.) He then dis-
missed his friends and spoke to some visitors from Rome, asking about the
health of Tiberius' granddaughter Julia, who was ill. The most serious discrepancy arises over the part that Tiberius might have played during the emperor's
final hours. Dio preserves one tradition, which he says he found in most
authorities, including the better ones, that the emperor died while his adopted
son was still in Dalmatia, and that Livia for political reasons was determined to
keep the death secret until he got back. Tacitus reflects a similar tradition,
reporting uncertainty about whether Tiberius found Augustus dead or alive
when he reached Nola. The house and the adjoining streets had been sealed
off by Livia with guards, and optimistic bulletins were issued, until she was
ready to release the news at a time dictated by her own needs. The story is
reminiscent of Agrippina's arrangements after the death of Claudius. She was
similarly accused of keeping the death secret and posting guards as Claudius
lay dying (see appendix 1). The suspicions about Livia do not appear in the
other extant accounts. Velleius reports that Tiberius rushed back and arrived
earlier than expected, which perked up Augustus for a time. But before too
long he began to fail, and died in Tiberius' arms, asking him to carry on with
their joint work. Suetonius is even more emphatic about Tiberius' role. He
says that Augustus detained Tiberius for a whole day in private conversation,
which was the last serious business that he transacted. His final moments were

spent with Livia. His mind wandered as he died — he thought that forty men were carrying him away — but at the last instant he kissed his wife, with an affectionate farewell, *Livia nostri coniugii memor vive, ac vale* (Livia, be mindful of our marriage, and good-bye), then slipped into the quiet death that he had always hoped for.[58]

That Livia might have kept the news of Augustus' death secret for a time is certainly plausible — there are all sorts of sound reasons why the announcement of a politically sensitive death might be postponed, although the similar delay after Claudius' death is disturbingly coincidental.[59] She also may well have put pickets around the house, but no sinister connotation need be placed on the action. The final hours of Augustus would doubtless have attracted the concerned and the curious, who in such situations follow a herd instinct to keep crowded vigils. After Agrippina the Younger had been shipwrecked near Baiae in AD 59, crowds of well-wishers streamed up to her house, carrying torches. The same would surely have happened in Nola, and some sort of control might have become necessary to give the dying emperor some peace. The house certainly became a place of pilgrimage afterwards, and was converted into some sort of shrine.[60] The romantic account of Augustus expiring in Tiberius' arms may be highly coloured, and Suetonius' claim that Augustus and Tiberius spent a whole day together sounds exaggerated, given that Augustus' health was fading so fast. But it is difficult to see how that whole sequence of events could simply have been invented if it did not have at least a basis of truth.

In any case, rumours surrounding the events at Augustus' deathbed were totally eclipsed by dramatic developments across the water. As an immediate consequence of the emperor's death, Postumus also lost his life: *primum facinus novi principatus fuit Postumi Agrippae caedes* (the first misdeed of the new principate was the slaying of Agrippa Postumus), as Tacitus words it. The events of this first and possibly murkiest episode of Tiberius' reign have been much debated, and it is probably now impossible to disentangle fact from rumour and innuendo, since there is considerable ambiguity in the ancient accounts of the incident.[61]

The general *outline* of the events is not particularly controversial. The officer commanding the guard at Planasia executed Postumus after he had received written instructions *(codicilli)* to carry out the deed. Postumus had no weapons other than his powerful physique, and he put up a valiant but ultimately futile struggle. A desperate attempt by a loyal slave, Clemens, to save him was frustrated when the would-be rescuer took a slow freight ship to

Planasia and arrived too late. After the execution, the officer then reported to Tiberius, presumably still at Nola, that the action had been carried out. He did so, as Tacitus describes it, *ut mos militiae* (in the military manner), presumably in the sense of a soldier reporting to his commander that his orders have been discharged.[62] Tiberius denied vehemently that he had given any such orders. According to Tacitus, he claimed that Augustus had sent the order, to be put into force immediately after his death, and insisted that the officer would have to give an account to the Senate.

Tacitus at this point adds a new wrinkle to the story, and gives a role to a figure not mentioned in any of the other sources in the context of this incident. The codicilli, he claims, had been sent to the tribune by Augustus' confidant Sallustius Crispus. This man was the great-nephew and adopted son of the historian Sallust. Although his family connections had opened up the opportunities for a brilliant senatorial career, Sallustius chose to fashion himself after Maecenas and seek real influence rather than the empty prominence of the Senate. He rose to the top through his energy and determination, which he managed to conceal from his contemporaries by pretending a casual or even apathetic attitude to life. He acquired considerable wealth, owning property in Rome, and among other landed estates he could list a copper mine in the Alps producing high-grade ore. More importantly, at least until his later years, he had the ear of both Augustus and Tiberius, as a man who bore the *imperatorum secreta* (secrets of the emperors).[63] When Sallustius learned that Tiberius wanted the whole matter brought before the Senate, he grew alarmed, afraid that he personally could end up being charged. He interceded with Livia, alerting her to the danger of making public the *arcana domus* (the inner secrets of the house), with all that would entail — details of the advice of friends, or of the special services carried out by the soldiers — and urged her to curb her son.[64]

Beyond this general framework the details are highly obscure, and, it seems, totally speculative. Tacitus says that Tiberius avoided raising the issue of Postumus' death in the Senate, and Suetonius observes that he simply let the matter fade away. There would thus have been no official source of information. Yet fairly detailed narratives have been passed down, which could have come only from eyewitness accounts. In particular one has to wonder how the supposed secret dealings between Livia and Sallustius could ever have become known. This uncertainty over the source and reliability of the information clearly makes it impossible to determine who was ultimately responsible for Postumus' death.

Suetonius summarises the problem nicely. He states that it was not known whether Augustus had left the written instructions, on the verge of his own death, to ensure a smooth succession, or whether Livia had dictated them (*dictasset*) in the name of Augustus, and, if the latter, whether Tiberius had known about them. Dio categorically insists that Tiberius was directly responsible but says that he encouraged the speculation, so that some blamed Augustus, some Livia, and some even said that the centurion had acted on his own initiative. Tacitus found Tiberius' claim that Augustus had left instructions for the execution hard to believe, and describes this defence as a posture (*simulabat*), suggesting that the more likely scenario was that Tiberius and Livia hastily brought about the death, Tiberius driven by fear and she by *novercalibus odiis* (stepmotherly hatred). Velleius may have been aware of these speculations, for he is very cagey about Postumus' death. He insists that "he suffered an ultimate fate" (*habuit exitum*) in a way that was appropriate to his "madness" (*furor*). Velleius may well have been deliberately ambiguous to avoid becoming enmeshed in a contentious and sensitive issue that might reflect badly on Tiberius.[65]

Scholars have generally been inclined to exonerate Livia, and only Gardthausen has held that Livia was totally responsible, without even Tiberius' complicity. Syme accuses Tacitus of supporting an imputation against Livia "which he surely knew to be false." The implication of Livia has been challenged by Charlesworth in particular. He sees it as emanating from the same tradition that had her poisoning Augustus. Certainly Pliny's brief summary imputes no criminal action against her. She seems on principle to have refrained from taking independent executive action. (The picket she set up around Augustus' house would be the only known counterexample.) At most, it is possible that she knew of such an order, but it seems highly unlikely that she initiated it.

Even if a meeting did actually take place between Sallustius and Livia, as Tacitus alleges, this need not mean that anything sinister had necessarily been underfoot. Sallustius may have wished simply to appeal to the wisdom and experience of Livia to counter the political naïveté of a son who had spent his career on military campaigns and had not yet become adept in the complexities of political intrigue. The suppression of information about the activities of the soldiers could just as easily have been meant to refer to Augustus' instructions as to Livia's, in a system where secrecy for the sake of secrecy was considered a vital element in the fabric of efficient government. If Livia had somehow been involved with Sallustius in carrying out Augustus' instructions, there would have had to be secret and dangerous communication between Rome and Nola, unless Sallustius was also with Augustus at the end (and Tacitus would surely have mentioned his presence).[66]

Tiberius seems largely exonerated by his own conduct. If he had been guilty, he would hardly have wanted an investigation by the Senate, and could simply have claimed that the execution was carried out on Augustus' orders or even have reported officially that Postumus had died from natural causes.[67] We can surely eliminate Dio's barely tenable suggestion that the guard might have executed Postumus on its own initiative, and the hardly more convincing notion that Sallustius Crispus similarly might have acted on his own initiative.[68] On balance, the most plausible suspect is Augustus, although plausibility is far different from conviction. Augustus might well have issued standing orders to the tribune to execute Postumus the moment news of his own death arrived. Sallustius could well have sent the announcement of the emperor's death in Tiberius' name (with or without his knowledge), which could account for the centurion's coming to Rome to make a report to Tiberius.[69] When he needed to, Augustus could behave quite ruthlessly against those who threatened him. He put to death Caesarion, the supposed son of Julius Caesar and Cleopatra, for purely political motives. He also could be harsh towards his own family. He swore that he would never recall the elder Julia from exile, refused to recognise the child of the younger Julia, and would not allow either Julia burial in his mausoleum. It was he who had set the armed guard over Postumus. Moreover, Augustus did make meticulous preparations for his own death. He left behind three or four *libelli*, with instructions for his funeral, the text of the *Res Gestae*, a summary of the Roman troops, fleets, provinces, client-kingdoms, direct and indirect taxes — including those in arrears — the funds in the public and in the imperial treasuries, and the imperial accounts. There was also a book of instructions for Tiberius, the Senate, and the people. Augustus went into considerable detail, with such particulars as the number of slaves it would be wise to free and the number of new citizens who should be enrolled. He was clearly a man determined not to leave any issues hanging in the balance, and the future of Postumus would have been an issue of prime importance.[70]

Postumus' death was the final blow for Julia the Elder. From this point on, she simply gave up and went into a slow decline, her despair aggravated by her destitution. She received no help from Tiberius, although he had earlier tried to win leniency for her from her father. According to Suetonius, Tiberius, once emperor, deprived her of her allowance, using the heartless argument that Augustus had not provided for it in his will. As we have seen, Livia might well have helped the exiled Julia at one point by giving her one of her slaves, and she certainly helped Julia's daughter when she was sent away from Rome. But she does not seem to have tried to intercede on this occasion. Julia died in late AD 14 from weakness and malnutrition.[71] The new reign had got off to a bloody start.

A NEW REIGN

The death of Augustus brought about a dramatic and inevitable change in Livia's situation. For the previous half-century or so her role had depended essentially on her personal bond with her husband. She was now the mother of a princeps whose notion of the principate differed greatly from his predecessor's and certainly from her own.

It is difficult to get a clear picture of the relationship that had developed between mother and son in the years before Tiberius came to power. Although the sources suggest that her husband had found Tiberius' personality tiresome and irritating, they give little insight into what Livia thought of her son. It might be suspected that she had favoured his brother, Drusus. Certainly, Drusus' death caused her, and Augustus, intense grief. But an early death will always be a catalyst for affection. There is no serious indication of any contest between Tiberius and his brother for their mother's regard. Suetonius claims some sibling antagonism, supposedly proved by Tiberius' making known a letter in which Drusus had revealed his republican sympathies. But Tiberius' reaction to his brother's death must surely belie any deep hostility. In the same general context Suetonius says that Tiberius showed his ill-will towards his *necessitudines* (close kin), but the examples he adduces to illustrate animosity towards Livia all belong to the period after the accession. That said, it must be conceded that there are no real signs of a close attachment, either. Livia did on occasion take up Tiberius' case, as when he was anxious to leave Rhodes, but she was in fact prepared to intervene for Romans of all classes and conditions.

Nor is there any recorded instance of any actual display of affection between them. This should not, however, occasion any surprise. Open displays of affection were not in their nature, and they both made clear their deep distaste for flaunting private feelings in public.

After Tiberius' accession, the sources paint a picture of deep antipathy between him and Livia, and there is no reason to doubt that there must have been considerable strain, given the ambiguity of her new status and a princeps who had firm ideas on the exclusion of women from affairs of state. These differences are considered in some detail in chapter 8, but it can be noted at the outset that whatever tensions may have existed between Tiberius and his mother, both were astute enough to appreciate that they were natural allies in the political battlefield of the early empire. Unlike Nero, who resorted to murder to rid himself of an interfering parent, Tiberius had the basic common sense to recognise that Livia was of great value to him. Suetonius notes that for all his effort at a public show of independence, he in fact at times sought from his mother the very guidance that he pretended to forswear, and, into the bargain, often followed her suggestions.[1]

Tiberius threw himself into action on Augustus' death. There was no serious rival hovering in the wings, but his situation was entirely without precedent, and he could clearly leave nothing to chance. Curiously, although the sources give Livia a prominent role in ensuring that Tiberius would be on the scene when Augustus died, and that the transmission of power would be a smooth one, they record no involvement by her in the immediate aftermath. That said, it seems inconceivable that she would not have been at her son's side, guiding and advising him, given that his own political experience was at this stage very limited. The public announcement of the old emperor's death carried with it the explicit statement that authority had devolved onto Tiberius. As an important symbolic gesture, it was he who passed on the watchword to the praetorian guard. He then sent letters to all the legionary commanders informing them of his accession. He also wrote to the Senate to tell them that he would be accompanying the body back to Rome. More importantly, he left the senators in no doubt about his own position, informing them that he intended, by virtue of his tribunician authority, to convene a meeting when he reached Rome. It was a diplomatic, yet emphatic, statement that henceforth he was in control.[2] With the transition smoothly under way, Augustus' body could be returned from Nola to Rome in a solemn procession, accompanied by Tiberius and almost certainly by Livia, although the sources, in their preoccupation with the new emperor, omit to mention her. The occasion can hardly have failed to remind both how more than twenty years earlier they had similarly accompanied Drusus' body to Rome. They would have reached the city in early September.[3]

When the Senate was convened, business was limited. The first item was the reading of the will. Augustus had made his last will on April 3, 13, when he was seventy-four, and had deposited it with the Vestal Virgins.[4] Drusus Caesar, Tiberius' son, now brought it into the Senate. After the witnesses examined the seals, it was read out to the senators by a freedman. Two heirs were instituted: Tiberius to two thirds of the estate, and Livia to one third. As heirs in the second grade (people who would inherit if the primary ones for any reason failed to do so) Augustus named Drusus Caesar to one-third of the estate and Germanicus and his sons to the other two-thirds. This must mean that Germanicus and his sons were to be the substitutes to Tiberius, and Drusus Caesar to Livia. The arrangement was advantageous to Germanicus, but it would be foolish to read any political significance into it. Drusus Caesar was still childless when the will was written, and his responsibilities were accordingly fewer. The third grade was made up of relatives and friends. To be named in this way brought them little practical benefit, because the chances of their inheriting were negligible. Their inclusion was really a declaration of *amicitia*, and they would almost certainly have been covered elsewhere in the will by individual legacies. Augustus explained that although he had taken in 1.4 billion sesterces from inheritances, he had spent it for the public good, along with what he had inherited from his father and from Caesar. Thus his actual estate would be considerably smaller than his income might have led people to expect. He left a number of legacies, in two groups. There were those given in bulk to the people and the army, to a total of about ninety million. Then there were individual bequests, the sums not recorded.[5]

Tiberius and Livia as his heirs would receive 150 million, a third of which would go to Livia. To enable her to inherit this substantial amount, special exemption from the financial disabilities suffered by women in inheritances had to be secured from the Senate (see chapter 9). This exemption, however, was to be the least remarkable of the arrangements made for her. By the terms of the will she was to be adopted by her late husband and entered into the Julian family. Moreover, just as Tiberius received the name of Augustus, she would receive the name Augusta, and be known henceforth as Julia Augusta. These extraordinary arrangements are discussed in detail in chapter 8.[6]

Once the will was settled, the arrangements for the funeral could go ahead. Tiberius was insistent that proper decorum should be observed. The Senate asked that members be allowed to act as pallbearers. The new emperor, who had an aversion to extravagant public gestures, declined their request. He also resisted the pressure to allow the body to be cremated in the Forum rather than in the Campus Martius, where Augustus' mausoleum had been built. He was particularly concerned about the risk of a repetition of the wild excesses following the cremation of Julius Caesar. To ensure public order, troops were lined up to guard the procession. Drusus and Tiberius delivered the funeral addresses. Then the body was placed on the pyre in the Campus Martius, to be lit by the centurions. An eagle was released and allowed to fly off, as if it were bearing his spirit to heaven. As it soared aloft, Numerius Atticus, a man of praetorian rank, swore that he saw the form of Augustus on its way to heaven, a claim supported by the Senate when later that year they declared Augustus a god. Numerius was rewarded by Livia with a million sesterces for his acute observation. At this point the chief mourners left, except for Livia. She displayed her devotion to the very end, remaining on the spot, along with the most prominent of the equestrians, for five days of mourning. She then gathered up Augustus' ashes and placed them in his mausoleum.[7]

The literary sources place much emphasis on the difficulties that soon arose between Tiberius and his mother. These differences were almost certainly philosophical, rather than personal, and caused by the impossible constitutional dilemma created by Augustus through his special arrangements for Livia (see chapter 8). In fact, the early years of the reign were dominated not by the Tiberius-Livia tensions but by the issue of Germanicus. In AD 12 he had general authority over the military districts on the Rhine frontier and command over the four legions stationed there. His wife, Agrippina, spent the summer in Antium, where Augustus owned a favourite villa, and on August 31 she bore her third son, Gaius.[8] She joined her husband in Germany, taking with her their new son, who was kitted out in a little soldier's uniform and boots and given the affectionate nickname of "little boots" — Caligula — a name that would later eclipse even that of his famous father. This domestic serenity was broken by the report of Augustus' death. The news caused considerable unrest among the northern legions, where severe conditions of service and unfulfilled commitments had already had an unsettling effect on morale, leading to scattered mutinies. Of considerable relevance to the story of Livia, the disaffection of the German legions is invested with a political flavour in the literary sources, which assert that the troops wanted Germanicus to usurp power. This idea is implausible, and difficult to reconcile with the trouble Germanicus later had in getting the soldiers to obey him. But once the notion had taken hold, it came to haunt Livia and Tiberius.[9]

Germanicus' handling of the mutiny seems to have been weak and incompetent, in contrast to the firm handling of a similar situation by Tiberius' son,

Drusus Caesar, who was sent to deal with military riots in Pannonia. Germanicus appealed unsuccessfully to the loyalty of the troops, and when he then dramatically threatened to kill himself was jokingly encouraged to go ahead. His final desperate move was to produce a bogus letter from Tiberius, supposedly offering to meet some of the concessions demanded. The gesture was backed up by bribes drawn from official funds. This bought a very brief respite. In the end only the theatrical gesture of his wife Agrippina resolved the crisis. Her threat to leave the camp with her children to seek the protection of neighbouring peoples shamed the mutinous troops into submission.[10]

Germanicus quickly set about removing the stain on his men by vigorous military actions. He would have felt a natural desire to pattern himself on his much-admired father, Drusus, by seeking to extend the Roman frontier as far as the Elbe. But his ambitions were not matched by a sound sense of strategy. His troops were forced to withdraw, and as they retreated hurriedly to the Rhine, Agrippina once again saved her husband's bacon. Tacitus tells us that the "great-spirited woman" (*femina ingens animi*) took on the duties of a commander (*munia ducis*) and met the retreating soldiers as they poured over the Rhine bridge at Vetera (Xanten). Although she was at an advanced stage of pregnancy (with her daughter and namesake, Agrippina the Younger), she came to their assistance by handing out clothing and supplying dressings for the wounded. Only later did they learn that her real contribution had been far more crucial. When news reached the military zone that the Romans had been trapped and that the Germans were teeming west, even threatening Gaul, panic broke out and there were frantic demands that the Vetera bridge be destroyed to stem the invasion. Agrippina stepped in to stop the demolition and saved the Roman troops from being trapped on the east bank of the river. At the same time she saved Germanicus' reputation from a fatal blow. Tacitus paints a vivid picture, derived from Pliny (probably from his work on the German wars), of the dramatic figure of Agrippina at the bridge, greeting the returning soldiers, praising them and expressing gratitude on behalf of the Romans for their sacrifices.[11] The whole incident infuriated Tiberius, who was deeply offended by the notion of women usurping the role of commanders or provincial legates (*duces* and *legatos*).

Tacitus brings in the lengthy description of Germanicus' campaigns almost as a digression, to emphasise his loyal devotion to Tiberius in spite of the jealousy and hostility of the princeps and his mother. The historian insists that the mutual antipathy between Livia and her son was put aside in their common cause of opposition to Germanicus, who, he claims, felt harassed (*anxius*) by a hatred that was both unfair and irrational. The reason given for their enmity was the suspicion that Germanicus had inherited the republican tendencies of his father and wanted to see an end to the imperial system *(libertatem redditurus)*. Tacitus revives this theme later, when we learn of Germanicus' final illness and the resentment it ignited in Rome. He cites a belief that both father and son, Drusus and Germanicus, had been cut down because they desired to restore *libertas*. Germanicus no doubt did inherit his father's popularity, but nothing he did even hinted at an interest in restoring the republican system (and the same is true of Drusus). In fact, Germanicus' rapidly accelerated career suggests a privileged representative of the imperial system and not a champion of the old republic.[12]

The claims of hostility should be treated with caution. Although the special circumstances of Germanicus' popularity and the high regard in which he had been held by Augustus might have been a source of embarrassment for Tiberius, there is certainly no real evidence of personal animosities before his accession. Even after it Germanicus remained perfectly loyal to the new emperor, and Tiberius' conduct, certainly to all outward appearances, was proper and even positive. Both Livia and Tiberius had been devoted to Germanicus' father, and all the sources agree that there were close bonds of friendship between Germanicus and Tiberius' son, Drusus Caesar. Hence Tacitus is obliged to suggest that the hatred of Livia and Tiberius was concealed *(occultis odiis)*.[13] Is it plausible that Livia would have felt hostility towards Germanicus? Tacitus seems to contradict himself. He notes that Livia and Augustus had no children of their own, but thanks to Germanicus and his wife, Agrippina, had the consolation of sharing great-grandchildren. Moreover, Suetonius says that Germanicus was much loved by Augustus, to say nothing of the rest of his family *(omitto enim necessitudines reliquas)*, which implies very strongly that Livia had the same warm feelings towards him. Her treatment of Germanicus' children was exemplary. She assumed responsibility for looking after Caligula, and probably his sisters also, when Germanicus was dead and Agrippina in forced detention. Suetonius reports that when one of the children of Germanicus and Agrippina, a particularly loveable child, died in early boyhood, Livia dedicated a statue of him as Cupid in the temple of Venus on the Capitol. (Augustus had this statue or a replica placed in his bedroom and would kiss it when he entered the room.) Germanicus named two of his daughters, Livia Drusilla and Julia Livilla, after his grandmother. Tacitus relates that in AD 16, during a crucial part of his campaign in Germany, Germanicus had a dream that he was offering a sacrifice and his special vestments became spattered with blood. In the dream Livia then handed him another, more beautiful, robe. Germanicus was elated by the omen. We are not told what it actually portended, but Livia's role is clearly supportive. When Germanicus took the auspices, he found that they confirmed the message of the dream. So he called his men together and gave them a rousing speech to engage the enemy. This would have been an odd dream indeed if Germanicus' sleep was disturbed, as is claimed, by anxiety over Livia's supposed hatred for him.[14]

Germanicus conducted further campaigns in 16, moving his legions by boat down the Weser. A devastating storm scattered the vessels, and the survivors were cast up along the shoreline of the North Sea, some carried as far as Britain. Undaunted, he made further incursions into Germany, and Tacitus asserts that AD 16 closed with the morale of the Rhine legions at a peak and their commander fully convinced that with one further thrust he could advance the Roman boundary to the Elbe. Hope seems to have taken over reality, but in the event he was denied his final great opportunity to prove (or perhaps humiliate) himself. Tiberius recalled him to Rome, a gesture ascribed by some, surely unfairly, to jealousy and spite.[15] If Germanicus saw his recall from Germany as a private snub, he kept his thoughts to himself, and Tiberius went to every length to convey a public image of official approval. A posture of great military success was maintained, and on his arrival he was treated as a returning hero. On May 26, AD 17, he celebrated a magnificent triumph for his supposed victories.[16] The lavish triumph and the assurance of a consulship for the next year might not in themselves have been seen by Germanicus as adequate compensation for the loss of his German command. But Tiberius more than made up for any disappointment by offering him a responsibility that seemed perfectly suited to his diplomatic skills, a crucial mission in the East to deal with a number of problems, but primarily to mediate with Parthia over the controversial status of Armenia. Rome was resolved to ensure that this small mountainous country should remain in friendly control as a buffer state, and to foil Parthia's aim of controlling the territory. Velleius acclaimed the commission as a considerable distinction. Tacitus predictably saw it as a typical piece of Tiberian hypocrisy, designed to get Germanicus out of the way.

One of the problems that Germanicus would have to deal with was the status of the kingdom of Cappadocia, whose king, Archelaus III, had died in captivity in Rome not long before Germanicus' departure.[17] By AD 17 Archelaus had been in possession of Cappadocia for fifty years. There had been long-standing ill feeling between him and Tiberius. The emperor as a young man had responded to Archelaus' urgent appeal to act as his advocate, when an action was brought against the king by his own subjects. Archelaus clearly had an undeveloped sense of gratitude and gave Tiberius the cold shoulder when he was in Rhodes. Tacitus notes that this happened in the golden days of Gaius Caesar, who had been sent to settle affairs in the East, and Archelaus had clearly been given to understand that friendship with Tiberius could be dangerous. Once he became princeps, Tiberius had the satisfaction of getting his own back, but Dio makes it clear that the basic motive for his action was not in fact personal. Archelaus was accused of plotting rebellion. The precise indictment is unclear. He may have interfered in the confused affairs of Armenia, and Levick has suggested that his crime might have been that he helped a relative, Zeno, to the throne of Armenia without consulting Rome. Philostratus talks obscurely of intrigue between Archelaus and the governor of Cilicia. Whatever the basis of the charge, the incorporation of Cappadocia, an area of considerable military importance, was almost certainly a matter of state politics rather than private spite.

But how to get Archelaus to Rome? At this point Tacitus informs us that Tiberius turned to Livia to write to the king to entice him from his kingdom. She was quite frank in her letter to the king about Tiberius' anger, but she promised that if he came to Rome to make amends, he would receive clemency. Suetonius does not mention Livia in the context of Archelaus' being lured to Rome, but he does speak of Tiberius having recourse to *blanditias atque promissa* (blandishments and promises).

Archelaus took Livia at her word, but no sooner was he in Rome than he found himself brought before the Senate on what Tacitus describes as fictitious charges. He died in the city. It was not the charges that broke him but rather his old age — he was decrepit and suffered from gout. So frail was he that he could not sit straight; he was carried into the Senate and spoke from a litter. This physical weakness was aggravated by anxiety, for he had in the past been offended by anyone presumptuous enough to treat him as an equal, and straight humiliation was a novel experience. He seems to have suffered a nervous breakdown, creating the impression that he had lost his mind. Dio claims that during the trial he knew full well what he was doing and just pretended to be gaga. He would have been put to death, but one of the witnesses testified that Archelaus had declared that when he got back to Cappadocia he would show them that he was a man of muscle. This disclosure caused much mirth, and Tiberius saw that his execution was hardly necessary. Eventually he died, possibly a suicide. His kingdom was incorporated into the empire, a process that allowed for a reduction of the unpopular sales tax imposed by Augustus to finance his military treasury. Modern claims that Tiberius spared Archelaus' life because of the intercession of Livia cannot be substantiated by any ancient source, although a promise of support might be implied in the letter that she initially wrote to him. Nor is it clear that she was conscious that in corresponding with Archelaus she was laying the foundations for his ruin. Perkounig suggests that the whole incident has been distorted to associate Livia in a sordid affair for which Tiberius should bear the responsibility, just as Livia and Tiberius would later be associated in guilt in the death of Germanicus. Certainly, if she deliberately tricked Archelaus into coming to Rome, this would contradict Velleius' claim that those who associated with her only benefitted by her intervention. But Archelaus might have damned himself by his own conduct after his arrival, because Livia's letter did indicate to him that clemency would have to be preceded by contrition. Moreover, if one takes the broader view, it might be argued that Livia's conduct was directed towards the common good. Archelaus had fallen foul of Rome. He might have faced military action in Cappadocia, which could have proved disastrous for his people and his kingdom. Thus Livia's conduct would be seen as directed towards a constructive end. That said, the incident should serve to alert us to the danger of excessive naïveté in interpreting political affairs. It is clear that when political reality demanded it, Livia was prepared to place the interests of the state before any personal rapport she might have developed with a client-king.[18]

In autumn 17 Germanicus set out with a large retinue, including his wife, Agrippina, and his son Caligula. Technically, he was a functionary going to his *provincia*, but his journey to the East had all the atmosphere of a grand progress, as cities tried to outdo one another in the lavishness of their hospitality. On the island of Rhodes, Germanicus met the man who was to dominate the final months of his life, Gnaeus Calpurnius Piso. At about the same time as he had entrusted Germanicus with his eastern commission, Tiberius had appointed Piso, described by Tacitus as naturally violent (*ingenio violentum*), as legate of Syria. The appointment was to have major consequences for both Tiberius and Livia. Piso belonged to a prominent Roman family. His father had been a bitter opponent of Julius Caesar, conducting a campaign against him in Africa, and after the dictator's death he had become an adherent of Brutus and Cassius. Following the amnesty he had refused to serve under Augustus until approached with a personal request to do so. He went on to hold the consulship in 23 BC and was entrusted with the accounts of the Roman armies and finances in the same year, when the emperor fell seriously ill and thought he was on the point of death.[19] Tacitus asserts that the younger Piso inherited the father's arrogance; he served in Spain and held the consulship with Tiberius in 7 BC, and at some point was governor of Africa, where Seneca claims that he acted with unwarranted brutality towards his own men.

Towards the end of his life Augustus supposedly held a discussion in which he pondered the names of potential successors. In some accounts Piso was included in the list, and it is implied that the emperor considered him a serious contender and bold enough to take on the responsibility if offered it. Certainly his stock was high enough for him to be co-opted not much later into the *sodales Augustales*, the priestly body charged with the cult of the deified Julius and Augustus.[20] Piso clearly felt, if Tacitus is to be credited, that his mission was to clip Germanicus' wings, and there were some who believed *(credidere quidam)* that he had received secret instructions to that effect. None of this is provable, of course, and even if true it does not mean that there was anything sinister afoot — Germanicus' conduct in Germany provided ample evidence of a tendency to recklessness, and it might have been felt that he would benefit from a steadying influence. We simply do not have enough information about his career to be sure why Tiberius thought Piso was the right man for the key position of legate of Syria at this particular time. His wife, Plancina, was a close friend of Livia's, but Tiberius' aversion to petticoat politics would have made him immune to any maternal pressure in such a matter. If Tacitus is correct that Piso, like his father, was the kind of man who could scarcely admit the superiority even of the princeps, his strength of will might have been a quality that was felt to be needed in the circumstances.

Whatever unfortunate family traits Piso might have inherited from his father, they were supposedly aggravated by the malign influence of his wife. Munatia Plancina was the daughter (or granddaughter) of Lucius Plancus, censor of 22 BC, and the sister of Lucius Munatius Plancus, who had held the consulship in AD 13. Judging from Livia's close ties to Plancina, Lucius Munatius may well have enjoyed the imperial patronage, and he was appointed to head a commission sent to help deal with the mutinies on the Rhine frontier in 14. Tacitus claims that Livia, inspired by the usual female spite to want to harass Agrippina, gave Plancina her own set of instructions, but he offers no clue about what, specifically, she was supposed to do. Perhaps Livia was anxious to avoid in Syria another theatrical performance like the episode at the bridge over the Rhine. Agrippina's gesture there may well have benefitted the distressed troops but would have been deeply offensive to conservative Romans, not least conservative Roman women, and would have been uncomfortably reminiscent of the worst aspects of the notorious Fulvia's behaviour (see chapter 7).[21]

On his journey to Syria, Piso stopped off in Athens, where he reputedly behaved with considerable rudeness, supposedly as a reproof of Germanicus for showing such deference to the riffraff that made up contemporary Athens, people who had supported Mark Antony against Augustus.[22] From there he took the fast route to Rhodes and then to Syria. Once in the province he reputedly pandered to the soldiers, bribing them and relaxing their good order (a claim difficult to reconcile with his reputation for brutal discipline in Africa). He also removed veteran officers and replaced them with men of his own choosing. Of course, after Germanicus' adventures in Germany, Tiberius might have considered it an important priority that Piso should keep the Syrian legions under his very tight control. Plancina also did her bit, and supposedly at Livia's direction used every opportunity to denigrate Agrippina, but at the same time she was prepared to imitate her earlier activities in Germany, taking part in the cavalry drills and the infantry exercises. She thus, as Tacitus observes, failed to observe the limits of female decorum (*decora feminis*), although the historian omits to mention that the precedent had been set by Agrippina herself. Tacitus does not explicitly come out and say that this happened with the knowledge of Tiberius, but by stating that people increasingly believed the rumour that he knew, in his usual way he leaves an impression of Tiberius' culpability.[23]

Germanicus was supposedly aware of Piso's game but refused to let the awkward situation affect his performance. He dealt first with Armenia, where Zeno was installed — he was to last sixteen years in power. He then absorbed a number of old kingdoms into the empire, including Cappadocia, whose king Livia had helped remove.[24] With these tricky administrative issues settled, Germanicus returned to Syria. Late in 18 Germanicus and Piso had their first encounter in the province, at Cyrrhus, in the camp of the tenth legion. It was not a warm meeting. There was a clash over Piso's unwillingness to accept Germanicus' instructions, possibly because of a genuine misunderstanding over their respective authority.[25] In the winter of 18–19 Germanicus visited Egypt. He enjoyed a rapt reception at Alexandria, where he ordered a grain distribution to relieve a famine. He then took a cruise up the Nile, visiting the antiquities and the standard tourist destinations, such as the pyramids. The trip may have been quite innocent; indeed he owned estates there jointly with Livia (see chapter 9), which he may have wanted to visit. Moreover, in Alexandria, Germanicus went out of his way to demonstrate his loyalty to, and affection for, Tiberius and Livia, as revealed in two surviving papyri that preserve speeches to the people of Alexandria. In one he refers to the personal hardships caused by the prolonged absence from those close to him, including his "father and grandmother." In another he rejects any notion of special honours for himself but declares their appropriateness for Tiberius, the *soter* and *euergetes* (saviour and benefactor) of the world, and for Livia, whom

Germanicus again refers to as his grandmother *(mamme)*. But for all his declarations of loyalty, his actions were at the very least imprudent. Egypt was an imperial province different from all the others, in particular because of its importance as a source of grain. As a consequence, Augustus had banned visits by senators without express permission, a prohibition that was still in effect. When Germanicus returned to Alexandria, he found a stern rebuke awaiting him, along with a minor reprimand for dressing like a Greek. It is hardly likely that he had any designs on Egypt, but the episode does highlight Tiberius' concern — probably well-founded — about his adopted son's undeveloped sense of responsibility.[26]

When he got back to Syria, Germanicus discovered that Piso had rescinded the orders given to the legions and to the civilian communities. The tension now reached boiling point, and Piso recognised that the most diplomatic course would be for him to take his leave. In the meantime, Germanicus had fallen ill, and the discovery in his house of spells and curses, such as lead tablets carved with his name, along with other evidence of witchcraft, strengthened his suspicions that his illness was not natural. Piso was on the island of Cos when word was brought that his rival had breathed his last, on October 10, AD 19.

As Germanicus' condition had worsened, he had become increasingly convinced that he had been poisoned, and his dying wish was to ask his friends to make sure that Piso and Plancina would be brought to justice. He also asked them to exploit the high regard that Romans felt for his wife, Agrippina, while begging her to be more tactful and diplomatic. Tacitus cleverly relates Germanicus' conviction that he was dying *muliebri fraude* (through female treachery), presumably with reference to Plancina but deliberately ambiguous enough to associate Livia in the charge. That said, Germanicus also suggested in his final words that the notion of secret instructions given to Piso and Plancina was essentially a fiction: *fingentibus scelesta mandata . . . non credent homines* (people will not believe them if they pretend that there were wicked instructions).[27]

The funeral was conducted on a lavish scale in Antioch. The body was placed in public view, then cremated, and the fact that the heart could not be destroyed by the flames was taken as proof of poisoning, available for all the world to see. Finally, the ashes were collected for transportation to Rome.[28] When news began to filter to the city that Germanicus was ill, the gossip mill was sent into high gear. Tacitus claims that there was a widespread conviction that like his father, Drusus, he was paying the price for his republicanism, and suspicions were voiced about Piso's appointment to Syria and supposed secret discussions between Livia and Plancina. Suetonius also reports the general opinion *(creditur* and *opinio fuit)* that Tiberius had been in league with Piso to trick Germanicus. The usual appeal to rumour and mindreading confirms the suspicion that the speculation reflected in the sources over Tiberius and Livia's conduct and motives was based on little or no concrete evidence.²⁹

When Rome was finally hit by the stunning news of Germanicus' death, there was near-hysteria in the city, and lavish posthumous honours were bestowed on him.³⁰ Passions rose even higher when the grieving Agrippina landed at Brundisium on Italy's east coast in early AD 20, clutching the urn containing Germanicus' ashes. As she proceeded along the Appian Way towards Rome, she was met by a stream of officials and ordinary people. Amidst pomp and ceremony the ashes were deposited in the Mausoleum of Augustus, and that night the Campus Martius was illuminated by blazing torches. There was an overwhelming outburst of emotion and sympathy for Agrippina. Livia, who had tried both publicly and privately to make her life a model of what was right and fitting, must have seen a cruel irony in the praise that Agrippina received as an "ornament to her country" *(decus patriae)*, and must have felt incensed to hear her described as "an unequaled example of old-fashioned virtues" *(unicum antiquitatis specimen)*. Politically, it was even more ominous when people acclaimed Agrippina as the last representative of the line of Augustus.³¹

Conspicuously absent from the public ceremonies were Tiberius and Livia. As often, Tacitus tries to put the worst possible complexion on their behaviour. He does concede that they probably felt it "undignified" *(inferius)*, but goes on to suggest that the paramount reason for their absence was that if they were seen in the act of mourning, it would be recognised for the hypocrisy that it was. Thus Tacitus, who regarded Tiberius as the master of deception, and his mother as a good match for him in this sphere, felt that they were afraid that their faces would give them away. Tacitus' conclusion runs into a serious obstacle. He concedes that he checked earlier historians and the official records *(diurna actorum scriptura)*, where the attendance of Germanicus' relatives was recorded by name, but was unable to find any evidence that Antonia, Germanicus' mother, played any role in the ceremony, nor could he find any clue for why she failed to attend. He admits that she might have been prevented by ill health but goes on to say, without any apparent basis for his suspicion, that he finds it "easier to believe" *(facilius crediderim)* that she was detained by Livia and Tiberius at the palace. Holding her there would confer some respectability on their absence by giving them the cover that they had stayed at home out of a sense of duty and respect for Drusus' widow. In fact, with the discovery of the *Tabula Siarensis*, which documents the posthumous

honours voted to Germanicus, we now know that Tiberius was actively involved in selecting the tributes from among those proposed by the Senate, in
consultation with his mother, his son Drusus, Agrippina, and Antonia. Thus
Tiberius, Livia, and Antonia were not totally detached from the general process of honouring Germanicus.[32]

According to Tacitus, the people of Rome were struck by the comparison
between Drusus' funeral in 9 BC and the rites arranged for Germanicus in AD
20. The absence of Livia and Tiberius from the ceremony aggravated the
public displeasure, and there were rumblings that Germanicus had not even
enjoyed the send-off that any respectable run-of-the-mill member of the nobility could rightly expect. But again, the *Tabula Siarensis*, with its wealth of
honours for Germanicus, illustrates the general unfairness of the charge and
shows that Tacitus' report of the official reaction to Germanicus' death is
abbreviated and incomplete. His short account of the *honores* for the deceased
hardly reflects what the Senate voted, such as the detailed sculptural montage
for the arch to be erected in the Circus Flaminius, with the statue of Germanicus flanked by statues of his family. One of the specific complaints noted
by Tacitus was the absence of panegyrics *(laudationes)*. The *Tabula* shows that
such panegyrics in fact took place earlier, within the Senate, delivered on
separate occasions both by Drusus Caesar and by Tiberius, and that the full
text of both was to be inscribed in bronze. But Tacitus is surely right in his
assertions of popular discontent. Tiberius felt obliged to issue a public statement in what proved to be a vain effort to defuse feelings. He declared that he
shared the general sense of loss but believed that his response should be
restrained (the Latin text is somewhat ambiguous at this point), because the
same licence was not allowed ordinary people and rulers. The Roman world
had endured in the past the destruction of armies, the deaths of generals,
and the complete eradication of historic houses. Tiberius ended with the
commonplace that their leaders were mortal, but the state was immortal. Although we cannot assume that the text as recorded by Tacitus is precisely
accurate — there was a convention among ancient historians to invent plausible speeches — the thoughts are completely in character for Tiberius, who
might well have felt that the public displays of mourning for Germanicus had
turned into something of a circus. Tiberius later showed the same restraint
during the funeral rites of his son Drusus, keeping his expression unmoved
while those around him wept. He declared to the Senate on this later occasion
that he found it easier to handle grief by an attitude of "business as usual," adding, significantly, that he recognised that he would be criticised for taking such
a position. Also, Romans seemed to have forgotten that some years earlier Ti-

berius had expressly limited the mourning over his brother Drusus, on the grounds that "discipline had to be preserved" not only in warfare but also in grief. Livia, too, was commended for her dignity and restraint in dealing with the death of the elder Drusus, her son. But Tiberius' pronouncements about the need for a dignified response to Germanicus' death probably did little to win over the general public to him or his mother. Nor should this be surprising. Nearly two thousand years later the House of Windsor, mother and son, learned the cost of maintaining a reserve and dignity amidst fanatical displays of grief for a departed icon. It should finally be noted that a decade later Tiberius neglected to attend even his mother's funeral (see chapter 11).[33]

It appears that while Piso was lurking in Cos, it had devolved upon the senators in the province to appoint a new temporary legate, without the need to secure the authority of Germanicus (who perhaps had been too ill to take part). Their ultimate choice was Gnaeus Sentius Saturninus, who had been suffect consul in AD 4. To judge from a fragmentary inscription from Neopolis, Syria, dated between 21 and 30, where Sentius is described as *legatus Caesaris*, his position in Syria was confirmed by Tiberius, a detail that was to prove significant for Piso.[34] When news of Germanicus' death reached Cos, Piso received differing advice on his best next step. His son Marcus sensibly pressed him to return to Rome to face what would be inevitable unpopularity, but nothing more serious. Others with less foresight urged that he should exercise his authority as the true legate of Syria. These same men, as Tacitus relates their argument, reminded Piso that once he returned to Rome he would have no support. He had enjoyed the complicity of Livia and the backing of Tiberius. But that complicity could be acknowledged only in private. In public no one would put on a bigger show of distress over Germanicus than those who were secretly overjoyed by what had happened. This slur on Tiberius and Livia is contradicted, of course, by the earlier report that they in fact avoided a public display of grief. Piso chose to listen to the activists rather than to his son, and in doing so committed a literally fatal error. He set sail for the province but soon realised that he had seriously misread the situation in Syria, where he had anticipated that he would win the loyalty of the legions. In the event, the bulk of the army in Syria remained loyal to Sentius Saturninus. The beleaguered Piso was ultimately driven to find refuge in the fortress of Celendris in Cilicia, where after a brief siege he surrendered unconditionally. The only concession he secured was a safe passage to Rome, where he would now have to face far more serious consequences than the unpopularity that his son Marcus had predicted for him if he returned to Rome at the outset.[35]

Piso was full of self-confidence when he reached the city, early in AD 20. He threw a dinner party and gaily decorated his house.[36] But the euphoria was short-lived. The day after his arrival, charges were laid against him of murder, extortion, and treason, and Plancina was charged along with him. Until the 1990s evidence for the trial that followed consisted essentially of Tacitus' account, with brief notices in other sources. Recently discovered epigraphic material of major significance, consisting of bronze fragments found in various locations in Baetica in Roman Spain, has thrown new dramatic light on many of the issues raised in the trial. Although these sources vary in some small details, they represent the text of a summary of a senatorial decree (strictly speaking, several decrees), the *Senatus Consultum de Cn. Pisone Patre* (hereafter, the *Piso Decree*), enacted in connection with the trial, ending with a *subscriptio* of Tiberius in which he instructs that the document is to be posted in the major provincial centres and the army camps.[37]

Tiberius declined to hear the case himself *in camera* and remitted it to the Senate, where he presided over the proceedings. This arrangement, according to Tacitus, was to Piso's satisfaction, because he felt that the princeps had the integrity to discard rumours, and his confidence was boosted by what Tacitus calls Livia's guilty participation in the affair. This, of course, represents only Tacitus' conjecture of what was going on in Piso's mind — he makes no suggestion that Piso communicated any such thoughts to a third party.[38] The trial was convened in the portico of Apollo's temple on the Palatine. Piso made no progress on the more serious charges either in the Senate hearing or outside, where the public mood grew distinctly nasty. A lynch mob came up to the Palatine and collected outside the temple, baying for his blood. They hurled his statues down the Gemonian stairs, and Suetonius says that Piso himself came close to being torn to pieces.[39]

Tacitus notes that the *invidia* felt for Plancina was just as bitter, but that she enjoyed *maior gratia* (bigger support), and it was unclear how far Tiberius would be able to act against her. Plancina had insisted that she would stand by Piso. But as the trial progressed, she could see the writing on the wall and decided to look out for herself. She prevailed on Livia to intercede on her behalf and then began to dissociate her defence from Piso's.[40] At this stage Piso was ready to concede defeat, and only the urging of his sons convinced him to resume his defence. But he could sense the hostility of the Senate. After returning home, he wrote a few notes, which he handed to his freedman, then closed the door to his room. Next morning he was found with his throat cut. A sword lay on the floor. Conspiracy theorists denied suicide.[41]

Piso's last letter was read out in the Senate. In it he declared his loyalty to Tiberius and Livia, and begged that his sons not be made to suffer for their father's behaviour. The letter was perhaps most striking for what it omitted to say. As Tacitus laconically observes, *de Plancina nihil addidit* (he said not a word about Plancina). In his final hours Germanicus had demonstrated clearly his devotion to Agrippina, giving her fond if anxious farewells. The contrast between that scene of matrimonial bliss and tragedy and Piso's ultimate disdain for his wife is self-evident.[42]

The suicide of Piso did not bring an end to the trial. The Senate was instructed by Tiberius to reach findings on the case against Piso himself, his son Marcus, his wife, Plancina, and his chief lieutenants in Syria. The final resolution ensured that Piso's name would remain under a shadow. His statues were to be removed from public places, and his image was banned from funeral processions. Marcus was treated with understanding; part of the family property, although confiscated, was even returned to him as a generous gesture. The chief lieutenants were exiled and their property confiscated.[43] The treatment of Plancina is perhaps the most interesting. She spoke in her own defence to the Senate, although she may well have been obliged to stand at the entrance to deliver her speech. There are other examples of such personal appearances by women, although they are rare. Annia Rufilla, for instance, had on one occasion stood at the threshold of the Senate shouting abuse at one of the members yet was able to claim immunity because she held the portrait of the emperor as she did so.[44] In her speech Plancina was no doubt more restrained than Annia, but she did not mount a proper rebuttal. She would have found herself very vulnerable if she had been obliged to do so, for among other actions she had made her slaves available to Piso when he went into Syria, an action that would be difficult to defend. It was the intervention of Tiberius that saved her. He spoke on her behalf, and Tacitus describes his speech as a shameful performance, adding that it caused the emperor considerable embarrassment. In his defence he pleaded the intercession of his mother. The decree makes plain that Plancina was not in fact acquitted of the charges. Rather, the Senate acceded to Livia's wishes and decided to waive the penalty in her case.[45] (The issue is considered in chapter 8.) The proceedings wrapped up with a motion from Valerius Messalinus that the family of Germanicus be thanked for their efforts to ensure that he was avenged. Livia's name is included among those cited. The *Decree* sets out this *gratiarum actio* in some detail. In Livia's case it links the praise for her to that for Drusus, observing that they matched their devotion to the memory of Germanicus with their fairness in reserving judgement until the case was concluded. Unlike the other relatives of Germanicus, Drusus and Livia had been involved (in Livia's case indirectly) in the trial. The *actio* was perhaps intended to some degree to deflect the criticism that had been levelled against Livia and to argue that what had been perceived as bias was in fact the exercise of judicious balance. Again, when praising the moderation shown by Germanicus' children and his brother Claudius in their grief, the Senate gave full credit to the training (discipulina) that they had received from Tiberius and Drusus, and from Livia.[46]

The end of the trial did not bring an immediate end to the controversy. Tacitus observes, in perhaps his most insightful comment on the affair, that the Germanicus issue was a battleground of conflicting rumours (vario rumore iactata) and notes further that the frenzied speculation did not abate as time passed but perverted and confused the issues. Livia's conduct, Tacitus claims, was the object of savage but secret criticism, because she had consorted with the murderess of her grandson and had then rescued her from the Senate. The next step, it was feared, would be for her to turn the same poisons against Agrippina and her children. The expression used here is among the most powerful in the Tacitean corpus. Tiberius and Livia, it was believed, would seek to sate their hunger on the blood of a family reduced to calamity. As often on these occasions, the criticisms were supposedly made secretly, and thus were unprovable. That said, given the mood of the time, Livia's reputation must have suffered, at least in the short term, through her support of Plancina.[47] A hint of the strength of feelings may be found in the actual circumstances of the Piso Decree. In Tacitus' account the trial of Piso is followed by the ovation of Drusus, which had been voted earlier but postponed. The ovation is securely dated by the fasti to May 28, and the trial must have preceded that date. If Tacitus' sequence is chronologically correct, the decree must have been issued considerably later than the actual trial, for it is dated to December 10. The problem is far from settled, but the decision to promulgate the decree so long after the event might be evidence of anxiety about continuing unrest among the troops and throughout the provinces. That said, it is hard to imagine that it could have done much good. The self-serving nature of the document and its adherence to a strict party line would surely have been apparent even to the least cynical.[48] Although many of the inferences that Tacitus draws may arouse scepticism, the very decision to distribute the decree in a permanent medium outside Italy confirms his picture of the resentment stirred up by Germanicus' death.

Although Tacitus insists, not too convincingly, that Livia and Tiberius were racked by a seething hatred of Germanicus and his family, he concedes that relations between Germanicus and Drusus Caesar, brothers by adoption, had been strikingly amiable and harmonious (egregie concordes). It comes as no surprise, then, that after their father's death, Germanicus' two eldest sons,

Nero and Drusus, were given a home by Drusus Caesar, who treated them as kindly as he would his own children. It is possible that the hand of Tiberius or Livia lay behind this gesture, as a public declaration that Livia's great-grandsons (and Tiberius' grandsons by adoption) would be accorded their due recognition when the issue of the succession came to the fore. In addition, Drusus Caesar had a personal cause to celebrate, in an otherwise gloomy year. His wife bore him twin sons. Tiberius was delighted by the happy event but did not allow his joy to cloud his judgement. Although his own bloodline now seemed assured, he remained punctilious in advancing the prospects of Germanicus' sons. But despite his efforts to be scrupulously fair, things began to go terribly wrong.

The blame for the domestic crisis that divided the imperial house in the twenties cannot be laid at the door of Tiberius or Livia. The distrust within the family was so deep that there would probably have been little prospect of reconciliation, and Agrippina, with her smouldering sense of injustice, did little to help. But this difficult situation was made immeasurably worse by the intrigues of the one man whose interests were best served by continued tension and infighting. Lucius Aelius Sejanus, later to become the most notorious figure of Tiberius' principate, had first entered the record while serving in an unspecified capacity in the retinue of Gaius Caesar. He became joint prefect of the praetorian guard with his father in AD 14 and sole prefect in 16 or 17. By that time he had the ear of Tiberius, playing on the emperor's insecurities during Germanicus' Rhine campaigns in the early days of his reign. Sejanus is given an active, if vague, role in the Piso affair, in arranging the suppression of incriminating documents.[49] He was clearly someone who could work well behind the scenes. Despite his very brief appearances in the public record, he had by AD 20 become the emperor's right-hand man, close enough to be described by Tiberius as the "partner of his labours" *(socius laborum)*. He had also built up a power base both in the army and in the Senate. He spread his net widely and reputedly sought to enlist Livia, among others, to further his cause.[50]

Livia was very conscious of the importance of staying in good health and seems to have reached her eighties unscathed. In AD 22, however, she received, perhaps for the first time, a clear and dangerous intimation of her mortality when she was brought down by a serious, unspecified, illness. Tiberius had left Rome for Campania in the previous year, pleading his own ill health. Tacitus is sceptical about his excuse but is less than helpful on what might have been the true reason. He cannot decide whether Tiberius wanted to prepare himself for a later, more protracted, absence from Rome or to allow his son Drusus

Caesar, who was to hold the consulship in 22, to get on with the job without his father's brooding presence. In any case, Livia's situation was precarious enough for her son to rush back to be at her side. This was a touching gesture, something of a speciality for Tiberius. Some thirty years earlier, in 9 BC, he had hastened to Germany from Ticinum to be at the sickbed of his brother Drusus, and he had also rushed from Illyricum to Nola in AD 14 to attend Augustus in his final hours.[51]

Ever the cynic, Tacitus claims that Tiberius' show of concern was a sham, that deep down he was furious with his mother because of her constant attempts to steal the limelight from him. He was particularly incensed over the recent dedication of a statue of Augustus during which she had tried to claim precedence (see chapter 8). To put on the proper public face, Tiberius suppressed his irritation, and her illness was officially treated as a matter of great communal concern. When she recovered, the Senate decreed *supplicia* (acts of thanksgiving) to the gods and *ludi magni* (great games), to be put on by the pontifices, the augurs, the quindecimviri (officials entrusted with the charge of the Sibylline books and the general supervision of the foreign cults), and the septemviri, whose historic role was the congenial one of managing the banquets. These four constituted the great priestly colleges, and to make the occasion especially grand they were to be assisted by the Sodales Augustales, a body that had been formed in AD 14 on the death of Augustus and charged with the cult of the two *divi*, Julius and Augustus. The fact that the celebrations were in honour of the mother of the emperor invested the occasion with a special solemnity, which brought out the worst pedantry in everyone involved. Lucius Apronius moved that the presidency of the games should fall to the Fetials, a quaint body whose functions had become largely obsolete and who were concerned with such formalities as declarations of war and conclusions of treaties. Apronius, who is ranked by Tacitus as a sycophant of the first order, was clearly keen to curry favour, but the actual nature of the flattery is rather elusive. In any case, the attempt backfired. Tiberius opposed the inclusion of the Fetials, giving a short lecture on the precedence and prerogatives of the priesthoods (the Fetials did not really make the grade). This hardly seemed consistent, for he included the "junior" Augustales. He justified their presence with the very best of reasons, their family connections. He could have added that Livia's status as priestess of Augustus (see chapter 8) would have made the participation of this particular college highly appropriate. The issue, in any case, is hardly likely to have aroused great passions.[52]

Between July 22 and July 23 Tiberius issued a dupondius, depicting on its obverse a draped bust of Salus, her hair parted in the centre and falling in waves at the side of the head, and identified by the legend SALUS AUGUSTA (fig. 4) The reverse carries no image, only Tiberius' names and titles. The date and the reference to Salus (Well-being) leave little doubt that the coin alludes to Livia's illness. But the allusion is indirect. Salus Augusta does not mean the well-being of (Julia) Augusta. Feminine abstractions, like Salus or Pietas, modified by the adjective Augusta, refer not to Livia but rather to the association of the personified abstraction with the Augustan house. In the case of Salus, this association had a long history. In 16 BC Augustan coins celebrate vows taken for the emperor's salus, and identify it with the salus of the *respublica*, and oaths were sworn by the *Salus Augusti*, where the genitive indicates that the *salus* belonged to Augustus specifically. There was a cult of Augustus' salus during his lifetime, and a priest is attested at Alabanda. Although Valerius Maximus calls Tiberius the Salus of the country, that emperor may have discouraged dedications to his personal Salus; instead, they are made to the broader Salus Augusta. Inscriptions of the Tiberian period at Nasium in Gallia Belgica speak of the perpetual Salus of the divine house (*pro perpetua salute divinae domus*), and at Interamna there were dedications in AD 31 to Salus Augusta, along with Libertas Publica, the municipal *genius* and Tiberius' *providentia*, to celebrate the downfall of Sejanus. That said, the intention of the salus dupondius may be more nuanced. Although the legend does not refer overtly to Livia, and although the portrait technically is not hers, the head does have a human personality, and common sense dictates that in the year of her illness the coin would at the very least have been associated by the public with the emperor's mother.[53]

The equestrians were faced with a particularly knotty religious dilemma. They wanted to do their bit and to mark Livia's recovery by making an offering to equestrian Fortuna (*equestri Fortunae*). But in what temple would they make it? There were many shrines to Fortuna in Rome, but none that alluded specifically to the equestrians. One had indeed been vowed in 180 BC and dedicated in 173 to honour the achievements of the Roman cavalry. It was apparently still visible in the Augustan period, for the architect Vitruvius, the emperor's contemporary, speaks of seeing it. By AD 22 it had clearly been demolished, and the equestrians had no choice but to select a site outside the capital. The pleasant resort town of Antium to the south of Rome offered an ideal alternative. It had close associations with the cult of Fortuna, and could even boast a temple to Fortuna Equestris. Moreover, it was the location of one of the most important imperial villas, the birthplace of Caligula, and later of Nero. As a favourite summer residence of Augustus, Antium would certainly have been well known to Livia.[54] It is noteworthy that in their accounts of the outpouring of regard and affection for Livia the sources say nothing of the ill will aroused earlier by the death of Germanicus. The public resentment seems to have been short-lived, perhaps assuaged to some degree by Piso's suicide. The affair clearly had no long-term impact on Livia's reputation.

There is some evidence that the Senate made an additional gesture to honour Livia in the year of her illness by drawing attention to her sons' *pietas*, a peculiarly Roman concept that embraced duty both to the gods and to the family. They voted for the erection of a structure to *Pietati Augustae*, long referred to by modern scholars as the Altar of Pietas Augusta. It was not completed for another twenty years, when its dedication was recorded in a Claudian inscription. The original stone is lost, but the text is preserved in a transcription, one of the many made by the itinerant and anonymous monk of Einsiedeln in the middle ages. Koeppel has pointed out that the notion of an Ara Pietatis was dreamt up by Mommsen in the nineteenth century, and since then its existence is simply taken for granted. In fact, we have no idea what the structure was or how large it was — it could have been something as small as a statue base or as large as a temple. The text records the dedication of the building, whatever it was, by Claudius in AD 43, though in fulfillment of a *senatus consultum* passed during the consulship of Decimus Haterius Agrippa and Gaius Sulpicius Galba — that is, more than twenty years earlier, in AD 22. The reason for the long delay between the original vote and the final dedication is puzzling. Tiberius left Rome within four years of the decree, and interest in the project might have fallen into abeyance for a time. It would be revived later by Claudius, who was keen to establish his own ancestral credentials and had arranged the consecration of Livia in the year immediately preceding the dedication.[55]

In 23 Sejanus further strengthened his position by concentrating the cohorts of the praetorian guard into one set of permanent barracks at the Porta Viminalis.[56] The main obstacle to his growing influence over the emperor was removed in September of the same year. Tiberius suffered a crushing personal blow when his son, Drusus Caesar, died. (It was revealed some years later that he may well have been poisoned by his wife, Livilla, who had become Sejanus' lover.) The emperor delivered a dignified speech in the Senate to mark the sad occasion and made it clear that he would now turn to Germanicus' sons, Nero and Drusus, to provide him with the support he would need to perform the duties required by his office. His mother, Livia, he pointed out, had reached *extremam senectutem* (extreme old age).[57] She was now eighty or eighty-one, and his thoughts were no doubt prompted by her serious illness in the previous year. There might also have been a quiet hint to Livia to yield to the conventional demands of years as advanced as hers, and to take more of a back seat (something of a vain hope). But she did not lack for honours. She was granted the privilege, whenever she entered the theatre, of taking her place with the Vestals. At one time men and women had been allowed to mix freely at the games. Augustus, who thought this promiscuity improper, had restricted women to the very highest seats. Only the Vestal Virgins were assigned decent seating, opposite the dais of the praetor. Caligula as emperor extended this entitlement, offering it to his grandmother Antonia and to his sisters. Claudius in turn granted it to his wife Messalina. There is also good reason to believe that Livia might at the same time have been offered the privilege of travelling in the *carpentum*, or covered carriage. Coins of AD 22 or 23 (dated by reference to Tiberius' twenty-fourth tribunician year) carry the device of the carpentum drawn by two mules, with its front and sides decorated with Victories and other figures (fig. 5). That these coins are associated with Livia's Vestal honours is strongly suggested by Dio's testimony that Messalina in 43 received the right to sit with the Vestals, and was at the same time allowed the use of the carpentum. The coin issue may, on the other hand, be related directly to Livia's illness, and the scene could relate to the procession of the supplicationes which the Senate decreed.[58] Also in AD 23 an honour came from farther afield, when with Tiberius' permission the cities of Asia decreed a temple to Tiberius, his mother, and the Senate (considered in some detail in chapter 8).[59]

These displays of family devotion would have helped to conceal a domestic atmosphere of increasing tension. Tiberius did go out of his way to treat Germanicus' boys with kindness and goodwill, and had their mother, Agrippina, reciprocated she might have been able to withstand the assault that Sejanus was preparing. In the event, her behaviour was the very opposite to what the situation demanded. Convinced, like her mother, Julia, that Tiberius was an unworthy *arriviste*, and embittered by the death of her husband and the exile of her mother and sister, she promoted the interests of her sons with a single-minded obsession. Sejanus was more than willing to encourage Agrippina on this suicidal course, and worked hard to isolate her, drawing on the help of Livia to bring this about. Clearly the prefect still thought Livia vigorous enough to be of use to him. She was supposedly urged through agents to go to Tiberius and persuade him that Agrippina was casting ambitious eyes on his position, which she had earmarked for one of her sons. Sejanus' task, Tacitus says, was made all the easier because Livia was antagonistic towards Agrippina, thus enabling Sejanus to exploit her *vetus odium* (old contempt). Livilla, Drusus' widow and Sejanus' mistress, helped her paramour. The *Piso*

Decree describes the bonds between Livilla and her grandmother as close. This could be an empty formula, but we do know that Livia provided a nurse from her own staff for Livilla. The young woman seems to have identified a way of winning Livia's support. She enlisted the aid of Julius Postumus, possibly the future prefect of Egypt in 47. He was supposedly known to Livia through his adulterous affair with her friend Mutilia Prisca, the wife of Livia's protégé Gaius Fufius Geminus, consul in AD 29. Julius is said to have worked hard to alienate Livia from Agrippina, and Tacitus observes that he was helped by the fact that she was herself *anxiam potentiae*, which could mean that she was desperate either to retain or to regain her influence, because Sejanus would by now have replaced her as Tiberius' closest advisor. Inevitably, Agrippina's ill-tempered zealotry would have created an atmosphere of rivalry in the imperial household. But we have no way of telling how successful Julius was, and there is no real evidence that Livia worked actively against her daughter-in-law. Her supposed intrigues may be little more than speculation.[60]

By now Livia was in her eighties and had been seriously ill. But she still remained involved, and that she was still a power in the land is suggested by a bizarre series of events dated to AD 24. In that year the praetor Plautius Silvanus entered in his modest way into the annals of history when he threw his wife out of their window to her death. He was charged before Tiberius. His answers to the emperor's questioning were rather fuzzy, and he claimed that he had been asleep at the time and unaware that his wife had committed suicide. Tiberius went to the house to examine the evidence on the spot and found signs of a struggle. He referred the case to the Senate. The case was a mysterious one, and it might be explained by the possibility that Silvanus was acting "under the influence." At any rate, his first wife, Numantina, was later charged with sending him crazy with drugs and spells (she was acquitted). As he awaited trial, Silvanus' grandmother Urgulania sent her grandson a dagger. Given Livia's close friendship with Urgulania, this was taken as tantamount to *monitu principis* (by guidance from the princeps), a clear sign that to the outside world Livia still carried much weight. The impression might have been reinforced by the prosecution and death (possibly suicide), about the same time, of Lucius Piso, who had shown contempt for Livia's potentia in acting against Urgulania some years earlier (see chapter 8). Silvanus attempted suicide but found that it was easier to finish off a wife than himself, and had to get help to do it properly.[61]

Meanwhile, within the imperial household the clashes between Tiberius and Agrippina grew, both in frequency and intensity. The emperor had by now endured enough of the strife and intrigue of palace life in Rome, and had come to the sober realization that it was time to take his leave. At some point in 26 he departed for Campania, and went from there to his villa on the island paradise of Capri. He was not destined to return to Rome, except for his own funeral. Why did he leave? The literary sources offer a wide range of suggestions.[62] There was the suspicion that Tiberius wanted a quiet spot to indulge in his acts of cruelty and lust. Another school of thought suggested that he left because of his appearance — he was by now totally bald, with an ulcerous face covered with plasters. The majority view of historians, according to Tacitus, ascribed the decision to leave to the relentless urging of Sejanus. The prefect kept bringing up the problems of life in the capital — the crowds, the endless petitioners — and stressed the pleasures of a quiet, peaceful life (but made no mention of Livia as an obstacle to a happy life). He also used the argument that Tiberius could rule from a distance, and would increase his popularity if Romans were not constantly reminded by his very presence that they were subject to his power. Tacitus does confront one obvious objection, that Tiberius stayed away from Rome after the prefect's fall. Of course, by then the aged emperor might simply have got used to the pleasure of being away from it all. All the main sources add another plausible reason: his desire to get away from his mother. Dio hedges a little, noting that it was chiefly because he found Livia such a handful even when she restricted herself to domestic matters that Tiberius removed himself to Capri. Tacitus records a common belief *(traditur)* that Tiberius could not stand his mother's uncontrollable passion for power *(matris impotentia)*. Suetonius is more specific. He reports that Tiberius was sorely put out that his mother had preserved letters of Augustus critical of him, and brooded over her behaviour, which seemed especially spiteful. Some thought, according to Suetonius, that this was the strongest of the reasons for his retirement.

It is clear that the sources are indulging in nothing more than speculation. In many ways the departure seems psychologically sound, the action of a man who found political life thoroughly distasteful yet who throughout his life had demonstrated an inability to resist the appeal of power. As an absentee emperor he could enjoy the best of both worlds. Tiberius no doubt was disgusted by the imperious behaviour of Agrippina, and the tension between the women of the house certainly may have influenced his decision. Syme points out that in the period before his departure Tiberius found himself in what he calls a nasty predicament, "being encompassed by no fewer than four widows" — Livia, Antonia, Agrippina, and Livilla (widow of Drusus).[63] All of this may simply have compounded his ongoing frustration over the insoluble problem that the complex constitutional situation of his mother had created, a problem that had dogged him since the beginning of his reign (see chapter 8).

Whatever motivated Tiberius' departure for Capri—and Livia personally was probably not the only cause—it is clear that little true affection remained between mother and son. They met on a single further occasion, and that was for only a few hours. History has not recorded where or when the meeting took place, or what was discussed. It certainly did not happen in Rome, which Tiberius never visited again. We do know that in 28 the emperor crossed from Capri to the mainland. Possibly during that visit he presided over the betrothal of Agrippina the Younger and her first husband, Gnaeus Domitius Aheno-barbus, parents of the future emperor Nero. Livia might well have been present in Campania, either specifically for the ceremony or to spend time at one of the imperial villas. But this is speculation.[64]

Tiberius had left behind a family rent by conflict. How closely involved Livia was in the internal wrangling is unclear. Intrigues there certainly were, but they seem mainly to have been instigated by Sejanus. The prefect's ultimate ambitions are a matter of some debate, but there can be no doubt that he would have seen Agrippina and her sons as their chief obstacle. His first efforts, once he had the field free to himself, seem to have been directed against Agrippina's sons. The oldest, Nero, suffered the common failing of young princes of the imperial house, an inability to hold his tongue. Sejanus bribed those close to him to egg him on. He made rash and injudicious statements, which were noted down and duly reported to Tiberius. At the same time the crafty prefect worked his way into the favour of Drusus, exploiting his resentment of his older brother, whom he saw as his mother's favourite.[65] Livia seems to have had little if any role in these family feuds. Nor in reality is there concrete evidence of a serious clash with Agrippina. To the contrary, Tacitus suggests very strongly that the presence of Livia in Rome to some degree protected Agrippina and her family.[66]

In the year following Tiberius' departure, AD 27, Sejanus finally made his move against his main target—Agrippina herself. He ordered his praetorians to keep watch over Agrippina and her son Nero and to make detailed reports on their activities. At some stage, probably in early 28, Agrippina was placed in a form of custody, possibly under house arrest. In another context Seneca remarks that she had a luxury villa at Herculaneum where she was once held under guard (the villa was later destroyed on the orders of Caligula).[67] Unfortunately, he does not indicate the date but it could well have been in AD 27. We do not know where Nero might have been, but he very possibly was subjected to similar restrictions. Livia was able to afford some limited degree of protection to Agrippina's family. Caligula, now aged fifteen, moved into his great-grandmother's home. The later role and wild reputation of Caligula have ensured that the ancient sources would take a lively curiosity in his whereabouts and record them in detail. But his younger sisters did not arouse the same interest. Thus if Livia took in his sisters Drusilla and Livilla also (Agrippina the Younger no doubt would have left home after her marriage in 28), it would not be remarkable for her gesture to go unmentioned. At any rate, we do know that after Livia's death, when Caligula was looked after by his other great-grandmother, Antonia, at least one of the sisters, Drusilla, lived with them (and reputedly engaged in incestuous underage sex with her brother). It is therefore a reasonable inference that Caligula and his two unmarried sisters had also lived together under Livia's roof.

Whatever Livia's personal feelings about the outspoken and headstrong Agrippina, a woman so different in temperament from herself, she clearly maintained a strong sense of family obligation. While Livia was still on the scene she could counter the influence of Sejanus, who, as Tacitus concedes, felt restrained by her presence from acting against his opponents in the imperial household. But Livia was not immortal. She had suffered a serious ailment in 22, and in 29 she fell ill again. This second illness proved to be fatal. It would prove in the end to be no less fatal for Agrippina and her oldest sons.

1 Denarius of Tiberius
(enlarged). Numismatica
Ars Classica, Zurich

2 Dupondius of
Tiberius. Numismatica
Ars Classica, Zurich

3 Dupondius of
Tiberius. Numismatica
Ars Classica, Zurich

4 Dupondius of
Tiberius. Numismatica
Ars Classica, Zurich

5 Sestertius of Tiberius.
Numismatica Ars
Classica, Zurich

6 Dupondius of
Claudius. Numismatica
Ars Classica, Zurich

7 Aureus of Nero
(enlarged). Numismatica
Ars Classica, Zurich

8 Denarius of Galba
(enlarged). Numismatica
Ars Classica, Zurich

9 Sestertius of
Antoninus Pius.
Numismatica Ars
Classica, Zurich

10 Lead tessera (Tiberius).
From Rostovtsev (1900)

11 Cameo, Tiberius and Livia.
Soprintendenza Archeologica di
Firenze

12 Head of Livia from Fayum. Ny Carlsberg Glyptothek, Copenhagen

13 Basalt head of Livia. Musée du Louvre, Paris

14 Head of Livia. Deutsches Archäologisches Institut, Rome. Inst. Neg. 78.1937

15 Head of Livia. Ny Carlsberg Glyptothek, Copenhagen

16 Giant head of Livia. From
Aurigemma (1940)

17 Head of Livia. Musée Saint-
Raymond, Toulouse

18 Bronze bust of Livia. Musée du
Louvre, Paris

19 Sardonyx, Livia and Augustus.
Kunsthistorisches Museum, Vienna

20 South frieze of Ara Pacis. Deutsches Archäologisches Institut, Rome. Inst. Neg. 72.2403

21 Detail of fig. 20. Deutsches Archäologisches Institut, Rome. Inst. Neg. 72.2403

22 Detail of statue of Livia as Ceres. Musée du Louvre, Paris

23 Statue of Livia as Ceres. Musée du Louvre, Paris

24 Statue of Livia as priestess.
Monumenti, Musei e Galerie
Pontificie, Città del Vatticano

25 Statue of Livia as priestess.
Deutsches Archäologisches Institut,
Rome. Inst. Neg. 67.1593

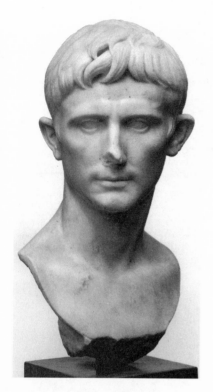

26 Head of Augustus. Ny Carlsberg
Glyptothek, Copenhagen

27 Head of Tiberius. Ny Carlsberg
Glyptothek, Copenhagen

28 Wall painting, Primaporta. From Antike Denkmäler (Berlin 1891)

29 Reconstruction of Mausoleum of Augustus. From Cordingley and Richmond (1927)

II

LIVIAN THEMES

THE PRIVATE LIVIA

Livia was a prominent figure in Roman society for most of her long adult life. Yet we have surprisingly little direct information about Livia the person, as opposed to Livia the wife or mother of the princeps. To some extent this was doubtless her own doing. Although she was capable of considerable charm and affability, to the extent of earning a mild rebuke from Tacitus for displaying these qualities more than was traditionally expected in women of the old school, behind her public persona Livia maintained a deliberate reserve. She may not have been so inclined by nature, but she certainly was by circumstance. Seneca calls her a *feminam opinionis suae custodem diligentissimam* (woman who was the most diligent protector of her reputation). She felt obliged to conduct herself always in such a way that there could be no criticism of her, not only on major issues but also on trifling matters. She thus created a protective shell which few would manage to penetrate.[1]

The dearth of information cannot be attributed totally to Livia's conscious effort to discourage public curiosity. We are told almost nothing even about her external appearance, which she can hardly have kept concealed. The ancient literary sources generally did not trouble to give detailed descriptions of individual women, nor do women figure in the various physiognomic treatises that began to appear in the fourth century BC.[2] When ancient authorities do provide information about how prominent women looked, their reliability is highly suspect. Ovid in his exile poetry describes Livia as having the form of

Venus and the face of Juno. At the time she was in her seventies, and the description surely reflects the poet's desire to please rather than Livia's physical appeal. By implication Dio also suggests an attractive appearance, for he relates a story that Augustus was so besotted by Terentia, Maecenas' wife, that he made her enter a beauty contest with Livia (the outcome is not recorded). Both Tacitus and Velleius speak of Livia's *forma*, which without modification has a straightforward positive connotation, and means essentially "beauty." Velleius' general enthusiasm for Livia, of course, should make us wary of his testimony, and Tacitus often links physical beauty to spiritual corruption. But a more serious problem is that all such descriptions, whether friendly or hostile, of aristocratic Roman women tend to be formulaic.[3]

Potentially a more reliable source of information should be the contemporary depictions of Livia that appear in various media, especially coins and sculpture. The general importance of this evidence will be dealt with in some detail in appendix 1; here we shall limit ourselves specifically to what it tells us about her appearance. The first problem to be faced is that no portrait explicitly identified as Livia's appears on any of the imperial coins—that is, on coins minted in Rome or in "official" mints outside the capital for distribution throughout the empire. There are possible depictions of her seated, and identified by name, more than a decade after her death, but the image is on such a small scale that it offers no insight into her appearance (figs. 1, 6). There are abstract personifications on coins during her lifetime, portraits of such figures as "Salus," "Iustitia," and "Pietas," which might obliquely reflect Livia's appearance (figs. 2–4). We must be cautious. Abstract personifications such as Salus that are grammatically feminine and modified by the adjective Augusta are not a direct allusion to Livia's name Augusta and in a formal sense have nothing specifically to do with Livia. This would not, of course, preclude Livia's being identified informally with whatever virtue is depicted, just as the public might well have associated the abstract virtues represented with the virtues of Livia, or at least an idealised concept of Livia. Only the Salus issue has idiosyncratic personalised features. Certainly outside of Rome the Salus coin was used as a type for Livia's portrait, and although this does not prove that it was a precise record of her appearance, it is likely that it broadly reflected her features.[4]

Sculpture is a little more helpful, but while a large body of sculpted portraits have been assigned to Livia, the evidence they provide has to be treated with caution, because the facial features that are repeated as established elements of her iconography do not necessarily represent her appearance precisely, and only the broadest generalizations should be drawn. In early portraits Livia sports the nodus hairstyle, in which the hair rolls forward over the forehead and is then drawn back to form a distinctive topknot. This style was seen by Ovid as a useful corrective to a very round face.[5] Generally in the heads of this group the face is a regular oval with broad cheekbones. The eyes are large and the brow above them arches slightly. The nose is large and aquiline, while the curving mouth and the chin are very small. The portraits project an image well suited to Livia — one of ageless and elegant beauty, calm and dignified, perhaps strangely emotionless (figs. 12–13). The severity of the nodus style would be less appealing with age. Thus the hair in portraits of the Tiberian period generally has a centre parting, and falls from either side in waves (fig. 17). The head is still relatively youthful, given that Livia must have been now in her seventies, a tradition maintained by modern aging monarchs, whose images on stamps and coins tend to be frozen for several decades. It could be argued that the elusive issue of Livia's appearance is irrelevant in a political biography. But it has some historical importance. The sources suggest that Augustus was drawn to Livia initially by basic sexual attraction. Some knowledge of her physical appearance would help us place that claim in a proper context.

Whatever attributes Livia was granted by Nature she could enhance by Art. When it came to dress, Ovid attributes to Livia a surprisingly progressive attitude, that she was simply too busy to spend a lot of time on her appearance. The assertion has to be seen against the background of a large household and an enormous staff, whose task it would have been to pay attention to those details deemed unworthy of their mistress's time and effort.[6] The evidence for the wide range of functionaries operating within the household of Livia is dealt with in chapter 9. At this point we can limit ourselves to noting the surprising number of helpers devoted to Livia's personal appearance. Inevitably there were several *ornatrices* (dressers), as well as staff *a veste/ad vestem*, whose task it was to keep her clothes in good order. In addition, the *ab ornamentis* would have had responsibility for her ceremonial garments and accessories, along with a specialist who looked after those she wore as priestess of Augustus, a freedman *ab ornamentis sacerdotalibus*. Her *calciator* made her shoes. Augustus liked to boast that his clothes were made by his wife and sister. Perhaps, but they would have had help. Livia employed both *lanipendi* (wool weighers) and *sarcinatores / sarcinatrices* (sewing men / women). For her comfort she had an *unctrix* (masseuse). Perhaps most striking are the skilled craftsmen who would have been employed for the manufacture and maintenance of luxury items. Her *aurifex* (goldsmith) and *inaurator* (gilder) might have been occupied mainly with furniture, but the *margaritarius* (pearl setter) sounds like someone who would have been employed to work on her personal jewellery.[7]

Elizabeth Bartman has noted the absence of jewellery from the sculpted images of Livia, which she describes as "bordering on the ascetic." This, of course, may have been a deliberate fabrication of Livia's image in the sculptural prototypes that she allowed to be distributed. There was a tradition of Roman women making a sacrifice of luxury items for the good of the state, such as the women who donated their jewellery to help fund the war against Veii in the early republic. But it may be that Livia aimed for understated elegance, to be *simplex munditiis*, as Horace expressed the concept in his famous poem. This could explain why Augustus aroused amused disbelief among the senators when he held up Livia as an example of womanhood and, when pressed to explain, cited as evidence her appearance and dress and her *exodoi* (her public forays) as illustrations of moderation to be emulated.[8] Augustus had the evidence of his own eyes, and he admired her for avoiding extravagance. But the senators perhaps may have seen a kind of elegant *moderatio*, the appearance of simplicity that only the best dressmakers, coiffeurs, and jewellers can produce, using the finest and most expensive material.

Livia's energies would have been channelled mainly into her role as wife of Augustus and as mother of Tiberius. We know little of her private interests, or of how she tried to relax. Only one scrap of evidence survives for anything remotely approaching frivolity. She seems to have competed inanely with Julia, the granddaughter of Augustus, over the record for owning the smallest dwarf. This was settled honourably, as Julia owned the smallest male, at two feet, one palm (about sixty-seven centimetres), but Livia could boast the smallest female dwarf, Andromeda, height not recorded.[9] We might also detect perhaps a hint of a certain silliness when she was a young woman. The story of her trying to foretell her child's sex by means of a hen's egg is noted in chapter 1. After Tiberius' birth she seems to have consulted an astrologer *(mathematicus)*, Scribonius. He was able to forecast that her son would govern, but without the trappings of monarchical rule, an especially impressive performance, because he anticipated this before the principate had been established and before Livia had even met Augustus.[10] But this kind of behaviour should be viewed in the context of its age, and Livia was probably no more unsophisticated in such matters than the great mass of her contemporaries. Otherwise her interests are likely to have been more serious, and she seems to have been a literate and educated woman. At any rate, in one of his letters to her Augustus quotes frequently and extensively in Greek, presumably on the assumption that she would understand him. She did of course spend some time in the Greek world during the period of her first husband's exile, but she would at that time have moved mainly in a Latin-speaking milieu. It is more than likely that she learned the language through formal tuition.

Given her family background, we can assume that Livia would have been well educated as a child. Roman girls shared domestic tutors with their brothers before their marriage. There are many examples of the happy result of this practice. Pliny the Younger was flattered to find his young wife reading and memorizing his works, and setting his verses to music. Cornelia, the wife of Pompey, was educated in literature, music, and geometry, and enjoyed attending philosophical discussions. The existence of the highly educated woman, at least at a slightly later date, is confirmed by the caustic observations of the atrabilious Juvenal, who proclaims horror at females who speak with authority on literature, discuss ethical issues, quote lines of verse the rest of humanity has not even heard of, and even correct your mistakes of grammar.[11] Apart from Livia's knowledge of Greek, however, we have no concrete evidence of her intellectual pursuits, in contrast to her great-granddaughter Agrippina, whose memoirs survived and were read by Tacitus (see appendix 1). But we do have some testimony about Livia's intellectual sophistication. Philo was a contemporary and, though a resident of Alexandria, very familiar with Rome and the imperial house. For example, he met Caligula in person when he headed a delegation to Rome to represent the case of the Jews of his native town. In a speech that he attributes to Caligula's Jewish friend Herod Agrippa, he has Agrippa cite the precedent of Livia, whom he represents as a woman of great mental ability and untypical of her sex, for he contended that women were generally incapable of grasping mental concepts (whether this is Agrippa's or Philo's prejudice is not made clear). Agrippa supposedly attributed Livia's superiority in this sphere to her natural talents and to her education (*paideia*). Livia was well disposed to the Jews and generous to the Temple, and we might expect some gilding of the lily. But Philo's characterization of her could clearly not have been absurdly wide of the mark, or the arguments attributed to Agrippa would have been discredited. The Corinthian poet Honestus describes Livia as fit company for the muses, a woman who saved the world by her wisdom. The inflated language traditional in such a dedicatory piece, however, means that it has little historical value. Apart from the uncertain case of Honestus, we have no other case of Livia's supporting any cultural or intellectual endeavour, although she was an active patron in many other areas. In this sphere she was eclipsed by Augustus' sister Octavia, who was a sponsor of the architect Vitruvius and to whom the Stoic philosopher Athenodorus of Tarsus dedicated a book of his work.[12]

Although Livia's interest in fostering artistic and cultural undertakings might have been limited, there was one field in which her enthusiasm seems to have been boundless: the issue of healthy living, both physical and psychological. Despite her general reserve in most other matters, she seems to have been willing, even eager, to impart her views on the issue of how to live a long and robust life. She was ahead of her time in her use of what would now be called a grief counsellor. When her son Drusus died in 9 BC, she was devastated. That she managed to handle the situation with dignity was due to no small extent to the counselling given her by the philosopher Areus (or Areius) Didymus of Alexandria. Areus was basically a Stoic but kept an open mind to other schools and ideas, the kind of eclectic pragmatist that the Romans found appealing. He was clearly a man of great charm, and at the time of Actium, Octavian described him as his mentor and companion. Octavian reputedly spared all the Alexandrians after the battle and stated publicly that he did so because of the fame of Alexander the Great, the beauty of the city, and his regard for one of its citizens, Areus. In the event Alexandria did not emerge totally unscathed, for Octavian followed up his generous gesture by visiting the corpse of Alexander, where he behaved like the worst kind of bad tourist, touching the nose and breaking it off.[13]

According to Seneca's account, to which the author undoubtedly added his own imaginative touches, Areus, in giving his advice to Livia, described himself as an *assiduus comes* (constant companion) of her husband and claimed to know not only their public pronouncements but also the *secretiores animorum vestrorum motus* (the deeper emotions of the two of you). He clearly knew his patient well, and in the event proved a highly effective consultant. He gently observed that Livia had been in the habit of repressing her feelings and of being constantly on guard in public. He encouraged her to open up when dealing with the subject of Drusus, to speak to her friends about the death of her son, and to listen to others when they praised him. She should also dwell on the positive side of things, particularly the happiness that he brought her when he was still alive. The advice may have the shallow ring of the popular psychology handed out in the modern media, but it worked. Seneca observed how well Livia coped with her loss by following this advice, in contrast to the morbidly obsessive Octavia, sister of Augustus, who never ceased to be preoccupied with thoughts of her dead son Marcellus.[14]

Livia lived a long and, by her own description, healthy life, with only one serious illness recorded, when she was already eighty. Her formula for her robust constitution seems to have been proper diet and the use of "natural" remedies. She clearly had the irritating habit of healthy people who insist on inflicting on others their philosophy of wholesome living. For history this has proved fortunate, because some of her dietary recommendations are recorded. In her early eighties she anticipated a trend that was to reemerge almost two thousand years later, attributing her vigorous condition to her daily tipple. She drank exclusively the wine of Pucinum. This was a very select vintage, grown on a stony hill in the Gulf of Trieste, not far from the source of the Timavo, where the sea breezes ripen enough grapes to fill a few amphorae. Pliny confirms its medicinal value, which he suspects might long have been recognised, even by the Greeks.[15]

It need not be thought that in following this regimen Livia had simply invented a formula for healthy living. In fact, she was echoing a nostrum that had become very trendy in her youth, and in doing so marked herself as an acolyte of one of the master-gurus of health-faddists, Asclepiades of Prousias. According to tradition, Asclepiades started as a poor professor of rhetoric before turning to medicine. During his career he acquired considerable fame (Pliny speaks of his *summa fama*) and provoked the animosity of other medical writers — he was still being attacked by Galen almost three hundred years after his death. The anger of his fellow healers is not hard to explain, because he turned ancient medicine on its head by distancing himself from dangerous pharmacological and surgical procedures, even describing traditional medicine as a "preparation for death." Instead, he placed emphasis on more humane and agreeable treatments — diet, passive exercise, massages, bathing, even rocking beds. Pliny felt that he mainly used guesswork but was successful because he had a smooth patter. How effective he was cannot be gauged now. He is said to have recovered a "corpse" from a funeral procession and then to have successfully treated it. But famous doctors in antiquity routinely restored the dead to life. Perhaps more impressive, and more alarming to the medical profession, was Asclepiades' pledge that by following his own prescriptions he could guarantee that he would never be ill, and that if he lapsed, he would retire from medicine. He was apparently never put to the test, and eventually died by accident, falling from a ladder.

It is not hard to believe that Asclepiades might have exercised an influence on Livia, especially in that Pliny remarks that he almost brought the whole human race round to his point of view, and Elizabeth Rawson argues that a case can be made that he was the most influential Greek thinker at work in Rome in the first century BC. Pliny notes a dilemma that has a strangely contemporary ring — whether wine is more harmful or helpful to the health. As the champion of the latter belief Pliny cites Asclepiades, who wrote a book on wine's benefits, based to some extent on the teaching of Cleophantus.

Asclepiades received a familiar nickname *oinodotes* (wine giver), although to avoid being cast as someone who encouraged inebriation, he did advocate abstinence under certain circumstances. As Pliny words it, Asclepiades stated that the benefits of wine were not surpassed by the power of the gods, and the historian, like Livia, seems to have been won over, conceding that wine drunk in moderation benefitted the sinews and stomach, and made one happy, and could even be usefully applied to sores. Livia might have become acquainted with Asclepiades' teaching while he was still alive (it is uncertain when he died), but in any case Pliny makes it clear that after his death his ideas took a firm hold on the population, and would still have been in circulation for many years after he made his ultimate precipitous descent from the ladder.[16]

Apart from her views on the benefits of fine wines, Livia was known for other health tips. Pliny adds his personal recommendation for one of her fads, a daily dose of *inula* (elecampane). The elecampane, with its broad yellow petals, is a common plant throughout Europe, and its root has long been a popular medicine. Because it is bitter and can cause stomach upset if eaten alone, it is usually ground up, or marinated in vinegar and water, then mixed with fruit or honey. It was supposedly useful for weak digestion. Horace describes its popularity among gluttons, who could overdo safely by using elecampane afterwards. Then, as now, celebrity endorsements helped; Pliny observes that the use of the plant was given a considerable boost by Livia's recommendation. In some modern quarters it is still promoted as an effective tonic and laxative.[17]

Livia's views on a healthy lifestyle seem to have been cherished by the devotees of natural cures, and the evidence for their abiding appeal is that her recipes were still used nearly four centuries later. Marcellus Empiricus of Bordeaux, who served as *magister officiorum* under Theodosius I (AD 379–95), composed his *De Medicamentis Liber* in the first decade of the fifth century. In some respects Marcellus resembles Asclepiades of Prousias in trying to teach people to do without doctors and surgery and essentially to cure themselves. He set out to collect all he could from such writers as Pliny and Scribonius Largus, whose entries he simply copied out in their entirety. He brought together a rich mix of popular remedies, charms, and herbal folklore, which in his preface he describes as "the uncomplicated and effective remedies of ordinary country dwellers." As a final colourful touch he added verses (either his own or someone else's) describing the contents of the work and ending with the hope that the reader will live a year for each line (seventy-eight of them).

This "extraordinary mixture of traditional remedies and conjuring" as Rose describes it, has preserved among other fascinating tit-bits the formula for toothpaste used by Livia's sister-in-law Octavia, as well as two recipes of Livia herself.[18] They are perhaps trivial in themselves, but they do offer an intriguing glimpse of a side of Livia not apparent in other sources. The first is for inflammation of the throat. Note the apothecary's use of coins as measures of weight.

This medicine has proved beneficial to many:

2 denarii of each of the following:
costus [an oriental aromatic plant]
opium
anis
aromatic rush
red cassia
1 denarius of coriander
1 victoriatus of amomum
2 denarii of seed of hazelwort
1 denarius of split alum
5 grains the size of chickpeas from the centre of oak-apple
2 denarii of saffron
1 victoriatus of saffron residue
1 victoriatus of myrrh
4 denarii of Greek birthwort
3 denarii of cinnamon
5 denarii of the ash of baked chicks of wild swallows
1 victoriatus of a grain of nard.

All these ingredients, thoroughly ground up, are mixed with skimmed Attic honey. When there is a need to renew the medicine, a sufficient amount of the same honey is added and in that medium it is inserted into the jaws.

Livia always had this ready on hand, stored in a glass vessel, for it is amazingly effective against quinsy and inflammation of the throat. [Marc. *De Med.* 15.6]

The second was intended to relieve nervous tension:

Salve for chills, tiredness and nervous pain and tension, which when applied in winter prevents any part of the limbs from being chilled. Livia Augusta used this:
Ingredients:

1 sextarius of marjoram
1 sextarius of rosemary

1 lb of fenugreek
1 congium of Falernian wine
5 lbs of Venafrian oil

Apart from the oil one should steep all the ingredients in the wine for three days, then on the fourth day mix in the oil and cook the medicine on a moderate coal, until the wine vanishes, and the next stage is to strain through two layers of linen and to add a half-pound of Pontic wax while the oil is warm. The medicine is stored in a clay or tin vessel. It is effective when rubbed gently into all the limbs. [Marc. *De Med.* 35.6]

These curiosities do provide a possible context for one of the charges levelled against Livia, which the scholarly world generally agrees was groundless: that of using poison to remove those who blocked her ambitions. The accusation is one that powerful women in competitive political situations throughout antiquity and the middle ages found difficult to refute, because poison has traditionally been considered the woman's weapon of choice. Because women took the primary responsibility for family well-being, they would have been the inevitable targets of suspicion if a person died of something brought on by gastric problems.[19] If Livia had insisted on inflicting her home cures on members of her family, it is not difficult to imagine that a malign reputation could have arisen after a death that was advantageous to her. One also should not discount the possibility that the combination of birthwort and ash of swallows did more harm than good, and that she might indeed have helped despatch some of her patients, despite the very best of intentions.

Allied to Livia's preoccupation with herbal remedies is her passionate interest and regular involvement in various aspects of horticulture. The most vivid illustration of this comes from her villa at Primaporta (see chapter 9). The highlight of the complex is the garden room, built and decorated around 20 BC in the form of a partially subterranean chamber nearly 12 metres long by 6 metres wide, perhaps a dining room intended for summer use. The most impressive feature of the room is the magnificent wall painting, unparalleled for its scale and detail (fig. 28). It creates an illusion of a pavilion within a magical garden, teeming with flowers and birds. Unusually for the Pompeian Second Style of painting, all structural supports have been dispensed with, even at the angles, although along the tops of the walls there is a rocky fringe, which conveys the impression of the mouth of a grotto. In the foreground stands a wicker fence. Behind that is a narrow grassy walk, set with small plants, bordered on its inner side by a low stone parapet. A small recess is set in the wall at intervals to accommodate a bush or tree. Behind it stands a rich tangled forest of carefully painted shrubs and trees, with various types of laurel predominating. The rich mass of foliage is framed at the top by a narrow band of sky. The painting is detailed and accurate, with flowers and fruit and birds perched on the branches or on the ground. The birds, of many species, range freely, with the exception of a single caged nightingale. Flowers and fruit of all seasons are mingled together.[20] This rich extravaganza belonged clearly to an owner who exulted in the richness and variety of nature.

But Livia's horticultural interests went beyond a mere feast for the eye — she had a direct and practical interest in produce. She developed a distinctive type of fig that bore her name, the Liviana, mentioned by agricultural writers and recommended by Columella and Athenaeus, and which may have contributed to the tradition that she eliminated Augustus by specially treated figs grown in their villa at Nola. They could well have been found on the estate, for Athenaeus describes them as grown near Rome, although they could not have been ripe at the time of Augustus' death because Columella places their ripening in the autumn.[21] In Egypt she gave her name to a class of papyrus. The top grade was called the Augustus, the third class the hieratic. Between them, in the second grade, was the Livia.[22] She probably cultivated the Pucine wine that she drank every day, and in Rome, Valerianus Cornelius considered it worthy of record that the single vine in the Portico of Livia (see chapter 9) provided shade and at the same time produced twelve amphorae of must each year.[23]

On her estate at Primaporta, Livia was said to be personally responsible for planting a laurel grove. It produced a low-growing shrub with crinkly leaves, quite rare, and was the source of the laurels carried by triumphatores in their processions.[24] This genus is distinct from another laurel to which Livia gave her name, originally called the royal laurel, then renamed the Augusta, with large leaves and berries and without a harsh taste. The form of this word is grammatically ambiguous, for it could simply be a feminine adjective agreeing with *laureus*, the "Augustus laurel." But it is worth noting that when Pliny introduces Livia a few paragraphs after describing the plant, he rather pedantically refers to her as Livia Drusilla *quae postea Augustam matrimonii nomen accepit* (who later received the name Augusta as a result of her marriage), a totally unnecessary clarification and explicable only in the context of how the laurel got its name.[25] Recent excavations at the villa have revealed perforated pots found mainly at the edge of the hill overlooking the Tiber. These were produced in a kiln from the villa itself, and offer good evidence for a laurel grove. They would have been used for the planting of laurels by the process known as layering, a form of propagation mentioned both by Cato and Pliny, the latter with specific reference to the Augusta laurel.[26]

From what we can glean about Livia's personality from the scant evidence available, the picture that emerges is not a remarkable one, and at first sight better suited to our modern notion of middle-class respectability than to an active if understated role at the very centre of Rome's political life. In reality, the very ordinariness of Livia as a private individual was one of her strongest assets. Romans had watched with alarm during the final years of the republic as women with powerful personalities asserted themselves on the political scene. Livia's dull normalcy was reassuring, and perfect for the times.

WIFE OF THE EMPEROR

By the early empire the image of women of past times was clouded by a nostalgic romanticism. The Roman woman was by tradition devoted to her husband, whom she would not think to cross, and she spent her time and energies on the efficient running of her household, a paragon of impeccable virtue, a perfect marriage partner. The realm of the woman was strictly the *domus*. A famous and familiar tomb inscription of the end of the second century BC expressed the most fulsome praise that could be bestowed on a deceased wife: *Domum servavit. Lanam fecit* (she kept house; she made wool). The qualities of this ideal wife were those of Amymone, wife of Marcus, as described in another inscription, *pulcherrima lanifica pia pudica frugi casta domiseda* (very beautiful, woolmaking, pious, modest, frugal, chaste, stay-at-home). The women of Augustus' domus, including Livia, were expected at least in their public personas to conform to this semimythical image. It was in this spirit that Augustus made it known that his simple clothes were all woven by his sister, wife, or daughter.[1] It cannot be an accident that those imperial women who were seen to embody such ideals — Antonia, Octavia, Livia — were in the long run honoured and rewarded. Those who contradicted them — both Julias, mother and daughter, both Agrippinas, mother and daughter — suffered the dire consequences of their wilfulness.

By Augustus' day the image of the Roman woman as a mere wife and mother was in practice becoming difficult to sustain, at least among the upper classes. The traditional form of Roman marriage, through which the bride was committed to the complete authority *(in manu)* of her husband, had become by the late republic little more than a vestige of a quaint past. Roman women had by then acquired the power to inherit, own, and bequeath property and had attained a level of independence still unmatched in many modern-day states. Their privileges were still in theory dependent on the authority of a man. A daughter was subject to the *potestas* (power) of her paterfamilias (the oldest surviving "head" of the household, usually her father, but possibly the paternal grandfather or even great-grandfather). On the death of the pater-familias, authority passed technically to a guardian, *tutor,* usually the closest male relative. The activities of wealthy and prominent women in the late republic, however, show that this curb was more theoretical and apparent than real, and control could always be voided by a number of devices, such as an appeal to a magistrate. Even those formal restrictions were eventually re-moved by Augustus from those women who had borne three children.

The line between the independent woman and the ideal woman who ex-cluded herself from involvement in political matters became increasingly less well defined. By the final century of the republic the aggressive political woman had become a familiar feature of the political landscape. As often as not, her ability to manipulate events came through her influence over her husband or lover. Chelidon, mistress of Verres, the notorious governor of Sicily (73–70 BC), for instance, was able to use her hold on the governor to control contracts and settle civil cases for a price. After Verres had reached a decision, a whisper in his ear was all that was needed for him to summon the parties back and alter his judgement.[2] One of the most celebrated of these powerfully corrupt women was the beautiful and aristocratic Sempronia, a well-read, witty woman of considerable intelligence, who appears in Sallust's account of the conspiracy of Catiline (63 BC). He asserts that Catiline won the adherence of several women whose extravagance had led them into debt, and he planned to use them for various nefarious activities. Sempronia turned her assets to bad purposes to cheat and to escape her debts, and even became involved in murder. She may also have been a victim of the paranoia noted earlier. When we look closely at Sallust's account of the conspiracy, we find that he does not in fact assign Sempronia any substantive role, nor is there any reference to her in other accounts of the conspiracy that have survived. No formal charges were made against her and there was no punishment—she simply fades from view. Her broadly defined image was intended to exploit fear of the damage that could arise when women became involved in public affairs. She illustrates yet another facet of the depiction of powerful women

that reemerges in the accounts of Livia, especially in Tacitus: the use of innuendo in the absence of ascertainable facts.[3]

Throughout the republic, men tended to display an irrational anxiety about
the threats they saw in growing female independence. Perhaps the most sinister characteristic of the ambitious woman was her ruthless willingness to
murder her opponents, and her preferred method was supposedly poison. The
first recorded case goes back as far as the great series of poison trials of 331 BC,
when the deaths of a number of leading citizens were blamed on what Livy
calls *muliebris fraus* (female treachery), an expression identical to the one used
by Tacitus to explain the death in AD 19 of Germanicus, reputedly despatched
by poison on the secret instructions of Livia.[4] Moreover, an incident in 180 BC
is reminiscent of the claims made about Livia nearly two centuries later, as
someone determined to clear the decks to make way for her son Tiberius. In
that year the consul died, supposedly poisoned by his wife, Hostilia, to create a
vacancy for her son.[5] There can be little doubt that such stories, handed down
as popular lore from generation to generation, would have in turn influenced
popular beliefs about the deaths of Augustus and Claudius, who, it was hinted,
had similarly to make way for Livia's son Tiberius and Agrippina's son Nero.

If any precedent might have preoccupied Livia, especially in her early career, when she was attempting to mould an image fitting for the times, it would
have been a negative one, provided by the most notorious woman of the late
republic and, most important, a woman who clashed headlong with Octavian
in the sensitive early stages of his career. Fulvia was the wife of Mark Antony,
and his devoted supporter, no less loyal than Livia in support of her husband,
although their styles were dramatically different. Fulvia's struggle on behalf of
Antony, Octavian's archenemy, has secured her an unenviable place in history
as a power-crazed termagant. While her husband was occupied in the East in
41, Fulvia made an appearance, along with Antony's children, before his old
soldiers in Italy, urging them to remain true to their commander. When Antony's brother Lucius gathered his troops at Praeneste to launch an attack on
Rome, Fulvia joined him there, and the legend became firmly established that
she put on a sword, issued the watchword, gave a rousing speech to the soldiers, and held councils of war with senators and knights. This was the ultimate sin in a woman, interfering in the loyalty of the troops.

In the end Octavian prevailed and forced the surrender of Lucius and his
armies at Perusia. The fall of the city led to a massive exodus of political
refugees. Among them were two women, Livia and Fulvia. Livia joined her
husband, Tiberius Claudius Nero, who escaped first to Praeneste and then to

Naples. Fulvia fled with her children to join Antony and his mother in Athens. Like Octavia later, she found that her dedicated service was not enough to earn her husband's gratitude. In fact, Antony blamed her for the setbacks in Italy. A broken woman, she fell ill at Sicyon on the Gulf of Corinth, where she died in mid-40 BC. Antony in the meantime had left Italy without even troubling himself to visit her sickbed.[6]

Fulvia's story contains many of the ingredients familiar in the profiles of ambitious women: avarice, cruelty, promiscuity, suborning of troops, and the ultimate ingratitude of the men for whom they made such sacrifices. She was at Perusia at the same time as Livia, and as wives of two of the triumvirs, they would almost certainly have met. In any case, Fulvia was at the height of her activities in the years immediately preceding Livia's first meeting with Octavian, and at the very least would have been known to her by reputation. Livia would have seen in Fulvia an object lesson for what was to be avoided at all costs by any woman who hoped to survive and prosper amidst the complex machinations of Roman political life.

In one respect Livia's career did resemble Fulvia's, in that it was shaped essentially by the needs of her husband, to fill a role that in a sense he created for her. To understand that role in Livia's case, we need to understand one very powerful principle that motivated Augustus throughout his career. The importance that he placed in the calling that he inherited in 44 BC cannot be overstressed. The notion that he and the house he created were destined by fate to carry out Rome's foreordained mission lay at the heart of his principate. Strictly speaking, the expression *domus Augusta* (house of Augustus) cannot be attested before Augustus' death and the accession of Tiberius (see appendix 9), but there can be little doubt that the concept of his domus occupying a special and indeed unique place within the state evolves much earlier. Suetonius speaks of Augustus' consciousness of the *domus suae maiestas* (the dignity of his house) in a context that suggests a fairly early stage of his reign, and Macrobius relates the anecdote of his claiming to have had two troublesome daughters, Julia and Rome. When Augustus received the title of Pater Patriae in 2 BC, Valerius Messala spoke on behalf of the Senate, declaring the hope that the occasion would bring good fortune and favour on "you and your house, Augustus Caesar" *(quod bonum, inquit, faustum sit tibi domuique tuae, Caesar Auguste)*.[7] The special place in the Augustan scheme enjoyed by the male members of this domus placed them in extremely sensitive positions. The position of the women in his house was even more challenging.[8]

In fashioning the image of the domus Augusta, the first princeps was anxious to project an image of modesty and simplicity, to stress that in spite of his extraordinary constitutional position, he and his family lived as ordinary Romans. Accordingly, his demeanour was deliberately self-effacing. His dinner parties were hospitable but not lavish. The private quarters of his home, though not as modest as he liked to pretend, were provided with very simple furniture. His couches and tables were still on public display in the time of Suetonius, who commented that they were not fine enough even for an ordinary Roman, let alone an emperor. Augustus wore simple clothes in the home, which were supposedly made by Livia or other women of his household. He slept on a simply furnished bed.[9] His own plain and unaffected lifestyle determined also how the imperial women should behave. His views on this subject were deeply conservative. He felt that it was the duty of the husband to ensure that his wife always conducted herself appropriately. He ended the custom of men and women sitting together at the games, requiring females (with the exception of the Vestals) to view from the upper seats only. His legates were expected to visit their wives only during the winter season. In his own domestic circle he insisted that the women should exhibit a traditional domesticity. He had been devoted to his mother and his sister, Octavia, and when they died he allowed them special honours. But at least in the case of Octavia, he kept the honours limited and even blocked some of the distinctions voted her by the Senate. Nor did he limit himself to matters of "lifestyle." He forbade the women of his family from saying anything that could not be said openly and recorded in the daybook of the imperial household.[10]

In the eyes of the world, Livia succeeded in carrying out her role of model wife to perfection. To some degree she owed her success to circumstances. It is instructive to compare her situation with that of other women of the imperial house. Julia (born 39 BC) summed up her own attitude perfectly when taken to task for her extravagant behaviour and told to conform more closely to Augustus' simple tastes. She responded that he could forget that he was Augustus, but she could not forget that she was Augustus' daughter.[11] Julia's daughter, the elder Agrippina (born 19 BC?), like her mother before her, saw for herself a key element in her grandfather's dynastic scheme. She was married to the popular Germanicus and had no doubt that in the fullness of time she would provide a princeps of Augustan blood. Not surprisingly, she became convinced that she had a fundamental role to play in Rome's future, and she bitterly resented Tiberius' elevation. Her daughter Agrippina the Younger (born AD 15?) was, as a child, indoctrinated by her mother to see herself as the destined transmitter of Augustus' blood, and her whole adult life was devoted to fulfilling her mother's frustrated mission. From birth these women would have known of no life other than one of dynastic entitlement. By contrast, Livia's background, although far from humble, was not exceptional for a woman of her class, and she did not enter her novel situation with inherited baggage. As a Claudian she may no doubt have been brought up to display a certain hauteur, but she would not have anticipated a special role in the state. As a member of a distinguished republican family, she would have hoped at most for a "good" marriage to a man who could aspire to property and prestige, perhaps at best able to exercise a marginal influence on events through a husband in a high but temporary magistracy. Powerful women who served their apprenticeships during the republic reached their eminence by their own inclinations, energies, and ambitions, not because they felt they had fallen heir to it.

However lofty Livia's station after 27 BC, her earlier life would have enabled her to maintain a proper perspective. She did not find herself in the position of an imperial wife who through her marriage finds herself overnight catapulted into an ambience of power and privilege. Whatever ambitions she may have entertained in her first husband, she was sadly disappointed. When she married for the second time, Octavian, for all his prominence, did not then occupy the undisputed place at the centre of the Roman world that was to come to him later. Livia thus had a decade or so of married life before she found herself married to a princeps, in a process that offered time for her to become acclimatised and to establish a style and timing appropriate to her situation. It must have helped that in their personal relations she and her husband seem to have been a devoted couple, whose marriage remained firm for more than half a century. For all his general cynicism, Suetonius concedes that after Augustus married Livia, he loved and esteemed her *unice et perseveranter* (right to the end, with no rival). In his correspondence Augustus addressed his wife affectionately as *mea Livia*. The one shadow on their happiness would have been that they had no children together. Livia did conceive, but the baby was stillborn. Augustus knew that he could produce children, as did she, and Pliny cites them as an example of a couple who are sterile together but had children from other unions.[12] By the normal standards obtaining in Rome at the time they would have divorced — such a procedure would have involved no disgrace — and it is a testimony to the depth of their feelings that they stayed together.

In a sense, then, Livia was lucky. That said, she did suffer one disadvantage, in that when the principate was established, she found herself, as did all Romans, in an unparalleled situation, with no precedent to guide her. She was the first "first lady" — she had to establish the model to emulate, and later imperial wives would to no small degree be judged implicitly by comparison to her. Her success in masking her keen political instincts and subordinating them to an image of self-restraint and discretion was to a considerable degree her own achievement. In a famous passage of Suetonius, we are told that Caligula's favourite expression for his great-grandmother was *Ulixes stolatus* (Ulysses in a stola). The allusion appears in a section that supposedly illustrates Caligula's disdain for his relatives. But his allusion to Livia is surely a witty and ironical expression of admiration.[13] Ulysses is a familiar Homeric hero, who in the *Iliad* and *Odyssey* displays the usual heroic qualities of nerve and courage, but is above all *polymetis:* clever, crafty, ingenious, a man who will often sort his way through a crisis not by the usual heroic bravado but by outsmarting his opponents, whether the one-eyed giant Polyphemus, or the enchantress Circe, or the suitors for Penelope. Caligula implied that Livia had the clever, subtle kind of mind that one associates with Greeks rather than Romans, who were inclined to take a head-on approach to problems. But at the same time she manifested a particularly Roman quality. Rolfe, in the Loeb translation of Suetonius' *Life of Caligula*, rendered the phrase as "Ulysses in petticoats" to suggest a female version of the Homeric character. But this is to rob Caligula's sobriquet of much of its force. The stola was essentially the female equivalent of the toga worn by Roman men. A long woollen sleeveless dress, of heavy fabric, it was normally worn over a tunic. In shape it could be likened to a modern slip, but of much heavier material, so that it could hang in deep folds (figs. 20, 23, 24, 25). The mark of *matronae* married to Roman citizens, the stola is used by Cicero as a metaphor for a stable and respectable marriage. Along with the woollen bands that the matron wore in her hair to protect her from impurity, it was considered the *insigne pudoris* (the sign of purity) by Ovid, something, as he puts it, alien to the world of the philandering lover. Another contemporary of Livia's, Valerius Maximus, notes that if a matrona was called into court, her accuser could not physically touch her, in order that the stola might remain *inviolata manus alienae tactu* (unviolated by the touch of another's hand). Bartman may be right in suggesting that the existence of statues of Livia in a stola would have given Caligula's quip a special resonance, but that alone would not have inspired his bon mot. To Caligula's eyes, Livia was possessed of a sharp and clever mind. But she did not allow this quality to obtrude because she recognised that many Romans would not find it appealing; she cloaked it with all the sober dignity and propriety, the gravitas, that the Romans admired in themselves and saw represented in the stola.[14]

Livia's greatest skill perhaps lay in the recognition that the women of the imperial household were called to walk a fine line. She and other imperial women found themselves in a paradoxical position in that they were required to set an example of the traditional domestic woman yet were obliged by circumstances to play a public role outside the home — a reflection of the process by which the domestic and public domains of the domus Augusta were blurred.[15] Thus she was expected to display the grand dignity expected of a person very much in the public eye, combined with the old-fashioned modesty of a woman whose interests were confined to the domus. Paradoxically, she had less freedom of action than other upper-class women who had involved themselves in public life in support of their family and protégés. As wife of the princeps, Livia recognised that to enlist the support of her husband was in a sense to enlist the support of the state. That she managed to gain a reputation as a generous patron and protector and, at the same time, a woman who kept within her proper bounds, is testimony to her keen sensitivity. In many ways she succeeds in moving silently though Rome's history, and this is what she intended. Her general conduct gave reassurance to those who were distressed by the changing relationships that women like Fulvia had symbolised in the late republic. It is striking that court poets, who reflected the broad wishes of their patron, avoid reference to her. She is mentioned by the poet Horace, but only once, and even there she is not named directly but referred to allusively as *unico gaudens mulier marito* (a wife finding joy in her preeminent husband).[16] The single exception is Ovid, but most of his allusions come from his period of exile, when desperation may have got the better of discretion. The dignified behaviour of Livia's distinguished entourage was contrasted with the wild conduct of Julia's friends at public shows, which drove Augustus to remonstrate with his daughter (her response: when she was old, she too would have old friends). In a telling passage Seneca compares the conduct of Livia favourably with even the universally admired Octavia. After losing Marcellus, Octavia abandoned herself to her grief and became obsessed with the memory of her dead son. She would not permit anyone to mention his name in her presence and remained inconsolable, allowing herself to become totally secluded and maintaining the garb of mourning until her death. By contrast, Livia, similarly devastated by the death of Drusus, did not offend others by grieving excessively once the body had been committed to the tomb. When the grief was at its worst, she turned to the philosopher Areus for help. Seneca re-creates Areus' advice. Much of it, of course, may well have sprung from Seneca's imagination, but it is still valuable in showing how Livia was seen by Romans of Seneca's time. Areus says that Livia had been at great pains to ensure that no one would find anything in her to criticise, in major matters but also in the most insignificant trifles. He admired the fact that someone of her high station was often willing to bestow pardon on others but sought pardon for nothing in herself.[17]

Livia was not completely successful in evading the criticism of her contemporaries. We know that she attracted the censure of one of the leading Greek writers active in Augustan Rome. Timagenes of Alexandria was captured in 55 BC by Aulus Gabinius and taken back to Italy. He attained his freedom and gained a reputation as a teacher of rhetoric and as a prolific writer, composing a universal history down to the time of Julius Caesar. Initially he was friendly to Antony, but he switched his allegiance and came to enjoy the special favour of Augustus. His close relationship with the imperial house soured, and it was then that he made an unspecified attack on Livia. We should not read too much into his reported anomosity towards her. Seneca reports that he was a man who was inherently hostile to Rome and resented its success. He developed a particular aversion to the imperial family, and after the quarrel with Augustus destroyed the account he had written of his achievements by consigning it to the flames. He attacked not only Livia but also the emperor and the whole of the imperial family *(in totam domum)*. It is fair to conclude that his criticisms of Livia would have been made as a matter of course, given that she was the wife of the emperor, and Timagenes' unsympathetic views cannot be taken to represent a widely or even narrowly held opinion in the Rome of the time. Timagenes was banished from Augustus' house and went to live with another historian, Asinius Pollio. He eventually choked to death.[18] His attacks on Livia seem to have had no harmful effect on her reputation.

Perhaps most important, it was essential for Livia to present herself to the world as the model of chastity. Apart from the normal demands placed on the wife of a member of the Roman nobility, she faced a particular set of circumstances that were unique to her. One of the domestic priorities undertaken by Augustus was the enactment of a programme of social legislation. Parts of this may well have been begun before his eastern trip, perhaps as early as 28 BC, but the main body of the work was initiated in 18.[19] A proper understanding of the measures that he carried out under this general heading eludes us. The family name of Julius was attached to the laws, and thus they are difficult to distinguish from those enacted by Julius Caesar. But clearly in general terms the legislation was intended to restore traditional Roman gravitas, to stamp out corruption, to define the social orders, and to encourage the involvement of the upper classes in state affairs. The drop in the numbers of the upper classes was causing particular concern. The nobles were showing a general reluctance to marry and, when married, an unwillingness to have children. It was hoped that the new laws would to some degree counter this trend. The Lex Iulia de adulteriis coercendis, passed probably in 18 BC, made adultery a public crime and established a new criminal court for sexual offences. The Lex Iulia de maritandis ordinibus, passed about the same time, regulated the validity of marriages between social classes. The crucial factor here, of course, was not the regulation of morality but rather the legitimacy of children. Disabilities were imposed on the principle that it was the duty of men between twenty-five and sixty-five and women between twenty and fifty to marry. Those who refused to comply or who married and remained childless suffered penalties, the chief one being the right to inherit. The number of a man's children gave him precedence when he stood for office. Of particular relevance to Livia was the *ius trium liberorum*, under which a freeborn woman with three children was exempted from *tutela* (guardianship) and had a right of succession to the inheritance of her children. Livia was later granted this privilege despite having borne only two living children.

This social legislation created considerable resentment — Suetonius says that the equestrians staged demonstrations at theatres and at the games. It was amended in AD 9 and supplemented by the Lex Papia Poppaea, which seems to have removed the unfair distinctions between the childless and the unmarried and allowed divorced or widowed women a longer period before they remarried. Dio, apparently without a trace of irony, reports that this last piece of legislation was introduced by two consuls who were not only childless but unmarried, thus proving the need for the legislation.[20]

Livia's moral conduct would thus be dictated not only by the already unreal standards that were expected of a Roman matrona but also by the political imperative of her husband's social legislation. Because Augustus saw himself as a man on a crusade to restore what he considered to be old-fashioned morality, it was clearly essential that he have a wife whose reputation for virtue was unsullied and who could provide an exemplar in her own married life. In this Livia would not fail him. The skilful creation of an image of purity and marital fidelity was more than a vindication of her personal standards. It was very much a public statement of support for what her husband was trying to achieve. Tacitus, in his obituary notice that begins Book V of the *Annals*, observes that in the matter of the *sanctitas domus*, Livia's conduct was of the "old school" (*priscum ad morem*). This is a profoundly interesting statement at more than one level. It tells us something about the way the Romans idealised their past. But it also says much about the clever way that Livia fashioned her own image. Her inner private life is a secret that she has taken with her to the tomb. She may well have been as pure as people believed. But for a woman who occupied the centre of attention in imperial Rome for as long as she did, to keep her moral reputation intact required more than mere proper conduct. Rumours and innuendo attached themselves to the powerful and prominent almost of their own volition. An unsullied name required the positive creation of a public image. Livia was despised by Tacitus, who does not hesitate to insinuate the darkest interpretations that can be placed on her conduct. Yet not even he hints at any kind of moral impropriety in the narrow sexual sense. Even though she abandoned her first husband, Tiberius Claudius, to begin an affair with her lover Octavian, she seems to have escaped any censure over her conduct. This is evidence not so much of moral probity as of political skill in managing an image skilfully and effectively. None of the ancient sources challenges the portrait of the moral paragon. Ovid extols her sexual purity in the most fulsome of terms. To him, Livia is the Vesta of chaste matrons, who has the morals of Juno and is an exemplar of pudicitia worthy of earlier and morally superior generations. Even after her husband is dead she keeps the marriage couch (*pulvinar*) pure. (She was, admittedly in her seventies.) Valerius Maximus, writing in the Tiberian period, can state that Pudicitia attends the couch of Livia. And the *Consolatio ad Liviam*, probably not a contemporary work but one at least that tries to reflect contemporary attitudes, speaks of her as worthy of those women who lived in a golden age, and as someone who kept her heart uncorrupted by the evil of her times. Horace's description is particularly interesting. His phrase *unico gaudens marito* is nicely ambiguous, for it states that Livia's husband was preeminent (*unicus*) but implies the other connotation of the word: that she had the moral superiority of an *univira*, a woman who has known only one husband, which in reality did not apply to Livia. Such remarks might, of course, be put down to cringing flattery, but it is striking that not a single source contradicts them. On this one issue, Livia did not hesitate to blow her own trumpet, and she herself asserted that she was able to influence Augustus to some degree because she was scrupulously chaste. She could do so in a way that might even suggest a light touch of humour. Thus when she came across some naked men who stood to be punished for being exposed to the imperial eyes, she asserted that to a chaste woman a naked man was no more a sex object than was a statue. Most strikingly, Dio is able to recount this story with no consciousness of irony.[21]

To reinforce this image of moral probity, an effort was clearly made to ensure that Livia's public activities should relate especially to the centrality of the family, such as the restoration of the temple of the Bona Dea or the dedication of her *aedes* to Concordia (see chapter 10). By her association with the religious rites of women she could promote her husband's moral legislation and help him to revive the old ideal of Roman womanhood, with its focus on the sanctity of marriage and the crucial place of the family in Roman life.[22] The role of Concordia in this process was important. *Concordia* could convey two notions, of harmony in both public and marital life. When Livia located her aedes to Concordia in her portico, she would have declared publicly that her own marriage was harmonious and that she wished to set an example for other wives to follow.[23]

Probably the first public declaration of the importance of the place of the Augustan family in the state comes in the form of the Ara Pacis, voted in 13 BC to commemorate the emperor's return from Gaul and Spain, and finally completed in 9 BC. It provides the perfect expression of Augustan ideology. The altar itself was decorated, but its reliefs are overshadowed by those on its surrounding rectangular precinct wall, with mythological panels on its east and west fronts, Roma and another female (Italy or Mother Earth?) on the east, and Mars and Aeneas on the west. On the north and south walls, long friezes portray a procession of religious officials intermingling with members of the Augustan house. The occasion depicted is the *supplicatio*, the celebration that followed Augustus' safe return, an event in which women and children were able to participate. There had been an earlier tradition of depicting ancestors within Roman houses, but public statues of women and children were rare, and Bartman characterises the inclusion of mortal women in a state ceremony as an "iconographic revolution."

There is not complete certainty about the identification of some of the family members depicted, but there seems to be little doubt that we have a grand dynastic portrait. Livia can probably be fairly securely identified as the first foreground figure on the frieze after Augustus, not because of any family likeness — the portraits generally are idealised — but because she and Augustus wear veils and laurel crowns (figs. 20, 21). Although the altar is dedicated to *Pax* (Peace), it cannot be said that Livia was ever closely associated with this particular concept. She is identified at Corinth as *Diana pacilucifera* (Diana bringing peace at dawn), but the inscription is securely dated to the Tiberian period, more than twenty years later than the Ara Pacis. The intention of the frieze is rather to present the family of Augustus and Livia symbolically, less in association with Pax than as examples of the virtues that Augustus was trying to promote through his marriage legislation. The prominence of children throughout the monument reinforces this idea. Thus Augustus and Livia appear as the symbolic father and mother of the Roman state. The depiction of Livia here constitutes the one exception to the rule of the prevailing modest coiffure in her likenesses during Augustus' lifetime (see chapter 6). Here she has the middle parting, and her hair falls in long waves to below her shoulders. The hairstyle, as Wood points out, gives a Livia a strong similarity to the goddess who appears on the east face. She, like Livia, is veiled and garlanded and has her hair parted in the middle. Similarly, Augustus is reminiscent of Aeneas on the west frieze.[24]

Livia was clearly expected to play an important role in the state as the emperor's consort, as a woman who embodied the values and qualities that he felt important. But did she have a role in her own right? Within the family circle, of course, she certainly did, and after her obligations to her husband, her first obligation would have been as materfamilias to the members of the domus Augusta. She certainly earned the esteem of her daughter-in-law, the venerable Antonia. We are told that after Drusus' death Antonia chose to live with Livia and resolved not to marry again, preferring the company of her mother-in-law over a second marriage.[25] Moreover, how seriously Livia took her family duties is illustrated by how conscientiously she met her obligations to her grandson, Antonia's son Claudius, whose physical handicaps and perceived mental limitations were considered an embarrassment to his family. As a child, Claudius lived for much of the time at his grandmother's home, presumably while Antonia accompanied Drusus on his military campaigns. Although Livia's attitude may fall far short of acceptable modern standards, it is only fair to observe that her intolerance was no worse than that shown by his own mother. Antonia, a woman universally admired, called him a *portentum . . . non absolutum a natura sed tantum incohatum* (a monster, only started and not finished by nature), and as a byword for stupidity she would call someone *stultiorem . . . filio suo Claudio* (more foolish than her own son Claudius). If we are to take Suetonius at his word, Livia was no different, treating her grandson with utmost contempt and rarely speaking to him, communicating with him through short letters or through messengers.[26] But after providing this broad characterisation of her attitude, Suetonius goes on to offer evidence for Augustus' opinions on Claudius, quoting extensively from his correspondence, and in the process furnishing a quite different picture of Livia's attitude. She, in fact, went to considerable trouble over his welfare, and it is little wonder that the *Piso Decree* praises her for the *discipulina* that she provided him.[27]

Suetonius has preserved extracts from three letters written by Augustus to his wife which show that Livia had assumed a general charge for Claudius. Augustus clearly wanted to evade any responsibilities in the matter, stressing in his letters that Claudius is Livia's grandson. The first extract indicates that Livia had asked her husband to speak to Tiberius about what should be done with Claudius at the games of Mars Ultor, celebrated in AD 12. Augustus felt that the family should come to a final decision about whether the young man was fit to be advanced. The letter shows clearly that Livia had made some specific request on behalf of her grandson and indicates that despite her supposed contempt for him, she was prepared to make an effort to help him towards some limited progress. Augustus was willing to go along with her suggestion that he be allowed to take part in the banquet of the priests, provided someone was there to make sure that he behaved himself. But the emperor drew the line at two other suggestions. He refused to allow Claudius to take a seat in the imperial box at the circus — he did not want to risk public embarrassment. He was also opposed to the idea of his taking part in the ceremonies in the Latin festival, either in Rome or on the Alban mount. It is interesting that he gives her leave, *if she should so wish*, to show that part of the letter to Antonia, Claudius' mother, who thus was recognised as having a legitimate interest but not the final responsibility in the matter. Livia also seems to have been concerned that there be proper supervision of Claudius during her absences, for in a second letter Augustus promises to invite him to dinner every day while she is away. Finally, in the third extract Augustus acknowledges that no matter how awkward his conversation in private, when it came to public speaking, Claudius could declaim splendidly. What is especially striking about this last passage is that its positive tone suggests strongly that it is just what Livia wanted to hear.[28]

Whatever his physical limitations, Claudius had a good mind. He took to writing history, with the active encouragement of the famous historian Livy. Among his projects was an account of events in Rome from the time of the death of Julius Caesar. The period was a political minefield, and he was persuaded by his mother and Livia to skip the civil-war phase and to start with the Augustan settlement. The advice was wise and well meant. The passions felt about the end of the republic had not yet calmed down, and Claudius' account, especially as coming from within the imperial family, was likely to rekindle some of the old resentments.[29] Livia's ongoing interest in Claudius' progress extended even to making the choice of his first wife. His bride, Plautia Urgulanilla, was the granddaughter of Livia's close friend Urgulania (see chapter 10), and the two women no doubt worked closely together to bring about the match.[30]

Livia's relationship with Claudius might in one sense be called neutral, in that, ironically, no one could have remotely imagined that he could play a role in the succession issue. Accordingly, it might be argued that there was no compelling reason why Livia should not have been willing to help his career. But she also seems to have concerned herself with those other members of the imperial family who might have been in a position to thwart the ambitions she entertained for Tiberius. The children of Julia would seem ideal candidates for this role. Yet Julia the Younger, who died in AD 28 after twenty years of exile, was sustained during this period of hardship by the charity of Livia. Tacitus is obliged to acknowledge her benevolence, although he insists that it was hypocritical, that she worked to bring down her "stepchildren" and then advertised her compassion to the world once they had been destroyed.[31] While Tacitus claims that she hated the same Julia's daughter, Agrippina the Elder, and used Piso's wife, Plancina, as a weapon against her, he admits that it was Livia who in her later years protected Agrippina from Sejanus, and that Livia's death opened up the field for a full-scale attack on her.[32] Livia seems to have involved herself with the well-being of Agrippina's children, as we might reasonably expect, for they were also her great-grandchildren. She took care of Caligula, and possibly two of his sisters, after his mother's removal from the scene, and seems to have treated them kindly (see chapter 5). Despite mischievous comments about Livia (he made similar comments about all his relatives), when it came to a more practical demonstration of his feelings, as in the honouring of her will, suppressed by his predecessor, Caligula demonstrated that he held his great-grandmother in high regard.[33]

Seneca called Livia a *maxima femina*.[34] But did she hold any real power outside the home? According to Dio, Livia believed that she did not, and claimed that her influence over Augustus lay in her willingness to concede whatever he wished, not meddling in his business, and pretending not to be aware of any of his sexual affairs.[35] Tacitus reflects this when he calls her an *uxor facilis* (accommodating wife). She clearly understood that to achieve any objective she had to avoid any overt conflict with her husband. It would do a disservice to Livia, however, to create the impression that she was successful simply because she yielded. She was a skilful tactician who knew how to manipulate people, often by identifying their weaknesses or ambitions, and she knew how to conceal her own feelings when the occasion demanded: *cum artibus mariti, simulatione filii bene composita* (well suited to the craft of her husband and the insincerity of her son) is how Tacitus morosely characterises that talent.[36] Augustus felt that he controlled her, and she doubtless was happy for him to think so. Dio has preserved an account of a telling exchange between Augustus and a group of senators. When they asked him to introduce legislation to control what was seen as the dissolute moral behaviour of Romans, he told them that there were aspects of human behaviour that could not be regulated. He advised them to do what he did, and have more control over their wives. When the senators heard this they were surprised, to say the least, and pressed Augustus with more questions to find out how he was able to control Livia. He confined himself to some general comments about dress and conduct in public, and seems to have been oblivious to his audience's scepticism.[37] What is especially revealing about this incident is that the senators were fully aware of the power of Livia's personality, but recognised that she conducted herself in such a way that Augustus obviously felt no threat whatsoever to his authority.

Augustus would have been sensitive to the need to draw a line between Livia's traditional and proper power within the domus and her role in matters of state. This would have been very difficult. Women in the past had sought to influence their husbands in family concerns. But with the emergence of the domus Augusta, family concerns and state concerns were now inextricably bound together. We know that Agrippina the Younger's transgression of this boundary in the Claudian period caused deep offence, and on his accession her son Nero, no doubt at the prompting of his tutor Seneca, promised that he would keep *discretam domum et rempublicam* (his house and the state separated). During Augustus' lifetime Livia certainly had a keen appreciation of where the line of demarcation lay, and her determination to observe it won the admiration of the next generation. Hence the poet of the *Consolatio* admired her because, as he worded it, she did not allow her powers to range over the Campus Martius or the Forum, but established her domus within the permitted limits: *nec vires errasse tuas campove forove / quamque licet citra constituisse domum.* The allusions are clear enough. The Campus Martius had been the traditional gathering place for the popular assembly, the *comitia centuriata*, and the name was in fact was used by contemporary writers figuratively to mean the elections themselves. The Forum was the centre of Roman legal life, and the scene also of many political events. It, similarly, has a figurative use, to denote state and legal affairs. Cicero uses the phrase *forum attingere* (to come in contact with the forum) to denote his entry into public life.[38] Livia thus was admired for maintaining traditional domesticity and not trying to play an unwarranted role in public affairs.

Although Livia did not intrude in matters that were strictly within Augustus' domain, her restraint naturally did not bar communication with her husband. Certainly, Augustus was prepared to listen to her. That their conversations were not casual matters and were taken seriously by him is demonstrated by the evidence of Suetonius that Augustus treated her just as he would an important official. When dealing with a significant item of business, he would write things out beforehand and read out to her from a notebook, because he could not be sure to get it just right if he spoke extemporaneously. Moreover, it says something about Livia that she filed all Augustus' written communications with her. After his death, during a dispute with her son, she angrily brought the letters from the shrine where they had been archived and read them out, complete with their criticisms of Tiberius' arrogance.[39] Despite Tacitus' claim that Livia controlled her husband, Augustus was willing to state publicly that he had decided not to follow her advice, as when he declined special status to the people of Samos (see chapter 10). Clearly, he would try to do so tactfully and diplomatically, expressing his regrets at having to refuse her request. On other issues he similarly reached his own decision but made sufficient concessions to Livia to satisfy her public dignity and perhaps Augustus' domestic serenity. On one occasion Livia interceded on behalf of a Gaul, requesting that he be granted citizenship. To Augustus the Roman citizenship was something almost sacred, not to be granted on a whim. He declined to honour the request. But he did make a major and telling concession. One of the great advantages of citizenship was the exemption from the tax (*tributum*) that tributary provincials had to pay. Augustus granted the man this exemption. When Livia apparently sought the recall of Tiberius from Rhodes after the Julia scandal, Augustus refused, but did concede him the title of *legatus* to conceal any lingering sense of disgrace. He was unwilling to promote Claudius to the degree that Livia wished, but he was willing to allow him some limited responsibilities. Thus he was clearly prepared to go out of his way to accede at least partially to his wife's requests. But on the essential issues he remained very much his own man, and on one occasion he made it clear that as an advisor she did not occupy the top spot in the hierarchy. In AD 2 Tiberius made a second request to return from exile. His mother is said to have argued intensively on his behalf but did not persuade her husband. He did, however, say that he would be willing to be guided by the advice he received from his grandson, and adopted son, Gaius.[40]

The most extensive account of any aspect of Livia's whole life and career relates to the advice she gave Augustus on how to deal with a supposed conspiracy by Cornelius Cinna, described in considerable detail by both Seneca and Dio (see appendix 10). Cinna was the grandson of Pompey the Great, and a man of limited natural intellect, if we are to believe Seneca (*stolidi ingenii virum*). His offence is hard to determine, a difficulty complicated by the fact that Dio and Seneca differ on his name (Dio calls him Gnaeus; Seneca calls him Lucius) and on the date (Dio places the incident in AD 4, Seneca between 16 and 13 BC, while Augustus was in Gaul). Shotter suggests that the suspected conspiracy might have been related to some event during Tiberius' time of exile, because by a curious twist Cinna was not punished, but according to Dio was rewarded by the consulship, which he held in AD 5, the year after Tiberius' recall. The whole story is of less value for offering us an insight into Livia's mentality and her relationship with Augustus than might be expected from the degree of detail. The discussion supposedly took place at night, in private. Eavesdropping retainers would have needed formidable powers of memory to retain the particulars. As we have seen, Augustus did normally make extensive notes before any important discussion, which Livia retained. But in this case we are told that the exchange was unpremeditated.[41]

The plot involving Cornelius Cinna is absent from all the recorded lists of conspiracies against the emperor. The intrigue was apparently exposed in all its details, and Augustus was determined to punish Cinna. He summoned a council of his advisors, but before they met he consulted Livia. Seneca and Dio have the princeps pass a sleepless night, concerned about the young man's otherwise blameless record, his distinguished family, the fact that he had been proscribed by Mark Antony, and the question of whether his punishment would prevent new plots. Livia noticed his troubled state, and Seneca has her break in and ask if he would entertain advice from a woman (*muliebre consilium*). Dio reflects the same idea, when he has Livia apologise for the fact that she, a woman, is about to express an idea that even his closest friends would not be bold enough to give voice to. She points out that nothing has been achieved by harsh treatment in the past, and to prove her point lists a succession of conspirators whose punishments were followed by further conspiracies — his friend Salvidienus Rufus, a man of humble origin whose only achievement noted in the record other than his consulship was that when he was tending his herds his head caught fire; Marcus Aemilius Lepidus, son of the triumvir, who headed a plot against Augustus soon after Actium; Varro Murena, brother or half-brother of Maecenas' wife Terentia, coconspirator of the otherwise unknown Faenius Caepio; and Egnatius Rufus, who in 19 seems to have intended to use his firefighting crew to spearhead a popular uprising.[42] With some men there was no hope — they were incurably depraved. But that said, in dealing with the others it was time to try *clementia*. Dio has Livia launch into a relatively long but well-observed psychological account of the strong sense of loyalty of those who are forgiven. She also shows a remarkably progressive attitude in speaking against the death penalty in a case like this, and in advocating rehabilitation. Cinna could do Augustus no harm, but the pardon would do the emperor's reputation a lot of good. Dio adds some further details, with Livia showing good common sense and demonstrating a shrewd understanding of political realities. She assured Augustus that opposition was inevitable to a figure of his importance. He was bound to displease some, and even those who had no axe to grind would aspire to his position. In the event, Augustus was relieved to receive her advice and cancelled the planned meeting of his consilium. Then he called in Cinna, and according to Seneca they spoke for two hours. Augustus rehearsed the favours he had bestowed on him and the benefits Cinna had received, and finished by offering friendship, an offer the other could hardly refuse. In fact, he became one of Augustus' most loyal followers and even received the consulship. On his death he bequeathed his estate in its entirety to the emperor. Livia's advice proved to be sound, and from then on, according to Seneca and Dio, there were no further plots against Augustus. They are mistaken in this, of course, in that they ignore the murky conspiracy of AD 6, which possibly involved Lucius Aemilius Paullus, husband of Augustus' granddaughter Julia.[43]

Even if we allow considerable exaggeration in the report of the Cinna case, there can be no doubt that Livia would have had some influence over Augustus' policies. But is there any evidence that he gave her a formal and institutional voice? It has been skilfully argued by Purcell that Livia's position in the state involved more than being a willing helpmeet of her husband in furthering his ethical and social aims. The principate was in itself an experiment, without precedent, evolved by Augustus with considerable skill and a canny knowledge of human nature. If there was to be further revolutionary change in the place of women in the governance of the Roman world, now might be seen to be the time. But on close examination it seems that while Augustus was prepared to allow his wife to assume something very close to an official role, he was careful to ensure that during his own lifetime her role was still securely defined by the traditional expectations of a woman's position within the domus.[44]

In the Cinna incident Dio has Livia point out that while Augustus is safe and sound she could continue *sharing in part of the rule (to meros archousa)*. Little faith should be placed in this striking assertion, for much of the Cinna episode has clearly been created from the imagination. Nor should we be influenced by allusions by the poets to Livia as *princeps*. Ovid calls Livia a *femina princeps*, but the expression appears in poems addressed to a woman, Ovid's wife, who was to look to Livia as her model and teacher. The *Consolatio* refers to her as *princeps* and as *Romana princeps*, but applies the term also to Drusus, her son, and uses Ovid's phrase, *femina princeps*, of Antonia. Clearly the word *princeps* could at this period still connote "prominent person" without necessarily implying any constitutional status.[45]

References to Livia's *potentia* are common throughout the literature, but they provide no insight into her constitutional position, for the term applies generally to extralegal power, generally when it is abused. Scribonia, for instance, complained about the potentia of Octavian's mistress, almost certainly

Livia, more than a decade before the Augustan settlement. When people were supposedly fearful of Livia's influence in the period before Augustus' death, they saw her as someone with *muliebri potentia*, implying the sinister influence of a woman exercising private pressure. Seneca speaks of mothers who exploit their sons with *muliebri impotentia* specifically because they are legally barred from exercising direct power themselves. To charge, then, that Livia enjoyed potentia tells us little, because in itself the word did not necessarily connote the formal exercise of power. More significantly, she did not exercise *potestas*, in the sense that the word usually conveyed in constitutional contexts — namely, the legal authority that was attached to a magistrate. In fact, at no point in Roman history did a woman have such authority. If Livia is indeed a "political woman" as Mommsen calls her, we must understand *political* in a very limited sense.[46]

There was a quality that Livia could lay claim to, a quality that was deeply embedded in the Roman political consciousness, that of *maiestas*.[47] In the broadest sense maiestas alludes to the dignity or honour of whatever individual, group, or institution it is attached to. Publius Scipio Africanus is said by Velleius to have possessed it, and Livy can refer to the maiestas of Roman matrons *(maiestas et pudor matronarum)*. But in the republic the concept is particularly associated with the Roman people, in the sense of the sovereign majesty of the state. Hence Cicero can talk of Gaul loyally defending the *maiestatem populi Romani*.[48] By a process that is complex and not fully understood, but all the same clearly inevitable, the "majesty" associated with the Roman people came to be embodied in the person of the princeps. Thus some ten years or so after the settlement of 27 BC, Horace could state that his modest verse could not do justice to Augustus' maiestas. Ovid, about a year after his exile in AD 8, can describe Augustus' maiestas as gentle. It is important to recognise that in the case of the princeps, maiestas was much more than simply the quality inherent in the offices he held. Thus when Augustus demanded two colleagues in the consulship, he met public resistance on the grounds that his maiestas would be diminished *(maiestatem eius imminui)* by having even one colleague. Also, Livy notes that in the early days of the republic it was confirmed that the people's maiestas was superior to the maiestas of consuls.[49] It was also inevitable that Augustus' maiestas would attach itself to members of his family. Hence we are told that he always addressed his troops by the formal expression, *milites* (soldiers), and insisted that his sons or stepsons do the same, believing that a more familiar term would not be appropriate to his own maiestas or that of his domus *(quam . . . aut sua domusque suae maiestas postularet)*. Tiberius was one of the most important beneficiaries of this development. After his adoption by Augustus nothing was spared to enhance his maiestas — *nihil ex eo tempore praetermissum est ad maiestatem eius augendum*. In fact, it soon became difficult to imagine that maiestas could repose in anyone outside the imperial family. Velleius states that when Tiberius was in Rhodes, he was treated with deference by the visiting officials, a deference that was remarkable for a private citizen, if indeed the maiestas he possessed was ever present in a private person *(si illa maiestas privata umquam fuit)*.[50]

Another beneficiary was Livia. The *Consolatio* words the concept indirectly, *non eadem vulgusque decent et lumina rerum* (the same things are not right for the ordinary people and for the world's glories). Ovid, in exile, becomes increasingly explicit. Livia alone, he says, is Augustus' equal and not overawed by his maiestas. Later the poet anticipates that his wife Fabia will feel overwhelmed and hardly able to speak when she comes into the presence of Livia. This, he feels, is not a serious problem, for Livia will recognise that Fabia stands in awe of her maiestas: *(sentiet illa / te maiestatem pertimuisse suam)*.[51] That Livia was conscious of sharing this very special quality is suggested by Tacitus' comment on the events of AD 20. When Germanicus' remains were returned to Rome, Livia and Tiberius held themselves aloof from the general lamentation, one explanation being that they thought that their involvement would be beneath their maiestas *(inferius maiestate sua rati)*.[52]

Violation of the maiestas of the emperor or his family *(maiestas laesa* or *minuta)* and the trials that ensued became one of the most hated aspects of the principate. The process by which this legal concept evolved is unclear and the subject of much controversy. It can certainly be traced back to at least 100 BC. Because the campaign against the Cimbri and Teutones had been conducted incompetently, a Lex Appuleia de Maiestate was passed, probably to punish incompetence rather than criminal action against the state. Sulla later passed a Lex Cornelia de Maiestate, designed to deter ambitious legionary commanders from taking their troops beyond the borders of their provinces. Caesar followed this with a Lex Julia de Maiestate, but unfortunately the offences covered by his law are not known. It might have been modified or perhaps even replaced by a Lex Julia passed under Augustus; at the very least the practical application of the preexisting law had to deal with the novel situation of the principate. Most important, because the state and the imperial domus were becoming more and more difficult to disentangle, Augustus' law covered not only attacks "committed against the Roman people and its security," as the the great legal code, the Digest, defines the term, but also attacks against the emperor and his family, and the punishments imposed became increasingly more stringent. Augustus initiated prosecutions for written libel under this law, and Tacitus cites the first case as that of Cassius Severus. Severus was sentenced in AD 8 or 12 (the sources are in disagreement), as a result of which he was exiled and his books burned. His case shows that women were also protected, for the prominent citizens whose defamation led to Severus' conviction are said to have included both men and women.[53]

In 35 BC we are told by Dio (the information appears in no other source) that Octavian granted his sister Octavia and his wife Livia security and protection against verbal insult *(adees kai anubriston)* similar to that provided for the tribunes *(ek tou homoiou tois demarchois)*, along with two other privileges: honorific statues and the right to administer their own estates without a guardian.[54] Dio seems to suggest that the privileges were granted by Octavian personally, but there must have been a formal grant. Whether it took the form of a lex or a senatus consultum or a tribunician edict, we cannot tell, nor can we be sure that the tribunician protection and the other distinctions were voted at the same time.

A year earlier, according to Dio, a formal law had granted Octavian protection against verbal and physical attacks and had stipulated that offenders would be liable to the same penalties as were applied in the case of the tribunes. This in turn might have had a precedent in similar privileges granted to Julius Caesar in 44 BC, although both of these supposed earlier grants have been much disputed.[55] Certainly, never before had such a status been enjoyed by a Roman woman. The grant of *sacrosanctitas* analogous to that of the tribunes was to give Livia and Octavia rights that lay at the very heart of the Roman system. Later emperors embraced the principle of tribunician privilege as a potent symbol of their office.

The legal and constitutional basis of the protection described by Dio is difficult to define. In the first place, it is not clear whether the reference to the tribunes is the historian's own gloss or whether his language reflects that of the enactment, in whatever form it appeared. If the latter, we cannot be sure from Dio's paraphrase whether the process involved detaching part of the tribune's authority. This seems very unlikely indeed. The grant of the powers of an office separated from the office itself had been recognised since 211 BC, and it was possible to separate office and powers to empower someone who was technically ineligible, as happened when the patrician Octavian received tribunician powers.[56] But Octavian was not dramatically ineligible, and he could, if necessary, have had himself adopted into a plebeian family. Nothing, however, could make a woman eligible, and it is more likely that the protection accorded Livia and Octavia was merely defined as analogous to that enjoyed by the tribunes. Even so, it is remarkable. Mommsen saw the measure as the extension of tribunician protection to the closest members of the emperor's family. But at this early stage there was no real concept of the principate, and it is doubtful that such a programme could have been in Octavian's mind in the mid-thirties. Purcell describes the arrangement as "traditional in flavour and nuance, in substance . . . revolutionary and novel." Its application to women, the wives of the triumvirs, is without precedent, and perhaps best seen as a specific response to the peculiar conditions of the period, with the primary intention being to protect Octavia rather than Livia (see chapter 3). It is difficult to know what the measure tells us about Livia's constitutional position. Nor is it clear whether the grant is to be regarded as an extension of the *maiestas populi Romani* to the wives (or wife and sister) of triumvirs. Resolution of this last question depends on the relationship between tribunician sacrosanctity and the *crimen maiestatis*, about which there is no unanimity.[57] Nor can the arrangement be explained satisfactorily as analogous to the privileges of the Vestal Virgins, as was first suggested by Willrich. As we shall see, the association between Livia and the Vestals seems to have developed gradually. Moreover, the Vestals received their immunity because of their virginity, and Vestal sanctity was as much an obligation as a privilege, for infractions could lead to punishment under the jurisdiction of the pontifex maximus, hardly a precedent that would have been sought after for Livia and Octavia.[58]

Although tribunician protection continued to be assumed by later emperors, the experiment was not to be repeated for the women. It was perhaps seen as coming too close to the admission of women into a formal role in Rome's governance, because it implies that a person who has a right to public protection must be fulfilling a public role. Different forms of protection evolved later. Women came to be included in the oath of allegiance sworn to the emperor, and the imperial family was after AD 8 protected by the law of maiestas when verbal insults were included. It may be that the legislation of 35 BC was an isolated but bold initiative by Octavian, one that may not have been received well and was not repeated. We do have one slightly bizarre instance of the protection of Livia's maiestas. On one occasion, noted earlier, not precisely defined and thus left to the imagination, she found herself in the presence of naked men. For the misfortune of being in the wrong place at the wrong time, they were condemned to death. Livia saved their lives by interceding on their behalf. In Octavia's case the only known instance of the apparent application of the law is in the case of a man condemned to the galleys for claiming that he was her son and that her real son, Marcellus, was a changeling.[59]

In practical terms, for Livia the most useful of the honours bestowed in 35 would have been the freedom from *tutela* (guardianship), because she was on course to becoming a very wealthy woman (see chapter 9). This privilege generally reflects the increasing independence of women in managing their property, a process that had been begun under the republic, when in theory the disposition of a woman's property was at the discretion of her *tutor* but in practice was very largely under her own control. Augustus' social legislation made the exemption formal for any woman who had borne three children. Livia was granted the *ius trium liberorum* in 9 BC, but this does not mean that Dio's testimony about 35 BC should be doubted. The Vestals had not been subject to the tutela and were similarly awarded the ius trium liberorum, in AD 9.[60]

It may well be that the award of the statues was meant to mark the receipt of the two other privileges. This honour did have precedents, but they were far from numerous. There were a few legendary examples, commemorating some special service rendered by women to the state. A public equestrian statue of Cloelia, a heroine of the sixth century BC, is described by Livy as an unprecedented honour for an unprecedented act.[61] The first concrete historical case is that of Cornelia, who received a statue honouring her, according to the report of Plutarch, as "the mother of the Gracchi." The information appears in the context of a report on a speech of 184 BC in which Cato the Elder condemned the erection of statues to women in the provinces. Pliny remarks that Cato was not effective, to the extent that there was a statue to Cornelia in Rome. But the very fact that Pliny mentions only this one example several generations after Cato's speech suggests that the honour was indeed rare, and there is no evidence of a public statue erected for a woman between Cornelia's and those of Livia and Octavia in 35 BC.[62] No known representations of Livia (or Octavia) can be assigned to this special grant, but they would almost certainly have been of the Marbury Hall type (see appendix 1, fig. 14), which comes closest to republican models. The earliest known evidence for a Livian statue comes a little later, from a group in the sanctuary of Demeter and Kore (Persephone) at Eleusis, dated perhaps to 31 BC. An inscription there records statues of her and Octavian (the actual figures are lost).[63]

Livia receives no mention in the *Res Gestae*, the great document in which Augustus recorded his achievements for publication after his death. Moreover, if she had enjoyed a formal institutional status during her husband's lifetime, we would expect it to be reflected in some of the traditional marks of distinction that the state bestowed on its official and semiofficial dignitaries. As an example, the birthdays of Tiberius, on November 16, of Germanicus, on May 24, and of Drusus Caesar, son of Tiberius, on October 7, are recorded in the *Feriale Cumanum*, a fragmentary calendar of festivals found at Cumae recording the honours paid to Augustus and the imperial house. Tiberius and his son

Drusus are named Caesars on the calendar, and the entry cannot have been made before AD 4, the date of Tiberius' adoption and his right to that cognomen. Augustus is not identified as Divus, and there is no reference to his death, which seems to place the calendar no later than AD 14. Thus there is evidence that the birthdays of the male members of the imperial family were being honoured in the latter part of Augustus' reign. There is no corresponding indication that this honour was bestowed on Livia, even though the parts of the calendars that would have covered her birthday have survived.[64] Livia, in fact, is not mentioned at all in any of the extant calendars until eight years after Augustus' death, when she dedicated a statue to him at the Theatre of Marcellus and caused a controversy by listing her name before Tiberius' (see chapter 8). There is no evidence that Livia's birthday was marked before AD 14, and the first extant recognition is, again, later than Augustus' death, in the record of the Arval Brethren in AD 27.[65]

Augustus did, of course, honour Livia indirectly on her birthday. The dedication of what was arguably the most important monument of his regime, the Ara Pacis, took place on the anniversary of her birth, perhaps her fiftieth, and was celebrated annually and entered accordingly in the calendars. The coincidence is an illustration of Augustus' adeptness in promoting his own image of himself, and, indirectly, acknowledging the regard in which Livia was held, without violating Roman tradition by honouring a woman publicly and officially. He seems to have demonstrated the same sleight of hand in timing the dedication of the altar to his Numen — carried out by Tiberius probably between AD 6 and 9 — on January 17, the date of his wedding to Livia. As Fishwick has pointed out, the dedication of the altar to Augustus' Numen marked a radical step, far more significant than the cult of the emperor's *genius*, because it marked a recognition in Rome of a divine presence within the emperor. The altar probably stood on the Palatine and is presumably the one where Caligula carried out sacrifices on the day of his assassination. Once again Augustus sought to honour Livia indirectly, by timing a highly significant state event to coincide with the anniversary of one that had special significance for her (see appendix 11).[66]

It is striking that Livia is absent from her husband's official coinage.[67] This reticence cannot be attributed to a long Roman tradition that frowned upon the numismatic depiction of women. Any such tradition had been thoroughly violated by the time that Livia came to prominence. The first step had in fact been taken by Mark Antony. After the formation of the triumvirate in 43, Antony received Gaul (apart from Narbonensis) and placed his headquarters at Lugdunum, where his mint was established. Silver coins minted in the late forties BC in Lugdunum, some with Antony's name on the reverse, depict a winged bust. The type had appeared in earlier Roman coins, but in this case the figure has a nodus hairstyle, which seems to suggest a mortal woman, possibly Fulvia, Antony's wife. The type seems to be echoed in the Roman East. The Phrygian city of Eumenea was renamed Fulvia in honour of Antony's wife. Its bronze coins of the very late forties depict the same motif of a winged female bust with nodus. Also in the late forties, coins of the Roman mint depict the same Victory bust with nodus, although it may be that the Roman moneyer was inspired by the coins of Lugdunum without any deliberate intention of invoking the image of Fulvia. Indeed, there is far from general agreement on whether any of these busts is of a real woman, and if so, whether she is Fulvia, and the issue is complicated by uncertainty about the coins' dates. Wood has suggested that the winged Victory is probably best seen as a divine personification who subtly resembles a living woman, rather than as a deified portrait of that woman. If the bust is Fulvia's, it marks the first depiction of a historical female on a Roman coin and would represent a truly dramatic innovation, because even the triumvirs themselves had begun to appear on coins only in the mid-forties.[68]

Antony may or may not have put Fulvia on his coins. About the representations of Octavia, his second wife, there can be no serious doubt, even though she is nowhere identified by name. Some of the coins in question were struck in eastern mints under Antony's control and follow his marriage to Octavia in 40. On these the portrait of the woman with the nodus hairstyle is not winged, and in fact does not have any divine attributes. She is found in the company of mortal men, Antony and / or Octavian. Silver cistophori of Miletus and the aes coinage of Pergamum (dated before the mid-thirties) depict Octavia in a jugate position with Antony — that is, facing in the same direction with his head superimposed over hers, a type of portrait common in eastern ruling houses in the Hellenistic period. On silver cistophori of Pergamum, Antony's bust appears on the obverse, while on the reverse there is a small bust of Octavia rising above the sacred *cista* (basket).[69] Bronze tresses (three asses) minted in Rome show Octavia facing jugate portraits of the two important men in her life, her husband Antony and her brother Octavian. Other aes coins, sestertii, and dupondii show them facing, which is an innovation.[70] Gold aurei depict Antony on one side and Octavia on the other.[71]

Perhaps the most remarkable of Antony's coins in this context followed his breakup with Octavia and his open association with Cleopatra. He minted official denarii with his own bust on the obverse and Cleopatra's on the reverse and thus broke yet again with tradition, this time by portraying a foreign monarch, his consort, on Roman coins. But he went even further. Neither Fulvia (if indeed it is she who is depicted) nor Octavia was identified by name. The Cleopatra coins carry the legend *Cleopatrae reginae regum filiorum regum* (to Cleopatra queen of kings and of her sons-kings).[72]

Augustus did not follow the precedent established by Antony. Only one female portrait appears on his official coinage, that of his daughter Julia. Nor can even this one instance be called a true likeness. On denarii of 13 BC her bust appears in tiny scale between those of Gaius and Lucius, clearly celebrating her role in continuing the dynasty. Augustus' reluctance to portray his wife surely cannot have simply been a fear of being associated with an innovation of Antony's. The injunction was maintained to the end of the reign, more than forty years after Antony's death, and in any case some of the most striking portraits of Livia in local mints were struck in Alexandria. If there was any lingering sensitivity about the Roman coins depicting Cleopatra, it would have surely been felt in Egypt even more strongly than in Rome. Augustus' unwillingness to give Livia official recognition on his coinage doubtless arose from his conviction that such an honour would move her formally out of the domus into an unacceptable formal and public role in the state.

Only one official coin issue of Augustus has a potential Livian association. Precious metal coins that are generally assigned to the closing years of his reign depict a seated figure on their reverse. This motif reappears on the reverse of undated precious metal issues of his successor Tiberius (fig. 1), and some years later reappears on dupondii of Claudius, where there is no doubt about the identity, made clear by the legend DIVA AUGUSTA, balancing the radiate head of Divus Augustus, identified as such, on the other side (fig. 6).[73] Unfortunately, the identity of Livia is not confirmed on either the Augustan or the Tiberian coins, and there is no consistency in the depiction of the figure, which seems to speak against a representation of a statue of Livia. On the Augustan coins she is seated on a chair and holds a sceptre in her right hand, while on some of the Tiberian pieces the sceptre is replaced by an inverted spear. In her left she holds a branch or ears of wheat. On the Claudian pieces, which have a larger flan, she holds a torch in her right, and ears of wheat in her left. There is also the difficulty that we cannot be certain of a true Livian image even on the larger Claudian coins. As we shall see, she was closely associated in inscriptions and sculpture with the goddess Ceres (see also chapter 10). Claudius could well have adapted an established image of Ceres, identified as such by the ears of corn, to present Livia in this guise. Nor does the fact that contemporary provincial coins identify the same seated image as Livia's carry any special weight. Provincial mints regularly adopted and adapted the issues of the Roman mint and would not have hesitated to see nonexistent identifications or even create them. We have no way of telling what was in the minds of provincial engravers, or of those who commissioned their work. That said, the ubiquity of the type, with the clear identification of Livia, in the provincial mints indicates a widespread tendency to associate Livia with the image, apparently without official disapproval. Once again we seem to have a clever way in which Augustus sought to honour his wife without giving her an official institutional role, by using a type that would have suggested her without overtly depicting her. This stands in powerful contrast to the forceful and incontrovertible depiction of Agrippina the Younger on the coins of Claudius and on the early issues of her son Nero.

If Livia was to seek an institutional role within the state, there was one group of contemporary women who should in a sense provide a model. Up to this period, the institutional involvement of Roman women in public life was limited essentially to certain priestly offices, particularly to membership in the Vestal Virgins. There are good reasons to believe that the Vestals were one of the oldest religious organizations in Rome and their early standing was still noted in late antiquity by St Augustine.[74] Vesta was the goddess of the hearth. Her round temple near the Regia in the forum housed a sacred fire, and the community of Vestals (numbering six in the Augustan period) was charged with tending it.[75] A Vestal was required to stay chaste during her period of service, which was normally thirty years, after which she was then free to marry, although few seem to have exercised this option. While in service she did not stay under the authority of her paterfamilias but was responsible to the pontifex maximus, who could sentence her to death for violation of her chastity, although that penalty seems to have been imposed only rarely.[76]

The Vestal enjoyed several privileges. She possessed sacrosanctity, for example, which made her person inviolate. She also had the right to make a will without the consent of a tutor. Some of her entitlements were ancient. The freedom from tutelage, for instance, was guaranteed in the Twelve Tables. Others were more recent, such as the use of a lictor (see chapter 8), granted in 42 BC by members of the Second Triumvirate.[77] The Vestals' privileges were enhanced by Augustus, who held them in high regard. After the battle of Actium they headed the procession that greeted him on his return to the city. They carried out sacrifices on the anniversaries of the day of his return from Syria in 19 BC and to commemorate his return from Spain and Gaul in 13. They participated in the annual sacrifices at the anniversary of the dedication of the Ara Pacis, where they appear on an inner frieze.[78] Suetonius claims that Augustus once declared that if any of his granddaughters had been at the right age (Vestals were usually chosen between the ages of six and ten), he would have put them forward as candidates for the order. He never took the step, but he did increase the Vestal entitlements. Two specific examples are known. Vestals were given the exclusive right to watch shows from lower seats in the arena opposite the praetor's tribunal. Also, in AD 9 they received the privileges of women who had borne three children *(ius trium liberorum)*. Tiberius also increased their entitlements, and to encourage interest in the order and to raise its prestige he made an award of two million sesterces to a Cornelia on her becoming a Vestal in AD 23.[79]

After Caesar's death the triumvir Lepidus had seized the office of pontifex maximus, which he succeeded in holding on to until his death in 13 BC. The position was now open to Augustus, who was duly elected on March 6 of the following year, a spectacular occasion when more people came to Rome for an election than ever in its recorded history.[80] The pontifex maximus was traditionally required to live in an official house in the Forum next to the precinct of the Vestals. Julius Caesar had acceded to this requirement. Augustus was unwilling to move out of his house on the Palatine, but he devised a way to make part of his own house public property. Two months after the election, a statue and possibly a shrine or temple of Vesta were dedicated in his house on the Palatine (see appendix 12). The public hearth of the state was in a sense moved to the private hearth of the emperor. This act was of great symbolic importance, because it now could be said that the emperor's house and the state were in a sense synonymous.[81]

The cult of Vesta became increasingly important to Augustus as the domus of the emperor became increasingly identified with the state. Perhaps not surprisingly, there has been a general tendency to argue that Augustus used Livia's association with Vesta to reinforce his wife's image as a symbol of chastity and a fitting representative of the home of the princeps and, in a sense, the home of the nation. Had such a connection arisen in the public mind, then Augustus would surely have done nothing to discourage it. But there are some serious objections to the notion of a deliberate policy to create a special connection between Livia and Vesta.[82]

The claim that the cult of the Palatine Vesta might have been entrusted to her is little more than speculation. The only concrete evidence for her close association with the Vestal ritual is her restoration of the shrine of Bona Dea and Ovid's allusion to her carrying out sacrifices in the Vestals' company. She did involve herself in trying to extinguish two fires that threatened the temple of Vesta in the Forum Romanum; but her role there can be explained by her status as wife, on the first occasion, and mother, on the second, of the pontifex maximus. Ovid most strikingly calls her the "Vesta of chaste matrons." But this last expression postdates his exile in AD 8, after which his imagery had become generally extravagant, and his inflated expressions cannot be used to offer insight into official policy. In any case, Vesta is not the only divine figure drawn into an analogy with Livia, for Ovid compares her also with Venus and Juno.[83]

It is also important to note that an association with the Vestals was not the exclusive preserve of Livia. The grant of sacrosanctitas and exemption from tutela as early as 35 BC may well have made people associate Livia's new rights with the similar privileges of the Vestals, but these entitlements were also conferred on Octavia, and indeed it is generally argued that Octavia, not Livia, was intended as the main target of the benefactions. The sacrosanctitas bestowed in 35 is, in fact, the only "Vestal" privilege that Augustus granted his wife. She did indeed share with them the ius trium liberorum, but this privilege was granted to her in 9 BC to compensate for the death of Drusus. At the time this was still not a Vestal privilege, and they did do not seem to have acquired it until AD 9 and the passing of the Lex Papia Poppaea. Three other Vestal privileges are commonly linked to Livia, all after Augustus' death. She was granted a lictor, probably in AD 14. In 22 she may have been allowed the use of the *carpentum* (covered carriage), a privilege, albeit not an exclusive one, of the Vestals. In AD 23 she was granted the right to sit in the same lower seats in the theatre.[84] It should be noted, however, that these analogous distinctions are not so significant as they may seem at first sight. In the first place, the use of the lictor was almost certainly connected with Livia's role as priestess of the Divus Augustus, and in fact it seems that she was prohibited from employing one except in strict connection with her priestly duties. Nor were these privileges exclusively hers for long. Caligula allowed his sisters to occupy the special seats in the theatre. Indeed, Caligula conferred the rights and privileges of the Vestals en masse on his grandmother Antonia. Claudius granted his wife Messalina the special seating, as well the use of the carpentum.[85] Also, note that in any case these last entitlements were conferred on Livia not by Augustus but by Tiberius, who was resistant to the idea of her playing an institutional role. Hence when Claudius placed the cult of the deified Livia in the hands of the Vestals after her consecration, this should perhaps be seen not so much as a declaration of a special association of Livia but rather as a gesture appropriate to one of the women of the imperial family, all of whom were somehow seen as having an association with Vesta.[86]

Inscriptional evidence is similarly misleading if taken at face value. It is true that as early as the twenties BC Livia was included in the cult of Hestia, the Greek equivalent of Vesta, at Athens. But she shared the cult with Julia, Augustus' daughter, and they were served by the same priestess, documented by a theatre seat belonging to that priestess. Between 27 and 11 Livia, along with the Vestals, was thanked by the ambassadors of Mytilene. But being diplomats, they also passed on the same thanks to Augustus' sister Octavia, as well as to his children, relatives, and friends. At Lampsacus, Livia is given the cult name Hestia. But the inscription, as we can see from her name (Ioulia Sebaste), is at the earliest Tiberian and may be much later. Moreover, in the same inscription Livia also has the cult name *nean Demetera*. Demeter (Ceres) is in fact far more commonly identified with Livia than is Hestia, and the first record of a Livian statue is from the sanctuary at Eleusis, with its strong associations with Demeter. In her catalogue of cult names of Livia in the eastern provinces, Hahn notes that she is identified with nine goddesses other than Hestia on coins and inscriptions (quite apart from abstractions like Tyche and Pronoia). In addition to the obvious candidates, the list includes less common figures like Mnemosyne, Maia, and Isia.[87]

In any case, it can be noted that even the men of the Augustan house were associated with Vesta. Thus on the birthdays of Tiberius, Germanicus, and Drusus, son of Tiberius, special thanksgivings were offered to Vesta.[88] On his way to his Rhodian retirement Tiberius persuaded the Parians to part with the statue of Vesta and sent it to be placed in the Temple of Concord in Rome, which was associated in the public mind as a joint venture between Tiberius and his brother Drusus.

It is clear that while Augustus was happy to exploit Livia's standing and image to strengthen his own political position, and was willing to listen to her advice and to be influenced by it, he was punctilious during his own reign in keeping the boundaries of the domus and the respublica separate. He was not so willing to bequeath this important distinction to the next reign, and his apparent decision to elevate Livia's official position posthumously was to be the source of endless friction between her and her son, a problem not finally resolved until her death in 29.

MOTHER OF THE EMPEROR

In many respects Tiberius was eminently unsuited to the task he assumed in AD 14. Up to that point he had been trained primarily as a soldier, and even after being acknowledged unequivocally as Augustus' successor, and thus marked out for a future political role, he still continued to serve, with considerable distinction, with the troops on the frontiers, rather than in an administrative apprenticeship in Rome. Nor had he any taste, or instinct, for political life, which he viewed as inevitably corrupting. More than once he commented on the increasing perils facing any man the higher he climbed in the hierarchy of the state. The posture that Augustus adopted in 27 BC, that he was essentially an ordinary magistrate with extraordinary responsibilities, had been to no small degree an exercise in public relations. But that principle would have been genuinely in character for Tiberius, and it seems that, at least at the outset, he took it seriously and tried to see himself as an ordinary individual. Suetonius observes that, if anything, he behaved even less assertively than a private citizen (*civilem admodum inter initia ac paulo minus quam privatum egit*). But this stance would have been difficult to maintain even for someone endowed with consummate political and diplomatic skills. Augustus had been just such a superb manager of people. Tiberius by contrast was "aloof and austere amid the grace and ease and smooth perfidy of fashionable society," as Syme describes him.[1]

It was inevitable that once he became princeps, tensions would arise between Tiberius and his mother. In the minds of many Romans she would have represented continuity after the death of Augustus in a way that her son was not able to do. It is noteworthy that in the earliest days of the reign it was to her that Sallustius Crispus reputedly expressed his concern over Tiberius' intention to refer all matters to the Senate, following the report of Agrippa Postumus' execution (see chapter 4). There are signs that such thinking was not limited to Sallustius. When Tiberius at his first meeting with the Senate behaved peremptorily with the obsequious Quintus Haterius, it was Livia who was called upon to calm the matter down. This kind of involvement would not have been viewed as a threat by Augustus, who had sought to find an informal role for women like his wife and sister in the state and was happy to listen to Livia's advice — and if necessary to reject it. But for Tiberius such a situation was difficult to accept, and he would have felt a natural reluctance to continue in his mother's shadow. Moreover, the idea of backroom politics was alien to his nature. His reaction to his mother is consistent with his vision of the principate, and his treatment of her is in line with his treatment of others he now had to deal with. Suetonius says that he avoided frequent meetings and long confidential conversations with Livia so as not to seem dominated by her. He may well be right, but one should not read anything dramatic or unusual into the situation. This principled stand would have been totally in character for Tiberius. Moreover, he was particularly averse to the intervention of women in matters he felt were properly the exclusive reserve of men. Hence his injunction against Livia's involving herself in "serious matters unsuited to a woman" *(maioribus nec feminae convenientibus negotiis)*. It is no surprise that, as Dio observes, Tiberius became very defensive about the part that Livia had played in his elevation to the principate and that he went to some effort to downplay her contribution. This had little to do with Tiberius' feelings for his mother. It tells us more about how Tiberius visualised the proper conduct of any princeps.[2]

In any case, the notion of mother-son conflict should not be pushed too far. To some extent the sources would have been instinctively inclined to exaggerate the differences between Tiberius and his mother, because they could not pick on a powerful wife — a Messalina or Agrippina the Younger — to denigrate as the sinister power behind the throne. The unavoidable difficulties that arose between Livia and Tiberius might have been expected to resolve themselves as his principate evolved and he became more experienced and self-confident. The fact that this did not happen probably has very little to do with their personalities or mutual feelings. Their situation was in fact irretrievably confounded by a fundamental complexity that would overtax the political skills and patience of both of them. In AD 14 Livia's quasi-legal status changed dramatically. The nature of the change was not spelled out precisely, and its consequent ambiguity laid the foundation for major confrontation between mother and son over their respective roles in the new order. Ultimately, they failed to reach a modus operandi, and the constitutional tension, if anything, grew more serious as the reign progressed. The problem was Augustus' doing, and it arose from his attempt after his death to grant Livia what he had denied her during his lifetime, a form of institutional status. In taking this action he bequeathed a problem to Tiberius that he himself had been unwilling to face and which his successor, as Augustus should have been able to anticipate, was temperamentally ill-suited to handle.[3]

The change in Livia's status was achieved in two stages. In his will Augustus specified that she was to be adopted, as his daughter, into the Julian gens. In addition, she was to assume the name Augusta *(nomen Augustum)*.[4] Despite its significance, Livia's adoption has attracted virtually no attention in the ancient literary authorities. It is of the type classed as testamentary, in that it was enacted in the adopter's will. This process is mentioned at times by ancient authors, but is never discussed by the jurists, and it is difficult to know what its strict legal consequences would have been. Known cases of individuals adopted by this means seem to betray a strange anomaly in the adoptee's filiation. He will be described as the son of his natural father, and not by the normal (for the Romans) designation as son of his adoptive father. Gnaeus Domitius Afer (consul AD 39), for instance, adopted in his will Titius Lucanus. Epigraphic evidence shows that Lucanus took the full name of his adoptive father but continued to call himself the son of Sextus *(Sexti filius)*. The famous Pliny the Younger was adopted by his uncle, the Elder Pliny, Gaius Plinius Secundus, but kept the filiation "son of Lucius." Scholars argue plausibly that because the original filiation is maintained, testamentary adoption is not real adoption, but rather a device to institute an heir on the condition that he take the testator's name. One must be cautious, however, about drawing inferences from such limited data, especially in a period where Roman nomenclature was undergoing considerable change.[5] In inscriptions dated clearly after AD 14, all from outside Rome, Livia is identified as the daughter of Marcus Drusus, but this may reflect the awkwardness of designating someone as the daughter of her husband. There is only one certain case of an inscription (from Velleia, dated to the Caligulan period) where she is identified as the daughter of Augustus. On the other hand the *Fasti Praenestini* record her dedicating a statue in Rome itself, in AD 22, to her father Augustus.[6] After the adoption, although Livia's freedmen took her new nomen Julius or Julia, they adopted the praenomen of her natural father, Marcus. This, however, may be a deliberate device to distinguish them from the slaves freed by Augustus.[7]

The issue of testamentary adoption is generally problematic at the best of times. It is especially complicated in Livia's case, for two primary reasons. Nothing is known about the testamentary adoption of females. Indeed, little is known even about conventional female adoption. Moreover, the principle of the adoption of a wife is especially problematic. Only one parallel has been suggested, from the so-called *Laudatio Turiae*, an inscription, dated to the Augustan period, in the form of an obituary addressed by a husband to his departed wife, Turia. The analogy is not persuasive. In one much-discussed passage the husband wishes that he had predeceased his wife *[super]stite te* and then wishes that he had adopted a daughter, or, as Wistrand has argued, had been survived by his wife in the role of a daughter *[f]ilia mihi supstituta*. Unfortunately, both the text and the general meaning of this segment of the *Laudatio* are so controversial that they cannot be used to provide a convincing precedent for Livia's new status.[8]

The dubious status of testamentary adoptions would not have presented an insuperable obstacle in Livia's case. Augustus took no chances when he came to write his will, leaving minute and almost comically detailed instructions on his funeral arrangements, on who should be allowed entry into his mausoleum, on the number of soldiers on active service, on the arrears in the treasury accounts, and more of the same. For good measure, he added the names of people who could provide the necessary information should further particulars be needed. We can therefore feel sure that he would have made meticulous and explicit provisions to ensure that Livia's adoption would be regularised. His task would have been made easier by the fact that he himself could provide the compelling precedent. He had in 44 BC been adopted by Julius Caesar in the late dictator's will. When he became consul in the following year, his top priority was to present to the popular assembly a law which he had been trying hard to enact for many months but had been blocked by the stalling tactics of Mark Antony. This *lex curiata* ratified his adoption and secured its legal basis. Appian notes that through the procedure Octavian, as he then was, acquired exactly the same legal status as would natural sons. There is no proof that Augustus made such an arrangement in AD 14, but it seems inconceivable that he would not have benefitted from his experience to ensure that Livia's adoption would be unimpeachable.[9]

The adoption could have been recognised by a *senatus consultum*, which would be passed on to the popular assembly to be enacted as a formal *lex*. We do at any rate have indirect evidence that the Senate was involved in the adoption process. To mark the fact that Livia had become Augustus' daughter, the senators voted for an Altar of Adoption (Ara Adoptionis). The gesture was not as dramatic as it may appear. Such an altar would been intended as a commemorative monument, not a place for worship, and altars in honour of the imperial family are a relatively common phenomenon. Their sponsors often looked on them as a harmless device to curry favour. In 28 the Senate sycophantically voted to honour Tiberius and Sejanus with an Ara Amicitiae and an Ara Clementiae, possibly never built. Altars were erected to celebrate the births of Agrippina's children. An Ara Ultionis, proposed to mark Germanicus' death, was turned down by Tiberius. He also rejected the Ara Adoptionis in AD 14, although there is no hint that he challenged the actual adoption provision in the will. Tiberius behaved as he did on other occasions, honouring to the wishes of his late adoptive father, but rejecting excessive reaction to those wishes.[10]

What could Augustus have intended in adopting his wife? There might have been several considerations. He had demonstrated from early in the principate a desire to be succeeded by someone from the domus Augusta. This determination sprang from a deep sense of his past, a feeling enhanced by his adoption by Caesar. That adoption had brought him his fair share of Caesar's political support. But it enabled him also to lay claim to a much greater legacy. Caesar belonged to a famous family, the Julians, whose name was invoked repeatedly by generations of his successors and attached for all time to the first ruling dynasty in Rome. When Caesar gave the funeral oration for his aunt Julia in 68 BC, he took the opportunity to remind his audience that the Julian gens had endured since the earliest days of the Roman people and could trace their descent from the goddess Venus, through her son Aeneas, and his son Julius, who had given the gens its name. The court poet Vergil converted this from a family tradition to a national myth in Rome's great epic, the *Aeneid*, in which the role to be played by Augustus and his family are laid out in prophecy.[11] The emphasis that Augustus placed on this legendary ancestry was later manifested in the decoration of the Forum of Augustus, which Zanker has described as a showplace of the Gens Iulia. Its centrepiece, the Temple of Mars Ultor, as Ovid noted, looked down upon the statue of Aeneas with his son and father, surrounded by the ancestors of the Julian house.[12] Denied a descendant of his own blood, Augustus was obliged eventually to adopt his stepson. Through his adoption Tiberius became a Julian. It will be remembered that the way had in a sense been prepared when Julian as well as Claudian images were carried in the funeral of Livia's Claudian son Drusus. When Livia was adopted into the

Julian house, Tiberius could claim Julian descent on both sides of his parent-age, and his right to the principate would rest on stronger foundations. Thus the adoption of Livia, far from putting Tiberius in the shade, as some have argued, if anything strengthened his position.[13]

Livia's new status as a Julian would no doubt have helped to place Tiberius' principate on a surer footing. Yet its full impact would have been on Livia herself, and may have been intended primarily to provide the right conditions for Augustus' other, no less dramatic and far-reaching measure, the conferring on her of the name Augusta. Flory has aptly observed that if the emperor had granted her new name without a change in her gens, it would mean that the designation of Augustus or Augusta could pass to someone from any family. Livia Drusilla's transformation into Julia Augusta was a remarkable event. There was no precedent in Rome for the transfer of what was in effect an honorific title from a man to a woman.[14] Octavian had received the cognomen of Augustus, with its powerful religious associations, in 27 BC, in preference to the alternative Romulus. By AD 14 it had acquired the force of a title that marked the holder as princeps. This process may well have begun in the East. In AD 1 Augustus instructed the Parthian king to withdraw from Armenia and wrote to him as Phrataces, deliberately dropping the title of king. The Par-thian rose to the occasion and wrote back haughtily, addressing the princeps simply as Caesar. The implication is that Augustus was thus a title, not a name, like Caesar, a title that belonged not to the individual but to his position.[15] This notion was reinforced by Augustus himself in AD 9 when the Senate sought to offer Tiberius various titles, such as Pannonicus, for his victories. The princeps observed that Tiberius would have to remain content with the one that he would assume after Augustus' death. Thus Ovid in the *Fasti* antici-pates that when Tiberius takes on the burden of the world, it will be as *tanti cognominis heres* (inheritor of such a great cognomen).[16]

Even under normal circumstances the assumption of an honorific cogno-men that had been granted by the Senate to a predecessor was unusual. Sueto-nius notes that among the honours originally decreed for Tiberius' brother Drusus, the Senate bestowed Germanicus on him and his descendants, imply-ing that the latter would not have happened automatically, and may have been enacted because Drusus was dead and could not enjoy the honour himself. Later, after Claudius' successful campaign in Britain, the Senate in AD 43 made a similar gesture and bestowed on Claudius and his son the title of Britannicus. Dio claims that Tiberius did not allow the Senate to vote the title of Augustus to him. This injunction may have been purely legalistic, if he felt that it was part of his inheritance and did not need to be conferred by the Senate, and

Suetonius does indeed describe it as *hereditarium* (inherited). The Senate is unlikely to have raised any objection to the title in Tiberius' case, however it was technically acquired, because such a development had been anticipated since at least AD 9. Suetonius and Dio say, in fact, that in AD 14 Tiberius did not regularly name himself Augustus, although he did not object to others using it of him, either in speech or in writing, and he used it when addressing kings. Tiberius' hesitation must have had a very limited application. The title appears in official documents, letters to communities in the East and in the *Piso Decree* of AD 20, where the emperor, writing in the first person, alludes to himself as Augustus. It appears regularly on his coins from the beginning of the reign. If the claim of abstinence is serious, then it can refer only to Tiberius' more private communications.[17]

The fact that Tiberius acquired the legal right to the title of Augustus, whether or not he chose to use it, would not have been considered remarkable. But the same could not have been true of the transmission of the title not only to the successor of Augustus but also to his widow and adopted daughter. It is probably safe to assume that the Romans did not have an exact notion of what Augusta was meant to convey in AD 14. Precedents in the East would have been of little help. Even during Augustus' lifetime the feminine form Sebaste was applied to Livia, but it was used also of his daughter Julia and seems to have been intended there only as a general honorific.[18] The later force of Augusta seems to vary from reign to reign. Claudius made a point of not allowing it to be bestowed on his wife Messalina. Agrippina the Younger assumed it when she solidified her power (see appendix 13). Claudius posthumously bestowed the title on his mother, Antonia; she may already have received it during her lifetime under Caligula and may have refused to use it (see appendix 14). After studying the Augustae of the first two centuries, Temporini has argued that they had certain things in common — they were the props of the dynasty, and the title came to be intended for the mothers of emperors when the sons had succeeded.[19] Temporini may be correct that the concept evolved in this way. But we must avoid the temptation to project the later development in the meaning of a word back to its very beginning. Certainly Antonia, if she received the tile from Caligula, could not be seen as the mother of the emperor.

What were the consequences of the very first bestowal of the title Augusta, and what role did it presage for the Augusta? In 1864 Ashbach argued the extreme view — which unsurprisingly seems to have won no adherents — that the Augusta was the true ruler and that Tiberius was second to her. Mommsen's more moderate and more influential view, which he later discarded, was tentatively that while the bestowal of Augusta on Livia did not formally grant her joint rule with Tiberius, it did not exclude it. Mommsen's initial thesis has since been developed and refined by some scholars, on the principle that because the title of Augustus was limited to the princeps and his descendants and not allowed for private persons, the granting of the feminine equivalent, Augusta, must similarly suggest that Livia was no longer a *privata* and either was expected to have some share in governing or exploited the opening that Augustus' will inadvertently created.[20] To such scholars the term Augusta signified real political power. They see the senatorial behaviour in AD 14, when they competed to honour Livia in her new role as Julia Augusta, as a response to the new constitutional situation, in which Tiberius had a partner in the principate.

Other scholars have argued that the award of the name was intended to be purely honorary.[21] That certainly is how Tiberius sought to understand it, whatever Augustus' intentions. But if such was Augustus' intention, it is hard not to conclude that he behaved either naively or irresponsibly, and he was not generally subject to either of these failings. Although the notion of joint rule is surely an overstatement of his intentions, it is hard to believe that Augustus did not intend Livia to have some kind of formal constitutional role. He must have understood the emotive power of the title Augustus, and have been aware that its female equivalent would raise Livia to a level well beyond traditional honours. The fact that Augusta later became attached regularly to imperial women does not mitigate the impact that this unprecedented award of the title would have had in AD 14. It is surely telling that Augustus did not dare make Livia the Augusta during his lifetime. That reluctance was certainly not due to an obsessive possessiveness about the title — he was more than happy to declare publicly that Tiberius was earmarked to receive it. Of course, Tiberius could not be allowed to hold the title during the incumbent's lifetime. Similarly, giving Livia the name during his lifetime might have been felt to signal that she was some sort of coruler, at least at the symbolic level, in the manner of the Hellenistic rulers of the East. The fact that Agrippina the Younger managed to acquire it while Claudius was still alive is remarkable, but her ultimate fate and her reputation among succeeding generations show that Agrippina was willing to claim rights for which the Romans were quite unprepared.[22]

The key to the problem lies not so much in Livia's status after AD 14 as in Augustus' intentions. Unfortunately, for all that has been written on him, Augustus still remains something of an enigma — Syme was right to draw attention to the symbol that he used on his seal, the sphinx, the ultimate enigmatic icon.[23] And nowhere did he prove more of an enigma than in the arrangement made for his widow. In a sense he made it inevitable that after his

death Livia would be seen in many quarters as someone who had been bequeathed a formal institutionalised position within the state. He was unwilling
to proceed to the next logical step, to define what that position should be.

Ritter has recently argued with some vigour that Livia received no constitutional powers by her elevation to Augusta, because the position of the princeps
rested not on his title of Augustus but on his specific powers, such as *imperium
proconsulare* and the *tribunicia potestas*, which a woman could not possess. Livia
was a powerful woman, but her power lay in her pragmatic effect on matters of
state, not on her constitutional position. Ritter is technically correct, but
Augustus may well have intended a constitutional status that would comple-
ment, not subsume, the official role of the magistrates. As Purcell observed,
"there was a graded range of activities lying between the totally domestic and
the completely public, not a sharply defined boundary." Augustus seems to
have wished by his final gesture to his wife to move that boundary, but left it to
the Senate and to Tiberius to define where it should lie. His action, inevitably,
sowed seeds of confusion. The Senate and Livia understood his intentions to
be directed to one end. Tiberius saw them quite differently. This placed the
new emperor in an unenviable position. Tacitus paints his predicament in the
darkest colours. He asserts that Tiberius rejected Livia's attempt to claim a
share of his power, but at the same time he could not depose her because he
had received that power from her as her gift *(donum)*. This is a very crude
summation of Tiberius' dilemma. He was no Nero. He recognised the *pietas*
due to his mother and he appreciated that she was entitled to certain distinctions. Moreover, Tiberius did not demand of his mother anything that he did
not demand of himself. This is stated explicitly by Tacitus and is reflected in
Dio's comment that Tiberius told his mother to conduct herself in a restrained
manner. It was right and proper, he insisted, that she should imitate him.[24]
Tiberius also had a respect, if not awe, for the figure of Augustus, whose wishes
he could not easily countermand. But his sense of filial obligation could not
move him to accept a form of constitutional arrangement that offended his
very basic principles. We should also add to the formula the mundane observation that Tiberius was presented with this difficulty when his mother was in
her seventies, and perhaps less willing to be as flexible and accommodating as
when she was a young woman.[25]

Dio has Livia seek a substantial and formal role in the government of the
state after Augustus' death. He says that she was not satisfied with the position
of ruling as an equal partner *(ex isou archein)* but she sought precedence over
Tiberius, and involved herself in government affairs *(pragmata)* as if "sole
ruler" *(autarchousa)*. One sign of this, Dio informs us, was that she wrote and

received official letters. Correspondence of Tiberius for a time supposedly bore her name as well as his, and communications were addressed to both alike. But we have no corroborating evidence to support Dio's claim, and in fact those examples of letters that have survived, written to the people of Cos and Gytheum, are in Tiberius' name only. We do know of a specific instance in which Tiberius exploited Livia's *amicitia* with Archelaus of Cappadocia (see chapter 5) to persuade her to write on his behalf, but this was the action of a willing servant of the princeps rather than a coregent, and probably involved a separate, independent letter. In any case, as Dio notes, the practice of joint letters lasted for a short time only. It may have involved only a small fraction of the total correspondence.[26]

Dio may well have been influenced by the conduct of Julia Domna in his own day. As a consequence, he could have developed an exaggerated view of Livia's political activism. Moreover, Goodyear suggests that in his depiction of Livia's exercise of power, Dio might well be working back from Agrippina the Younger. Although other sources recognise Livia's influence over her husband, Dio is the only one to give her a de facto share in the actual rule. In his version of the speech that she supposedly gave on behalf of Cinna in AD 4, she herself speaks of how even while Augustus is alive she has a share in ruling *(meros archousa)*. In fact, Dio seems to undercut his own thesis. He insists that Livia tried to exercise this autocratic power, except that she did not enter the Senate chamber, or the camps, or the public assemblies. But these in fact are the very places where power could be exercised. In one telling passage Dio describes measures passed by the Senate in honour of Augustus. He says that in reality they were carried by both Tiberius and Livia. The senators would pass their suggestions in writing to Tiberius, who then chose from them. Remarkably, Dio admits in his explanation that he added the name of Livia simply because of his general thesis that she was involved in public business. Thus he seems to have no formal evidence for his claim, but adds her anyhow, in a circular, though warped, argument. Suetonius sees the situation quite differently. He is very careful not to claim that Livia enjoyed or sought to enjoy an equal share in the rule *(partes aequas potentiae)*, a phrase that is reminiscent of Dio's *ex isou*. He states rather that Tiberius in his anger claimed it to be so, an assertion possibly made in a fit of pique and of little value in assessing Livia's constitutional role. Tacitus emphasises that after the death of Augustus, Livia had excessive influence, calling her a *mater impotens*, but as has been shown, this term did not necessarily connote the formal and legal exercise of power.[27]

Although the claims that Livia sought to share executive power are clearly exaggerated, this does not mean that Augustus did not intend to elevate her to

some kind of public role. No matter how intensely scholars may debate the
nature of Livia's status after AD 14, the Senate clearly had no doubts. Their
response to the new order shows that in their view Livia now occupied a
formal, no matter how ill-defined, position in the state. Tacitus reports that
she received *multa . . . adulatio* (excessive adulation) from the members. There
is nothing remarkable in that.[28] Far more significant, they voted that she
should be given the title of *mater patriae* (mother of the nation), or of *parens
patriae* (parent of the nation), a tribute by now associated, in its masculine
form, exclusively with the person of the princeps.[29] The concept of *pater
patriae*, familiar among the titulature of Roman emperors, goes back to the last
century of the republic. The earliest extant evidence for the term is in connection with the great military figure Marius, who, Cicero said, should have
received the title. The first recipient in the event was Cicero himself, after he
had suppressed the famous conspiracy of Catiline, when in addition it was
proposed that he should also receive the *corona civica*, the oak-wreath granted
to a soldier for saving the life of a comrade in action. Suetonius and Appian
record the title among the honours enjoyed by Caesar, on whose coins the
legend *parens patriae* appears in 44 BC.[30] Augustus first declined the distinction when a delegation of senators went to his villa at Antium to offer it to him,
and did the same afterwards at the theatre in Rome. Finally he yielded to the
Senate's insistence, and formally assumed it on February 5, 2 BC. He made
it clear that he considered this to be his most important attribute, and in his
Res Gestae he emphasised that it had been bestowed by the Senate, equestrians, and people as a whole. Seneca sees the title as standing above any other
given to a leader, even Augustus, and that it was intended to let the princeps
know that he had been entrusted with *patria potestas* over the nation.[31] Augustus' hesitation in accepting explains why, even though the people repeatedly
pressed it upon him, Tiberius consistently and characteristically refused the
title. It is not found on his official Roman coinage (although it is found on
coinage of Carthage and on non-Roman inscriptions). Contemporary writers
avoided the expression but would use phrases that suggested it; Valerius Maximus, for instance, twice calls Tiberius *princeps parensque noster*.[32] Caligula declined the appellation of pater patriae when in March 37 the titles and powers
of Augustus were assigned to him en bloc, and did not in fact assume it until
September 21, 38, as we know from recently discovered Arval records.[33]

Whether a serious distinction was intended between parens patriae and
mater patriae in Livia's case is not made clear. Some sort of difference between
the two concepts is preserved in the earlier instances. Suetonius records that
Caesar received the title pater patriae during his lifetime, but in a different

context he notes that on the columns erected in the Forum to honour him after his death, the inscription *parenti patriae* was added.[34] *Parens patriae* did not catch on. As Flory notes, it was never a state title for emperors, as pater patriae was to become after 2 BC. It may be that in AD 14 it was used by the Senate to avoid mater patriae, which might have been taken to rival Augustus' title. Bauman argues the opposite, that *parens* as a common noun would have equated Livia with male rulers, while *mater* would have put her on a somewhat lower level.[35]

Whatever the precise form of the title, it is beyond doubt that the Senate voted for Livia a distinction intended by now only for the princeps himself, perhaps the clearest sign that the senators recognised that some form of public function had been intended by Augustus for his widow. It should not be considered remarkable, nor any evidence of serious dissension between himself and his mother, that Tiberius refused this honour for Livia. He fully understood its implication. Nor did his refusal mean that the title was not attached to her unofficially. The enthusiasm of the senators was echoed throughout the empire. A coin of Leptis Magna calls Livia mater patriae, and an issue of Romula designates her as *genetrix orbis*.[36] That said, until the time of Julia Domna, in the Severan period, no woman was officially recognised as mater patriae, not even the forceful and ambitious Agrippina the Younger.

In AD 14 the Senate did not limit itself to this innovation. Tacitus reports that in their enthusiasm a majority of the members wanted the phrase "son of Julia" to be added to Tiberius' official nomenclature, along with the regular formulaic phrase "son of Augustus." To do so would, again, have raised her in a sense to the status of the princeps himself, or in this case, the late princeps, and would have been an innovation at least as remarkable as the title of Augusta. Dio even seems to suggest that there was a proposal to bounce Augustus' name entirely, and to use the matronymic exclusively. Suetonius carelessly records the phrase as "son of Livia" (instead of "son of Julia"), but nothing should be read into this anachronism, for he is generally inconsistent in his use of Livian nomenclature, and on this issue is otherwise in general accord with Tacitus and Dio. Moreover, Tacitus probably took his material from the senatorial records, or from a source that used the records, for he provides the information in the context of the senatorial debates, while Suetonius sees it as a general element of the tense relations between Tiberius and his mother.[37]

The proposal to call Tiberius *Iuliae filius* is totally alien to Roman practice, and it might seem hard to believe that it was expected that the proposal could be accepted. Dio and Suetonius both report that Tiberius was annoyed by the suggestion, and some scholars have taken the measure to be provocative, a deliberate affront to Tiberius, perhaps intended to needle him. The senators might even have wanted to give him a gentle reminder that he came to power because Augustus had married his mother. Flory sees a possible analogy to 44 BC, when some senators voted for immoderate honours to deride Caesar.[38] But there is no need to see the gesture as a studied insult, and Tacitus certainly does not take it that way, for he places the offer in the context of senatorial *adulatio*. The mood of the Senate in general seems to have annoyed Tiberius by its sycophancy rather than its provocation.[39] The Senate's action doubtless reflected what they interpreted as the wish of Augustus rather than any desire to rile Tiberius. The matronymic, along with the title of Augusta and of mater patriae, would elevate Livia's status to something approximating that of her late husband. Not surprisingly, Tiberius turned down this proposal also.

Tiberius similarly turned his thumbs down on another measure that would have moved Livia's status yet closer to his and Augustus', the suggestion that the month of October be renamed Livius (along with the proposed renaming of September as Tiberius). It is likely that Roman months had originally been arranged by simple numbers and began gradually to acquire the names of gods. The Greeks after the time of Alexander had a tradition of naming months after individuals, who eventually came to include Roman generals. At Mytilene, for instance, it seems that a month was named after Pompey. This practice was eventually adopted in Rome also. The first authenticated case of an eponymous month in Rome belongs to 44 BC, when it was decreed that Quintilis should henceforth be called Iulius because Caesar was born in that month. Later, Sextilis was renamed Augustus, a choice made by the emperor on the grounds that his great achievements and first consulship belonged to it, rather than to September, the month of his birth. As the modern calendar demonstrates, both of these innovations have proved to be permanent. The intent of the motion for Tiberius and Livia was simply to link the two new holders of Augustus' name with their two predecessors. But Tiberius saw it differently, as the elevation of the princeps, and more important, his mother, to a station to which mortals should not aspire. He handled the situation deftly, and with considerable humour — he asked the Senate what they would do when the time came that there were thirteen Caesars.[40]

Tiberius was not adamantly opposed to all the honours directed towards Livia, and was clearly prepared to recognise that her preeminence as the widow of the former princeps and the mother of the incumbent deserved its proper recognition. During his reign, she was included with her son in the yearly vows for the safety of the ruler (*pro salute et incolumitate . . . Iuliae Augustae*) made by the Arval Brethren. This ritual had its origins in the practice of the consuls, who would offer *vota pro salute reipublicae* when entering office on January 1. According to Dio, annual public vows for Caesar's welfare were enacted in 44 BC, and similar vows were decreed for Octavian in 30 BC, and for emperors and their family after that. Although these vows for the imperial family no doubt continued to be made by the consuls, they were also added to the calendars of the priesthoods and are a standard feature of the Arval record.[41] Moreover, in line with a privilege enjoyed by male members of the domus Augusta, Livia's birthday was now officially celebrated in Rome. The earliest extant notice of her inclusion in the annual vows seems to belong to the Arval rites of AD 21, and her birthday celebrations to those of AD 27, but there is no reason to assume that both honours were not accorded in earlier years, where the record is incomplete. Outside Rome, birthday celebrations were registered at the Forum Clodii in AD 18, when honey, wine, and pastries were distributed.[42]

Tiberius, moreover, did not block what proved to be the most concrete manifestation of the willingness of Romans to see Livia in some form of official and public role. This arose from the consecration of Augustus. The Senate had assembled on September 17, AD 14, following the emperor's death, and it was probably on this occasion that the formal accession of Tiberius was confirmed. But the only item of business securely assigned to this date by the fasti was the consecration of his predecessor. Tiberius expressed no public opposition to this measure, and in some respects he must have found it satisfying. Despite his impatience about such honours when offered directly to him, the title of *Divi Filius* (son of a deified one) was an important but indirect means for him to strengthen the legitimacy of his accession. Augustus' worship was now ordained as a state cult, and he was voted the usual accoutrements of a god — that is, a temple and priesthood. The temple was a joint undertaking of Livia and Tiberius, in the sense that they would supply the funds (see chapter 9).

In the organization of the cult of Augustus the pattern of traditional Roman religion provided a model of sorts. Some of the individual Roman deities had personal *flamines*, who numbered fifteen by the late republic. They were not elected or co-opted, as were other priests, but chosen from a slate of candidates by the pontifex maximus. Three were considered senior *(maiores)*, the most important being the Flamen Dialis (Jupiter); the other two had responsibility for Mars and Quirinus. The Flamen Dialis's life was regulated by a number of quaint and cumbersome rules. To compensate for the inconvenience of not being allowed to touch a goat, and similar restrictive taboos, he enjoyed certain privileges, such as the right to a *sella curulis* and the *toga praetexta*, the garb and special chairs of higher magistrates, as well as a seat in the Senate and a lictor.[43]

Germanicus was appointed flamen of Divus Augustus. An immediate precedent was provided by Mark Antony, who was Julius Caesar's first flamen, and, if we are to believe Dio, selected by Caesar himself, in the capacity of pontifex maximus, to be his flamen during his lifetime. In the event, Antony was not inaugurated until after the Peace of Brundisium in October, 40 BC.[44] Germanicus' career does not seem to have been impeded by his appointment. On his death it was laid down that he could be succeeded only by another member of the Julio-Claudian house. It was a rule that proved impossible to maintain, for the office of Flamen Divi Augusti continued for two more centuries.[45]

In addition, a college of priests, the Sodales Augustales, was appointed to serve the cult of Divus Augustus. The most revolutionary innovation, however, was the role assigned to Livia. Before AD 14 we find her involved in activities that are associated with priesthoods, such as making offerings for Tiberius' safe return from Germany. The consecration of Divus Augustus took the process an important stage further, in that Livia was appointed *sacerdos* (priestess). This position was unprecedented. Outside the Vestal order, the major priesthoods at Rome were all held by men. Livia's relationship to the flamen and the sodales is not clear, and her closest model may have been the wife of the Flamen Dialis. This woman held the position of flaminica.[46] Like her husband, the flaminica was bound by a rigid set of prohibitions, aimed mainly at avoiding the exposure of her person to public view, even down to regulations against going up a ladder by too many rungs at a time. The precise rituals in which the flaminica was involved, according to Aulus Gellius, were the same as those of her husband. We hear very little of specific duties, although it is recorded that she, not her husband, sacrificed a ram on the *nundinae* (market days).[47] The parallelism should not be drawn too closely — Livia was certainly not bound by the arcane restrictions that must have bedeviled the life of the flaminica (and her husband).

Livia's appointment is little short of remarkable. It is not clear why, from the narrow point of ritual, her special office was needed, for the flamen and the Sodales Augustales were available to look after the cult of Augustus, and the Arval Brothers to carry out the appropriate sacrifices. It may be that the assignment represented the one concession Tiberius was willing to make in recognizing her right to a public role, choosing the one that would cause conservative Romans the least offence.[48] The appointment of Livia to a priesthood brought with it a concrete manifestation of her new place within the state. As a symbol of her new status, she was allowed a lictor.[49] The lictors were

the attendants of magistrates, usually of the rank of freedmen, and their numbers varied according to the status of the official they served (consuls had
twelve each in Livia's day). They went ahead of the magistrate when he was on
the move, announcing his arrival and clearing bystanders from his path. The
privilege was extended to the Vestals in 42 BC by members of the Second
Triumvirate, supposedly because one of the Vestals on returning home from
dinner was not recognised and was subjected to insulting behaviour. Dio states
that Livia was granted a lictor, and in this claim seems to be flatly contradicted
by Tacitus, who insists the opposite, that Tiberius refused his mother this
privilege. Tacitus' claim may represent another example of his facility for
presenting material about Livia that, while not strictly inaccurate, was intended to mislead. Dio makes his statement in the context of Livia's appointment as priestess and notes that she was granted the lictor *en tais hierourgiais*
(in the exercise of her sacred offices). We might see a parallel in Agrippina's
similarly being granted a pair of lictors strictly in her capacity as priestess of
Claudius. Tiberius' injunction seems to have been against the general use of a
lictor for other functions, an understandable concern, because the lictor was a
symbol of office, and its general use would suggest to Tiberius a further violation of the important line between the state and the domus.[50]

Livia would have viewed her new role as one of great consequence. Ovid
refers to her as "wife and priestess" *(coniunx sacerdos)*, while Velleius calls her
"priestess and daughter of Augustus" *(sacerdotem ac filiam)*.[51] Her elevation to
this novel duty may well be commemorated in a statue now in the Vatican,
found in the basilica at Otricoli, apparently near a nude statue of Augustus.
The archaeological context places it after Augustus' death, although she continues to sport the traditional nodus hairstyle. Her upturned gaze and out-
stretched raised hands suggest her priestly role (fig. 24).[52] A statue in the
Louvre seems to combine Livia's priesthood of Augustus and her association
with Ceres (fig. 22). Her veiled head is crowned with a floral wreath. In her left
arm she holds a cornucopia, in her right, wheat and fruit, but much of this is
modern restoration. In addition she has a very human attribute — the beaded
woollen infula or band hanging from the floral crown inside the veil, generally
taken to be an allusion to her role as priestess, for it is worn by women carrying
out sacrifices.[53] But the most striking representation of the new Livia is on a
sardonyx cameo in Vienna (fig. 19). Livia invokes the figure of Cybele, for she
is enthroned, wears a turret crown, and holds a shield embossed with a lion.
Thus she is presented as the protectress of the state. The foliage she holds
includes wheat as well as poppies, thus suggesting simultaneously a reference
to Ceres, goddess of rich abundance. The unique feature of the sardonyx,

however, is that she is gazing at a bust of Augustus, whose radiate crown identifies him as a god.[54]

Tiberius must have felt himself beleaguered in dealing with the Senate in AD 14. The ghost of Augustus seemed to hover over the proceedings, and the Senate fell over itself in its zeal to implement what it saw as his posthumous wishes. Tiberius understood Augustus' intentions differently, or at least pretended to, and was determined to resist the dangerous tendencies he saw lurking in the measures the Senate proposed. He took the public position that Livia's role should reflect the status of women as it had been envisaged during the republic. Dio is surely right when he says that the emperor sought to restrict his mother's sphere to the domus. But defining this sphere now became a serious challenge, and at the outset Livia demonstrated that she did not share Tiberius' strictly conservative understanding of her role. The first recorded difference in outlook arose from a relatively innocuous incident, a celebration in honour of Augustus. In the festivities that followed Tiberius' ovatio in 9 BC, Livia and Julia together had invited the women to a banquet. Also on the dedication of the Porticus Liviae in 7 BC, Livia gave a party for women, while Augustus gave one for senators on the Capitol.[55] In AD 14, when Livia dedicated an image to Augustus in her house, she felt herself now entitled to break with tradition and to invite the senators and the equestrians, along with their wives, to mark the occasion. For a woman to host such an event, particularly on her own initiative, would have been a serious breach of protocol. Tiberius was tactful enough not to deny permission outright, but he insisted on observing the established proprieties. Livia was not allowed to proceed with the invitation until the Senate had given its formal approval, and even then she was not permitted to invite the men. Tiberius tactfully undertook to entertain them, and Livia was limited to carrying out the same function for the women.[56] The first potential crisis had passed over smoothly. Things would only get worse.

Tiberius' determined views on the proper role for women in general, and the proper constitutional role for Livia in particular, should not be taken, as they often are by the ancient sources, as a sign of personal animosity towards his mother. While reluctant to grant her a place in the governance of the state, he did not begrudge her the recognition her status demanded, as is demonstrated by the widespread homage to Livia recorded throughout the empire. In fact, on some occasions Tiberius actually shared that homage. Coins from eastern mints depict facing heads of Livia and Tiberius. At Smyrna a dedication to both of them has survived, with Livia specified as Tiberius' mother. At Tralles mother and son shared a priest.[57] Livia's divine status is widely attested in numerous inscriptions and coins in all quarters of the empire, and this process did not abate with the accession of Tiberius; in fact, it seems to have increased. The striking colossal statues of Livia, for instance, most familiar from examples at Leptis Magna, all belong to the period after Tiberius' accession.[58] Although this provincial veneration was certainly not orchestrated from Rome, it doubtless reflected what was locally perceived as the wish of the emperor. The persistence of such expressions of regard for Livia demonstrates that Tiberius made no consistent effort to try to suppress them. On the one occasion when we have evidence of his involvement in the resolutions, his response to the Gytheans to accord divine honours to the imperial family, he expressly allows Livia to make her own decision (see chapter 10). Tiberius did once decline to allow the worship of his mother, but that refusal must be seen in its context. In AD 25 a deputation came from Baetica in Spain to Rome. Citing the precedent of the Temple to Tiberius, Livia, and the Senate that had been given imperial sanction in Asia (see chapter 10), they sought permission to erect a shrine in honour of Tiberius and his mother. Tiberius refused the request, fully aware that he would appear inconsistent. As often happened when he was in a difficult corner, he was careful to spell out the precedent created by Augustus. His predecessor had allowed the city of Pergamum to build a temple to himself and to Rome, and Tiberius had consequently felt impelled to follow his example in Asia, especially in that the worship of his own person was to be linked with the worship of the Senate. But, as he argued, to yield that once was acceptable. If the process were to be repeated throughout the Roman world, the honour would become vulgar. In fact, he followed the pattern he had set down in Tarraconensis and Lusitania, which restricted divine honours to the consecrated members of the imperial house. Clearly, Tiberius' refusal on this occasion should be seen in the context of his general aversion to divine honours, especially when offered at the provincial rather than a merely local level; it should not be viewed as a deliberate attempt to deprive his mother of further distinction.[59]

The sheer number of the distinctions, divine and otherwise, that Tiberius allowed to be heaped on Livia in all quarters of the empire is clear evidence that he did not resent his mother's eminent stature. These distinctions were even extended to her family, for it is under Tiberius that we find honorific statues to her parents in such widely separated locations as Baetica in Spain, Marruvium in Italy, and Samos in the Aegean. Tacitus' claim that Tiberius behaved towards her as he did because he was consumed by envy (*anxius invidia*) is thus difficult to sustain.[60] But as fair-minded as Tiberius tried to be, the uncertainty about how to handle his mother's position in Rome constantly bedeviled him. In AD 16 an issue arose that illustrates perfectly how ambiguous her position was in her son's eyes. Dio reports under that year that Livia, as well as Tiberius, gave assistance to the victims of various fires. Her action would have been totally in keeping with her well-established tradition of a public display, whether genuinely heartfelt or not, of behaving generously to the unfortunate. But Livia's help came not only after the fire but during it. Suetonius reports that Tiberius took his mother to task for meddling in affairs unsuitable for a woman and was especially annoyed that she had played a role in a fire near the temple of Vesta, urging and encouraging people, as she had done when Augustus was alive. The allusion to Augustus' reign suggests that she might have been involved in helping to suppress the famous fire that broke out in the Basilica Aemiliana in 14 BC, when the flames threatened the temple of Vesta and the sacred relics were carried up to the Palatine to safety.[61] Certainly, during Augustus' life Livia had been involved in giving aid during fires herself, doubtless as a recognised duty, just as Agrippina the Younger later joined her husband Claudius in similar situations. Tiberius' annoyance seems at first sight uncharacteristically irrational. Her conduct could not reasonably be seen as a serious attempt to usurp his position, and she may well have found it offensive to be reprimanded for rendering such a worthy service. At the same time, Tiberius' sensitivity over the issue can be appreciated. In Rome the fire service was essentially a military operation, provided by the seven *cohortes vigilum*. After a serious conflagration in AD 6 Augustus created this unit of seven thousand vigiles, all freedmen, organised in seven cohorts, each commanded by a tribune, under the general command of a praefectus vigilum of equestrian rank appointed by the emperor. They could be asked from time to time to perform military duties, as in the arrest of Sejanus, when it would have been dangerous or impolitic to use the praetorians. There was also a serious potential for abuse. Tiberius would not have forgotten the conspiracy of Egnatius Rufus, who organised a private fire brigade in Rome and had the units at his disposal when he made his private bid for power around 20 BC. This sensitivity would be compounded by Tiberius' particular aversion to the idea of women being involved in military matters, as shown by his fury over Agrippina the Elder's defence of the bridge over the Rhine in AD 15.[62]

To illustrate the basic validity of his claim that Livia enjoyed an exalted status far above women of former days, Dio cites a custom that doubtless did cause Tiberius much unease, in that it gave her a formal, institutionalised role: the "salutation." Augustus was much given to these morning receptions, when people could come to the palace to greet him. His events were open affairs, which included ordinary citizens, and he was very affable when dealing with the requests of the participants. Hence his famous quip when a star-struck petitioner approached him nervously, that it was as if he was "giving a penny to an elephant." In addition to the "popular" salutations, regular appearance at a senatorial *salutatio* was expected of all members of the Senate. From 12 BC Augustus had dispensed with that ceremony on days when the Senate met, so that sessions should not be delayed, and in extreme old age he asked that the senatorial ritual be dropped altogether. Livia assumed the tradition of the salutatio, even reviving the senatorial gatherings, although in fairness it must be said that Augustus had not curtailed their visits out of deference but rather because he was too frail to take part. Livia's receptions, as Dio notes, were even entered in the public record, the *acta publica*. This contained items of public importance but also many items for which the border between private and public was not a sharp one, such as the birth of Livia's son Drusus.

It might have been argued by her defenders that Livia's willingness to engage in the salutations represented a selfless act of duty on her part rather than ambitious self-promotion. All the same, the activity was one that would have caused a Roman with traditional male views some concern. It is surely not coincidental that at the very time Agrippina received the title of Augusta, she also received the distinction of participating in the daily salutatio, so that when courtiers and clients paid their daily homage to the emperor, they would henceforth do the same to her. When Nero wanted to clip his mother's wings in 55, he made her move out of the palace into a private house once owned by Antonia, to prevent her from holding large salutations. Julia Domna, who under the Severans revived the notion that women could aspire to positions of power and influence, similarly made a point of receiving the Senate after she had been widowed.[63]

During Augustus' reign Livia had been a model of self-effacement. Now that the regime had changed, she did not take very long to make clear her conviction that as the Augusta she had certain quasi-legal entitlements. In AD 16 Lucius Calpurnius Piso, who later defended his brother Gnaeus in the famous trial in AD 20, managed to create a considerable stir. He was angered by the corruption of the judicial process and by the ruthlessness of the prosecutors. In disgust he finally announced that he would leave Rome forever and live out his days in some quiet backwater. Tiberius made every effort to dissuade him from leaving, and even called in members of the imperial family to help in the task. Piso was won over, and with a new sense of confidence proceeded to demonstrate his independence by summoning Plautia Urgulania to court to recover a sum of money. It was a bold act, because, as Tacitus puts it, he recognised that the friendship (*amicitia*) of Livia had raised Plautia above the law *(supra leges)*. Plautia may have enjoyed an additional degree of security if she was a Vestal Virgin — Tacitus' text seems to imply that she was, although his words are ambiguous. In any event, she refused Piso's summons and went to take refuge in the palace, where Livia championed her cause, even though Vestals were not exempt from giving testimony in court. Piso was not perturbed by Livia's *potentia* — he pursued Plautia there, and was prepared to remove her from the imperial quarters. Tiberius offered a compromise, calculating that it would not be a serious abuse of his power to promise to appear on Plautia's behalf in order to break the deadlock. He procrastinated on the way to court, telling his bodyguard to keep its distance while he broke off his journey to speak to the public. Tacitus implies that the delay was deliberate. Piso grew more and more impatient and increasingly insistent that Plautia turn up. But the tactic proved effective. Before Tiberius had arrived at the court, Livia paid the fine. Both Tiberius and Piso gained credit from the incident.[64]

The passage raises some interesting points. The notion that the amicitia of Livia had raised Urgulania above the law emerges as an issue, although it is not clear whether this was the belief of Piso or Tacitus' own gloss on events. *Amicitia* means more than just friendship — it implies reciprocal obligations. It is a very Roman concept, used in the political sphere of states or individuals who exploited their nexus of connections to advance their mutual interests. It is a word that helps to elevate Livia to the level of powerful men in the state. But if Livia felt that she had the right to protect friends from prosecution, then she would have put herself on a par with the emperor. Moreover, Tacitus states that the incident led Livia to complain that she personally *(se)*, not Urgulania the Vestal, was violated and humiliated *(violari et imminui)*. The wording here is striking, associated as it is with the language of offences against maiestas, which had been extended to cover members of the imperial family beyond the emperor.[65] This passage allows us considerable insight into Livia's own sense of her status. Her maiestas had not been violated by physical or verbal abuse. She had suffered only from Piso's determination to take her friend out of her house to court. No longer the self-effacing Livia of the previous reign, she let her indignation be known. The passage also shows that at this stage Tiberius was caught in the dilemma that Augustus had bequeathed him, and that he made every effort in the early part of his reign to resolve such issues in a diplomatic and nonconfrontational manner. He was therefore prepared to compromise and to indulge his mother up to a point. He took a considerable risk in doing so. There was nothing untoward in a man appearing for a client in a court case, nor for the head of a house to appear for a family member's client. But if the trial had gone ahead, the emperor's presence would have been interpreted as a clear signal to find on behalf of his mother's friend.

Urgulania did not learn to yield. She was later summoned as a witness in a case being tried before the Senate. She refused to appear, and a praetor was sent to her home to take her testimony. She might, however, have taken some comfort in the fate of her bête noire, Lucius Piso. He did not prosper. He faced prosecution for violation of maiestas in AD 24, possibly an act of revenge against the relatives and supporters of his late brother Gnaeus Calpurnius Piso, following his notorious trial. Before his case came up, Lucius died, either of natural causes or from suicide (*mors opportuna*, as Tacitus describes it).

The issue of Livia's maiestas arose again in the following year, AD 17. Appuleia Varilla, niece of Augustus' sister Octavia, was foolish enough to voice some outrageous indiscretions to companions who were equally indiscreet. She was found out and accused of insulting the Divus Augustus, as well as Tiberius and Livia, to which was added a charge of adultery, perhaps for security in view of the uncertainty of the law covering maiestas. In the event only the charge of adultery was proceeded with, under Augustus' Lex Julia de Adulteriis. On the other issues Tiberius instructed the senators that if she had made insulting comments against Augustus, which would have been tantamount to sacrilege, she should be punished. But he wanted no inquiry into comments made about himself. Tiberius was then asked about the attacks on his mother. After some thought he responded that no one should be made legally accountable for words uttered against Livia. He gave this as his own opinion, but represented it as her view also. This accords with Suetonius' comment that at the beginning of his reign Tiberius was an advocate of freedom of speech and thought, and prepared to tolerate verbal abuse of himself and his family. Bauman suggests the possibility that there was a formal cessation in maiestas proceedings at this point. If so, it was short-lived. The case was not carried forward, but the groundwork had clearly been laid for a legal response to insults against the emperor and against his family, and in time Tiberius proved unable to live up to his early high ideals. Dio notes that when eventually Tiberius pushed maiestas cases for slanderous attacks to the bitter end, these included attacks not only on Augustus but also on himself and his mother.[66]

The handling of the case of Appuleia is difficult to reconcile with the claim made by Tacitus that two years earlier, in AD 15, Tiberius was prepared to see a proceeding for verbal abuse go forward under the Lex Maiestas, because he had been irritated that verses were circulating taking him to task for his *saevitia* and *superbia* (cruelty and haughtiness) and claiming a rift between him and his mother *(discordem cum matre animum)*. The allusion is surprising, and seems to be contradicted by the verdict reached in the later case. Syme suggests that Tacitus has presented his information in the wrong order, and that such verses could not have not appeared so early in the reign. But the discord ridiculed in the lampoons need be based on little more than the charges made in the literary sources and attributed by those sources to the beginning of the reign, that Tiberius had refused certain honours for Livia out of personal antipathy. Also, Tacitus seems to have chosen his words carefully. The basis for Tiberius' reply when questioned by the praetor, that there was no reason that actions involving maiestas should not be proceeded with, was that the law should be followed. There is nothing in his response to indicate whether such actions involved attacks on himself or on the late Augustus. Tacitus adds, almost as an afterthought, that Tiberius had been annoyed by the satirical lampoons. But the association of that specific instance of annoyance with his position on the maiestas cases may well be Tacitus' own gloss.[67]

The discovery of new epigraphic material relating to the trial of Gnaeus Cornelius Piso in AD 20, following the death of Germanicus, has thrown important fresh light on many aspects of this period, including the unique status enjoyed by Livia. It appears from the *Piso Decree* that the Senate passed a separate *senatus consultum* in the case of Plancina, who faced *pluruma et gravissima crimina* (many very serious charges). These are not spelled out, probably intentionally, because, as Eck notes, the contrast between the punishment and the crime would have been made too self-evident.[68] Despite the discreet silence on this specific issue in the *Decree*, it is possible to reconstruct with some confidence the broad charges from Tacitus' narrative. In two instances it can be assumed that the indictments would have echoed those levelled against her husband. The *Decree* specifically notes that Germanicus testified against Piso (line 28). Tacitus provides the further detail that on his deathbed Germanicus in fact accused both Piso and Plancina of working against him. The *Decree* records also that Piso rejoiced at Germanicus' death (lines 62–80), and among other manifestations of this conduct it cites his sacrifices and visits to temples. Tacitus mentions these also, but he adds that Plancina's joy was even more shocking and demonstrated by the fact that she gave up the mourning garb that she had been wearing for her dead sister (we do not know, of course, how long previously her sister had died). This last was perhaps the weakest plank in the prosecution's case. Speaking at the opening of the trial, Tiberius made it clear that even if the alleged celebration had taken place, it would be morally reprehensible, but not criminal.[69] Much more serious charges were to follow. Plancina committed the cardinal sin of a woman meddling in military matters, and taking part in the army manoeuvres and suborning the soldiers' loyalty.[70] She received gifts from Vonones, the claimant to the Parthian throne and short-lived ruler of Armenia, at the time in question under Roman surveillance in Syria. Tacitus, perhaps reflecting the general view, claims that the gifts she accepted influenced Piso to support Vonones' cause.[71] The most serious, and probably irrefutable, charge was that Plancina had made her slaves available to Piso, to be joined up with his motley units of deserters and mercenaries in the ill-conceived effort to regain Syria by military force.[72] At any rate, whatever the precise indictments against her, the public seems to have been fully aware of them. In 33, with Livia dead for four years, Plancina died at her own hand after the very same charges had apparently been revived, charges which, according to Tacitus, were widely known *(haud ignotis)*.[73]

Plancina placed herself at the mercy of the emperor and the Senate. Her protection would ultimately rest upon Livia, but Livia could not address the Senate herself. That depressing duty fell upon Tiberius. The decree states that Tiberius spoke *saepe* and *accurate* (wisely and pointedly; line 111) in putting her case. Tiberius seems not to have addressed the legal question of the strength of the charges but to have made a special intercession on Plancina's behalf. The *Decree* uses the technical term *deprecari*, the same word used by Tacitus to describe Tiberius' intercession on behalf of Appuleia Varilla when he asked the Senate not to proceed against her on a maiestas charge in AD 17.[74] Tacitus describes Tiberius' speech as a shameful disgrace *(cum pudore et flagitio)*, in which he used his mother's request *(preces)* as his cover. In his account of Plancina's death thirteen years later, Tacitus levels the same charge, and in fact uses the same word, *preces*. Tacitus' version of events receives a strong endorsement from the *Piso Decree*, which explains (line 114) that Tiberius had received *iustissimas causas* (very just reasons) from Livia why she should have her way in this matter. Naturally enough, the decree does not echo Tacitus' thesis that Livia was asking the favour for Plancina for services against Agrippina.[75]

Even the language of the decree is striking and surprising. When Tiberius sought to intercede for Plancina, in accordance with his mother's wishes, the Senate declared its obligation to accede to the request of Livia, for *optume de r(e) p(ublica) merita* (having served the state excellently). The concept of *meritum* had been associated with women before this. Pliny illustrates its use from unspecified "Annals" that recorded the gratitude of the state for the Vestal Virgin, Gaia or Fufetia, who donated the Campus Martius to the Romans. But the actual formula used in the *Piso Decree* was one conventionally applied to men, and to men who had held office. Caesar uses the phrase *bene de republica meritum* of himself to describe the sterling qualities that convinced the decurions of a town that he should be allowed to enter. Cicero in a letter to Munatius Plancus at the end of 44 BC wrote that *de republica bene mereri* was the highest ideal his friend could aspire to (Plancus was to disappoint Cicero by throwing in his lot with Mark Antony).[76] The application of such a phrase to Livia in AD 20 was to accord recognition of signal public service to the state.

The decree notes that the Senate determined that they should acquiesce in Tiberius' requests for clemency on the basis that they were Livia's requests, which they were bound to honour. Livia was entitled to such respect, on two grounds (lines 115–19). The first argument was that she had benefitted the world. She had done so in her capacity as the mother of Tiberius, a sentiment expressed also in less formal documents. The *Consolatio* refers to her as "one woman who has given so many benefits through her two offspring" *(tot bona per partus quae dedit una duos)*.[77] Moreover, she had bestowed favours upon men of every rank. This is a familiar theme in all the literary sources, but it is striking to find it given a formal status in the decree. But even more remarkable is the pronouncement that Livia's wishes should be granted because she was entitled to a supreme influence *(plurumum posse)* in any request that she might put to the Senate, by right and deservedly *(iure et merito)*, even if in practice she chose to exercise that right sparingly. The phrase *iure et merito* does not have the strict juridical force it might seem at first sight to possess, and is in fact commonly used in Latin in a figurative sense, just as "rightfully" is used in English. It is found as early as Plautus, where one of his characters is said to find fault with himself *iure optimo merito*, and Juvenal in an obscure passage applies the phrase to people who, when they criticise moral humbugs, do so *iure ac merito*. Even in the political sphere the expression has a moral rather than a legal force, as when Cicero observes that the praetors, because of their loyal support in the Catiline crisis, deserve to be praised *merito ac iure*.[78] All the same, the expression is remarkable in a formal decree, and gives Livia an authority which would never have been given public and official sanction while Augustus was alive.

Conflict between Tiberius and his mother over her right to intervene in public issues plagued the two of them until Tiberius' departure for Capri. There were occasions when he had to admit essentially that he was beaten, that he could not prevent his mother's involvement in issues of governance. In these cases he could do little more than acquiesce, while disassociating himself as far as possible from what had transpired. Suetonius describes an incident, which he dates very vaguely to the period just before the departure for Capri, that nicely captures Tiberius' frustration. For much of the republican period judges were taken from the senatorial order, and traditionally their names, along with those of priests and other officials, had been made public by being posted in black letters on a white board, the *album*. The exclusive hold of the senatorials was broken by Gaius Gracchus when he selected the judges for his extortion court from the equestrian order. The issue became something of a political battleground in 70 BC when the Lex Aurelia established a balanced system by which the panels *(decuriae)* were made up of distinct socioeconomic divisions, the first consisting of senators, the second of equestrians, and the third taken from the *tribuni aerarii*, whose precise status is not clear. Modifications were introduced, and by the time of Tiberius' reign there were four panels, serving in both civil and criminal cases. In the early empire the decuriae consisted of about a thousand members each, all Roman citizens. Equestrians seem to have predominated, for with reference to the twenties AD both Tacitus and Suetonius allude loosely to the *decuriae equitum* (panels of equites). Membership was eagerly sought, and was limited initially under Augustus to citizens from Rome or Italy. By the end of the Julio-Claudian period the panels were opened up to provincials, but a strict rule was still maintained that a newly enfranchised citizen could not be appointed immediately (the qualifying period is not made clear).[79]

Suetonius records that Livia placed Tiberius in a difficult position when she sponsored the request of an unnamed individual to be empanelled, even though he had only recently acquired Roman citizenship. Livia was insistent, and Tiberius found himself on the horns of a dilemma, torn by the petition of the Augusta and by the time-honoured rule against accelerated elevation. His patience at trying to reach a diplomatic compromise seems by this stage to have been exhausted. With ill grace he allowed the appointment to go ahead but insisted that when it was gazetted, an entry should be added that he had acted under pressure from his mother. In the event, Livia was not assuaged and found it impossible to retain the poise and *comitas* of her more youthful days. The incident produced the one specific serious clash between Tiberius and his mother that is recorded in the sources. Suetonius claims that on hearing what had happened, Livia flew into a rage *(commota)*. She proceeded to a shrine where letters written to her by Augustus had been deposited. In Tiberius' presence she read out some of them, dredging up her late husband's views on Tiberius' sour nature and his intolerance. Tiberius was put out less by the opinions expressed by Augustus (he can hardly have been unaware of them) than by the fact that his mother had held on to the letters and used them so vindictively.[80]

At some point after the end of April, AD 22, Tiberius had hastened back to Rome on news of his mother's illness. Tacitus reports that at that time their relations were harmonious *(sincera adhuc inter matrem filiumque concordia)*, or that they were hypocritically keeping their mutual hatred well concealed *(sive occultis odiis)*. Bad feelings had supposedly arisen over an incident that occurred just before the illness. Tacitus explains that in AD 22, at some point before Tiberius' return, Livia, in dedicating an effigy *(effigies)* to Augustus at the Theatre of Marcellus, had put her son's name after her own in the inscription.[81] It was believed *(credebatur)* that Tiberius had felt that his dignity as princeps had been offended, although he had kept the insult to himself.[82] The essentials of this anecdote, in particular the order of the names, are confirmed by a notation in the *Fasti Praenestini* that on April 23 *sig(num) divo Augusto patri ad theatrum Marc(elli) Iulia Augusta et Ti. Augustus dedicaverunt* (Julia Augusta and Tiberius Augustus dedicated a statue to [their] father, the deified Augustus, by the Theatre of Marcellus).[83] Some also see an allusion to the statue in a contemporary coin, a sestertius minted in Tiberius' twenty-fourth tribunician year, in AD 22 or 23. On the reverse, Augustus, identified by the legend *Divus Augustus Pater,* wears a radiate crown and toga and sits on a throne, facing left, with his feet on a stool. He holds a branch in his right hand and a long sceptre in his left. In front of him, on the left, is an altar.[84]

The statue was dedicated in the names of both Livia and Tiberius, but because the emperor was absent from Rome, it is to be assumed that arrangements for the commemorative inscription were left to Livia. The entry in the fasti is almost certainly based on the dedication stone that she commissioned. It confirms the order of the names. That same sequence may be reflected in Dio's reference to Livia and Tiberius "making" a temple to Augustus in AD 14; Dio puts the names in that order. Dio's order may reflect the temple's dedicatory inscription, now lost, which could well have been the ultimate source for his entry. If so, it may have little significance for the Livia-Tiberius relationship, because the temple was finally completed only under Caligula in AD 37, and the word order could have reflected that emperor's choice rather than Livia's. The painted images recorded in the Gytheum decree are listed as those of Augustus, Livia, and then Tiberius, in that order, suggesting that the Gytheans gave Livia the place of honour after Augustus (see chapter 10).[85] If Tiberius was in fact offended in AD 22, his indignation was unwarranted. Livia was priestess of Augustus, and this office would justify her precedence. In any case, the most striking feature of the fasti inscription is the reference to *patri* after Augustus' name. The participation of Livia in a dedication to someone identified as a father may seem incongruous, but could in fact be a recognition of her adoption by her husband. Livia may have felt that on this occasion she had gone out of her way to observe strict protocol. For his part Tiberius clearly saw her action as an arrogation of rights properly his. Eight years after the death of Augustus and the opening of his will, the problem that he created had still not resolved itself.

With Tiberius' departure for Capri in AD 26 the stress over the constitutional issue abated. Livia was now in her eighties, and for the last three years of her life she almost disappears from the historical narrative, eclipsed by Sejanus and his efforts to exercise a de facto control over the affairs of state in Rome during the emperor's absence. Yet in the minds of the Romans she still enjoyed a status not normally associated with women. This was demonstrated after her death, when the Senate passed an extraordinary measure for an arch in her honour, in recognition of her acts of kindness and generosity. This vote was indeed an extraordinary gesture. As Dio notes, this was the first time that such a distinction had been bestowed on a woman, and indeed there is no known example of the Senate's ever again voting for an arch for a woman. The first to be set up to an individual man seems to be the one erected on the Via Sacra in 120 BC to Quintus Fabius Maximus for his victory over the Allobroges. The first recorded use of public funds voted for such a purpose was for the arch granted to Drusus on the Appian Way in 9 BC, as a posthumous honour. A grieving Senate voted for three arches for Germanicus after his death, and similarly, when Drusus Caesar, the son of Tiberius, died in AD 23, the Senate seems to have erected a memorial arch in his honour. Thus even in the case of men the grant of a posthumous arch financed from public funds in Rome was far from common. Livia's arch was never built, skilfully sidelined by Tiberius. But it did provide a final and dramatic opportunity for the senators to demonstrate that they had remained faithful to Augustus' intentions, when fifteen years earlier he had elevated her to the unprecedented position of the Augusta.[86]

WOMAN OF SUBSTANCE

Despite Livia's public image as a woman who lived soberly and unpreten-tiously, the evidence indicates that by the time of her death she had become one of the most wealthy women in Rome. The terms of her will, if correctly reported, seem to leave no doubt on this issue. In it she left a legacy of fifty million sesterces to her favourite, Galba.[1] Romans were restricted in the pro-portion of their estate that they could leave in individual legacies. The Lex Falcidia stipulated that at least one quarter of the whole inheritance had to be reserved for the heir(s) of the estate. This would mean that Livia's estate must have been worth at least sixty-eight million. But in fact Suetonius notes that Galba was only one of the legatees to receive bequests, albeit the most hand-somely rewarded. The total value must have been considerably larger, though how much larger is a matter of speculation. Tiberius reduced Galba's bequest to 500,000, using the argument that the sum had not been written out and the numerical symbol was erroneous (see chapter 11). But it is significant that Tiberius did not argue that the amount violated the terms of the Lex Falcidia.[2]

It is unlikely that Livia could have owned much of this wealth before her marriage. She was the daughter of a proscribed Roman, and the wife of some-one who had fled into exile. When she returned to Rome in 39 BC, she proba-bly possessed very little, beyond perhaps a family estate near Veii (see chap-ter 3). This situation would have been transformed by her second marriage. She could not have benefitted by direct contributions from Augustus during his lifetime — Roman law prohibited gifts between husbands and wives. On his death, however, the financial benefits of her marriage were substantial indeed. Augustus in his will named Tiberius and Livia as his heirs. They were to receive 150 million sesterces, a third of which, 50 million, would go to Livia. The heirs were given a year's grace to pay out the bequests. This must mean that the cash in hand, which would obviously not represent the full value of the estate, was not sufficient to meet the demands of the legacies. These were made up of the gross amount of about 90 million to be paid to the army and the people, and a number of individual bequests whose amounts are not known.[3] In order for Livia to inherit her 50 million sesterces from her husband, special provisions had to be made for her, and Augustus in his will asked the Senate to allow him to leave her a sum that, strictly speaking, was prohibited by law. The capacity of women to inherit was restricted by two groups of legislation, the Lex Voconia of 169 BC and the Lex Iulia of 18 BC (amended by the Lex Papia Poppaea of AD 9). The latter restricted the right of women with fewer than three children to benefit from inheritances. The *ius trium liberorum* that Livia acquired on the death of her son Drusus in 9 BC protected her against this disability. But the Lex Voconia could have remained a problem. This law had been introduced in 169 at the behest of Cato the Censor. Its details are unclear, but it did contain a provision that a person whose property was valued in the census at 100,000 asses could not name a woman as heir, and it was presumably from this clause that Livia was given exemption.[4]

While Augustus was still alive, the indirect benefits of the marriage would have been enormous. Livia's position would have enabled her to create an extensive network of *amici*, and much of her wealth would have come in return for the favours she had shown to families. She would be rewarded by gifts, by legacies, and by being named heir. By tradition the Roman will was seen as a device for indicating friendship and esteem, and it was assumed that clients would bequeath their patrons a legacy. The potential benefits of this tradition are illustrated by the case of Augustus himself, who recorded in his will that he had received legacies worth 1.4 billion sesterces (and had spent them).[5] Augustus' prestige would have increased Livia's clientele and the potential for similar bequests for her. In this she benefitted from a special provision enacted sometime before AD 9 to allow certain women, doubtless including Livia, to inherit property worth more than 100,000 sesterces.[6] Unfortunately, we have no direct evidence for any legacies received by Livia in Rome. She owned a number of slaves who can be traced to distinguished Romans, but there is no way of telling whether they were inherited directly from the original owners. As an example, the name of one her freedmen, Timotheus Maronianus, indicates that he, like other slaves or former slaves similarly named, had once been owned by the poet Vergil (Publius Vergilius Maro). But Timotheus is recorded as the freedman of Livia as Julia Augusta, thus after Augustus' death, and had probably been bequeathed first to Augustus, who passed him on to Livia in his will.[7]

What direct evidence we have of Livia's legacies comes from outside Rome, especially Judaea. We know that she shared the five hundred talents that Herod the Great left Livia, his friends, and freedmen in his will. (Augustus received a thousand talents, but supposedly gave back most of it to Herod's sons.) As we shall see, some years later Herod's sister Salome on her death left Livia the major part of her estate. Both legacies could have included slaves. Tiberius at any rate later inherited from his mother a slave who had belonged to Herod or Salome.[8]

When Amyntas, king of Galatia, died in 25 BC, his kingdom was incorporated into the empire and Augustus received much of his personal property. Some of Amyntas' slaves may have been bequeathed to members of the imperial family. One has the name Marcus Livius Aug(ustae?) l(ibertus) Anteros Amyntianus — he possibly became a freedman of Livia's, while an Epinicius Caesar(is) ser(vus) Amyntianus became a slave of Augustus'. One must, however, be cautious in extracting information from the pattern of servile names. There are other inscriptions at Rome that mention individuals with the cognomen Amyntianus (or Amyntiana) without indication of any connection with the imperial family.[9]

Livia had lived a generally rootless existence with her first husband, passing from pillar to post as a wandering exile. When she returned to Rome and met Octavian, this wandering lifestyle changed. She moved into an established residence, and a very well-appointed one. Octavian had come to Rome in late summer 44 BC to claim his political inheritance after the death of Caesar. His first home, near the Forum Romanum, had belonged to the orator Gaius Licinius Calvus, probably best known through his friendship with the poet Catullus.[10] Calvus' property, though probably not humble, did not live up to Octavian's aspirations. In the late republic the choice residential district for the status-conscious was without question the Palatine hill. Octavian moved there and offered Livia a home in an area where she was to stay for the remainder of her long life. The Palatine, rising some forty metres to the south of the Forum Romanum, was closely associated with Rome's early history, especially in the southwest corner, where Livia resided. By tradition it contained Rome's oldest settlement, and in Vergil's *Aeneid* it was a place of veneration even before the founding of the city. The earliest private residence recorded there is that of Vitruvius Vaccus, which was destroyed in 330 BC. By the late republic Palatine residents could at one time or another rub shoulders with Cicero, the demagogue Clodius, and almost certainly Mark Antony. Octavian was born in the district, and Livia's first husband owned a Palatine residence, where she was certainly living in 42 BC, when her first son, Tiberius, was born there.[11]

We cannot be certain when Octavian obtained his Palatine address. We know from Suetonius that at some point he acquired (by what means remains unknown) the house of the celebrated orator Quintus Hortensius. This might have happened after his return from the battle of Philippi, in 42 BC, during a period of widespread proscriptions. It would have been into this fine residence that Livia moved (see appendix 15). In 36 BC their house was hit by a thunderbolt, and the priests declared this a divine sign that the god desired the site. Accordingly Octavian made that part of the house public property. He consecrated it to Apollo, whom he had adopted as his patron god as a consequence of his naval victory at Naulochus, and promised to build a temple with a portico, which he did in splendid style. This generous act was reciprocated. In return the public granted him another house at public expense.[12]

It was now politically opportune for Octavian to project an image of simple living. Suetonius describes his house as very modest, both in its size and in its decoration, with small colonnades of peperino (hard grey volcanic stone) and rooms without marble decorations or pavements. The same bedroom was used by Augustus in summer and winter, according to Suetonius, for more than forty years.[13] There is general agreement that the house is represented by remains on the south brow of the hill, south of the Domus Tiberiana, between the Scalae Caci and the Temple of Magna Mater on the west, and what is clearly identified as the Temple of Apollo to the east (plan 1). Livia spent the more than half-century of her marriage in the complex of public and private buildings that had this house at its core.

It was possible for a husband to bequeath to his widow the use of a house or part of a house until her own death, when it would revert to his heir.[14] It is likely then that on Augustus' death in AD 14, Livia moved from the main part of the imperial residence to her own quarters. The so-called Casa di Livia was discovered by Rosa in 1869 in the part of the Palatine behind the Domus Tiberiana, between the Temple of Magna Mater and the House of Augustus (plan 2). The Casa has a complicated history of construction and was decorated by an important series of paintings that are at a stage of development similar to those of the House of Augustus (Pompeian Second Style), and can be dated to about 25–20 BC. When the Roman authorities undertook conservation of the paintings, it was discovered that behind them there were

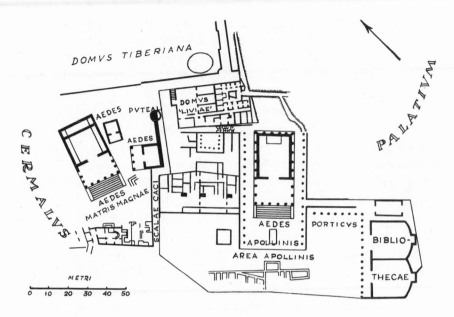

Plan 1. Augustus' Palatine residence. After Lugli, 1938 (Domus Liviae = Casa di Livia)

irregular reticulate-faced walls (a facing of bricks made up of a network of small blocks in diagonal lines), with doorways that had been blocked with masonry before the plaster was put down. Hence the building is earlier than the paintings and could have been erected in the mid-first century. The attribution to Livia is based on a lead pipe found in the excavations bearing the name of Iulia Augusta. This is strong evidence of her ownership, but not definitive proof.[15]

The house has a large lobby (atrium) onto which three halls open. The central larger hall has been called a *tablinum*, and the rooms at the side are designated as *alae* (wings), identified as right and left from the perspective of facing southeast. A room at the west corner has been called the *triclinium*. None of these labels is strictly valid, but because they have become established in the literature, they are retained for convenience. Beyond the tablinum was a yard flanked by a portico supported on heavy pillars. (The yard was later replaced by a number of small service rooms.) The main rooms of the house were underground. There is no evidence of windows, and there was perhaps a source of light through the ceiling. These lower rooms were reached by a stair and a ramp with a vaulted roof. Inside the atrium a stair led to a narrow corridor, along the southwest side of which was a series of small rooms.

There are traces of fine mosaic pavement throughout the house. The tri-

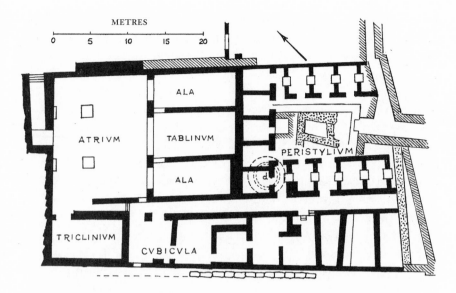

METRES

0 5 10 15 20

ALA

ATRIVM

TABLINVM

PERISTYLIVM

ALA

d

TRICLINIVM

CVBICVLA

Plan 2. The "Casa di Livia." After Lugli, 1938

clinium was paved with white mosaic interspersed with irregular shapes of coloured marble and alabaster. More important are the paintings, conserved in the 1950s. It has been suggested that they and the stuccowork of the House of Livia, the House of Augustus, the Farnese Villa, and others, are the work of one main workshop, charged with commissions by Augustus and Marcus Agrippa. In the tablinum the most elaborate paintings are part of an architectural scheme with large central pictures, two of which survive, depicting Polyphemus and Galatea on the rear wall, and Argos and Io on the right. They are set in mainly closed structures with wall surfaces painted red. Narrow openings at the end of the long (right) wall and in the upper part of the scheme allow views onto further buildings which have small figures. There are typical features of the Second Style: elongated columns with vegetal sheaths around their shafts, grotesque creatures on the entablatures, chains of stylised floral ornaments, fanciful motifs such as a Gorgon head flanked by a pair of volute-tailed lion-griffins. The triclinium has a similar architectural scheme with pictures of rustic sanctuaries. The right ala depicts a repeating scene with a screen of columns linked by fruit garlands in front of orthostates, with a frieze portraying an idealised landscape with Greek and Egyptian elements interwoven, with boats, temples, statues, and animals (including a camel) in yellow monochrome. Ling calls this the "crowning achievement of monochrome painting," with a "ghostly, dream-like effect somewhat akin to that of Japanese prints." The left ala is basically similar, except that the garlands are omitted, the colour scheme is much richer, the columns have more vegetation, and the yellow landscapes are replaced by pairs of monsters facing in heraldic posture.[16]

Within her residence Livia would have been served by a large corps of retainers. The richest evidence for her household comes from the *Monumentum Liviae*, a form of sepulchral monument called a columbarium (dovecot), where the containers for ashes were deposited in the pigeonholes. The monumentum was excavated in 1726, but little of it, other than the inscriptions, has survived. Accounts from the time of the excavation indicate that it contained 550 niches, generally with two urns sunk into the floor of each niche. The inscriptions, supplemented from other columbaria, have been closely studied by Susan Treggiari, who offers us a vivid impression of the size and scope of Livia's domestic staff. The whole upper hierarchy can be reconstructed (menial jobs would tend not to have been identified), beginning with the *dispensator*, the steward of the household, chiefly involved with the expenditure of cash; the *arcarii* (keepers of the chest) and *tabularii* (accountants), whose task was aided by a slave *ad possessiones*, an office, it seems, unique to Livia's household, or at least not known elsewhere; and a *custos rationis patrimoni*, who would have looked after the accounts of her inheritance from Augustus. (It has been suggested that he was a member of Tiberius' rather than Livia's staff.) At the more personal level we find a surprising number of *ornatrices*, individuals devoted to her appearance; staff *a veste / ad vestem, ab ornamentis, ab ornamentis sacerdotalibus;* and a *calciator, lanipendi,* and *sarcinatores/-rices* (see chapter 6). For her comfort she had an *unctrix* (masseuse). She employed *pedisequi/-ae* (footmen / women) and a *puer a pedibus*, perhaps a head footman.[17] Livia seems to have been particularly attentive to her health, and her household contained many medical men for her own use and for that of her staff. Several *medici* are attested, as well as a *supra medicos*, or medical supervisor.[18] Finally, perhaps the most striking group are the skilled craftsmen who would have been employed for the manufacturing and maintaining of luxury items — her *aurifex* (goldsmith), *inaurator* (gilder), *margaritarius* (pearl setter), *colorator* (perhaps furniture polisher), *ab supellectile* (in charge of furniture), and *a tabulis* (in charge probably of pictures).[19]

A large household would also have its share of entertainers. Roman matrons liked to keep naked boys *(delicia)* in their company to amuse them. Dio describes an exchange between such a lad and Livia at a banquet shortly after her betrothal to Augustus (see chapter 2). One is attested for Livia, Gaius Julius Prosopas, whom she shared with her granddaughter Livilla. He died at the age of nine. Apart from this the only other entertainer recorded is a reader *(lector)*. Perhaps Livia felt that Augustus and Tiberius provided sufficient amusement. As we have seen (chapter 6), the imperial house considered it fashionable to own dwarfs, and Livia could boast the record for the smallest female.[20] It might just be argued, of course, that Livia maintained her Palatine residences as the wife or mother of the princeps and that a certain level of opulence had to be maintained, consonant with the dignity of the Roman state. This might have been at odds with an essentially personal frugality and modesty, but would be a burden she had no choice but to bear. There is evidence, however, that in addition to the Palatine residences, Livia seems to have owned property in the city, where she had blocks *(insulae)* with apartments and slaves who managed them.[21]

Although the possession of urban properties might have appealed to the basic capitalist instinct of wealthy Romans, the ownership of country estates was the ultimate goal of the aristocratic classes in the Roman world, as in other societies. Livia seems to have acquired a large number of rural properties during her lifetime in the form of land, homes, and commercial activities. We do not have a complete picture by any means — Josephus and Pliny are the only literary sources to make reference to her landed property, and most of our knowledge is based on papyri and inscriptions.

Some of Livia's holdings were spread throughout Italy. She had a fine home only a few kilometres from the city, near Veii, where the Via Tiberiana forks from the Via Flaminia (see chapter 3). The modern Primaporta was called Rubra or Saxa Rubra in antiquity, from the red colour of the surrounding earth. A track leads up from the road to the plateau on which Livia's villa stood in a delightful location. Cooled by a constant gentle breeze, it commands spectacular views, and the Alban Hills and the Appenines are visible in the distance. The best-known part of the complex is what might be called a pavilion, located at the westernmost edge of the plateau. Stairs lead down to a small vaulted vestibule, at the left of which an arched doorway opens into a large room with splendid wall paintings (fig. 28).[22] Suetonius refers to Livia *Veientanum suum revisenti* (revisiting her property at Veii) immediately after her marriage to Octavian. The fact that she was returning to her villa, described as suum (her own) at this time, suggests that she owned it before the marriage. There is general agreement that the *opus reticulatum* of the boundary walls of the villa and substructures belong to about 50 BC, and the estate may have come to Livia from her father, Marcus Livius Drusus Claudianus. His property was confiscated in the proscriptions at the end of 43. The villa might have passed to her earlier than that, possibly at her wedding to Tiberius Claudius Nero.[23]

Livia owned brickworks in Campania which were probably part of a great estate. Stamped tiles bearing the names of her household staff have been found at Herculaneum and Stabiae. She possessed estates on the island of Lipari just north of Sicily, where a Cornelius Manuetus is identified as the procurator of the Augustus and Augusta *(proc[urator] Aug[usti] et Aug[ustae])*. The term *procurator* is used for a number of quite distinct offices, one of which was the manager of the private imperial properties. Thus Livia and Tiberius presumably owned an estate there that they inherited jointly from Augustus. In the area of Tusculum she shared ownership of another estate with Tiberius. Because of the presence of house slaves on Capri, Willrich concluded that she had possessions there. A slave belonging to her is attested at Scolacium in Lucania.[24]

Outside Italy the record is even more impressive. One of the administrators of Livia's property would acquire considerable fame afterwards: Publius Afranius Burrus, who became the commander of the praetorian guard just before Nero's accession and played an important if shadowy role in the early years of his reign. Burrus was born in Vaison, and an inscription honouring him in that town records that for a time he was Livia's procurator in Gallia Narbonensis. She was by then Julia Augusta, indicating that Burrus held the office after Augustus' death in 14, although she may have acquired the property before that.[25] In Gaul, Livia owned land with copper deposits, which she would have been legally entitled to mine. In his general section on copper, Pliny the Elder indicates that the highest quality deposits of the mineral had by his time long been worked out. Of those remaining he ranked the best as the Sallustianum in the Alpine region of Haute Savoie, named after the Sallustius linked with the execution of Agrippa Postumus. Next was ranked the Livianum, found on Livia's estate in Gaul. Her deposits were all but exhausted by Pliny's day and were producing only a small output, but the fact that the product acquired a name of its own, *aes Livianum*, attests to its high quality. Davies tentatively suggests that Livia's mine was in the Rhône area at Chessy or St. Bel.[26]

Her holdings in Judaea were extensive. On Salome's death (c. AD 9–12), the major part of her estate, Jamnia on the coast and Phasaelis and Archelais with their palm groves in the Jordan Valley, passed under her will to Livia. Archelais in particular was noted for the size of its palm plantations and the high quality of its dates. Salome had been allowed to accept a bequest from Herod on his death, and Augustus may have given his permission on the understanding that she make an imperial disposition in turn. Livia's property would be administered by procurators resident in Jamnia. We know that the estate passed to Tiberius on Livia's death. It passed ultimately to Caligula, during whose reign it was the scene of violent disturbances between Greeks and Jews. The procurator in Caligula's day was Gaius Herennius Capito, who may have been appointed originally by Livia to that office.[27]

During Augustus' lifetime Livia acquired a large estate in the neighbourhood of Thyateira in Asia Minor, which still existed in the time of Caracalla. An *arke Leibiane* or *Liouiane* (Livian treasury) with its own procurator was still in use under that emperor and is mentioned in third century inscriptions. It presumably collected the rents of property which had belonged to Livia and had passed into imperial patrimony. Augustus inherited property from Lucius Sempronius Atratinus in AD 7. A freedman of Atratinus is recorded in Thyateira, and Shatzman concludes that Livia inherited the estate there from Augustus when he died in AD 14. The inscriptions refer to her as Leibia or Liouia rather than Ioulia Sebaste, but strict consistency in her nomenclature is not always maintained (see appendix 4). Huntsman notes that Tiberius took his first career steps representing the citizens of Thyateira (as well as Laodicea and Chios), who had suffered from an earthquake in 24 BC and were in Rome seeking help. He might have been discharging patronal obligations on behalf of clients. Other inscriptions at Thyateira mention Julia Augusta, but we cannot be certain that they do not refer to Julia Domna and the Severan period.[28]

In Egypt, Dio records that Cleopatra's land was confiscated after Actium. This would have enabled Augustus to acquire property there without incurring the unpopularity that would have followed widespread seizure of private holdings. It is generally assumed that it was these estates that were passed from Augustus to friends and family, although we cannot rule out the possibility that they might have been acquired on the open market.[29] Livia owned considerable property in Egypt, including papyrus marshes, grain lands, vineyards, vegetable farms, granaries, and olive and wine presses.[30] The earliest reference to her holdings dates to AD 5, when we hear of an estate owned jointly by Livia and Germanicus in the Arsinoite district (the modern Fayum). As seems to have happened frequently on estates in Egypt, a dispute broke out, in this case when a hired donkey driver stole some of the equipment and caused one of the donkeys to die. A petition referring to the incident has survived in which Callistratus, Livia's estate superintendent, writes to the senior police official (*epistates phulakiton*) of the area seeking redress for the lost equipment and the dead donkey, and even for the time lost for the other donkeys made idle by the misbehaviour. One piece of secondary information from this papyrus, provided that it has been restored correctly, is that the estate was large enough to have a donkey gaffer *(prostates ton onikon ktenon)*. It is possible that Germanicus' share was inherited from his father, Drusus, who might have held it in joint ownership with Livia.[31] Joint ownership with Germanicus is attested also at Bakkhias, where a labourer on one of the estates was similarly involved in some sort of petition to the *strategos* of the nome — the bad state of the papyrus prevents further details.[32] After Germanicus' death in AD 19, his share would have passed to his children. In fact, we find Livia and his children, or at least the sons, Nero, Drusus, and Caligula, in joint ownership of a long section of the papyrus marshes at Theadelphia, where they seem to have held a monopoly, and of grain lands at Philadelphia.[33] Also, there is a reference at Tebtynis to a treasury of their jointly held estate.[34] Livia seems to have continued to acquire properties in Egypt right to the end. In 28 or 29 she is recorded as owning lands for cultivating wheat and barley at Euhemeria, where a neighbouring farmer allowed his sheep and cattle onto the land, and they ate some of her grain.[35] There are also references to her Egyptian estates after her death.[36]

Livia's prominent position helped her acquire a considerable fortune, but it also imposed many obligations. Her generosity to individuals and to communities is noted in chapter 10. She would also have incurred many expenses relating to her own family, falling in the grey area between public and private liberality. Thus when Tiberius put on gladiatorial shows in honour of his father and of his grandfather Drusus, the cost was carried by Livia and Augustus.[37] Apart from the public honours voted for Divus Augustus, there would have been numerous gestures made by individual citizens in a private capacity. These included Livia, and at her own expense she established a private festival on the Palatine in Augustus' honour, probably beginning in AD 15. It was destined to continue for several centuries. Originally it lasted for three days, but this period seems later to have been extended, and at some point the festival became a public one, through an undated senatorial decree (see appendix 16).[38] By Caligula's day the event was not attracting the best people — Josephus seems to have viewed the assembled crowds essentially as riffraff, although he may just have been irritated that they were upset to hear of Caligula's assassination during the festivities in AD 41. There are hints that a low tone might have been set at the very outset. In AD 15 charges were brought against a knight, Falanius. It was claimed that he had allowed an actor and catamite by the name of Cassius to participate in the organised worship of Augustus that took place in the larger private homes in Rome. Tiberius took no action against Falanius, making the point that Cassius and other actors had taken part in Livia's Palatine celebrations, presumably the first ones, in that same year.[39]

When the Senate voted for Augustus' consecration, they approved a temple (*heroon*) to be erected in Rome. The responsibility for its construction was assumed by Livia and Tiberius. The building in question was presumably the Temple of Divus Augustus that stood in the depression between the Capitoline and the Palatine. If so, neither of its sponsors lived to see it completed. It reached an advanced stage under Tiberius, but he died before its dedication, and the honour (and excellent publicity) fell to his successor, Caligula, who carried out the dedication at the end of August 37. When finished, it was a splendid building, depicted on a sestertius of Caligula, where it is identified by the inscription DIVO AUGUSTO. It has a facade of six columns and various statue groups on its pediment. It was restored by Antonius Pius in 158–59, and it appears on his coins, now with a range of eight columns, in the Corinthian order (fig. 9).[40]

Probably separate from the temple eventually completed by Caligula is a second structure, mentioned by Pliny, who refers to a *templum* erected by Livia (with no mention of Tiberius) to Divus Augustus on the Palatine. Pliny visited the Palatine in person, where he saw an enormously heavy cinnamon root placed on a golden dish. Every year until the shrine was destroyed by fire (probably the major fire of AD 80) drops fell from the root and hardened into grains.[41] After Livia's own deification in AD 42, Claudius put her statue in the same temple and it was there that each January 17 (and also on other dates, such as Augustus' birthday), the Arvals sacrificed to her and to Divus Augustus. We have inscriptions alluding to servants attached to Divus Augustus' Palatine Temple, including one in service after Livia's own deification: *aeditus templi divi Augusti et divae Augustae quod est in Palatium* (the aeditus [steward] of the temple of Divus Augustus and Diva Augusta which is on the Palatine).[42]

FRIEND, PATRON,
AND PROTECTOR

By Livia's time Romans were well acquainted with the phenomenon of women playing an influential, if indirect, role in public life. Their influence came not through military command or through political office — these were still very much male preserves — but through the exploitation of family connections in the complex personal process by which political business was often conducted in Rome.[1] Precedents of sorts could be cited from the earliest period of Roman history and tradition. The Sabine women, abducted by a subterfuge, interceded between their new Roman husbands and their former families and persuaded the two groups to form an alliance. Then there was the deputation of women in 491 BC, led by the wife and mother of Coriolanus, which is said to have persuaded the renegade commander against leading an army on Rome. In more recent times there was the example of Cornelia, mother of the Gracchi brothers. Gaius Gracchus introduced a law that would prevent a deposed magistrate from holding office again. It was aimed at a Marcus Octavius, who had been deprived of the tribunacy in 133 BC by Gaius' brother Tiberius. Cornelia interceded and succeeded in persuading Gaius to abandon his motion.[2]

There were certain limitations that could not be transgressed, and there had always been women who transgressed them, supposedly from sexual depravity or in the reckless pursuit of power. But provided the boundaries were respected, it was recognised that a woman could freely offer helpful and positive private advice to a male relative or exploit her influence with family friends. In the turbulent period of the triumvirate we find numerous instances of women being recruited to work on behalf of their husbands or sons. In 40 BC Sextus Pompeius despatched Antony's mother, Julia, to Athens to help him form an alliance with her son. (Livia and her husband sailed with him on the same ship.) Octavian responded by using Sextus' mother, Mucia, to make an approach on his behalf to Sextus. Antony's mother played a further role in the negotiations between Octavian and Antony that led to the peace of Brundisium, even applying a degree of maternal pressure on a reluctant Antony. Not long after, Mucia was sent at popular demand to urge Sextus Pompeius to conclude peace, and she was joined by his wife, Scribonia, in pressuring him to conclude the treaty of Misenum with Antony and Octavian in 39.[3]

Besides helping members of their own family, women could also properly intervene on behalf of those linked by a bond of *amicitia*. There are many instances of this kind of intercession in the late republic.[4] When Sextus Roscius sought refuge in Rome, under suspicion of murdering his father, he asked for the help of Caecilia Metella, who had been a friend of his father's. She chose Cicero to represent Roscius, which he did successfully in a case that had powerful political overtones. Cicero went out of his way to pay tribute to the way Metella met her obligations to her old friend's son.[5]

If there was one particular model for Livia to emulate, it would have to be Octavia, who through her diplomatic skills combined the qualities of the loyal wife with those of the devoted sister and mediated tirelessly between her husband Antony and her brother (see chapter 3).[6] But Octavia's activities were not limited to bridging the gap between husband and brother. Even before her marriage to Antony, she gained the reputation of someone who made positive use of her influence with Octavian. She is portrayed as the heroine of a bizarre episode dated to 43 BC. Among those proscribed by the triumvirs was a Titus Vinius. His wife, Tanusia, gave it out that he had been killed, and hid him in a chest at the house of one of their freedmen. This was a courageous gesture, for concealing a proscribed person was itself a capital offence. Tanusia now brought Octavia into the plan. She for her part supposedly engineered matters during a festival so that her brother would enter the theatre without the other two triumvirs. At the right moment, Tanusia dramatically produced the chest, as well as her husband. The ruse worked. Octavian, as his sister had anticipated, was so impressed by Tanusia's courage that he absolved both her and her husband. For good measure he even co-opted their freedman into the equestrian order. This is the first instance on record — even if that record is perhaps not totally reliable in all its details — of an admirable trait that can be observed later in Octavia, a willingness to intervene on behalf of worthy

Romans who found themselves at risk.[7] Even after her estrangement from
Antony and her humiliating return to Rome, Octavia continued to work as a
mediator. When her scurrilous husband's associates came to the city, she gra-
ciously welcomed them into her house and spoke to her brother on their
behalf.[8] In addition, she was prepared to promote the careers of deserving
people who had no link with politics. The architect Vitruvius, for instance,
seems to have owed the continuation of his appointment under Augustus to
Octavia's support, for which he thanks her in the preface to his famous treatise
on architecture.[9]

Syme observed that under Augustus politics was managed "through a persuasive system of patronage and nepotism."[10] The emperor was expected to
intervene on behalf of worthy citizens in need of help, and to assist them by
such devices as access to office. He was also expected to show generosity on a
lavish scale by bestowing his largesse on the Roman people or on the Roman
army at large, and also on an individual basis on people of high or low rank
facing personal crisis. Such blatant subsidies were an accepted part of Roman
tradition. When an upper-class family got into difficulties, contributions were
commonly made by the father's friends: Pliny the Younger made benefactions
of this type. The princeps assumed this responsibility on a broad scale, as, for
example, in the case of Quintus Hortensius, to whom Augustus gave a million
sesterces to help raise his family and prevent his line from facing extinction.[11]
Because they had the ear of the emperor, or simply because of the prestige of
the family name, the emperor's close relatives were in a position to arrange
similar help and support. Octavia's activities on behalf of her own and Antony's
friends presaged a role that would become routine among women of the
imperial family. They would look after not only their own relatives but also
their extended nexus of contacts, from senatorials to foreign rulers.

As the wife of the princeps, Livia would be expected to be a generous
patron, and there are numerous cases of individuals who were helped by her
benefactions. It is to her credit that her amicitia did not limit itself to helping
the upper classes. She extended her magnanimity to all orders. She gave financial help to the victims of fires. She was particularly attentive to the need to
help families that had fallen on hard times. She paid the dowries of daughters
when the relatives could not afford it, and assumed the obligation for the
upbringing of children of respected but impoverished parents. Most of these
individuals are now unknown, like the unnamed individual she tried to have
empanelled as a juryman, or the Gaul for whom she sought Roman citizenship.[12] Broadly speaking, her interventions were seen to be directed to a positive end. According to Dio, she once astutely observed that people could be

won over by good treatment and also by the good treatment they saw bestowed on others. He notes that she lived up to this worthy principle, and through her mediation saved the lives of many senators. Although it would be a mistake to argue a close causal connection, it is to be noted that after her death there was a surge in the number of treason trials. In his final comment in his history (apart from a brief envoi), Velleius states that no one felt Livia's *potentia* except for the alleviation of danger or for the promotion of rank. This is a sentiment echoed also in the *Consolatio*, that she had the power to harm but harmed no one, and no one had reason to fear her power *(nec nocuisse ulli et fortunam habuisse nocendi / nec quemquam nervos extimuisse tuos)*. Livia's altruism was recognised by a grateful Senate when she died, in the honours it tried to extract for her from a no less ungrateful son. Moreover, on at least one occasion her public spirit was proclaimed openly in an official document sent out to the Roman provinces. The *Piso Decree* speaks of her many great acts of generosity *(beneficia)* shown to men of all orders *(cuiusque ordinis homines)*.[13]

It is worthy of note that some of the people who enjoyed Livia's favour, or whose family enjoyed it, later rose to positions of considerable power, including the principate itself.[14] Sextus Afranius Burrus, the celebrated prefect of the praetorian guard who played a key role in the elevation and early reign of Nero, began his career as a procurator in her service.[15] The most prominent beneficiary was the future emperor Galba, who capped a distinguished military career with a brief reign as emperor in AD 68. According to Plutarch, Galba was related to Livia and owed his consulship to this family connection. We are provided with no further information on this connection, and it may well be that Plutarch confused Livia with Galba's stepmother, Livia Ocella, second wife of his father. At any rate, he was certainly highly regarded by Livia, who left him 50 million sesterces in her will, eventually paid out by Caligula. Her special favour seems to have encouraged a tradition that Galba had long been seen as a man earmarked for the principate.[16]

Galba's short-lived tenure of power was followed in January 69 by the even shorter-lived term of Marcus Salvius Otho, the old friend of the emperor Nero, and at one time husband of Nero's second wife, Poppaea. Here again there was a Livian connection, for Otho, grandfather of the emperor, had been raised in the home of Livia and reached the praetorship through her influence. The bond was obviously a close one, and the elder Otho seems to have been a childhood chum of Tiberius. At any rate his son Lucius Otho (father of the emperor) was on such warm terms with Tiberius that people thought Lucius was Tiberius' son.[17]

Not all of Livia's protégés, of course, attained such eminence. Quintus

Haterius, born about 63 BC, was a novus homo married to a daughter of Marcus Agrippa, when he assumed the suffect consulship in 5 BC. As an orator he was popular, but noted for his excessively fluent verbalism, and Augustus at one point expressed the opinion that he needed to be "cooled down" *(sufflaminandus)*.[18] Haterius was inclined to use his fluency to ingratiate himself with the important and powerful. When in AD 22 Tiberius sought the tribunicia potestas for his son Drusus Caesar from the Senate, Haterius' proposal that the Senate's resolution should be set up in the curia, inscribed in letters of gold, provoked mockery and the observation that he was a *senex foedissimae adulationis* (an old man given to disgusting flattery) who would gain nothing but *infamia* for his efforts.[19] He died in AD 26, the prophecy more or less proven true.

Haterius came to prominence early in Tiberius' reign. At the meeting of the Senate following the death of Augustus, the princeps designate displayed considerable hesitation about assuming authority. A number of senators spoke, including Mamercus Scaurus and Haterius. Scaurus ventured to hope that Tiberius' forbearance from using his tribunicia potestas to veto the motion of the consuls (who had sworn allegiance) meant that he would accede to the Senate's wishes. Scaurus' observation was received with nothing more damaging than a stony silence. Haterius, his natural obsequiousness fortified by his remote connection by marriage to the imperial family, asked in full rhetorical flow, *quo usque patieris, Caesar, non adesse caput* [as emended] *rei publicae?* (How long, Caesar, will you allow the state to be without a head?) Tiberius, who was contemptuous of the Senate's general lack of spine, took his irritation out on Haterius and turned his full invective on him. It seems that later he actually felt ashamed of his lack of self-control, if this was the occasion when he apologised to Haterius for speaking in language more blunt *(liberius)* than was proper for someone of his rank. The apology did not reassure the sycophantic senator, who was desperate to make amends and followed Tiberius to the palace to do so. At this point there ensued a scene of considerable chaos and even more embarrassment. Seeing Tiberius walking through the palace, Haterius threw himself down before the emperor and grabbed his knees, with such fervour that Tiberius fell flat on his back. The senator came very close to being despatched by the guards. Tiberius would not give him the time of day, and Haterius now had to turn to Livia for help. She perhaps was more willing than the unfortunate Haterius to see the humour in it all, and was at first inclined to brush the incident aside. But Haterius begged her to help, with increasing urgency. Finally she relented, and spoke to Tiberius on his behalf. This is the first recorded example of Livia's intervention under the new regime, and it is not clear how much should be read into it. We have no prior information on Haterius' relations with Livia, and Tacitus indicates no previous link. His approach to the emperor's mother may have been inspired by her general reputation for being helpful in such cases. The incident probably represents nothing more significant than Livia putting in a word for a silly but essentially harmless man.[20]

Livia continued to advance the careers of her friends in Rome, literally until her death in AD 29. The consul for that year was Gaius Fufius Geminus, possibly the son of the Gaius Fufius attested as suffect consul in 2 BC. According to Tacitus, Fufius the son owed his advancement to Livia's favour. After her death Tiberius criticised Fufius, attacking his *amicitiae muliebres* (friendships with women).[21] Fufius was married to Mutilia Prisca, who had earlier found herself caught up in one of the more sordid episodes of court politics (see chapter 5). On the death of Tiberius' son Drusus Caesar, Sejanus made serious efforts to isolate Agrippina, and part of this campaign involved working on Livia through agents to persuade Tiberius that Agrippina was scheming to replace him with one of her sons. The agent employed for this scheme was Julius Postumus, known to Livia through the adulterous affair he had conducted with her friend Mutilia.[22] We are unfortunately given no further information on this odd connection. Fufius and Mutilia were forced to commit suicide not long after Livia's death (see chapter 11).

Other female friends of Livia's are attested. There is Plancina, the wife of Calpurnius Piso, who supposedly acted against Germanicus and his wife in Syria as Livia's agent. Livia was loyal to her friend in the trial that followed, and secured the successful intercession of Tiberius. The death of Livia stripped Plancina of her protection; she was subjected to fresh charges in 33 and committed suicide (see chapter 11). The list would also include Marcia, the wife of Fabius Maximus. Fabius, a close friend of Augustus', was reputedly involved in Augustus' plan to seek a rapprochement with Agrippa Postumus. Marcia is said to have passed on the information to Livia but was afterwards smitten by conscience, and committed suicide. This Marcia is a rather shadowy figure. A far more distinct personality can be attached to another Marcia, also a friend of Livia's. This second Marcia was the recipient of a *Consolatio* from Seneca, probably at some time in the reign of Caligula (AD 37–41). From Seneca's account we can deduce that she had four children — two sons and two daughters — of whom only the daughters survived, and she was comforted by Seneca over the loss of one of her sons, Metilius. More important from a historical perspective, she was the daughter of the writer Cremutius Cordus. Cremutius composed a history of the civil war to the year 16 BC (and possibly beyond). He did not glorify Augustus, although he does not seem to have gone out of his way to criticise him, and he had good words for the tyrannicides, praising Brutus and calling Cassius the "last of the Romans." At the instigation of Sejanus he was charged, in AD 25, with treason, and committed suicide. His writings were burnt, but copies were preserved by his daughter, who was clearly a woman of some courage. They were republished under Caligula, when the memory of the earlier attempt to suppress them served to raise public interest.[23] Seneca speaks of a close friendship between Marcia and Livia (*quam familiariter coluisti*). Marcia's influence is said to have helped Metilius secure an appointment to a priesthood, and it is probably safe to assume that she worked through Livia.[24] Livia's father had, of course, been an adherent of Brutus and Cassius; he had loyally followed them on their final campaign and died with them. While this might have provided a deep-seated psychological reason for Livia's willingness to support Marcia, whose family cannot have been especially popular, common family experience could hardly have been an overt reason and is unlikely to have been even a subconscious one. If a political motive is to be sought, it is more likely to have been Livia's urgent need to thwart the excessive influence of Sejanus over Tiberius.

Of all the female friends of Livia, none stands out so vividly as Plautia Urgulania. She was a member of a prominent Etruscan family who attained some distinction in the early empire. She was also the grandmother of Urgulanilla, the future wife of the emperor Claudius. Her son Plautius Silvanus, consul in 2 BC, may well have owed his office at least in part to Livia's friendship with his mother. Urgulania attained a certain notoriety two years after Tiberius' succession when she enlisted Livia's aid in taking a stand against the praetor Lucius Piso in AD 16 (see chapter 9).

Those who enjoyed Livia's patronage have not left any extant writings, and we are not given the opportunity to subject their public declarations of gratitude or loyalty to close scrutiny. But we do have a remarkable insight into the whole atmosphere of imperial patronage from the works of the poet Ovid. Admittedly we have no evidence that Ovid ever benefitted from Livia's support, but he clearly sought to do so, and he framed his efforts to win her backing in language that is extraordinarily fulsome. Ovid's early literary career saw him as the sophisticated observer of Rome's sexual mores and Roman institutions, and even the imperial family could be drawn in as targets for his clever and good-natured wit. In AD 8 he was banished to Tomi on the Black Sea in circumstances that are exceptionally murky but hint at political improprieties connected with the imperial family. From the time of his exile, his clever repartee was replaced by an often nauseating sycophancy, as he tried desperately to secure his recall.[25]

In the few references Ovid addresses to Livia before the exile, she appears as the model Roman wife, restoring the Bona Dea shrine or dedicating a temple to Concordia, and generally trying to emulate her husband in all respects, while providing a fine example of matronly virtue.[26] The picture is favourable, but moderate and reasonable. In the postexile period, Livia is assaulted by extravagant expressions of adulation. To communicate this adulation Ovid made extensive use of what we have seen as a time-honoured Roman tradition, employing a female relative as an intermediary, in this case his wife. Ovid's third wife, possibly called Fabia, was a kinswoman of the Fabius Maximus who reputedly accompanied Augustus to Planasia. Fabius' wife, the suicidal Marcia mentioned above, was a friend of both Fabia and Livia, and Ovid implies that the last two were also acquainted. The poet was clearly devoted to his wife. In the *Tristia* he suggests that if Homer had written about her she would have outclassed Penelope, the model wife of Odysseus, who patiently and dutifully awaited her husband's return. These qualities she derives from her own inner character, but also from the example that she is set by Livia, a woman she has regarded highly for many years and whom Ovid describes as a *femina princeps*. Livia is the only woman fit to be the wife of Augustus, and but for her the emperor would have remained unmarried.

In the slightly later *Ex Ponto*, by which time Ovid was feeling increasingly desperate, the tone is more dramatic. Fabia is still a model wife and a rival of Penelope, but Livia does more than just provide an example to her; Livia is now the universal exemplar of chastity for all time, with the beauty of Venus and the character of Juno, alone worthy of Augustus' couch. She is once again the femina princeps, but by now is also the most splendid thing in the universe, from the sun's rising to its setting (apart from Augustus, of course). She has to be approached at just the right time — she has weighty matters to deal with and those rare moments when she is idle allow her to snatch some brief time for herself.[27]

Ovid ascribes to Livia the divine qualities of Venus and Juno. He also associates her closely with Vesta, as the symbol of chastity. Thus in anticipating the triumph that Tiberius was to celebrate in October, AD 12, the poet pictures Livia carrying out sacrifices in the presence of the matrons and the Vestal Virgins, whose purity he emphasises. In the later *Ex Ponto* he expresses the idea in even stronger language, calling Livia the Vesta of chaste matrons (*pudicarum Vesta matrum*).[28] These comparisons are harmless enough, but in other passages Livia's divine association becomes much more powerful. The worship of the imperial family was not officially sanctioned in Rome, but it is clear that on an informal and unofficial level people thought of the emperor in terms that came very close to the divine. The poets seem generally to have been reluctant to express the same feelings about Livia. In Vergil and Horace there are frequent laudatory allusions to Augustus, even to divine attributes that the poets observed in him. But Livia is mentioned only in passing by Horace, in a single innocuous context, and Vergil says nothing of her. By contrast Ovid throws restraint to the winds, and his special circumstances and desperate need for her intercession must surely lie behind the difference.

Ovid tells his wife that she must have the gods on her side, and to that end must light a fire on the altar, and offer incense and wine. Above all she must worship the *numen* (divine power) of Augustus and his pious son, and of the woman who shares his couch, Livia. The numen signifies the power residing in any person or thing, but tends to be associated with the power of a god, and by a natural process in Ovid's time it had become virtually synonymous with "god." To worship the numen of Livia is, strictly speaking, to worship the divine properties within her without technically acknowledging that she is divine, although one wonders how conscious the Romans were of the proper distinction. Elsewhere Ovid seems to drop even this reserve, and in another poem in the *ex Ponto* Livia is called worthy *(digna)* of Caesar, and offerings are made to them as true gods *(dis veris)*. This fulsome language, with its divine overtones, is not reserved exclusively for letters to his wife. In a poem to his bon vivant friend Cotta Maximus, Ovid speaks of receiving silver images of Augustus, Tiberius, and Livia and observes that their presence in the metal gives it numen. These statuettes are his most precious possessions, and he would suffer any torment rather than be deprived of them. In his eyes the three images are *praesentes deos*, to whom he offers prayers. In another piece, to the soldier-litterateur Pomponius Graecinus, he describes how he has set the effigies in a shrine, adding to them images of Tiberius' two sons, Drusus and Germanicus.[29]

The tone of these verse-epistles is echoed also in the section of the *Fasti* that Ovid reworked after going into exile. In his commentary on the festival held on January 24 in honour of Concordia, whose temple Tiberius restored and dedicated, Ovid calls Livia the consort of mighty Jupiter, hence drawing another association with Juno. But he introduces another clever touch. By the time that he wrote, or revised, this section of the *Fasti*, Livia had been adopted into the Julian line. Ovid refers to her not as *mater* but as *genetrix*, an epithet particularly associated with Venus, the mother of Aeneas and the mythical ancestress of the Julian line. He makes an even more remarkable statement in his section on the Carmentalia, celebrated on January 11. This festival commemorates the arrival in what later became Rome of the divine prophet Carmentis and her son, the future King Evander. The parallelism is striking. Evander, like Tiberius, was distinguished by his ancestry, especially on his mother's side. Carmentis, according to Ovid, prophesies that Augustus will be succeeded by his son and declares that one day Julia Augusta will be a new divinity, to be worshipped just as Carmentis is worshipped. Ovid proved to be prescient, although the consecration had to wait for more than a quarter-century and the accession of Claudius.[30] For all his efforts, in the end Ovid's petitions failed, and he died in lonely exile. This outcome might well reflect the cynicism of the age. Ovid's limited potential usefulness as an ally to Livia perhaps did not merit the serious effort that would have been needed to have him recalled. Moreover, Livia was not always successful in her appeals either to Tiberius or to Augustus, and she may have felt that his cause was just not winnable. His fulsome efforts may have served merely to alienate Tiberius further. And of course we do not know what transgression led to his exile in the first place. It could be that in Livia's eyes Ovid's earlier sins simply placed him beyond the pale.

The protective range of Livia's patronage extended even beyond the confines of the empire.[31] In the course of her long life she developed a nexus of friendships with rulers on the fringes of the Roman world. She seems to have had especially close ties with two areas, the Bosporus and Judaea. Polemo I was established by Mark Antony as king in Pontus, on the south coast of the Black Sea. This arrangement was confirmed by Augustus, and in about 19 BC the Romans helped Polemo seize the Cimmerian Bosporus in the Crimea area. The inhabitants were restive, but Polemo calmed things to some degree by his marriage in 14 BC to the Bosporan Dynamis, granddaughter of the old king Mithridates. The union had the full backing of Augustus.[32] Something went wrong—the details are not clear—and eventually Dynamis, with the help of Sarmatian warriors, expelled her husband. Despite her estrangement from the pro-Roman Polemo, Dynamis pursued a policy friendly to Rome, as her inscriptions demonstrate. She dedicated statues to Augustus, calling herself *philoromaios* (friend of Rome) and calling him *soter* and *euergetis* (saviour and benefactor). Moreover, she dedicated a statue of Livia in her native town of Phanagoria in 9–8 BC, once again calling herself philoromaios and honouring Livia as her euergetis.[33] The act that inspired the gesture is unknown, but it could be that Livia was helpful in persuading Augustus to recognise Dynamis' then-husband, Polemo, as king.

After his expulsion Polemo married a Pythodoris and continued fighting in the Bosporus. In 8 BC he lost his life there, and Pythodoris succeeded him, to become queen of Pontus. She refounded the cities of Sebaste (Cabeira) and Sebastia (Megalopolis), where she built a royal residence.[34] Pythodoris dedicated a statue of Livia, on this occasion at Hermonassa in the Bosporus, probably in 8–6 BC. In her dedication she uses the same familiar language to express her gratitude, calling her euergetis. We do not know when Pythodoris died. She may very well have outlived Livia; at any rate, one coin shows that she was still queen in AD 28.[35]

The daughter of Polemo and Pythodoris, Antonia Tryphaena, married the king of Thrace, Cotys. The uncle of Cotys, Rhescuporis, had designs on the throne and murdered his nephew at some point shortly before AD 19. Tryphaena took her three sons to Rome, where they stayed with Antonia and became friends of the future emperor Caligula (a friendship from which they later benefitted). Given that Antonia had apartments in Livia's house, it seems inevitable that Tryphaena would have made the acquaintance of Livia, who might well have championed her cause (see chapter 7).[36] Rhescuporis no doubt thought that he was now in an unassailable position, but he was lured to Rome, where Tryphaena, with the help of powerful patrons, possibly including Livia, had him charged with the murder of her husband. He was exiled to Alexandria and later killed "while attempting to escape." The whole of Thrace was temporarily placed under a Roman official, acting as regent for Tryphaena's children. She made her way eventually to the prosperous city of Cyzicus, where she settled down and became a benefactress of the city.[37] She held the position of priestess of Livia and dedicated a statue (agalma) to her patron in the Temple of Athena Polias in Cyzicus, as Nikephoros (bringer of victory). This epithet had earlier been granted to Athena for her help to Cyzicus during the siege of the city in the third Mithridatic war, and suggests that Livia was similarly seen as performing great, if unspecified, service to the city, although that service presumably had been delivered indirectly, through Tryphaena.[38] These dedications are surely more than simply an attempt by foreign rulers to curry favour with Livia. Their sponsors are all women who at one time or another had enlisted the aid of Rome, and almost certainly had benefitted from Livia's active intervention.

Another area where Livia clearly had strong connections was Judaea. Like other women of the imperial household, she formed close ties to the Jewish ruling family. She was a friend of Salome, sister of Herod the Great. This Salome, not to be confused with the infamous enemy of John the Baptist, seems to have perfected the arts of sinister intrigue that Tacitus unfairly ascribed to Livia. A bitter enemy of Herod's wife, Mariamme, Salome exploited her brother's natural suspicions and poisoned his mind against his wife. In the end Herod executed Mariamme, her two sons, her brother, her grandfather, and her mother. Livia and Salome might have met during the imperial visit to Syria in the late twenties BC. The two women became close confidantes, and Salome called on Livia's assistance at a time of great personal stress. Salome fell in love with the Nabataean Arab Syllaeus and needed Herod's permission to marry him. She tried to persuade Livia to intercede on her behalf. Herod had made no secret of his opposition to the match, given Syllaeus' refusal to convert to Judaism, and in fact had told his sister that he would consider her his bitterest enemy unless she gave up the idea. Livia had the good judgement to recognise that there was a danger of a serious rift in the Herodian family and joined others in urging Salome to give in. According to Josephus, it was Livia's advice, with all the prestige inherent in her role as the consort of the princeps, that persuaded Salome to accede to Herod's wishes, and, albeit reluctantly, agree to marry one of his friends, Alexas. Salome died a year or two before Augustus and demonstrated in a concrete way her regard for Livia, making her the heir to much of her estate (see chapter 9).[39]

These close political connections created the inevitable risk that Livia would be drawn inadvertently into political intrigues to which she was not a real party. Acme was a Jewish freedwoman of Livia's, much involved in Jewish issues. She became caught up in the dynastic machinations of Antipater against his father, Herod. Antipater forged a letter purportedly written by Salome to Livia, creating the impression that Salome had made abusive comments about Herod and his conduct in the Syllaeus affair. Antipater bribed Acme to pretend that she had found the letter among Livia's papers, and to send it to Herod. She was not the most astute of conspirators, and committed the elementary mistake of writing to Antipater to confirm to him that she had carried out his instructions, a communication that, unfortunately for both of them, came to light. Acme was put to death by Augustus, shortly before Antipater suffered the same fate at the hands of Herod, only five days before Herod's own death.[40]

In addition to her efforts for individual friends and protégés, Livia could also on occasion act on behalf of whole communities. The most tangible evidence of this practice is found in Aphrodisias on the west coast of Caria, in Asia. This city was to prove a most loyal supporter of Augustus and his descendants. It could boast a lavish *sebasteion* (sanctuary) to Aphrodite and the imperial family; its upper stories contained 180 relief panels flanked by columns. It is possible that the fragmentary remains of one the panels depicts Livia carrying out a sacrifice, perhaps in her capacity as priestess of Augustus.[41] The

Aphrodisians mounted important archives on the wall of their theatre, and so seriously did they seek to maintain their image that they included texts of any communications between the emperor and other cities that contained a favourable reference to Aphrodisias. One such document is in the form of a letter from Augustus to the people of the island of Samos, in response to their petition for free status. In turning down their petition (he eventually allowed it, in 20–19), Augustus explains that he is not disposed to grant freedom without good cause, and notes that he has allowed such a privilege to no community other than Aphrodisias (which explains why they had the text on display). His objection was not to the consequent loss of tribute, in that freedom would grant them exemption from taxes, but rather to the indiscriminate handing out of such entitlements.[42] Augustus clearly feels embarrassed at refusing the request. He notes that he is well disposed to the Samians, but even more remarkably he says that he would like to please his wife, who has been most energetic on their behalf. This reveals two aspects of Livia (Scribonia can be ruled out as the unnamed wife) and her relationship with her husband. It shows that she was prepared to act as the patron for a community and to intercede on its behalf with the emperor. It shows also that the level of collaboration between Augustus and Livia was so well established that he felt obliged to apologise in public when he was unable to accede to her requests. Unfortunately, this valuable evidence for relations between Augustus and his wife cannot be precisely dated (see appendix 17).

There is other evidence that Livia saw herself as a friend and patron of the Samians, in the form of two inscriptions discovered recently on the island. Both came originally from the Heraeum, the sanctuary of Hera, and record the dedication of statues of Livia to the goddess, one before 27 BC, the other after. Although married, she is in both cases called Drusilla. In public inscriptions Livia generally avoided her original cognomen after her marriage, but she may have continued to use it in private, and its use here might express her close personal ties with the Samians, also suggested by other inscriptions from the island honouring her parents.[43] She may well have stayed at Samos as a place of refuge with her first husband, Tiberius Claudius Nero, just as they had stayed at Sparta, which belonged to Tiberius' clientele. Livia, along with other members of the imperial family, also had strong personal links with the island of Lesbos, witnessed in coins and inscriptions. There is epigraphic evidence hinting that when ambassadors came from Mytilene some time shortly after 27 BC, Livia was of some assistance to them in their mission, although it is to be noted that in addition to recording their gratitude to Livia, they thank Octavia, Augustus' sister, as well as his children and his friends.[44]

A wealthy and powerful patron would give service not only by interceding with third parties on behalf of individuals or communities but also by the use of private wealth for communal welfare. There was much evidence of such activity on Livia's part in the physical reminders of her liberality scattered throughout Rome. Not all of these would be grandiose and showy — some, though valuable, were on a miniature scale. Pliny the Elder, who had a keen eye for such things and a good sense of anecdote, provides a history of just such a gift. Polycrates of Samos, we are told, had a passion for gems. This pleasure was offset by his obsession with the idea that he was so wealthy that he might provoke nemesis, so he decided to atone for his prosperity by making a major sacrifice. He put out in a boat and threw a ring with a splendid sardonyx stone into the water. The ring was swallowed by a huge fish *natus regi*, fit for a king, which appropriately ended up due course on the king's plate. Its reappearance seemed a bad omen for Polycrates, implying that Fortune had not been appeased. The gem eventually came into Livia's possession, possibly a gift from the grateful Samians. She decided on a more permanent home for it and donated it to the Temple of Concord, where it was set in a golden horn. Pliny expresses sensible reservations about its legendary provenance and also comments that even though splendid by normal standards, it would be ranked quite low in the context of such a grand collection.[45] In fact, the Temple of Concord seems to have been a kind of museum depository, with numerous dedications from Augustus and others, as well as the statue of Vesta that Tiberius had persuaded the Parians to part with when he stopped at the island on his way to his Rhodian exile.[46] Pliny also records that the largest mass of rock crystal he had ever seen was one dedicated on the Capitol by Livia — it weighed about seventy kilograms.[47]

Livia did not limit herself to gifts of objets d'art. She beautified Rome by involving herself in the construction or restoration of a number of important buildings.[48] Women are often associated with prestigious building projects in the Roman empire. One of the most impressive structures in the Forum of Pompeii, for example, is the one given to a workers' association by Eumachia, who advertises her name and her office on the building inscription, *sacerdos publica*.[49] Rome benefitted from similar largesse. Polla, the sister of Marcus Agrippa, began the construction of the Porticus Vipsaniae near the Aqua Virgo in the Campus Martius. It was completed by Augustus and used to house Agrippa's map of the world.[50] Polla also built a racecourse. Octavia, patron of the architect Vitruvius, was particularly associated with the beautification of the city. The most famous of the landmarks that she built, or that Augustus built in her name, were the Theatre of Marcellus, built to honour her son, and the nearby Porticus Octaviae.[51] Strabo expresses excitement over the new buildings of Augustan Rome, and he gives credit to Livia, among others. Her major contribution to the landscape of Rome, the Porticus Liviae, was strictly speaking not her gift, because Augustus paid for it, but some credit for the construction, and for the design, is clearly owed to Livia, and she certainly paid for the small shrine housed within the portico. The background of the portico is a colourful one. The site had at one time belonged to Vedius Pollio, an outrageously wealthy member of the equestrian class, descended from a freedman. He is not remembered for any noteworthy accomplishments but had somehow managed to become an intimate associate of Augustus. This close friendship was a source of embarrassment for the emperor, who was discomfited both by Vedius' great wealth and by his grim reputation for cruelty. In his home he maintained reservoirs with giant lampreys trained to eat men — he reputedly chose lampreys rather than savage land animals for the thrill of seeing people torn apart in an instant. If a slave was unfortunate enough to fall out of favour, he was at great risk of being tossed into the lamprey tank. On one occasion, according to Dio, while Augustus was dining at Vedius' home, one of the servants dropped and broke a crystal goblet. He was ordered into the tank but had the presence of mind to beg for mercy not from his master but from the emperor. Even Augustus was unable to secure a pardon, so he resorted to cunning. He asked Pollio to bring his valuable goblets, which he proceeded to break — thus putting his host in the position where he could not in fairness punish the slave without pitching the emperor into the tank to join him. Pollio had been taught a lesson, and to bring it home Augustus instructed him to put the tanks out of commission by filling them in.

Deep down, Pollio no doubt realised that he could never enjoy the emperor's true regard while he was alive, and he clearly made up his mind that the best time to secure it would be posthumously. When he died, in 15 BC, he left Augustus much of his estate, both in Rome and elsewhere, notably in Campania. In the city Pollio had an enormous house on the Esquiline Hill. Ovid describes it as so massive that it could have swallowed up the ground area of many a city. Augustus ordered that the house be razed, in part to atone for his earlier connections with Pollio and also to show his disapproval of private extravagance. There would have been the added bonus, mentioned by Dio, of guaranteeing that Pollio would leave no monument in Rome. Dio seems to imply that the razing of the structure took place almost immediately after the owner's death, although this does not necessarily tell us when work was begun on the portico that replaced it. At any rate, the new monument was not dedicated until 7 BC. Clearly embarrassed by the political support of a man whose abiding image was so negative, Augustus named it in honour not of Pollio but of Livia.[52]

The portico is an example of Augustus' general policy of creating public spaces in Rome, and it gave him an excellent opportunity to associate his wife Livia with a demonstration of his concern for the communal welfare. Two *cippi* (stone markers) in the area of S. Martino ai Monti, in the general area of Vedius' house, referring to the transfer of private to public land by Augustus, have been connected by Grimal to the conversion of Vedius' estate. Other than that possible link, no physical trace of the portico has survived. It is represented, however, on four adjoining fragments of the Severan Marble Plan, where its name, Porticus Liviae, is preserved, and if we assume that it was symmetrical, the overall design can be recovered (plan 3). Although it seems that Augustus financed the project, Livia may well have had a hand in its design. It was rectangular in shape, about 120 × 90 m, enclosing a garden, as we might expect in a building linked with Livia. It thus fits into the general category of portico and garden, a common feature of the later republic and early empire, both in Rome and in smaller towns. It was fronted internally by a double colonnade, behind which were open niches, themselves fronted by columns. The larger of these niches were rectangular, the smaller a mix of rectangular and semicircular. Pliny the Elder uses as his authority Valerianus Cornelius, who was particularly impressed by the way a single vine stock planted in the portico had spread to cover all the walkways and produced a dozen amphorae of wine, very much in keeping with Livia's close personal interest in horticulture. Ovid also reveals that the portico housed an art gallery, and Strabo describes the building (it is not clear whether he meant the gallery or the whole complex) as one of the great spectacles of Rome. The surrounding area seems to have been cleared of buildings. The very luxury of the project would in itself have had great propaganda value, for it would have drawn attention to the contrast between the private extravagance of Pollio and the fine building for the public sponsored on behalf of Livia. A century or so later Pliny the Younger was still meeting his smart friends there.[53]

More was to come. Ovid in his *Fasti* records that on June 11 of an unspecified year Livia dedicated a *magnifica aedes* to Concordia, to honour her husband. He follows this entry with an immediate reference to the Porticus Liviae, suggesting that the two structures are very closely related, but implying also that their dedication dates were different. Augustus, according to Dio and Suetonius, had taken responsibility for the financing of the portico, but Ovid makes it clear in this passage that it was Livia alone who dedicated and paid (*praestitit*) for the aedes. The term *aedes* is a fairly neutral one, and could refer to anything

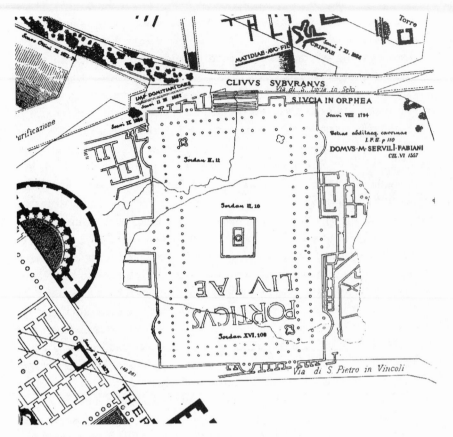

Plan 3. The Porticus Livia. After Lanciani (1893–1901)

from a small shrine to a larger temple. In the space within the portico on the Marble Plan there is a large square structure, with small features at its corners. It may well be Livia's building. Platner and Ashby objected that it was not suited to Ovid's description of *magnifica*. Coarelli, however, has noted the resemblance between the plan of this central structure and of the Ara Pacis. If its decoration also matched that of the earlier building, then Ovid's *magnifica* would be justified.[54]

Livia is associated with other buildings in Rome. A market, *macellum Liviae*, named after her, was restored by Valentinian, Valens, and Gratian (AD 364–78) and is recorded in the regionary catalogues under the sightly different name of *macellum Liviani*. Unfortunately, nothing more is known about the complex, although there have been many attempts to identify it in excavations.[55] There has also been speculation that Livia might somehow have been involved in the restoration of a shrine of Pudicitia Plebeia (Plebeian Chastity). The building was by tradition associated with a Verginia, who abandoned her patrician background to marry a plebeian, Lucius Volumnius, consul in 296 BC. Banned from the shrine of Patrician Chastity because of the marriage, she established a shrine in her husband's house on the Vicus Longus. Propertius in a poem written by 28 BC refers to temples to pudicitia, and Palmer takes this to mean that Augustus restored the two shrines, and links the restoration to Suetonius' use of the expression *de pudicitia* to describe Augustus' moral legislation. A man could not be involved in the cult of chastity, and accordingly a woman would have had to be called on to sponsor the restoration. Palmer bases Livia's supposed involvement on evidence that in the early fifth century there existed what was called a Basilica Libiana in the Vicus Longus, which he suggests was connected with the general provision of amenities and linked with Livia's restoration of the shrine of Pudicitia Plebeia there. But there are problems with the general theory, and also with Livia's supposed role. The most serious difficulty is the suggestion that Augustus' social legislation should be placed before 28 BC, the date of Propertius' poem, and thus even before the settlement. Also, Livia was patrician, and although Augustus was plebeian by birth, he had been enrolled as a patrician by the time of his marriage to Livia.[56]

Another contribution of Livia to the landscape of Rome was her restoration of the Temple of Bona Dea Subsaxana. The evidence for this work is found in the *Fasti* of Ovid, in his account of the celebration of Bona Dea held on May 1. Ovid locates the shrine of the goddess below the Saxum or Remoria (on the northeast Aventine), where Remus supposedly stood when he carried out the auguries for the founding of the city. He reveals that it was restored by Livia (it was later repaired yet again by Hadrian).[57] The cult was exclusive to females, and there were various explanations of its origins. The third-century AD authority Labeo cites the books of the pontiffs for evidence that Bona Dea was identical with Terra (Earth). Others link her with Faunus (either the Roman form of Pan or an early king of the Latins), as his wife or as his daughter. They claim variously that he committed incest with her (in the form of his daughter) or beat her to death (as his wife). Yet others associate her with Juno, Proserpina, or Hecate.[58] No doubt the secret nature of the rites account to a large degree for the great confusion about exactly who and what was being worshipped.

Ovid states that the Temple of Bona Dea was originally dedicated by a chaste Vestal of a distinguished family. In describing the rites, he calls their founder an inheritor of a famous name *(veteris nominis heres)*. Unfortunately, the manuscripts differ about the spelling of the name, either Clausorum or

Crassorum. If the former reading is accepted, the allusion to the Clausi would provide a pointed connection with Livia, for Clausus, according to legend, was the founder of the Claudians and was supposed to have helped Aeneas in establishing himself in Italy.[59] Thus Livia would be seen as restoring a temple that had been founded by an unknown ancestor (see appendix 18). It had fallen into disuse by the late republic, and, perhaps because of its disrepair, the December rites were carried out by the Vestals not in the temple but in the house of a magistrate with imperium. By restoring this building, as Ovid expresses it, Livia could imitate Augustus and follow him in every respect (*imitata maritum . . . et ex omni parte secuta*). Thus Livia would have had a number of motives. At the simplest level she could show her generosity by repairing a public monument. She was able also to associate herself with something that in certain aspects symbolised chastity, through linking herself with the Vestal Virgins. Finally, she could be seen as a willing partner of her husband in helping to restore traditional Roman religious practices. Certainly Augustus was particularly proud of the large number of temples that he had refurbished, and no doubt delighted to see his wife involved in the same activity.[60]

Livia's gesture would have carried another powerful political message. The celebration of the Bona Dea ceremony had by her day become linked in the public mind with a notorious scandal involving another Claudian. A short time before Livia's birth, the disreputable demagogue Publius Clodius Pulcher, dressed in women's clothing, had made his way into the house of Julius Caesar, the pontifex maximus. Here the Vestal Virgins were performing December sacrifices to the goddess. Clodius' motives were not spiritual — he was lusting after Pompeia, Caesar's wife. Indeed, as a result of the scandal, Caesar had to divorce her, with a pronouncement later destined to become famous, that Caesar's wife had to be above suspicion.[61]

After he became pontifex maximus, Augustus' duties would have included the supervision of the Vestals, whose allowances and privileges he increased. The earlier scandal had taken place in the house of his adoptive father, Julius Caesar, in the official home of the pontifex on the Sacra Via. After assuming his priestly office, Augustus pointedly showed no interest in installing himself in that residence. He wanted to avoid any slur on his authority threatened by his own past association with Clodius — he had at one time been betrothed to Clodius' daughter Claudia. Thus Augustus would have been anxious to re-habilitate the good name of the cult. It is worth noting that the date of the celebration of Livia's restoration of the temple as provided by Ovid, May 1, would be appropriately removed from the month of December, indelibly associated with scandal. Thus Livia could in a sense atone for the behaviour of her kinsman Clodius.[62] Her association with the Bona Dea persisted into the next reign. An important inscription from Forum Clodii in Etruria, dated to AD 18, describes the honours to be paid to Augustus, Tiberius, and Livia on their birthdays. In Livia's case, wine and cakes were to be offered to the women who lived in the community near the shrine of the Bona Dea.[63]

Remains discovered at the fourth milestone on the Via Latina have been identified as those of a temple of Fortuna Muliebris. An inscription records its restoration by *Livia Drusi f(ilia) uxs[or Caesaris Augusti]* — Livia, daughter of Drusus and wife of Caesar Augustus — as well as a later restoration by Severus and Caracalla. This cult had been established early in the fifth century BC and was connected to the legend surrounding Coriolanus. He had been banished from the city for his supposedly tyrannical behaviour and placed himself at the service of the hostile Volscians, leading an army which threatened Rome. He was dissuaded only through the entreaties of his wife, Volumnia, and mother, Veturia, who had set out from Rome with a delegation of women. The temple to Fortuna Muliebris was established by the Senate to honour this event and the women who had taken part in it, supposedly at the very spot where Coriolanus had turned back. Dionysius of Halicarnassus, a contemporary of Livia's, indicates that the story of Coriolanus and the origin of the cult were very familiar to Romans in his (and Livia's) day. She could thus associate herself with women who had served the state, and who had served it by acting within the family, either as wives or as mothers, roles which Livia combined. It is striking that in the inscription she identifies herself by her father as well as by her husband, perhaps showing that her contribution was to be seen as an independent act, carried out in her own right.[64]

Her generosity is attested outside Rome and continued to the end of her life, and we see evidence for this in the aqueducts that she built with Tiberius in southern Etruria in Vicani Matrini.[65] Beyond the borders of Italy most of the information about her liberality relates to Herod and Judaea. Gifts were given to the Temple at Jerusalem. Herod travelled to Rome in about 16 BC to bring back his sons, who had been sent there to study. It is possible that after this visit he took home with him a donation that Livia, and probably Augustus, made to the rebuilt Temple in the form of gold vessels, destined to be melted down during the later Jewish War.[66] Another beneficiary was Caesarea. This city was one of Herod's greatest achievements, built to replace the old Phoenician settlement of Strato's Tower and to provide a major new port. It was an outstanding engineering feat, one which took some ten years to complete. On its inauguration (in either 12 or 10–9 BC), a festival was celebrated in Augustus' honour, with musical and athletic contests, along with beast and gladiatorial shows. Delegates from outside Herod's kingdom came. Augustus helped to defray expenses, and Josephus notes that Livia sent some of her best treasures from Rome, and that the total contribution was five hundred talents.[67]

Patronage and amicitia were at their heart reciprocal concepts, and Livia's generosity and support would be expected to bring her something in return. This return could take the form of simple material benefits—the extensive estates that she inherited from Salome, for instance (see chapter 9). She could also be honoured by statues or monuments, confirmed by the numerous dedicatory inscriptions that have survived. Often, however, the rewards could be less tangible, though no less important for that. These more abstract benefits, which continued after her death, would have constituted a recognition of Livia's importance and standing, a powerful element in the Roman consciousness.

We get glimpses from time to time in the fragmentary evidence of the expressions of respect for Livia that must have been frequent and familiar. In AD 13, for instance, Augustus received a deputation of envoys from Alexandria in the Roman library of the Temple of Apollo on the Palatine. We do not know the substance of the embassy's business—the papyrus that records the event is too fragmentary—but enough text has survived to show that one of the leaders of the deputation, Alexander, expressed the high regard in which the Alexandrians held Livia. The attestation may, of course, be largely formulaic, but even so, the very repetition of a formula represents a form of esteem and respect.[68]

Other communities celebrated festivals that honoured Livia. She was the patron of poetry competitions held in various parts of the Greek world. Such competitions are recorded in Corinth, where Gaius Cassius Flaccus Syracusius recited a poem dedicated to Livia at the Caesarea. More than a century after her death we hear of a triennial contest held in her honour in Egypt, also quite possibly artistic rather than athletic (see chapter 11). Nowhere were such contests more actively pursued than in Boeotia, the traditional home of the muses, and accordingly claiming a long association with music and poetry. In Chalcis in Boeotia, a festival, again almost certainly artistic, was held in Livia's honour, the Leibidea. But no Boeotian city prided itself more on its artistic heritage than Thespiae, famous for its nearby shrine of the muses. Mouseia — poetry festivals — were celebrated there, and inscriptions from the town mention Livia, one of them addressing her as the Muses' mother, Mnemosyne.[69] A possible competition piece has been preserved in the epigraphic record at Thespiae in the form of a poem by Honestus of Corinth. During the reign of

Tiberius this poet sought, perhaps successfully, the patronage of the imperial family. His poems are found inscribed on the statue bases of the Museion. One of them refers to an Augusta (Sebaste) who can boast of two Caesars, possibly Augustus and Tiberius, who are sceptred gods and twin lamps of peace. She is the proper company for the muses, and her wisdom saved the world.[70]

Not all cities, of course, could claim the artistic associations of Boeotia, but they could honour Livia in a number of other ways. One of these was by adopting her name. Among her links with the Herodian family, she may have been a friend of Herod the Great's son, Herod Antipas, who on the death of his father in about 4 BC was appointed tetrarch of Galilee and Peraea. Antipas was a close friend of Tiberius, who used him as an honest broker to mediate between the Romans and Parthians. Under Caligula he fell foul of the intrigues of his nephew, the emperor's favourite, Herod Agrippa. Among the strongholds of Antipas severely damaged during a rebellion in 4 BC were Sepphoris, the capital of Galilee, and Betharamphtha in Peraea. Antipas renamed the former Autocratoris (city of the emperor) in honour of Augustus (the change did not last long). Betheramphtha, on the east bank of the Jordan, was rebuilt as a major stronghold against the Nabataeans and was renamed in honour of Livia. The new name is given as Julias by Josephus, Livias by other sources. This suggests that the rebuilding might have taken place early in Antipas' reign and that he assigned the name of Livias from the start, but it was changed to Julias after the accession of Tiberius and the adoption of Livia into the Julian house. The original name might have taken too firm a hold to be replaced, and for that reason have continued in use. One of the administrative regions on the east side of the Jordan valley was still called Livias into the sixth century.[71]

The city of Augusta in Cilicia Pedias, mentioned by Pliny, was founded in AD 20, as indicated on its coins. Its name clearly derives from Livia's. The coins, carrying the legend *Augustanon*, bear the head of Livia until the Trajanic period. Its location is not known for certain, but it has been identified with Gübe, north of Adana.[72] Almost certainly one of the Bosporan rulers who had benefitted from Livia's friendship founded, or renamed, in honour of Livia the fortress city of Liviopolis on the southern shore of the Black Sea between Pharnaceia and Trapezusia.[73]

The most common expression of regard and respect for Livia comes in the form of divine honours, and she found fervent and enthusiastic worshippers throughout the empire. The tradition in the East of honouring Roman officials by revering them as gods had already become well established during the republic and was a continuation of the practice of venerating the Hellenistic rulers who had preceded them. Thus men like Titus Flamininus, Sulla, and Pompey had been treated as divine or quasi-divine figures, paving the way, as it were, for the widespread cult of the emperors.[74] As attention was increasingly focussed on the domus Augusta it was inevitable that similar honours would be accorded the women of the imperial family. Not only Livia but Octavia, Augustus' sister; Julia, his daughter; and Antonia, Livia's daughter-in-law, were much honoured, as indeed were the later imperial women, throughout both the eastern and, very quickly, the western provinces.[75] In Livia's case this process began during Augustus' lifetime and continued well after her death. Unfortunately, it is not always possible to date the evidence, especially in the East, where divine standing preceded Livia's official consecration in Rome. But it is clear that the process began early. Divine status is made explicit on a coin from Thessalonica dated 21–19 BC, and in the twenties BC Livia joined Julia as objects of a cult in Athens.[76] From at least that time on, the phenomenon manifested itself through the Roman world, and Livia is explicitly recognised as a goddess at numerous sites, both before and after her death. In the festivals at Corinth, for instance, the poems of Flaccus Syracusius are recited *eis thean Ioulian Sebasten* — to the goddess Julia Augusta. At Eresos on Lesbos, where she was worshipped as Livia Providentia (Pronoia), she had her own temple and a sanctuary.[77]

While attestations to Livia's divinity are more numerous in the East, probably the most visibly striking manifestations of the phenomenon are actually from the West, in the form of the huge statues familiar from Leptis Magna in Africa. One of the most arresting is a colossal (68 cm) head of Livia associated with the Temple of Augustus and Roma, in the Forum Vetus of Leptis (fig. 16).[78] Inscriptions in the temple and on two statue bases show that Livia appeared in a family group, set up at the same time, to judge from the inscriptions, which included Germanicus and Drusus, son of Tiberius, in chariots, along with their wives and mothers. Towering over the others were enormous heads of Augustus, Dea Roma, Tiberius, and Livia. The large statues were acrolithic — that is, the head, hands, and feet were made of marble attached to a frame of wood or metal covered with fabric. It is noteworthy that Livia in this grandiloquent form was distinguished from the other imperial women, and her likeness was grouped with the emperors and the personified Roma.

Another colossal statue from Leptis was found in fragments in the theatre. Now reconstructed, the figure is buxom and heavy, and stands just over three metres high. In the same theatre an inscription was found which, given its findspot, may be associated with this statue. It tells us that the proconsul Gaius

Rubellius Blandus (in office AD 35–36) dedicated the shrine to Ceres Augusta and was joined in making the dedication by a local woman, Suphunibal, perhaps a priestess of the cult or a wealthy patron, for she is described in the inscription as *ornatrix pa[triae]* (adorner of her country). It is possible, of course, that the statue is later than the dedication of the shrine.[79]

As Livia received divine honours, it was inevitable that she would come to be identified with existing deities. In her catalogue of cult names of Livia in the eastern provinces, Hahn records an identification with ten goddesses on coins and inscriptions.[80] Her associations with Vesta / Hestia are noted elsewhere, but two of the other more important identifications might usefully be noted here. First, Juno / Hera. Even in Rome, Livia is associated with this goddess by, for example, Ovid and Valerius Maximus, an inevitable comparison to balance Augustus' association with Jupiter. The connection is found throughout the empire. On coins of Tarsus, Eumenea, Pergamum, and Thessaly she is identified with Hera.[81] At Mylai (Thessaly), Aphrodisias, and Mytilene inscriptions assimilate her to that goddess, while at Assos she is called the "new Hera."[82] A similar assimilation seems to take place in the West, but the allusions in the western Latin inscriptions are ambiguous. At Falerii a dedication is recorded to the *genius* of Augustus and *Iunoni Liviae*, which in this case almost certainly conveys the notion of "to the Juno of Livia" rather than "to Livia Juno." From immediately after the battle of Actium, tributes were paid to Augustus' genius, the spirit with its own divine qualities that every Roman possessed, a useful device to avoid explicitly according divine honours to Augustus himself. The "Juno" of a woman, given the association of this goddess with childbirth, could be seen as the equivalent attendant spirit. Exactly the same grammatically ambiguous phrase, *Iunoni Liviae*, is found in inscriptions in Aeclanum, Zara in Dalmatia, and El Lehs in Africa.[83]

In Egypt, and perhaps elsewhere, Livia actively assumed the function of *Juno pronuba*, and her name is mentioned in marriage contracts as a goddess of marriage well into the mid-second century. These surviving contracts state that the document was concluded *epi Ioulias Sebastes* (in the presence of Julia Augusta), very likely before her statue (see chapter 11).[84]

Livia's most striking assimilation is with Ceres / Demeter, goddess of fruitfulness and abundance. In fact, the first known evidence for any Livian statue is from a group in the sanctuary of Demeter and Kore (Persephone) at Eleusis, recorded in an inscription dated perhaps to 31 BC (see appendix 1).[85] Livia's full identification as Ceres comes later, probably in the Tiberian period, although already under Augustus we get a close association between her and the abstraction Abundantia. Hence on Alexandrian coins of AD 10–11, Euthenia (the Greek equivalent of Abundantia) appears on the reverses of coins with Livia's portrait on the obverses.[86]

With the accession of Tiberius there is plentiful evidence for an assimilation of Livia and Ceres. Winkes has suggested that this identification was a spontaneous one in the provinces, perhaps meant as an alternative to the official designation of *mater patriae* that Tiberius refused to grant her (see chapter 8). Whatever the inspiration, this link with Ceres created an enduring association, one that would carry through and persist among later imperial women. Livia is often named in the epigraphic record as Ceres Augusta (or its Greek equivalent) in Asia and in Africa, and even in Malta, suggesting a large number of statues, now lost, in which she was given the goddess' attributes.[87] Of the surviving representations, one of the most striking is preserved on a cameo in Florence, almost certainly cut during her lifetime, depicting the jugate heads of Livia and her son (fig. 11). Tiberius wears a laurel crown, his mother, who bears a physical resemblance to him, a garland of poppies and ears of corn, held in place by a crescent diadem.[88]

Even in Rome the link between Livia and Ceres was recognised. A dupondius of Claudius depicts a draped seated female figure wearing a wreath of wheat and holding ears of wheat and a long torch (fig. 6). The figure is clearly meant to suggest Ceres, but the legend is that of the Deified Augusta, DIVA AUGUSTA. Moreover, the coin type suggests that the identification was an old one in Rome, for it is reminiscent of types of precious metal coins of Augustus that portray a similar seated female figure, holding a sceptre and a branch.[89]

When assimilated to Ceres, Livia often took on other attributes. In the fragmentary statue found in the theatre at Leptis Magna, she adopts various roles. She wears the poppy and wheat ears of Ceres, and also the turret crown of Cybele (this combination of the two is common). The turret crown can also be seen as an attribute of Tyche / Fortuna. Similarly, the striking representation of Livia on the Vienna sardonyx (fig. 19), where she gazes at the deified Augustus, reminds us of Cybele, with her turret crown and lion shield. But she holds wheat and poppies, symbols of Ceres. On the statue in the Louvre commemorating her priesthood, Livia's head bears a floral wreath and, if the restoration is correct, she carries a cornucopia and a bunch of wheat and fruit, all symbols of Ceres (fig. 22).

Such veneration, of course, tells us much about the social and religious life of the Roman empire, and the cult of Livia as an individual. But it should not be seen as having great political significance in Rome, where she did not receive divine recognition until after her death. There are only two recorded instances, in fact, of direct involvement of Rome in the issue of divine honours for Livia, although the incidents do not relate to honours in the city itself. Both occur during the reign of Tiberius.

Deeply opposed to the notion of veneration directed towards his own person, Tiberius after his accession declared that he would allow no sacred precinct to be set aside for him, or priests to be appointed, and no statue to be erected, unless the sponsors had obtained his permission. He added as an afterthought, "I won't grant it!" *(ouk epitrepso).*[90] But for all his opposition to personal divine honours, he recognised the need to acknowledge the long-standing traditions outside Rome, as illustrated by the fascinating letter that he wrote to Gytheum, the port of Sparta, at a date now difficult to determine, but possibly in the spring or early summer of AD 15, less then a year after coming to power. His letter was in response to one sent by the town to Tiberius and his mother, laying out the honours that it was proposing in a forthcoming festival for Divus Augustus and his family, which included the commissioning of a set of statues (or painted images). In his carefully worded reply Tiberius approved the divine honours for Augustus, justifying them by his predecessor's contribution to the world, but he stated that he, Tiberius, would be satisfied with more modest tributes, on a human scale. Significantly, he added that he would leave it to his mother to send her own reply when she had received the communication. (Livia seems to have received a separate letter and was expected to make a separate response.) Tiberius' ambiguous language has been seen as a reflection of his supposed hypocrisy, and Rostovtsev has argued that he worded his refusal so vaguely that he left it open to the Gytheans essentially to ignore what he purported to be instructing. But his tone more likely reflects an effort to be particularly diplomatic, given that Sparta had long been part of the Claudian clientele and had offered hospitality to his mother and himself as an infant during their time of exile.

The festivities to which the Gytheans had alluded were laid out in a "sacred law" *(hieros nomos)* inscribed on a stone column in the town, with a copy held in the record office. Much of this inscription has survived. It enumerates the honours intended for Tiberius, which had presumably been toned down on receipt of his reply. That the townspeople did to some degree accede to his wishes is generally assumed, for it is unlikely that they would simply have ignored the imperial will, although there are in fact instances when communities went their own way in the teeth of imperial objections. Price notes that Thasos, whose divine honours Claudius had refused, had a priest of that same emperor. Clearly, local enthusiasm could make it difficult for some groups to accept a simple refusal. At any rate, as it stands, the festival could not have caused Tiberius serious offence. None of the living members of the imperial family in the document as recorded receives divine honours, and the sacrifices are made on their behalf, not to them. It is also possible that Tiberius' nomenclature had been much grander in the version originally sent for his approval.

Much of the "sacred law" is taken up with an account of the penalties to be suffered by the officials for financial incompetence or embezzlement, but it also provides a detailed account of the festival itself. The celebrations were to last for eight days. The initial five would be dedicated to members of the imperial house, the first to Divus Augustus, son of a god; the second to Tiberius Augustus, imperator and pater patriae (the relatively restrained language is to be noted); the third to Livia, the Tyche (Fortune) of the province and the city (representations of her in the turret crown of Tyche have been noted); the fourth to Aphrodite / Drusus; the fifth to Nike / Germanicus. The sixth was devoted to the legendary Titus Quinctius Flamininus, consul of 198 BC, revered by the Greeks as their liberator from Macedonian domination. Two further days honoured worthy locals. During the festival painted images (*graptas eikonas*) of Augustus, Livia, and Tiberius were placed in the theatre, where a burner was also set up so that officials could offer incense before the start of the performances. The procession was to make its way from the temple of Asclepius and Hygeia to the imperial temple, where a bull would be sacrificed for the well-being of the imperial family, both living and deified. Another sacrifice was to be carried out in the town square, and from there the procession would go to the theatre, where offerings of incense would be made before the imperial statues. The use of incense, as opposed to animals, might reflect the modesty advocated by Tiberius (as well as the frugality that loomed large in the town's deliberations). Moreover, the incense was to be burnt for the well-being of the imperial family, which fell far short of direct worship. The fact that Livia is honoured as Tyche suggests that her answer was different from Tiberius' and that she did not feel the need for a show of restraint and modesty, especially in a community where she was so highly revered.[91] It also suggests that Tiberius was not committed to blocking honours for Livia if they did not set awkward precedents for Rome or other parts of the empire.

Tiberius seems to have been equally flexible in other instances, as in his response to the request of the cities of Asia to establish his cult in the province. In 29 BC a temple to Rome and Augustus had been constructed in Pergamum. Some fifty years later a request for a second cult centre was to follow. In AD 22, two corrupt officials of Asia had been brought to justice. Gaius Silanus, governor of the province, had been convicted of extortion, and in the following year Lucilius Capito, procurator of the imperial estates in Asia, sustained a similar conviction. In gratitude for the way Tiberius had handled these cases, the cities of the province decreed a temple to him, his mother, Livia, and the Senate. Tiberius felt obliged to relax his embargo on such major initiatives and granted the request, recognising that the authorisation previously given by Augustus constituted a precedent of sorts. The matter did not stop there, however, for the cities fell into an unseemly dispute about which would have the honour of providing a home for the new temple. The wrangling went on for three years, at the end of which they agreed to submit the issue to the Senate, sending representatives to Rome to plead their cases. The sessions were contentious and the arguments ingenious, and Tiberius, who had a taste for pedantic disputations, made a point of attending. The Pergamenes shot themselves in the foot by parading the fact that they already possessed the Temple to Rome and Augustus. (They were told essentially not to be greedy.) Sardis produced a convoluted historical claim (which was taken quite seriously) that it had an ancient link with Etruria. Halicarnassus took a practical line: it could offer solid rock foundations and an earthquake-free environment. In the end, Smyrna won the day, with its claim of loyal service to Rome over two centuries. A special commissioner was appointed by the Senate to supervise the construction. Coins of Smyrna minted under Tiberius depict the three parties to the cult in a single issue. One side illustrates a simplified temple with four columns, enclosing Tiberius as pontifex. The other side carries a draped bust of a personified Senate (legend: *synkletos*) facing Livia (legend: *sebaste*).

Thus the only officially sanctioned temple to Livia during her lifetime was built in this wealthy and beautiful city, which was to boast the coveted title of *neocoros* (literally "temple warden"), bestowed on those cities that were homes to an imperial temple. The monument might well have remained a permanent reminder of the high regard in which the Roman world held Livia, and the gratitude felt for her services. Unfortunately, in the end Halicarnassus would have proved a better location. Symrna was virtually destroyed by earthquakes in the second century.[92]

It is difficult not to be cynical when analysing the expressions of public regard for officials who are in a position to bestow largesse and favours on a grand scale. Yet even though self-interest and ambition are bound to affect the record, it must surely be seen as remarkable that in the nearly seventy years during which Livia occupied a place close to the centre of power in Rome, there is hardly a hint of criticism that would seriously detract from her reputation for generosity and service. Velleius may well have been sycophantic and self-serving, but he seems to have come very close to the truth when he asserted that when people were affected by Livia's influence, they always came off for the better.[93]

II

DEATH AND REPUTATION

Laxatives and red wine had provided Livia with a healthy life, but they could not, of course, guarantee immortality. She had been seriously ill in AD 22. In 29, probably early in the year, she fell ill again, and finally passed away, at the age of eighty-six.[1] Tiberius did not attend his mother in her final illness, but because we have no idea how long it lasted, or whether its true seriousness had been appreciated, it would be dangerous to join Suetonius in ascribing unfilial motives.[2] That said, Tiberius' conduct certainly seems to conflict with his behaviour on previous similar occasions. During the illnesses of Augustus and of Drusus, his brother, he went to desperate efforts to be with them, and in AD 22 he hurried back to Rome to be at his mother's sickbed. Velleius proudly records that when on campaign, no soldier was too low in rank for Tiberius to take a personal responsibility for his well-being. We might expect some exaggeration from Velleius, but Suetonius does give some support to this rosy image in reporting an excellent example of Tiberius' high-minded sense of duty. Visiting a city on Rhodes, the emperor expressed a desire to visit all the sick people. This led to an embarrassing scene when overzealous attendants brought all the infirm they could find in the area to a public arcade and organised them according to their complaints. Tiberius was taken aback but went through with it, dutifully speaking to each individual in turn. Dio also comments on how punctilious he was in visiting friends when they were sick.[3]

Circumstances may have prevented Tiberius from getting to his mother's side in time to see her alive. But they could hardly have prevented him from going to her funeral. Indeed, the ceremony was actually postponed for a few days because, according to Suetonius, the emperor held out the prospect of coming over to attend. It was not to be, and nature in the end dictated the timetable. The body started to decompose, and the funeral had to go ahead, Tiberius or no Tiberius.[4] Tacitus implies that he was unwilling to give up the comforts of Capri to take the trouble to see his mother off, and that he simply wrote to say that the pressure of state affairs prevented his attendance. This might seem hypocritical, but it is at any rate quite in keeping with Tiberius' (and Livia's) aloofness during the funeral of Germanicus. Velleius is as loyal as ever. He skips over Livia's illness and funeral, simply observing that the loss of his mother added to Tiberius' other tribulations: *aegritudinem auxit amissa mater*. Tiberius did arrange in absentia for public rites, with the traditional procession of attendants wearing ancestral death masks. Dio, without specifying them, adds that he also ordered some other minor honours. Otherwise the funeral was extremely simple. Tiberius had always sought to model himself on Augustus, but in this case the contrast between the rites of Livia and of Octavia, Augustus' sister, in 11 BC, are painfully evident. Although Augustus did block some of the honours voted Octavia, he gave the funeral oration himself, with a second one delivered by Livia's son Drusus from the rostra in the forum. Moreover, Octavia's body lay in state in the Temple of Divus Julius and was carried in procession by her sons-in-law, Drusus and Lucius Domitius Ahenobarbus.[5] Hatzl has argued that the simple arrangements for Livia reflect Tiberius' own *modestia*. This may well be the case — he certainly did not approve of public demonstrations of emotion. But Hatzl claims further that the modest scale matched the wishes of Livia herself, and according to Suetonius the arrangements were made by Livia as she lay dying. This idea is more difficult to sustain — it is the same excuse that Tiberius used later to justify not granting her deification. Livia had never been averse to honours, and it is hard to believe that a funeral on the cheap would have been in her plans.[6]

Roman tradition called for the funeral address to be given by a young man of the family. In Livia's case the oration was given by her great-grandson Caligula, who had considerable oratorical skills. (As a child, he had delivered a speech to the people of Assos in Asia Minor.)[7] She was then laid to rest in the Mausoleum of Augustus (fig. 29).[8] The mausoleum was the first building begun by Augustus in the Campus Martius. It is dated by Suetonius to 28 BC (Augustus' sixth consulship) but had clearly not been completed by then, for Dio indicates that it was still in the process of construction in 23 BC when the remains of Marcellus were placed there. The building was intended to be impressive, and the flatness of the area, in the northern reaches of the campus between the via Flaminia and the Tiber, would have added to this impressiveness. It stood in a paved rectangular precinct, and the surrounding area was designed as a public park with trees, including a grove of black poplars and fine walks.[9] The mausoleum complex took the form of an earthen mound, rising from a concrete drum eighty-eight metres in diameter, faced with travertine limestone. There is no clear consensus on what stood above the base. Strabo suggests a single sloping knoll, planted with evergreen trees, rising to a point surmounted by a colossal bronze statue of Augustus. Modern reconstructions generally favour a stepped formation. Apart from the statue the structure seems to have been undecorated, its very simplicity probably intended for effect (unless the decorative elements were plundered in later years). The entrance was located to the south, and in front of the door stood two obelisks in red granite.[10] Augustus' *Res Gestae*, inscribed on tablets, stood somewhere outside the structure.

The base took the form of a central burial chamber surrounded by four concentric rings. The outer ring was broken into semicircular compartments, divided again by radial walls to create quarter-circles, the second into trapezoidal compartments. Neither the trapezoids nor the quarter-circles were accessible, and the purpose of the radial walls and divisions was presumably to support the mass of earth above. From the entrance a vaulted passage traversed two of the rings to a large inner circular ambulatory — perhaps for a ritual circuit of the burial chamber before the deposition of the remains. From the ambulatory one passed into a circular burial chamber, which had a large pier in the centre with a square niche, probably containing the ashes of Augustus, and possibly those of Livia (plan 4).

The mausoleum was the final resting place of the Julio-Claudian high and mighty and their associates. Marcellus was the first to gain admittance. He was followed by his rival Agrippa, and then by his mother, Octavia. (The gravestones of Octavia and Marcellus have survived.) Drusus the Elder and his son Germanicus followed. Augustus was joined there by Livia after her death, followed by Tiberius. On his accession Caligula brought the remains of Agrippina from her island of exile and rejoined her with her husband, Germanicus. He performed the same service for his brother Nero. (The ashes of his other brother could not be recovered.) Almost certainly Antonia would likewise have joined her husband, Drusus, in the mausoleum. Claudius followed. The mausoleum retained its cachet when the Julio-Claudian dynasty came to an end. As a special favour, Nerva's ashes were placed in it. Exclusion could be used as a weapon of disfavour, as when Augustus refused entry to the two Julias, his daughter and granddaughter. If Livia hoped for peace and quiet in

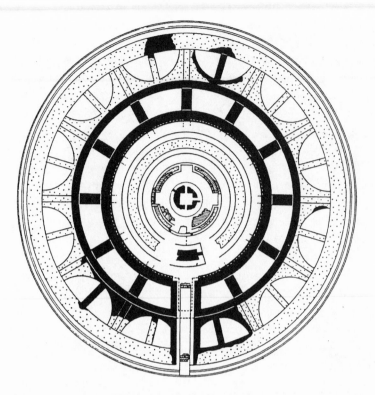

Plan 4. Mausoleum of Augustus. After Gatti (1938)

the next life, she would have been disappointed. The mausoleum, or at least its physical shell, has remained in continuous use, with functions ranging from a concert hall to a bullring.[11]

Although Livia's actual influence in her later years is legitimately questioned, there can be no doubting the high regard in which she was held right up to the end. Any unpopularity that she might have suffered in AD 19 as a consequence of the death of Germanicus and her support of Plancina in the subsequent trial seems to have been completely effaced by 29. The Senate responded to her death with striking generosity, but if we are to believe Tacitus, they faced an uphill battle against an almost totally unyielding Tiberius. He issued no coins to mark his mother's death. He did sanction some minor tributes, but they failed to satisfy the senators, who, according to Dio, went well beyond the emperor's instructions. They ordered an official period of mourning for a whole year for the women. During this time they were to don black clothing, wear their hair loose, and avoid any kind of adornment. Under pressure from Tiberius, the Senate conceded that this would not be a formal *iustitium*, during which all public business would have been suspended.[12] More dramatic was their vote for an arch in her honour, in recognition of her acts of kindness and generosity (see chapter 8). The arch, in common with the other unprecedented distinctions selected by the Senate, came to nothing. Tiberius did not oppose it head-on. As described by Dio, his method was much more devious (perhaps uncharacteristically so for Tiberius). Instead of annulling the senatorial decree, he promised to erect the arch at his own rather than public expense, but then never got around to building it. It is only fair to note that Tiberius took a very jaundiced view of all luxury building projects. Even the important Temple of Divus Augustus, constituted in AD 14, was not finished at the time of his death in 37 and had to be completed by Caligula.[13]

Most significant, the Senate moved to vote Livia divine honours. Her cult had been widespread throughout the empire during her lifetime (see chapter 10). The proposal of the Senate would have involved something much more dramatic, the official recognition of her divinity in Rome, with her own temple and her own priesthood. She would thus have become the first woman to be consecrated and worshipped officially as a goddess in Rome itself. Tiberius was adamant in refusing this honour, saying that it was not what she would have wished and that she had given specific instructions that it should not be allowed to happen. Although his reaction demonstrates a commendable restraint and common sense, it may not have met with popular approval. It is noteworthy that Velleius, Tiberius' ardent admirer, ends his history, apart from a very brief exordium, with the death of Livia, who, he says, in all details resembled the gods more than humans — *per omnia deis quam hominibus similior femina*. Some scholars have detected a modest reprimand of Tiberius in these words.[14]

We know of at least one contemporary Roman who got into hot water over the issue. Cotta Messalinus was a man noted for his generosity and his gluttony. (He invented a recipe for pickling the feet of geese.) According to Tacitus, he specialised in outrageous proposals, usually intended to ingratiate himself with the powers that be. It was he who had proposed after the suicide of Scribonius Libo, suspected of treason in AD 16, that his effigy should not be carried in the funeral of his descendants, and that they could not carry the cognomen Drusus. He also moved that governors of provinces be penalised for the misdeeds of their wives, and demanded a motion of the Senate condemning Agrippina and her son Nero. He was a protégé of Tiberius' and referred to him by the affectionate diminutive *Tiberiolus meus*. He also seems to have had a penchant for putting his foot in his mouth. After Livia's death he found himself in jeopardy on two grounds. He made snide comments about the sexual inclinations of Agrippina's surviving son, Caligula, who had been taken to Capri and placed under his grandfather's wing. Also, in AD 32, when dining with the priests on Livia's birthday, he made the witty comment that it seemed more like a *novendialis*, a feast for the dead held nine days after the funeral. Presumably the point of the joke was that a feast celebrating the birthday of a dead but undeified person was essentially a wake under another name.[15] Messalinus was charged before the Senate. The precise accusation is not specified. Bauman suggests that an alert accuser thought that Tiberius could be identified as the target of criticism implicit in the remark. At any rate, the case was so strong that Messalinus had to beg Tiberius' protection. The emperor obliged and wrote to the Senate noting Messalinus' past services and asking that a naughty witticism over dinner not be used as evidence of guilt. The incident was perhaps a trivial one in itself, but it does serve to show that the issue of divine honours for Livia was a sensitive one and could still strike a nerve three years after her death.

Livia's death may well have had an immediate impact on the contemporary political situation. Dio notes that during her life she had saved the lives of several senators. After her death there was a surge of treason trials. Between AD 15 and 28, thirty trials took place. In AD 30, six were charged; in 31, seven; in 32, eighteen; in 33, ten known by name and twenty anonymous. These figures might suggest a trend, but the relationship between cause and effect is unproved.[16] Suetonius levels the serious charge that Tiberius took action against Livia's close friends, even those who had been entrusted with her funeral arrangements, and condemned one of them, an equestrian, to the treadmill. Only one identifiable case is known, and the later fate of those of her supporters like Galba, whose careers are a matter of record, certainly proves that there was no general witch hunt.

Tacitus limits Tiberius' attacks in the immediate aftermath of Livia's death to a verbal assault on "feminine friendships," aimed at the consul Fufius. The emperor may have felt a personal antipathy for him beyond the mere fact that the consul had been a protégé of his mother's. Fufius seems to have combined a flair for ingratiating himself with elderly women and a clever talent for witticisms, which unfortunately he used to ridicule Tiberius, and which the emperor resented. By the following year, AD 30, Fufius had been charged with a violation of maiestas. He tried to make amends, even reading his will in the Senate to show that he had shared his estate between his children and the emperor. It did him no good. He was now criticised for being a coward as well as a traitor. He returned home and stabbed himself before the Senate could take a vote. He arranged beforehand for a report to be sent to them that he had died like a man. His wife, Mutilia Prisca, was also charged with some unspecified offence. She showed more style, reputedly managing to smuggle a dagger into the Curia, where she dramatically committed suicide before the assembled senators. Dio is our source for these events, and his account at this point survives only in epitomes. The version of John of Antioch (assuming that his "Mucia" is an error for "Mutilia") alleged that Tiberius also destroyed their two daughters because of the family's friendship with Livia. Tacitus reports that Fufius' aged mother, Vitia, made the mistake of mourning for her son, for which she also paid with her life.[17]

Another who ultimately suffered was Piso's widow and Livia's friend Plancina, who had emerged relatively unscathed from the turmoil of the celebrated trial that followed Germanicus' death. That respite proved temporary. The death of Livia in 29 removed her main support. Her hostility towards Agrippina continued to offer her a degree of protection for a time after that, according to Tacitus. Agrippina's death in 33 removed that last line of defence. Plancina was charged on counts that Tacitus describes as well known, perhaps implying that they were the old charges, on which she had never been given a formal acquittal. She took her own life, suffering a penalty that was *sera magis quam immerita* — postponed rather than undeserved.[18]

The main target of Sejanus and his backers after Livia's death would have been Agrippina and her sons. In the minds of the ordinary people there was a firm belief that Livia had continued to exercise a strong influence over events right up to the end. After her death, when the attacks on Sejanus' enemies were unchecked, a letter denouncing Agrippina and Nero was sent (from Capri) to Rome. The popular view was that the letter had been delivered much earlier but had been suppressed by Livia. Admittedly, the opinion of the public on this matter could hardly be called informed, and they seem to have based their inference on the simple fact that the letter was read out so soon after her death. But the anecdote itself does indicate that in the popular mind Livia could to the very end still have an impact on important decisions, and also that she had taken on a role as protector of Agrippina and her children, despite her supposed secret intentions to destroy Germanicus' family.[19] The chronology of what happened to Agrippina's family at this time is confused, and there are contradictory versions of what occurred. The basis for the sequence of events adopted here is laid out in the appendices.[20] What is clear is that after Livia's death Sejanus pulled no punches in his offensive. Formal charges were launched, coinciding with a frustrating lacuna in Tacitus' text and major gaps in Dio's account. Both Agrippina and Nero were proclaimed public enemies and banished, Nero to Pontia and Agrippina to Pandateria. Agrippina was a difficult and courageous prisoner. She lost an eye during a fracas with one of her guards and had to be force-fed after a hunger strike. Nero died in mysterious circumstances, shortly before Sejanus' own fall in late 31. Drusus, who had remained unscathed while Livia was alive but who was similarly arrested after her death, was starved to death in his prison in AD 33. He was survived by his mother for only a few months.[21]

Although Caligula made sarcastic comments about his great-grandmother Livia's relatively humble maternal origins, she was honoured during his reign, and the Arvals celebrated her birthday in 38 and 39, and probably in the other Caligulan years, for which the Arval record is lost.[22] His high regard for her is demonstrated by the belated execution of her will. Although Tiberius had not questioned the validity of Livia's will, which named him heir, he refused to honour the various individual legacies that she provided. Suetonius reports that one of her legatees was Galba, the future emperor, whose bequest, at 5 million sesterces, was the largest that she made. But there was a technical problem in the way the will was drawn up. It was written in figures and not spelled out verbally, presumably as $\boxed{\text{D}}$. By claiming that it should be $\overline{\text{D}}$, Tiberius was able to reduce the sum to 500,000, and in the event did not pay even that amount.[23] Galba fared better under Caligula. On his accession in AD 37 the young emperor proved irresponsibly generous. Although he excluded Tiberius' natural grandson and heir from the late emperor's will on dubious legal grounds, even invalidating the will itself, all Tiberius' bequests were honoured, and the legacies earlier bequeathed by Livia but withheld by Tiberius were now, eight years later, finally paid. Whether Galba received his full amount or the drastically reduced figure is not stated.[24]

Livia's consecration would have to await Caligula's assassination in AD 41 and the accession of his uncle. For all his image as a scholar and harmless eccentric, Claudius had taken power efficiently and coolly, essentially by a military coup. He would doubtless have been keen to give himself respectability by emphasising the eminence of his own family line. The enhancement of his grandmother Livia's status would by necessity mean the enhancement of his own. Among his early measures, divine honours were voted to Livia on January 17, 42, the anniversary of her wedding to Augustus, and, if she was born in 59 BC, the one hundredth anniversary of her birth. At the circus games her image was to be carried in a chariot drawn by elephants. Her statue was set up in the Temple of Augustus that she had founded on the Palatine, and the Vestals were charged with the task of making the appropriate sacrifices. As a further manifestation of her divine status, it was ordered that women should use her name in taking oaths. In an extant fragment of the Arval chronicle for a year between 43 and 48, sacrifices to her and to Divus Augustus at the temple on the Palatine are recorded at the beginning of the year and on the anniversary of her consecration. Another fragment from between 50 and 54 records sacrifices to her and Divus Augustus on September 24 as part of the celebration of Augustus' birthday. Nor was this high regard limited to Rome. A dedication recorded in Egypt (Abydos?) on January 30, 49, seems to allude to a local celebration of her birthday. Bartman has noted that dynastic statuary groups including Livia become very popular during the Claudian period.[25] Moreover, she continued to be venerated under Nero, to judge from the frequency of the honours in the Arval record.[26] The fact that Seneca sought her out for praise during the reigns of the last three Julio-Claudian emperors suggests very strongly that at the official level she was continuously held in high esteem.

Livia enjoyed an abiding regard even after the Julio-Claudian dynasty had came to an end in AD 68. Galba saw the powerful propaganda effect of her image and issued several series of coins honouring her. She appears in the Arval record for Galba, Otho, and perhaps Vitellius.[27] Trajan reissued Tiberius' type with a reverse that depicts Livia, or at least strongly suggests her. A Trajanic inscription from an unknown colony, perhaps Trebula, securely dated by the names of consuls to AD 108, records that her birthday was still being observed then, with games and gladiatorial shows and a public banquet given to the local councillors (decuriones) and the seviri Augustales, the board responsible for the worship of Augustus.[28] Livia's and Augustus' birthdays were still being celebrated under Trajan at Pergamum. The complete calendar of the imperial choir in that city has survived. Its list of activities includes among the celebrations for imperial birthdays three-day events for Livia and Augustus.[29]

Livia's name was used in the marriage oath for more than a century after her death. The evidence for this comes from Egypt, in the form of marriage contracts preserved on papyri, and it may have been a custom observed throughout the empire, in places where the evidence has not survived. The most useful document in this context is a contract between Serapion and Thais, concluded in the reign of Hadrian in AD 127. It is almost complete and provides much interesting information on the dowry of Thais and the property brought into common stock by Serapion, as well as a prenuptial agreement about the disposition of the property in the event of a divorce (an extra sixty drachmae if Thais is pregnant at the time!). Most important for our purpose is the formula near the beginning of the text, agathei tychei, epi Ioulias Sebastes. Wilcken has pointed out the formula agathei tychei (for good luck) occurs in the body of the contract, not in its prescript, and that the following phrase, *epi Ioulias Sebastes*, does not, accordingly, allude to the location or the date. His conclusion, generally accepted, is that the phrase means something like "in the presence of Julia Augusta," in the sense of a general reference to her, or, more likely, because the contract is sworn before her statue (a common force of *epi* in oaths). Wilcken notes that the same reference to Livia occurs in other papyri of the first and second centuries, and, although the *agathei tychei* is missing, the context must surely be the same.[30]

Livia was still held in special honour in Egypt during the Antonine period. An edict of Marcus Petronius Honoratus, prefect of the province in 147–48, has survived on a fragment of papyrus from Oxyrhynchus. It records the particulars of a triennial contest held in honour of Livia and of another deified member of the imperial family, whose name is lost (Germanicus would be a good candidate). No further details about the contests have survived, and it is not known whether they were athletic or artistic. But it is clear that they were of considerable local interest. Some ten years later, Antoninus Pius depicted Livia along with Augustus on his coins of 157–59.[31]

Her cult seems to have lapsed by the end of the second century, if not before. Records of the garrison at Dura Europus on the Euphrates from the first quarter of the third century have survived on papyri. They include the observation of the birthdays of divi from Augustus to Caracalla, as well as of four divae, deified female members of the imperial family: Marciana, sister of Trajan; Matidia, niece of Trajan and mother-in-law of Hadrian; Faustina (which one is meant is not certain — either the wife of Antoninus Pius or the wife of Marcus Aurelius); and Maesa, grandmother of Severus Alexander. The list is not complete, for there are gaps in the papyri and some months are missing. But there is a complete record for January, and Livia's name does not appear there.[32]

Although her cult had lapsed by the time of Feriale Duranum, Livia's prestige seems to have persisted. Perhaps the most vivid demonstration of her lingering presence comes from Prudentius, the Christian poet born in the middle of the fourth century. In 384 the distinguished orator Symmachus had made an appeal to the Senate to tolerate pagan beliefs. The attempt was thwarted by Ambrose, bishop of Milan, but Symmachus published his appeal anyhow. Some twenty years later Prudentius, concerned about the unwillingness of the upper classes to abandon paganism, wrote a verse rebuttal of Symmachus (already dead by then). Prudentius illustrates the evils of paganism from various periods of Roman history but reserves some of his heaviest ammunition for Livia. He revives at length the old antipathy over her second marriage while she was pregnant by her first husband, and castigates the Romans for making a goddess of her along with the likes of Flora and Venus. Prudentius was deadly serious in his intentions, and he would not have wasted his time flogging a dead horse. The vehemence of his attack must have had a purpose. Clearly, in the dying days of ancient Rome, five centuries after Livia's own lifetime, her name was still a potent force among a broad section of the populace, and she remained a figure widely revered and admired.[33]

APPENDICES

APPENDIX 1: SOURCES

LITERARY SOURCES

The ancient literary sources present us with all the problems associated with any historical era, for written material cannot help but be tainted, to a greater or lesser degree, by the prejudices of its author. But the historian of classical antiquity faces additional difficulties generally spared researchers of more recent periods. The ancient texts are often fragmentary or incomplete, and, more seriously, employ a more flexible concept of objective truth than we now feel acceptable in a historical writer. For the Julio-Claudian period there are further hurdles to be overcome. The writers are inevitably preoccupied with the central figure of the emperor. This concentration can come at the expense of political analysis, a serious problem in itself. But it can create a further problem for the study of someone like Livia, in that secondary figures tend to be of interest primarily for what they tell us about the emperor. They rarely emerge as individuals in their own right, unless their public personas were vivid enough to enable them to carve out their own independent niche. Germanicus would be a prime example of this kind of rare exception. Consequently Livia, like most of her contemporaries, tends to move in and out of the historical narrative, temporarily dominating the scene when an emperor dies or a prince is intrigued against, but otherwise hovering in the background and making surprisingly little impression on the historical narrative.

One potential source of information on Livia should be the writings of the emperors themselves and of their family. In fact, surprisingly little overt use is made of this medium by the ancient authorities. Suetonius is happy to quote Augustus' correspondence and provides some insight into the emperor's relationship with Livia through the letters he wrote to her, presumably stored in the imperial archives. He also quotes from Augustus' will. But he was reluctant to use his more formal writings, and in fact is dismissive about imperial memoirs in general. It is not easy to understand why. Such personal reminiscences would have been self-serving, of course, but the ancient sources are generally more than happy to cite the self-serving views of rulers, if only to deride them.

Augustus, like many of the other Julio-Claudians, was an accomplished man of letters. He composed poetry and penned an unfinished play, as well as a number of scholarly works, of which he tired, passing them on to Tiberius to finish. He was also a historical writer of sorts. His most famous contribution in this sphere is his *Res Gestae*, the record of his achievements that he ordered to be set up outside his mausoleum and in the provinces. Whether this work should be classed as a memoir or public monument is perhaps moot for the present purpose, for Livia receives no mention in it. Augustus' *Commentaries* covered his career down to the Cantabrian War (27–24 BC), and Suetonius seems to make occasional use of them, as in his account of the emperor's family background. They must have contained allusions to Livia. Augustus committed to writing *(ut scribit)* his decision to divorce Scribonia because of her shrewish habits, and if this information was found in his *Commentaries*, we would have a likely context there for an appearance by Livia. Also, we would certainly expect Livia to have been featured in the biography of her son Drusus, which Augustus wrote after the young man's death in 9 BC.[1]

Tiberius left two sets of writings. Suetonius refers to the *Commentarii*, of an unspecified nature, and to his *Acta*, presumably an account of his political achievements. They were Domitian's favourite reading matter.[2] Apparently separate from these was his *Commentarius*, a brief and sketchy autobiographical narrative. This last doubtless had a great deal to say about Tiberius' mother, but none of the sources ever cites it, and Suetonius is in fact the only one even to indicate a knowledge of it.[3]

Claudius was a prolific writer. Suetonius refers to a contemporary history in forty-one books, which seems have covered the period from the settlement of Augustus down to his death (27 BC–AD 14). It would have dealt with the preceding civil wars, had Claudius not been frightened off this earlier period by his grandmother Livia and his mother, Antonia. The history doubtless contained much material of potential interest, but the sole reference to its contents is in Pliny the Elder, who cites Claudius on the qualities of an exotic tree resembling the cypress, with the information that it had powerful aromatic qualities and that the Parthians sprinkled it in their drink.[4] Claudius also wrote an autobiography in eight volumes, which would no doubt have contained information on Livia, who seems to have played a significant role in his early life. Suetonius scathingly describes the work as nonsense, although he admits that it had a certain literary charm. We know of only one apparent allusion to it: Nero stated that he had read in the *Commentarii* of Claudius that his predecessor had never forced anyone to undertake prosecutions.[5]

Probably the most familiar imperial memoirs, and potentially the most important in the present context, are those of Agrippina the Younger, now lost. We do know that they were available. Tacitus, under the year AD 26, cites information he found in her commentarii, where she left a record for later generations "of her own life and of the misfortunes of her family" — *quae Neronis principis mater vitam suam et casus suorum posteris memoravit.* The item in question involved the request of her mother, Agrippina the Elder, for permission from Tiberius to remarry. As further evidence of the neglect of imperial memoirs, Tacitus pointed out that this information had been overlooked by all other historians (*scriptores annalium*). In fact, in the extant record only one other citation seems to originate from Agrippina's memoirs: Pliny the Elder records that Nero was delivered by a breach birth.[6]

It is far from certain when Agrippina put together the memoirs. When Tacitus alludes to her authorship he describes her as *mater Neronis*, but he may not necessarily mean that Nero was already born when she wrote them. (He was born, almost certainly, in 37.) Scholarly views on this question vary. Some have argued that Agrippina wrote them during Claudius' reign, when planning Nero's succession, and even used them as propaganda to balance Messalina's hostility. In this case the text would presumably have ended at the point when Agrippina became Claudius' wife. Most scholars, however, have Agrippina imitating Cicero, making use of her forced absence from political activities after 55 to engage in writing. Nor is there agreement on what they might have contained, or how influential they were. More than a century ago Stahr, without further elaboration, suggested that they contained attacks on Livia and Tiberius. Motzo has expanded on this suggestion and claims that they were the source for Tacitus' material on Agrippa Postumus, the involvement of Livia and Tiberius in his death, the story of Augustus' voyage to Planasia to visit Postumus, the story of Claudius Clemens and his impersonation of Postumus, and the death of Augustus, with its negative portrayal of

Livia. Motzo's thesis would thus make the memoirs the key source for the more controversial episodes in Livia's life. But at the other extreme Fabia has argued that Agrippina the Elder's petition to remarry is the only information borrowed by Tacitus from that particular source. In support of Fabia, Walker points out that Tacitus introduces the citation in a way that suggests that the memoirs were not used regularly by him.[7]

Consolatio ad Liviam

Although frequent passing reference is made to Livia in the literary sources, the only two surviving detailed accounts of her activities have to be treated with the utmost caution. One of those is the exhaustive description found in Seneca and Dio of the exchange between her and Augustus over how to handle the suspected conspirator Cornelius Cinna (see chapter 7). Livia's advice has the ring of a standard school exemplum, with a historical event lying only at the core of a highly elaborated rhetorical flight of fancy. The other example is more complex and at first sight potentially more valuable. The *Consolatio ad Liviam* was purportedly written to offer Livia consolation following the death of her son Drusus in 9 BC. It takes the form of a poem of 474 lines, composed in elegiac couplets, and is preserved in a number of late manuscripts, which ascribe it to Ovid. The manuscript text is highly corrupt, and it is often hard to distinguish between the errors of a careless copyist and the idiosyncracies of a mediocre poet.

Modern scholars universally agree that the poem is not what it represents itself to be — namely, a work written in or shortly after 9 BC. This view did not always prevail. In the late sixteenth century Scaliger was willing to accept it at face value. For some time his position held sway, but it was eventually demolished in the nineteenth century by Haupt, who went so far as to argue that the poem was confected during the Renaissance. Haupt's extreme position has not found favour, but his general principle of a later composition is now widely accepted, although there is no consensus on when it was written. The resemblances to Ovid suggest that it could not be earlier than he, on the assumption that it is hardly likely that Ovid would have imitated an unknown poetaster and have continued to do so after his exile. There are also resemblances between the *Consolatio* and Seneca's writings, dated after AD 43, but this may be because they share a common source.

The very strong likelihood that the *Consolatio* is not contemporaneous with the events it describes makes its value as a historical document questionable, because we do not know whether the author is drawing on personal observation. Richmond, for instance, observes that the poet might have made use of the historian Livy, who, we know, wrote on the death of Drusus and on his funeral in Rome.[8]

Contemporaries of Livia

Only a small portion of the contemporary accounts of the Julio-Claudian period have survived — no serious loss, according to Tacitus, who observes that records were falsified through cowardice when the emperors were still alive and infected with hatred after their deaths.[9] It is indeed the case that the writers active while Livia was on the scene are generally obsequious, or had a personal motive for winning her over specifically.

Velleius Paterculus

Velleius Paterculus was born in about 19 BC, of equestrian stock. Like his grandfather and father, he pursued a military career, serving first under Gaius Caesar and Tiberius, latterly as *legatus* in Germany and Pannonia. After this he moved up into the senatorial order, reaching the praetorship in AD 16. His *Historiae Romanae* is a compendium of Roman history from the legendary past, as far back as the Trojan War, down to AD 30, and is dedicated to his friend Marcus Vinicius to honour Marcus' consulship in that year. The earlier parts are missing and must have been summary indeed. He becomes more detailed as he reaches his own day, focussing very much on the figure of Tiberius.

Velleius' esteem for his old commander has won him many detractors. Summer, for instance, calls him an "obsequious royalist." Syme speaks of his "loyal fervour" and describes him as "voluble and unscrupulous." But his enthusiasm must be placed in its proper context. His coverage of Tiberius is limited to his successful period as an imperial prince and the earlier part of his reign, before things started to go awry. Although Velleius' account contrasts with the darker picture given by Tacitus, it is surely the case that Tacitus' impressions are coloured by the excesses that mark the later years. Velleius also can be subtly critical, as on the death of Livia, when he implies that she should have enjoyed consecration. He was an eyewitness to many of the events that involved Livia, and his admiration for her is patent.[10]

Valerius Maximus

Valerius Maximus published his volumes on memorable deeds and sayings (*Factorum ac Dictorum Memorabilium Libri IX*) in AD 31 and dedicated his work to Tiberius. He maintains an obsequious tone throughout, as in his description of Livia attended by Pudicitia.[11]

Philo Judaeus

Similarly, the Jewish writer Philo of Alexandria (30 BC–AD 45) much admired Livia and praised her for her intelligence and judgement. This is hardly surprising, for she had shown herself to be well disposed to the Jews and was a benefactress of the Temple at Jerusalem.

Ovid

The poet Ovid, born 43 BC, was a witty and impertinent observer of Roman life and morals, until his exile in AD 8 to Tomi on the Black Sea, for reasons still not understood and much debated. He had good reason to heap flattery on Livia, for his slender hope of recall depended entirely on regaining the favour of the imperial family. Before his exile he praised her as the model Roman wife and paragon of Roman virtue, a fairly conventional description and even echoed in Tacitus' obituary portrait. But after his exile Ovid's compliments become sickeningly fulsome, addressed to a goddess-in-the-making. His flattery was ultimately to no avail, for he remained in exile until his death, in about AD 17.

Seneca the Younger

Seneca's early career played out while Livia was still alive, but he wrote about her after her death. Born in Cordoba, Spain, towards the end of the first century BC, he was taken as a child to Rome. There he gained a reputation during the reigns of Caligula, Claudius, and Nero as a writer and a seducer of the imperial women. He died by suicide in AD 65. His writings cover a wide range — letters, essays, plays — and tend to be characterised by sycophantic flattery of the reigning emperor accompanied by denigration of his predecessor.

Livia appears in the works of Seneca three times. All three references come after her death; indeed, all are post-Tiberian. In each case her role is positive. This is surprising and uncharacteristic of Seneca. It may suggest genuine admiration on his part, but more likely it reflects the high regard in which Livia was held in the latter part of the Julio-Claudian era, a personage to be criticised at one's peril, while the lewd and adulterous Julia, as an example, was fair game and a safe target. In *De Ira* Livia's role is secondary. Seneca in describing rulers who have been able to control their anger relates that Timagenes the historian attacked Augustus and Livia and the rest of the imperial family but suffered no retribution, beyond being barred from the emperor's

home (see chapter 7). Although Livia's role in this work is essentially inciden-
tal, she does at least by implication garner Seneca's admiration.[12]

In the *De Clementia* Seneca provides a detailed account of Livia's efforts to
secure clemency for Cornelius Cinna. Although we can assume much rhetorical exaggeration, Vidén argues that if Seneca had wanted to persuade his pupil
Nero to a sound philosophy of life, he would not have chosen examples that
were incredible. In fact, the general image of Livia here comes very close to
that found in Suetonius, of a woman who involved herself in her husband's
business but did not control him. It is interesting that the disparaging term
muliebre consilium (advice offered by a woman) is self-deprecatingly put by
Livia into her own mouth.[13]

Livia's third appearance is in the *Consolatio ad Marciam*, as the *maxima
femina* to be emulated by Marcia in dealing with her grief.[14] Seneca claims that
after Drusus' death in 9 BC, Livia behaved with stateliness and moderation,
unlike the traditionally impeccable Octavia, whom he describes as excessive in
her behaviour and catty towards Livia. It is interesting here to contrast the inferences drawn from Seneca's description of Livia in the aftermath of Drusus'
death, and her similar moderation following Germanicus', from which Tacitus
draws the most negative conclusions.[15]

Pliny the Elder

The most important sources are not in fact contemporaries of Livia but
come later. Pliny the Elder was born in AD 23 or 24, actually before Livia died,
but he would have been too young to form a personal firsthand impression of
her. After a varied and active life, he died during the eruption of Vesuvius in 79.
Pliny was a diligent collector of facts and a prolific writer. His history of the
German Wars in twenty books, as well as his annalistic history in thirty-one
books, are both lost. His only surviving work, the extraordinary *Natural History*, comprises thirty-seven books. Pliny provides much information on Livia
that reflects his encyclopedic approach to the world's varied wonders: details
about her fertility, diet, drinking habits, and the size of her dwarf. But he also
provides useful information of a more conventional historical nature, in which
a relatively benign view of Livia emerges. The stories about the deaths of
Gaius and Lucius distressed Augustus — but he was upset by the rumours, not
by a belief in Livia's guilt. In his account of the death of Agrippa Postumus,
Pliny attributes no responsibility to her, and limits his criticism to a reference
to her *cogitationes* (intrigues) at the close of Augustus' life. This restraint does
not reflect a bias in favour of imperial women and in fact is in telling contrast

to Pliny's depiction of Agrippina the Younger, where his information is almost uniformly hostile, describing her as a misfortune for the whole world.[16]

Suetonius

Suetonius was born in about AD 70, probably in Africa. He held a number of imperial appointments under Trajan and Hadrian and was a productive writer, most famous for his *Lives of the Caesars*. He died in about 140. He had access to the imperial archives, and at his best can be the most impressive of the major authorities of the period on points of detail. Unfortunately, when he uses the material of others, he often lacks serious judgement, and he is unable to resist a lively anecdote.

Suetonius wrote biography, not history, and tended to handle his material by theme, not by chronological sequence. His subject was the lives of the emperors, and as a general principle he describes women only if they add something to the portrait of the emperor in question, usually in terms of the influence they had over them, or their place in their dynastic plans.[17] This does not imply that Suetonius was slighting towards the imperial women. Rather, he saw the literary advantage of focussing almost exclusively on his main subject. Generally speaking, Livia does not leap to the attention in Suetonius' writings. She emerges as someone who more or less kept within the bounds of what was suitable for a woman. As a consequence, Suetonius' depiction of her is far less savage than the one offered by Tacitus or even by the more restrained Dio. Suetonius says nothing of crimes or poisoning. The theme of cunning and hypocrisy that is so prevalent in Tacitus is perhaps reflected in only one place, Suetonius' report of Caligula's dictum that she was a *Ulixes stolatus* — Ulysses in a stola — in a context that is intended to illustrate Caligula's mischievous habit of denigrating his relatives and his facility for bon mots.[18] At worst, we are allowed a few glimpses of her ambition, her attempt to secure citizenship for a Gaul, her advancement of Otho's grandfather. Tiberius does express annoyance at Livia for claiming an equal share of the rule. But Suetonius' focus in this context is on Tiberius' view of things, such as his odium towards members of his own family and his conviction that women should not meddle in men's affairs. That the notion of her seeking an equal share in power is a rhetorical exaggeration is demonstrated by Tiberius' reaction to her engaging in the efforts to prevent the fires, something that in the past she had always done. Any criticism of Livia on the issue of her ambitions is at best muted and implied, rather than overt.[19]

Suetonius takes the position that Livia might have sought to sway Augustus from time to time but that her influence on political events was relatively slight. In a particularly telling passage he mentions the claims made by others that Augustus had been personally inclined not to adopt Tiberius but was won over by pressure from his wife. Suetonius emphatically states that in a matter of such great importance it is hardly credible that Augustus would not have given the issue very careful thought. He suggests that the princeps in fact weighed up the advantages and disadvantages of Tiberius very carefully and decided in the end that the advantages predominated. Livia's intercession, he suggests, was not the deciding factor. He backs up his claim by quoting letters from Augustus to Tiberius.[20]

Suetonius passes over opportunities to besmirch Livia's name. He reports the general opinion (*creditur* and *opinio fuit*) that Germanicus met his end through Tiberius' treachery, aided by Piso, but he does not associate Livia in the scandal. Often he follows the tradition that actually favours her. On the issue of whether she suppressed the news of Augustus' death to allow Tiberius time to return, Suetonius takes the unequivocal position that Tiberius reached the emperor's bedside before his death and that the two were able to hold a fairly lengthy conversation. This contrasts with Tacitus, who characteristically clouds the issue by raising doubts which he does not resolve, and Dio, who suggests that the most reliable authorities have Augustus dead before Tiberius' arrival. Suetonius makes no mention of a visit by Augustus to Agrippa Postumus or of any suspicion that Livia may have poisoned her husband. In only one place does he seem to take a Tacitean approach in characterizing Livia's actions. Suetonius reports the uncertainty about who wrote the letter that ordered the slaying of Agrippa Postumus. But the death of Agrippa was clearly an incident that left the ancient historians genuinely baffled, and Suetonius simply lays out the variants, without giving any opinion.[21]

Cassius Dio

Cassius Dio came from the province of Bithynia and held consulships in about AD 205 and in 229. He wrote a history in Greek, from the early kings down to the time of Severus Alexander (222–35). He was essentially an accumulator of information and gave little thought to broad synthesis or serious analysis. At times he claims acquaintance with several sources, but he rarely names them, and never with reference to Livia. He generally lacks serious critical judgement in assessing his material, and often fails to distinguish between the preposterous and the plausible, although he does in fact seem to go out of his way to suggest a sensible assessment of the various traditions about Livia.

Dio can in places be useful, in that he treats events in broad sequence, unlike

Suetonius, and thus provides the only extant annalistic account of Augustus'
reign. Unfortunately, there are major gaps in his text, which are to some
degree filled by Byzantine epitomes. This term is rather misleading, for the
epitomators tend to excerpt rather than to summarise, and often simply omit
significant events.

There is extensive material on Livia scattered throughout Dio's account,
and he is our sole source for such important information as the grant of quasi-
tribunician *sacrosanctitas* in 35 BC. His judgements on her are very much of a
mixed bag. He depicts her as giving Augustus sound and moderate counsel on
how to handle the Cinna conspiracy. Yet he claims that amidst the universal
sadness, Tiberius and Livia were alone in their joy at Germanicus' death. He is
also preoccupied more than any other of the extant sources with the notion
that Livia saw herself as a coruler after the death of Augustus. Goodyear has
suggested that Dio may have worked back from Agrippina the Younger in
portraying an excessive desire for power on Livia's part. Moreover, it is possible that he was influenced by the reemergence of the powerful imperial
women during the Severan period. He states as fact that Augustus sailed secretly to see Agrippa Postumus. He also repeats without comment the speculation that Livia was involved in the deaths of Gaius and Lucius. But he
expresses scepticism over the claim that she brought about the death of Marcellus, the son of Octavia. Although he inclines towards the view that she
postponed making public the news of Augustus' death, he concedes that there
is a contrary tradition. He is our only source for the claim that Livia despatched Augustus by means of poisoned figs, but he demonstrates a noticeable
ambivalence about the story. In none of these accounts does one detect the
enthusiastic venom of Tacitus, but rather a general incuriosity.[22]

Dio made use of source material not found in Tacitus and other earlier
extant writers. In the account of the debate over the conspiracy of Cornelius
Cinna he echoes Seneca in a number of places. Both accounts clearly have
elements in common. They use the same imagery, for instance, such as Livia's
analogy between Augustus and the doctor who is forced to find a new cure
when all else has failed. Because Seneca had a good reason for preserving the
full form of the story, given that he was writing on the general topic of clemency, it might be expected that he would have been Dio's main source, and
there certainly is evidence that Dio had read other works of Seneca, such as the
ad Polybium. But Dio's version of the incident is in fact much longer, and it
differs in a number of details, such as Cinna's name and the date of the incident. He clearly had access to a source independent of Seneca.[23]

Tacitus

Tacitus is the primary literary source for the Julio-Claudian period. His general qualities as a historian have already been treated in exhaustive detail and need not be entered into here. In particular his celebrated claim that he wrote impartially — *sine ira ac studio* — has been subjected to much scrutiny. It would be foolish to deny his bias against the imperial system, but unlike many other ancient writers he is not so naive as to accept as feasible every bit of nonsense passed down to him.

In assessing Tacitus' portrayal of Livia, we must note his general hostility towards ambitious women of the imperial family. There have been those who, like Wuilleumier and Bardon, have claimed that Tacitus was a misogynist, motivated by a basic hatred of females.[24] But he can surely be cleared of a general charge of misogyny, in the sense of an irrational and consistent hatred of women. He does recognise female qualities such as *constantia* and *fides*, and his women are at times capable of heroism.[25] The problem is not Tacitus' overall view of women but his view of a particular class of women, in a particular context. He was deeply offended by those women who were placed in positions of power and influence through their family connections and sought to use this power to manipulate the political process for their own ends, a process that in any case rightly belonged to the Senate and people and not to an autocrat or his relatives. For Tacitus, this corrupt use of power was manifested primarily in continuous manoeuvres to promote the interests of a potential successor, leading to inevitable factional feuds.

In the obituary notice that begins the fifth book of the *Annals*, Tacitus' assessment of Livia is commendably restrained. He depicts her as a woman of old-fashioned virtue and of impressive noble lineage. On the negative side he observes that she was more affable (*comis*) than women of the old school would have thought right, that she was a match for her husband's craftiness and her son's insincerity, and that she was a domineering mother (*mater impotens*). This restrained tone is notably absent, however, from the allusions to Livia in the preceding narrative. Here Tacitus' hostility is blatant. He can scarcely mention her name without a touch of malice, and he creates a portrait of a scheming and ruthless manipulator that is glaringly at variance with the general picture that appears in the other historical authorities. As noted earlier, Suetonius' and Dio's criticisms of Livia are relatively measured; Suetonius in particular finds only vague gossip to use against her. Apart from an allusion to Augustus' distress over her intrigues, Pliny has nothing critical to say, while

Velleius, not surprisingly, and Seneca, somewhat remarkably, are unashamed admirers.[26]

This is not to suggest that Tacitus fabricated information. Rather, the problem is that where he has two sources and one is unfavourable, he either will follow the adverse account or will at the very least cloud the issue by raising it as a possibility. There would certainly have been a large body of anti-Tiberian (and anti-Livian) material for him to call upon. Tacitus himself alludes to the wide range of hostile charges made against Tiberius *cum omnia . . . conquirerent intenderentque* (when [writers] were collecting and exaggerating all sorts of things). The memoirs of the younger Agrippina were certainly known to him, and they are unlikely to have had many kind things to say about Livia. He knew of bitter letters denouncing Tiberius, sent to Augustus by Julia during her husband's stay in Rhodes.[27]

Apart from using information hostile to Livia, Tacitus was most skilful at presenting information that, while strictly accurate, created a damaging effect. Outside the early period of her marriage, it is probably fair to say that he never makes a substantial allusion to Livia that is not designed to arouse animosity, often by presenting the details in such a way that one cannot help drawing an unfavourable inference. Often he will avoid doing this explicitly, but will protect his historical integrity by citing public opinion or speculation. The trip to Planasia provides an excellent illustration of this technique. The story is implausible. Tacitus no doubt recognised it as implausible. He could defend himself by pointing out that he was presenting it only as a rumour. But in the end he would have been fully satisfied no doubt with the insinuation that he had deliberately planted.

Tacitus skilfully employs certain words that carry a powerfully negative connotation when characterising Livia. Thus he applies to her the term *potentia*, with its associations of unauthorised and improper power, often manifested by excessive influence. When Calpurnius Piso defies Livia and hauls her friend Urgulania into court, he does so *spreta potentia Augustae* (with Augusta's power thwarted), implying that her potentia was of such a malign nature that it was the duty of an intrepid official to stand up against it. When Sejanus uses Mutilia Prisca to stir up Livia's animosity towards Agrippina, Livia is described as *anum . . . natura potentiae anxiam*, a very powerful phrase suggesting not simply a love of power but a desperate innate desire for it (*natura . . . anxiam*), and even more, an unhealthy unwillingness to give up that power even in old age (*anum*).[28] Even more damning in its effect is the word *impotentia*, whose force is quite different from its English derivative, and conveys the sense of a lust for power that is completely out of control. Recording public opinion and the supposed anxiety about Tiberius taking over, Tacitus adds the problem of a mother driven by *muliebri impotentia* (a woman's passion for power), with the result that *serviendum feminae* (they would have to be slaves to a woman). Tiberius supposedly left Rome because his mother was desperate to share his rule, which Tacitus skilfully calls *dominatio*, implying an insatiable craving for a tyrannical form of control that was alien to Roman tradition, and echoing the supposed earlier concerns of the public. In his obituary notice Livia is described as a *mater impotens*, a cleverly ambiguous phrase because it can convey the notion of a woman desperate to control her son, but also a mother uncontrollable in advancing her son's ambitions.[29]

Tacitus suggests that as a woman Livia achieves her ends not by overt action but by devious underhand methods, usually involving intrigue. When Lucius and Gaius Caesar died he declined to commit himself about the cause, noting that it might have been simply the working of fate or it might have been the *dolus* (treacherous scheme) of Livia. Augustus was persuaded to promote the interests of Tiberius *obscuris . . . matris artibus* (by the murky devices of his mother), a convenient charge because by its nature it could not be refuted. When Livia helped Julia the Younger in her exile, it was part of a pattern of making a public show of concern for her stepdaughter's children while she worked to undermine them "in secret" *(per occultum)*. When word reached Rome of Germanicus' ill-health, Tacitus again used the shield of public opinion to express outrage over Livia's conduct and her secret conversations with Plancina *(secretos sermones)*. While Livia's conversations with her friends would naturally be expected to be private, the adjective *secretos* has an emotional impact, for it connotes intrigues, and especially devious and underhand intrigues. When Germanicus died in Syria, and Piso was considering his options, there were those who encouraged him to be bold, assuring him that Tiberius and Livia were making a loud show of grief for Germanicus *(iacantius)* but in their hearts were glad, and that he could count on Livia's secret complicity *(conscientia)*. Again Tacitus avoids making an explicit statement about someone's secret thought and protects himself by attributing what are in reality absurd, but prejudicial, statements to other parties.[30]

Perhaps the most vivid illustration of Tacitus' skill in arousing antipathy towards Livia is the way he applies the word *noverca* to her. The concept of stepmother had sinister connotations for the Romans as for other societies. Quintilian might have protested at the use of the stock evil stepmother in legal exercises *(declamationes)*, a stereotype he claimed belonged to the realm of fantasy, but in the popular mind the notion was firmly set, particularly in the association of stepmothers and poison, and stepmothers as the murderers of their stepchildren. So Ovid can describe how in the Iron Age the *terribiles novercae* mixed their dark poisons, and the boy in Horace's Epode who is carried into the witches' den so that they can use his body for a magic potion asks why they look at him "like a stepmother" *(ut noverca)*.[31] When Livia is first introduced, it is with the speculation that the deaths of Gaius and Lucius were caused by the *novercae Liviae dolus* (craftiness of their stepmother Livia). Quite apart from the unfairness of the stereotype, Livia was their stepmother only in a very technical sense, after Augustus' adoption of his grandchildren for political purposes. But the prejudicial damage of the word was deliberate. Similarly, in the speculation over the blame for the death of Agrippa Postumus, Tacitus suggests that it was likely caused by Tiberius and Livia, the latter from a stepmother's hate *(novercalibus odiis)*. Livia is said to be hostile towards Agrippina for exactly the same reason, novercalibus odiis. Here the stretch is even greater. Livia was in fact the stepmother of the elder Julia, Agrippina's mother. Finally, among the burdens that Augustus had to bear, Tacitus adds his wife, *gravis in rempublicam mater, gravis domui Caesarum noverca* (a stepmother who was a burden on the state, a burden to the house of the Caesars), a line of brilliant artistry. It shows the way in which state and domus had become intertwined. On the one hand she was mater reipublicae, standing as the counterpart to the pater patriae, whose obligations to and power over the state reflect a Roman man's position within his family. (It reminds the reader of the attempt to have Livia declared mater patriae on Augustus' death.) But in the purely domestic situation she was a noverca, and a gravis one at that, reminding us of the rumours about the deaths of Gaius, Lucius, and Agrippa Postumus. As a footnote, it might be added that Suetonius never calls Livia *noverca*.[32]

Livia's supposed intrigues against the rival members of the imperial family might be a legitimate theme, given that they would potentially have had serious consequences. But Tacitus continues his campaign of denigrating Livia after her son's accession. He speaks of the rift between Tiberius and his mother over the supposed struggle for power. This is mentioned in other sources, but we should be cautious about the weight and importance that Tacitus gives to the disagreement. As Syme has observed, the potentia of Livia and the effect on Tiberius barely correspond with the "sinister intimations" that Tacitus ascribes to them. He says at first that Tiberius held down Livia through envy *(anxius invidia)*. It is only later that the notion of discord arises, none of which is matched by what he says in Livia's obituary notice. Syme suggests that some of the incidents implying conflict may have been added after the obituary was written. Tacitus makes the plain statement that when Tiberius rushed back to Rome at the time of his mother's illness in AD 22 the *concordia* between the emperor and his mother was still *sincera*. Then he adds, almost as an after-thought, that the explanation could be that they were concealing their mutual antipathy — *sive occultis odiis*.[33]

The most dramatic Livian episodes in Tacitus' *Annals* belong to his account of the death of Augustus and its immediate aftermath, the execution of Agrippa Postumus and the succession of Tiberius. There are enough close parallels to make a case that Tacitus, Dio, and Suetonius had access to one or more common source for the events surrounding Tiberius' accession. The basic narrative is the same in Tacitus and Dio. It is also possible that Dio drew on Tacitus but had access also to other sources, possibly later than Tacitus.[34] Suetonius certainly drew from the same source as Tacitus (if not actually drawing on him directly), as is evidenced even by the similarity of their language. In describing the tribune in charge of the guard, for instance, Suetonius writes *tribunus . . . custos appositus*, Tacitus, *tribuno custodiae adposito*. Tiberius' response to the soldier who brings the information is described by Suetonius as *renuntianti tribuno . . . rationem respondit* and by Tacitus as *nuntianti centurioni . . . rationem . . . respondit*. We cannot now know what this source might have been, but the anti-Tiberian passages of the memoirs of Agrippina the Younger have been suggested as a candidate.[35] Although Tacitus may have used the same sources as Dio and Suetonius, he drew more fully from them, or supplemented them by other information or perhaps even by his own speculations.

Perhaps the most striking aspect of this part of the narrative is the way that Tacitus' portrayal of Livia's behaviour is echoed in the chronologically later account of Agrippina the Younger's role in the death of Claudius, separated by some forty years. The general parallels between Agrippina and Livia in the major sources are marked to a degree that raises suspicions. Both sons take power through the scheming of a mother, the removal by the mother of rival claimants, and possibly the poisoning of the incumbent emperor, her husband. In each case the mother tries to rule through her son but is rebuffed. Worn out by his mother's interference, Tiberius left Rome, and Nero threatened to leave for similar reasons. Livia's claim that she reminded Tiberius where he got his power from is echoed by Agrippina's assertion that she made Nero emperor and she could unmake him too. Both new emperors at the outset of their reigns seemed moderate, but after their mothers' deaths exercised evil tendencies without restraint. Interestingly, an explicit comparison between the two women is made only once by Tacitus, in an innocuous context, when Agrippina is said to have emulated Livia in providing the exact funeral arrangements that Augustus had enjoyed.[36]

To put this whole issue into perspective, some account must be given of

Claudius' death in October 54. The question of whether or not he was indeed murdered by his wife Agrippina is not important in this particular context. Much more important is that people believed she was guilty, and on this question there is almost complete unanimity among the ancient sources. There are only minor expressions of caution. Josephus twice notes tentative reservations, and Philostratus, in his life of Apollonius of Tyana, does the same. But these two are in a lonely minority, and the major sources express no doubt. Thus, quite apart from the question of actual guilt, it is clear that there was a strong tradition that Agrippina murdered Claudius. The notion that Livia had committed a similar crime was far less firmly established and reported as nothing more substantial than a rumour.[37]

It need cause no surprise that Claudius should have died when he did. He had always suffered from ill health, and the possibility of a natural cause of death, from, say, gastroenteritis and heart failure, cannot be ruled out.[38] The mere fact that a charge is made against Agrippina is not in itself significant, for such accusations tended to follow the deaths of prominent members of the Julio-Claudian family. There would have been no compelling motive for her to remove her husband. It is true that the longer the succession was delayed, the stronger would be the claim of the youthful Britannicus, Claudius' natural son. But we have to balance this with the fact that in 54 Nero, though Britannicus' senior, was himself still very young, probably only sixteen.

In the absence of a compelling motive, a tradition viciously hostile to Agrippina would have had no trouble concocting one. The sources agree that by 54 Agrippina's cunning plans were under suspicion and that there had been a reconciliation between Claudius and Britannicus. Suetonius and Dio give the initiative in this to Claudius. Tacitus, who generally sought to portray Claudius as a fool, the dupe of his wives and freedmen, gives the credit for smoking out Agrippina to the freedman Narcissus, who then became reconciled to Britannicus. Narcissus had been largely responsible for the execution of Britannicus' mother, Messalina, and believed that he had enough evidence similarly to undo Agrippina. Supposedly, he was so lacking in discretion that he revealed his plans to his friends, thereby conveniently offering his archenemy the chance to discover what he was up to.[39]

The opportunity for murder came about in October 54. Agrippina first made sure that Narcissus was off the scene, persuading him, according to Dio, to take the cure at the hot baths of Sinuessa in Campania.[40] The story of Claudius' subsequent death is familiar and famous. At a palace banquet, on the night of October 12, the emperor was served a poisoned mushroom. Tacitus and Dio provide the tradition that the poison was sprinkled on a particularly succulent sample, and Dio adds the further detail that Agrippina cunningly ate the rest herself.[41] The details of later events vary, and the sources note variant traditions. In the version reflected in both Suetonius and Tacitus, Claudius fell ill, then rallied, to be given a second dose, which finished him off. The news of the death was supposedly kept secret. The Senate was convened and the priests made their vows for the emperor's recovery, at the very time when his corpse was being wrapped up in warm coverlets to prevent the onset of rigor mortis. Otherwise, Agrippina blocked admission to the palace and gave out regular bulletins that maintained the fiction that there was hope for recovery. Tacitus and Suetonius provide the reason for the delay, which was to keep the news from the main body of the praetorians until the preparations for Nero's succession were completed.[42] Shortly after midday on October 13, 54, the emperor's death was reported, and the *Apocolocyntosis* indicates that the official report stated that he died happy, watching the performance of the comic actors brought in to entertain him.[43]

There is a solid core of fact in both successions — it is indisputable that each emperor had adopted a stepson as his heir and was succeeded by him. But beyond this, the common themes of the two deaths as they appear in the major sources should be viewed with caution. Each emperor regrets his decision and decides that he will restore the rightful heir. His wife gets wind of the scheme and decides to eliminate her husband before his plan can be implemented. The emperor dies but the event is kept secret until the stepson's position is secure. In each case the death is followed by the murder of a prominent Roman. There are disturbing resemblances of detail also. In the background hover the loyal retainers, who happen to be in the wrong place at the wrong time — Narcissus, the freedman of Claudius, and Clemens, the devoted slave of Agrippa. There is the powerful emotion of the reconciliation with the rival claimant, followed by the betrayal of the secret, by Narcissus and Marcia, both behaving indiscreetly. The means are strikingly similar, in that in each case the poison is introduced by a clever device intended to trick the emperor, on a succulent mushroom or on a fig still on the tree. Comic actors are brought in for Claudius' last hours, and Augustus likens himself to a comic actor in departing life's stage. There is the delay that follows each death, hard to explain if the emperor had been removed by a premeditated murder. In each case the wife barricades the house where the dead emperor lies and issues reassuring reports about his health until the political situation is right for her.[44]

While the general parallelism is striking, more remarkable are the verbal echoes evident in Tacitus' accounts of both incidents. Tacitus certainly can sometimes be an *imitator sui* in that he will use the same language to describe what he sees as similar events.⁴⁵ But there are no other episodes in Tacitus in which the verbal echoes and parallelism of incidents extend over so considerable a portion of continuous narrative. The actions of Livia and Agrippina are both described as *scelus*. Augustus and Claudius are both *exanimis*. Livia blocked the house *custodiis domum et viam saepserat*, and Agrippina did the same, *aditus custodiis clauserat*. The verbal parallels continue after the account of each death, and do so with powerful effect. Thus Tacitus follows the death of Claudius with a dramatic introduction to book 13 of the *Annals*, asserting that the first victim in the new regime of Nero was Marcus Junius Silanus, governor of Asia *(prima novo principatu mors Iunii Silani proconsulis)*, and thus echoes his claim at the beginning of Tiberius' reign that "the first misdeed of the new principate was the slaying of Agrippa Postumus" *(primum facinus novi principatus fuit Postumi Agrippae caedes)*. The link is reinforced by the sentence that immediately precedes the reference to Postumus' death. In reporting that Tiberius had taken power, Tacitus calls him Nero *(Neronem)*, although that name was no longer correct after his adoption by Augustus in AD 4. The deliberate anachronism is intended to insinuate that the accession of Tiberius is associated with the same infamy as Nero's. Also, Agrippina supposedly had Marcus Silanus killed *ignaro Nerone* (without Nero knowing), just as Tiberius claimed ignorance over the death of Agrippa.⁴⁶

Which of these accounts influenced the other? The death of Claudius occurs later in Tacitus' narrative and might seem logically to have been inspired by the earlier incident. But as noted earlier, there can be no doubt that in the popular tradition the case against Agrippina is by far the stronger. Thus it seems very possible that Livia was depicted as a murderer on the analogy of Agrippina, and that the rumours about Augustus' death did not circulate until after AD 54.⁴⁷ This possibility is strengthened by the fact that Dio's reference to the poisoned fig is likely to have been inspired by the well-known story of Agrippina's poisoned mushroom. The notion that Livia murdered her husband, in the manner that would associate her with Agrippina, suits very well Tacitus' theme that in AD 14 power was in effect seized, not transmitted.

Goodyear suggests that Tacitus might not in fact have worked out the significance of the similarities. But they are likely to have been deliberate. Mellor describes the situation nicely: "Tacitus is content to use the rumours to besmirch by association Livia and Tiberius who, whatever their failings, never displayed the deranged malice of an Agrippina and a Nero. It is good literature but it can be irresponsible history."⁴⁸

Livia is mentioned by other writers, but only incidentally. A list of literary citations follows. It will be noted that although there is no shortage of information, with the exception of the episodes relating to the marriage of Livia and Augustus, the death of Augustus and its immediate aftermath, and Livia's own death, relatively few of the references can be tied to precise dates.

Literary Citations

Anonymous, *Consolatio ad Liviam*

1–12:	Address to Livia.
13–20:	Drusus provides an *exemplum* through his military achievements.
21–40:	Livia anticipated a triumph but must prepare a funeral.
41–58:	Even Livia's virtues could not prevent the disaster.
59–74:	Despite his achievements, Augustus was not immune to grief, for Drusus' death was preceded by those of Marcellus, Agrippa, and Octavia.
75–84:	Drusus' great merits, matched by Antonia's.
85–94:	Tiberius is devastated by his brother's death.
95–118:	Livia's grief.
119–66:	Livia addresses Drusus.
167–78:	The return of Drusus' body to Rome.
179–98:	The people mourn and seek answers from the gods.
199–220:	The funeral.
221–52:	Mars and Tiber express their grief.
253–64:	The cremation.
265–70:	The immortality of Drusus' achievements.
271–82:	Germany will be punished.
283–98:	The temple to Castor and Pollux that Drusus would have dedicated with Tiberius.
299–328:	Antonia's grief.
329–40:	Drusus' departed ancestors will greet him.
341–78:	Livia has a duty to accept Fate and not to yield to grief.
379–92:	Livia has been blessed by her status, sons, and husband.
393–410:	Livia had time to cope with the news.
411–16:	Long life for Livia and Tiberius are wished for.
417–26:	Augustus and Tiberius have given their support, despite Livia's reluctance.
427–44:	No one can escape death.
445–70:	Drusus would not want Livia to grieve.
471–74:	Livia can draw comfort from Tiberius and Augustus.

Cornelius Nepos, *Atticus*

19.4:   The granddaughter of Atticus was betrothed to the son of Livia.

Strabo

5.3.8:   Livia and Octavia are credited with fine buildings in Rome, including the Porticus Liviae.

Horace, *Odes*

3.14.5–6:   Livia carries out sacrifices to mark Augustus' return to Rome.

Ovid, *Tristia*

1.6.25–27:   Ovid's wife's qualities might be derived from Livia, *femina princeps*, who was revered through the years.

2.161–4:   Livia alone was worthy of Augustus. But for her he would have remained unmarried.

4.2.11–14:   Livia makes offerings for the safe return of Tiberius in company with the matrons and the Vestals.

Ovid, *ex Ponto*

1.4.56:   Livia is worthy of Caesar, and offerings are made to them as true gods *(dis veris)*.

2.2.69:   Livia keeps the couch pure.

2.8.4:   Ovid possesses a silver image of Livia.

2.8.29:   Livia alone is equal *(par)* to Augustus.

2.8.45:   Ovid prays for Livia's support and hopes that her family will prosper.

3.1.114–18:   Ovid's wife must approach Livia, whose chastity overshadows that of previous ages. Livia has the beauty of Venus and the morals of Juno and alone is worthy of the celestial couch.

3.1.125–26:   Livia is a *femina princeps* who proves the efficacy of Fortune.

3.1.139–45:   Livia might be involved in major matters; she scarcely has time for her own person. Ovid's wife will approach the countenance of Juno.

3.1.163–64:   Ovid's wife is asked to worship the *numen* of Augustus, his son (Tiberius), and his wife.

3.4.95–96:   Livia is urged to prepare for Tiberius' triumph.

4.9.107:   Beside the image of the Divus Augustus stands that of his priestess wife *(coniunxque sacerdos)*.

4.13.29:   Livia is the Vesta of chaste matrons, and it is hard to tell whether she is more worthy of her father or of her son.

Ovid, *Fasti*

1.536:   Ovid prophesies the deification of Livia.

1.640:   Livia alone is worthy to share the couch of great Jove.

1.649:   Livia, alone worthy of the bed of mighty Jove, established (?) *concordia.*

5.157–58:   Livia restored the Bona Dea shrine to imitate her husband in all respects.

6.637:   Livia dedicated a temple to Concordia.

Philo, *Legatio*

291:        Livia was generous to the Temple in Jerusalem.

319–20:   Livia gave golden bowls to the Temple. She was a woman of education and intellect.

Seneca, *De Ira*

3.23.4:   Timagenes the historian said damaging things about Augustus and Livia.

Seneca, *De Clementia*

1.9:   Livia advocates clemency towards Lucius Cinna.

Seneca, *Consolatio ad Marcium*

2–5:   Livia, grief stricken over the death of Drusus, was advised by the philosopher Areus. Octavia hated Livia. Livia accompanied the corpse of Drusus to Rome.

Anonymous, *Apocolocyntosis*

9.5:   Claudius ordered that Livia be made a goddess.

Honestus

SEG 13.348: Augusta has borne two sceptred sons. She is fit to accompany the learned muses, and her mind has preserved the whole world.

Velleius

2.75.2:   Livia's family background, distinction, and marriages.

2.79.2:   Tiberius Nero gave Livia to Octavian for marriage, which boded well for the state.

2.94.1:   Tiberius Nero gave Livia to Octavian for marriage.

2.95.1:   Livia bore Drusus in the house of the Caesars.

2.130.4–5: Tiberius grieved over the death of his mother, a preeminent woman. Her influence was always beneficial.

Valerius Maximus

4.3.3:   After the death of Drusus, Antonia went to live with Livia.
4.5.3:   The victorious Tiberius came to Ticinum to greet Augustus and Livia.
6.1.1:   Pudicitia attends the couch of Livia.

Columella, *de re Rustica*

5.10.11:   The Livian fig is recommended.
10.141:   The Livian fig ripens when Arcturus rises.

Pliny, *Natural History*

7.57:   Augustus and Livia are an example of an otherwise fertile couple who could not have children together.
7.75:   Livia owned the smallest dwarf, Andromeda.
7.150:   Among Augustus' misfortunes were the intrigues of his wife and Tiberius.
10.154:   Livia used an egg to determine the sex of her baby.
12.94:   Livia erected a temple to Augustus on the Palatine, containing a cinnamon root.
14.11:   The Porticus Liviae produced wine.
14.60:   Livia died at the age of 82 [*sic*], after drinking Pucine wine exclusively.
15.129:   The "Royal" laurel is now called the *Augusta*.
15.136–37: An eagle dropped a chick with a laurel sprig in Livia's lap. The sprig grew into a laurel grove.
19.92:   Livia ate elecampane salad.
34.3–4:   Livia owned copper mines in Gaul.

Josephus, *Antiquities*

16.139:   Livia contributed to the celebrations for the founding of Caesarea.
17.10:   Livia dissuaded Salome from marriage to Syllaeus.
17.134–41: A plot involving forged letters from Salome to Livia was exposed.
18.27:   Herod Antipas renamed Betheramphtha after Livia.

Josephus, *Jewish War*

1.566:   Livia advised Salome about her passion for Syllaeus.
1.641:   Antipater forged letters to Livia.
2.168:   Herod Antipas built the city of Julias.

5.562–63:   Vessels sent to the Temple by Augustus and Livia were melted down.

Tacitus, *Annals*

1.3.3–4:   Livia might have been involved in the deaths of Gaius and Lucius. She openly promoted Tiberius' claims and arranged the exile of Agrippa.

1.4.5:   Livia had a female lack of control. People would have to obey a woman.

1.5:   Some suspected Livia of causing Augustus' final illness; she had found out about his plans from Marcia. Livia concealed the death of Augustus until Tiberius could reach the scene.

1.6:   Livia and Tiberius were responsible for the death of Agrippa. Livia was advised to dissuade Tiberius from revealing all the details.

1.8.1:   Livia was Augustus' heir and was adopted into the Julian family and took the Julian name.

1.10.5:   Octavian abducted Tiberius Nero's wife and consulted the pontiffs whether she could be legally married despite her pregnancy.

1.13.6:   Livia saved Haterius.

1.14.1–4:   The Senate voted honours for Livia but Tiberius out of envy insisted on restraint.

1.33.1:   Germanicus was the grandson of Livia.

1.33.3:   Livia had a stepmother's hatred for Agrippina.

1.71.3:   Libellous poems spoke of stress between Tiberius and Livia.

1.72.4:   Satirical verses claimed tension between Livia and Tiberius.

1.73.3:   Actors took part in Livia's Palatine celebrations in honour of Augustus.

2.14.1:   Germanicus dreamt of Livia.

2.34.2–3:   Urgulania was protected against legal action by Livia.

2.42.3:   Livia wrote to Archelaus, but only at the request of her son.

2.43.4:   Livia instructed Plancina to undermine Agrippina.

2.50:   Livia was verbally attacked by Appuleia Varilla, but Tiberius asked that no action be taken.

2.77.3:   Piso enjoyed Livia's secret support.

2.82.1:   Livia intrigued secretly with Plancina.

3.3:   Livia and Tiberius abstained from mourning for Germanicus. They might have prevented Antonia from participating in the ceremonies.

3.15.1:   Plancina acquired a pardon through Livia.

3.16.3:   Piso declared that he had been loyal to Livia.

3.17.1–2:   Tiberius pardoned Plancina through Livia's intercession. This
               caused much offence.

3.34.6:   Livia accompanied Augustus to the East and the West.

3.64:   Tiberius returned to Rome because of his mother's illness, and
               games were instituted. Livia had caused offence over the dedi-
               cation of the Theatre of Marcellus. Games were decreed for her
               recovery.

3.71.1:   The equestrians made vows for Livia's recovery.

4.8.3:   Tiberius made reference to Livia's extreme old age.

4.12:   Livia was drawn into Sejanus' intrigues against Agrippina.

4.15.3:   Asia was given the right to build a temple to Livia, Tiberius, and
               the Senate.

4.16.4:   Livia was granted the right to sit with the Vestals in the theatre.

4.21.1:   Lucius Piso scorned Livia's *potentia*.

4.22.3:   Plautius Silvanus committed suicide after a supposed hint by
               Livia.

4.37.1:   Tiberius refused to allow a temple to be built in Spain for him-
               self and his mother.

4.40.3:   Tiberius cited Livia as an appropriate advisor to her grand-
               daughter Livilla.

4.57.3:   Tiberius could not reject his mother because he owed his power
               to her as her gift. She may have driven him to Capri.

4.71.6:   Livia supported Julia the Younger in her exile.

5.1.1–4:   Livia died in AD 29. Claudian by birth, she was adopted into the
               Livian and Julian houses. Her first husband was Tiberius Nero.
               Smitten by Livia's beauty, Octavian took her from her husband
               and brought her to his home, despite her pregnancy. After this
               she had no offspring. She had old-fashioned virtues. She was a
               demanding mother and an accommodating wife. She matched
               her husband's subtleties, her son's insincerity. Her funeral was
               simple. Her will for a long time was not executed. The funeral
               eulogy was delivered by Caligula.

5.2.1–2:   Tiberius curtailed the tributes paid to Livia and refused her
               divine honours, claiming to act in accordance with her wishes.
               Tiberius attacked the consul Fufius, who had risen through
               Livia's favour.

5.3.1:	The death of Livia removed a restraint on Tiberius, who was instinctively deferential towards his mother. It was believed that she had suppressed a letter from Tiberius denouncing Agrippina and her son.
6.5.3:	Cotta Messalinus commented adversely on Livia's birthday celebration.
6.26.3:	Plancina was protected by Livia.
6.51.3:	While Livia was alive, Tiberius displayed a mixture of good and evil.
12.6.2:	Vitellius told the Senate how they had heard from their fathers that women had been snatched from husbands on the whim of the Caesars.
12.69.4:	Agrippina imitated Livia in arranging the funeral of Claudius.

Plutarch, *Antony*

| 83.4: | Cleopatra hoped that Livia and Octavia would intercede for her. |

Plutarch, *Galba*

| 3.2: | Galba was related to Livia and owed his consulship to her. |

Plutarch, *De garrulitate*

| 508A–B: | Livia learned of Augustus' plans to recall Agrippa Postumus. |

Plutarch, *Peri tou Ei tou en delphois*

| 385F: | Livia dedicated the golden *E* at Delphi. |

Athenaeus, *Deipnosphistae*

| 3.75: | The highly recommended Livian fig grew near Rome. |

Suetonius, *Augustus*

29.4:	Augustus constructed the Porticus Liviae in his wife's name.
40.3:	Livia asked Augustus to grant a Gaul citizenship.
62.2:	Octavian divorced Scribonia and married the pregnant Livia. He remained devoted to her up to his death.
63.1:	Livia bore Augustus no children. There was a conception followed by premature birth.
69.1–2:	Mark Antony charged Octavian with a hasty marriage to Livia and later questioned his marital fidelity.
70.1:	Augustus and entourage celebrated a banquet of the Twelve Gods.

71.1:   Livia reputedly provided Augustus with young girls.

73:            Livia made Augustus' clothes.

84.2:   Augustus wrote out beforehand what he would say to Livia.

99.1:   Augustus died in the arms of Livia, bidding her farewell.

101.2:   Augustus appointed Livia as chief legatee, with one-third of the estate.

Suetonius, *Tiberius*

4.3:   After returning from exile, Tiberius Nero gave up the pregnant Livia to Octavian.

6.1–3:   Livia endured many perils during her first husband's exile.

7.1:   Tiberius put on gladiatorial shows in honour of his father and of his grandfather Drusus at Livia and Augustus' expense.

10.2:   Livia begged Tiberius not to go to Rhodes.

12.1:   Livia secured a *legatio* for Tiberius while he was in Rhodes.

13.2:   Livia lobbied for Tiberius' return from Rhodes.

14.2:   Livia sought an omen for Tiberius' birth by hatching an egg.

21.2:   Livia begged Augustus to adopt Tiberius.

21.7:   Augustus and Livia were concerned for Tiberius' well-being.

28:            Tiberius was tolerant of verbal abuses against him and his family.

50.2–3:   Tiberius was angry at his mother's demands to share power, avoided meeting her, and avoided confidential conversations so that he would not seem to be guided by her advice — though in fact he did sometimes follow it. He refused her honorific titles and was annoyed when she helped during a fire.

51.1–2:   Tiberius appointed a man as juror at his mother's bidding. Livia read out letters of Augustus complaining to her about Tiberius. This may have been why he left Rome. Tiberius gave Livia a modest funeral. The decomposing body hastened the rite. Tiberius disregarded her will and punished her followers.

Suetonius, *Caligula*

7:             Livia dedicated a statue of her dead great-grandson.

10:            Caligula lived with Livia and gave her funeral eulogy.

14.2:   Livia's privileges were given also to Antonia.

16.3:   Caligula paid out Livia's bequests.

23.2:   Caligula referred to Livia as Ulixes Stolatus and claimed that she had a humble grandfather.

Suetonius, *Claudius*

1.1: Drusus was born within three months of the marriage of Livia and Octavian, and there was speculation that he was the latter's son. People joked about a "three-month child."

3.2–4.6: Augustus corresponded with Livia on family matters.

11.3: Claudius arranged divine honours for Livia and a chariot drawn by elephants in the circus.

41.2: Livia discouraged Claudius from writing on the civil war period.

Suetonius, *Galba*

1: An eagle dropped a chick with a laurel sprig in Livia's lap.

5.1: Livia bequeathed a legacy to Galba which Tiberius did not pay.

Suetonius, *Otho*

1.1: Otho's grandfather was reared by Livia.

Marcus Aurelius, *Meditations*

8.31: Livia and all the court of Augustus are dead.

Dio

48.15.2: Livia accompanied her husband out of Campania, then out of Sicily.

48.34.3: Augustus was beginning to fall in love with Livia.

48.44: Livia was six months pregnant when she married Octavian, who sought clearance from the pontiffs about the wedding. Tiberius Nero gave Livia in marriage just as a father would. At a party a slave boy confused Octavian and Tiberius Nero as husbands of Livia. When Drusus was born after the marriage Octavian returned the child to his natural father. People coined a proverb about the lucky having a child in three months.

48.52.3–4: An eagle dropped a chick with a laurel sprig in Livia's lap.

49.15.1 (cf. 49.18.6): Livia was granted the right to host a banquet in the Temple of Capitoline Jupiter (or Temple of Concord) on the anniversary of the battle on Naulochus.

49.38.1: Livia and Octavia were granted statues, the right to administer their own affairs without a guardian, and the same *sacrosanctitas* enjoyed by the tribunes.

51.13.3: After Actium, Cleopatra pretended to hope for Livia's intercession.

53.33.4:	Livia was suspected of causing the death of Marcellus.
54.7.2:	Augustus rewarded Sparta for its hospitality towards Livia.
54.16.4–5:	Augustus claimed to instruct Livia on matters of dress and deportment. The senators did not believe him.
54.19.3:	Augustus made Terentia and Livia compete in a beauty contest.
55.2.4:	Livia and Julia organised a feast for women for Tiberius' *ovatio*.
55.2.5:	On Drusus' death, Livia was granted statues and the *ius trium liberorum*.
55.8.2:	With Tiberius, Livia dedicated the Porticus Liviae and held a banquet for the women.
55.9.8:	Before departing for Rhodes, Tiberius opened his will in front of Augustus and Livia.
55.10a.10:	Livia was suspected of the deaths of Gaius and Lucius.
55.11.3:	Thrasyllus predicted that a ship would come to Rhodes with a message from Livia and Augustus.
55.14–22.2:	Livia counselled Augustus in the Cinna case.
55.32.2:	Agrippa Postumus spoke ill of Livia as a stepmother.
56.17.1:	When it came to the bestowing of honours on the dead Augustus, Livia played a full role as if she were sole ruler.
56.30.1–2:	Livia was suspected of murdering Augustus with poisoned figs because of his rapprochement with Agrippa.
56.31.1:	Some say that Livia postponed announcing the death of Augustus.
56.32.1:	Livia inherited one-third of Augustus' estate, more than she was allowed by law.
56.42.4:	Livia placed Augustus' bones in his mausoleum.
56.46:	Livia became a priestess of Divus Augustus, with a lictor. She gave money to a man who had seen Augustus' soul on the way to heaven. With Tiberius she built a temple to Augustus. She founded the Ludi Palatini.
56.47.1:	Tiberius and Livia were responsible for the decrees passed to honour Augustus on his death.
57.3.3:	Tiberius rejected the notion that he had received power from Livia, whom he hated.
57.3.6:	Some thought that Livia put Agrippa to death.
57.12.1–6:	Tiberius tried to keep Livia in check. Livia was in a position of unprecedented power for a woman. She received senators at her home. Tiberius' letters bore her name. Without any overt show

she exercised power. She sought to have precedence over Tiberius. Special honours were sought for Livia, which irritated Tiberius. Tiberius forbade her from celebrating at her house because of the expense. He removed Livia from public life, but she continued to be a nuisance. She was the main cause of his leaving Rome for Capri.

57.16.2: Livia helped the victims of fires.

57.18.6: Livia and Tiberius were pleased by Germanicus' death.

57.19.1: Tiberius prosecuted *maiestas* cases involving his mother.

58.2.1–6: Livia died at the age of eighty-six. Tiberius did not visit her when she was ill and took no measures other than arranging the funeral. He forbade deification. The Senate voted mourning by women for a year. The Senate voted an arch in Livia's honour, because she had reared the children of many and had helped to pay daughters' dowries. Some called her mother of the country. She was buried in the mausoleum. Tiberius did not pay her bequests. Livia claimed that for a chaste woman naked men had no appeal. Livia claimed that she exercised influence over Augustus by playing the role of the proper Roman wife. Tiberius did not build her arch because of the expense.

58.4.5–6: Tiberius destroyed Fufius Geminus and his family because of their friendship with Livia.

59.1.4: Tiberius did not pay out Livia's bequests.

59.2.3: Caligula finally paid out Livia's bequests.

60.2.5: Claudius lived for a long time with Livia.

60.5.2: Claudius consecrated Livia and entrusted her worship to the Vestals.

60.22.2: Messalina was granted some of Livia's privileges.

60.33.12: All Livia's privileges were bestowed on Agrippina the Younger.

63.29.3: On Nero's death, the laurels planted by Livia died.

Porphyry on Horace's *Odes*
4.4.28: Livia was pregnant when she joined Octavian.

Aurelius Victor, *Caesares*
1.7: Augustus was unlucky in his marriage.

5.17: With Nero's death, the laurel groves and white chickens died also.

Anonymous, *Epitome de Caesaribus*

1.23:   Octavian married Livia from passion, with her husband essen-
            tially approving. Livia had two sons.

1.27:   Some ascribe Augustus' death to Livia, because of his rap-
            prochement with Agrippa Postumus, whom she had exiled.

Macrobius, *Satires*

5.2.6:   The entourages of Livia and of Julia are contrasted.

3.20.1:   Cloatius is cited on the Livian fig.

Prudentius, *Contra Symmachum*

1.251–70,   The worship of Livia as Juno is attacked, especially in light of

292:        her disgraceful marriage.

Marcellus Empiricus, *De Medicina*

15.6:   Livia's recipe for a sore throat.

35.6:   Livia's recipe for chills.

MATERIAL SOURCES

Portraits

Sculpture

Before Livia's time, Romans had been distinctly unenthusiastic about the
notion of erecting statues to women. It comes as no surprise that in 194 BC the
redoubtable Cato the Elder, always thoroughly reliable when we need to see
Rome at her most reactionary, condemned the notion of women's statues in
the provinces.[49] It was only with the emergence of the *domus Augusta* that this
attitude changed, and the turning point can be seen as early as 35 BC, when
statues of Livia and her sister-in-law Octavia received official sanction. As the
wife of the first princeps, Livia became the first woman in Roman history to be
honoured on a major scale by sculpted portraits.

It is now accepted that the surviving portraits of members of the imperial
families go back to a limited number of types, probably produced under official supervision in Rome and distributed throughout the empire, to be copied
locally. At the initial stage there could be firm control over the likenesses
produced, but once the process of replication had begun, individual artists
would no doubt add their own idiosyncratic variations to their commissioned
works. There will never be unanimity about what constitutes a "type" in the
case of any given individual, and the process of defining the prototypes on the

basis of their replicas is charged with difficulties. The basic principle is simple enough. We assign to types those portraits that seem to share common features. But typology is not an exact science, and ultimately instinct and aesthetic sensibility will influence, or even be part of, scholarly judgement. The situation is further complicated by the inevitable idealization of revered figures like Livia. Her images showed a dogged reluctance to reflect Livia's increasing age. Also, given the prominence of Livia, artists outside of Rome might well have been influenced by the pervasive familiarity of her portraits when they undertook commissions to depict her contemporaries. Consequently, it may at times be difficult to distinguish Livia's image from those of other Julio-Claudian women, particularly Octavia and Julia the Elder.

It is rare indeed for any Roman sculpted portrait still to be accompanied by its identifying inscription. Only one possible Livian example is known, and as we shall see, it is much disputed. The identification of portraits of the male members of the imperial house, especially the emperors themselves, is much aided by comparison with their heads on imperial coins. This procedure can be of some limited use for the women, but in the case of Livia there is no indisputable representation on official coins. She is identified on provincial coins, but their value for precise portraiture is more limited.

The first scholar to attempt a systematic approach to the study of representations of Livia's portraits was Bernoulli, in 1886. Later generations have built on his work, and in recent years there has been much active scholarship of high quality in this field. In 1962 Gross produced an important and useful monograph on Livia's portraits, which was supplemented by the weighty contributions of Vagn Poulsen in 1973 and of Fittschen and Zanker in 1983. Bartman and Winkes have both recently published valuable catalogues and studies of Livia's portraits. Although not devoted exclusively to Livia, Rose's work on sculptural groups and Woods' on the portraits of Julio-Claudian women have made further very useful contributions to Livian iconography.

In light of the high calibre of recent contributions to the subject, I present just a brief summary of the current thinking on Livian typology here. Two broad principles can be applied to her portraits. One is simple, perhaps crude, but valid. There is a massive corpus of portraits of the early imperial period that share common features and can generally be taken to represent the same woman. Their sheer number precludes for practical purpose their assignment to any other person. The second principle is one already recognised by Bernoulli. Livia could be expected to be found in family groups, where often other members have been securely identified. A valuable illustration of this last point is provided by a group from Arsinoe, in the Fayum region of Egypt. Three marble busts have survived, two of which can be securely assigned to Augustus and Tiberius. The third is of a woman who so closely resembles Tiberius that she can hardly be anyone other than his mother (figs. 12, 26, 27). The head is a familiar one of the period (the Fayum type), and comparable replicas can similarly be attributed to Livia.[50]

There are two basic groups of Livian portraits.

The Nodus Group

Scholars are in broad agreement that this group is the first of the two, generally in vogue 38 BC–AD 14, although the temporal range is by no means rigid. It is named for the wide knot (nodus) created when the hair is rolled forward at the middle of the head, then drawn back to form a topknot. At the sides the hair is rolled back in plaits to behind the head, where it is bound in a bun. To soften its severity, short wisps may be allowed to appear on the forehead and temples, at the front of the ears, and at the back of the neck.

Within the nodus group different types have been identified. There is a general scholarly consensus about an early Marbury Hall type, named after the country house in Cheshire that once held a striking example. Here the nodus is broad and flat and the hair at the side is woven tightly into twisted braids. Winkes notes that this type is closest to Livia's portraits on Alexandrian coins (fig. 14). Close to this, most scholars (although not Bartman) recognise another major type, probably chronologically later than Marbury Hall, the Albani-Bonn type, named after two examples in the Villa Albani in Rome and the Akademisches Museum in Bonn. Here the nodus is larger and the hair around the face is thicker (fig. 13). The Marbury Hall and Albani-Bonn types tend to show Livia with a rather elongated oval face.[51]

The Fayum type is the most representative in terms of surviving examples. It broadens Livia's head and makes the lower part more triangular. The nose is strong, the lips small and very curved. The chin is small and firm. The details of the hair are reduced.[52] Wood notes that this type gives Livia a facial shape much closer to that of Augustus, with his characteristically Julian triangular face, and allows a fictitious resemblance of Augustus to his adoptive son Tiberius.

One group of nodus portraits is identified by some scholars as a separate type, the Zopftyp, in which two braids cover the sides of the heads, sometimes instead of, sometimes in addition to, the usual twisted plaits of hair that run along the same area. The earliest examples of the type are found on coins of Pergamum, where Livia is clearly identified by name, and it may represent a local creation in Asia Minor (fig. 15).[53]

The Centre-Parting Group.

The hair now has a centre parting and falls down at each side to frame the face in a series of waves (figs. 17, 21). The tresses at the back are drawn into a tight bun at the neck. There are no shoulder locks. (The head on the Ara Pacis [a representation of Livia, rather than a likeness] is a notable exception.) The centre-parting coiffure is widely adopted in portraits from AD 14. But the nodus style continues, for not all the sculptors would have had access to the new type, and many would simply have preferred the traditional old-fashioned style. The centre-parting group is a large one, and a wide range of varieties have been detected. It is less easy to categorise than its predecessor and there is much disagreement about precise types and precise dating, and general uncertainty in applying terms such as *type* or *group*. It seems unlikely that in her sixties Livia would have sat for a new type in the strict sense, and the sculptors may have adapted existing models. It is commonly referred to as the salus group or type, the name being derived from the portrait in the Salus Augusta dupondius of Tiberius (fig. 4).[54]

Among the earlier examples is a group sometimes classed as the Kiel type, in which the locks at the side of the centre parting bulge more heavily than the rest of the hair and rise to create almost a halo effect. The ends are drawn back into a bun that is split horizontally, a relic of the nodus style. Others, possibly of this early group but perhaps later, arrange the waves into a series of parallel bands.[55] These examples might be considered transitional, before what Winkes call the core group *(Kerngruppe)*. This last consists of the posthumous portraits that follow Livia's consecration under Claudius. The hair now waves back from the centre parting in parallel lines. The face is idealised and very regular, with wide cheeks and large, wide-set eyes.

Inscribed Bronze Busts

Two small bronze busts have survived from the town of Neuilly-le-Réal, which, if genuine, are a remarkable, indeed unique, find, for they represent a matched set of Livia and Augustus, identified by inscriptions. These read, *Caesari Augusto / Atespatus Crixi fi. v.s.l.m (votum solvit libens merito)* and *Liviae Augustae / Atespatus Crixi fil. v.s.l.m. . . .*, purporting to record that Atespatus, the son of Crixus, fulfilled the dedications, to Caesar Augustus and Livia Augusta (fig. 18).[56] The fortunate combination of a matched pair, identified by name, seems almost too good to be true, and indeed the absence of a proper archaeological context and the very fine state of preservation of these items have led some scholars to question their authenticity. Adding to this doubt is the oddity of the name, Livia Augusta, not otherwise known in any inscription.

The fact that this casual form is favoured by Suetonius is not reassuring, for Suetonius would have been an obvious literary source for a forger.[57] Balancing these doubts, however, it must be noted that there is no positive evidence indicating a forgery, and analysis conducted at the Louvre has revealed that the metallic content of the bronze is consistent with ancient pieces. Most modern scholars are willing to accept their genuineness.

The pieces are of inferior provincial workmanship, intended for the private ownership of someone of limited means, perhaps similar to the bronze statuette of Augustus as a boy, with the cognomen Thurinus, obtained by Suetonius.[58] Their provincial origin and modest workmanship would explain their "realism," because they would not have adhered to patterns of the official idealised portraits. Hence they show signs of aging, although their precise dates are difficult to determine. The absence of Divus in Augustus' name should mean that they were sculpted during Augustus' lifetime, but the presence of Augusta in Livia's would place them after his death. Livia's cheeks are drawn, she has bags under her eyes and deep folds from the sides of the nose to the outer edges of the lips. These features are matched by the lines on Augustus' forehead.

Livia's bust has a nodus hairstyle, of a variant that is not typical of sculpted heads but is found in more casual media. The nodus style is usually combined with small wisps of hair that fall behind the ears. The long shoulder locks on the Neuilly bust are unknown in other freestanding portraits securely identified as Livia's. This feature, again, might point to a provincial origin.

Other Media

It is safe to assume that Livia would have appeared in a wide range of media: on cups, lamps, and various items of domestic function. Most of these ephemeral items will now be lost, and among those that have survived it is likely that the image of Livia, often crudely executed, will not be recognised.

Gems

The most significant of this subgroup is represented by carved gems made from semiprecious stones. They would not have circulated widely but have remained in the private ownership of their well-to-do owners, allowing much more freedom in the subject matter.[59] This has produced some striking images. The most famous is probably the Grand Camée. There has been much debate about the meaning of the scene, but many accept that it represents the departure of Germanicus for his eastern mission, although the piece may have been engraved in the Claudian period. On this interpretation the seated central figure is Tiberius, who bestows the task on Germanicus, who faces him. Livia, seated by Tiberius, holds the poppies and corn ears of Ceres and dominates the centre of the composition.[60]

A striking gem in Vienna, made from gilded green glass, perhaps in imitation of carved stone, depicts a jugate pair of Augustus, wearing a laurel, and Livia, who has the nodus hairstyle.[61] Also in Vienna, a sardonyx depicts a diademed Livia as Cybele and priestess of Divus Augustus, holding a bust of Augustus and ears of corn, to create an allusion to Ceres also. She wears a stola and wisps of hair hang down the neck (fig. 19).[62] Livia is given the attributes of Ceres on a cameo in Florence, where she is portrayed jugate with Tiberius. He wears a laurel crown; his mother has a garland of poppies and ears of corn held in place by a crescent diadem. She wears a stola, the costume of a living woman. Her type is one that is generally dated early, further suggesting a living rather than posthumous portrait (fig. 11).[63]

A less expensive form of glass is represented by a number of flasks shaped like a female head. The hair is arranged in a severe style, with a nodus over the forehead and corkscrew curls falling from the bun at the back of the head. The flasks are meant to be seen in profile, for a seam runs down the centre of the face. The heads have been identified as those of Livia, perhaps as a personification of a goddess such as Hera.[64]

Tesserae

Token coinage, usually in the form of lead *jetons* (tesserae), but also in other metals or materials, was widely used in the Roman empire, sometimes by officials to regulate such activities as the distribution of grain or entry into the public games, and sometimes privately, presumably for business reasons. These tesserae often bore the portraits of the imperial family. Livia is depicted on a lead tessera in very poor condition now in the Terme Museum in Rome, with a female head on the obverse identified as Augusta. A carpentum appears on the reverse, drawn by two mules. This is clearly in imitation of the Tiberian carpentum sestertius of AD 22–33 (fig. 10). A lead example in Berlin depicts a bust of Livia, identified as Iulia Augusta, in the guise of Demeter, with a crown of grain.[65]

Gaming Counters

One fascinating subgroup of Livian portraits identified by inscriptions comprises those that appear on small game counters of bone or ivory. It is generally recognised that they originated in Alexandria, although the precise nature of the game is far from clear. It seems that it required counters numbered 1–15 and that the "fronts" had a series of pictures, such as sets of animals or

Egyptian landmarks or famous people, including rulers. Examples have been found with Livia's portrait for pieces numbered 2, 4, and possibly 6, thoughtfully provided in both Roman and Greek numerals.[66] An example of a Livian counter is preserved in the National Museum in Naples.[67] In the game it is numbered 4. The portrait is identified by the name (in Greek) LIBIA. It is unquestionably genuine, but of little value for determining Livia's portrait, as the quality of the carving is quite poor. The hair has the centre parting. A well-preserved example has survived in Knossos, from the Roman colony level, with the legend in Greek *Libia* and the number 2. The head has the nodus hairstyle, with thick shoulder locks. The carving is detailed, but the features are very heavy, and very stylised.[68] Another piece found in Oxyrhynchus in Egypt and now in Alexandria has been the object of some debate. The figure is identified, in Greek, as *Ioulia*, and is numbered 6, again in both Latin and Greek. The carving is better than in the earlier examples, and the face has more personality. It has full cheeks and lips, and a small chin. The hair is in the nodus style with the characteristic strands falling down the neck, thicker and longer than on most nodus types, but less so than on the Neuilly bronze. The head may be intended to be Julia's rather than Livia's, but as Alföldi-Rosenbaum points out, a later owner of the game would certainly have assumed the head to be that of Augustus' wife.[69]

Ceramic and Metalwork

Boschung has identified as Livia the profile bust of a woman on a first-century ceramic lamp found at Belo near Cádiz. She has a nodus hairstyle and faces the profile laureate bust of Augustus. Imperial portraits on lamps are very rare.[70] It has been suggested that Livia is depicted on one of the two splendid silver vessels known as the Boscoreale cups.[71] An Arretine drinking vessel from Vetera bears a diademed bust of a woman on a column facing left towards a man's bust on a column, identified by Lehner as Augustus and Livia.[72] Also from the Rhine area is another piece of provincial workmanship, a bronze plaque intended to decorate a sword sheath. It represents a frontal Livia with the nodus hairstyle and shoulder locks arranged to flow along her shoulders above the drapery. She appears between two young men, facing slightly towards her. The figure to the right bears a resemblance to known heads of Tiberius, and the other must represent Drusus. This item presumably belongs to the lifetime of Drusus, and is thus earlier than 9 BC.[73]

Paintings

We know that painted images of Livia and other members of the imperial family were carried at the festival at Gytheum (see chapter 10), and similar items for Livia and her grandsons are recorded at Ephesus.[74] She may have been honoured in the paintings that decorated the villa in Boscotrecase on the Bay of Naples, thought to have belonged to Marcus Agrippa, possibly commissioned shortly after his death by the widowed Julia.[75] Livia and Julia have been identified in the roundels inserted into the tops of elegant corner columns, possibly meant to replicate full-scale tondi. They have the nodus hairstyle and the long shoulder locks seen at Neuilly.

INSCRIPTIONS

Inscriptions are an important historical tool. They are particularly valuable for social history and for the reconstruction of the careers of prominent individuals. With some notable exceptions, the value of inscriptions for more narrowly political history may be limited. The majority involve dedications or other distinctions for the imperial family in the provinces, where the nomenclature does not always conform to official Roman practice (as in the striking example from Mytilene, where during the early phases of Augustus' reign Livia is called Julia). Moreover, they often reflect local interests and as such cannot be taken necessarily to reflect an official programme from Rome. There is a large corpus of inscriptions relating to Livia, their chief value being to show how highly she was regarded by the communities of the empire, and how consistently this was expressed, from the relatively early years of her marriage to beyond her death.

Frequent reference is made to the "Arval record." The cult centre of the Arval Brotherhood lay to the west of Rome, just outside the city limits, at the shrine of Dea Dia, but their rites were also carried out in the city. The college kept a record of its rituals inscribed on stone. These texts have survived in fragmentary sections from 21 BC to AD 304 and provide valuable information on the activities of the imperial family, who occupy a prominent place in the rituals.

The following is not meant to be an exhaustive catalogue. Nor does it offer any sophisticated epigraphical analysis. It is intended essentially as a checklist, and the basis for further study. Place names are given in either the ancient or modern form, whichever is the more familiar or the more conventional. Where the province is not named, a location in Italy should be assumed. The dating is added if internal content provides information not already obvious from material provided. Allusions to Divus Augustus or to Julia Augusta, for example, can normally be assumed to postdate Augustus' death. The list does not include the numerous sepulchral inscriptions for slaves, freedmen, and freedwomen who adopted Livia's name or identify her as their mistress.

Reference is generally limited to the most widely available source material. Abbreviations refer to the catalogues in the following works: H=Hahn (1992); M=Mikocki (1995); R=Rose (1997); B=Bartman (1999). Curved brackets (...) are used to fill out abbreviations. Square brackets [...] are used in the original text to indicate restorations. Square brackets are used in the translations only, to indicate where the translation is dependent on a major restoration.

Neo-Punic

Leptis Magna, Africa

Translation: Rose (1995), 182–84, Cat. 125; G. L. della Vida, "Due iscrizioni imperiali neo-puniche di Leptis Magna." *AfrIt* 6 (1935): 1–29.
Group portrait dedication to Rome and Augustus, Tiberius, Julia Augusta, Germanicus, Drusus Caesar, Agrippina the Elder, Livilla, Antonia and Vipsania Agrippina.
AD 23–31
B 57; R 125; Kokkinos (1992), 45

Bilingual (Latin and Greek)

IGR 4.1392, *CIL* 3.7107: Smyrna, Asia
Augustae Caesaris Augusti Matri (Latin)
Sebastei Kai[saros Sebastou metri (Greek)
Augusta, wife of Caesar Augustus, mother (of Tiberius)
B 64

IGR 1.1033, *CIL* 3.8: Cyrenae, Cyrene
Iuliae Augustae (Latin)
Ioulian Sebasten (Greek)
Julia Augusta
Tiberian
B 41

Latin

Arval Record, Rome

CIL 6.32340.17
Iulia[e Augustae
January 11, 21

AFA xxxiii*a*.7
Iuliae Augustae
January 4, 27

AFA xxxiii*a*.11
[Iulia Augusta]
January 4, 27

AFA xxxiv*e*.2
Iuliae A[ugustae]
January 30, 27

AFA xxxviii.3
[Iuliae Augusta]e
January 3, before 29

AFA xliii*c*.2
Iuliae Augustae
January 30, 38

AFA lv.10
Di[vae] Augustae
January 6–12, 43–48

AFA lv.16
Divae Aug(ustae)
January 17, 43–48

AFA lv.19
Divae Augusta]e
January 17, 43–48

AE (1969–70), no. 1 (Arval fragment)
Divae Au]g(ustae)
September 23, 43–48
Restoration uncertain.

AFA lxiii.6
Div[ae Augustae]
57

AFA lxvii*d*.18
Divae [Aug](ustae)
January 3, 57

AFA lxix.12
Divae Aug(ustae)
October 13, 58

AFA lxxi.45
Divae Aug(ustae)
January 3, 59

AFA lxxv.44
Divae Aug(ustae)
October 12, 59

AFA lxxvii.29
Divae Aug(ustae)
January 3, 60

AFA xcd.15
[Diva]e Aug(ustae)
January 3, 69

AFA xcii.52
Divae Aug(ustae)
January 30, 69

AFA xciii.80
Divae Aug(ustae)
March 14, 80

Fasti

EJ, p. 46 Fasti Verulani, Verulae
Augusta
January 17
Referring to an event of 38 BC.

EJ, p. 48 Fasti Praenestini, Praeneste
Iulia Augusta
April 23, AD 22

CIL 6.1178: Rome
ma]cello Liviae
market of Livia (on Esquiline)

ILS 4995 (EJ 125): Rome
aeditus templi divi Aug(usti) [e]t Divae Augustae
superintendent of the temple of Divus Augustus and Diva Augusta

CIL 11.3859: Rome
Dianae Augustae
Augusta Diana

CIL 6.883: Rome
Livia (D)rusi f. uxs[or
Livia, daughter of Drusus, wife (of Augustus)
Dedication of Temple to Fortuna Muliebris.

CIL 5.6416 (Codex Einsidlensis 326): Rome(?)
Livia[e] / Drusi f./uxori Caesaris Aug
Livia daughter of Drusus wife of Caesar Augustus
Long thought to belong to an arch at Pavia, but now see Rose, *JRA* 3 (1990),
    163–69.
AD 7–8
B 18

CIL 15.7264: Rome, Palatine "Casa di Livia"
Iuliae Aug(ustae)
Julia Augusta
After AD 14

CIL 14.399: Ostia
Flaminicae / D[i]vae Aug(ustae)
Priestess of Goddess Augusta

CIL 9.787: Luceria
[Iuliae] / Augusta[e] / Divi Augu[sti
[Julia] Augusta wife of Divus Augustus
B 58

EJ 225; Smallwood (1967), 255: Teate Marrucinorum
C. Herennius . . . Capito . . . proc(urator) Iuliae Augustae
Gaius Herennius Capito, procurator of Julia Augusta
After AD 37

CIL 9.3304: Superaequum
L]iviae Drusi f(iliae) / Augusti / ma]tri Ti (berii) Caesaris et / [Drusi Ger-
    manici

Livia the daughter of Drusus, wife of Augustus, mother of Tiberius Caesar and
     [Drusus Germanicus]
After AD 4
B 22

CIL 15.7814: Tusculum
T]i(berii) Caesaris et Iuliae Augu[stae
of Tiberius Caesar and Julia Augusta
After AD 14

ILS 157: Interamna
saluti perpetuae Augustae
the perpetual health of Augusta
or the health of the perpetual Augusta
B 54; Gross (1962) 19 n. 32 (not Livia); see Hahn (1992), 96 n. 338

CIL 10.7489: Lipari, Sicily
procurator(i) Ti Caesar(is) / Aug(usti) et Iuliae August(ae)
the procurator of Tiberius Caesar Augustus and Julia Augusta

CIL 2.3320, 11.3322: Forum Cassi
[au]gusta Iuli[a]
Julia Augusta

CIL 11.1165: Velleia
[Iuli]ae Divi / A[ugusti] f(iliae) Augustae / matri Ti Caesaris / [Di]v[i Au]gusti
     f(ilii) / Aug[usti e]t Neronis / [C]lau[di] Dru[si]
[Julia] Augusta daughter of Divus Augustus, mother of Tiberius Caesar Au-
     gustus, son of Divus Augustus and Nero Claudius Drusus
Caligulan
B 76

ILS 123: Herculaneum
Divae Augustae
Diva Augusta
B 74

ILS 125: Marruvium
Alfidia M. f(ilia) mater Augustae
Alfidia, daughter of Marcus, mother of Augusta
After AD 14

ILS 122: Pompeii
Augustae Iulia[e] / Drusi f(iliae) / divi Augusti
To Julia Augusta, daughter of Drusus, wife of Divus Augustus

CIL 10.1023 (= 2340): Pompeii
Iunoni / Tyches Iuliae / Augustae
Julia Augusta, Juno, Fortune
M 61

CIL 6.29681: Trebula(?)
natali Iuliae August(ae)
on the birthday of Julia Augusta
AD 108

ILS 1.118 = *CIL* 14.3575: Tibur
Liviae Caesaris / Augusti
Livia the wife of Caesar Augustus
B 25

CIL 9.4514: Ager Amiternus
Augustae Iuliae / Drusi f(iliae) / Divi Augusti
Julia Augusta, daughter of Drusus, wife of Divus Augustus
B 29

AE 1927, no. 158: Cumae
Iuliae Augustae
(statues) of Julia Augusta
B 40; Rose 8

CIL 10.7340: Himera, Sicily
Iul(iae) Matri Imp(eratoris) Cae(saris)
Julia mother of Imperator Caesar

ILS 119 = *CIL* 10.7464): Haluntium, Sicily
Liviae Augusti / deae
Livia, wife of Augustus, goddess
Claudian
B 73

ILS 121 (EJ 126): Malta (Gaulos)
Cereri Iuliae Augustae / divi Augusti, matri / Ti. Caesaris Augusti / Lutatia ...
   sacerdos Augustae / ... consacravit

Lutatia the priestess of Augusta consecrated . . . to Julia Augusta Ceres wife of
 Divus Augustus mother of Tiberius Caesar Augustus
B 50; M 1

AE 1976, no. 185: Furcona
[Iuliae A]ugustae / [Drusi f(iliae) uxori Divi Au]gusti, Germanico / Caesari, Ti
 Augusi / [f(ilio)
[Julia] Augusta [daughter of Drusus, wife of Divus] Augustus and to Ger-
 manicus Caesar [son of] Tiberius Augustus
AD 14–19
B 49

ILS 154 (EJ 101): Forum Clodii, Etruria
natali Augustae
dedicatione statuarum Caesarum et Augustae
on the birthday of the Augusta
on the dedication of statues of the Caesars and the Augusta
AD 18
B 47; R 11 (with translation)

CIL 11.7552: Forum Clodii, Etruria
[Aug]ustae Iuliae / Drusi f(iliae)/[Divi] Augusti
Julia Augusta, daughter of Drusus wife of [Divus] Augustus
B 58

AE 1988, no. 422: Corfinum
[flaminica] Iulia(e) Augusta(e)
[priestess] of Julia Augusta

CIL 11.7416: Ager Viterbiensis, Etruria
Iuliae Drusi [f. Augustae] Ti. Caesaris [Aug(usti) et] Drusi Germani[ci matri]
Julia [Augusta] daughter of Drusus, mother of Tiberius Caesar [Augustus] and
 Drusus Germanicus

CIL 10.459: Buxentum, Lucania
Augustae Iulia(e) Drusi f. divi Augusti
Augusta Julia, daughter of Drusus, wife of Divus Augustus

CIL 10.8060: Herculaneum
Aug(usta)
Augusta
Attested by Bayardi (1755), 403 on a inscribed cornelian, now apparently lost

and clearly not the same as the cornelian from Herculaneum recorded by
Pannuti (1983), no. 213; see Winkes (1995), no. 172.

CIL 10.1620: Puteoli
[Iu]lia August[a]
Julia Augusta

CIL 11.6709.33: Falerii
Liv[ia] Caesar[is
Livia wife of Caesar

CIL 11.7488: Falerii
Livi[a] Caesari[s]
Livia wife of Caesar
B 12; M 60

CIL 6.882a: Falerone
Augustae Iuliae Drusi f(filiae)
to Julia Augusta daughter of Drusus
B 46

CIL 9.1098: Aeclanum
Iononi Augustae
Juno Augusta or Augustan Juno
B 4

CIL 9.1155: Aeclanum
Divae Augustae
Goddess Augusta
Original lost, texts offer variants *Augustinae* and *Faustinae*.

CIL 9.1105: Aeclanum
Juliae Aug(ustae)
To Julia Augusta
B 28

Inscr. It. 10.3.1, no. 113: Polla
Insteia . . . sacerd(os) Iuliae / Augustae
Insteia priestess of Julia Augusta

Inscr. It. 10.5.1, no. 247: Brixia, Venetia
[P]ostumi[ae] . . . Paullae . . . sacerd(oti) Div[a]i August(ae)
To Postumia Paulla priestess of the Goddess Augusta

CIL 10.6309: Suara, Tarracina
C]aesari Divi Aug f. Augusto . . . Divae Augus[tae
Caesar Augustus son of Divus Augustus, Goddess Augusta

CIL 11.6172: Suara, Tarracina, Latium
Divae Augustae
Goddess Augusta

AE 1975, no. 403: Albengo / Albingaunum, Liguria
D[ivae Aug(ustae]
Goddess Augusta
Heavily restored.

AE 1982, no. 415: Gualdrasco, Transpadana
Divae Aug(ustae)
Goddess Augusta

AE 1988 no. 607: Collegno, Transpadana
[. . . divae Dru]sillae et divae Augu[stae
Goddess Drusilla and goddess Augusta
As restored, the worship of Drusilla, Caligula's sister, is linked with Livia's.

ILS 1321: Vasio, Narbonensis
proc[uratori] Augustae
to the procurator of Augusta
Dedication to Sextus Afranius Burrus, recorded as procurator of Livia.
After AD 51

ILS 6991: Vasio, Narbonensis
flam(inicae) / Iul(iae) Aug(ustae)
priestess of Julia Augusta

CIL 12.4249: Baeteris, Narbonensis
flaminica / Iuliae Augustae
priestess of Julia Augusta

CIL 12.1845: Vienne, Narbonensis
[Divae Augustae]
Deified Augusta
Preserved in a drawing of holes left after the removal of letters.
AD 42–45

ILS 112: Narbo, Narbonensis

imp(eratori) Caesari . . . Augusto . . . coniugi liberis gentique eius senatui / poluloque Romano et colonis incolisque

Imperator Caesar Augustus and his wife and children and family and the Senate and the Roman people and the colonists and inhabitants

AD 12–13

CIL 13.1366: Neuilly-le-Réal, Aquitania

Liviae Augustae

to Livia Augusta

On the base of inscribed bronze statues to Livia (with matching item for Augustus).

Fishwick (1987–92), II.1, 535

ILS 3208 (*CIL* 13.4769): Lugdunum, Lugdunensis

Mercurio Augusto et Maiae Augustae sacrum

Sacred to Mercury Augustus (or Augustan mercury) and Maia Augusta (or Augustan Maia)

M 103

AE 1980 no. 638: Lugdumum, Lugdunensis

[Augusta Iuli]a / [Drusi] f

Augusta Iulia daughter of Drusus

Massively restored.

CIL 2.3102: Segobriga, Tarraconsesis

Liviae [Drusi f. uxori Caesaris Aug(usti) matri Ti(berii) Caesaris] / aviae [Germanici et Drusi Iuliorum Tiberii) f.

Livia [daughter of Drusus, wife of Augustus mother of Tiberius Caesar] grandmother [of Germanicus and Drusus, Julii, sons of Tiberius]

AE 1966, no. 177: Santarem, Lusitania

flamen provinc(iae) Lusitaniae Divi Aug(usti) [et] Divae Augustae

Priest of Divus Augustus and Diva Augusta for the province of Lusitania

AD 48

AE 1915, no. 95, Emerita, Lusitania

[C]n. Cornelio . . . [fl]amini Iuliae Augustae

Cnaeus Cornelius priest of Julia Augusta

AD 14–29

CIL 2.473: Emerita?, Lusitania
flamen Divae Aug(ustae) provinciae Lusitan(iae)
Priest of Diva Augusta for the province of Lusitania
Soon (?) after AD 42

SC de Cn.Pisone Patre (Piso Decree) Various locations, Baetica
115, 133, 150
Iuliae Augustae
Julia Augusta
143
avia
grandmother (of Livilla)
December 10, AD 20

Tabula Siarensis I.7: Siarum, Baetica
Augusta mater eius
Augusta his [Tiberius'] mother
AD 19–20

CIL 2.1667: Tucci, Baetica
Alfidiae Mat(ri) Augustae (heavily restored)
Alfidia, mother of Augusta
After AD 14

CIL 2.2108: Arjona, Baetica
Iuliae Augustae
Julia Augusta

CIL 2.1571: Castro el Rio, Baetica
sacerdos div[ae / Augustae
Priest of Diva Augusta

CIL 2.2038: Anticaria, Baetica
Iuliae Aug(ustae) Drusi [fil(iae)] Div[i Aug] matri Tiberii / Caesaris Aug(usti)
    principis et conservatoris et Drusi / Germanici [g]en[etric]is orbis
Julia Augusta, mother of the world, daughter of Drusus wife of Divus [Au-
    gustus] mother of Tiberius Caesar Augustus princeps and conservator, and
    of Drusus Germanicus
B 31; EJ 123

ILS 6896 (= *CIL* 2.194): Olisipo, Lusitania
Flamini Germ(anici) Caesaris Fla / mini Iuliae Aug(ustae)
Priest of Germanicus Caesar, priest of Julia Augusta

AE 1976, no. 185: Mytilene, Lesbos, Asia

[Iuliae A]gustae / [Drusi f.uxor divi Au]gusti Germanico / Caesari Ti. Augusti / [f

[Julia] Augusta [daughter of Drusus, wife of Divus] Augustus (and) Germanicus Caesar [son of] Tiberius Augustus

AE 1904, no. 98: Ephesus, Asia

Liviae Caesaris Augusti

Livia wife of Caesar Augustus

ILS 8897, EJ 71: Ephesus, Asia

Liviae Casaris Augusti . . . patronis

their patrons (Augustus and) Livia the wife of Caesar Augustus

Inscription to Livia and Augustus from the gate of the agora, to identify statues.

4–3 BC

B 9; R 112

CIL 11.3196: Nepet, Africa

Cereri August(ae) / Matri Agr(orum)

Augusta Ceres, mother of the fields

AD 18

B 63

CIL 8.6987: Colonia Iulia Cirta, Africa

Divae Au(gustae) . . . flaminica Di[vae Augustae

Priestess of Diva [Augusta] to Diva Augusta . . . Claudian

B 71

AE 1948, no. 13: Leptis Magna, Africa

Divae Augu(stae)

Diva Augusta

AD 45–46

B 75

ILS 120 (EJ 127): El Lehs, Africa

Iunoni Liviae Augusti sacrum

Livia Juno (or the Juno of Livia), wife of Augustus

AD 3

B 27; M 62

AE 1948, no. 13: Leptis Magna, Africa

Divae Augu(stae)

Diva Augusta
After AD 29, probably after AD 42

IRT no. 269: Leptis Magna, Africa
Cereri Augustae sacrum
Sacred to Ceres Augusta
AD 35–36
M 2; Wood (1999), 121

AE 1914, no. 171: Thugga, Africa
Iulia Divi Augusti
Julia wife of Divus Augustus

CIL 3.12037: Gortyn, Crete, Cyrene
Iuliae (Aug(ustae)
Julia Augusta
B 51

Inscriptiones Creticae I.137, no. 55: Lebena, Crete, Cyrene
Iuliae Au[gustae / matr[i
Julia Augusta mother (of Tiberius)
B 56

ILS 7160: Salonae, Dalmatia
flamini / Iuliae Augustae
Priest of Julia Augusta

CIL 3.9972: Corinum, Dalmatia
Iuliae August(ae) divi / Augusti matri Ti. Cae / saris Aug(usti)
Julia Augusta wife of Divus Augustus mother of Tiberius Caesar Augustus

ILS 2.3089: Zara, Dalmatia
Iunoni Augustae
the Juno of Augusta (or Juno Augusta
B 26

CIL 3.651: Philippi, Macedonia
Sac(erdos) divae Aug(ustae)
Priestess of the goddess Augusta
H 51

AE 1991.1428a: Philippi, Macedonia
sacerdoti divae / Aug(ustae)

priestess of the Goddess Augusta
This and the next three belong to a base for statues for five women of whom at
   least four are priestesses of Livia.

AE 1991.1428b: Philippi, Macedonia
sacerd(oti) [divae Augustae)]
priestess of [the Goddess Augusta]

AE 1991.1428c: Philippi, Macedonia
Aug(ustae)
Augusta

AE 1991.1428d: Philippi, Macedonia
sacerd(oti) divae Aug(ustae)
priestess of the Goddess Augusta

AE 1941 no. 142: Antiocheia, Psidia
Deae Iul[iae / Au]gustae
Goddess Julia Augusta
H 50

EJ 130: Corinth, Achaea
[Dianae] Pacilucifer[rae Aug]ustae sacrum
Sacred to [Diana] Augusta, bringer of light and peace
B 39; H 69

Corinth 8.3 (1966), 33 no 55: Corinth, Achaea
Div]ae Aug[ustae av]ae / [Ti C]laudi Cae[saris / Aug]u[sti Germanici
[The goddess] Augusta [grandmother] of [Tiberius] Claudius Caesar [Au-
   gustus Germanicus
Claudian
B 72; H 53

Corinth 8.3 (1966), no. 55: Corinth, Achaea
div]ae Aug[ustae av]ae / Ti C[laudi Cae[saris / Aug]u[sti Germani]ci
[The goddess] Augusta [grandmother of Tiberius Claudius Augustus Ger-
   manicus
About AD 25
H 52

Corinth 8.3 (1966), no. 153: Corinth, Achaea
ad Iulia]m diva[m Au[gustam
to [Julia] Augusta, goddess

About AD 25
H 52

AE 1994.1757 (*CIL* 3.12105): Salamis, Cyprus
[Iulia Augusta Drusi f(ilia) c]oniuge div[i / Augusti matre Ti. Caesa]ris Aug(usti)
[Julia Augusta, daughter of Drusus] wife of Divus [Augustus, mother of Tinberius Caesar] Augustus
Heavily restored; earlier restorations assigned the inscriptions to Julia Domna.

R. Egger, *Carinthia* 156 (1966), 467, fig. 126: Magdalensberg, Noricum
Liv[i]ae Caeasaris Augu[st(i) uxori]
Livia wife of Caesar Augustus
One of three inscriptions, the other two honouring Julia the Elder and Younger.
10–9 BC
B 15

Greek

Miranda no. 40: Naples, Italy
kai Iouliai Sebaste[i
and Julia Augusta
Miranda (1990), 58–60, identifies Julia as the daughter of Titus; P. Hermann, *Gnomon* 66 (1994), 24, argues for Livia.

Lindos 2.2 *Inscriptions* (1941), 739, no. 387: Lindos, Rhodes, Asia
[Libi]as gunaikos / [Aut]okratoros / [Kaisaros] theou huiou / [Seabstou]
Livia the wife of Imperator [Caesar Augustus] son of a god
B 14

IGR 4.249: Assos, Asia
thean Leiouian Heran n[ean] / ten tou Sebastou the[ou gunaika
The goddess Livia, the new Hera, wife of the god Augustus
M 66

IGR 4.250: Assos, Asia
Euergetis tou Kosm[ou]
Benefactress of the world
Identified as Livia because of *IGR* 2.249
B 5; H 19

G. Bean, *Belleten* 29 (1965), 593, no. 3; Elaea, Asia
Leibian Sebasten
Livia Augusta
B 44; Rose 111

IGR 4.144: Cyzicus, Mysia, Asia
agalma tes metros autou / sebast[es Nei]ke[ph]orou
Statue of his (sc. Tiberius) mother, Augusta, Bringer of Victory
Dedicated by priestess Antonia Tryphaina
B 43; H 97; M 107; Price (1980), 63–64

SEG 33.1055, *AE* 1983, no. 910: Cyzicus, Mysia, Asia
[Liouian] thean Demeter[a
The goddess [Livia] Demeter
fragmentary inscription to Livia and Augustus
B 7; H 17; M 5

TAM 5.2.906: Thyateira, Asia
[thea]n Ioulian / [Se]basten
[The goddess] Julia Augusta
Possibly refers to Julia Domna.
B 68; H 37

IGR 4.1203: Thyateira, Asia
thean Ioulian Sebasten
The goddess Julia Augusta
Possibly refers to Julia Domna.
B 67; H 35

IGR 4.1193: Thyateira, Asia
thea[n Iou]lian / Se[b]asten
The goddess Julia Augusta
Possibly refers to Julia Domna.
B 66; H 36

ILS 8853: Thyateira, Asia
arches Leibianes
The Livian demesne
Also read as *arkes*, treasury.
cf. *CIG* 2.3484
Severan?

AE 1988.1025: Mahmudiye (near Troy), Asia

Autrokratori / Kaisari / theoi theou huioi / Sebastoi / Tiberioi Kaisari / Seabastoi / theoi Iulioi / Iulia Sebastei / Gaio kai Loukioi / Sextoi Appoleioi

Imperator Caesar Augustus, god, son of a god, Tiberius Caesar Augustus, the god Julius, Julia Augusta, Gaius and Lucius, Sextus Appuleius.

A Sextus Appuleius was consul in 29 BC; his son was consul in AD 14, and is probably the proconsul of the inscription.

IG 12 suppl. 50: Mytilene, Lesbos, Asia

Sebasten Her[en

Augusta Hera

B 62; H 76

IGR 4.39: Mytilene, Lesbos, Asia

tei te sug[kle]toi kai tais iereais tes Hes[ti] / as kai Iouliai tei gunaiki autou / kai Octaiai tei adelphei kai tois / teknois kai suggenensi kais phi / lois

(Thanks to) the Senate and the priestesses of Vesta and Julia his (Augustus) wife, and Octavia his sister and his children and relatives and friends

Soon after 27 BC; the name Julia may be a mistake.

SEG 15 (1958), no. 532: Brontados, Chios, Asia

[Sebast]es Theas Aphrodites Libias

[Augusta] Goddess Aphrodite Livia

H 23; M 124

IG 12 suppl. 124, 20: Eresos, Lesbos, Asia

[Lio]u[iai] Seb[astai / [Pro]noiai ta gunaiki to Sebasto theo Kaisaros

[Livia] Augusta Pronoia (Providentia), wife of the God Augustus Caesar

H 86; M 105

IGR 4.319: Pergamum, Mysia, Asia

Se[ba]sten Iou[lian Hera Ne]an Ba[sileian

Augusta Julia [New Hera] Queen (?)

H 74; M 64

AE 1969/70 no. 594: Elaea, Asia

Leibian Sebasten Deibon Kaisara

Livia Augusta Divus Caesar

MDAI(A) 75 (1960), 105 n. 12: Tigani, Samos, Asia

[D]rousil[l]an gunaika tou / [Autokrato]ros theou hiou Kaisaros dia / [ten pros t]en thean eusebeian Herei

(The people dedicated a statue) to Hera of Drusilla wife of the Imperator
  Caesar because of her piety towards the goddess
27 BC–AD 14
B 3; H 24

MDAI(A) 75 (1960), 104 n. 11: Heraeum, Samos, Asia
Drousillan Au[tokrato] / ros Kaisaros [theou uiou] / Sebastou gu[anaika
  Herei]
(The people dedicated a statue) [to Hera] of Drusilla, the wife of the Impera-
  tor Caesar Augustus, [son of a god]
27 BC–AD 14
B 20

IGR 4.982: Samos, Asia
Markon Libion Drouson, ton / patera Theas Ioulias Seba / stes
Marcus Livius Drusus, the father of the Goddess Julia Augusta
After AD 14
H 27

IGR 4.983: Samos, Asia
Alphidian ten metera Theas Iulias Seabst[e]s megiston agathon aitian ge-
  gonuian toi kosmoi
The mother of the Goddess Julia Augusta, Alfidia who has been been the cause
  of the greatest benefits to the world.

IGR 4.984: Samos, Asia
ten iereian tes Archegetidos Heras kai The / as Ioulias Sebastes Lollian Koin-
  tou thu / gatera
(the people honour) Lollia, daughter of Quintus, priestess of Archetis Hera
  and of the Goddess Julia Augusta
After AD 14
H 25

AE 1980, no. 870: Aphrodisias, Caria, Asia
Iouliai Sebastei
Julia Sebaste
Accompanies dedications to Augustus as Zeus Patroos and to Tiberius.

SEG 30 (1980), no. 1248: Aphrodisias, Caria, Asia
I]ouliai Sebaste[i
Julia Sebaste
Reynolds (1980), 79, no. 10

SEG 30 (1980), no. 1249: Aphrodisias, Caria, Asia
Io]ulian Sebaste[n
Julia Sebaste
Reynolds (1980), 82, no. 17
M 65

Reynolds (1982) Doc. 13: Aphrodisias, Cara, Asia
tei gunaika mou
My (Octavian / Augustus) wife
Dated disputed, see appendix 17

AE 1980, no. 877: Aphrodisias, Caria, Asia
[Io]ulian Sebaste[n] / Sebastou thugate[ra] / Heran
Julia Augusta, Hera, daughter of Augustus
Reynolds (1980), 79–80, 82, no. 17
Caligulan
B 70; H 77; R 104

Le Bas II.1611: Aphrodisias, Caria, Asia
[Th]ea Ioulia Sebaste
The Goddess Julia Augusta
H 28

CIG II.2815: Aphrodisias, Caria, Asia
Theas Ioulias, neas Demetros
The Goddess Julia, New Demeter
Possibly Julia Domna
H 31; M 3; Wood (1999), 112

IG 12.5, no. 628: Ioulis, Ceos, Asia
Leibian Autokratoros / Kaisaros gunaika
Livia wife of Imperator Kaisar
31–27 BC
B 2; R 71

IGR 4.584: Aezani, Asia
ton sebaston neon homobomion
the Augusti (Livia and Augustus) recently sharing an altar
Sebastes Pronoias
Augusta Pronoia (Providentia)
After AD 41
M 106

BCH 10 (1886), 516, no. 6: Tralles, Lydia
hiereus Tiberiou Kaisaros / kai Hekates Sebastes
the priest of Tiberius Caesar and Augusta Hecate
AD 4–14
H 71; M 55

IGR 4.1183: Apollonis, Asia
Thea[n Iouli]an S[eba]sten
The Goddess [Julia] Sebaste
May be Julia Domna.

SEG 37 (1987) no. 1007: Alexandreia Troas, Asia
Autokratori / Kaisari / Theoi Theou uiowi / Sebastoi / Tiberioi Kaisari /
   Sebastoi / Theoi Iulioi / Iouliai Sebastei / Gaioi kai Loukioi / Xestoi Ap-
   poloeioi
Imperator Caesar, God, son of a God; Tiberius Caesar Augustus, the God
   Julius, Julia Augusta, Gaius and Lucius, Sextus Appuleius

IGR 4.257: Assus, Asia
Aphroditei Juliai
Julia Aphrodite
The allusion to Augustus as Theos in the same inscription inclines it to Livia,
   but not conclusively.

IGR 4.180 (EJ 129): Lampsacus, Asia
Ioulian Sebasten / Hestian nean Deme / tra
Julia Augusta, new Hestia Demeter
B 55; H 60; M 4

SEG 4.515: Ephesus, Asia
Serbilia de Sekounda / tes Sebastes Demetros Karpo / phorou
Servilia Secunda (priestess of) Augusta Demeter Bringer of Produce
AD 19–23
B 45; H 63; M 6

Smallwood (1967) 380.viii.26: Ephesus, Asia
Iouliai Sebastei
Julia Augusta
Hymnodes of the deified Livia at Ephesus are entitled to same rights as those
   of Augustus.
After AD 42

AE 1993.1469: Ephesus, Asia
[. . . iereo]s [Tiberio]u K[aisaros] Sebastou kai Iouli[as] Sebastes
[priest] of Tiberius Caesar Augustus and Julia Augusta
AD 30/31
See Knibbe et al. (1963), no. 9, p. 117.

IGR 3.157: Ancyra, Asia
Iulias / Sebastes
(statue) of Julia Augusta
AD 19–20 (based on priests names)
B 30

AE 1940, no. 184: Attouda, Caria, Asia
Libian thean gu[naika Autokratoros] / Kaisaros theou [huiou theou Sebastou]
The goddess Livia wife of the god [Imperator] Caesar [Augustus, son of a god
AD 3–10
B 6; H 32

IG 3.460: Athens, Achaea
Sebaste Hugeia
Augusta Hygeia (= Salus)

IGR 1.821: Athens, Achaea
Ioulia Thea Autokratoros / Kaisaros Theou Sebastou
Julia, Goddess, [?] of Imperator Caesar Augustus, the god
May be for Julia the Elder.

IG 3.316: Athens, Achaea
Hiereas Hesti[as] kai Leibias kai Iulias
Priestess of Hestia, Livia and Julia

IG 3.381: Athens, Achaea
L[ei]bias
Livia
The text is not certain.

IG 2/3 3241: Athens, Achaea
[Lio]uian Seb[asten] . . . ten eat[es euergetin]
Livia Augusta . . . her [benefactress]
B 33; H 7

SEG 22 (1967), no. 152: Athens, Achaea
[Artemis] Boula[i]a Iulia Sebaste

[Artemis] Boulaia Julia Augusta
H 56; M 46

Hesperia 6 (1937), 464: Athens, Achaea.
Ioulian Sebasten Boulai[i]an Tiberiou Sebastou metera
Julia Augusta Boulaia mother of Tiberius Augustus

IG 2/3 3239: Athens, Achaea
Ioulian th[ean] / Seb[asten]
The goddess Julia Augusta
B 35; H 6

IG 2/3 3238 = *IG* 3.461 (EJ 128): Athens, Achaea
Ioulian thean Sebasten Pronoian
The goddess Julia Agusta Pronoia (Providentia)
B 36; H 5; M 104

IG 2/3 3240: Athens, Achaea
Sebast]ei Hygeiai
Augusta Hygeia
B 37; H 81

AE 1933, no. 2: Rhamnous, Attica, Achaea
Thea Leibia
The Goddess Livia
H 8
AD 45/46

AE 1971, no. 439: Eleusis, Achaea
Libian Drousillan [Au]tokratoros Kaisaros gunaika
Livia Drusilla wife of Imperator Caesar
Statue base of Livia accompanying one for Augustus.
31–27 BC
B 1; Rose 71

IG 4.1393: Epidauros, Achaea
Libian Kaisa / ros Sebastou / gunaika
Livia the wife of Caesar Augustus
B 10

IG 4.1394: Epidauros, Achaea
Leibia[n K]aisaros Sebastou / gunaika

Livia the wife of Caesar Augustus
B 11

SEG 23.472: Dodona, Achaea
Libian ten . . . / Kaisaros Se[bastou
Livia (the wife of) Caesar Augustus
B 8

IG 7.65: Megara, Achaea
Ioulian
Julia
B 59; H 9

IG 7.66: Megara, Achaea
Ioulian Thean Sebasten
The Goddess Julia Augusta
B 60

SEG 41 (1991), no. 328: Messenia, Achaea
l. 26 Tiberiou de Kaisaros
ll. 28–29 kai thean Leibian tan matera autou kai g[unaika theou sebastou
    kaisaros] / kai Antonian kai Libillan
Tiberius Caesar . . . and the Goddess Livia his mother and wife [of Divus
    Augustus Caesar] and Antonia and Livilla
AD 14

IG V.2.301: Tegea, Arcadia, Achaea
Theas Ioulias Sebastes (Ioulias added later)
The Goddess Julia Augusta
H 13

AE 1920, no. 1: Corinth, Achaea
Tiberion Kaisara Theou Sebastou hu(ion) Sebaston . . . Thean Ioulian
    Sebasten
Tiberius Caesar Augustus, son of Augustus the God . . . Goddess Julia Sebaste
The Goddess Julia Augusta
21–23 AD
H 11

Corinth 8.1, no. 19: Corinth, Achaea
eis thean I[o]ulian Sebasten
To the goddess Julia Augusta

AE 1928 no 50: Thespiae, Boiotia, Achaea
[Libian Autokratoros] / Kaisaros [Sebastou / gun[aika
[Livia] wife of [Imperator] Caesar [Augustus]
B 24; Rose 82

SEG 13, 348: Thespiae, Boeotia, Achaea
Sebaste
Augusta
From poem of Honestus.
Probably Livia rather than Julia; see Jones (1970), 249–55.
B 65; H 85

SEG 31 (1981), no. 514: Thespiae, Boiotia, Achaea
Sebasten Ioulian Mnemosunen
Sebaste Julia Mnemosyne
H 84; M 108

P. Jamot, *BCH* 26 (1902), no. 18: Thespiae, Boiotia, Achaea
Sebastes Ioulias
Julia Augusta
Probably Livia rather than Julia; see Jones (1970), 226.

BCH 3 (1879), 443: Chalcis, Boeotia, Achaea
en Chalkidi Leibidea
Contests in honour of Livia in Chalcis

SEG 24 (1969), no. 212: Eleusis, Attica, Achaea
Libian Driusillan / [Au]tokratoros Kaisaros / gunaika
Livia Drusilla wife of Imperator Caesar
Accompanies inscription to Octavian, perhaps 31 BC.

SEG 31 (1981), no. 409: Lebadeia, Boiotia, Achaea
Sebast[es Ioulias]
Augusta [Julia]

Kornemann (1929), no. 4: Gytheum, Laconia, Achaea
Epiphanestata / Thea Tyche tes Po / leos
Very present goddess Fortune of the city
Kornemann states that the goddess is "sicher Livia."
H 12

SEG 11.923 (EJ 102)
(a) ll. 3, 10, 35: Gytheum, Laconia, Achaea

Ioulias Seba]stes . . . Iulias Sebaste[s] / tes tou ethnos kai poleos hemon
   Tuches . . . Iulias tes Sebastes
(Statue of) [Julia] Augusta . . . of Julia Augusta the Fortune of our people and
   city . . . of Julia the Augusta . . . (b) l. 13: ten emen metera
My (Tiberius) mother
B 52; Rose 74; H 87; M 48

IG 12.8.65: Imbros, Asia
Ioulian Sebast[en Hygeian
Julia Augusta [Hygeia]
after AD 22/23
B 53; H80

SEG 24 (1969), no. 613: Mekes, Macedonia
Tiberiou Kaisa]ros kai Iulias Sebaston
[Tiberius Caesar] and Julia, Augusti
AD 21/22

IGR III 1507: Oinoanda, Lycia
ierasamenen theas Seb / astes
Priestess of the goddess Augusta
H 44

IGR III 540: Telmessus, Lycia
hiereia . . . theas Sebastes
Priestess of the goddess Augusta
H 45

IGR 3.720: Myra, Lycia
Ioulian thean Sebasten / gunaika theou Sebastou / Kaisaros metera de Tibe-
   riou / theou Sebastou K[ai]saros
The goddess Julia Augusta wife of the god Augustus Caesar mother of the god
   Tiberius Augustus Caesar
B 61; H 43; Rose 102

IGR 3.721: Myra, Lycia
Tiberion Kaisara theon Sebaston theon Sebaston huion autok[r]ator
Tiberius Caesar Augustus Imperator, son of Augustus and Augusta

SEG 38 (1988) 914: Cnossus, Crete, Cyrene
Libia
Livia
On gaming counter, with portrait.

SEG 38.1887: Cyrenae, Cyrene
[Ioulian Sebasta]n Sebasto gunaika
[Julia Augusta] wife of Augustus

AE 1967 no. 491: Antioch, Galatia
Iul[ia Augusta]
Julia [Augusta]
Heavily restored; may be Severan, see Levick, *Anatolian Studies* 17 (1967), 101
n. 1.

Ditt. 533,25: Ankyra, Galatia
Kaisaros [Sebastou] kai Iulias Sebastes
Caesar Augustus and Julia Augusta

IGR 3.312: Apollonia Sozopolis, Galatia
[Theai Iouliai] or [Iouliai Sebastei]
[The goddess Julia] or [Julia Augusta]
Completely restored.
B 32; R 107; H 47

IGR 1.1150: Athribis, Egypt
Huper Tiberiou] Kaisaros Sebastou theou / huiou Autokratoros kai huper
    Ioulias Seba[stes neas / Isidos / metros autou] kai tou oikou auton
On behalf of [Tiberius] Caesar Augustus Imperator son of god and on behalf
    of Julia Augusta [the new Isis] and their house
B 38; H 82

IGR I. 1109: Pelusium, Egypt
Hyper Autokratoros Kaisaros Theou huiou Sebastou kai Leiouas Sebatou kai
    Gaiou Kaisaros kai Leukiou Kaisaros ton huion tou autokratoros kai Ioulias
    tes thugatros tou autokratoros
On behalf of Imperator Augustus son of Caesar the God and Livia, wife of
    Augustus, and Gaius Caesar and Lucius Caesar, the sons of the Imperator,
    and Julia, the daughter of the Imperator
4 BC

SEG 38.1678: Akoris, Egypt
Huper Tiberiou Kaisaros Sebastou kai Iul / ias Sebastes
On behalf of Tiberius Caesar Augustus and Julia Augusta
AD 29
B 69

ILS 8784: Thasos, Thrace
Leibian Drousillan ten tou Seabstou Kaisaris / gunaika thean euergetin
Livia Drusillan wife of Augustus Caesar goddess and benefactress
Dedication shared with Julia the Elder and Younger.
19–12 BC
H 4

IGR 1.835: Thasos, Thrace
Leibian Drou[sillan ten tou Sebastou Kaisaros] / gunaika thean euergetin
Livia Drusilla wife [of Augustus Caesar] goddess and benfactress
16–13 BC
B 23; R 95

IG 12.8.381: Thasos, Thrace
Leibian Drou[sill]an t[e]n tou Sebastou Kaisaros gunaikan Thean Euergetin /
  Ioulian Markou Ag[r]ippou Thugatera
Livia Drusilla the wife of Augustus Caesar goddess, benefactress; Julia daugh-
  ter of Marcus Agrippa

IG 14.2414.40 (= *CIL* 10.8069.9): Naples
Libia
Livia
On gaming counter. May have originated in Egypt.

IGR 3.1086: Abila, Syria
Kyrion Sebaston
Lords Augusti (Tiberius and Livia)
H 96

IGR 3.1344: Gerasa, Syria
huper tes Sebaston soterias
For the welfare of the Augusti
Possibly AD 22, referring to Tiberius and Livia.

IG IX.2.333: Mylai, Thessaly
Iou / lias Heras Sebastes
Julia Hera Augusta
H 72; M 63

IGR 3.984: Salamis, Cyprus
Libian ten gunaika tou / [Au]tokratoros Kaisaros / [S]eb[a]stou

Livia, the wife of Imperator Caesar Augustus
B 19

JHS 9 (1988), 242, no. 61: Paleapaphus, Cyprus
Liouian thean nea[n Aphroditen]
The goddess Livia the new [Aphrodite]
B 16; H 49; M 123

IGR 1.902: Phanagoria, Pontus
[Lioui]a[n] ten tou Sebastou gunaik[a / basilissa] Dunamis philoromaios / [ten
  heau]tes euergetin
[Queen] Dynamis, friend of the Romans, (dedicated this statue) of [Livia] wife
  of Augustus, her benefactress
9–8 BC
B 17; H 92

SEG 39.695, 44.658: Hermonassa, Black Sea
[Puth]odoris Leiouian ten / heau[tes euergetin
Pythodoris [dedicated this statue of] Livia her own [benefactress]
Probably 8–6 BC
B 13; H53

PAPYRI

Much valuable historical material has been preserved in papyri unearthed in
Egypt. The surviving documents provide an unparalleled insight into the
details of commercial and social life, and contain the occasional item of political history, usually associated in some way with activities in the province.
References to Livia in papyri consist of either expressions of gratitude, oaths in
marriage contracts, or, most commonly, details of her commercial enterprises
in the province.

P. Oxy 2435 verso, 45 AD 13 (EJ [1976] 379.1)
epai]non de kai Libias
praise(?) also of Livia

P. Oxy 2435 recto, AD 19 (EJ [1976] 379.2
dia to apestasthai patros kai mammes
because of my [Germanicus'] separation from my father and grandmother

P. Berol. SBA (1911), 796–97, 37–38: Alexandria, AD 19
tei metri autou, emei de / mammei
to his [Tiberius'] mother, my [Germanicus'] grandmother

P. NYU inv. 18.47 (= SB 9150): Arsinoite, AD 5
ousi]as Libias [kai] Germani[ikou Ka]isaros
[estate] of Livia and Germancius Caesar

P. Lond. II. 445: Bakkhias, AD 15/15
edaphon Ioulias Sebastes kai Germanicou Kaisaros
property of Julia Augusta and Germanicus Caesar

PSI 1028: Tebtynis, AD 15
thesaurou Libuias Sebastes
the treasury of Livia Augusta

P. Mich. inv. 735 (= SB 10536): Tebtynis, AD 25/6
thesaruou Ioulias Sebastes kai teknon Germanikou Kaisaris
the treasury of Julia Augusta and the children of Germanicus Caesar

P. Sorbonne inv. 2364: Philadelphia, AD 25/26
georgou Ioulias Sebastes kai teknon Germanicou Kaisaron
farmer of Julia Augusta and the children of Germanicus, Caesars

P. Med. 6: Theadelphia(?), Theoxenis, AD 26
biblou Iulias Sebastes kai tekno(n) Germanikou Kaisaros
the papyrus of Julia Augusta and the children of Germanicus Caesar

Pap. Ryl. 126: Euhemeria, AD 28/29
Ioulias Sebastes ousias
property of Julia Augusta

P. Mich. 560: Karanis AD 46
ousi]as Libianes
Livian [estate]
Might refer to an estate of Livia or Livilla.

P. Vindob. Tandem 10: Euhemeria, AD 54
proteron . . . Ioul[ia]s Sebastes
(an estate) previously of Julia Augusta

BGU 252, 2/3 (December 24, AD 98)
epi Ioul(*ias*) [*Sebastes*]
before Julia Augusta

P. Oxy. 17.2105, AD 147–48
timei theon Libias kai [. . .
in honour of the divine Livia and . . .

P. Oxy 3.496, AD 127
e[pi] Io]lias S[eba]stes
before Julia Augusta

P. Oxy 604, early second century
epi Ioulias Sebastes (published as restored)
before Julia Augusta

CPR 24.2, AD 136
. . .]i tes Ioulias Sebastes
before Julia Augusta

COINS

Coins are a useful tool of the historian of the ancient world, for they fulfilled a double function: they were units of currency or bullion and also a device by which the current ruler could project his image to the people at large and keep his policies and concerns in the public eye.

Apart from providing information on political issues, coins can often tell us much about the appearance of their subjects. This is particularly true of official issues — that is, coins produced in the imperial mint under the direct control of the central Roman authorities, although not necessarily in Rome itself, and intended for distribution throughout wide areas of the empire. Local coins, on the other hand, were intended for much more limited distribution, in either a province, a region, or a city. Their portraits tend to be far less individualised. Unfortunately, in the case of Livia there are no official coins on which a head is identified by her legend, although it is possible that one or more of the abstractions that appear on Tiberius' issues may be intended to represent her.

Official Coins

Augustus

*RIC*² 219–20
Aurei and denarii, 13–14
Obverse: Head of Augustus
Legend: Caesar Augustus Divi F. Pater Patriae
Reverse: Seated draped female figure holding a sceptre and a branch
Legend: Pontif Maxim

Tiberius

*RIC*² 25–30 (fig. 1)
Aurei and denarii, undated
Obverse: Head of Tiberius
Legend: Ti Caesar Divi Aug F Augustus
Reverse: Seated female figure holding a sceptre or spear and a branch
Legend: Pontifex Maximus
Probably associated with *RIC*² 23–24 with Divus Augustus on reverse.

*RIC*² 33–37
As, AD 15–16
Obverse: Head of Tiberius
Legend: TI CAESAR DIVI AUG F AUGUST / AUGUSTUS IMP VII
Reverse: Draped seated female figure, holding patera and sceptre between S
   and C
Legend: PONTIF MAXIM TRIBUN POTEST XVII

*RIC*² 71–73
As, undated
Obverse: Radiate head of Augustus, with star above and thunderbolt in front
Legend: DIVUS AUGUSTUS PATER
Reverse: Draped seated female figure holding patera and sceptre, between S
   and C
Legend: None
The seated female figure type is one of the most persistent and widespread
   features of aes coinage during Tiberius' principate. Local coinage at Hippo
   (*RPC* 711), Emerita (*RPC* 40), Caesaraugusta (*RPC* 341), and Italica (*RPC*
   66–67) confidently identify the type as Julia Augusta; many scholars assume
   the same identification on official asses of Tiberius and suggest that the
   seated figure may represent Livia in her new capacity as priestess of Divus
   Augustus. There is less confidence that the same was intended in precious
   metal issues introduced under Augustus and copied by Tiberius. See Grant,
   Aspects (1950), 115; *Anniversary* (1950), 62; Sutherland (1951), 84, (1976),
   109 n. 67; Wood (1998), 89.

*RIC*² 43 (fig. 2)
Dupondius, 22–23
Obverse: Veiled and diademed bust of Pietas
Legend: PIETAS
Reverse: No image

Legend: DRUSUS CAESAR TI AUGUSTI AUG TR POT ITER, round SC

Panormus depicts a similar head (*RPC* 642–43), which it simply identifies as Augus(ta); Gross (1962), 18–19; Fittschen-Zanker (1983), III.3–3, 3. Mikocki (1995), 25–28, 164, nos. 94, 95, accepts Pietas and Iustitia (see next) as portraits of Livia. Kokkinos (1992), 90–95, suggests that these two and the salus issue (below) depict Antonia Minor.

*RIC*² 46 (fig. 3)

Dupondius, 22–23

Obverse: Draped and diademed bust of Iustitia

Legend: IUSTITIA

Reverse: No image

Legend: TI CAESAR DIVI AUG F AUG TR POT XXIIII, round SC

*RIC*² 47 (fig. 4)

Dupondius, 22–34

Obverse: Draped bust of Salus, hair parted in centre

Legend: SALUS AUGUSTA

Reverse: No image

Legend: TI CAESAR DIVI AUG F AUG TR POT XXIIII, around SC

Gross (1962), 58, 62–66, notes that the salus type resembles local issues with Livia's head and so should be taken as having her features. Wood (1999), 109, notes that the arched nose, small mouth, and soft chin line are in contrast to the ideal features of Iustitia and Pietas.

See also Sutherland (1951), 96–97, 191–92; Weinstock (1971), 171–72; Torelli (1982), 66–70; Sutherland (1987), 51–52; Purcell (1986), 86, n. 45.

*RIC*² 50–51 (fig. 5)

Sestertius, 22–23

Obverse: Carpentum drawn by two mules, the sides decorated with victories and other figures

Legend: SPQR LIVIAE AUGUSTAE

Reverse: No image

Legend: TI CAESAR DIVI AUG F AUGUST P M TR POT XXIIII, round SC

The carpentum coins are dated on the reverse to Tiberius' twenty-fourth tribunician year, AD 22–23, and are presumably associated with Livia's illness. The scene may relate to the procession of the *supplicationes* decreed as a thanksgiving for her recovery. The coin could have another meaning. In 22 Livia received the right to sit with Vestal Virgins at public games. It is possible that at the same time she received another Vestal privilege, the right to be transported by the carpentum, and that the grant is alluded to in the coin. Carpentum types are generally posthumous, and it is argued by Grant, *Aspects* (1950), 123, that it is unlikely that Tiberius would have thus honored Livia in her lifetime. He notes that certain coins of Tiberius were issued some time after the date represented by the tribunician years, and he puts the carpentum type in that category, dating it shortly after Livia's death. See Sutherland (1951), 192–93; (1974), 151; Flory (1984), 321; Winkler (1995), 53–54; Winkes (1995), 24; Wood (1999), 82.

Claudius

*RIC*² 101 (fig. 6)
Dupondius, 41–50 (?)
Obverse: Radiate head of Augustus, between S and C
Legend: DIVUS AUGUSTUS
Reverse: Draped seated female figure with wreath of corn ears holding corn ears and long torch
Legend: DIVA AUGUSTA
This coin bears a certain resemblance to the Aurei and Denarii of Augustus depicting a seated female figure holding a sceptre and a branch. It may be that Claudius simply adopted a previously existing type and continued a tradition already established; see Sutherland (1951), 124–25, 131.

Nero

*RIC*² 44–45, 56–57 (fig. 7)
Aurei and denarii, dated 64/65, 65/66, respectively
Obverse: Head of Nero
Legend: NERO CAESAR AUGUSTUS
Reverse: Standing radiate male holding patera and sceptre, beside a standing veiled and draped female figure holding patera and cornucopia
Legend: AUGUSTUS AUGUSTA
Hahn (1994), 76 n. 85, suggests that the reverse might depict Nero and his wife, probably Poppaea.

Galba

*RIC*² 13–14, 36, 52 (fig. 8)
Aurei and Denarii, minted in Spain (Tarraco), April–late 68
Obverse: Head of Galba
Legend: GALB IMP / GALBA IMPERATOR / SER GALBA IMP CAESAR AUG P M TR

Reverse: Draped standing female holding patera, leaning on sceptre
Legend: DIVA AUGUSTA

*RIC*² 65–67
As, minted in Spain (Tarraco), April–late 68
Reverse: Draped standing female holding patera, leaning on a sceptre
Legend: DIVA AUGUSTA
Obverse: Galba riding
Legend: SER GALBA IMPERATOR / SERVIUS GALBA IMPERATOR

*RIC*² 331–38, 432–33
Sestertius
Obverse: Head of Galba, laureate or oak-wreathed
Reverse: IMP SER GALBA CAE AUG TR P / SER GALBA IMP AUGUSTUS
Reverse: Livia, seated holding patera and vertical sceptre between S and C
Legend: AUGUSTA
Kraay (1956), 58, says that Augusta is clearly Livia, but notes that the title Diva
   is omitted and that the type perhaps suggests Livia as the priestess of Divus
   Augustus.

Titus

*RIC*² 218–24
Dupondius
Draped and diademed bust (of Livia?)
Legend: Iustitia
Under Titus the Iustitia and Pietas coins were revived (*RIC* 2: 144, 145, nos.
   218–24)

Trajan

*RIC*² 821: one of Trajan's "restored" issues, on which Trajan's legend was
   added to earlier dies and the coins reissued as an aureus with head of Tiberius on obverse and Livia (?) seated, facing right on reverse. Cf. *RIC*² 25–
   30
Hahn (1994), 76 n. 87

Antoninus Pius

*RIC*² 973–75, 978, 998, 1003–4 (fig. 9)
Sestertius, AD 157/58, 158/59

*RIC*² 988, 1013, 117, 1021

Dupondius, AD 157/58, 158/59

*RIC*² 1024–25
As, AD 158/59
Octastyle temple in which seated figures of Augustus and Livia appear

Local Coins

B = Bust or head of Livia / S = Seated image of Livia / v = veiled / p = holding patera / s = holding sceptre / c = holding earns of corn.

JA = jugate with Augustus / JT = jugate with Tiberius / FA = facing head of Augustus / FT = facing head of Tiberius / FS = facing head of personified Senate

/ = other side occupied by member of family / A = Augustus / DA = Augustus with Divine attributes / T = Tiberius / C = Claudius / N = Nero. Greek legends in italics.

Augustus

Sparta *RPC* 1105: B
Chalcis *RPC* 1346: B / Hera, 1348: B / Hera
Thessalian League *RPC* 1427: B *Hera Leiouia* / DA
Thessalonica *RPC* 1563: B *Thea* or *Theou Libia*
Thrace: Rhoemetacles I *RPC* 1708–10: JA *Kaisaros Sebastou* / Rhoemetacles and Queen Pythodoris
Bithynia *RPC* 2097: JA Imp.Caesar Augustus Pontif / Max. tr. p./S
Methymna *RPC* 2338: B *Thea Libia* / A
Pergamum 2359: B *Libian Heran* / *Ioulian Aphroditen* Bust of Julia
Magnesia AD Sipylum *RPC* 2449/Gaius and Lucius Caesar: FA *Sebastoi*, 2450 B / A *Sebastoi*
Magnesia AD Maeandrum H 57: B Livia as Artemis?
Smyrna *RPC* 2464, 66: JA *Sebastoi*, 2467: Livia as Aphrodite, standing, holding sceptre and nike, leaning on column *Libian Zmurnaion Koronos*
Clazomenae *RPC* 2496: B *Thea Libia* / A *Seabstos Ktistes*
Nysa *RPC* 2663: JA
Ephesus *RPC* 2576, 2580: B, 2581–85, 2587, 2589–91, 2593–96, 2599–606, 2608–12: JA
Tralles 2647: Livia as Demeter holding corn and poppy *Kaisareon Libia* / A *Sabastos*, 2648: as 2647/head of Gaius Caesar *Gaios Kaisar*
Antioch AD Maeandrum *RPC* 2829: B / A *Kaisar Sebastos*
Eumenea *RPC* 3143: B *Hera Libia*

Alexandria *RPC* 5006: B: *Liouia Sebastos* / double cornucopia, 5008 (as 5006) / eagle, 5027: B / cornucopia *Patros Patridos*, 5042, 5046, 0554: B / oak wreath 5043, 5047, 5058, 5064, 5068 B / modius 5053, 5063: bust of Euthenia *Euthenia* 5055, 5065, 5072 B / Athena

Tiberius

Emerita *RPC* 38: B Salus Augusta, 39: B Salus Augusta / S Iulia Augusta, 40: B Iulia Augusta / T Ti Caesar Augustus Pox Max Imp

Italica *RPC* 66, 67: S with sceptre and pater Iulia Augusta / A Divus Augustus Pater

Romula *RPC* 73: B on globe Iulia Augusta Genetrix Orbis / A Divi Aug(usti)

Tarraco *RPC* 233: Facing heads of Drusus and Livia Drusus Caes Trib Pot Iul Augusta / T Ti Caes Aug Pont Max Trib Pot

Caesaraugusta *RPC* 341: S Iulia Augusta / T Ti Caesar Divi Augusti f Augustus

Gaul (city uncertain) *RPC* 538: B in diadem and veil in wreath of corn / A Divus Augustus Pater

Paestum *RPC* 604: Svsp / T

Panormus *RPC* 642–43: Bv Augus, 645: Ssp

Hippo *RPC* 711: Ssp Iul Aug / T Ti Caesar Divi Augusti f Augustus

Utica *RPC* 721–26: Svps / T Ti Caesar etc., 731–32: S / T Ti Caesar Divi f Aug Imp viii, 733–34 S

Carthage *RPC* 754–55: Svps / T Ti Caesar Imp PP

Paterna *RPC* 763–69: Svcs / T TiCae Divi Aug F Aug Imp viii cos iiii

Thapsus *RPC* 795: Ssc Cereri Augustae / T Ti Cae Divi Aug F Aug Imp vii, 796 Bv / as 795, 797 Sps / as 795

Oea *RPC* 833: B, between peacock and ear of corn, 835: B

Lepcis *RPC* 849: B Svsp Augusta Mater Patria / T Imp Caesar Au, 850: as 849/T Imp Ti Caes Aug COs iiii

Cnossus *RPC* 986: S Iulia Augus / A Divos Aug, 988: B Iulia Aug, 989: as 988/T Ti Caesar Aug

Corinth *RPC* 1149–50: S with sp or p or cs

Dium *RPC* 1506: Sps / T Ti Caesar Divi F Augustus

Edessa *RPC* 1525–27: B *Sebaste* / T *Ti Kai* or *Kaisar Sebastos*

Thessalonica *RPC* 1566: *Sebaste* Demeter in car, 1567–68: B *Sebaste* / T *Ti Kaisar Sebastos*, 1569: Sps *Sebaste* / as 1569, 1570–71: Bv *Sebaste* / as 1569

Amphipolis *RPC* 1634: Bv *Ioulia Sebaste Thea*; H 55 B (Livia or Artemis)

Byzantium *RPC* 1779: B *The Sebaste* / A *Theos Sebastos*

Sinope *RPC* 2126: S / A

Mytilene *RPC* 2345–6: B *Iou Thea Sebaste* / T *Ti Theos Sebastos*

Pergamum *RPC* 2368: Ssc *Thean* . . . *Menogenes* / TA *Sebastoi* 2369: FT *Sebastoi* / statue of Augustus in temple, *Theon Sebaston* H 62: Ss(and ähren) *Sebaste*

Magnesia AD Sipylum *RPC* 2453: B *Thean Sebasten* / bust of Senate *Sunkleton*

Smyrna *RPC* 2469: FS *Sebaste sunkletos* / statue in temple *Sebastos Tiberios*

Mastaura *RPC* 2673: FT *Sebastous*

Magnesia *RPC* 2699: B *Ioulia [Seb]ste*

Aphrodisias *RPC* 2840: B *Sebaste RPC* 2842: JT *Sebastoi*

Apollonia *RPC* 2865: B *Sebaste*

Cibyra *RPC* 2886: B *Sebaste* / Zeus, 2888: as 2886/T *Sebastos*

Sardis *RPC* 2991: Ssc *Sebaste* / togate Tiberius *Sebastos*

Tripolis *RPC* 3053: B *Sebaste*, 3054 JT *Sebaston Kaisara*

Aezani *RPC* 3071: B *Sebaste* / T *Kaisar*

Apamea *RPC* 3132: B *Sebaste*

Eumenea *RPC* 3148: B *Sebaste;* H

Eucarpia *RPC* 3160: B *Sebaste*

Cyprus *RPC* 3919–20: Sps Iulia Augusta / T Ti Caesar Augustus

Tarsus *RPC* 4005: Sc & poppies as Hera: *Sebastes Ioulias Heras Metr* / T *Tiberiou Kaisaros Sebastou*

Augusta *RPC* 4006–8, 4011: B 4009–10 *Iouliae Sebaste*

Mopsus *RPC* 4049: B *Thea Sebaste* / A *Theos Seb[astos]*

Judaea — Philip *RPC* 4949: B Ioulia Sebaste / *Karpophoros*, 4951: JT(?) *Sebas[*

Judaea — Procurators *RPC* 4959, 4961, 4963: *Ioulia*, 4964–66: *Ioulia* / *Tib Kaisar*, 4967: *Ioulia Kaisaros* / *Tiberiou Kaisaros*

Alexandria *RPC RPC* 5079–80, 5086: B

Unknown city *RPC* 5435: B *Sebaste*

Unknown city *RPC* 5447: B *Se]b* / T *Tib*

Claudius

Crete *RPC* 1030: B *Thea Sebasta* / C *Ti Klaudios Kaisar Germanikos Sebatos*

Thessalonica *RPC* 1577: B / C *Ti Klaudios Germanikos Sebatos*

Nero

Augusta (Syria) *RPC* 4013–14: B *Ioulia Sebaste* / veiled Tyche

Uncertain Emperor

Mysomakedones *RPC* 2568: Ss & branch *Sebaste* / cult statue of Artemis

Mallus *RPC* 4016: B / Athena

APPENDIX 2: THE ROMAN SYSTEM OF GOVERNMENT

Many of the institutions that evolved during the republic were maintained more or less intact through the imperial period. The following description applies to the years immediately after the Augustan settlement.

The chief deliberative and legislative body in Rome was the Senate, made up of about six hundred former magistrates of the rank of quaestor or above. A man (public offices were not open to women) could enter the quaestorship if he had reached at least his twenty-fifth year. Twenty quaestors were elected annually and were concerned with financial matters. The quaestorship might be followed by one of two offices, that of aedile, charged with certain aspects of municipal administration, or that of tribune, appointed originally to look out for the interests of the plebeians but by the Augustan period concerned chiefly with minor judicial matters. Alternatively, the quaestorship might lead directly to the next office in the hierarchy, the first major one, the praetorship (twelve elected annually, at least five years after the quaestorship). This involved responsibility for the administration of justice, and could in turn lead to one of the two consulships, the highly prestigious senior offices in the state. Strictly speaking, consular rank was attainable only after the candidate had reached the age of forty-two, but having an ex-consul in the family history made it possible to seek the office much sooner, possibly by thirty-two, and members of the imperial family achieved it at an even younger age. From 5 BC it was common for consuls to resign office during the year to make way for replacements (suffects). Technically, the Senate could not pass legislation in this period. For its decrees to have the force of a law *(lex)* they had to be passed by the popular assemblies, although the popular ratification tended to be something of a formality. Membership in the Senate was generally permanent, subject to the approval of the censor. This official maintained the citizen list and could expel senators on moral grounds or if they fell below the requisite property qualification.

Consuls and praetors exercised a special form of higher power, *imperium*. When their terms had expired, they would often be granted one of the "public" provinces, where they exercised their imperium in the capacity of their previous offices, as *propraetor* or *proconsul*. In the "imperial" provinces — generally those where the Roman legions were stationed — the governors *(legati Augusti)* and the legionary commanders *(legati legionis)* were appointed by the emperor, who thus effectively commanded the Roman armies. Accordingly, the high point of the soldier's career, the great military parade or "triumph" that followed a major victory in the field, became the prerogative of the imperial family. Lesser beings had to remain content with triumphal *insignia*. Egypt and some of the smaller provinces were governed by imperial appointees from the equestrian order (broadly, the commercial middle class) with the rank of prefect or (most common later) procurator. The latter term is used also for financial officers in the provinces, as well as for administrators of imperial estates.

Augustus acquired two of the privileges of the plebeian tribunes. Tribunician *sacrosanctitas* made any attack on his person sacrilegious. His tribunician *potestas* gave him a number of entitlements, including the right to convene the Senate and the popular assemblies, and to introduce or to veto legislation. This special authority was a symbolically important element of the principate, and emperors dated their reigns from the point when it was assumed.

APPENDIX 3: LIVIA'S
MATERNAL ORIGINS

In the letter of Caligula to the Senate cited by Suetonius, in which the emperor charges that Livia's maternal grandfather was no more than a decurion of Fundi, the name of her grandfather is given as Aufidius Lurco. This slur on her birth is refuted by Suetonius. He knew that a good historian goes to the sources, and he reveals that the public records show that far from being a humble municipal functionary, Aufidius Lurco held important offices in Rome (Suet. *Tib.* 5, *Cal.* 23.2; Ollendorff [1926], 901). Unfortunately, for all his diligence at research, especially in family history, Suetonius might have got things wrong on this occasion. He may have confused Livia's grandfather with a senator and tribune of the plebs named Aufidius Lurco, who lived in Rome in the late republic and was probably the Marcus Aufidius Lurco mentioned by Pliny the Elder (Pliny *NH* 10.45; *RE* 2.2. [1986], 2293, no. 26 [E. Klebs]). This Aufidius made his mark on history by being the first to fatten peacocks for the market, making a nice profit from the trade. Unfortunately, inscriptions show that Livia's mother was not Aufidia but Alfidia, and Livia's maternal grandfather, if a Lurco, would thus be an Alfidius Lurco, quite unconnected with the Roman tribune and possible peacock rancher (*CIL* 2.1667 [Tucci, Baetica], *ILS* 125 [Marruvium], *IGR* 4.983 [Samos]). Some scholars argue that Aufidius and Alfidius are one and the same: see Broughton, *MRR* 2.529, 535, 647; Shackleton-Bailey (1965), 1.323. Huntsman (1997), 30, notes that a Marcus Alfidius without a cognomen is attested for the period: Asconius in his commentary on Cicero's *in Milonem* (55.8) notes that the Sextus Clodius who had Clodius' body taken into the Senate house was convicted by a prosecution conducted by Marcus Alfidius and Gaius Caesennius Philo. According to Asconius, he prosecuted Sextus Cloelius in 51 BC.

We cannot be completely certain that Livia's mother actually came from Fundi. Wiseman draws attention to the statues honouring Alfidia and her husband erected at Marruvium, a town originally settled by the Marsi. Livius Drusus, who probably adopted Livia's father, had been a friend of Quintus Poppaedius Silo, the leader of the Marsi during the Social War. It is suggested that her father might have continued the connection with the Marsi by marrying a woman from Marruvium. Wiseman has suggested that in the letter cited by Suetonius, Caligula might have impishly referred to Aufidius Luscus, an ex-scribe who had become praetor of Fundi in 37 BC and puffed himself up — to be much derided by Horace *Sat.* 1.5.34–36 for his pomposity; see *PIR*[2] A528 (Stein); Wiseman (1965), 334, (1971), 57, 211; Perkounig (1995) 31–32. But Suetonius is consistent in his references to Fundi, and it is know that there were Alfidii from that town (*CIL* 10.6248), which has to remain the favourite for Livia's maternal origins.

APPENDIX 4: LIVIA'S NAME

By the imperial period Roman men allowed themselves considerable flexibility in their nomenclature. The naming of Roman women was even more varied. It seems that Livia was originally named by the feminine form of her *gens* (her father's gens by adoption, that is) and a feminine diminutive form of her father's *cognomen*, hence Livia Drusilla (*CIL* 6.13179). This name is used in Pliny, Suetonius, and Dio for Livia before she married Octavian (Nep. *Att.* 19.4; Pliny *NH* 15.136; Suet. *Aug.* 62.2, *Tib.* 4.3; Dio 48.15.3). In the literary sources relating to the period after this marriage, she is usually called Livia. The notion that the element Drusilla was dropped completely after her marriage to Octavian is not tenable (Ollendorff [1926], 900, Kienast [1990], 84; cf. Hahn [1994], 67 n. 13). An inscription from Eleusis dated before 27 (Octavian is not yet Augustus) refers to her as *Libian Drousillan* (*SEG* 24 [1969], 212); an inscription from Samos, possibly relating to her visit to the East (22–19 BC), calls her *Drousillan Autokratoros Kaisaros Sebastou gunaika* (Drusilla, wife of Imperator Caesar Augustus) (*MDAI[A]* 75 [1960] 104 n. 11); an inscription from Thasos dated 19–12 BC refers to *Leibia Drousilla Sabastou Kaisaros* (Livia Drusilla, wife of Augustus Caesar) (*ILS* 8784, EJ 77). Moreover, the name Drusilla can be attested in Rome, at least in private communications. Antony, for instance, uses it in a letter to Octavian (Suet. *Aug.* 69.2).

After her adoption in AD 14, she is officially called Julia Augusta. She is widely attested as such, but it sometimes is difficult to distinguish among her and Julia, daughter or granddaughter of Augustus, Julia daughter of Titus, and Julia Domna, wife of Septimius Severus. In the literature she is called Julia by Valerius Maximus 6.1.1, Augusta at Suet. *Claud.* 3, and throughout Tacitus, except in the more formal obituary, where she is Julia Augusta (Tac. *Ann.* 5.1.1). Similarly, Ovid *Fast.* 1.536 calls her Julia Augusta, presumably as a mark of respect. Suetonius inconsistently calls her Livia Augusta (Suet. *Cal.* 15.2, 23.2, *Galb.* 5.2, *Oth.* 1.1), as does Marcellus Empiricus in the early fifth century (Marc. *De Med.* 15.6).

APPENDIX 5: LIVIA'S BIRTHDATE

The year of Livia's birth must be calculated back from the information given by Dio and Tacitus for the year of her death, placed securely in AD 29 (Tac. *Ann.* 5.1.1; Dio 58.2.1). Dio adds the precise information that at the time of her death she had lived for eighty-six years, by which he means that she had completed eighty-six whole years; cf. 56.30.5 (Augustus), 58.28.5 (Tiberius), 60.34.3 (Claudius). Pliny the Elder says that Livia attributed her eighty-*two* years to her exclusive consumption of Pucine wine (Pliny *NH* 14.60), but we are not told that this remark was uttered in the year of her death (Nipperdey [1851–52] on Tac. *Ann.* 5.1.1 suggests emending Pliny's LXXXII to LXXXVI).

As we have seen, Livia's birthday was January 30, in the Julian system. When this is linked with Dio's evidence that she had passed her eighty-sixth birthday in AD 29, her year of birth could be either 59 or 58 BC, depending when in 29 she died. This uncertainty is not reflected in modern sources, which give the year 58 for her birth.

There are good grounds for allowing that she might have died before January 30. One of the *consules ordinarii* for AD 29 was Gaius Fufius Geminus, who was clearly in office when Livia died and was criticised, as consul and favourite of Livia, by Tiberius after her death (Tac. *Ann.* 5.2.2). Inscriptional evidence proves that Fufius and his colleague Lucius Rubellius Geminus had completed their terms by July 6 at the latest and been replaced by that year's suffects,

309

Lucius Nonius Asprenas and Aulus Plautius (*ILS* 6124; *CIL* 4.15555). Tacitus notes Livia's death as the very first item of AD 29. This is not in itself definitive, but enough of *Annals* 5 survives to show that the events of 29 as presented by Tacitus naturally follow, rather than precede, the announcement of Livia's passing. Thus a death before January 30, AD 29, is a serious possibility, with the consequence that Livia would already have reached her eighty-sixth birthday on January 30, AD 28, and thus have been born not in 58 BC, but in the previous year, 59.

(See Barrett [1999].)

APPENDIX 6: HUSBANDS
OF SCRIBONIA

The identities of Scribonia's first two husbands have constituted the object of much scholarly debate, and the problem is considered by Syme to be "insoluble" (Syme [1939], 229; [1986], 246, Stemma XX). As we have seen, Suetonius reports that, before Octavian, Scribonia had been twice married, to two ex-consuls, and had borne children to one of them, whom we know to have been the second. This second husband was of the Scipionic line. One of their sons, Publius Cornelius Scipio, was consul in 16 BC. (His son in turn may have been the Scipio involved in a scandal later with Octavian's daughter, Julia.) Their daughter Cornelia, who died in the year of her brother's consulship, has achieved immortal fame through one of the most famous poems of Latin literature, the lament of the dead Cornelia for her husband Paullus Aemilius Lepidus (consul 34 BC) in the Fourth Book of Propertius' *Elegies* (4.16). The poet pays Cornelia a great compliment in saying that her death caused much grief to Octavian, who regarded her as a worthy sister to his daughter Julia. Syme argues for Publius Cornelius Scipio, consul of 35 BC, as the candidate for this second husband. If so, Suet. *Aug.* 62.2 made a slight mistake, or is misleading. Although he could be correct in stating that Scribonia's previous husbands both reached consular rank, the second could not have done so until after their divorce.

Scribonia's first husband may well have been Gnaeus Lentulus Marcellinus (consul 56 BC). An inscription refers to freedmen of Scribonia (after the marriage to Octavian) and her son Cornelius Marcellinus (*CIL* 6.26033: *Libertorum et familiae Scriboniae Caes. et Corneli Marcell. f. eius*). This indicates that she had a son from the first marriage, too, and that the young Marcellinus was still living in his mother's household after her marriage to Octavian. He may have died young and have been ignored by Suetonius.

APPENDIX 7: THE BIRTH
OF DRUSUS

The birth of Drusus presents a historical problem. The marriage between Octavian and Livia took place on January 17, 38 BC (EJ, p. 46). Suet. *Claud.* 1.1 says that Livia married Octavian while pregnant and gave birth to Drusus *intra mensem tertium* (within three months); Dio 48.44.1 similarly says that Augustus married *(egemen)* Livia in her sixth month of pregnancy. The quips reported by Dio and Suetonius about the three-month pregnancy are consistent with these reports.

But the above statements cannot be reconciled with the evidence for the birth of Drusus. If Livia was six months pregnant when she married, this would logically mean that Drusus would have needed to be born by the end of March at the earliest. Suetonius informs us that Drusus and Mark Antony shared the same birthday, and that Claudius, when emperor, proclaimed that the birthday of his father, Drusus, would be marked with added intensity because it coincided with Antony's (Suet. *Claud.* 11.3; see also Dio 60.5.1). The *Fasti Verulani* put Antony's birthday, and thus by implication Drusus', on January 14 (EJ, p. 45), three days before the wedding.

A possible explanation is that Claudius might have officially placed the celebration of Drusus' birthday on a date different from the actual birth. Sumner makes the point that Dio's allusion to the grant of games to Drusus belongs to AD 41, yet the games could not have been held on January 14 of that year because Claudius did not succeed until close to the end of the month (Jos.

Ant. 19.77; Suet. *Cal.* 56.2; Dio 59.29.5–6; Barrett [1990], 169–70). Sumner's chronology is correct, but Dio in fact indicates only that the legislation was passed in 41 — he does not actually say that the event was celebrated in that year. Sumner also makes the point that it would have been difficult for Livia to go through a wedding three days after the delivery. Difficult perhaps, but not impossible.

The notion of an alternate "official" birthday seems implausible. After nearly half a century Claudius would hardly have wanted to go out of his way to mark the official birthday of his father three days before the celebration of the marriage of his grandmother Livia and Octavian. Also, he would hardly have voluntarily chosen a day that was considered a *dies vitiosus* (cursed day) in the calendars because of the birthday of Antony. Moreover, celebration of Drusus' birthday caused some disruption, according to Dio, because Claudius had to move the established (unidentified) festivals on that day to another time to avoid a clash (Dio 60.5.1).

The concrete evidence of inscriptions and birthdates must, other things being equal, be considered more reliable than literary information that derives ultimately from gossip and propaganda. In the textual narrative I make the assumption that the confusion, perhaps deliberately fostered, between the wedding and the betrothal lies at the heart of the apparent contradiction. Octavian presumably was betrothed to Livia in early October, when she was six months pregnant, but made a point of delaying the actual marriage until Drusus was born. The liaison, scandalous in its own right, was presented by Antony in the most lurid terms available, presumably to deflect criticism of his own affair with Cleopatra.

References: Carcopino (1958), 73; Radke (1978), 211–13. Willrich (1911), 10, suggests that the marriage took place in the year 39 and that Drusus was born three months later; Sumner (1978), 424 n. 1, argues for March or April 38 as the birthdate; Hahn (1994), 34, puts it in March or July 38; Bleicken (1998), 209, places the birth in April; Gardthausen, I.2.1021; II.2.634; III.2706; and Ollendorff (1926), 902, between the end of March and the beginning of July 38.

APPENDIX 8: LIVIA'S *AEDES* AND THE TEMPLE OF CONCORD

In considering Livia's *aedes* to Concordia, it is important to keep two events distinct:

(a) Tiberius' pledge to restore the Temple of Concord, which took place about the time he participated with Livia in the dedication of the Porticus Liviae (in January, 7 BC), and

(b) Livia's dedication, at an unknown date, of the shrine (aedes) to Concordia within the portico.

It is probably inevitable that although two separate buildings were involved, the two dedications would come to be associated in the public mind, because both were made to Concordia. This connection seems to be reflected in Ovid. In a section of the *Fasti* not related to his account of the aedes inside the portico, Ovid describes the dedication of the Temple of Concord by Tiberius, on January 16 (AD 10). Because he calls Tiberius *dux venerande*, the lines must have been written after AD 14, at least four years after the temple's dedication. Ovid notes the republican precedent for the temple, which had come about as a result of partisan political tensions. Tiberius' gesture was far more noble — his restoration would come about from the spoils of the German wars. "You made a temple," Ovid says to Tiberius, "for the goddess you yourself worship" *(templaque fecisti, quam colis ipse, deae)*. In the final couplet the poet seems to allude to the other building, Livia's aedes, when he adds, almost as an

afterthought, *hanc* (some mss *haec*) *tua constituit genetrix et rebus et ara* (*Fasti*
1.649). This is a difficult line to translate. *Constitutio* is the technical term by
which a temple, altar, or the like was initially decreed. *Rebus* is unclear — it
must mean something like "by her actions" (Frazer in the Loeb edition of *Fasti*
translates as "by her life," hence "your mother set up [a shrine] for this goddess
[sc. Concordia], by means of her [Livia's] actions and an altar." Ovid has
already in an earlier section of the *Fasti* referred to the dedication of the aedes
in the Porticus Liviae, and perhaps does not feel the need for any further
explanation. In this later reference he speaks of an altar (*ara*), not a shrine
(*aedes*), but that does not present an insuperable problem — presumably an
altar would have been located inside the aedes. It is important to note, however, that there is a serious problem in the manuscripts. Some editors accept
the reading *haec*, rather than *hanc*, a change of only one letter but one that
completely alters the meaning of the passage. *Haec* would refer not to the
goddess but to her temple, restored by Tiberius, and give Livia a role in the
"constitutio" of that temple. Levick (1978) has shown that the controversial
ideological associations of the temple would make it very difficult for any
woman to be involved. Herbert-Brown (1984), 165 n. 72, accepts *hanc*, and her
lead is followed here.

If Livia had no role in the restoration of the temple, why does Ovid tack on
her name here? Herbert-Brown (1984), 167, suggests that in his description of
the dedication of the portico by Livia and Tiberius in 7 BC, the poet had to be
very careful about what he said of the dynastic problems. After AD 10, in a
section of the *Fasti* that he revised in his exile, he can make up for that restraint
by associating Livia with the harmony that the state now enjoys. There is no
unanimity on the question. Simpson (1991), for instance, has argued that Ovid
meant to indicate that Livia took part with Tiberius in the constitutio or
ceremonial (re)inauguration of the temple, an occasion that would often involve the dedication of an altar. The insertion of Livia in this later passage of
the *Fasti*, if she were not closely associated with Tiberius in the Temple to
Concord, is, at the very least, awkward.

APPENDIX 9: THE *DOMUS AUGUSTA*

The first official recognition of the expression *domus Augusta* is in the text of the *senatus consultum* passed in December, AD 19, and preserved in the *Tabula Siarensis*. It stipulated that a marble arch honouring Germanicus should be put up, at public expense, near the statues of Divus Augustus and of the Domus Augusta that had previously been dedicated by Gaius Norbanus Flaccus in the Circus Flaminius: *ad eum locum in quo statuae Divo Augusto domuique Augus[tae iam dedicatae es]sent ab C(aio) Norbano Flacco* . . . Norbanus Flaccus' dedication no doubt occurred during his consulship, in the first half of AD 15, the year after Augustus' death, when Drusus, son of Tiberius, was his colleague (Tac. *Ann.* 1.55.1; Norbanus was still in office at the end of July when he was named in connection with the *ludi victoriae Caesaris: CIL* 6.37836). Flory (1996) believes that the group would have included Livia. The statues then were almost certainly voted by the Senate among the honours following the death of Augustus, and if the *Tabula* reflects the actual wording of the senatus consultum, the term *domus Augusta* was already in use by at least AD early 15. The first instance of the literary use of the exact term may be Ovid *Pont.* 2.2.74, written shortly before Augustus' death.

APPENDIX 10: THE CONSPIRACY OF CORNELIUS CINNA

Dio 55.14.1 gives Cinna the names Gaius Cornelius and describes him as the son of the daughter of Pompey the Great. Seneca *Clem.* 1.9.2 calls him Lucius (Cornelius) Cinna, grandson of Pompey the Great. Dio places the incident in AD 4. Seneca says that it occurred *cum annum quadragensimum transisset et in Gallia moraretur* (when [Augustus] had passed his fortieth year and was staying in Gaul). It is generally assumed that Seneca must be referring to Augustus' stay in Gaul from 16 to 13 BC. But there is an internal discrepancy. Augustus was born September 23, 63, and would have completed his fortieth year in 23 and have been in his late forties during this stay in Gaul.

Lucius Cornelius Cinna, praetor in 44 BC and an anti-Caesarean, was the husband of Pompey's daughter Pompeia (*RE* 4 [1900], 1287 [F. Münzer]). He had two sons:

(a) Lucius Cornelius Cinna junior, by an earlier wife (*PIR* C. 1338). This son was suffect consul in 32 BC and was not the grandson of Pompey; thus unless the sources are seriously confused, he could not be the conspirator.
(b) Gnaeus Cornelius Cinna Magnus, Lucius' son by Pompeia (*PIR* 1339; *RE* 4 [1900], 1288–89, and *Suppl.* 1 [1903], 328). This individual was a supporter of Antony and thus fits the description in Seneca (*Clem.* 1.9.11) of someone who was once an enemy *(prius hosti)*. Cinna is called an *adulescens* by Seneca (*Clem.* 1.9.3, 5), possibly applicable to him in 16–13 BC but

impossible in AD 4. Nor was this Cinna consul in the year following this stay or indeed any of the stays in Gaul.

Fitzler and Seeck (1918), 370–71, find it impossible to reconcile the inconsistencies and point out that the conspiracy is not mentioned by Velleius, Livy, or Suetonius and that in his other reference to Cinna (*Ben.* 4.30.2), Seneca does not mention it. They suspect that the incident may be fictitious.

   The general consensus is that Dio's account is the more reliable and taken from a source independent of Seneca, who may have confused Gnaeus with his father or his half-brother. Bauman (1967), 196, believes that Seneca was basically correct, in that Lucius was the conspirator, but that he distorted the events somewhat, which in turn misled Dio.

APPENDIX 11: THE CELEBRATION OF LIVIA'S MARRIAGE

An entry in one of the calendars, the *Fasti Verulani* (produced in the reign of Tiberius), seems to indicate that a festival was decreed by the Senate to mark Livia's marriage *(feriae ex s.c. quod eo die Augusta nupsit divo Aug[us]t[o])* on January 17. Livia is identified as Augusta and her husband as Divus Augustus, which seems to place the public celebration of the marriage in the post-Augustan period. But that later celebration has been called into question. In a different calendar, the *Fasti Praenestini*, there is a record of a dedication of some sort by Tiberius, presumably between AD 6 and 9, the period when the initial entries in this calendar seem to have been made. The record is fragmentary, but Mommsen's supplement, *n[umini Augusti ad aram q]uam dedicavit Ti. Caesar* ([sacrifices were carried out] to the Numen of Augustus at the altar that Tiberius dedicated), is generally accepted. The reference is followed by an entry in the same calendar, added probably soon after Augustus' death, revealing that the Senate decreed that the anniversary of the dedication of the altar was to be celebrated with a festival *(fe[riae ex s.c. q]u[od e.d. Ti. Caesar aram divo] Aug. patri dedicavit)*.

Degrassi (1963), 401 (see also Grether [1946], 235), suggests that the entry relating to the marriage in the *Fasti Verulani* was made in error, based on the erroneous belief that the festival established for the dedication of the altar had been established for the marriage.

APPENDIX 12: PALATINE VESTA

Calendars show that in 12 BC, on April 28, a dedication took place in Augustus' house on the Palatine (EJ, p. 48). The day and month are recorded also by Ovid (*Fast.* 4.949–50), who observes that on that date Vesta was received within the threshold of her kinsman (*cognati Vesta recepta est / limine*).

The dedicator is not named by the calendars, but it is almost certainly Augustus. The *Fasti Caeretani* state that a *signum* was dedicated *in domo P(ala-tino)* (in the Palatine house). The *Fasti Praenestini* give the location as *in domu imp. Caesaris* (in the house of Imperator Caesar), but there is no real inconsistency in the two statements. Unfortunately, the stone of the latter is damaged, and we do not know what was dedicated. The text reveals only gaps connected by the word *et (eo di[. . .]a? et [. . .] Vestae)*. Mommsen on *CIL* 1, 226, 317, assumed the existence of an actual temple to Vesta on the Palatine, although there was no physical evidence for a specific structure, nor is it specifically mentioned in the literature. He restored the word *aedicula* before *et* (whatever the correct reading, it has disappeared completely except for its final *a*), and added *ara* after *et*, hence *aedicula et ara* (shrine and altar). Degrassi (1955), 146, decided that an *m* precedes *et* and restored *signum et ara* (statue and altar). Guarducci (1964) read *signum et aedis* (statue and temple), on which see Fishwick (1992). The issue has been much debated since; see Kolbe (1966–67); Weinstock (1971), 275–76; Radke (1981), 363; Fishwick (1987–92), 88 n. 37; (1993); Simpson (1991); McDaniell (1995), 81–83; Capelli, *LTUR* 5.128–29.

APPENDIX 13: THE TITLE AUGUSTA IN THE JULIO-CLAUDIAN PERIOD

It is possible that the much-revered Antonia was granted the title of Augusta by her grandson Caligula in 37. If so, the gesture would have been in keeping with a number of other revolutionary measures carried out by Caligula, such as the extraordinary privileges extended to his sisters and the consecration of one of them, Drusilla. In a sense Caligula's measure was less dramatic than it seems at first sight. Antonia could not represent a challenge to the emperor's authority. She was by Caligula's accession a very elderly woman and was to die within months (see appendix 14).

The title became a serious issue in the reign of Caligula's successor, Claudius. The birth of a son, Tiberius Claudius Caesar Germanicus (Britannicus), probably in 41, was a great occasion for Claudius, who delighted in displaying the infant in public to the applause of the masses or in showing him off to the praetorians. In gratitude to his wife, Messalina, he eagerly heaped distinctions on her. Her birthday, for instance, was officially celebrated, and statues were erected in public places. His generosity in this sphere was repeated later. After the British campaign in AD 43 she was granted the privileges — both enjoyed earlier by Livia — of occupying the front seats at the theatre and of using the carpentum, or covered carriage, on sacred occasions, a privilege previously limited to individuals like Vestals and priests. But this was as far as Claudius would go. Significantly he refused to allow Messalina to be granted the title of Augusta, offered by the Senate possibly when she produced a male heir. The emperor doubtless felt that such an award would have gone beyond honouring her merely as his consort and have elevated her to a quasi-constitutional position that was out of character with Roman tradition. Nor did he allow Britannicus the title of Augustus (Dio 60.12.4–5, 22.2; Suet. *Claud.* 17.3; note that Messalina is called Sebaste on coins of Nicaea [*RPC* 2033–34, 2038], Nicodemia [*RPC* 2074], and Aegae [*RPC* 2430], and Augusta at Sinope [*RPC* 2130]).

The first usurpation of the title of Augusta by the wife of a living emperor was by Agrippina (the Younger), wife of Claudius. She was much more skilled than her predecessor Messalina in laying claim to power. As a Julian and blood descendant of Augustus, she recognised that she could be a considerable political asset to Claudius. By the end of 49 she had married the emperor and betrothed her son Nero to his daughter Octavia. Her success was crowned in the following year, when she officially became Augusta (Tac. *Ann.* 12.26.1; Dio 60.33.2a; Levick [1990], 71). From then on her official name in coins and inscriptions was Iulia Augusta Agrippina, a change of great symbolic importance. It seemed to elevate her to the status of empress — not, of course, in the technical sense of a woman with authority to make legally binding decisions, but in the sense of a woman who could lay equal claim to the maiestas that the office of emperor conveyed. For the first time the portraits of the emperor and his consort appear on the same official coin of Rome: Claudius is depicted on the obverse, a draped bust of Agrippina, identified as Agrippina Augusta, on the reverse (*RIC*[2] Claudius 80–81). An official silver coin of Ephesus, dated 50 or 51, similarly carries an obverse head of Claudius, and a reverse of Agrippina Augusta. Another Ephesian issue depicts jugate heads of Claudius and Agrippina Augusta (*RIC*[2] Claudius, 117, 119, erroneously described). The heads of the emperor and his wife appearing together on the same face of a coin is a remarkable first for Roman official (as opposed to local) coinage. The jugate heads, a type first developed by Ptolemy II to celebrate his marriage to his sister Arsinoe, signal strikingly the official sanction of the role of Agrippina as Claudius' partner. After Agrippina, the application of the title to a woman was no longer considered revolutionary. Poppaea, the wife of Nero, became Augusta when her daughter Claudia was born at Antium in January 63, and Claudia received the title at the same time (Tac. *Ann.* 15.23; *AFA* lxxix.6–7, lxxxii.27; *ILS* 234; Griffin [1984], 103). Vitellius named his mother Augusta, and it became the regular title for the wife of the princeps from the accession of Domitian in 81 (Tac. *Hist.* 2.89.2).

APPENDIX 14: ANTONIA
AS AUGUSTA

Suet. *Cal.* 15.2 claims that Caligula gave Antonia all the rights enjoyed by Livia; Dio 59.3.4 states that he gave Antonia the title of Augusta, made her priestess of Augustus, and granted her the privileges of the Vestal Virgins.

If Caligula offered Antonia such honours, she appears to have declined to use her new title during her lifetime. The *Fasti Ostienses*, recording her death on May 1, 37, describe her simply as Antonia. The first evidence for the application of the title of Augusta to Antonia in Rome is on an Arval fragment of January 31, 38, honouring her birthday in the year following her death (*AFA* xliii.7 [Smallwood 3.7]). The reference in Suet. *Claud.* 11.2 to *cognomen Augustae ab viva recusatum*, with Lipsius' emendation of the manuscript's *avia* to *viva*, suggests that Antonia had refused the distinction during her lifetime and that Claudius had the Senate bestow it on her after death. Unemended, reading *ab avia*, the text seems to suggest that Claudius' grandmother Livia had refused the honour, which clearly is nonsense. If Antonia declined the title during her lifetime, Caligula might have conferred it on her after her death (although Dio implies that he bestowed it at the very outset [*euthus*]). Claudius cancelled all Caligula's *acta* and may afterwards have reconfirmed the honour, as an act of piety towards his mother. The title appears in a fragmentary inscription from Corinth involving Tiberius (Gemellus) and Antonia Augusta, generally dated to the beginning of Caligula's reign, early 37 (Corinth 8.2.17; Kokkinos [1992], 46–47). Also, local coins of Corinth (*RPC* 1176–77) and of

Thessalonica (*RPC* 1573–74) of Caligula's reign call her Augusta / Sebaste, the only mints to do so. There is an undated coin of Tomi with the legend *Antonia Sebaste* (*RPC* 1833; see Kokkinos [1992], 87–89). The evidence of local coinage is of little value, if any, in deciding such questions. The coins of Thessalonica of the Claudian period do not give Antonia the title (*RPC* 1581–82, 1584–86). But Messalina is identified as Augusta / Sebaste on the local coins of Aegeae (*RPC* 2430), Nicaea (*RPC* 2033–34), Nicomedia (*RPC* 2074), and Sinope (*RPC* 2130), even though the title was officially withheld from her. On the question see Barrett (1996), 62, 268; Kokkinos (1992), 93.

APPENDIX 15: AUGUSTUS'
PALATINE RESIDENCE

The assumption is made on page 177 that the modest residence excavated on the Palatine and identified as the house of Augustus is not the property that Suetonius claimed Octavian acquired from Hortensius (Suet. *Aug.* 72.1). It seems unlikely that Hortensius would have lived in a modest house (Claridge [1998], 128, suggests that he owned the "Casa di Livia"); he was noted for his collection of objets d'art, which included a sphinx that he had acquired in partial payment for the defence of the rascal Verres, and a painting of the Argonauts by Cydias for which he paid 144,000 sesterces. He built a special shrine in his villa at Tusculum to hold it (Pliny *NH* 34.48, 35.130). Moreover, soon after the initial acquisition, Octavian used agents to buy properties that were adjacent to his own (Vell. 2.81.3). This expansion probably embraced the house of Catulus, one of the finest on the Palatine, said by Pliny to surpass even the splendid *(magnifica)* house of Crassus (Pliny *NH* 17.2), and adjacent to a public portico with plantations of trees, donated by Catulus from the spoils of the campaigns against the Germanic Cimbri (Cic. *Dom.* 62). This house was used by the famous teacher Marcus Verrius Flaccus, who stimulated effort in his pupils by the offer of glittering prizes. Flaccus was employed by Augustus at 100,000 sesterces a year to teach his grandsons Gaius and Lucius, probably early in the last decade of the century. The instruction took place in the atrium of Catulus' house, identified at that time as part of the imperial palace (Suet. *Gram.* 17).

The surviving house was decorated probably not long after 30 BC, to judge from the painting style. This would fit a residence voted for in 36, after the lightning damage, and built on a modest scale, not suited to the neighbour-hood but suited instead to Augustus' temperament. Suetonius may well have based his description of the simple residence on what had survived of it in his day, and may have mistakenly attributed it to Hortensius because he knew that Augustus had at one point acquired Hortensius' house. There is another com-plication. In AD 3 there was a serious fire on the Palatine. The Temple of Magna Mater to the west of the imperial palace was burnt down and rebuilt by Augustus. The imperial residence was also destroyed; at any rate, it was de-stroyed in the same year — whether in same fire is not known. Augustus' house was said to have been rebuilt at public expense after AD 3 (*RG* 19; Ovid *Fast.* 4.348; Val. Max. 1.8.11). But the surviving house was certainly not rebuilt after the early twenties — the paintings show us that. Moreover, Suetonius, *Aug.* 72.1, states that Augustus slept in the same room for more than forty years. This claim may exaggerate the emperor's true sleeping habits, but it does suggest continuous occupation of the same private residence for forty years, uninterrupted by the destruction in AD 3 and the replacement by a different residence. Otherwise the assertion would be self-evidently absurd. Nor need Augustus have named the forty-year figure — he may simply have made a general boast towards the end of his life, and Suetonius could have made the calculation.

It is likely, then, that the house that now survives was built for Augustus to take up residence after his return from Actium, in compensation for the land made over for the Temple of Apollo, and was in continuous occupation from then to the emperor's death, when it might have been abandoned. The fine residences of Hortensius and Catulus must have lain elsewhere in the imperial complex (Degrassi [1966–67]). The public aspects of the Roman house, par-ticularly those at the upper end of the social scale, have been laid out in some detail by Wallace-Hadrill (1988). Also, Zanker (1988) 49–53, 67–68, 85–89, has observed that Augustus seems to have taken his lead from Hellenistic rulers, for at sites like Pergamum and Alexandria the structures adjacent to the palace served as a kind of showplace. The fine residences of Hortensius and Catulus could have formed the kernel of the public area. But where were they located? Ovid may provide a clue. The poet seems to give the shrine of Vesta that Augustus established in his home a prominent place in the landscape of the Palatine, seeing it as almost equal in importance to Apollo's temple, one unit in a tripartite arrangement (Ovid *Fast.* 4.949–51, *Met.* 15.864–65; see also Dio 54.27.3). The shrine could not lie to the west of the Temple of Apollo, for that was bounded by the Temple of Magna Mater. It may be that the public part of Augustus' residence, originally made up of the houses of Hortensius and Catulus, lay to the east, and was framed by the section that housed Vesta's shrine to the east. This part of the house was severely damaged and rebuilt in AD 3 at the time of the destruction and rebuilding of the Temple of Magna Mater, although not necessarily as part of the same event. This area to the east has been overlaid by later building. One might, however, note a room that has survived the Domitianic rebuilding, the Aula Isiaca, a large vaulted hall, with decoration in apparently Egyptianizing motifs. This building used to be assigned to Caligula, largely on account of the Egyptian themes, but is now generally recognised as dating to the Augustan period (R. Ling, *CR* 35 [1985], 218; *JRS* 89 [1999], 248; Iacopi [1997].

APPENDIX 16: LIVIA'S FESTIVAL
ON THE PALATINE

The fourth-century calendar of Philocalaus and the fifth-century calendar of Silvius indicate that the Ludi Palatini began on January 17 (Grant [*Anniversary*, 1950], 156; Degrassi [1963], 239, 264). Although no ancient source mentions the connection, this date is significant as the anniversary of the wedding of Augustus and Livia in 38 BC.

Dio 56.46.5 states explicitly that the festival was established as a three-day event, and had been continued under every emperor down to his own day. Already by the reign of Caligula it had been extended. Dio 59.29.5–6 notes that Caligula added three extra days in the year of his death, AD 41. The assassins waited for five, and then struck on the last. This testimony seems to be corroborated by a contemporary source, Josephus (Jos. *Ant.* 19.77), who alludes to three extra days, although his text is so corrupt that his precise meaning eludes us (see Wiseman [1991], 56). Thus Dio and Josephus imply that the assassination took place on January 23. Suetonius says that it happened on January 24 (VIIII Kal. Febr.), although manuscript variants allow January 25 or 26. None of these dates matches January 23, six days after January 17. This might suggest that the games began originally on January 19. On the other hand, Degrassi suggests that the VIIII of Suetonius manuscripts might represent a confusion of XI for IX (numerals were notoriously prone to scribal errors). If he is right, Suetonius, Dio, and Josephus would be in harmony. Whether the six days instituted by Caligula remained in force after his day is not clear, but certainly by the fourth century the festival appears as a

six-day event in the calendar of Philocalaus. The extension certainly seems to
have occurred before the reign of Gordian III, whose birthday celebrations on
January 20 seem to have interrupted the Palatine festival.

Dio asserts that initially the festival was a private one *(idian)* (Fishwick
[1987–92] I.1, 163 n. 83). At some point the private celebration became a
public festival, as recorded in the calendars of Silvius and Philocalaus. The
date of this change is not known.

APPENDIX 17: DATE OF THE
LETTER TO THE SAMIANS

The date of the document discussed on page 198 is uncertain. The text is in Greek, but the letter's author is called *Augustos* (*sic*), a rare transliteration at this period and possibly added later — thus it is not necessarily safe to assume that the name proves that the text was originally written after 27 BC. The document must precede 20–19, when the Samians did in fact receive their freedom, and can hardly be earlier than late 39, when Octavian began to adopt the *praenomen imperatoris* (that is, placed *imperator* before his other names). The document speaks of Aphrodisias having supported Octavian and having been taken by storm *en to polemo* (in the war). Reynolds (1982), no. 13, assumes that the reference is to the campaign waged by the renegade Labienus in 40–39 BC, and she suggests a date of 38 for the inscription, because the general allusion to the war without further specification would be confusing if the document were dated after the Actium campaign in 31. The Samians might also have sought in 38 BC to take advantage of the recent marriage of Octavian to Livia to make their request. Not everyone has accepted Reynolds' dating. It has been argued that to the Aphrodisians there would have been no confusion about the reference to the war of Labienus, and contexts have been suggested from immediately after Actium in 31 (Badian [1984]) to the late twenties (Bowersock [1984], 52); see also Millar and Segal (1984), 42, 58 n. 9; (1992), 431–32; Flory (1993), 303 n. 27. To this might be added the consideration that 38 seems very early in the marriage for Livia to have lobbied her husband so seriously that he feels obliged to explain publicly his refusal of the request. On this basis the request could belong to the trip to the East that Augustus and his wife took in 22 or 19. It is conceivable that the petition of the Samians was turned down in 21, but on the repeated urging of Livia was granted in the following year.

APPENDIX 18: THE CULT OF BONA DEA AND LIVIA

There is some uncertainty over the identity of the Vestal *veteris nominis heres*, associated by Ovid with the establishment of the cult of Bona Dea. If we are to read *Clausorum* in his text at *Fasti* 5.155, we have an allusion to an unknown legendary founder of the same gens as Livia, a situation which would suit the tone of Ovid's poem and give an excellent context to Livia's restoration of the goddess' temple. As Herbert-Brown (1984), 135 n. 15, has pointed out, however, the superior reading of the manuscripts is not *Clausorum* but *Crassorum* (of the Crassi). If this reading is correct, it will be difficult not to see a reference to Licinia Crassi, a Vestal of noble birth, who is mentioned by Cicero as dedicating *ara, aedicula et pulvinar sub Saxo* in 123 BC (Cic. *Dom.* 136; Herbert-Brown [1984], 135 n. 15). Licinia's Vestal office and the location of her dedication argue strongly for the identification of her as the benefactor of the shrine of Bona Dea, although it must be noted that Cicero does not specify to whom she actually dedicated her foundation.

The role of Licinia would, however, present a problem. It seems that her dedication in 123 BC was later declared invalid because of her personal impropriety. She was accused of incest and tried before the pontifices in 114 BC (Dio 26.87.3). Herbert-Brown (1984), 139–41, does point out that, in his allusion to Licinia, Cicero seems deliberately to have avoided giving precise details about her, and it may be that her connection with Bona Dea was relatively unfamiliar by Livia's day. That said, it is difficult to see why Ovid should have gone out of his way to remind the reader that a woman who had "known" no man *(virgineo nullum corpore passa virum)* was the very member of the family of the Crassi who, according to Dio, had entertained a host of lovers. Johnson (1997), 409, sees the allusion to Licinia as a "clumsy . . . act of historical revisionism."

APPENDIX 19: AGRIPPINA AND
LIVIA IN AD 28-29

According to Tac. *Ann.* 5.3.1, the final attack on Agrippina the Elder and her son Nero was not made by Sejanus until after Livia's death — that is, in 29. Suet. *Cal.* 10.1, however, seems to contradict Tacitus, claiming that Caligula was taken to the home of Livia, still very much alive, after his mother, Agrippina, had been banished. Suetonius seems to gain some support from Pliny's account of the trial of Titius Sabinus, who had been an old friend of Germanicus and a frequent visitor to Agrippina's home (*PIR* T 202; *RE* 6 [1937], 1569 [A. Stein]). The reports of the soldiers on the headstrong and outspoken Nero had apparently been detailed enough to bring some sort of proceeding against the young man. As a result of what was disclosed there (we have no details), Sejanus began to investigate Sabinus. In early 28 Sabinus was convicted on the evidence of spies, who had kept him under surveillance by concealing themselves in his attic. He was executed and his body thrown down the Gemonian stairs (Tac. *Ann.* 4.68–70; Dio 58.1.1–3). When speaking of Sabinus' trial, Pliny *NH* 8.145 says that it came about *ex causa Neronis* — as a consequence of Nero's case. Because the trial of Sabinus belongs to 28, Nero must have been charged at least by that date and thus before Livia died. Velleius 2.130.4–5 is less specific, but he does strongly imply that Livia died after Agrippina and Nero had been brought down. The conflicting evidence has been the subject of much scholarly debate, and the most satisfactory explanation is probably that of Eckhard Meise, who argues that Sejanus' final attack was broken into two stages, the first before Livia's death in 29, when Agrippina and Nero were placed under house arrest on the mainland, and the second and more serious one when Livia was no longer on the scene and they could be banished to small islands. Admittedly, Suetonius does state that the children went to Livia's house after Agrippina had been banished *(ea relegata)*, but given that his narrative is very condensed at this point, events might well have been telescoped, and the phrase might have been used loosely not of the banishment proper but of her forced confinement in Herculaneum: Meise (1969), 240. Other modern treatments include Gardthausen, *RE* 10 (1918), 475; Gelzer, *RE* 10 (1918), 511; Charlesworth (1922), 260–61; Petersen, *PIR* I.217; Marsh (1931), 184–87; Rogers (1931), 160; (1935), 101; (1943), 57–59; Colin (1954), 389; Syme (1958), I.404–5; Koestermann (1963–68), on Tac. *Ann.* 5.3; Bauman (1992), 151.

ABBREVIATIONS

ANCIENT AUTHORS AND WORKS

AP	*Anthologia Palatina*
Apoc.	*Apocolocyntosis Divi Claudii*
App. *BC*	Appian, *Bella Civilia*
App. *Mith.*	Appian, *Bella Mithridatica*
Apul. *Apol.*	Apuleius, *Apologia*
Ath. *Deip.*	Athenaeus, *Deipnosphistae*
Aug. *Civ. Dei*	Augustine, *De Civitate Dei*
Aul. Gell. *NA*	Aulus Gellius, *Noctes Atticae*
Aur. Vict. *Caes.*	Aurelius Victor, *Caesares*
Bell. Afr.	*Bellum Africum*
Boethius, *Cons.*	Boethius, *De Consolatione Philosophiae*
Calp. Sic.	Calpurnius Siculus
Cato *De Agr.*	Cato, *De Agri Cultura*
Caes. *BC*	Caesar, *Bellum Civile*
Cic. *ad Att.*	Cicero, *ad Atticum*
Cic. *ad Fam.*	Cicero, *ad Familiares*
Cic. *ad Q. fr.*	Cicero, *ad Quintum Fratrem*
Cic. *Brut.*	Cicero, *Brutus*
Cic. *Cael.*	Cicero, *Pro Caelio*
Cic. *Cat.*	*In Catilinam*

Cic. *De Orat.*	Cicero, *De Oratore*
Cic. *De Rep.*	Cicero, *De Republica*
Cic.*Div.*	Cicero, *De Divinatione*
Cic. *Dom.*	Cicero, *De Domo Sua*
Cic. *Har. Resp.*	Cicero, *De Haruspicum Responso*
Cic. *Inv.*	Cicero, *De Inventione Rhetorica*
Cic. *Mil.*	Cicero, *Pro Milone*
Cic. *ND*	Cicero, *De Natura Deorum*
Cic. *Off.*	Cicero, *De Officiis*
Cic. *Phil.*	Cicero, *Orationes Philippicae*
Cic. *Pis.*	Cicero, *In Pisonem*
Cic. *Rab. Perd.*	Cicero, *Pro Rabirio Perduellonis Reo*
Cic. *Rosc.*	Cicero, *Pro Sexto Roscio*
Cic. *Sest.*	Cicero, *Pro Sestio*
Cic. *Tusc.*	Cicero, *Tusculanae Disputationes*
Cic. *Verr.*	Cicero, *in Verrem*
C. Th.	*Codex Theodosianus*
Col. *RR*	Columella, *De Re Rustica*
Cons. Liv.	*Consolatio ad Liviam*
Diod. Sic.	Diodorus Siculus
Dion. Hal.	Dionysius of Halicarnassus
Dem. *In Neaer.*	Demosthenses, *In Neaeram*
Donatus, *Vit. Verg.*	Donatus, *Vita Vergilii*
Eleg. in Maec.	*Elegia in Maecenatem*
Epit. de Caes.	*Epitome de Caesaribus* (anonymous)
Euseb. *Onom.*	Eusebius, *Onomasticon*
Eutrop.	Eutropius
Fast. Ant.	*Fasti* Antiates
Fast. Ost.	*Fasti* Ostienses
Front. *Aq.*	Frontinus, *de Aquaeductibus*
Gaius *Inst.*	Gaius, *Institutes*
Hor. *Epod.*	Horace, *Epodes*
Hor. *Odes*	Horace, *Odes*
Jer. *Chron.*	Saint Jerome, *Chronica*
Jos. *Ant.*	Josephus, *Antiquitates Judaicae*
Jos. *Ap.*	Josephus, *Contra Apionem*
Jos. *BJ*	Josephus, *de Bello Judaico*
Juv. *Sat.*	Juvenal, *Satires*
Lact. *Inst. Div.*	Lactantius, *Institutiones Divinae*

Livy *Per.*	Livy, *Periochae*
Lucan *BC*	Lucan, *Bellum Civile*
Lysias *In Diog.*	Lysias, *in Diogeiton*
Macrob. *Sat.*	Macrobius, *Saturnalia*
Marc. *De Med.*	Marcellus Empiricus, *De Medicina*
Marc. Aurel. *Med.*	Marcus Aurelius, *Meditations*
Martial, *Spect.*	Martial, *Liber de Spectaculis*
Nep. *Att.*	Nepos, *Atticus*
Nic. *Vit. Caes.*	Nicolaus Damascinus, *Vita Caesaris*
Obseq.	Obsequens
Ovid *AA*	Ovid, *Ars Amatoria*
Ovid *Fast.*	Ovid, *Fasti*
Ovid *Met.*	Ovid, *Metamorphoses*
Ovid *Pont.*	Ovid, *ex Ponto*
Ovid *Trist.*	Ovid, *Tristia*
Philo *Flacc.*	Philo, *Contra Flaccum*
Philo *Leg.*	Philo, *Legatio*
Philost. *Apoll.*	Philostratus, *Via Apollonii*
Phlegon, *Mir.*	Phlegon, *Miracula*
Plaut. *Most.*	Plautus, *Mostellaria*
Pliny *Ep.*	Pliny, *Epistulae*
Pliny *HN*	Pliny, *Historia Naturalis*
Pliny *Paneg.*	Pliny, *Panegyricus*
Plut. *Ant.*	Plutarch, *Antonius*
Plut. *Caes.*	Plutarch, *Caesar*
Plut. *Cat. Mai.*	Plutarch, *Cato Maior*
Plut. *Cat. Min.*	Plutarch, *Cato Minor*
Plut. *Cic.*	Plutarch, *Cicero*
Plut. *Cor.*	Plutarch, *Coriolanus*
Plut. *De garr.*	Plutarch, *De garrulitate*
Plut. *Gai. Gracc.*	Plutarch, *Gaius Gracchus*
Plut. *Galb.*	Plutarch, *Galba*
Plut. *Lucull.*	Plutarch, *Lucullus*
Plut. *Pomp.*	Plutarch, *Pompeius*
Plut. *Publ.*	Plutarch, *Publicola*
Plut. *QR*	Plutarch, *Quaestiones Romanae*
Plut. *Sull.*	Plutarch, *Sulla*
Plut. *Tib. Gracc.*	Plutarch, *Tiberius Gracchus*
Prop.	Propertius

Prud. *Con. Symm.*	Prudentius, *Contra Symmachum*
Ptol. *Geog.*	Ptolemy, *Geographia*
Quint. *Inst. Or.*	Quintilian, *Institutio Oratoria*
RG	*Res Gestae Divi Augusti*
Sall. *BC*	Sallust, *Bellum Civile*
Sall. *Cat.*	Sallust, *Catilina*
Schol. Juv. *Sat.*	Scholiast, on Juvenal's *Satires*
Sen. *Ben.*	Seneca, *De Beneficiis*
Sen. *Brev.*	Seneca, *De Brevitate Vitae*
Sen. *Clem.*	Seneca, *De Clementia*
Sen. *Cons. Helv.*	Seneca, *Consolatio ad Helviam*
Sen. *Cons. Liv.*	Seneca, *Consolatio ad Liviam*
Sen. *Cons. Marc.*	Seneca, *Consolatio ad Marciam*
Sen. *Cons. Polyb.*	Seneca, *Consolatio ad Polybium*
Sen. *Cons. Sap.*	Seenca, *De Constantia Sapientiae*
Sen. *Contr.*	Seneca, *Controversiae*
Sen. *Ep.*	Seneca, *Epistulae*
Sen. *Ira*	Seneca, *De Ira*
Sen. *QN*	Seneca, *Quaestiones Naturales*
Serv. on Verg. *Aen.*	Servius, on Vergil's *Aeneid*
SHA	*Historia Augusta*
Simplicius, *In cat.*	Simplicius, *In Categoria*
Stat. *Silv.*	Statius, *Silvae*
Suet. *Aug.*	Suetonius, *Augustus*
Suet. *Cal.*	Suetonius, *Caligula*
Suet. *Claud.*	Suetonius, *Claudius*
Suet. *Div. Jul.*	Suetonius, *Divus Julius*
Suet. *Dom.*	Suetonius, *Domitianus*
Suet. *Galb.*	Suetonius, *Galba*
Suet. *Gram.*	Suetonius, *De Grammaticis*
Suet. *Nero*	Suetonius, *Nero*
Suet. *Oth.*	Suetonius, *Otho*
Suet. *Tib.*	Suetonius, *Tiberius*
Suet. *Vesp.*	Suetonius, *Vespasianus*
Suet. *Vit.*	Suetonius, *Vitellius*
Sym. *Rel.*	Symmachus, *Relationes*
Tac. *Ag.*	Tacitus, *Agricola*
Tac. *Ann.*	Tacitus, *Annales*
Tac. *Dial.*	Tacitus (?), *Dialogus*

Tac. *Germ.*	Tacitus, *Germania*
Tac. *Hist.*	Tacitus, *Historiae*
Ulp. *Dig.*	Ulpian, *Digesta*
Ulp. *Reg.*	Ulpian, *Institutiones Regulae*
Val. Max.	Valerius Maximus
Varro, *LL*	Varro, *Lingua Latina*
Varro, *RR*	Varro, *Res Rusticae*
Vell.	Velleius Paterculus
Verg. *Aen.*	Vergil, *Aeneid*
Vitr. *Arch.*	Vitruvius, *De Architectura*
Zosim.	Zosimus

MODERN TITLES

AA	*Archäologischer Anzeiger*
AAAH	*Acta ad Archaeologiam et Artium Historiam Pertinentia*
AAntHung	*Acta Antiqua Academiae Scientiarum Hungaricae*
AC	*L'Antiquité Classique*
ACD	*Acta Classica Universitatis Scientiarum Debrecenensis*
AE	*L'Année Epigraphique*
AFA	*Acta Fratrum Arvalium*
AFLPer	*Annali della Facoltà di Lettere e Filosofia*
AfrIt	*Africa Italiana*
AHR	*American Historical Review*
AJA	*American Journal of Archaeology*
AJAH	*American Journal of Ancient History*
AJP	*American Journal of Philology*
Anc. Soc.	*Ancient Society*
ANRW	*Aufstieg und Niedergang der römischen Welt*
Arch. Class.	*Archeologia Classica*
BASP	*Bulletin of the American Society of Papyrologists*
BC	*Bulletino della Commisione Archaeologica Communale di Roma*
BCH	*Bulletin de Correspondence Hellénique*
BGU	*Berliner griechische Urkunden*
BICS	Bulletin of the Institute of Classical Studies
BJ	*Bonner Jahrbücher*
BMC	H. Mattingly, *A Catalogue of the Roman Coins in the British Museum* (London, 1923)

BMCR	*Bullettino del Museo della Civiltà romana*
BMCRR	H. A. Grueber, *Coins of the Roman Republic in the British Museum* (London, 1910, rpt. 1970)
BVAB	*Bulletin van de Vereeniging tot Bevordering de Kennis de Antieke Beschaving*
CAH	*Cambridge Ancient History* (Cambridge 1996), vol. 10
CB	*Classical Bulletin*
CIG	*Corpus Inscriptionum Graecarum*
CIL	*Corpus Inscriptionum Latinarum*
CJ	*Classical Journal*
C&M	*Classical et Mediaevalia*
Corinth	*Corinth: Results of Excavations conducted by the American School at Athens* (Cambridge, Mass., 1929–)
CP	*Classical Philology*
CPR	*Corpus Papyrorum Raineri*
CQ	*Classical Quarterly*
CR	*Classical Review*
CRAI	Comptes Rendues de l'Académie des Inscriptions et Belles-Lettres
CSCA	*California Studies in Classical Antiquity*
CT	*Les Cahiers de Tunisie*
CV	*Classical Views*
CW	*The Classical World*
DAW	*Denkschriften der Akademie der Wissenschaften*
Degrassi	A. Degrassi, *I fasti consolari dell'impero romano dal 30 avanti Cristo al 613 dopo Cristo* (Rome, 1952)
Ditt.³	W. Dittenberger, ed., *Sylloge Inscriptionum Graecarum*, 3d ed.
EClás	*Estudios Clásicos*
EJ	V. Ehrenberg and A. H. M. Jones, *Documents Illustrating the Reigns of Augustus and Tiberius* (Oxford, 1952)
EMC	*Échos du Monde Classique*
FGH	*Fragmente der Griechische Historiker*
FIR	*Fontes Iuris Romani*
FOS	M. T. Raepsaet-Charlier, *Prosopographie des femmes de l'ordre sénatorial* (Louvain, 1987)
FUR	*Forma Urbis Romae*
GNS	*Gazette Numismatique Suisse*

GR	Greece and Rome
GRBS	Greek, Roman, and Byzantine Studies
GS	Th. Mommsen, *Gesammelte Schriften* (Berlin, 1905–13)
HSCP	Harvard Studies in Classical Philology
HThR	Harvard Theological Review
IG	Inscriptiones Graecae
IGR	Inscriptiones Graecae ad Res Romanas pertinentes
IJCT	International Journal of the Classical Tradition
ILN	Illustrated London News
ILS	Inscriptiones Latinae Selectae
Inscr. Ital.	Inscriptiones Italiae
Inst.	Institutiones
IRT	Inscriptions of Roman Tripolitania
JDAI	Jahrbuch des Deutschen Archäologischen Instituts
JEA	Journal of Egyptian Archaeology
JNG	Jahrbuch für Numismatik und Geldgeschichte
JÖAI	Jahrshefte des Österreichischen Archäologischen Instituts
JRA	Journal of Roman Archaeology
JRS	Journal of Roman Studies
KölnJb	Kölner Jahrbuch für Vor- und Frühgeschichte
LEC	Les Études Classiques
LTUR	M. Steinby, *Lexon Topographicum Urbis Romae* (Rome, 1993)
MAAR	Memoirs of the American Academy in Rome
MDAI(A)	Mitteilungen des Deutschen Archäologischen Instituts. Athenische Abteilung
MDAI(R)	Mitteilungen des Deutschen Archäologischen Instituts. Römische Abteilung
MEFRA	Mélanges de l'Ecole française de Rome, Antiquité
MH	Museum Helveticum
MMAI	Monuments et Mémoires publiés par l'Académie des Inscriptions et Belles-Lettres
MRR	T. R. S. Broughton, *Magistrates of the Roman Republic* (New York, 1951, rpt. Chico, Calif., 1984)
NAC	Numismatica e Antichità classiche
NC	Numismatic Chronicle
NS	Notizie degli Scavi
NZ	Numismatische Zeitschrift

OCD	*Oxford Classical Dictionary*
ORF	*Oratorum Romanorum Fragmenta*
Pap. Ryl.	*Catalogue of the Greek Papyri in the John Rylands Library at Manchester*
P. Berol.	*Berlin Papyri*
P. Bour.	*Le Papyrus Bouriant*
PBSR	*Papers of the British School at Rome*
PCPhS	*Proceedings of the Cambridge Philological Society*
PIR	*Prosopographia Imperii Romani*
Piso Decree	*Senatus Consultum de Cn. Pisone Patre*
P. Lond.	*Greek Papyri in the British Museum*
P. Med.	*Papiri Milanesi*
P. Mich.	*Papyri in the University of Michigan Collection*
P. NYU	*Papyri in New York University*
P. Oxy.	*Oxyrhynchus Papyri*
PP	*La Parola del Passato*
PSI	*Papiri Greci e Latini*
P. Sorb.	*Papyrus de la Sorbonne*
P. Vindob.	*Papyrus Vindobonensis*
QAL	*Quaderni di Archeologia della Libia*
RA	*Revue Archéologique*
RAL	*Rendiconti dell'Accademia dei Lincei*
RBS	*Roman Brick Stamps*
RCCM	*Rivista di Cultura classica e medioevale*
RdA	*Rivista di Archeologia*
RE	*Paulys Real-Encyclopedie der classischen Altertumswissenschaft*
REA	*Revue des Études Anciennnes*
REL	*Revue des Études Latines*
Rev. Hist.	*Revue Historique*
RH	*Revue Historique*
RhM	*Rheinisches Museum für Philologie*
RFIC	*Rivista di Filologia e di Istruzione Classica*
RIA	*Rivista dell'Instituto Nazionale di Archeologia*
RIDA	*Revue Internationale des Droits de l'Antiquité*
RIC²	C. H. V. Sutherland and R. A. G. Carson, *The Roman Imperial Coinage* (London, 1984, 2d ed.)
RIL	Instituto Lombardo. Rendicanti. Classe di Lettere Morali e Storiche

RM	*Rheinisches Museum*
RN	*Revue Numismatique*
RPAA	*Rendiconti della Pontificia Accademia di Archeologia*
RPC	A. Burnett et al., *Roman Provincial Coinage* (London, 1991)
RPh	*Revue de Philologie*
RSA	*Rivista storica dell'Antichità*
SB	*Sammelbuch griechische Urkunden aus Ägypten*
SBA	*Sammelbuch griechischen Urkunden aus Ägypten*
SchNR	*Schweizerische numismatische Rundschau*
SEG	*Supplementum Epigraphicum Graecum*
Smallwood	E. M. Smallwood, *Documents Illustrating the Principates of Gaius, Claudius, and Nero* (Cambridge, 1967)
SO	*Symbolae Osloenses*
SR	Th. Mommsen, *Römisches Staatsrecht* (Lepizig, 1887, rpt. Graz, 1963)
StudClas	*Studii Clasice*
StudRom	*Studi Romani*
Syme *Papers A*	Syme, R. *Roman Papers* (Oxford, 1979–84) vols. 1–3
Syme *Papers B*	Syme, R. *Roman Papers* (Oxford, 1988) vols. 4, 5
Syme *Papers C*	Syme, R. *Roman Papers* (Oxford, 1991) vols. 6, 7
Tab. Heb.	*Tabula Hebana*
Tab. Siar.	*Tabula Siarensis*
TAM	*Tituli Asiae Minoris*
TAPA	*Transactions of the American Philological Association*
TZ	*Trierer Zeitschrift*
WS	*Wiener Studien*
Würz. Jhb	*Würzburger Jahrbücher*
YClS	*Yale Classical Studies*
ZÖG	*Zeitschrift für die Österreichen Gymnasien*
ZPE	*Zeitschrift für Papyrologie und Epigraphik*
ZSS	*Zeitschrift der Savigny-Stiftung*

NOTES

1. FAMILY BACKGROUND

1. Tac. *Ann.* 5.1.1.
2. Verg. *Aen.* 7.706.
3. Livy 2.16, see also Dion. Hal. 5.40.3, Suet. *Tib.* 1.1. On the consul of 495, see Wiseman (1979), 60–61.
4. Suet. *Tib.* 2.1 mistakenly calls Hasdrubal's opponent Tiberius.
5. Tac. *Ann.* 6.51; Suet. *Tib.* 3.1 (erroneously naming Publius as Appius). A plebeian branch of the family, the Claudii Marcelli, was descended, according to Cic. *De Orat.* 1.176, from a freedman of the patrician family.
6. Huntsman (1997), 41, argues that the eclipse of the Nerones may be more apparent than real, and simply reflect gaps in the sources. On the Pulchri during the triumvirate and Augustan periods: Wiseman (1970).
7. Tac. *Ann.* 1.4.3; cf. Livy 2.56.7; Suet. *Tib.* 2.4; Wiseman (1979), 113–39, attributes the hostile tradition to Valerius Antias, the annalist of the Sullan period; Alföldi (1965), 159–64, to Fabius Pictor; see also Ogilvie (1965), 217; Goodyear (1972), 121.
8. Livy *Per.* 19 (cf. 22.42.9); Cic. *ND* 2.7 (cf. *Div.* 1.29, 2.20, 71); Val. Max. 1.4.3, 8.1.4; Suet. *Tib.* 2.2.
9. Obseq. 21; Dio 22 fr. 74.1; Orosius 5.4.7; Livy *Per.* 53; Suet. *Tib.* 2.4; *RE* 3.2 (1899), 2848, no. 295 (F. Münzer).
10. Suet. *Tib.* 2.2; the name Clausius Russus is conjectured by Ihm (1901), 303–4. On the story: Premerstein (1937), 18; Taylor (1960), 137; Brunt (1988), 413. Taylor notes that the cognomen Drusus must be wrong, because it derived from Livia's ancestry. She suggests that the story was concocted by detractors of Appius the Censor (see also Mommsen [1864–69], 1.308–10).

11. Claudia, sister of Claudius Pulcher: Livy *Per.* 19; Suet. *Tib.* 2.3; Aul. Gell. *NA* 10.6; Val Max. 8.1.4; *RE* 3.2 (1899), 2885, no. 382 (F. Münzer). Claudia, daughter of Appius: Cic. *Cael.* 34; Suet. *Tib.* 2.4 (described as sister, not daughter); Val. Max. 5.4.6; *RE* 3.2 (1899), 2886, no. 384 (F. Münzer). Clodia: Cic. *Cael.* 14, 34.

12. Suet. *Tib.* 3.1 (Suetonius occasionally confuses the Claudii Pulchri and Nerones). Marcus: *ILS* 124; *IGR* 4.982; *RE* 13.1 (1926), 881–84 (F. Münzer), no. 19; Drumann-Groebe (1964), *Claudii*, no. 30; Willems (1878), I. 515, no. 308; Shackleton-Bailey (1991), 77, calls him a Pulcher. Münzer ("Claudianus," 1926), 882, claims that Livia's father was a Nero (and that Suetonius got it wrong); he suggests that there had been some earlier intermarriage between the Pulchri and Nerones, and thus the father had both ancestries. Huntsman (1997), 22, 39, 67, 69, supports the notion of Marcus being a Nero because it makes Livia's first marriage (to a Claudius Nero) more intelligible and is supported, he claims, by evidence of her property holdings (that evidence is very tenuous). If Marcus was in fact a Pulcher, there would be two known candidates for *his* father (and Livia's grandfather) — the consul of 92 BC, Gaius Claudius Pulcher (*RE* 3.2 [1899], 2856 no. 302 [F. Münzer]; Syme [1958], 424 n. 6) or Appius Claudius Pulcher, who held the office in 79 (*RE* 3.2 [1899], 2848–49 no. 296 [F. Münzer]). Pisaurum: Cic. *Sest.* 9; Catullus 81.3. Marcus' connection with Pisaurum: Cic. *ad Att.* 2.7.3.

13. *CIL* 2.1667 (Tucci, Baetica); *ILS* 125 (Marruvium); IGR 4.983 (Samos); see Syme (1939), 358 n. 1; Taylor (1960), 188–89; Linderski (1974), 465; Hurley (1993), 93–94; Huntsman (1997), 30. For marriage between senatorials and municipals: Taylor (1949), 39; Wiseman (1971), 53. For wealth as a possible attraction, Levick ("Tiberius," 1976), 13.

14. Suet. *Tib.* 5, *Cal.* 23.2; Ollendorff (1926), 901; Barrett (1990), 218–19.

15. Münzer ("Livius," 1926), 810; Huntsman (1997), 4–11.

16. Vell. 2.14.2.

17. Vell. 2.75.3, 94.1; Suet. *Tib.* 3.1; Tac. *Ann.* 5.1.1, 6.51.1.

18. But see Drumann-Grobe (1964), 2.158; Huntsman (1997), 3, 19–20. Note that Marcus was a *iudex quaestionis* presiding over cases under the Lex Scantina in 50 BC (*MRR* 248). If he did this as praetor *suo anno*, he would have to have been born in 89, two years after the famous tribune's murder. Livius Drusus might have adopted him as an infant: see Münzer ("Claudianus," 1926), 882. It is important to note, however, that there is no actual evidence that Livius Drusus the tribune was the adoptive father, as taken for granted in most modern sources. Huntsman (1997), 21, notes another candidate — Mamercus Aemilius Lepidus Livianus, consul in 77 (*RE* 1.1 [1893], 564 no. 80 [E. Klebs]); he was adopted by an Aemilius, but he could have adopted Livia's father before his own adoption.

19. Diod. Sic. 37.10.1; see also Dio 28.96.2.

20. Vell. 2.85.3.

21. Cic. *ad Att.* 2.7.3.

22. *AFA* xxxive.2 (AD 27); xliiic.2 (AD 38). With a different logic, Kienast (1990), 83, expresses Livia's birthday as January 28.

23. Cic. *ad Att.* 4.15.9, 16.5, 17.5; *ad Q.fr.* 2.16.3; Tac. *Dial.* 21.2.

24. Lex Scantinia: Cic. *ad Fam.* 8.14.4. Gardens: Cic. *ad Att.* 12.21.2, 22.3, 23.3, 25.2, 31.2, 33.1, 37.2, 38.2, 39.2, 41.3, 44.2, 13.26.1; Huntsman (1997), 43.

25. *CIL* 11.3517. Pirates: App. *Mith.* 95; Florus 1.41.9. Catilinarians: Sall. *Cat.* 50.4; App. *BC* 2.1.5.

26. The notion that Livia and her husband were cousins seems to be based on the assumption that Suetonius was in error in describing Livia's father as a Pulcher rather than a Nero: Willrich (1911), 8; Münzer ("Claudianus," 1926), 882; Ollendorff (1926), 901; Sirago (1979), 176; Winkes (1985), 56; Treggiari (1991), 129.

27. Cic. *ad Fam.* 13.64.

28. Cic. *ad Q. fr.* 3.1.15, 2.1; Gruen (1974), 322–24.

29. Cic. *ad Fam.* 13.64.

30. Cic. *ad Fam.* 3.12.2; *ad Att.* 6.6.1; Treggiari (1991), 127–34; Syme, *Papers C*, 239.

31. *Bell. Alex.* 25.3; Suet. *Tib.* 4.1; Dio 42.40.6.

32. On the possible colonies founded, see Christol and Goudineau (1987–88), 90–92.

33. Vell. 2.75.1; Suet. *Tib.* 4.1.

34. Age at marriage: Hopkins (1965, 1966); Weaver (1972), 182; Shaw (1987); Treggiari (1991), 399–402.

35. Suet. *Aug.* 2.

36. Priesthood and city prefecture: Cic. *Phil.* 2.71, 5.17; Caesar *BC* 3.99; Vell. 2.59.3; Nic. *Aug.* 5. Military posts: Nic. *Aug.* 9; Suet. *Aug.* 82.1.

37. Nic. *Aug.* 10; Vell. 2.59.3; Suet. *Aug.* 8 says nothing about Octavius' fighting in Spain; Dio 43.41.3 makes it sound as if he was there during the campaign.

38. App. *BC* 3.94; Dio 45.5.3–4; both claim that the main motivation was financial; Dio notes that Octavian would also benefit in other, unspecified, ways.

39. On coins of 43 BC he has started to call himself C. Caesar; Crawford (1974), no. 490.

40. Cic. *Phil.* 13.24.

41. Dio 47.18–19.3. Inscriptional evidence shows that Octavian was using the title after the Peace of Brundisium in 40 (Degrassi [1963], 1.87). Coins with the legend (Crawford [1974], nos. 525, 526) probably begin in the same year. Alföldi (1973) dates the coins to 43. See Weinstock (1971), 309 n. 12; Kienast (1982), 42; Pollini (1990), 346; Southern (1998), 219 n. 19.

42. Shackleton-Bailey (1960), 262 n. 2; Syme (1939), 199 n. 1, seems to incline towards Pompeian sympathies. Willems (1878), I. 515 n. 308, and Bruhns (1978), 47, suggest that there is no way to tell. Brutus: Cic. *ad Fam.* 11.19.1; cf. 11.14.2. Proscription and death: Dio 48.44.1; Vell. 2.71.3; see Hinard (1985), 485–86, no. 78.

43. On Marcus Libo: Weinribb (1968); Hallett (1984), 160 n. 8. Scheid ("Scribonia," 1975), 365–68, argues that Scribonia, wife of Octavian, was the daughter, not the sister, of L. Scribonius Libo, consul in 34 BC. On the penalties suffered by the proscribed: Hinard (1985).

44. Pliny *HN* 10.154; Suet. *Tib.* 14.2.

45. *ILS* 108; EJ, p. 54; Suet. *Tib.* 5 (date and year of birth), 73.1 (date of death: he died on March 16 in the seventy-eighth year of his life and in the twenty-third year of his reign); Tac. *Ann.* 6.50.5 (confirming March 16, 37, and the seventy-eighth year for death). Similarly Dio 58.28.5 reports that Tiberius had lived seventy-seven years,

four months, nine days. Dio had the day of death wrong as March 26 (cf. Dio 57.2.4).

46. Suet. *Tib.* 4.2; Vell. 2.75; Dio 48.15.3. Gaius Velleius: Vell. 2.76.1.

47. Rawson (1973), 226–27; (1977), 345; Bowersock (1984), 176–77. Huntsman (1997), 49, suggests that Tiberius Claudius went east before Octavian moved closer to Sextus Pompeius.

48. Tac. *Ann.* 6.51.1; Hinard (1985), no. 41.

49. App. *BC* 4.39–40 gives examples of wives who supported their husbands in time of exile. He notes also (*BC* 4.23) the case of a woman who added her husband's name to the proscription lists so that she could marry her lover.

50. App. *BC* 5.52; Dio 48.15.2.

51. Winkes (1985), 56; Huntsman (1997), 54: a Decius or Decimus Livius left a dedication at the Laconian port of Gytheum (*CIL* I² 2650). He was presumably the client of a prominent Livian. On Sparta as a client of the Claudii: Carteledge and Spawforth (1989), 94.

52. Suet. *Tib.* 6.2–3; Dio 54.7.2.

53. Vell. 2.77.2–3; Tac. *Ann.* 5.1; Suet. *Tib.* 4.3. On early summer 39 for the Treaty of Misenum, see Gabba (1970), 118, citing Gardthausen (1896), I.220; middle of summer: Carcopino (1958), 69.

2. MARRIAGE

1. See Scheid ("Scribonia," 1975), 365–68, for the alternative theory that Scribonia was Libo's daughter.

2. Scribonia: Sen. *Ep.* 70.10; Suet. *Aug.* 62.2, 69.1; Dio 55.10.14; *PIR* S220, *PIR* C1395; *RE* 2 (1921), 891–92 (M. Fluss); Hallett (1984), 161 n. 9; Bauman (1992), 246 n. 45. Marriage to Octavian: App. *BC* 5.53; Dio 48.16.3; Leon (1951), Levick (1975); Syme (1986), 248. Character: Suet. *Aug.* 62.2; Syme (1939), 219, 229, 378. Son's consulship: Prop. 4.11.66. Mistress: Suet. *Aug.* 69.1; Sen. *Ep.* 1.70.10; Puteal Libonis: Lugli (1947), 46; Richardson (1992), 322–23. Sentia: *CIL* 6.31276. Age: Syme (1986), 256 n. 9. Julia's birth: Dio 48.34.3; Macrob. *Sat.* 2.5.2. Accompanies Julia: Vell. 2.100.5; Dio 55.10.14. Livia's *comitas:* Tac. *Ann.* 5.1.3.

3. App. *BC* 5.72; Dio 48.36.4; Hinard (1985), 253–55.

4. Dio 48.34.3; Carcopino (1958), 71. Coins: Crawford (1974), nos. 534.3 (38 BC), 538.1 (37 BC), 540.1 (36 BC).

5. Suet. *Aug.* 69.1; Tac. *Ann.* 5.1.2.

6. Vell. 2.75.3; Tac. *Ann.* 5.1.2; *Epit. de Caes.* 1.23. Bridal beauty: Catullus 61.186–88.

7. Plut. *Ant.* 20.1; Suet. *Aug.* 62.1 actually says *duxit uxorem* of Claudia, even though she was under age; Dio 46.56.3 implies that Octavian had done no more than agree to the union; Carter (1982), 182–83.

8. Vell. 2.75.3, 79.2; Tac. *Ann.* 5.1.1; Flory (1988), 345–46. Antony's taunt: Cic. *Phil.* 3.15; Ferrero (1911), 54–55; Kienast (1982), 44. Agrippa's funeral: Dio 54.29.6; Syme (1939), 132, 344, *Papers C*, 338–45.

9. Tac. *Ann.* 5.1; Suet. *Aug.* 69.1; Dio 48.34.3.

10. Tac. *Ann.* 1.10.5; Dio 48.44.1–2.

11. Claudius and Agrippina: Tac. *Ann.* 12.5. Perturbatio partus: Tab IV.4 (= Gell.3.16.2); Gaius *Inst.* 1.55: *item in potestate nostra sunt liberi nostri, quos iustis nuptiis procreavimus;* Digest 3.2.11; Ulp. *Reg.* 14; Ulpian *Dig.* 38, 16, 3.9.11; Justinian Codex 5,17,8,4b; Corbett (1930), 249–50; Humbert (1972), 127–30; Suerbaum (1980), 344.

12. The approach to the pontiffs may have been largely a public relations exercise. Bauman (1992), 95, speculates that when Aemilius Lepidus was allowed to retain his office as pontifex maximus after being deposed from the triumvirate in 36 (App. *BC* 5.131), it was in recognition of his service in this particular matter. Of the fifteen pontiffs at the time of the consultation by Octavian, we know the names of seven. The most prominent were not in Rome. Marcus Aemilius Lepidus was in Africa, Mark Antony was in Athens, Publius Ventidius Bassus, an Antonian, was in the East, dealing with the Parthians, and Gnaeus Domitius Calvinus was in Spain. Publius Sulpicius Rufus, a Caesarian, may have been in Rome. The other two known pontiffs were Octavian and Tiberius Nero. Thus the timing of the question could not have been better from Octavian's point of view; see Huntsman (1997), 63 n. 50.

13. Tac. *Ann.* 1.10.5, 5.1.2. Caligula: Suet. *Cal.* 25.1; Dio 59.8.7, who gives the bride's name as Cornelia Orestina Vitellius. Claudius and Agrippina: Tac. *Ann.* 12.6.2. Antonian propaganda: Tac. *Ann.* 4.34.5; Suet. *Aug.* 69.1, 70.1; Flory (1988); Charlesworth (1933), 172–77.

14. Vell. 2.79.2; 2.94.1; Pliny *HN* 7.150; Suet. *Tib.* 4.3; Dio 48.44.3; *Epit. de Caes.* 1.23; Levick ("Tiberius," 1976), 15; Schilling (1977), 214. Tiberius' motives: Cic. *ad Fam.* 13.641; Carcopino (1929), 225.

15. Marcia: Plut. *Cato Min.* 25.5. Lollia: Dio 59.12.1.

16. Dio 48.44.3. On the delicia: Sen. *Cons. Sap.* 11.3; Stat. *Silv.* 2.1.72, 5.5.66 (emended); Quint. *Inst. Or.* 1.2.7; on the form of the word see Slater (1974), 134.

17. App. *BC* 5.67–68; Suet. *Aug.* 70. On the dodekatheos: Pike (1919); Scott (1929), 140; Taylor (1931), 119; Eitrem (1932), 42–43; Weinrich (1924–37), 804; Tondriau (1949), 128–40; Carter (1982), 92 (late 39 or early 38); Flory (1988), 353–59; Pollini (1990), 345. Bauman (1992), 95–96, 124, notes that in 36 Octavian received the honour of an annual banquet in the temple of Capitoline Jupiter — an excellent context for Suetonius' description of Jupiter abandoning his seat.

18. Suet. *Aug.* 69.1; see also Tac. *Ann.* 5.1. Antony had every reason to know better, because he was probably in Rome at the time of the betrothal. A report given before the Senate by Antony and Octavian concerning a senatorial decree relating to the city of Aphrodisias is preserved in an inscription found in the city. The decree is dated to October 2, 39. Antony's name precedes Octavian's, and it would be natural to assume that he made the statement of their joint views because of his agreed responsibilities for Asia. If so, this would place him in Rome in early October: Reynolds (1982), 75.

19. Vell. 2.95.1; date: EJ, p. 45; Suet. *Claud.* 11.3; see also Dio 60.5.1.

20. Dio 48.43.4, 44.1; cf. *Epit. de Caes.* 1.23.

21. Calendar references to January 17: EJ, p. 46; Suerbaum (1980), 346; Degrassi (1963), 401; Herz (1975), 10, 13; (1978), 1149, 1151, 1153; Temporini (1979), 69 n.

339. The further information, that the day was marked by a public celebration with *feriae* decreed by the Senate, must be regarded with some suspicion (see appendix 11).

22. Suet. *Claud.* 1.1; Tac. *Ann.* 1.10.5; Dio 48.44.5; Carcopino (1958), 65–82; Winkes (1985), 61. Caligula: Dio 59.23.7.

23. Dio 48.44.5; Treggiari (1991), 467–68; Huntsman (1997), 73. Willrich (1911), 11, identifies the hypomnemata with the *Res Gestae*, Blumenthal (1913), 285, with the *acta diurna*, Bardon (1968), 24, with Augustus' *Commentarii* (see appendix 1). Hallett (1984), 324, speculates that Augustus in fact might have been quite happy to foster the impression that he was Drusus' father and that this paternity would explain his favouring Drusus; see also Kuttner (1995), 295 n. 38.

24. Suet. *Tib.* 6.4; Dio 48.44.5. The date of Tiberius Nero's death can be calculated from Tiberius' age at the time. Treggiari (1991), 468, speculates that the husband of a divorced wife might have had the privilege of deciding where a child of a divorced wife should be brought up.

25. Dio 54.16.6: the anecdote is told under 18 BC but clearly refers to the earlier date.

3. IN THE SHADOWS

1. Huntsman (1997), 39, points out that the Primaporta villa was in the territory of the Arnense and that the Claudii Nerones were assigned to the tribe Arnensis; see Taylor (1960), 204–5, 285; Ashby and Fell (1921), 145. Millar (1992), 25, states that Primaporta was Augustus' property. Pliny *HN* 15.137 describes it as *villa Caesarum*, but perhaps from the perspective of his own day.

2. Suet. *Galb.* 1; Pliny *HN* 15.136–37; Dio 48.52.3–4; 63.29.3; Aur. Vict. *Caes.* 5.17 (following Suetonius closely and adding little); Alföldi (1973); Flory (1989); Reeder (1996). Suetonius places the event just after the marriage, Pliny after the betrothal *(cum pacta esset)*. Dio dates it to the next year, 37 BC, among disturbing omens, but in a rather imprecise context. Donatus in Serv. on Verg. *Aen.* 6.230 may be referring to a continuity of this tradition by saying that triumphatores crowned themselves from the laurel that sprang up on the Palatium on the day of Augustus' birth (Syme, *Papers A,* 1264).

3. Dio 48.52.4. Caesar: Suet. *Div. Jul.* 45.2; Dio 41.39.2, 43.43.1. Sterility: Col. *RR* 8.2.7.

4. Octavian had two sisters, both of whom carried the name Octavia. The elder, born to the first wife of Octavian's father, Ancharia, married Sextus Appuleius (*ILS* 8783); her son Sextus became consul in 29 BC. Plut. *Ant.* 31.1 clearly confuses her with her half-sister. The more famous Octavia Minor was born in about 69 BC to Octavius senior's second wife, Atia, some six years before Octavian junior was himself born; Suet. *Aug.* 4.1. Plut. *Ant.* 57.3 implies that she was the same age as Cleopatra.

5. Dio 48.31.4; Plut. *Ant.* 31.3.

6. App. *BC* 5.76.

7. App. *BC* 5.93–95; Plut. *Ant.* 31.2, 33.3, 35.1–4; Dio 48.54.1–5; Singer (1947).

8. Dio 49.51.1; cf. Dio 49.18.6, which suggests that the banquet was to be held in the temple of Concord, not in the Capitoline temple.

9. Dio 49.33.4.

10. Plut. *Ant.* 58; Suet. *Aug.* 69.2.

11. Plut. *Ant.* 53.1, 54–55.1.

12. Huntsman (1997), 81–82, suggests that Tiberius Nero might have seen further service with Octavian.

13. Nep. *Att.* 19.4, 22.3; cf. Sen. *Ep.* 21.4; Vell. 2.96.1; Dio 48.44.5; Willrich (1911), 18; Syme (1939), 345; *Papers C*, 258; Levick ("Tiberius," 1976), 18, 27. Vipsania: *ILS* 165. Marcella: Bauman (1992), 102. Atticus died on March 31, 32; he was still alive at the time of Tiberius' betrothal.

14. Plut. *Ant.* 83.4; Dio 51.13.3. Aschbach (1864), 11, assumes Livia's presence in Egypt. This is not likely, but Herrmann (1960), 105, suggests that she might have joined Augustus when he was in Samos after Actium in 31–30 or 30–29.

15. Cic. *ad Att.* 4.1.4, 7.2.2; *ad Fam.* 14.5.

16. Tac. *Ann.* 3.34.6; Suet. *Aug.* 24.1; Marshall ("Women," 1975; *Tacitus*, 1975). The issue of Livia's presence in Augustus' travels has been complicated by Sen. *Cons. Marc.* 4.3: Areus in addressing Livia calls himself the *assiduus viri tui comes* — that is, the constant companion of Augustus. This is read as *assidua comes* by a number of scholars, presumably as a vocative referring to Livia, making *her* the constant companion of her husband. The reading has no manuscript authority and suits the context less well than *assiduus;* Willrich (1911), 15; Ollendorff (1926), 905; Winkes (1985), 60; Hahn (1994), 34; Perkounig (1995), 70.

17. Hor. *Odes* 3.14.5–6; Halfmann (1986), 137; Calhoon (1994), 68; Perkounig (1995), 71.

18. EJ, p. 36; Vell. 2.93.1–2; Pliny *HN* 7.149, 19.24; Tac. *Ann.* 1.3.1; Suet. *Aug.* 66.1, 3, *Tib.* 6.4; Dio 51.21.3, 53.1.2, 28.3–4, 30.1–5, 31.1–4; Syme (1939), 342, 344.

19. Marcellus' death: Vell 2.93.1; Prop. 3.18.1–10; Verg. *Aen.* 6.860–86; Dio 53.30.4. Livia's involvement: Dio 53.33.4.

20. Dio 64.6–10; Gardthausen (1896), I.2.810; Ollendorff (1926), 905; Magie (1950), 469–76; Halfmann (1986), 22–24, 158–61, map 7O.

21. Ollendorff (1926), 905; Gardthausen I.2.810; Willrich (1911), 15; Bosch (1935), 22, assume the journey. Hermann (1960), 105, n. 114; Hahn (1994), 34, n. 20, are more cautious. An epigram by Crinagoras (*AP* 9.224) supposedly spoken by a milk goat, tells of Augustus' taking the goat on the journey, so addicted was he to its milk. Remarkably, some scholars identify the goat with Livia and take this as proof that Livia went to the East with him: Willrich (1911), 15; Ollendorff (1926), 905; Winkes (1985), 59; contra: Hahn (1994), 69 n. 20.

22. Dio 54.7.2; Clauss (1989), 89.

23. *IG* 3.316; Ollendorff (1926), 905.

24. Plutarch, *Peri tou Ei tou en delphois* 385F.

25. Augustus had passed the winters of 31–30 and 30–29 on Samos after Actium. Suet. *Aug.* 17.2, 26.3; Dio 51.18.1; Orosius 6.19.21 (Asia); cf. App. *BC* 4.42; Mommsen (1883), 136.

26. Strabo 14, p. 637; Magie (1950), 1331 n. 4.

27. Willrich (1911), 16; Ollendorff (1926), 905; Hahn (1994), 68 n. 20.

28. *IGR* 4.976 refers to a monument erected by Augustus in Samos dated to the fifth year of his tribuncia potestas, so before summer 19 BC.

29. *RG* 31; Suet. *Aug.* 21.3; Florus 2.62; Dio 54.9.8; Strabo 15.4, 73; Eutropius 7.10.1; Orosius 6.21.19 (who places the events in Spain). On the embassies, see Rich (1990), 185.

30. Dio 54.9.10; Strabo 15.4, 79, calls him a stoic and gives his name as Zarmanochegas; Bowersock (1965), 78 n. 3; Clinton (1989), 1507–9; Wood (1999), 92–93.

31. Donatus, *Vit. Verg.* 35.

32. *RG* 12.1; Dio 54.10.4.

33. Sen. *Cons. Marc.* 2.4; Willrich (1911), 18–19; Dixon (1988), 178, points out that Octavia had daughters, but it was as the mother of a potential princeps that they supposedly vied.

34. Sen. *Clem.* 9; Dio 54.19.3; Ollendorff (1926), 905; Fischler (1989), 47; contra, Perkounig (1995), 70; Bauman (1992), 249 n. 78.

35. Suet. *Aug.* 64.1; Plut. *Ant.* 87.3; Dio 54.6.5; 8.5, 12.4, 18.1, 28; Sutherland (1951), 58; Balsdon (1962), 73–74; Levick (1966), 229; ("Retirement," 1972), 798; ("Tiberius," 1976), 29–30, 233 n. 26; Roddaz (1984), 311, 351–81.

36. Her death was the cause of great grief to her brother (*Cons. Liv.* 442; Sen. *Cons. Polyb.* 15.3).

37. Drusus was younger than Germanicus, whose birthdate was May 24, 15 BC, and who was born before Tiberius' divorce from Vipsania, in 12. Month and day, October 7: EJ, p. 53 (Feriale Cumanum); year: Mommsen *GS* IV.262 places it between 15 and 12; Rogers (1943), 91, and Levick (1966), 236–38, favour 13; Sumner (1967), 427–29, and Seager (1972), 25 n. 2, argue for 14.

38. Marriage: Livy *Per.* 140; Vell. 2.96.1; Suet. *Aug.* 63.2, *Tib.* 7.2–3; Tac. *Ann.* 1.12.6, 53.2, 4.40.9; Dio 54.31.2, 35.4. Proculeius: Pliny *HN* 36.183; Tac. *Ann.* 4.40.9; Suet. *Aug.* 63.2; Gardthausen (1896), I.1028; Willrich (1911); Hanslik (1957), 73; Seager (1972), 72; Levick ("Tiberius," 1976), 31–32; Bauman (1992), 103. Marriage to Vipsania: 20 or 19: Levick ("Tiberius," 1976), 27; Roddaz (1984), 317 n. 44, thinks it took place before the Julia-Marcellus marriage.

39. Tac. *Ann.* 1.10.7; Suet. *Tib.* 21.4–7; Birch, "Correspondence" (1981).

40. Vell. 2.97.3; Tac. *Ann.* 1.33.3, 2.82.3; Suet. *Claud.* 1.4.

41. *RG* 12.2; EJ 46; Ovid, *Fast.* 1.710; Fishwick (1987–92) I.2. On the coincidence of the constitutio of the Ara Pacis and Livia's birthday, see Herz (1975), 11, 136; (1978), 1153 n. 104; Syme, *Papers B*, 419; Barrett (1999).

42. Winkes (1995), 97 no. 20; Rose (1997), plate 10.

43. Dio 55.2.4. The chronology is uncertain — the ovation may have followed Drusus' death; see Rich (1990), 220. Capitoline: Ehlers (1939), 510.

44. *Cons. Liv.* 89–90; Livy *Per.* 142; Val. Max. 5.5.3; Sen. *Cons. Marc.* 3.1; *Cons. Polyb.* 15.5; Pliny *HN* 7.84; Tac. *Ann.* 2.82.3; Suet. *Tib.* 50.1, *Claud.* 1.3–4; Dio 55.2.1.

45. Sen. *Cons. Marc.* 3, *Cons. Polyb.* 15.5; Tac. *Ann.* 3.5.1; Dio 55.2.1.

46. Tac. *Ann.* 3.5.1; Suet. *Claud.* 1.5; Dio 55.2. Junia: Tac. *Ann.* 3.76. Augustus: Dio 56.34.2.

4. THE PUBLIC FIGURE

1. Tac. *Ann.* 3.5.1; Muretus' emendation of *Iuliorumque* to *Liviorumque* is unnecessary. Augustus: Dio 56.34.2; Junia: Tac. *Ann.* 3.76.2. Suet. *Claud.* 1.5 mentions Drusus as potential joint heir with Augustus' "sons"; Flower (1996), 242.

2. Suet. *Aug.* 63.1; Dio 55.2.5; Bartman (1999), 3–4; she is identified as mother of Drusus on a base from Velleia (*CIL* 11.1165), but this belongs to the Caligulan period.

3. Flory (1993), 299.

4. Vell. 2.97.4; Dio 55.6; Eutrop. 7.9; Orosius 6.21.24. Date of dedication: January 16, EJ, p. 45. Motives: Levick ("Retirement," 1972), 803–5, (1978), 217–33; Rich (1990), 226.

5. Dio 55.8.2; Suet. *Tib.* 20. Gaul: Dio 55.6.1, 8.3. Banquet: Dio 55.8.2.

6. Ovid *Fast.* 6.637–38; Flory (1984), 313–14, 324, 329. Flory notes that *concordia* is a common theme on tombstones: *CIL* 6.7579.6: *vixit mecum tam concorde; CIL* 6.23137.5: *sunt duo concordes; CIL* 6. 26926: *cum quo concordem vitam . . . vixit.*

7. Dio 55.8.3, 9.1.

8. Tac. *Ann.* 1.3.3; Dio 55.9.2.

9. Behaviour of Gaius and Lucius: Dio 55.9.1–3. The applause for Lucius noted by Suet. *Aug.* 56.2 might best be assigned to this context. Tiberius' tribunicia potestas: Vell. 2.99.1; Tac. *Ann.* 3.56.3; Suet. *Tib.* 9.3; Dio 55.9.4. Gaius' consulship: *RG* 14.1; *CIL* 6.3748. Sequence: Levick ("Retirement," 1972), 780–91. Imperium: Levick ("Retirement," 1972), 781–82, ("Tiberius," 1976), 36; Rich (1990), 228.

10. Tac. *Ann.* 1.53.2; Velleius 2.99.2; Suet. *Tib.* 10; Dio 55.9.5–8; Sattler (1959), 511; Levick ("Retirement," 1972). Huntsman (1997), 119, suggests that Tiberius was sent away rather than leaving on his own accord, for when he wanted to return, he (unsuccessfully) sought the permission of Augustus. But any major decision within the imperial family would require the permission of the princeps.

11. Velleius 2.99.1; Suet. *Tib.* 10.2; Dio 55.9.8; Levick ("Retirement," 1972), 790.

12. Vell. 2.99.4; Suet. *Tib.* 11.1, 12.2; Dio 55.9.6; Sattler (1969), 513–14; Levick ("Retirement," 1972), 793, 805; Rich (1990), 228–29.

13. Pliny *HN* 7.45; Vell. 2.100.3; Suet. *Aug.* 64.2; Macrob. *Sat.* 2.5. On Julia's witticisms: Richlin (1992), 65–91. Much of the information on Julia's character comes from the much later author Macrobius but is generally accepted by scholars: see Sattler (1969), 75. Julia and Tiberius: Tac. *Ann.* 6.51.3; Suet. *Tib.* 8.2–3; Macrob. *Sat.* 2.5.8; Bauman (1992), 112. For the date of the estrangement: Levick ("Tiberius," 1976), 37.

14. Suet. *Tib.* 11.4.

15. Sen. *Ben.* 6.32.1–2, *Clem.* 1.10.3; Pliny *HN* 21.9; Tac. *Ann.* 1.53.1–4; Suet. *Aug.* 65.2, 101.3, *Tib.* 50.1; Dio 55.10.12–14, 13.1, 56.32.4. The modern scholarship on the topic is massive: for material before 1970, see Meise (1969), 3–34; since 1970 see, inter alios, Levick ("Retirement," 1972; 1975; "Julia," 1976); Ferrill (1976); Shotter (1971), 1120–21; Corbett (1974), 91–92; Lacey (1980); Syme, *Papers A* 912–36; (1978), 192–98 (also [1939], 427); Raditsa (1980), 290–95; Raaflaub

(1990), 428–30; Bauman (1992), 108–19. Fate of lovers: Vell. 2.100.4; Tac. *Ann.* 1.10.4, 4.44.3; cf. Dio 55.10.15.

16. Sen. *Ben.* 6.32.1, *Brev.* 4.5; Vell. 2.100.4; Tac. *Ann.* 3.18.1: *qui domum Augusti violasset;* 1.53.1, 3.24.2, 6.51.3 (impudicitia); 4.44.3 (adultery); 3.24.3 (excessive punishment); Suet. *Aug.* 65.1; Dio 55.10.12. Lists of conspirators: Sen. *Clem.* 1.9.6; Suet. *Aug.* 19.1; Sen. *Brev.* 4.5 (the "Paulus" of Seneca's manuscript is clearly an error for Iullus, caused by confusion with the affair of Julia the Younger); Pliny *HN* 7.149; Suet. *Aug.* 19.2; Tac. *Ann.* 1.10.5, 3.24.4; Dio 55.10.15. For a discussion of Pliny's evidence see Tränkle (1969), 121–23; Swan (1971), 740–41; Ferrill (1976), 344–45; Till (1977), 137. Bauman (1967), 198–245, argues that there was no political conspiracy, but that Julia and her paramours were convicted of a form of treason.

17. Suet. *Tib.* 11.4; Macrob. *Sat.* 5.2.6; Blaze de Bury (1874); Gardthausen (1896), I.1101; Syme (1939), 427; *Papers A,* 925; Sattler (1969), 524–25; Winkes (1985), 63; Bauman (1992), 126; contra, Willrich (1911), 24; Groag (1919), 82.

18. Gaius Gelus: *AE* 1975 (1978), no. 289; (1995), no 367; Suet. *Aug.* 65.3, Tac. *Ann.* 1.53; Linderski (1988); Gardner (1988). Linderski, 187, says that it is possible that the servile Julia, Thiasus, and Gaius Gelus were all three slaves of Julia, that the two men were manumitted but not Julia, who on her mistress' death would have passed to Augustus' heirs and could then have been manumitted by Livia. Portico: Herbert-Brown (1984), 155; Ollendorff (1926), 911, assumed that Livia's aedes and portico were dedicated at the same time.

19. Suet. *Tib.* 11.5–12.1; Suetonius calls him *quasi legatus.*

20. Vell. 2.102.1; Tac. *Ann.* 3.48; Suet. *Tib.* 13, 15.1; Pliny *HN* 9.118; Dio 55.11.3.

21. *RG* 14; Ovid *AA* 1.194; Tac. *Ann.* 1.3.2; Dio 55.9.9–10; Bowersock (1984).

22. Vell. 2.102.3; Suet. *Tib.* 70.2; Dio 55.10a.9–10; EJ, p. 50, no. 68.

23. EJ, p. 39, 47, no. 69; Vell. 2.102; Dio 55.10a.4–9.

24. Pliny *HN* 7.149; Tac. *Ann.* 1.3.3; Suet. *Aug.* 65.1; Dio 55.10a.10; Ollendorff (1926), 912.

25. *CIL* 10.1240, 11.3305, 6.31275; Dio 54.29.5.

26. Tac. *Ann.* 6.25.3: *aequi impatiens, dominandi avida;* Mellor (1993), 76–77.

27. Tac. *Ann.* 1.33.1, 2.73.2–3; Suet. *Cal.* 3–6. Walker (1960), 232, notes the resemblances between Tacitus' depictions of Germanicus and of his own father-in-law Agricola.

28. Germanicus was born on May 24 (EJ, 49; Suet. *Cal.* 1.1). Tac. *Ann.* 2.73.2 states that at his death Germanicus had not progressed much beyond thirty years. Suet. *Cal.* 1.1 says that he died on October 10, AD 19: *annum agens quartum et tricesimum* (during his thirty-fourth year). Sumner (1967), 413, takes this to mean that he was past his thirty-third birthday, hence born in 15 BC; Levick (1966) argues that it means that Germanicus had passed his thirty-fourth year.

29. Tac. *Ann.* 1.78.2 *(male consulta),* 2.8.2 *(erratum);* Mellor (1993), 75–76. For a recent analysis of Tacitus' depiction of Germanicus, see Pelling (1993). *Feriale Duranum* 12, reading *g[er]mani[c]ī cae[sa]ris;* Fink (1940), 136–38.

30. Tac. *Ann.* 1.3.3; 4.57.3; Suet. *Tib.* 21.4–7, *Cal.* 4. Velleius 2.103.2 says that Augustus did not have to think twice. A confused passage of Zonaras (Dio 55.13.1a)

seems to attribute Tiberius' success to Julia, who had been restored from banishment. Linderski (1988), 183, thinks that Zonaras' entry might contain a garbled allusion to a chronological link between Julia's recall to Rhegium and Tiberius' adoption.

31. Vell. 2.103.2 (period unspecified); Tac. *Ann.* 1.3.3; Suet. *Aug.* 65.1, *Tib.* 16.1 (five years); Dio 55.13.2 (ten years).

32. EJ, p. 49 (for the date); Tac. *Ann.* 1.3.3; Suet. *Aug.* 64.1, *Tib.* 15.2, *Cal.* 1.1, 4; Vell. 2.103.3 (June 27); Dio 55.13.2; Mommsen (1904), 4.272; Levick (1966), 232; Instinsky (1966); Birch ("Settlement," 1981).

33. Vell. 2.103.1, 4–5, 104.1; Suet. *Tib.* 21.3; Parsi (1963), 12; Instinsky (1966), 332; Seager (1972), 37–38; Woodman (1977), 136; contra, Sumner (1970), 269; Levick (1966), 229 n. 1.

34. Tac. *Ann.* 1.3.3.

35. Vell. 2.102.3. Toga: Dio 55.22.4; Pappano (1941), 32; Birch ("Settlement," 1981), 446–48. Birth: Levick (1966), 240 n. 4. Gardthausen (1896), II. 844 n. 1, argues that because Agrippa had not yet received the *toga virilis* when adopted by Augustus on June 26, AD 4, he must not yet have been fifteen years old.

36. The earliest hint of a more serious problem to come is in Velleius. After describing the campaign at the Volcaean marshes in Pannonia, fought in late AD 7, Velleius turns to the subject of Postumus, claiming that he had begun *qualis esset apparare* (to reveal what he was like) *iam ante biennium* (already two years before). Although this is surely not meant as a precise date, it does suggest that Postumus' behaviour started to cause real concern about late AD 5, more than a year after the adoption: Vell. 2.112.7; Woodman (1977), 170; Levick ("Tiberius," 1976), 57; cf. Hohl (1935), 350 n. 1.

37. Velleius 2.102.7; Tac. *Ann.* 1.3.4, 4.3; Suet. *Aug.* 65.1, 4; Dio 55.32.1–2. Drusus: Dio 57.14.9. Mad: Jerome (1912), 279; Charlesworth (1923), 148; H. von Hentig (1924), 20; Hammond (1933), 70; Hohl (1935), 350 n. 3. Sane: Pappano (1941); Norwood (1963), 152 ("a reckless temper"); Detweiler (1970), 290; Birch ("Settlement," 1981), 449 ("perhaps not overbright").

38. *Fast. Ost., Inscr. Ital.* 13.i.183; Velleius 2.102.7; Suet. *Aug.* 65.1, 4 (Suetonius is the only one of our sources explicitly to recognise two stages in the banishment); Tac. *Ann.* 1.3.4, 2.39.1; Dio 55.32.2; Pliny *HN* 7.149–50.

39. Tac. *Ann.* 1.3.4, 1.6.3, 12.1.1, 3.1; Ollendorff (1926), 915. Criticism of Germanicus: Tac. *Ann.* 1.4.4; Detweiler (1970), 290. Tacitus was perhaps just reporting the claims that the Julian side made; *Epit. de Caes.* 1.27 claims that Livia banished Postumus *odio novercali*.

40. Vell. 2.112.7; Dio 55.32.2; J. Crook, *CR* 4 (1954), 153; Levick ("Abdication," 1972; "Tiberius," 1976); Jameson (1975); Birch ("Settlement," 1981), 451. The "Agrippa as" (*RIC²* Caligula 58) depicts the bust of Agrippa on the obverse and Neptune on the reverse; for a summary of the arguments about the date: Barrett (1990), 250–51.

41. Tac. *Ann.* 1.6.2; Suet. *Aug.* 65.4. Pappano (1941), 37, suggests that the exile was made permanent by a decree of the Senate to ensure against a personal change of heart on Augustus' part. Jameson (1975), 303, says that if Postumus had just been relegated, he would have been able to make a claim against Augustus' will. This

would not be so if he had a sentence of *aqua et igni interdictio* (a more severe form of banishment, literally "exclusion from water and fire") passed on him, which Jameson thinks was the force of the *senatus consultum*.

42. Charlesworth (1923), 153; Pappano (1941), 40. On the Julian–Claudian division: Levick (1975).

43. For modern treatments, see, inter alios, Meise (1969), 35–48, with bibliography; Levick ("Julia," 1976); Syme (1978), 206–14; (1986), 117–22; Raaflaub (1990), 430–31; Bauman (1992), 119–24.

44. Pliny *HN* 7.75; Tac. *Ann.* 3.24.2, 4.71.6–7; Suet. *Aug.* 64.1, 65.4, 72.3, 101.3; Schol. Juv. *Sat.* 6.158.

45. Inheritance: Dio 55.32.2.

46. Dio 54.29.5, 55.32.2; Jameson (1975); Levick ("Abdication," 1972), 695; ("Tiberius," 1976), 245, no. 71; *CIL* 5.3257: at least one slave, Sex. Vipsanius M. f. Clemens, did not pass to Augustus but seems to have remained Agrippa's property (to be distinguished from the Clemens the conspirator).

47. *RIC²* Augustus, 235–48, 469–71; Suet. *Tib.* 17.2.

48. Vell 2.121.1; Suet. *Tib.* 21.1; Dio 56.28.1.

49. Pliny *HN* 7.150; Plut. *De garr.* 508A–B. Arria: Pliny *Ep.* 3.16; Martial 1.13.

50. Dio 56.30.1–2; one of Dio's epitimators, Xiphilinus, makes the comment that he does not trust the story.

51. Tac. *Ann.* 1.5.1–3 (Haase [1848] reads *ignarum*, to suggest that Livia brought about Fabius' death to suppress information about the reconciliation); Dio 56.30.1.

52. *AFA* xxx; Dio 56.26.2–3; Gardthausen (1896) I.1252; (1918), 184; Domaszewski (1909), Ia 247; Jameson (1972), 320 (Scheid [*Arvales*, 1975], 87, reaches the same conclusion independently). Levick ("Tiberius," 1976), 65, is willing to meet the hostile tradition halfway and suggests that Augustus might have made the journey, but that it did not lead to any change in his dynastic plans. Rejecting the story completely: Charlesworth (1923), 149, 155; Willrich (1927), 75–76; Dessau (1930), 1, p. 477; Pappano (1941), 41; Syme (1958), 483, 693, 688, 693; (1986), 415; (1978), 149–51 (historical fictions); Koestermann (1961), 332–33; Seager (1972), 48; Goodyear (1972), 131.

53. Suet. *Aug.* 19.2. Julia's relocation: Tac. *Ann.* 1.53.1; Suet. *Aug.* 65.3; Dio 55.13.1. Confusion over the place of exile: Meise (1969), 29–30; Rogers (1931), 147. Two separate plots: Norwood (1963), 354, suggests a confusion between the two Julias. Pappano (1941), 41, links this plot with the later plot of Clemens. Jameson (1972), 311 n. 118, says that Epicadus was a freedman of the Pollio family. She says that his origins might suggest that he was a freedman of Asinius Pollio the triumphator (*PIR* 1241). His son was Asinius Pollio, described among those deemed *capaces imperii* by Augustus, marrying Vipsania, and later becoming a suitor for Agrippina and a bête noire of Tiberius. Zonaras 10.38 states that Agrippa Postumus was exiled with his mother. There is a problem in Suetonius' version of events. He talks about Julia and Postumus being rescued from the islands, but by this time Julia was no longer on Pandateria. The confusion could have resulted from a simple slip, because islands were the traditional place for banishment. There is no need to assume that Suetonius has confused mother and daughter, or conflated two plots, one to

rescue Julia, the other Postumus. Linderski (1988), n. 10, observes that there is some evidence that a detachment of the fleet was stationed near Rhegium.

54. Suet. *Aug.* 97.2–3; Dio 56.29.1.

55. Journey: Vell. 2.123.1; Suet. *Aug.* 97.3, *Tib.* 21.1; Dio 56.29.2: Ollendorff (1926), 915, places the supposed visit to Planasia during this journey. Father: Suet. *Aug.* 100.1

56. EJ, p. 40, 50; Suet. *Aug.* 100.1; Dio 56.30.5.

57. Suet. *Aug.* 76.1; Tac. *Ann.* 1.5.1; Dio 55.22.2; 56.30.1–3; *Epit. de Caes.* 1.28; Charlesworth (1923), 155–56; Questa (1959), 48; Gafforini (1996), 134–36. Vespasian: Dio 66.17.1. Titus: Dio 66.26.2.

58. Vell.2.123.1; Suet. *Aug.* 98.5–99.1, *Tib.* 21.1; Tac. *Ann.* 1.5.3–4, 13.2 *(supremis sermonibus)*; Dio 56.30–31.1.

59. Levick ("Tiberius," 1976), 246 n. 1. Charlesworth (1927) notes that the death of King Ferdinand I of Roumania in 1927 was kept secret for political reasons.

60. Agrippina: Tac.*Ann.* 14.8.1. Shrine: Dio 56.46.3.

61. Velleius 2.112.7; Tac. *Ann.* 1.6.1, 2.39.1–2; Suet. *Tib.* 22; Dio 57.3.5–6; *Epit. de Caes.* 1.27; Charlesworth (1927), 55–57; Rogers (1931); Hohl (1935); Pappano (1941); Allen (1947); Martin (1955), 123–29, (1981), 162; Marsh (1959), 50–51; Questa (1959); Shotter (1965), 361; Lewis (1970); Detweiler (1970); Shotter (1971); Seager (1972), 49; Levick ("Abdication," 1972); ("Tiberius," 1976), 64–66, 245 n. 66; Shatzman (1974), 561–62; Jameson (1975); Birch ("Settlement," 1981), 455–56; Kehoe (1985), 247–54; Suerbaum (1990), 118; Sinclair (1995), 5–8; Watson (1995), 181–85; Gafforini (1996), 136–38; Woodman (1998). Shotter thinks that the purpose of Tacitus' account of the opening of the new reign is to illustrate Tiberius' character through his actions and to demonstrate the pressures that public opinion could place on a new ruler.

62. Suetonius and Tacitus agree that the report was sent to the tribune in Planasia. Suetonius states that the tribune then executed Postumus. Tacitus and Dio say that the blow was struck by a centurion. There need be no contradiction, if the centurion was simply acting on the tribune's instructions. Tacitus also has the centurion take the report to Tiberius. Perhaps more convincingly, Suetonius assigns that task to the tribune.

63. Tac. *Ann.* 3.30; Alps: Pliny *HN* 34.3. Rome: *CIL* 15.7508 (owned and probably inherited by his son); Syme, *Papers A*, 929.

64. Tac.*Ann.* 1.6.1–3, cf. 3.30.3.

65. Vell. 2.112.7. For the debate on Velleius' meaning, Woodman (1977), 177. In a careful analysis of Tacitus' account, Woodman (1998), 23–39, suggests that the "more likely scenario" was one proposed at the time, not a suggestion of Tacitus himself. Woodman argues that the sequence of Tacitus' narrative suggests that he did not in fact share the contemporary view, and considered Livia responsible.

66. Gardthausen (1918), 185; Charlesworth (1923), 156; Smith (1942), 16; Syme (1958), 306, 418; (1978), 149; Woodman (1998).

67. Detweiler (1970) argues that the ancient evidence seems to convict Tiberius; Marsh (1931), 50, and Hohl (1935) emphatically claim the contrary; Shotter (1971), 1120; (1965); Martin (1955), 123–29, (1981), 162.

68. Dio 57.3.5–6; Pappano (1941), 45; Jameson (1972), 314.

69. Charlesworth (1923), 156; Rogers (1935), 3; Hohl (1937), 323; Pappano (1941), 44; Norwood (1963), 163; Jameson (1972), 288; Seager (1972), 49–50; Levick ("Fortuna," 1972), 311; ("Tiberius," 1976), 65. The precise nature of the codicilli is not known. They might already have been on hand, left by Augustus, to be read when news of the emperor's death arrived. That would have been a highly risky procedure, because there would always be a risk that the instructions might come to light prematurely. Alternatively, they might have been signed by Augustus beforehand but kept in Rome ready for despatch when he died.

70. Suet. *Aug.* 65.3–4, 101.3; Dio 55.13.1. Arrangements in will: Tac. *Ann.* 1.11.4; Suet. *Aug.* 101; Dio 56.33.

71. Tac. *Ann.* 1.53.2; Suet. *Tib.* 50.1; Dio 57.18.1.

5. A NEW REIGN

1. Suet. *Tib.* 50.1–2.

2. Tac. *Ann.* 1.5.3, 7.3–5; Dio 57.2.1.

3. Tac. *Ann.* 1.7.4; Suet. *Aug.* 99.2; Dio 56.31.2–3.

4. Tac. *Ann.* 1.8.1; Suet. *Aug.* 101.2; Dio 56.32.1; Jos. *Ant.* 18.234. Julius Caesar also deposited his will with the Vestals: Suet. *Div. Jul.* 83.1. Dio 48.37.1 (see also 48.46.2) notes that the treaties negotiated between Sextus Pompeius and his opponents Octavian and Antony were stored in the same place. On the general practice, Vidal (1965), 555.

5. Tac. *Ann.* 1.8.1; Suet. *Aug.* 101.1, 3, *Tib.* 23; Dio 56.32.1, 4.

6. Vell. 2.75.3; Tac. *Ann.* 1.8.1; Suet. *Aug.* 101.2; Dio 56.46.1.

7. Tac. *Ann.* 1.8.5–6; Suet. *Aug.* 100.2–4; Dio 56.34.1–4, 42, 46.2.

8. Caligula: *Fasti Vallenses* and *Fasti Pighiani*; Suet. *Cal.* 8.1. On Antium as the birthplace of Caligula, see Barrett (1990), 6–7, 255 n. 10. Consulship: Suet. *Cal.* 1.1; Dio 56.27.5.

9. Vell. 2.125; Tac. *Ann.* 1.31–49; Suet. *Tib.* 25.2; Dio 57.5–6; Schove (1984), 4–6.

10. Tac. *Ann.* 1.40.3–44, 49.5–51.9; Suet. *Cal.* 48.1; Dio 57.5.6. On the different versions of the story, see Burian (1964), 25–29.

11. Tac. *Ann.* 1.69.3: *tradit C. Plinius, Germanorum bellorum scriptor ...*

12. Tac. *Ann.* 1.33, 2.82.2; Suet. *Cal.* 3.

13. Tac. *Ann.* 1.33.1: *causae acriores quia iniquae.* Drusus and Germanicus: Tac. *Ann.* 2.43.6; see especially Shotter (1968).

14. Tac. *Ann.* 2.14.1; 5.1.2; Suet. *Cal.* 4, 7; Willrich (1911), 36; Ollendorff (1926), 920; Perkounig (1995), 179.

15. Tac. *Ann.* 2.26; Suet. *Tib.* 52.2.

16. Tac. *Ann.* 2.41.2–4; Eck et al. (1993), 13.

17. Velleius 2.129.2; Tac. *Ann.* 2.42.1. Archelaus: *PIR* A 1023; *RE* 2 (1895), 451–52 (U. Wilcken). Two other kings had recently died: Antiochus III of Commagene: *PIR* A 741; *RE* 1 (1894), 2490 (U. Wilcken); Philopator of Amanus: *PIR* P 282; Tac. *Ann.* 2.42.7; Jos. *Ant.* 18.53.

18. Tac. *Ann.* 2.42, 5.1.3; Suet. *Tib.* 8, 37.4; Philost. *Apoll.* 1.12; Dio 57.17.3–7. There

is a chronological problem. Dio 49.32.3 begins the reign in 36 BC. App. *BC* 5.7 implausibly places its beginning in 41 BC; see Magie (1950), 1286. Tacitus' fifty-year reign might be a mistake, or fifty could simply be an approximation. If Tacitus' fifty years is correct, it may refer to Tiberius' accession, in AD 14. Date of the defence: Levick (1971), 478–86, ("Tiberius," 1976), 20, says 26 BC; Bowersock (1965), 157–61, argues for about 18 BC. Zeno: Levick ("Tiberius," 1976), 140. Livia's supposed intercession: Hardy (1975), 25; Perkounig (1995), 160; Tiberius and Livia seem to have inherited a slave from Archelaus, *CIL* 6.4776: *Dardanus Ti. Caesaris Aug(usti) et Augustae ser(vus) Archelaianus* (see Chantraine [1976], 302, 354). Velleius' compliment: 2.130.5. Sales tax: Tac. *Ann.* 1.78, 2.42.6; Dio 55.25, 58.16.2.

19. *Bell. Afr.* 3.1, 18.1; Dio 53.30.2; *PIR* C 286; *RE* 3.1 (1897), 1391–92, no. 95 (O. Groag).

20. *Piso Decree* 83; Sen. *Ira* 1.18; Tac. *Ann.* 1.13.3, 2.43.2, 3.12.1, 13.1, 16.4; Strabo 2.5.33; *PIR* C 287; *RE* 3.1 (1897), 1379–82, no. 70 (O. Groag).

21. Plancina: *PIR* M 737; *RE* 16 (1933), 556–57 (R. Hanslik); *FOS* 562. Munatius Plancus: *CIL* 10.6087; Vell. 2.83; Tac. *Ann.* 1.39.2; *PIR* M 729; *RE* 16 (1933), 551–59 (R. Hanslik). Secret instructions to Plancina: Tac. *Ann.* 2.43.4. Senate approval: Tac. *Ann.* 3.12.2. On Piso's qualifications: Shotter ("Piso," 1974), 234–36. Plancina's role: Shotter ("Piso," 1974), 242.

22. Tac. *Ann.* 2.54.1.

23. Tac. *Ann.* 2.55.5. Bribes: *Piso Decree* 54–55.

24. Tac. *Ann.* 2.56; Suet. *Cal.* 1.2; Dio 57.17.7.

25. *Piso Decree* 34–35; Tac. *Ann.* 2.43.

26. Absence: *P. Oxy.* 2435.1; EJ 379 (1976), 1. Honours: *P. Berol.* (*SBA* 1911, 796–97), 34–38 (see Goodyear [1981], 459–60); Tac. *Ann.* 2.59–61; Suet. *Tib.* 52.2.

27. Tac. *Ann.* 2.71.2–3.

28. *Fast. Ant.* (EJ, p. 53), *Tab. Siar.* IIa.1; Pliny *HN* 11.187; Tac. *Ann.* 2.69–72; Suet. *Cal.* 1.2; Dio 57.18.9. Tac. *Ann.* 2.83.3 says that he died in the suburb of Epidaphne, a garbled version of Antioch epi Daphne.

29. Tac. *Ann.* 2.82.1–3; Suet. *Tib.* 52.3, *Cal.* 2; Dio 57.18.6. The denigration of Livia and Tiberius might have come from the memoirs of Agrippina the Younger: Goodyear (1981), 327 n. 4; Perkounig (1995), 185.

30. Tac. *Ann.* 2.73, 83; Suet. *Cal.* 5–6. Honours: *Tab. Heb.*: EJ 94a; *Tab. Siar.*: González (1984), 55–100; revision by W. D. Lebek, *ZPE* 67 (1987), 129–48; 86 (1991), 47–78; 87 (1991), 103–24; 90 (1992), 65–86; 95 (1993), 81–120. For the complete text: Crawford (1966), 1.507–43.

31. Tac. *Ann.* 3.1–2, 4. *Tab. Siar.* IIb. 11 dates the approval of the honours to December 16, AD 19, and presupposes Agrippina's presence in Rome. Tacitus may be incorrect in his date of January, AD 20, for Agrippina's return.

32. Tac. *Ann.* 3.3; *Tab. Siar.* I.6–7 (Tiberius is added on the basis of secure restoration); Woodman (1996), 91–93; Kokkinos (1992), 23–24, 38–39; Flower (1996), 250–51.

33. *Tab. Siar.* IIb. 12–13, 18–19; Tac. *Ann.* 3.5–6; Millar (1988), 17–18. Drusus, son of Livia: Sen. *Cons. Marc.* 3.2 (Livia), *Cons. Polyb.* 15.5 (Tiberius). Drusus Caesar, son of Tiberius: Sen. *Cons. Marc.* 15.3; Tac. *Ann.* 4.8.

34. *CIL* 3.6703; *Eph. Ep.* v.1336; Tac. *Ann.* 2.74.1.

35. Tac. *Ann.* 2.75-81.

36. Tac. *Ann.* 3.9.

37. See, in particular, Eck et al. (1996); Damon (1999); Griffin (1997).

38. Tac. *Ann.* 3.10.2.

39. *Piso Decree* 1; Tac. *Ann.* 3.14.4; Suet. *Cal.* 2. Tacitus writes that the mob assembled outside the *curia*, the term presumably used loosely of whatever building the Senate occupied when in session (see Woodman [1996], 162).

40. Tac. *Ann.* 3.15.1.

41. Tac. *Ann.* 3.15-16; Suet. *Tib.* 52.3; Dio 57.18.10.

42. Tac. *Ann.* 3.16.4; Pelling (1993), 83-84.

43. *Piso Decree* 6-11, 80-84, 121-23; EJ 39 (erasure); Tac. *Ann.* 3.17.4, 36.3.

44. *Piso Decree* 6-12; Tac. *Ann.* 3.17.1-2 (see Woodman [1996], 182-83). Rufilla: Tac. *Ann.* 3.36.3; Talbert (1984), 157.

45. *Piso Decree* 110-20; Tac. *Ann.* 3.17.1. Plancina and Agrippina: Tac. *Ann.* 6.26.3. Livia never entered the Senate: Dio 57.12.3.

46. *Piso Decree* 132, 150; Tac. *Ann.* 3.18.3. Claudius was inadvertently left out of the first draft, according to Tacitus, a claim given support by the awkward position of his name in the decree.

47. Tac. *Ann.* 3.17.1, 19.3.

48. EJ, pp. 41, 49; Tac. *Ann.* 3.11.1, 19.3. For useful summaries of both sides of the issue see Woodman (1996), 69-77; Griffin 87 (1997), 258-60; Barnes (1981).

49. Dio 57.19.6. Documents: Tac. *Ann.* 3.16.1.

50. Tac. *Ann.* 2.84.1, 4.2.4, 8.4; Suet. *Claud.* 27.1; Dio 57.19.7, cf. Dio 58.4.3.

51. Tac. *Ann.* 3.31.2.

52. Tac. *Ann.* 3.64.3. Apronius: Tac. *Ann.* 2.32.2; Woodman (1996), 448, notes the curious use of the word *supplicium*. *Supplicatio* can mean both "propitiation" and "thanksgiving"; *supplicium* strictly conveys only the former, while it is the latter that is needed in this context, because the events took place after Livia's recovery, not before.

53. *RIC*² Tiberius 47. The imperial coin had many imitators — *RPC* 1154 Corinth, 1567-68 (Thessalonika), 1779 (Byzantium), 2840 (Aphrodisias); it is copied in a lead tessera now in the Terme Museum (see appendix 1). Augustus: *RIC*² 356-57: *ob r(em) p(ublicam) cum salut(e) imp(eratoris) Caesar(is) August(i) cons(ervatam)*. Alabanda: EJ 114. Nasium: EJ 137. Interamna: *ILS* 157. Oaths: *Inst.* 2.23.1: *Divus Augustus . . . per ipsius Salutem rogatus*. Tiberius: Val. Max. 1.13 *praef.* (cf. Ovid *Trist.* 2.574); Grant (*Principate*, 1950), 114; Sutherland (1951), 96-97, 191-92; (1987), 51-52; Gross (1962), 18-19; Torelli (1982), 66-70; Weinstock (1971), 172; Fittschen-Zanker (1983), III.3-3, 3; Purcell (1986), 86 n. 45; Fishwick (1987-92), II.1, 465; Mikocki (1995), 164 no. 94, 166 no. 109, accepts Pietas and Iustitia as portraits of Livia. Kokkinos (1992), 90-95, suggests that all three are of Antonia Minor.

54. Vitr. *Arch.* 3.3.2; Livy 40.40.10, 42.10.5; Obseq. 53; Hor. *Odes* 1.35.1; Tac. *Ann.* 3.71.1. On Fortuna Equestris, Champeaux (1982), 155-57, 176. Antium: Suet. *Aug.* 58.2; Barrett (1990), 6-7, 255 n. 10; (1996), 46.

55. *ILS* 202 (= *CIL* 6.562); Ollendorff (1926), 921; Koeppel (1982), 453–55; Levick (1990), 46; Richardson (1992), 291. Torelli (1977–78), 179–83; (1982), 67, 70, asserts that the Ara Pietatis was not connected with Livia but related to the grant of tribunicia potestas of Drusus, which Tiberius obtained from the Senate in this year (Tac. *Ann.* 3.57.1). The event was marked by the usual senatorial flattery and included a request for a series of memorials, including *aras deum* (altars of the gods).

56. Tac. *Ann.* 4.2.1; Suet. *Tib.* 37.1; Dio 57.19.6.

57. Tac. *Ann.* 4.8.3; Syme *Papers A*, 1378.

58. *RIC*² 1.97, nos. 50–51; Tac. *Ann.* 4.16.4; Sutherland (1987), 52. Augustus: Suet. *Aug.* 44.3; Caligula: 59.3.4; Messalina: Dio 60.22.2; Willrich (1911), 40–41. Tac. *Ann.* 12.42.2 describes the carpentum as an honour reserved since antiquity for priests and for sacred objects. Livy 34.1 notes that the old veto on women driving in the city under the Lex Oppia applied only *nisi sacrorum publicorum causa veheretur*. See Clay (1982), 28–29, on the difference between a carpentum and a *tensa* (which carried divine figures).

59. Tac. *Ann.* 4.15.

60. Tac. *Ann.* 4.12.3–4 (the text and Tacitus' meaning are uncertain), 5.2.2; Hardy (1975), 35. Postumus: *PIR* P 482; *RE* 10 (1918), 482 (A. Stein). Livilla and Livia: *Piso Decree* 143; *CIL* 6. 4352: *Prima Augusti et Augustae L. nutrix Iuliae Germanici filiae* (cf. 3998);

61. Tac. *Ann.* 4.22. Lucius Piso: Tac. *Ann.* 4.21.1.

62. Tac. *Ann.* 3.31.2, 64.1, 4.57.3; Suet. *Tib.* 51.1; Dio 57.12.6.

63. Syme, *Papers A*, 943.

64. Tac. *Ann.* 3.29.3, 4.74–5; Suet. *Tib.* 52.1. On the date of the betrothal: Barrett (1996), 40. Ollendorff (1926), 921, speculates that Livia might have been behind the marriage and suggests that she might also have been behind the marriage of Nero, the oldest son of Germanicus, and Julia, daughter of Drusus, son of Tiberius. That last marriage took place probably in late 20.

65. Tac. *Ann.* 4.60.5–6.

66. Tac. *Ann.* 5.3.1.

67. Sen. *Ira* 3.21.5; Tac. *Ann.* 4.67.5; see Scott (1939), 462.

6. THE PRIVATE LIVIA

1. Sen. *Cons. Marc.* 4.4; Tac. *Ann.* 5.1.3.

2. Evans (1935); Barton (1994), 115–18; Bartman (1999), 26.

3. Ovid *Pont.* 3.1.117, 145; Vell. 2.75.3; Tac. *Ann.* 5.1.2; Dio 54.19.3. The same kind of cliché would be applied to Agrippina the elder. Dio twice (60.31.6, 61.14.2) calls Agrippina *kale* (beautiful). Tacitus, when comparing her on separate occasions (*Ann.* 12.64.4, 13.19.2; 14.9.1) to two contemporary women (Junia Silana and Domitia Lepida), claims that the women were well matched in their moral depravity and were equals in their *forma*, where the context requires that this word be understood in a positive sense of "beauty."

4. *RIC*² Tiberius 4; Fishwick (1987–92) II.1, 465. Local issues: *RPC* 1154 (Corinth),

1567–68 (Thessalonica), 1779 (Byzantium), 2840 (Aphrodisias); Gross (1962), 58, 62–66.

5. Ovid *AA* 3.139–40.

6. Ovid *Pont.* 3.1.142.

7. Ornatrices: *CIL* VI. 3993, 3994, 8944, 8958. A veste / ad vestem: *CIL* VI. 3985, 4041–40, 4251. Ab ornamentis: *CIL* VI. 3992. Ab ornamentis sacerdotalibus: *CIL* VI. 8955. Calciator: *CIL* VI. 3939. Lanipendi: *CIL* VI. 3973, 3977. Sarcinatores/ -rices: *CIL* VI. 3988, 4028–31, 5357, 8903, 9038. Unctrix: *CIL* VI. 4045. Aurifex *CIL* VI. 3927, 3943–45, 3949. Inaurator: *CIL* VI. 3928. Margaritarius: *CIL* VI. 3981.

8. Livy 5.23; Hor. *Odes* 1.5.5; Dio 54.16.5; Bartman (1999), 44. Pliny *Paneg.* 83.7 praises Trajan's wife Plotina for her moderation in the number of her attendants.

9. Pliny *HN* 7.75.

10. Suet. *Tib.* 14.2. Augustus' letter: Suet. *Claud.* 4.2.

11. Pliny's wife: Pliny *Ep.* 4.19. Cornelia: Plut. *Pomp.* 55.1; Juv. *Sat.* 6.434–56.

12. Philo. *Leg.* 319–20; Gow and Page (1968), I.277; Jones (1970), 250–55. The identification of the Augusta in Honestus' poem is far from certain. Octavia: Plut. *Publ.* 17.5; Vitr. *Arch.* I praef. 2–3.

13. Plut. *Ant.* 80; Dio 51.16.3–5; *PIR* A1025; *RE* 2 (1895), 626 (H. von Arnim); Bowersock (1965), 33–34. Marc. Aur. *Med.* 8.31 cites Areus and Maecenas as prime examples of Augustus' friends.

14. Sen. *Cons. Marc.* 4.3. Suet. *Aug.* 89.1 speaks of the emperor's *contubernium* (close association) with Areus and with his sons Dionysius and Nicanor. Dio 51.16.1–4 says of Octavian that Areus *sunonti echreto* (he was in his company). Rawson (1985), 17, suggests that Areus might have come to Rome from Alexandria as a protégé of Caesar and might have taught Octavian before Caesar's death.

15. Pliny *HN* 3.127, 14.60, 17.31. Marchetti, "Del Sito dell'antico Castello Pucino e del vino che vi cresceva," *Archaeografo Triestino* 5 (1877–78), 431–50; 6 (1879–80), 58–59, places Castellum Pucinum in the neighbourhood of the small port of Duino, north of Trieste.

16. Cic. *de Orat.* 1.62 refers to a debate in which Asclepiades is mentioned as a great contemporary doctor. Cicero wrote in 55 BC, but the dramatic date of the passage is 91 BC. Pliny *HN* 7.124; 23.32, 37–40; 26.12–18 claims that Asclepiades was influential during the time of Pompey the Great (probably from the sixties to Pompey's death in 48). The nickname is provided by Anonymus Londinensis XXIV.30; Wellman (1896); Rawson (1982); Vallance (1990), 1–5 (1993), 694–95; Scarborough (1993).

17. Hor. *Sat.* 2.2.44, 2.8.51; Pliny *HN* 19.92.

18. Marcellus Burdigalensis, *De Medicamentis*, ed. M. Niedermann, trans. J. Kollesch and D. Niebel, *Corpus Medicorum Latinorum* 5 (Berlin: Akademie Verlag, 1968); Grimm (1865); Rouselle (1976); Rose "Superstition" *OCD* (1970); Brown (1981); Scarborough (1984), 224; Barton (1994), 144–45. Octavia's toothpaste: Marc. *De Med.* 13.1:2.

19. Bartman (1999); Wood (1999), 85.

20. Kellum (1994), 215; Ling (1991), 45, 135, 149–50.
21. Liviana: Pliny *HN* 15.70; Col. *RR* 5.10.11, 10.414; Cloatius in Macrob. *Sat.* 3.20.1; Ath. *Deip.* 3. 75.
22. Pliny *HN* 13.74.
23. Pliny *HN* 14.11.
24. Suet. *Galb.* 1; Pliny *HN* 15.136–37; Dio 48.52.3–4, 63.29.3. Pliny 15.136 says that the haruspices ordered the grove planted, but there is no real contradiction.
25. Pliny *HN* 15.129, 136; Reeder (1997), 95 n. 21.
26. Cato *De Agr.* 152 (133); Pliny *HN* 17.62; see Messineo (1984).

7. WIFE OF THE EMPEROR

1. *ILS* 8403. Amymone: *ILS* 8402; Suet. *Aug.* 73.
2. Cic. *Verr.* 2.1.120, 136–38; Hillard (1992), 42–46.
3. Sall. *BC* 24.3–25; Tac. *Ann.* 12.7.6; Balsdon (1962), 47–48; Syme *Papers A*, 1242–43; (1986), 198; Hillard (1992), 47.
4. Livy 8.18.6; Tac. *Ann.* 2.71.4. Tacitus also speaks of the imperial house being rent by *muliebres offensiones* (*Ann.* 1.33.5, 12.64.4).
5. Livy 40.37.5.
6. Vell. 2.74.3; Florus 2.16.2; Livy *Per.* 125; Martial 11.20; Plut. *Ant.* 10.3; App. *BC* 5.14, 55, 59; Dio 48.10.3–4, 28.3; Babcock (1965); Pomeroy (1975), 185, 189; Hallett (1977), 160–61; Dixon (1983), 109; Huzar (1986), 102; Delia (1991); Barrett (1996), 10–12.
7. Suet. *Aug.* 25.1, 58.2; Macrob. *Sat.* 2.5.3.
8. For general accounts, see Balsdon (1962); Pomeroy (1975); Hallett (1984); Gardner (1986); Bauman (1992).
9. Suet. *Aug.* 72–74.
10. Suet. *Aug.* 24.1, 44.2, 64.2; Dio 54.16.5. Funeral honours: Suet. *Aug.* 61.2; Dio 54.35.5; Flory (1984), 304.
11. Macrob. *Sat.* 2.5.8.
12. Pliny *HN* 7.57; Suet. *Aug.* 62.2, 63.1; Lacey (1996), 74. Correspondence: Suet. *Claud.* 4.1, 4.4, 4.6; one might compare similar expressions in Cicero *ad Fam.* 14.1.5: *mea Terentia;* 2.2 *mea lux;* 3.1: *mea Terentia.*
13. Suet. *Cal.* 23.2: *identidem appellans.* Syme *Papers A*, 1369, notes that the clever phrase is reminiscent of Caligula's expression "golden sheep" for Marcus Silanus (Tac. *Ann.* 13.1.1).
14. Suet. *Cal.* 23.2; Cic. *Phil.* 2.44; Ovid *AA* 1. 31–32; Val. Max. 2.1.5, 6.1 *praef.* Festus 112.26L. Caligula: Jos. *Ant.* 19.30; Sebesta (1994), 48–49; Bartman (1999), 42.
15. Fischler (1994), 122.
16. Hor. *Odes* 3.14.5; Syme (1939), 414.
17. Sen. *Cons. Marc.* 2.4–3.2, 4.4; Macrob. *Sat.* 5.2.6.
18. Sen. *Ep.* 91.13; Sen. *Ira* 3.23.4–6; *FGH* 88; *RE* 6A (1936), 1063–71; *PIR* T 156; Bowersock (1965), 109–10, 125–26.
19. Dio (54.10.5) states that in 19 BC Augustus was given the post of supervisor of

morals and (54.30.1) received the same office for another five-year term in 12 BC. Suet. *Aug.* 27.5 says that he was given the task for life, which seems to be contradicted by *RG* 6. The issue is much debated by scholars: see Rich (1990), 187.

20. Suet. *Aug.* 34.1; Dio 56.10.3. The differences between the Lex Julia and Papia Poppaea elude proper explanation. Sometimes the jurists cite what they call the Julian and Papian law, as if it were a single piece of legislation. The *ius trium liberorum* may well have been enacted at the later date.

21. *Cons. Liv.* 45–46, 343; Ovid *Pont.* 2.2.69, 3.1.115–16, 4.13.29; Hor. *Odes* 3.14.5 (cf. Flory [1984] 321); Val. Max. 6.1.1; Tac. *Ann.* 5.1.3; Dio 58.2.4, 5; Kunst (1998), 458.

22. Flory (1984), 322. On the marriage legislation: Frank (1975); Galinsky (1981).

23. Flory (1984), 313, has noted the significance of June 11, the dedication date of Livia's shrine to Concord. Ovid observes that June 11 was the *dies natalis* of the temple of Mater Matuta in Rome in the Forum Boarium and the day of the *Matralia*, a festival in her honour, and an occasion of importance to the family, with its emphasis on mothers and children (Ovid *Fast.* 6.479–807); Edwards (1993), 164–65.

24. Livy 3.7.7, 27.51.9; Simon (1967); Kleiner (1978); Pollini (1978), 75–172; Torelli (1982), 27–61; La Rocca (1983); Rose (1997), 15–17, 103–4; Bartman (1999), 86–92, plates 74, 75; Conlin (1992), 210–11; Wood (1999), 99–103, figs. 30–31, 53; Davies (2000), 111–14; Kleiner and Matheson (2000), 10–11, 46. The panels on the south frieze, where Livia appears, were reworked by Carradori, and we must accordingly be cautious about details.

25. Val. Max. 4.3.3.

26. Suet. *Claud.* 3.2; Dio 60.2.5.

27. *Piso Decree* 149–50.

28. Suet. *Claud.* 4.1–5. Technically, Claudius would have become *sui iuris* on the death of his father, and subject to a tutor only until his majority. Technically, Augustus was not his paterfamilias.

29. Suet. *Claud.* 41.2. Suetonius does not name Livia but refers to her as Claudius' grandmother *(avia)*. His maternal grandmother, Octavia, died a year before his birth (despite J. D. Rolfe's comment *ad loc.* in the Loeb translation); Syme, *Papers A*, 435.

30. Suet. *Claud.* 26.2.

31. Tac. *Ann.* 4.71.4; Phillips (1978), 75–76.

32. Tac. *Ann.* 5.3.1.

33. Suet. *Cal.* 10.1; 23.2. On Caligula and his relatives, Barrett (1990), 217–19.

34. Sen. *Cons. Marc.* 3.4; cf. Ovid *Pont.* 3.1.125.

35. Augustus' adulteries: *Eleg. in Maec.* 2.7–8; Suet. *Aug.* 69, 71.1 (with the rumour that Livia provided him with young women); Dio 54.16.3, 19.3, 19.6, 55.7.5.

36. Tac. *Ann.* 5.1.3; Dio 54.16.4–5, 58.2.5. See G. Williams (1958) on the traditional expectations that wives be obedient.

37. Dio 54.16.4.

38. *Cons. Liv.* 49–50; Lucan *BC* 1.180; Cic. *ad Fam.* 5.8.3.

39. Suet. *Aug.* 84.2, *Tib.* 51.1. Nero: Tac. *Ann.* 13.4.2.

40. Suet. *Aug.* 40.3, *Tib.* 12.1, 13.2.

41. Sen. *Clem.* 1.9; Dio 55.14-22.2; *PIR* C 1339; Speyer (1956); Millar (1964), 78-79; Bauman (1967), 196-97; Shotter (1971), 1118-19; ("Cinna," 1974); Manuwald (1979), 120-27; Giua (1981); Syme *Papers C,* 925, (1958), 404 n. 2; Raaflaub and Salmons (1990), 427-28.

42. Conspiracies: Suet. *Aug.* 19.1. Lepidus: Vell. 2.88; Dio 54.15.4; App. *BC* 4.50. Rufus: Dio 48.33.2. Murena and Caepio: Dio 54.3.4-7; Vell. 2.91.2. Egnatius: Dio 53.24.4-6; Vell 2.91.3-92.4.

43. On the conspiracy of AD 6: Suet. *Aug.* 19.1; Dio 55.27.2; Barrett (1996), 21, 256 n. 36.

44. Purcell (1986); see also Sirago (1979).

45. Ovid *Trist.* 1.6.25, *Pont.* 3.1.125. *Cons. Liv.*, Livia: 353, 365; Drusus: 285, 344; Antonia: 303. On the identification of Antonia in the *Consolatio* see the summary in Schoonhoven (1992), 24-25.

46. Dio 55.16.2. Potestas: Cic. *Tusc.* 1.30.74; *Phil.* 1.7.18; *Verr.* 2.4.5. Potentia: references to *(im)potentia* in the source are to actual power, not legal constitutional power; Sen. *Cons. Helv.* 14.2: *quia feminis honores non licet gerere;* Suet. *Aug.* 69.1: *nimia potentia* of Octavian's mistress (probably Livia); *Nero* 6.4: Agrippina's *potentia* while Messalina was alive; Tac. *Ann.* 12.57.2: Agrippina's *impotentia* as wife of Claudius; Suet. *Oth.* 2.2: Otho's *potentia* under Nero. Political: Mommsen *SR* II.664, 754, 1033.

47. On maiestas, see, inter alios, Kübler (1928); Drexler (1956); Burdeau (1964), 22; Bauman (1967), 228-29; Lear (1968), 49-72.

48. Cic. *Phil.* 3.13; Livy 34.2; Vell. 1.10.3.

49. Hor. *Epod.* 2.1.258-59: *sed neque parvum / carmen maiestas recipit tua;* Ovid *Trist.* 2.512: *maiestas adeo comis ubique tua est.* Two consuls: Suet. *Aug.* 37.

50. Vell. 2.99.4; Suet. *Aug.* 25.1, *Tib.* 15.2.

51. Ovid *Pont.* 2.8.30, 3.1.155-56; *Cons. Liv.* 347.

52. Tac. *Ann.* 3.3.1. For Tiberius' maiestas, see Ovid *Trist.* 4.9.68; Vell. 2.124.1; Tac. *Ann.* 1.47.2; 3.64.2.

53. Digest 48.4.1.1. See Allison (1962); Goodyear (1981), 141-50; Severus: Tac. *Ann.* 1.72.3; Jer. *Chron.* 176H: AD 8; Dio 56.27.1: AD 12.

54. Dio 49.38.1.

55. Octavian: Dio 44.5.3, 49.15.3-5, cf. App. *BC* 5.132.

56. Augustus had originally belonged to a plebeian family but was adlected to the patricians in accordance with the Lex Cassia by Julius Caesar: Suet. *Aug.* 2.1; Dio 45.2.7.

57. Mommsen (1899), 538-39, argues that the crimen maiestatis has its origins in the need to protect the maiestas of the tribunes. His view is not universally accepted; for a summary of the issues, Bauman (1967), 220-21.

58. Dio 44.5.3 (44), 49.15.5-6 (36), 49.38.1 (35). Ius trium liberorum: Dio 55.2.5; Mommsen *SR* II. 792 n. 2, 819; Sandels (1912), 12-13, 66-67; Bauman (1976), 217-20; Rheinhold (1988), ad loc.; Bauman (1981), 174-81; (1992), 93-98, 176; Scardigli (1982), 61-64; Purcell (1986), 85-87; Schrömbges (1986), 200; Flory (1993); Perkounig (1995), 55. Separation of powers of office: Siber (1952), 208, 214-18, 281. Analogy with Vestals: Willrich (1911), 54, followed by Hohl (1937).

Winkes (1985), 58, suggests that there was a deliberate ambiguity with reference both to the Vestals and to the tribunes.

59. Livia: Dio 58.2.4. Octavia: Val. Max. 9.15.2.

60. Dio 56.10.2.

61. Livy 2.13.11

62. *CIL* 6.10043: the bases have survived, possibly recut in the Augustan period; Plut. *Gai. Gracch.* 4.3. Pliny *HN* 34.31 says that the statue was to honour Cornelia not only as mother of the Gracchi but also as daughter of Scipio Africanus; see Flory (1993), 290, for a discussion and bibliography.

63. Suet. *Aug.* 93; Dio 51.4.1, 54.9.10; Rose (1997), 140–41 no. 71; Wood (1999), 92; Bartman (1999), 64. The emperor is still called Imperator Caesar (in the Greek form of the name) and not yet Augustus.

64. Tiberius: EJ, p. 54. Germanicus: EJ, p. 49. Drusus: EJ, p. 53; Degrassi (1963), 278.

65. Theatre of Marcellus: EJ, p. 48. Birthday: *AFA* xxxive.2; EJ, p. 46; Herz (1978), 1153. It is to be noted that AD 27 is the first year in the Arval record for which the section relating to the end of January has survived.

66. EJ, p. 46. Two famous early examples are known outside Rome, at Narbo (*ILS* 154) and Forum Clodii (*ILS* 154); Pippidi (1931), 100; Taylor (1937), 188–89; Fishwick (1987–92), 388; Wiseman (1991), 55.

67. See Kahrstedt (1910); Sutherland (1951), 53, 143; Kleiner (1992), 365–66.

68. Lugdunum: *RPC* 512–13. Eumenea: *RPC* 3139–40. Rome: Crawford nos. 494.40; 514.1; Kahrstedt (1910), 291–92; Kleiner (1992), 358–60; Woods (1999), 41; Bartman (1999), 37, 58. Earlier winged bust: Sydenham (1952), no. 747 (C. Valerius Flaccus, c. 82–81 BC).

69. Miletus: *BMCRR* 2.503, nos. 135–37. Pergamum, cistophori: *BMCRR* 2.502, nos. 133–34, pl. 114.1–2; Sydenham (1952), nos. 1197–98. Pergamum, aes: *BMCRR* 2.513, 516, 519, nos. 164–71.

70. *BMCRR* 2. 510–12, 515, 516, 518; Wood (1999), 50. The sestertii appear to depict on their reverses Antony and Octavia portrayed as Neptune and Amphitrite drawn in a carriage by sea creatures.

71. *BMCRR* 2, 1499; Sydenham (1952), no. 1196; Crawford (1974), no. 527/1, pl. 63: a unique aureus in Berlin. Obverse: head of Antony and inscription identifying him as triumvir; reverse: head of woman, without inscription. *BMCRR* 2, 507–8; Sydenham (1952), nos. 1200–1201; Crawford (1974), nos. 533/3a, b: aurei probably of 38–37 (later than the Berlin aureus). Obverse: head of Antony with inscriptions; reverse, an inscription describing further titles and a nodus head of Octavia, who is somewhat fleshier, perhaps because she had borne children, or possibly through assimilation to Antony. Recent discussion: Kleiner (1992), 362; Winkes (1995), 67–71; Wood (1999), 45.

72. *BMCRR* 2.525, nos. 179–82; Crawford (1974), no. 543, pl. 64. Cleopatra also appears on local issues: *BMC Ptolemies* 122–23; Kahrstedt (1910), 276–78, 292.

73. Augustus: RIC^2 219–220. Tiberius: RIC^2 25–30. Claudius: RIC^2 101.

74. Within the Roman empire it seems that only Rome had a temple to Vesta; *CIL* 6.2172, 14.2410 hints of a cult at Alba Longa (cf. Dion. Hal. 2.65), rejected by

McDaniel (1955); Aug. *Civ. Dei* 3.28: *nihil apud Romanos templo Vestae sanctius habebatur.*

75. On the ambiguity of the symbolic status of the Vestals: Beard (1980), (1993).

76. Cornell (1981), 28 nn. 5–7, claims only four historical cases.

77. *FIR* 37, 5.1. Lictor: Dio 47.19.4.

78. *RG* 10–12; Dio 51.19.2.

79. Suet. *Aug.* 31.3, 44.3; Dio 56.10.3. Hyginus 117 mentions land given to the Vestals, presumably by Augustus. Strictly speaking, the Vestals were chosen by lot from a list of twenty supplied by the pontifex maximus. Aul. Gell. *NA* 1.12 says that in his time (second century AD) anyone with correct social status could submit his daughter's name as a candidate; S. Price in *CAH*, 826–28. Cornelia: *PIR* C 1478; *FOS* 272; Tac. *Ann.* 4.16.4.

80. EJ, p. 47; *RG* 10.2; Livy *Per.* 117; Vell. 2.63.1; Ovid *Fast.* 3.415–28.

81. Weinstock (1971), 276–81.

82. On Livia and the Vestals, see especially Willrich (1911); Hohl (1939), and, among recent works, Bauman (1967), 217–18, (1981); Flory (1983), 320–21; Bartman (1999), 94–95.

83. Ovid *Fast.* 5.148–58, *Trist.* 4.2.11, *Pont.* 4.13.29. On the Palatine cult: Kienast (1982), 104, 196–97; C. Koch (1958), 1757. Fire: Dio 54.24.2, 57.16.2.

84. Seats: Tac. *Ann.* 4.16.4; Sutherland (1987), 51–53.

85. Antonia and Caligula's sisters: Dio 59.3.4. Antonia and Messalina: Dio 60.22.2.

86. Dio 60.5.2. It has been suggested that a relief depicting a Vestal banquet now in the Museo dei Conservatori in Rome was erected to honour Livia after her death: see Koeppel (1983), 114–16; Kampen (1991), 220–21, 222 fig. 3.

87. Athens: *IG* III 316; Grether (1946), 230 n. 43. T. Shear, *Hesperia* 50 (1981), 364, suggests that the Southwest Temple of the agora might have been dedicated to Livia. Mytileneans: *IGR* 4.39b. Lampsacus: *IGR* 4.180; Hahn (1992), 322–32. Mikocki (1995), who includes the abstractions, gives the total number as seventeen.

88. Tiberius: EJ, p. 54. Germanicus: EJ, p. 49. Drusus: EJ, p. 53.

8. MOTHER OF THE EMPEROR

1. Tac. *Ann.* 1.72.2; Suet. *Tib.* 26.1; Syme (1958), 425.

2. Tac. *Ann.* 1.6.3, 13.6, 1.14.3; Suet. *Tib.* 50.1–2, 3; Dio 57.3.3.

3. Tac. *Ann.* 5.1.3; Baldwin (1972), 94.

4. Vell. 2.75.3; Tac. *Ann.* 1.8.1; Suet. *Aug.* 101.2; Dio 56.46.1. Hoffsten (1939), 57 n. 37, says that Livia became Augusta when the title was conferred by the Senate. Tacitus uses *nomen* sometimes as an honorary name, sometimes as a simple title in association with an office. Tac. *Ann.* 1.9.2: *nomen imperatoris;* Tac. *Hist.* 1.62.2: *nomen Germanici;* Tac. *Ann.* 1.2.1: *triumviri nomine;* Tac. *Ann.* 12.4.1: *nomine censoris;* Tac. *Hist.* 5.9.2: *regium nomen;* Tac. *Hist.* 1.47.1, 2.90.2: *nomen Augusti;* 2.89.2: *Augustae nomine.*

5. Dio 45.5.4; von Premerstein (1923), 289; Schmitthenner (1952), 40–41; Weinribb (1968), 253–54; Syme, *Papers B* 159–70; Champlin (1991), 144–46; Perkounig

(1995), 123; Flory (1998), 134 n. 21; Kunst (1996); (1998), 470. Domitius: *ILS* 990; Pliny *Ep.* 8.18; Pliny: *ILS* 2927; Pliny *Ep.* 5.8.5.

6. Daughter of Marcus: *CIL* 6.882a; 2.2038, 3102; 5.6416.6; 11.7416, 7552. Daughter of Augustus: *CIL* 11.1165. A less certain example: Reynolds (1980), 82, no. 17.

7. *CIL* 6.3945,6. Treggiari (1975), 65 n. 11, for the suggestion that the filiation here was a distinguishing device.

8. *ILS* 8393, 52–53; Wistrand (1976), 64; Salomies (1992), 20 n. 1; Perkounig (1995), 122. Chatraine (1967), 221, argues that the adoption made it possible for Livia and Tiberius to inherit as joint Augusti, disputed by Weaver (1972), 63.

9. Augustus' will: Suet. *Aug.* 101. Lex curiata: App. *BC* 3.94.

10. Livia: Tac. *Ann.* 1.14.2; Goodyear (1972), 190. Agrippina: Suet. *Cal.* 8.1. Tiberius and Sejanus: Tac. *Ann.* 4.74.2. Germanicus: Tac. *Ann.* 3.18.2.

11. Verg. *Aen.* 1.288, 6.789; Serv. on Verg. *Aen.* 1.267, 2.166; Livy 1.30.1–2 (emended); Dion. Hal. 3.29.7; Tac. *Ann.* 11.24.2; Suet. *Div. Jul.* 6.1; Weinstock (1971), 5.

12. Ovid *Fast.* 5.563–64; Dio 55.10.6; Zanker (1988), 79–82, 113–14.

13. Ritter (1972), 323; Bauman (1992), 131; Perkounig (1995), 133, 136.

14. Flory (1998), 113, 117. Note that Suet. *Tib.* 26.2 calls Augustus a *nomen*.

15. Dio 55.10.20.

16. Ovid *Fast.* 1.615; Suet. *Tib.* 17.2.

17. Letters: EJ 102b, 318, etc.; *Piso Decree*, 174; Suet. *Tib.* 26.2; Dio 57.2.1; 57.8.1–2. Germanicus: Suet. *Claud.* 1.3. Britannicus: Dio 60.22.2; Scott (1932); Ritter (1972), 318–19. Flory (1998), 122, sees the influence of Hellenistic practice, and Ritter cites a Hellenistic precedent, noting that Ptolemy XII in his will made his son (Ptolemy XIII) and daughter (Cleopatra VII) his heirs, and they succeeded him as joint rulers. A copy of the will was sent to Rome (Caes. *BC* 3.108.6).

18. Ritter (1972), 316; *IGR* 3.940 (Palaepaphos, Cyprus): *I[ou]lian thean Sebasten, thugatera Autokratoro[s] Kaisaros* (Julia, goddess, Augusta, daughter of Imperator Caesar).

19. Tac. *Ann.* 12.26.1, 15.23.1; Dio 60.12.5; Temporini (1978), 23–36, 44; Perkounig (1995), 131; Flory (1998), 115.

20. Augustus' intentions: Aschbach (1864), 49; Mommsen, *SR* II.788 n. 4, 821–22; Gardthausen (1891), 46; Premerstein (1937), 269, 821; Willrich (1911), 56; Grether (1946), 233–34; Kornemann (1930), 35–36, 189; (1952), 205; (1960), 61; Gross (1962), 11; Königer (1966), 54; Pfister (1951), 20; Hatzl (1975), 23. Livia's exploitation of Augustus' will: Sandels (1912), 22, 76; Ollendorff (1926), 916; Ciaceri (1944), 58, 111.

21. Dessau (1926), 4; Ehrenberg (1946), 205; Grant (*Principate*, 1950), 126–28; Hardy (1972), 19.

22. Ritter (1972), 322–23; Flory (1998), 118.

23. Suet. *Aug.* 50; Syme (1939), 113.

24. Tac. *Ann.* 1.14.1; Dio 57.12.1.

25. Tac. *Ann.* 4.57.3; Ritter (1972), 313, 322 (also, Perkounig [1995], 130, 162); Purcell (1986), 87; Kunst (1998), 470.

26. Dio 57.12.2; Gytheum: EJ 102b; Cos: EJ 318; Ritter (1972), 328; Perkounig (1995), 151; Flory (1998), 115.

27. Tac. *Ann.* 5.1.3; Suet. *Tib.* 50.2; Dio 55.16.2, 56.47.1, 57.12.3; Goodyear (1972), 190.

28. Tac. *Ann.* 1.14.1; Suet. *Tib.* 50.2-3; Dio 57.12; Goodyear (1972), 190. On the honours bestowed on Livia: Schrömbges (1986), 191-221; Flory (1993), 302 n. 26; Kunst (1988), 451.

29. Tac. *Ann.* 1.14.1; Suet. *Tib.* 50.3; Dio 57.12.4, 58.2.3.

30. Cic. *Rab. Perd.* 27; *Pis.* 6; *Sest.* 121; Plut. *Cic.* 23.3; Aul. Gell. *NA* 5.6.15. Caesar: App. *BC* 2.106, 144; Crawford (1974), 491.

31. *RG* 35; *Fasti Praenestini*, EJ, p. 47; Sen. *Clem.* 1.14.2; Suet. *Aug.* 58.

32. Tac. *Ann.* 1.72.1 (under AD 15); Suet. *Tib.* 26.2, 67.2-4; Dio 57.2.1, 58.8.1 (under 14), 58.12.8 (under 31); Val. Max. 5.5.3, 9.11.4; Premerstein (1937), 166-75; Weinstock (1971), 200-205; Goodyear (1972), 138.

33. Scheid (1980), 225, lines 57-58.

34. Suet. *Div. Jul.* 76.1, 85; Juv. *Sat.* 8.243-44.

35. Bauman (1992), 250.4; Flory (1998), 121.

36. *RPC* 73 (Romula), 849-50 (Leptis).

37. Tac. *Ann.* 1.14.1; Suet. *Tib.* 50.2; Dio 57.12.4. The issue of Tacitus' use of senatorial records is hotly debated; for a summary of current views: Barnes (1998).

38. *IGR* 4.560 (restored) for an eastern parallel in an inscription from Aezani honouring Nero as natural son of Agrippina; Willrich (1911), 57; Kornemann (1952), 206; (1960), 66; Goodyear (1972), 190; Flory (1998), 120. Caesar: Dio 44.7.2-3, cf. 44.3.1-3; Ollendorff (1926), 916. Ritter (1972) sees Hellenistic influence.

39. Some have seen a parallel of the expansion of the names in Etruscan usage: Piganiol (1912), 163; Kornemann (1947), 206; (1960), 66.

40. Suet. *Tib.* 26.2. Dio 57.18.2 under AD 18 gives the month as November (Tiberius was born November 16); Scott (1931); Weinstock (1971), 154. Note that on a calendar from Cyprus between 21 and 12 BC a month beginning December 2 was named after Libaios, but the arrangement may have been only temporary (Scott [1931] 208; Grether [1946], 232). June: Macrob. *Sat.* 1.12.31; July: Dio 44.5.2; Macrob. *Sat.* 1.12.34; August: Suet. *Aug.* 31.2; Dio 55.6.6 (placing the event in 8 BC). Caligula renamed September as Germanicus: Suet. *Cal.* 15.2. Pompey: *IG* 12.2.59.18, restored as *menos Pom*[*peio*]. The actual numbering of the months Quintilis and Sextilis ("fifth" and "sixth"), our modern July and August, reflects the old Roman calendar, in which March was the first month.

41. *CIL* 6.32340.17; *AFA* xxxiiia.7; Dio 44.6.1, 50.1, 51.19.7; Weinstock (1971), 217-18.

42. Birthday: *AFA* xxxive.2; *ILS* 154.

43. Livy 1.20.2, 27.8.8; Plut. *QR* 113.

44. Cic. *Phil.* 2.110; Plut. *Ant.* 33.1; Dio 44.6.4; Weinstock (1971), 305-8.

45. *Tab. Heb.* (EJ 94a.50); Tac. *Ann.* 2.83.2. Germanicus was succeeded by Drusus Caesar, son of Tiberius, who was followed in turn by Germanicus' son Nero.

46. Wives of the other senior flamines may have held the same office: see Vanggaard (1988), 30-31.

47. Plut. *QR* 86 suggests that it was thought that the flaminica was priestess of Juno.

Aul. Gell. *NA* 10.15.26 *(eaedem ferme caerimoniae sunt)*; Serv. on Verg. *Aen.* 4.518; Macrob. *Sat.* 1.16.30.

48. EJ, p. 52; Vell. 2.75.3; 4.9.107; Tac. *Ann.* 1.10.8; Dio 56.46.1; Taylor (1931), 230; Grant (*Principate*, 1950), 119-20.

49. Taylor (1931), 230; Weber (1936), 92; Taeger (1960), 219; Ritter (1972), 324; Herz (1978); Fishwick (1987-92), 162-63. Gagé (1931), 15-20, argues that Livia was appointed to a domestic cult.

50. Tac. *Ann.* 1.14.2; Dio 56.46.2. Agrippina: Tac. *Ann.* 13.2.3; Sandels (1912), 30, Hoffsten (1939), 86; Weber (1936), 92; Ritter (1972), 324. Vestal privilege: Dio 47.19.4.

51. Ovid *Trist.* 4.2.11, *Pont.* 4.9.107; Vell. 2.75.3.

52. Fittschen-Zanker (1983), III.3.2.6; Winkes (1995), 39-41, 164-65; Rose (1997), 97-98, no. 25; Wood (1999), 114-15, fig. 37; Bartman (1999), 155-56, no. 22, dates it to the late republic.

53. Gross (1962), 106-7; Winkes (1995), 148-50, no. 74; De Kersauson (1986), 102-3, no. 45; Wood (1999), 115-16, fig. 38; Bartman (1999), no. 3, 146-47. On the infula see Small (1990), 224-28; Rose (1997), 77; Wood (1995), 478 nn. 79-84, suggests a broader significance, as a mark of sanctity.

54. Megow (1987), 254, no. B 15, pl. 9; Winkes (1995), 189, no. 113; Wood (1999), 119-20; Bartman (1999), 102, no. 110.

55. Dio 55.2.4, 8.2.

56. Dio 55.2.4, 8.2, 57.21.5; Willrich (1911), 59.

57. Pergamum: *RPC* 2369. Smyrna: *IGR* 4.1392, *CIL* 3.7107. Tralles: *BCH* 51 (1886), 516, no. 6; Bartman (1999), 108.

58. Kreikenbom (1992), 179-86.

59. Tac. *Ann.* 4.37; Fishwick (1987-92), I.1.158.

60. Tac. *Ann.* 1.14.2.

61. Suet. *Tib.* 50.2-3; Dio 54.24.2, 57.16.2; Agrippina: Dio 60.33.12.

62. Sejanus: Tac. *Ann.* 1.19.1, 69; Dio 58.9-13; Ritter (1972), 331; Perkounig (1995), 157.

63. Suet. *Aug.* 53.2-3; Dio 54.30.1, 56.26.2-3, 41.5, 57.12.2. Drusus: Dio 48.44.4. Nero: Tac. *Ann.* 13.18.3-5; Dio 61.33.1. Julia Domna: Dio 78.18.3; Ritter (1972), 329; Talbert (1984), 68; Kunst (1998), 455, 465-66.

64. Tac. *Ann.* 2.34; 4.21.1. Urgulania: *PIR* V 684; *RE* Suppl. 9 (1962), 1868-69 (R. Hanslik); *FOS* 619; see Syme (1939), 385; (1986), 375-76; Fischler (1989), 230.

65. Cic. *Inv.* 2.17.53: *maiestatem minuere.* Tac. *Ann.* 1.72.3: *maiestatem populi Romani minuisset.* Bauman (1992), 99, 135; Vidén (1993), 15; Fischler (1994).

66. Tac. *Ann.* 2.50.2; Suet. *Tib.* 28; Dio 57.19.1; Bauman (1967), 234; (1974), 77-78, 223; Goodyear (1981), 153.

67. Tac. *Ann.* 1.72.4; Syme (1958), 2.696.

68. Eck et al. (1996), 222.

69. Germanicus' claim: Tac. *Ann.* 2.71.2. Tiberius' statement: Tac. *Ann.* 3.12.2. Plancina's mourning: Tac. *Ann.* 2.75.2; Eck et al. (1996), 223.

70. Tac. *Ann.* 2.55.5.

71. Tac. *Ann.* 2.58.3.

72. Tac. *Ann.* 22.80.1.
73. Tac. *Ann.* 6.26.3.
74. *Piso Decree* 113; Tac. *Ann.* 2.50.3; cf. Quint. *Inst. Dr.* 5.13.5: *deprecatio . . . est sine ulla specie defensionis;* 7.4.18: *ubicunque iuris clementia est habet locum deprecatio.*
75. Tac. *Ann.* 3.17.1, 6.26.3.
76. *Piso Decree* 115; Eck et al. (1996), 228; Pliny *HN* 35.25; Flory (1993), 288; Cic. *ad Fam.* 10.5.2; *ad Att.* 10.4.5; Caes. *BC* 1.13, 3.39.
77. *Cons. Liv.* 82.
78. Plaut. *Most.* 3.2.23; Cic. *Cat.* 3.14; Juv. *Sat.* 2.34; Eck et al. (1996), 227.
79. Number and restriction to citizens: Pliny *HN* 33.30. predominance of equites: Tac. *Ann.* 3.30.2 (see also 14.20.7); Suet. *Tib.* 41; Galsterer (1996), 399–400.
80. Suet. *Tib.* 51.1. Wallace-Hadrill (1983), 94, suggests that Augustus' letters were kept in the imperial libraries. It was not unusual for correspondence to be kept in archives. Pliny *HN* 13.83 reports that he frequently saw documents in the hands of Cicero, Vergil, and Augustus, and that he had even seen documents in the hands of Tiberius and Gaius Gracchus written nearly two hundred years earlier and preserved in a private collection. Letters written in verse by Spurius Mummius were preserved by descendants (Cic. *ad Att.* 13.6.4). When charged with having won his wife Pudentilla by means of magic, the novelist Apuleius in his successful defence made use of letters of Pudentilla preserved by her son Pontianus and left by him to his archivist (Apul. *Apol.* 70.8, 78.6, 83.1, 84.5).
81. *RG* 21; *ILS* 5050.157; Pliny *HN* 8.65; Dio 54.26.1. This theatre was started by Julius Caesar, who acquired the land at the expense of the Temple of Pietas, for which he was much criticised. Augustus was obliged to buy up more land from private owners. After Marcellus' death in 23 BC, the theatre became a memorial to him. It was far enough advanced to house some of the celebrations of the secular games in 17 BC, but not dedicated until May 7, 13 BC. It appears on the Severan Marble Plan, between the Forum Holitorium and the Pons Fabricius.
82. Tac. *Ann.* 3.64.2.
83. EJ, p. 48; Degrassi (1963), 448. On April 23, AD 38, the Arvals sacrificed an ox before the simulacrum of Divus Augustus at the Theatre of Marcellus: AFA xliii. 25–26; Woodman (1981), 447. Torelli (1982), 69, argues that the statue was dedicated to commemorate the assumption of the toga virilis by Drusus, son of Tiberius, misdated according to Torelli to April 24. If we accept the sequence of events as provided by Tacitus, Tiberius could not have been present at the dedication ceremony, as the inscription implies he was.
84. *RIC*² Tiberius 49; Torelli (1982), 68, defining the Augustus side as the obverse.
85. Dio 56.46.3; see Degrassi (1963), 447. The incident has been seen by some scholars as a vindication of Tacitus' claim: Sandels (1912), 76; Ollendorff (1926), 50–58, 919; Hoffsten (1939), 15; Ciaceri (1944), 112; Kornemann (1947), 214; contra, Ritter (1972), 329. Mothers precede sons in grave inscriptions: *ILS* 1485, 1554. Gagé (1931), 16–17, says that Livia's claim to precedence was justified by her position as priestess of Augustus' cult and adoptive daughter of the divus. On the Gytheum decree, see Seyrig (1929), 91–92.
86. Dio 58.2.3–6; Kähler (1939), 378. Drusus, brother of Tiberius: Suet. *Claud.* 1.3;

Dio 55.2.3; *RIC²* Claudius: 69–72, 125–26. Germanicus: Tac. *Ann.* 2.83.2; González (1984), 58–69; Kleiner (1990), 511 n. 10. Drusus, son of Tiberius: Tac. *Ann.*
4.9.2 (Drusus received the same memorials as Germanicus). See Kleiner (1990),
512, for speculation that a posthumous arch was granted to Sabina, wife of Hadrian;
arches honoured Livia outside Rome. At Ephesus, Augustus and Livia, along with
Marcus Agrippa and Julia, were honoured on the south gate of the agora: *ILS* 8897,
EJ 71. A supposed arch in honour of Livia on the Via Valeria is linked with a
dedicatory inscription from Superaequum (*CIL* 9. 3304).

9. WOMAN OF SUBSTANCE

1. Thomas (1976), 192; Mratschek-Halfmann (1993), 45.
2. Suet. *Galb.* 5.2; Mratschek-Halfmann (1993), 279–80. Note, however, that Claudius' freedman Narcissus reputedly amassed a fortune of 400 million sesterces (Dio
   60.34.4).
3. *RG* 17; Suet. *Aug.* 101.3, *Claud.* 4.7; the text of Suetonius gives as a limit of each
   legacy 20,000 sesterces *(vicena sestertia)*. This is a very small amount, and Suetonius,
   who had seen the will, states elsewhere that Claudius received 800,000 as a legacy,
   which was considered niggardly. Thus there are grounds for accepting the proposed
   emendation to *vicies*, which would allow a maximum of two million; Shatzman
   (1975), 368 n. 561; Millar (1992), 191; Champlin (1989); Mratschek-Halfmann
   (1993), 280.
4. Cic. *De Rep.* 3.10.17 says the Lex Voconia was unjust to women. Dio 55.2.5,
   56.10.2, 32.1; Cato: *ORF* fr. 156–60; Steinwerter (1925), Astin (1978), 113–18;
   Bauman (1983), 176–78, (1992), 34. For the surviving terms of the Lex Voconia,
   see Thomas (1976), 487–88; Rogers (1947), 142, for individuals whose legacies to
   Augustus are known.
5. Suet. *Aug.* 101.3; E. Champlin (1989), 157, (1991), 11–17.
6. Dio 56.10.2 links the restriction to the Lex Voconia, but this is the only evidence
   that this Lex imposed such a constraint.
7. *CIL* 6.4173: Timotheus Maronianus; *CIL* 6.3952: Livia's slave Cascellianus, a legacy to the emperor from the distinguished lawyer Aulus Cascellius (*PIR* C 389); *CIL*
   6.4124: Eros Maecilianus, freedman of Livia, perhaps from Marcus Maecilius
   Tullus, triumvir monetalis in the last decade BC; *CIL* 6.4358: *Pelops Scaplian(us) Ti
   Caesar(is) tabularius et Augustae*, owned jointly by Livia and Tiberius; *CIL* 6.9066:
   Philadelphus Ti Caes(aris) Aug(usti) et Iuliae Aug(ustae) servus Scaplianus, slave of
   Tiberius and Livia; *CIL* 6.5226: Servilia Scapula, slave of Tiberius and Livia and
   Quintus Ostorius Scapula, one of the first pair of praetorian prefects in 2 BC and
   grandfather of Ostorius Scapula, who later won fame for his command in Britain;
   see Stein (1942), 1672; *CIL* 6.4095: Anna Liviae Maecenatiana, *CIL* 6.4016: *Par-
   meno Liviae a purpur. Maecenatian(a)*, both acquired from Maecenas; *CIL* 6. 5223:
   Castor Ti. Caesar(is) et August(ae) l. Agrippi(anus), acquired from Marcus Agrippa.
8. Jos. *Ant.* 17.146, 190; *AE* 1979, no. 33: *Idumaeus Ti. Caesaris maternus*; see Chantraine (1982), 132.
9. *CIL* 6. 4035: *M. Livius Aug(ustae?) Lib(ertus) Anterus Amyntian(us)*; from the *Monu-*

mentum Liviae: CIL 6. 8894: *Epinicius Caesar(is) ser(vus) Amyntianus.* With no connections to the imperial family: *CIL* 6. 4715, 8738 (= *ILS* 7866), 10395: Strabo 12.8.4; Dio 53.26.3 Shatzman (1975), 361. Because Anteros was a *supellectile,* it may be that his job was to look after fine furniture and works of art, and Huntsman (1997), 164, suggests that Amyntas might have left a fine collection to Livia. Magie (1950), 1304 n. 3, is dubious about using inscriptional evidence to establish an inheritance from Amyntas.

10. Suet. *Aug.* 72.1; *LTUR* 1.129; Richardson (1992), 130.
11. Varro. *LL* 5.54. Vitruvius: Livy 8.19.4; Cic. *Dom.* 101. Octavian: Suet. *Aug.* 5; Tamm (1963), 28–45, 47 n. 23; Coarelli (1983) II.25, 31; Richardson (1992), 279–82.
12. Ovid *Fast.* 1. 951; Dio 49.15.5; Suet. *Aug.* 29.3; Vell. 2.81.3.
13. Suet. *Aug.* 72.1.
14. Digest 33.2.32.2; Treggiari (1991), 390.
15. *CIL* 15.7264.
16. Lugli (1970), 167–74; Coarelli (1985), 129–30; Carettoni (1987), 775; Richardson (1992), 73–74; Claridge (1998), 128; Macciocca, Iacopi: *LTUR* 2. 130–32. Paintings: Ling (1991), 37–38, 113, 142, 216. Bragantini (1982), 30–33, suggests that the Egyptian motifs of the House of Livia, the Aula Isiaca, and the Farnese Villa suggest a unified scheme. Kokkinos (1992), 149–53, believes that this house was shared by Livia and Antonia.
17. All references are to *CIL* 6: dispensator: 3965b, 3966, 3968, 4237; arcarii: 3937, 3938, 8722; tabularii: 4250; slave ad possessiones: 4015; custos rationis patrimoni: 3962; ornatrices: 3993, 3994, 8944, 8958; a veste / ad vestem: 3985, 4041–43, 4251; ab ornamentis: 3992; ab ornamentis sacerdotalibus: 8955; calciator: 3939; lanipendi: 3973, 3977; sarcinatores / -rices 3988, 4028–31, 5357, 8903, 9038; unctrix: 4045; pedisequi / -ae: 4002–6; puer a pedibus: 4001.
18. All references are to *CIL* 6: medici: 3983, 3985–87, 8901. 8903, 8904; supra medicos: 3982.
19. All references are to *CIL* 6: aurifex: 3927, 3943–45, 3949; inaurator: 3928; margaritarius: 3981; colorator: 3953; ab supellectile: 4035, 4036, 5358; a tabulis: 3970.
20. Pliny *HN* 7.75.
21. *CIL* 6.3973: *Helenus Liviae ad insulam,* and *CIL* 6. 3974: *Clerdo insularius;* he is not necessarily a slave of Livia, but his ashes (as well as Helenus') were deposited in the *Monumentum Livia;* see Garnsey (1976), 128.
22. Lugli (1923); Gabriel (1955); Blake (1947), 272; Calci (1994).
23. Suet. *Galb.* 1; Dio 48.44.1. Huntsman (1997) suggests that the imperial villa at Antium was Livia's.
24. Campania: *CIL* 10.8042, 41, 60; Willrich (1911), 73. Sicily: *CIL* 10.7489; Willrich (1911), 72. Tusculum: *CIL* 15.7814. Capri: *CIL* 6.8958: Juno Dorcas is a freedwoman of Livia, her *ornatrix;* she died in Rome but was born *a Caprensis,* cf. 8409, Willrich (1911), 73. Lucania: *AE* 1972, no. 147: *Pancarpus Liv(iae servus);* D'Arms (1970), 84 n. 55. L. Jacono, *NS* (1926), 230 n. 5, notes that a tile stamp at Ponza with the name *Augustae* may refer to Julia; similarly R. Paribeni, *NS* (1902), 630, believes that a slave of *Julia August(a* or *i)* in Puteoli may be Julia's.

25. *ILS* 259. Huntsman (1977), 159, argues that he may not have administered the same property for all three.

26. Pliny *HN* 34.3–4. Ulp. *Dig.* VI.I.13.5 states that occupants had the right to exploit the minerals beneath their land; Ollendorff (1926), 906; Davies (1935), 3 n. 7.

27. Jos. *Ant.* 18.31, *BJ* 2.167; cf. Pliny *HN* 13.44; Smallwood (1976), 158 n. 56; Paltiel (1991), 67; Mratschek-Halfmann (1993), 269. Procurator: *AE* 1941, 105; Fracarro (1940).

28. *IGR* 4.1204, 1213 (= *ILS* 8853); Suet. *Tib.* 8; Hermann *DAW* LXXVII 1 (1959) no. 12; Hirschfeld (1902), 303, disagrees; Willrich (1911), 72; Broughton (1934), 220; Jones (1971), 84; Crawford (1974), 39; Shatzman (1975), 362; Huntsman (1997), 158. Some scholars have read *arches* for *arkes*, suggesting an administrative unit rather than a treasury. Pflaum (1960–61), 579, no. 218, argues for a treasury of an official, Livius, unconnected with Livia.

29. Dio 51.5.5; Frank (1940), 6; Parassoglou (1978), 6; Crawford (1974), 41.

30. Willrich (1911), 73; Parassoglou (1978), 15–29; Crawford (1974), 39–40; Lewis (1974), 52–54; Rostovtzev (1979), 145; Mratschek-Halfmann (1993), 280.

31. *SB* 9150; see Wolfe (1952).

32. *P. Lond.* II.445.

33. Theadelphia: *P. Med.* 6. Philadelphia: *P. Sorb.* Inv. 2364.

34. *PSI* 1028, *SB* 10536.

35. *Pap. Ryl.* 126; the land belonged to Gaius Julius Alexandros, whose death is put between AD 26 and 28 (on the death: Parassoglou [1978], 17).

36. *P. Vindob.* 560: Euhemeria (AD 54); *P. Mich.* 560 (AD 46): *Libiane ousia* could have belonged to Livia or Livilla (see Parassoglou [1978], 19 n. 46); Huntsman (1997) notes another possible estate at Drymos Hieras Nesou (*P. Bour.* 42).

37. Suet. *Tib.* 7.1.

38. EJ p. 46; Tac. *Ann.* 1.73.3; Dio 56.46.5. Caligula: Jos. *Ant.* 19.77; Suet. *Cal.* 56.2; Dio 59.29.5; Barrett (1989), 169–71; Fishwick (1987–92), I.1.162. On the date of the decree: Degrassi (1963), 13.2, p. 161.

39. Jos. *Ant.* 19.75; Tac. *Ann.* 1.73.3. Tacitus says *solitum interesse*, which is problematic in AD 15 because the festival can have been held only once. Cassius may have participated in other festivals connected with Augustus. On Falanius: Syme (1970), 68, *Papers B*, 630–31.

40. Caligula: *RIC*² 36. Antoninus: *RIC*² 973; Dio 56.46.3; Richardson (1992), 45; Fishwick (1992). Tac. *Ann.* 6.45.2 says that Tiberius finished the temple. Suet. *Tib.* 47; *Cal.* 21 claims it was unfinished. Dio 57.10.2 mentions only Tiberius' name in connection with the temple. Richmond (1913) argues that Caligula's sestertius depicts the Temple of Apollo on the Palatine. Hill (1979), 207, suggests that the temple on Antoninus' coins represents the building as restored by Domitian, after the fire of 80.

41. Pliny *HN* 12.94; Rehak (1990). Torelli (1982), 73, identifies this shrine with the *sacrarium* mentioned at Suet. *Tib.* 51.1, but surely a smaller structure is involved. Boatwright (1991), 519 n. 26, believes that Pliny's temple is the same as the one mentioned by Dio 56.46.3. Fishwick (1992) suggests that a single temple was in-

volved, and that the temple on the "Palatine," broadly defined, was the Temple of Divus Augustus.

42. *AFA* lv, lvi; *ILS* 4992, *ILS* 4993. Aeditus: *ILS* 4995; Dio 60.5.2; Hänlein-Schäfer (1985), 113–28; Fishwick (1987–92) II.1.485; Winkes (1985), 68; *LTUR* 1.143–6: *Aedes Augusti*.

10. FRIEND, PATRON, AND PROTECTOR

1. On this, see especially Dixon (1981); Hillard (1992).
2. Sabines: Livy 1.13; Dion. Hal. 2.30. Coriolanus: Livy 2.33–35, 37–40; Dion. Hal. 6.92–94, 7.19, 21–67; Plut. *Cor.* 34–36. Cornelia: Plut. *Gai. Gracch.* 4.1; Fischler (1989), 23.
3. App. *BC* 5.52, 63, 69, 72; Dio 48.15.2, 16.2–3; Cluett (1998).
4. See Dixon (1981–82), 94–96, for these and other examples.
5. Cic. *Rosc.* 27.
6. Fischler (1994), 117–18; Hallett (1977), 170–71; Pomeroy (1975), 186; Champlin (1989), 80.
7. Dio 47.7.4–5; Vinius: *RE* 9A (1961), 123 (H. Gundel).
8. Plut. *Ant.* 35.2.
9. Vitr. *Arch.* 1 pr. 2
10. Syme (1939), 386.
11. Tac. *Ann.* 2.37.1; Edwards (1993), 185.
12. Cic. *Off.* 2.56; Pliny *Ep.* 2.4.2, 6.32.2; Dio 58.2.2. Gaul: Suet. *Aug.* 40.3. Jury: Suet. *Tib.* 51.1; Talbert (1984), 49 n. 15. Fires: Dio 57.16.2.
13. Vell. 2.130.5; *Cons. Liv.* 48; Dio 55.19.5, 58.2.3; Seibt (1969), 14; Martin (1981), 141; Perkounig (1995), 163–64; Flory (1998), 120.
14. Syme (1986), 169, 172.
15. *ILS* 1321.
16. Tac. *Ann.* 6.20.2; Suet. *Galb.* 4–5; Dio 57.19.4. Consulship: Plut. *Galb.* 3.2; not mentioned by Suet. *Galb.* 6.1. Suet. *Galb.* 5.2 *paene ditatus* might suggest that Galba at best received a reduced amount of the legacy.
17. Tac. *Hist.* 2.50; Suet. *Oth.* 1; Syme (1986), 169; Saller (1982), 65.
18. Haterius: *PIR* H24; *RE* Suppl. 3 (1918), 889–90 (K. Gerth); Jer. *Chron.* 172H. Augustus: Sen. *Contr.* 4. *praef.* 7.
19. Tac. *Ann.* 3.57.2.
20. Tac. *Ann.* 1.13.6, 14.4–6. Suet. *Tib.* 27 says that the emperor fell on his back *supinus;* Tacitus, forward, *prociderat*. Apology: Suet. *Tib.* 29. Tacitus' text is corrupt; the "urgent appeals," in one reading of the manuscript, may be Livia's, but they suit Haterius better. Suetonius sees the episode as essentially humorous, Tacitus takes it more seriously.
21. Tac. *Ann.* 5.2.2. Father: EJ, p. 38.
22. Tac. *Ann.* 4.12.
23. Sen. *Cons. Marc.* 1; Tac. *Ann.* 4.34–35; Suet. *Aug.* 35.2, *Tib.* 61.3, *Cal.* 16.1; Dio 57.24.4.

24. Sen. *Cons. Marc.* 4.1, 24.3.
25. Ovid has been defended on the grounds that his references are ironical. For a summary and a balanced view: Johnson (1997).
26. Ovid *Fast.* 5.157–58, 6.637.
27. Ovid *Trist.* 1.6.25–27, 2.161–64; *Pont.* 1.4.56, 3.1.114–18, 125–28, 139–42. On the place of Livia in *Trist.* 1.6, see Hinds (1999), 139–41.
28. Ovid *Trist.* 4.2.11; *Pont.* 4.13.29. Syme (1978), 21–36, believes that the *Fasti* were written between AD 1 and 4, and revised in part after 14, 37–39; *Tristia* composed between AD 8–9 and 12, 39–44; *ex Ponto* I–III written in 12, published in 13, IV in 13–16.
29. Wife: Ovid *Pont.* 3.1.145–66. Images: Ovid *Pont.* 2.8.1–10, 51–52, 65–68, 4.9.105–8; see Scott (1931), 107, (1930), 43–69. Marcia: Ovid *Pont.* 1.2.126; Ovid also notes that she was highly regarded by Caesar's aunt Atia.
30. Ovid *Fast.* 1.461–586 (Carmentis), 649 (genetrix); Herbert-Brown (1984), 159.
31. Plut. *Gai. Gracch.* 19.2: Livia was not the first Roman woman to have such external connections. After Cornelia, the mother of the Gracchi, retired to Misenum, she maintained a lively contact with prominent individuals, and reigning kings exchanged gifts with her.
32. Dio 54.24.6; Paltiel (1991), 162.
33. Augustus: *IGR* 1.875, 901. Livia: *IGR* 1.902; Nawotka (1989), 326–28.
34. *RPC* 3803–7; Strabo 12.3.29, 8.16; Dio 49.25.4; Paltiel (1999), 138 n. 4.
35. *SEG* 39.695, Hahn (1992), 333 no. 91; Bartman (1999), 220 no. 13. Pythodoris married Archelaus, king of Cappadocia, after the death of Polemo, but the kingdoms of Pontus and Cappadocia were never united.
36. Val. Max. 4.3.3.
37. Tryphaena: *PIR* A 900; *RE* 1 (1894), 2641–42 (P. von Rohden).
38. *IGR* 4.144; Hahn (1992), 334, no. 97; Bartman (1999), 205, no. 43; Price (1984), 63–64. Athena: Plut. *Lucull.* 10; Magie (1950), 1208 n. 16.
39. Jos. *BJ* 1.566, *Ant.* 17.10. Date of Salome's death: Smallwood (1976), 156.
40. Jos. *Ant.* 17.134–41, 182, *BJ* 1.641, 661: Josephus' versions of the Acme-Antipater affair differs in some details in the *Antiquities* and the *Bellum*.
41. Smith (1897), 125–27.
42. Taxes: R. Bernhardt (1980).
43. Grant of freedom: Dio 54.9.7. Inscriptions: Herrmann (1960), 104–5, nos. 11, 12. Father: *IGR* 4.982. Mother: *IGR* 4.983. Priestess Lollia: *IGR* 4.984.
44. *IGR* 4.39: there may have been a later restoration of the inscription, for Livia is called Julia.
45. Pliny *HN* 37.3–4; the reading of the best MS, *Augustae*, with reference to Livia, is assumed in preference to *Augusti* (Augustus) of the inferior MSS.
46. Parian statue: Dio 55.9.6; Augustus dedicated four elephants made of obsidian (Pliny *HN* 36.196); statues of Apollo and Juno by Baton (Pliny *HN* 34.73); statue of Leto with the infants Apollo and Artemis by Euphranor (Pliny *HN* 34.77); statue of Asclepius and Hygeia by Niceratus (Pliny *HN* 34.80); statues of Ares and Hermes by Piston (Pliny *HN* 34.89); statues of Demeter, Zeus, and Athene by Sthennis (Pliny *HN* 34.90). The temple also contained a painting of Marsyas Bound by

Zeuxis (Pliny *HN* 35.66) and Nicias' painting of Father Bacchus (Pliny *HN* 35.131); see Becatti (1973–74); Kellum (1990), 278.

47. Pliny *HN* 37.27.

48. Eck, in Millar and Segal (1984), 139–42, notes that after 19 BC most public benefactions of the members of the senatorial order were outside Rome; in Rome such gestures were becoming the prerogative of the princeps and his family.

49. *CIL* 10.810.

50. Pliny *HN* 3.17; Martial 4.18.1; Dio 55.8.4.

51. Vitr. *Arch.* 1 pr. 2; Suet. *Aug.* 29.4; Dio 49.43.8; Livy *Per.* 138; Richardson (1976).

52. Ovid *Fast.* 6.640–48; Sen. *Clem.* 1.18.2, *Ira* 3.40; Suet. *Aug.* 29.4; Pliny *HN* 9.77; Tac. *Ann.* 1.10.5, 12.60.4; Dio 54.23.1–6; Syme, *Papers A*, 518–29; Edwards (1993), 164–65.

53. Suet. *Aug.* 29.3; Dio 55.8.2; Ovid *AA* 1.71–72; Pliny *HN* 14.11; Pliny *Ep.* 1.5.9; Strabo 5.3.8 (236); Grimal (1943), 155 n. 1; Boëthius and Ward-Perkins (1970), 327. Richardson (1976), 62, and (1978), 265–72, suggests that the land might have been donated by Augustus, but the building was paid for by Livia and Tiberius; Richardson (1992), 314; Flory (1984); Claridge (1998), 303; *FUR* pl. 18; Rodriguez pls. 7–9.

54. Ovid *Fast.* 6.637–38; Suet. *Aug.* 29.4; Dio 54.23.6; Flory (1984), 313–14, 329; Coarelli (1974), 206. Carettoni (1960), 69, tentatively suggests that the small structure is a fountain; see also Richardson (1992), 99–100, suggesting that the aedes and portico were "substantially identical."

55. *ILS* 5592; Coarelli (1974), 208; Richardson (1992), 241.

56. Propertius 2.6.25–26; Livy 10.23.1–10 (the cult had passed into disuse by Livy's time); Suet *Aug.* 34.1; Palmer (1974), 125–40. Palmer suggests that Julia might have been involved in the restoration of Pudicitia Patricia.

57. Ovid *Fast.* 148–58; *SHA Hadr.* 19.11; Wissowa (1899); Platner-Ashby (1929), 85; Coarelli (1985), 314; Richardson (1992), 59–60.

58. Propertius 4.9.23–74; Ovid *Fast.* 5.148–58 (pre-exile); Macrob. *Sat.* 1.12.21–22. Daughter: Macrob. *Sat.* 1.12.23–27. Husband: Sextus Clodius, Arnobius 5.18; Lact. *Div. Inst.* 1.22.11 (cf. Plut. *QR* 20). Theories on the origin of the cult are summarised by Herbert-Brown (1984), 132–33.

59. Verg. *Aen.* 7.706.

60. *RG* 19; Suet. *Aug.* 31; Dio 59.10.2–6; Hor. *Odes* 3.6.

61. Cic. *Dom.* 105, *Har. Resp.* 17.37.38, *ad Att.* 1.13.3; Plut. *Caes.* 9.

62. Vestals: Suet. *Aug.* 31.2. Caesar: Cic. *Har. Resp.* 3.4. Residence: Suet. *Div. Jul.* 46; Dio 54.27.3; Herbert-Brown (1984), 144.

63. EJ 101 (*ILS* 154): Rose (1997), 88–89.

64. *CIL* 6.883; Livy 2.40.1–12; Dion. Hal. 8.55–56; Val. Max. 1.8.4, cf. 5.2.1. Location: Ashby (1907), 79. Significance: Flory (1984), 318; Purcell (1986), 88; Wood (1999), 78–79. Filiation: Boatwright (1991), 520.

65. *CIL* 11.3322; Kornemann (1952), 209.

66. Visit: Jos. *Ant.* 16.6. Temple: Philo *Leg.* 157, 291. Philo *Leg.* 319 describes the bowls as a gift from Livia. Paltiel (1991), 84, prefers this account to the claim by Josephus (*BJ* 5.562–63) that they were donated jointly by Livia and Augustus.

67. Jos. *Ant.* 16.139. On the date see Smallwood (1981), 80 n. 62.

68. P. *Oxy.* 2435 verso, 45.

69. Corinth: *Corinth* 8.1, no. 19; 8.3, no. 153. Egypt: P. *Oxy* 17.2105. Chalcis, recording also *Caesarea* at Tanagra: *BCH* 3 (1879), 443. Thespiae: *AE* 1928, no. 50; *SEG* 13 (1956), 348; *SEG* 31 (1981) no. 514 (Mnemosyne); *BCH* 26 (1902), no. 18.

70. Jamot, *BCH* (1902), 153–55, no. 4; Gow and Page (1968), I. 277 (also II.309); Jones (1970), 249–55. Cichorius (1922), 356–57, argues for Antonia, and Caligula and Gemellus, her grandsons, both of whom were in line for the succession; see also Bowersock (1965), 141; D'Arms (1970), 85–86; Temporini (1978), 28–29; Kokkinos (1992), 42, 88–89, 92–93 (but Kokkinos suggests Germanicus and Drusus, or Caligula and Claudius).

71. Jos. *Ant.* 18.27, *BJ* 2.168. Josephus gives the name consistently as Julias: Jos. *Ant.* 20.159, *BJ* 2.252, 4.438. Livias: Pliny *HN* 13.44; Ptol. *Geog.* 5.16.9; Euseb. *Onom.* (Larson and Parthey), 112–13; Jones (1937), 275; Smallwood (1981), 118–19.

72. *RPC* 4006–11, 4013–14. Trajan: *BMC* 8; Pliny *HN* 5.93; Magie (1950), 1355 n. 14; Gough (1956); Jones (1971), 204, 438 n. 22.

73. Pliny *HN* 6.11; Pliny provides no information other than that Liviopolis did not stand on a river.

74. Taylor (1931), 35–57.

75. Livia's divine honours: Scott (1930), 57, 64–65; Ollendorff (1926), 907–23; Taylor (1933), 270–83; Grether (1946), 22–52; Grant (*Principate,* 1950), 108–29; Flory (1984), 320; Fishwick (1987–92); Hahn (1992); Mikocki (1995).

76. Thessalonica *RPC* 1563. Athens: *IG* 3.316.

77. *IG* 12 (Suppl.), 124, 18–24; Price (1984), 249, no. 5; Mikocki (1995), 105.

78. Gross (1962), 106–9; Fittschen-Zanker (1983), III.2.6; Kreikenbom (1992), 179 Cat. III.36; Winkes (1995), 181, no. 105; Rose (1997), no. 125, 182–84; Wood (1999), 110–12, fig. 35; Bartman (1999), 179, no. 72, 208. Aurigemma (1940), 21–27, argued that the group must belong to the lifetime of Germanicus; Trillmich (1988) deduces from the inscriptions on the bases that the group could not be earlier than 23 BC, Drusus' last year, and that it contained posthumous honours to both Drusus and Germanicus.

79. *IRT* no. 269; Fittschen-Zanker (1983), III.4.9; Sande (1985), 154–58; Kreikenbom (1995), 180–81, Cat. III.39; Winkes (1995), 184–85; Mikocki (1995), 156, no. 37, pl. 14; Rose (1997), 182–84; Wood (1999), 121–23, fig 43; Bartman (1999), no. 74, 179–80.

80. Hahn (1992), 322–32.

81. Tarsus: *RPC* 4005. Eumenea: *RPC* 3143. Pergamum: *RPC* 2359. Thessalian League: *RPC* 1427. Rome: Val. Max. 6.1.1; Ovid *Fast.* 1.650; *Cons. Liv.* 380. Association of Jupiter with Augustus: Alföldi (1970), 220–21.

82. Mylai: *IG* 9.2.333. Aphrodisias: *AE* 1980, no. 877. Mytilene: *IG* 12 Suppl. 50. Assos: *IGR* 4.249.

83. Falerii: *ILS* 116 (*CIL* 11.3076). Aeclanum: *CIL* 9.1098. Zara: *ILS* 2.3089. El Lehs: *ILS* 120 (*EJ* 127). The difficulty arises from the syntactical ambiguity of the form *Liviae,* whose case could be dative (to Livia) or genitive (of Livia).

84. Wilcken (1909); Flory (1984), 319–20.

85. Suet. *Aug.* 93; Dio 51.4.1, 54.9.10; Rose (1997), 140–41, cat. 71; Wood (1999), 92; Bartman (1999), 64.

86. Alexandria: *RPC* 5053, 5063.

87. Ephesus: *SEG* 4.515. Nepet, Africa: *CIL* 11.3196. Malta: *ILS* 121. Lampsacus: *IGR* 4.180. Aphrodisias: *CIG* 2.2815. The last two could be Julia Domna; Winkes (1988), 560–61; Mikocki (1995), 18–21, 141, 151–58; Wood (1999), 112–13.

88. The portrait type is one that is generally dated early: Winkes (1995), 103, no. 128; Mikocki (1995), 157, no. 40; Megow (1987), 179–80, no. A49; Wood (1999), 113, fig. 36.

89. Augustus: *RIC*² 219–20. Claudius: *RIC*² 101; Sutherland (1951), 124–25, 131.

90. Suet. *Tib.* 26.1; Dio 57.9.1; Charlesworth (1939).

91. *SEG* 11.922–23 (EJ 102): the letter of Tiberius is restored to indicate his sixteenth tribunician year (which lasted from July AD 14 to the following July), when he was already pontifex maximus — that is, after March 10, 15. Rose (1997), 269 n. 3, prefers a date closer to AD 17 and Germanicus' triumph; Sandels (1912), 41–44; Grether (1946), 238–40; Magie (1950), 502, 1360; Seyrig (1929), 92–102, 102; Kornemann (1929), (1952), 210, (1960), 106; Grether (1946), 240; Ritter (1972), 327; Price (1984), 60–61, 72, 103, 106, 109, 188, 210–11, 226; Winkes (1985), 67; Fishwick (1987–92), I.1.158–59; Mikocki (1995), 158, no. 48; Bartman (1999), 119 n. 77, 207, no. 52; Rose (1997), 142–44, no. 74. Thasos: Price (1984), 72 (cf. Veyne [1962], 62). Hypocrisy: Rostovtzev (1930), 23–24. Diplomacy: Charlesworth (1939), 3. Painted images: Blanck (1968).

92. *RPC* 2469; Tac. *Ann.* 3.68, 4.15, 37, 55–56, 51.20.7, 59.28.1; Magie (1950), 501, 1361; Price (1984), 64, 66, 185, 258, no. 45.

93. Vell. 2.130.5.

11. DEATH AND REPUTATION

1. Tac. *Ann.* 5.1.1; Dio 58.2.1 (Xiphilinus); Zonaras' summary is slightly different.

2. Suet. *Tib.* 51.2; Dio 58.2.1.

3. Vell. 2.114.1; Suet. *Tib.* 11.2; Dio 57.11.7.

4. Suet. *Tib.* 51.2; Dio 58.2.1.

5. Dio 58.35.4–5.

6. Suet. *Tib.* 51.2; Willrich (1911), 43; Hatzl (1975), 57; Flower (1996), 254.

7. *IGR* 4.251 (Assos); Suet. *Cal.* 53; Dio 59.19.4; Barrett (1990), 48.

8. Vell. 2.130.5; Tac. *Ann.* 5.1.4, 2.1; Dio 58.2.1, 2.

9. Strabo 5.3.8 (236); Suet. *Aug.* 100.4; Dio 53.30.5.

10. Pliny *HN* 36.69–74: the obelisks are not included in Pliny's account of the obelisks of Rome and perhaps were added later — they are first mentioned in the fourth century.

11. Marcellus: Dio 53.30.5, Octavia: Dio 54.35. Drusus: Suet. *Claud.* 1.4; Dio 55.2; 56.10; Aur. Vict. *Caes.* 12.12. Julias: Suet. *Aug.* 101.3; Cordingley and Richmond (1927); Boëthius and Ward-Perkins (1970), 197; Kokkinos (1992), 28; Richardson

(1992), 247–49; von Hesberg (1994); Claridge (1998), 181–84; von Hesberg, *LTUR* 3.234–37; Macciocca, *LTUR* 3.237–39.

12. Tac. *Ann.* 5.2.1; Dio 58.2.2.

13. Dio 58.2.3–6. On Caligula's completion of the Temple of Augustus, see Barrett (1990), 69–71.

14. Vell. 2.130.5 (see Woodman [1977], ad loc.); Tac. *Ann.* 5.2.2; Dio 58.2.1; Suet. *Tib.* 51.2.

15. Tac. *Ann.* 6.5.1; M. Aurelius Cotta Maximus Messalinus: *PIR* A 1488; *RE* 2.2 (1896), 2490–91 (P. von Rohden); Tac. *Ann.* 2.32.2, 4.20.4, 5.3.4. Gluttony: Persius 2.72; Pliny *HN* 10.52. Generosity: Ovid *Pont.* passim; Bauman (1974), 103.

16. Dio 58.2.3; Seibt (1969), 14; Perkounig (1995), 163–64.

17. Tac. *Ann.* 5.2.2, 6.10.1; Suet. *Tib.* 51; Dio 58.4.5–7.

18. Tac. *Ann.* 6.26.3.

19. Tac. *Ann.* 5.3.1; Martin (1981), 141.

20. Pliny *HN* 8.145; Tac. *Ann.* 5.3.1; Suet. *Cal.* 10.1. Martin (1981), 141, expresses serious doubts about any true role for Livia in holding back Sejanus from Agrippina, which he thinks is belied by the narrative of events between 23 and 29. He suggests that what influence Livia still possessed after 23 must have been confined to narrow family matters.

21. Suet. *Tib.* 53.2, *Cal.* 10.1.

22. *AFA* xliiic.2.

23. Tac. *Ann.* 5.1.4; Suet. *Tib.* 51.2, *Galb.* 5.2; Dio 58.2.3, 59.1.4, cf. Dio 59.2.4. Willrich (1911), 79.1, doubts that Galba was initially left such a large sum; see Perkounig (1995), 169 n. 945.

24. Dio 59.1.4, 2.4.

25. *Apoc.* 9.5; Suet. *Claud.* 11.2; Dio 60.5.2; *AFA* liv, lv; Torelli (1982), 74; Winkes (1985), 68; Bartman (1999), 131; *AE* 1969–70, 1 (43–48); *AFA* lix (50–54). Anniversary of birth: Grant (1950, *Anniversary*), 70. Abydos: *IGR* 1.1161; Snyder (1940), 234. Fishwick (1992) argues that the "Palatine" temple is in fact the Temple to Divus Augustus completed by Caligula.

26. *AFA* lxiii (57), lxvii (58), lxix (58), lxxi (59), lxxv (59), lxxvii (60).

27. Galba: *AFA* xc (69). Otho: *AFA* xcii (69). Vitellius?: *AFA* xciii (69).

28. Trajan: *RIC*[2] 821. Trebula (?): *CIL* 6.29681. Consuls Appius Annius Gallus and Marcus Atilius Bradua: Fishwick (1987–92) II.1, 576, 613.19. Taylor (1914), 240, identifies the colony as Trebula Suffenatium in Latium. The inscription apparently mentions both Augustales and seviri Augustales. On the difference, if any, see Taylor (1914).

29. *IGR* 4.353; Fishwick (1987–92) II.1, 569; Price (1984), 61, 118, 191; Bartman (1999), 140 n. 46. In the Asian calendar Livia's birthday fell on September 21.

30. *P. Oxy.* III.496 (AD 127). Other examples: *BGU* 252, 2/3 (December 24, AD 98): *epi Ioul(ias)* [*Sebastes*]; *CPR* 24.2 (AD 136); [. . .]*i tes Ioulias Sebastes*; *P. Oxy* III.604 (second century); Wilcken (1909); Grether (1946), 242; Temporini (1978), 69.

31. *P. Oxy.* 17.2105; Antoninus Pius: *RIC*[2] 973, 988, 998, 1003, 1013, 1017, 1024.

32. Fink et al. (1940), 187–90; Grether (1926), 251; Hahn (1992), 82 n. 124; Bartman

(1999), 140 n. 46. Oliver (1949), 36, suggests that Vespasian might have dropped Livia from the list of divi.

33. Sym. *Rel.* III; Prud. *Con. Symm.* 245–70.

APPENDIX 1. SOURCES

1. Suet. *Aug.* 2.3, 62.2, 85, *Claud.* 1.6; Blumenthal (1913); Bardon (1956), 99–100; (1968), 23–25.
2. Suet. *Dom.* 20.
3. Suet. *Tib.* 61.1: *quem de vita sua summatim breviterque composuit.*
4. Pliny *HN* 12.78; Suet. *Claud.* 41.2; Momigliano (1932), 317.
5. Suet. *Claud.* 41.3: *composuit et de vita sua octo volumina magis inepte quam ineleganter.* Nero: Tac. *Ann.* 13.43.4; Durry, in Latte (1956).
6. Pliny *HN* 7.46; in his preface Pliny also lists Agrippina as one of sources for book 7; Tac. *Ann.* 4.53.3.
7. Stahr (1867), 194; Raffay (1884); Fabia (1893), 331; Motzo (1927), 52; Paratore (1952), 41–42; Bardon (1956), 172; Syme (1958), 277; Kornemann (1960), 95; Walker (1960), 139; Balsdon (1962), 121; Michel (1966), 124; Wilkes (1972), 181; Hatzl (1975), 37; Clarke (1975), 50; Griffin (1984), 23, 28; Duret (1986), 3283; Syme (1986), 140; Wood (1988), 424; Eck (1993), 22, 52.
8. Scaliger (1572), 528; Haupt (1875), 315–57. Among recent theories: Herrmann (1951), AD 63, by Petronius; Shrijvers (1988), AD 20; Richmond (1982), 2780, some time before Tiberius' death in AD 37. Schoonhover (1992) argues that it was composed after the death of Claudius in the brief period before Britannicus died, to make the case for a Claudian succession; Kokkinos (1992), 99, suggests Ovid as author.
9. Tac. *Ann.* 1.2–3.
10. Summers (1920), 139, 147; Dihle (1955); Syme (1958), 367; Hellegouarc'h (1964); Sumner (1970). Woodman (1977), 28–56, for a well-argued defence of Velleius. Eck et al. (1996), 227, suggests that Velleius' final encomium about no one having suffered from her comes from the speech at Livia's funeral, which would have taken place shortly before Velleius' death.
11. Maslakov (1984), for a recent survey of Valerius Maximus.
12. Sen. *Ira* 3.23.4.
13. Sen. *Clem.* 1.9; Vidén (1993), 133.
14. Sen. *Cons. Marc.* 6.4.
15. Sen. *Ben.* 6.32, *Brev.* 4.
16. Pliny *HN* 7.45, 149, 33.63, 35.201.
17. Wallace-Hadrill (1983), 12–13.
18. Suet. *Cal.* 23.2; Vidén (1993), 89.
19. Suet. *Aug.* 40.3, *Tib.* 21.2–3, 50.2–3, *Oth.* 1.1.
20. Suet. *Tib.* 21.4–7.
21. Suet. *Tib.* 22.1, 52.3.
22. Goodyear (1972), 190. Sacrosanctitas: Dio 49.38.1. Gaius and Lucius: Dio

55.10a.10. Marcellus: Dio 53.33.4. Death announcement: Dio 56.31.1-2. Figs: Dio 56.30.1-2. Germanicus: Dio 57.18.6.

23. On the relationship between Dio's and Seneca's accounts: Adler (1909), 198; Smith (1951), 183. On Dio's general debt to Seneca: Giancotti (1956), 30.

24. Wuilleumier (1949), 79–80; Bardon (1962), 283; Syme (1958), 535; Riposati (1973). The issues are clearly set out in Wallace (1991).

25. Baldwin (1972), 84.

26. Exceptions are the later Aurelius Victor, *De Caesaribus*, and the anonymous *epitome de Caesaribus*, where the information seems to derive from Tacitus.

27. Tac. *Ann.* 1.53.5, 4.11.4. See Willrich (1911), 3; Harrer (1920), 57–69; Gafforini (1996), 129–34.

28. Piso: Tac. *Ann.* 4.21.1. Prisca: Tac. *Ann.* 4.12.4.

29. Accession: Tac. *Ann.* 1.4.5. Departure from Rome: Tac. *Ann.* 4.57.3. Obituary: Tac. *Ann.* 5.1.3 (see Vidén [1993], 17).

30. Gaius and Lucius: Tac. *Ann.* 1.3.3. Tiberius: Tac. *Ann.* 1.3.3. Julia: Tac. *Ann.* 4.71.4. Plancina: Tac. *Ann.* 2.82.1. Piso: Tac. *Ann.* 2.77.3.

31. Hor. *Epod.* 5.9; Ovid *Met.* 1.147; Quint. *Inst. Or.* 2.10.4-5; Gray-Fow (1988), 741–57; Vidén (1993); Watson (1995); Barrett (2001); Kleiner and Matheson (2000), 131.

32. Tac. *Ann.* 1.3.3, 6.3, 10.5, 33.3. Suet. *Galb.* 4.1 uses *noverca* of Livia Ocellina, the stepmother of Galba, but in a totally neutral context. Galinsky (1996), 78, suggests that Tacitus might be playing on the alternative meaning of *gravis*, pregnant, thus alluding to her scandalous wedding.

33. Tac. *Ann.* 1.14.2. Discord: Tac. *Ann.* 1.72.4. Illness: Tac. *Ann.* 3.64.1; Syme (1958), 308, 483 n. 4.

34. Syme (1958), 273. Marsh (1931), 278, feels that the discrepancies between Tacitus and Dio are so marked that they must have used different sources and that Tacitus had a different authority for the machinations in the palace.

35. Tac. *Ann.* 1.6.3; Suet. *Tib.* 22; Motzo (1927), 38; Martin (1981), 109.

36. Walker (1960), 70; Griffin (1984), 39. Nero's threat: Suet. *Nero* 34.1. Funeral: Tac. *Ann.* 12.69.4. Mother's claim to have made son emperor: Dio 57.12.3; 61.7.1-3.

37. Guilt: *Apoc.* 1–6; *Octavia* 31, 44, 64, 102, 164–65; Pliny *HN* 22.92; Juv. *Sat.* 5.146–48, 6.620–23 (with scholiast); Tac. *Ann.* 12.66–67; Martial 1.20; Suet. *Claud.* 44.2–46; *Nero* 33.1, 39.3; Dio 60.34.2-6, 35; Aur. Vict. *Caes.* 4.13; *Epit. de Caes.* 4.10; Orosius 7.6.18; Zosim. I.6.3. Reservations: Philost. *Apoll.* 5.32: *hos phasi* (so they say); Jos. *Ant.* 20.148: *logos ên para tinōn* (it was reported by some), 151: *kathaper ên logos* (according to report).

38. Illness: *Apoc.* 6–7; Suet. *Nero* 7.2; Dio 60.33.9. Death by natural causes: inter alios, Ferrero (1911), 450; Pack (1943); Bagnani (1946).

39. Tac. *Ann.* 12.65, 66.3; Suet. *Claud.* 43; Dio 60.34.1; Paratore (1952), 57; Barrett (1996), 138–39.

40. *Apoc.* 13; Tac. *Ann.* 12.66.1; Dio 60.34.4.

41. Suet. *Nero* 33.1; Dio 60.34.3, 35.4.

42. *Apoc.* 1, 3; Tac. *Ann.* 12.68.3; Suet. *Claud.* 45; Suet. *Nero* 8.1. See Pack (1943).

43. *Apoc.* 4.

44. Livia's role reflecting Agrippina's: Charlesworth (1923), (1927); Willrich (1927), 76–78; Martin (1955); Goodyear (1972), 125–29; Martin (1981), 109–10; Griffin (1984), 39; but see also Syme, (1958), 483, *Papers A*, 1036.

45. As an example, when a potential rival is eliminated, Tacitus seeks to emphasise that he was blameless. Drusus, the son of Tiberius, whom Sejanus supposedly got rid of with the help of Drusus' wife, Livilla, was *nullius ante flagitii compertum* (Tac. *Ann.* 4.11.1). This phrase clearly echoes Tacitus' description of Agrippa Postumus as *nullius tamen flagitii compertum* (Tac. *Ann.* 1.3.4).

46. Nero: Tac. *Ann.* 13.1.1. Tiberius: Tac. *Ann.* 1.5.6, 6.1; Benario (1975), 136; Mellor (1993), 118; Morford (1990), 1082, 1601. Tac. *Hist.* 2.64.2 notes the murder of Dolabella on the instructions of Vitellius, *magna cum invidia novi principatus*.

47. Two possible external influences on the account of Tiberius' succession have been suggested: first, the story of Tanaquil, who kept the death of Tarquinius Priscus secret until her son Servius Tullius could establish his position: Livy 1.41.5; Aur. Vict. *Caes.* 4.13; Charlesworth (1927); Martin (1981), 109–10; Goodyear (1972), 128; and second, the delay in the announcement of Trajan's death so that Hadrian's adoption could be established: *SHA Hadrian* 4; Dio 69.1.2–3; Syme (1958), 481–83; Syme, *Papers C*, 169; Koestermann (1963–68), 220. For reservations about the suggestions, see Goodyear (1972), 127–28.

48. Charlesworth (1927); Willrich (1927), 74–78; Hohl (1935); Weber (1936), 33–36; Martin (1955), 125 (arguing that the facts derive from Nero's accession but that the linguistic similarities derive from Tiberius' accession); Questa (1959); Koestermann (1961), 334–35; Timpe (1962), 29–33; Goodyear (1972), 126–27; Martin (1981), 253; Mellor (1993), 44; Barnes (1998), 140–41.

49. Pliny *HN* 34.31.

50. Ny Carlsberg Glyptothek, no. 615; Poulsen (1973), 65–71, no. 34; Gross (1962), 87–91, pls. 15–16; Winkes (1965), 114, no. 41; Rose (1997), 188–89, no. 129, pls. 237–40; Bartman (1999), 174–75, no. 64–65, pls. 161–62; Wood (1999), 93, pls. 22–23. Recent contributions: Kleiner (2000).

51. Poulsen (1968), 21, puts the Albani-Bonn first in the sequence; Winkes (1995), 32, 63, considers the Marbury Hall the earliest; Fittschen-Zanker (1983), III.1–2; Wood (1999), 94–95; Bartman (1999), 144–45.

52. Bartman (1999), 76, dates the Fayum type to the decade after Actium, against the prevailing view that would link it with adoption of Tiberius in AD 4.

53. Fittschen-Zanker (1983), III.4a–e; Winkes (1995), 35–38; Wood (1999), 95–96; Bartman (1999), 221, no. 2 (= Winkes, no. 2), 222, no. 7 (= Winkes, no. 40), considers two of the examples assigned to this type as not of Livia.

54. *RIC²* 47; Bartman (1999), 115, suggests that the Salus dupondius might have been inspired by the known sculptures, rather than the other way around.

55. Bartman (1999), 116, 182, no. 81 (Kiel), 156, no. 24 (Paestum); Winkes (1995), 46, 48; Rose (1997), 98, no. 26, pl. 95. Rose and Winkes consider the Paestum example post-Tiberian; Wood (1999), 118.

56. *CIL* 13.1366; Paris, Musée du Louvre, br. 22, inv. no. 3235: 21 cm. total height. Gross (1962), 85–86 (suspicious); Fittschen-Zanker (1983), 3.2.1, no. 1 (genuine); Fishwick (1976), 535, 545, pl. XCIX (genuine); De Kersauson (1986), 94–97, nos.

41–42 (genuine); Winkes (1995), 37–38, 146, no. 73 (genuine); Bartman (1999), 194–95, nos. 114, 189 (highly suspicious, perhaps eighteenth-century); Wood (1999), 105–6, nos. 32–33 (genuine).

57. Suet. *Cal.* 15.2, 23.2; Suet. *Galb.* 5.2; Suet. *Oth.* 1.1.

58. Suet. *Aug.* 7.1. Déjardins (1968), 3, 215–17, suggests that they are household spirits *(Lares)* meant to be kept in a domestic *lararium*. But Fishwick (1987–92), n. 363, notes that the inscriptions are in the dative, not the usual nominative (Latin) or accusative (Greek), and argues that the statues were dedicated in honour of Augustus and Livia. See also De Kersauson (1986), 94–97.

59. Bartman (1999), 12; Wood (1999), 91.

60. Paris, Bibliothèque de France, Cabinet des Médailles 264; Jucker (1977); Megow (1987), 202–7, no. A85; Mikocki (1995), 21, 157–58, no. 8; Winkes (1995), 49, 145, no. 71; Wood (1999), 137–38, 308–10.

61. Vienna, Kunsthistorisches Museum XII 1083; Winkes (1995), 188 no. 111; Bartman (1999), 12, 193, no. 109, pl. 8.

62. Vienna, Kunsthistorisches Museum IXA 95; Winkes (1995), 189, no. 113; Bartman (1999), 193, no. 110, pl. 79; Wood (1999), 119–20, pl. 41.

63. Winkes (1995), 103, no. 28; Mikocki (1995), 157, no. 40; Megow (1987), 179–80, no. A49; Wood (1999), 113, pl. 36.

64. Matheson (1980), 59–60; Stern (1992).

65. Rome: Rostovtsev (1900) III, p. 35, fig. 8; *(Bleitesserae*, 1905), 26, pl. 1; Winkes (1995), 164, no. 87. Berlin: Mikocki (1995), 152, no. 8; Grant *(Principate*, 1950), 111 (legend: *A Vitellius Cur*[*avit*] on reverse). Winkes (1995), 192, no. 120, notes another uninscribed (bronze) tessera in private ownership, possibly depicting Livia.

66. Rostovtsev ("Interpretation," 1905), 111, reads the legend LIV as *L(oco) IV*, on a bone counter from El Djem depicting an amphitheatre.

67. Naples Museo Nazionale, inv. no. 77129. *IG* 14.2414.40 (= *CIL* 10.8069.9); Rostovtsev (1904), pls. 3–4; Rosenbaum (1980), 32–33, nos. 9, 9.2; Winkes (1995), 140, no. 63.

68. *SEG* 38 (1988), 914; Warren (1987–88), 88–89, pls. 12, 13.

69. Alexandria, Graeco-Roman Museum, inv. no. 23869; Grimm (1973); Rosenbaum (1980), 31–32, no. 8, pl. 9.1. Winkes (1995), 81, no. 1, considers it Livian.

70. Boschung (1989), 121, no. 56. The subject was previously identified as Agrippina the Elder by Dardaigne (1981).

71. Héron de Villefosee (1899), 128; Kuttner (1995), 31. The cups are now lost.

72. Lehner (1912), 430–35, pl. 8. The vase is signed by the potter "Chrysippus."

73. Bonn, Rheinisches Landesmuseum 4320; Curtius (1935), 264; Kuttner (1995), 173–74; Winkes (1995), 97, no. 20; Rose (1997), pl. 10; Bartman (1999), 82–83, pl. 67; Wood (1999), 106–7. Identification as Livia is now generally accepted. Dressel (1894) hovers between Livia and Julia (with Gaius and Lucius); Kuttner maintains that Livia displays aspects of Venus Genetrix.

74. Ephesus: *SEG* 4.515. Gytheum: EJ 102.

75. New York, Metropolitan Museum, 20.192.1; Anderson (1987), 127–35; Kleiner and Matheson (1996), 35–36, pl. 6; Winkes (1995), 198, no. 134 (Livia), 221, no. 269 (Julia); Wood (1999), 107; Bartman (1999), 12.

BIBLIOGRAPHY

Abbott, F. F., and A. C. Johnson. (1926). *Municipal Administration in the Roman Empire*. New York.

Ackroyd, B. "Porticus Iulia or Porticus Liviae: The Reading of Dio 56.27.5." *Athenaeum* 80 (1992): 196–99.

Adler, M. "Die Veschwörung des Cn. Cornelius Cinna bei Seneca und Cassius Dio." *ZÖG* 60 (1909): 193–208.

Alföldi, A. (1965). *Early Rome and the Latins*. Ann Arbor.

———. (1970). *Die monarchische Repräsentation im römischen Kaiserreiche*. Darmstadt.

Alföldi-Rosenbaum, E. "Ruler Portraits on Roman Game Counters from Alexandria." In *Eikones. Studien zum griechischen und römischen Bildnis Hans Jucker zum Sechzigsten Geburtstag Gewidmet* (Bern, 1980: *Antike Kunst Beiheft* 12): 29–39.

Alföldy, G. (1973). *Flamines Provinciae Hispaniae Citerioris*. Madrid.

Allen, W. "The Political Atmosphere of the Reign of Tiberius." *TAPA* 72 (1941): 1–25.

———. "The Death of Agrippa Postumus." *TAPA* 78 (1947): 131–39.

———. "Imperial Table Manners in Tacitus' *Annals*." *Latomus* 21 (1962): 374–76.

Allison, J. E., and J. D. Cloud. "The Lex Julia Maiestatis." *Latomus* 21 (1962): 711–31.

Allmer, A. *Revue épigraphique du midi de la France* 2 (1884–89): nos. 513, 75–77, 138–39, 231–33.

Anderson, M. L. "The Portrait Medallions of the Imperial Villa at Boscotrecase." *AJA* 91 (1987): 127–35.

Andreae, B. "Wandmalerei augusteicher Zeit." In M. Hofter (ed.), *Kaiser Augustus und die verlorene Republik* (Mainz am Rhein, 1988): 283–86.

Antike Denkmäler (1891). Kaiserlich Deutsches Archäologisches Institut, Rome, vol. 1.

Archer, L. J., S. Fischler, and M. Wyke (eds.). (1994). *Women in Ancient Societies*. Rome.

Arthur, M. B. " 'Liberated' Women: The Classical Era." In R. Bridenthal and C. Koonz (eds.), *Becoming Visible: Women in European History* (Boston, 1977): 60–89.

Aschbach, J. (1864). *Livia. Gemahlin des Kaisers Augustus. Eine historisch-archäologische Abhandlung.* Vienna.

Ashby, T. "The Classical Topography of the Roman Campagna." *PBSR* 4 (1907): 1–160.

Ashby, T., and R. A. L. Fell. "The Via Flaminia." *JRS* 11 (1921): 125–90.

Astin, A. E. (1978). *Cato the Censor.* Oxford.

Aurigemma, S. "Sculture del Foro Vecchio di Leptis Magna raffiguranti la Dea Roma e principi della casa dei Giulio-Claudi." *AfrIt* 8 (1940): 1–92.

Baar, M. (1990). *Das Bild des Kaisers Tiberius bei Tacitus, Sueton und Cassius Dio.* Stuttgart.

Babcock, C. "The Early Career of Fulvia." *AJP* 86 (1965): 1–32.

Babelon, E. (1897). *Catalogue des Camées Antiques et Modernes de la Bibliothèque Nationale.* Paris.

Badian, E. "Notes on Some Documents from Aphrodisias Concerning Octavian." *GRBS* 25 (1984): 157–70.

Baldwin, B. "Women in Tacitus." *Prudentia* 4 (1972): 83–101.

———. (1983). *Suetonius.* Amsterdam.

Balsdon, J. P. V. D. (1934). *The Emperor Gaius* (Oxford).

———. (1962). *Roman Women: Their History and Habits* (London).

Bang, M. "Das gewöhnliche Älter der Mädchen bei der Verlobung und Verheiratung." In L. Friedländer (ed.), *Darstellungen aus der Sittensgeschichte Roms* 4 (1922): 133–41.

Bardon, H. (1956). *La Littérature latine inconnue.* Vol. 2, *L'Époque impériale.* Paris.

———. "Points de vue sur Tacite." *RCCM* 4 (1962): 282–93.

———. (1986). *Les Empereurs et les lettres latines d'Augustus à Hadrien.* Paris, 2d ed.

Barini, C. C. "La tradizione superstite e alcuni giudizi dei moderni su Livia." *RAL* (1922): 25.

Barnes, T. "Julia's Child." *Phoenix* 35 (1981): 362–63.

———. "Tacitus and the *Senatus Consultum de Cn. Pisone Patre.*" *Phoenix* 52 (1998): 125–48.

Barrett, A. A. "Gaius' Policy in the Bosporus." *TAPA* 107 (1977): 1–9.

———. "Polemo II of Pontus and M. Antonius Polemo." *Historia* 27 (1978): 437–48.

———. (1990). *Caligula: The Corruption of Power.* London and New Haven.

———. "Claudius' British Victory Arch in Rome." *Britannia* 22 (1991): 1–19.

———. (1996). *Agrippina: Sex, Power, and Politics in the Early Empire.* New Haven.

———. "The Year of Livia's Birth." *Classical Quarterly* 49 (1999): 630–32.

———. "Tacitus, Livia, and the Evil Stepmother." *RhM* 144 (2001), 171–75.

Bartels, H. (1963). *Studien zum Frauenporträt der augusteischen Zeit, Fulvia, Octavia, Livia, Julia.* Munich.

Bartman, E. (1999). *Portraits of Livia: Imaging the Imperial Woman in Augustan Rome.* Cambridge.

Barton, T. (1994). *Power and Knowledge: Astrology, Physiognomics, and Medicine Under the Roman Empire.* Ann Arbor.

Bastet, F. L. "Die grosse Kamee in Den Haag." *BVAB* 43 (1968): 2–22.

Bauman, R. A. (1967). *The Crimen Maiestatis in the Roman Republic and Augustan Principate*. Johannesburg.

——. (1974). *Impietas in Principem*. Munich.

——. "Tribunician Sacrosanctity in 44, 36, and 35 BC." *RhM* 124 (1981): 166–83.

——. (1992). *Women and Politics in Ancient Rome*. London.

Bayardi, O. (1755). *Catalogo degli antichi monumenti di Ercolano*. Naples.

Beard, M. "The Sexual Status of Vestal Virgins." *JRS* 70 (1980): 12–27.

——. "Re-reading (Vestal) Virginity." In R. Hawley (ed.), *Women in Antiquity: New Assessments* (London, 1995): 166–77.

Becatti, G. "Opera d'arte greca nella Roma di Tiberio." *Arch. Class.* 25–26 (1973–74): 18–53.

Becker, K. (1950). "Studien zur Opposition gegen den römischen Prinzipat." Diss. Tübingen.

Benario, H. W. "*Imperium* and *Capaces Imperii* in Tacitus." *AJP* 93 (1972): 14–26.

——. (1975). *An Introduction to Tacitus*. Athens, Georgia.

Bengston, H. (1967). *Grundriss der römischen Geschichte mit Quellenkunde*. Vol. 1. Munich.

Béranger, J. "L'Hérédité du Principat: Note sur la transmission du pouvoir impérial aux deux premiers siècles." *REL* 17 (1939): 171–87.

——. "Remarques sur la Concordia dans la propagande monétaire impériale et la nature du principat." *Festschrift Altheim* (1969): 470–91.

Bergener, A. (1965). "Die führende Senatorenschicht im frühen Prinzipat (14–68 n. Chr.)." Diss. Bonn.

Bernhardt, R. "Die Immunitas der Freistädte." *Historia* 29 (1980): 190–207.

Bernouilli, J. (1886). *Römische Ikonographie. Die Bilnisse der römischen Kaiser und ihrer Angehörigen*. Vol. 2, *Das jülisch-claudische Kaiserhaus*. Berlin.

Besnier, R. (1847–48). *Les Affranchis impériaux à Rome, de 41 à 54 P.C.* Paris.

Best, E. E. "Cicero, Livy, and Educated Roman Women." *CJ* 65 (1970): 199–204.

Bianchi-Bandinelli, R., et al. (1966). *The Buried City: Excavations at Leptis Magna* (trans. B. Ridgway). London.

Birch, R. A. "The Correspondence of Augustus: Some Notes on Suetonius, *Tiberius* 21.4–7." *CQ* 31 (1981): 155–61.

——. "The Settlement of 26 June AD 4 and Its Aftermath." *CQ* 31 (1981): 443–56.

Birt, Th. (1932). *Frauen der Antike*. Leipzig.

Blanck, H. "Porträt-Gemälde als Ehrendenkmäler." *BJ* 168 (1968): 1–12.

Blaze de Bury, H. "L'Impératrice Livie et la fille d'Auguste." *Revue des deux mondes* 44 (1874): 591–637.

Bleicken, J. (1998). *Augustus. Eine Biographie*. Berlin.

Bloomer, W. M. (1992). *Valerius Maximus and the Rhetoric of the New Nobility*. Chapel Hill.

Blumenthal, F. "Die Autobiographie des Augustus." *WS* 35 (1913): 113–30, 267–88; 36 (1914): 84–103.

Boatwright, M. T. "The Imperial Women of the Early Second Century A.C." *AJP* 112 (1991): 513–40.

Boëthius, A., and J. B. Ward-Perkins. (1970). *Etruscan and Roman Architecture*. London.

Bömer, F. (1958). *P. Ovidius Naso. Die Fasten*. Heidelberg.

Bonamente, G. (1987). *Germanico: La persona, la personalità, il personaggio. Atti del Convegno, Macerata-Perugia, 9–11 maggio 1986*. Facoltà di Lettere e Filosofia Università Macerata, 39, Rome.

Boschung, D. "Die Bildnistypen des Iulisch-claudischen Kaiserfamilie." *JRA* 6 (1993): 39–79.

Boulvert, G. (1970). *Les Esclaves et les affranchis impériaux sous le Haut-Empire romain: Rôle politique et administratif*. Aix en Provence, 1964.

———. (1974). *Domestique et fonctionnaire sous le Haut-Empire romain: La condition de l'affranchi et de l'esclave du prince*. Paris.

Bouvrie, S. D. "Augustus' Legislation on Morals: Which Morals and What Aims." *SO* 59 (1984): 93–113.

Bowersock, G. (1965). *Augustus and the Greek World*. Oxford.

———. "Augustus and the East: The Problem of the Succession." In Millar and Segal (1984): 169–88.

———. Review of Reynolds (1982). *Gnomon* 56 (1984): 48–53.

Braccesi, L. "Pesaro romana, moribunda e felix." *SO* 2–3 (1982–83): 77–98.

Bragantini, I., and M. de Vos (1982). *Museo Nazionale Romano. Le pitture II.1. Le decorazioni della villa romana dell Farnesina*. Rome.

Brisson, J.-P. "Achaicus ignis: Horace, Odes I, 15 et IV.6." *REL* 71 (1993): 161–78.

Broughton, T. R. S. "Roman Landholding in Asia Minor." *TAPA* 65 (1934): 207–39.

Brown, P. (1981). *The Cult of the Saints*. Chicago.

Bruhns, H. (1978). *Caesar und die römische Oberschicht in den Jahren 49–44 v. Chr*. Göttingen.

Brunt, P. "The Lex Valeria Cornelia." *JRS* 51 (1961): 71–83.

———. "Lex de Imperio Vespasiani." *JRS* 67 (1977): 95–116.

———. (1988). *The Fall of the Roman Republic and Related Essays*. Oxford.

Burdeau, F. "L'Empereur d'après les Panegyriques Latins." In F. Burdeau, N. Charbonnel, and M. Humbert (eds.), *Aspects de l'empire Romaine* (Paris, 1964).

Calci, C., and Messineo, G. (1984). *La Villa di Livia a Prima Porta*. Rome: *Lavori e studi di archaeologia 2*.

Calhoon, C. G. (1994). "Livia the Poisoner: Genesis of an Historical Myth." Diss. California, Irvine.

Cameron A., and A. Kuhrt (eds.). (1983). *Images of Women in Antiquity*. London.

Carandini, A. (1988). *Schiavi in Italia*. Rome.

Carcopino, J. "Le Marriage d'Octave et de Livie et la naissance de Drusus." *Rev. Hist.* 161 (1929): 225–36.

———. (1958). *Passion et politique chez les Césars*. Paris.

Carettoni, G., et al. (1960). *La Pianta marmorea di Roma antica: Forma urbis Romae*. Rome.

———. "The House of Augustus." *ILN* 255, no. 6790 (1969): 24–25.

———. "La X Regione: Palatium." In *L'Urbs. Espace Urbain et Histoire* (Rome, 1987): 771–79.

Carteledge, P., and A. Spawforth (1989). *Hellenistic and Roman Sparta*. London.

Carter, J. M. (1982). *Suetonius: Divus Augustus*. Bristol.

Castagnoli, F. "Note sulla topographia del Palatino e del Foro Romano." *Arch. Class.* 16 (1964): 173–99.

Champeaux, J. (1982). *Fortuna. Recherches sur le culte de la Fortuna à Rome et dans le monde romain*. Rome.

Champlin, E. "The Testament of Augustus." *RM* 132 (1989): 154–65.

———. (1991). *Final Judgments: Duty and Emotion in Roman Wills, 200 B.C.–A.D. 250*. Berkeley.

Chantraine, H. (1967). *Freigelassene und Sklaven im Dienst der römischen Kaiser. Studien zu ihrer Nomenklatur*. Wiesbaden.

———. "Zu AE 1979, 33." *ZPE* 49 (1982): 132.

Charlesworth, M. P. "The Banishment of the Elder Agrippina." *CP* 17 (1922): 260–61.

———. "Tiberius and the Death of Augustus." *AJP* 44 (1923): 145–57.

———. "Livia and Tanaquil." *CR* 41 (1927): 55–57.

———. "Some Fragments of the Propaganda of Mark Antony." *CQ* 27 (1933): 172–77.

———. "The Refusal of Divine Honours, an Augustan Formula." *PBSR* 15 (1939): 1–10.

Chastagnol, A. "Les Femmes dans l'ordre senatorial: Titulature et rang social à Rome." *RH* 103 (1979): 3–28.

Christ, K. "Tacitus und der Principat." *Historia* 27 (1978): 449–87.

Christol, M., and C. Goudineau, "Nîmes et les Volques Arécomiques au 1er siècle avant J.-C." *Gallia* 45 (1987–88): 87–103.

Ciaceri, E. (1944). *Tiberio, succesore di Augusto*. Rome, 2d ed.

Cichorius, C. (1922). *Römische Studien*. Leipzig.

Claridge, A. (1998). *Rome*. Oxford.

Clark, G. "Roman Women." In I. McAuslan and P. Walcot (eds.), *Women in Antiquity* (Oxford, 1996): 36–55.

Clauss, M. (1983). *Sparta, Eine Einführung in seine Geschichte und Zivilisation*. Munich.

Clay, C. L. "Die Münzprägung des Kaisars Nero in Rom und Lugdunum. Teil 1: Die Edelmetallprägung der Jahre 54 bis 64 n. Chr." *NZ* 96 (1982): 7–52.

Clinton, K. "The Eleusinian Mysteries: Roman Inititates and Benefactors, Second Century B.C. to A.D. 267." *ANRW* 18.2 (1989): 1499–1539.

Cluett, R. G. "Roman Women and Triumviral Politics." *CV* 42 (1998): 67–84.

Coarelli, F. (1974). *Guida Archeologica di Roma*. Rome.

———. (1981). *Dintorni di Roma*. Rome.

———. (1983). *Il Foro Romano*. Rome.

———. (1984). *Lazio*. Rome.

———. (1985). *Roma*. Rome, 3d ed.

Colakis, M. "Ovid as praeceptor amoris in Epistulae ex Ponto 3.1." *CJ* 82 (1987): 210–15.

Conlin, D. A. "The Reconstruction of Antonia Minor on the Ara Pacis." *JRA* 5 (1992): 209–17.

Corbett, J. H. "The Succession Policy of Augustus." *Latomus* 33 (1974): 87–97.

Corbett, P. E. (1930). *The Roman Law of Marriage*. Oxford.

Cordingley, R. A., and I. A. Richmond. "The Mausoleum of Augustus." *PBSR* 10 (1927): 23–35.

Corsaro, F. "Sulla relegatio di Ovidio." *Orpheus* 15 (1968): 5–49.

Cousin, J. "Rhétorique et psychologie chez Tacite." *REL* 29 (1951): 228–47.

Crawford, D. J. "Imperial Estates." In Finley (1976): 35–70.

Crawford, M. H. (1974). *Roman Republican Coinage*. Cambridge.

——— (ed.). (1996). *Roman Statutes*. London.

Crook, J. (1955). *Concilium Principis*. Cambridge.

Curtius, L. "Ikonographische Beiträge zum Porträt der römischen Republik und der Julisch-Claudischen Familie." *MDAI(R)* 50 (1935): 260–320.

Damon C., and S. Takács. *The Senatus Consultum de Cn. Pisone Patre*. Special issue, *AJP* 120 (1999).

Dardaigne, S. "Portraits impériaux sur une lampe de Belo." *Mélanges de la casa de Velazquez* 17 (1981): 517–19.

D'Arms, J. H. (1970). *Romans on the Bay of Naples*. Cambridge, Mass.

———. (1981). *Commerce and Social Standing in Ancient Rome*. Cambridge, Mass.

Davies, O. (1935). *Roman Mines in Europe*. Oxford.

Davies, P. J. E. (2000). *Death and the Emperor: Roman Imperial Funerary Monuments, from Augustus to Marcus Aurelius*. Cambridge.

Degrassi, A. "Esistette sul Palatino un Tempio di Vesta?" *MDAI(R)* 62 (1955): 144–54.

———. (1963). *Inscriptiones Italiae*. Rome: vol. 13.2.

Degrassi, N. "La Dimora di Augusto sul Palatino e la Base di Sorrento." *RPAA* 39 (1966–67): 77–126.

De Kersauson, K. (1986). *Catalogue des portraits romains*. Vol. 1, *Portraits de la République et d'époque Julio-Claudienne*. Paris.

Delia, D. "Fulvia Reconsidered." In S. Pomeroy (ed.), *Women's History and Ancient History* (Chapel Hill, 1991): 197–217.

Demougin, S. (1988). *L'Ordre Equestre sous les Julio-Claudiens*. Rome: Collection de l'École Français de Rome No. 108.

D'Ercé, F. "La Mort de Germanicus et les poisons de Caligula." *Janus* 56 (1969): 123–48.

De Serviez, J. R. (1752). *The Roman Empresses*. London.

Desjardins, E. E. A. (1885). *Géographie historique et administrative de la Gaule romaine*. Paris.

Dessau, H. (1924–26). *Geschichte der römischen Kaiserzeit*. Vol. 2.1. Berlin.

Dettenhofer, M. H. (ed.) (1994). *Reine Männersache. Frauen in Männerdomänen der antiken Welt*. Cologne.

Detweiler, R. "Historical Perspectives on the Death of Agrippa Postumus." *CJ* 65 (1970): 289–95.

Devillers, O. (1994). *L'Art de la persuasion dans les Annales de Tacite*. Collection *Latomus* 223.

Dixon, S. "A Family Business: Women's Role in Patronage and Politics at Rome, 80–44 B.C." *C&M* 34 (1981–82): 91–112.

———. (1988). *The Roman Mother*. London.

Dobbins, J. "Chronology, Decoration, and Urban Design at Pompeii." *AJA* 98 (1994): 648–49.

Domaszewski, A. von (1885). *Die Fahnen im römischen Heere*. Vienna.

———. (1909). *Geschichte der römischen Kaiser*. Vol. 2. Leipzig, 2d ed.

———. (1967). *Die Rangordnung des römischen Heeres*. Cologne-Graz, 2d ed.

Domenicucci, P. "La caratterizazione astrale delle apoteosi di Romolo ed Ersilìa nelle Metamorfosi di Ovidio." In I. Gallo and L. Nicastri (eds.), *Cultura, poesia, ideologia nell'opera di Ovido* (Salerno, 1991): 221–28.

Dorey, T. A. "Adultery and Propaganda in the Early Roman Empire." *University of Birmingham Historical Journal* 8 (1962): 1–6.

Downey, G. (1961). *A History of Antioch in Syria from Seleucus to the Arab Conquest*. Princeton.

Dressel, H. "Beschlag eine römischen Schwertscheide." *BJ* 95 (1894): 61–66.

Drexler, H. "Maiestas." *Aevum* 30 (1956): 195–212.

Drumann, W. (1964). *Geschichte Roms* (rev. P. Groebe). Rpt. Hildesheim.

Dudley, D. R. (1968). *The World of Tacitus*. London.

Duff, A. M. (1928). *Freedmen in the Early Roman Empire*. Oxford.

Duret, L. "Dans l'ombre des plus grands. II. Poètes et prosateurs mal connus de la latinité d'argent." *ANRW* 2.32.5 (1986): 3152–346.

Durry, M. "Le Mariage des filles impubères à Rome." *REL* 47 (1970): 17–24.

Duruy, V. (1885). *Geschichte des römischen Kaiserreichs*. Vol. 1. Leipzig.

Eck, W. "Senatorial Self-Presentation: Developments in the Augustan Period." In Millar and Segal (1984): 129–67.

———. (1993). *Agrippina, die Stadtgründerin Köhns: Eine Frau in der frühkaiserzeitlichen Politik*. Cologne.

Eck, W., A. Caballos, and F. Fernandez. (1996). *Das Senatus Consulto de Cn. Pisone Patre*. Munich.

Edwards, C. (1993). *The Politics of Immorality in Ancient Rome*. Cambridge.

Ehlers, W. "Triumphus." *RE* 7A (1939): 493–511.

Ehrenberg, V. (1946). *Aspects of the Ancient World: Essays and Reviews*. Oxford.

Eitrem, S. "Zur Apotheose." *SO* 10 (1932): 31–56.

Espérandieu, E. (1929). *Inscriptions Latines de Gaule*. Paris.

Esser, A. (1958). *Cäsar und die julisch-claudischen Kaiser im biologisch-ärztlichen Blickfeld*. Leiden.

Evans, E. "Roman Descriptions of Personal Appearances in History and Biography." *HSCP* 46 (1935): 43–84.

———. (1969). *Physiognomics in the Ancient World* Philadelphia.

Evans, J. K. (1991). *War, Women, and Children in Ancient Rome*. London.

Fabia, Ph. (1893). *Les Sources de Tacite dans les Histoires et les Annales*. Paris.

Fabbrini, L. "Livia Drusilla." *Enciclopedia dell'Arte Antica* (1961): 4.663–67.

Fau, G. (1978). *L'Empancipation féminine dans la Rome antique*. Paris.

Favro, D. (1996). *The Urban Image of Augustan Rome*. Cambridge.

Felletti Maj, B. M. (1953). *Museo Nazionale Romano*. Vol. 1, *Rittratti*. Rome.

Ferrero, G. (1911). *The Women of the Caesars*. London.

Ferrill, A. "Augustus and His Daughter: A Modern Myth." In *Studies in Latin Literature and Roman History* 2. Collection *Latomus* 168 (1980): 332–66.

Fink, R. O., A. S. Hoey, and W. F. Snyder, "The *Feriale Duranum*." *YClS* 7 (1940): 11–222.

Finley, M. (ed.). (1976). *Studies in Roman Property*. Cambridge.

Fischler, S. (1989). "The Public Position of Women in the Imperial Household in the Julio-Claudian Period." Diss. Oxford.

———. "Social Stereotypes and Historical Analysis: The Case of the Imperial Women at Rome." In Archer, Fischler, and Wyke (1994): 115–33.

Fishwick, D. "Prudentius and the Cult of Divus Augustus." *Historia* 39 (1990): 475–86.

———. "Ovid and Divus Augustus." *CP* 86 (1991): 36–41.

———. (1987–92). *The Imperial Cult in the Roman West: Studies in the Ruler Cult of the Western Provinces of the Roman Empire*. Vols. 1–2. Leiden.

———. "A Temple of Vesta on the Palatine?" *Mélanges Tadeusz Kotula* (Breslau, 1993): 51–57.

Fittschen, K. "Zur Panzerstatue in Cherchel." *JDAI* 91 (1976): 175–210.

Fittschen, K., and P. Zanker. (1983). *Katalog der römischen Porträts in den Capitolinischen Museen und den anderen kommunalen Sammlungen der Stadt Rom*. Mainz.

Fitzler, K., and O. Seeck. "Iulius Augustus." *RE* 10 (1918): 275–381.

Flaig, Egon. "Loyalität ist keine Gefälligkeit. Zum Majestätsprozess gegen C. Silius 24 n Chr." *Klio* 75 (1993): 289–98.

Flory, M. "*Sic Exempla Parantur*: Livia's Shrine to Concordia and the Porticus Liviae." *Historia* 33 (1984): 309–30.

———. "*Abducta Neroni Uxor*: The Historiographical Tradition on the Marriage of Octavian and Livia." *TAPA* 118 (1988): 343–59.

———. "Octavian and the Omen of the *gallina alba*." *CJ* 84 (1988–89): 343–56.

———. "Livia and the History of Public Honorific Statues for Women in Rome." *TAPA* 123 (1993): 287–308.

———. "Dynastic Ideology, the *Domus Augusta*, and Imperial Women: A Lost Statuary Group in the Circus Flaminius." *TAPA* 126 (1996): 287–306.

———. "The Meaning of *Augusta* in the Julio-Claudian Period." *AJAH* (1998): 113–38.

Flower, H. I. (1996). *Ancestor Masks and Aristocratic Power in Roman Culture*. Oxford.

Foley, H. P. (1981). *Reflections of Women in Antiquity*. New York.

Forbis, E. P. "Women's Public Image in Italian Honorary Inscriptions." *AJP* 111 (1990): 493–512.

Förschner, G. (1987). *Die Münzen der Römischen Kaiser in Alexandrien*. Frankfurt.

Forsyth, P. Y. "A Treason Case of A.D. 37." *Phoenix* 23 (1969): 204–7.

Fracarro, P. "C. Herrenius Capito di Teate: Procurator di Livia, di Tiberio e di Gaio." *Athenaeum* 18 (1940): 136–44.

Frank, R. I. "Augustus' Legislation on Marriage and Children." *CSCA* 8 (1975): 41–52.

Frank, T. "Livy's Deference to Livia." *AJP* (1998): 223–24.

Freyburger, G. "La Supplication d'action de grâces sous le Haut-Empire." *ANRW* 16.2 (1978): 1418–39.

Freyer-Schauenburg, B. "Die Kieler Livia." *BJ* 182 (1982): 209–24.

Friedrich, W.-H. "Eine Denkform bie Tacitus." In *Festschrift E. Kapp* (Hamburg, 1958): 135–44.

Fuchs, M. (1989). *Il teatro e il ciclo statuario giulio-claudio*. Rome.

Furneaux, H. (1896). *The Annals of Tacitus*. Oxford, 2d ed.

Gabba, E. (ed.) (1970). *Appian: Bellorum Civilium Liber V*. Florence.

Gabriel, M. M. (1955). *Livia's Garden Room at Prima Porta*. New York.

Gafforini, C. "Livia Drusilla tra storia e letteratura." *RIL* 130 (1996): 121–44.

Gagé, J. "Divus Augustus. L'Idée dynastique chez les empereurs julio-claudiens." *RA* 55 (1934): 11–341.

Galinsky, K. "Augustus' Legislation on Morals and Marriage." *Philologus* 125 (1981): 126–44.

——. (1996). *Augustan Culture: An Interpretative Introduction*. Princeton.

Galsterer, H. "The Administration of Justice." *Cambridge Ancient History* (Cambridge, 1996, 2d ed.): 397–413.

Gardner, J. F. (1986). *Women in Roman Law and Society*. London.

——. "Julia's Freedman: Questions of Law and Status." *BICS* 35 (1988): 94–100.

——. (1998). *Family and Familia in Roman Law and Life*. Oxford.

Gardner, P. "A New Portrait of Livia." *JRS* 12 (1922): 32–34.

Gardthausen, V. (1891). *Augustus und seine Zeit*. Leipzig, rpt. Darmstadt, 1964.

——. "Agrippa Julius Caesar." *RE* 10 (1918): 183–85.

Garlick, B., S. Dixon, and P. Allen (eds.). (1992). *Stereotypes of Women in Power: Historical Perspectives and Revisionist Views*. New York.

Garnsey, P. (1970). *Social Status and Legal Privilege in the Roman Empire*. Oxford.

——. "Urban Property Development." In Finley (1976): 123–36.

Garnsey, P., and R. Saller (1987). *The Roman Empire: Economy, Society, and Culture*. London.

Garzetti, A. (1974). *From Tiberius to the Antonines* (trans. J. R. Foster). London.

Gatti, G. "Nuove osservazioni sul Mausoleo di Augusto." *L'Urbe* 8.16 (1938): 1–17.

Ghedini, F. "Il dolore per la morte di Druso maggiore nel vaso d'onice di Saint Maurice d'Agaune." *RdA* 11 (1987): 68–74.

Giancotti, F. "La consolazione di Seneca a Polibio in Cassio Dione, LXI, 10.2." *RFIC* 34 (1956): 30–44.

Giua, M. A. "Clemenza del sovrano e monarchia illuminata in Cassio Dione, 55.14–22." *Athenaeum* 59 (1981): 317–37.

González, J. "Tabula Siarensis, Fortunales Siarenses, et Municipium Civium Romanorum." *ZPE* 55 (1984): 55–100.

González, J., and J. Arce (eds.). (1988). *Estudios sobre la Tabula Siarensis*. Madrid.

Goodyear, F. R. D. (1972). *The Annals of Tacitus, Volume I*. Cambridge.

——. (1981). *The Annals of Tacitus, Volume II*. Cambridge.

Gough, M. "Augusta Ciliciae." *Anatolian Studies* 6 (1956): 168–70.

Gow, A. S. F., and D. L. Page. (1968). *The Greek Anthology II: The Garland of Philip*. Cambridge.

Grant, M. (1946). *From Imperium to Auctoritas: A Historical Study of Aes Coinage in the Roman Empire, 49 B.C.–A.D. 14*. Cambridge.

——. (1950). *Aspects of the Principate of Tiberius: Historical Comments on the Colonial Coinage Issued Outside Spain*. New York.

——. (1950). *Roman Anniversary Issues*. Cambridge.

——. "The Pattern of Official Coinage in the Early Principate." In *Essays in Roman Coinage Presented to H. Mattingly* (Oxford, 1956): 96–112.

——. (1958). *Roman History from Coins*. Cambridge.

Gratwick, A. S. "Free or Not So Free? Wives and Daughters in the Late Roman Republic." In E. M. Craik (ed.), *Marriage and Property* (Aberdeen, 1984): 30–53.

Gray-Fow, M. J. G. "The Wicked Stepmother in Roman History and Literature: An Evaluation." *Latomus* 47 (1988): 741–57.

Grether, G. "Livia and the Roman Imperial Cult." *AJP* (1946): 222–52.

Griffin, M. "The Senate's Story." *JRS* 87 (1997): 249–63.

Grimal, P. (1943). *Les Jardins Romains*. Paris.

Grimm, G. "Zum Bildnis der Iulia Augusti." *MDAI(R)* 80 (1973): 279–82.

Grimm, J. "Über Marcellus Burdigalensis." *Kleinere Schriften* (Berlin, 1865): 121–25.

Groag, E. "Studien zur Kaisergeschichte III. Der Sturtz der Iulia." *WS* 41 (1919): 74–88.

Gross, H. W. (1962). *Iulia Augusta*. Göttingen.

Gruen, E. (1974). *The Last Generation of the Roman Republic*. Berkeley.

Guarducci, M. "Vesta sul Palatino." *MDAI(R)* 71 (1964): 158–69.

——. "Enea e Vesta." *MDAI(R)* 78 (1971): 73–118.

Guarino, A. "Il Coup de foudre di Ottaviano." *Labeo* 27 (1981): 335–37.

Haase, F. "Tacitea." *Phililogus* 3 (1848): 152–59.

Hahn, U. (1994). *Die Frauen des Römischen Kaiserhauses und ihre Ehrungen im Griechischen Osten anhand Epigraphischer und Numismatischer Zeugnisse von Livia bis Sabina*. Saarbrücken.

Halfmann, D. (1986). *Itinera Principum*. Stuttgart.

Hall, J. "Livy's Tanaquil and the Image of Assertive Etruscan Women in Latin Historical Literature of the Early Empire." *Augustan Age* IV (1985): 31–38.

Hall, M. D. "Eine reine Männerwelt? Frauen um das römische Heer." In Dettenhofer (1994): 207–8.

Hallett, J. P. "Perusinae Glandes and the Changing Image of Augustus." *AJAH* 2 (1977): 151–71.

——. (1984). *Fathers and Daughters in Roman Society*. Princeton.

——. "Women as Same and Other in Classical Roman Elite." *Helios* 16 (1989): 59–78.

Hammond, M. (1933). *The Augustan Principate*. Cambridge, Mass.

——. "Octavius (Octavia)." *RE* 17.2 (1937): 1859–68.

Hänlein-Schäfer, H. (1985). *Veneratio Augusti. Eine Studie zu den Tempeln des ersten römischen Kaisers*. Rome.

Hanslik, R. "Proculeius." *RE* 23.1 (1957): 72–74.

——. "Urgulania." *RE* Suppl. 9 (1962): 1868–69.

Hanson, J. A. (1959). *Roman Theater-Temples*. Princeton.

Hardy, L. E. (1976). "The Imperial Women in Tacitus' 'Annales.' " Diss. Indiana.

Harkness, A. G. "Age at Marriage and at Death in the Roman Empire." *TAPA* 27 (1986): 35–72.

Harrer, G. A. "Tacitus and Tiberius." *AJP* 41 (1920): 57–68.

Hatzl, Ch. (1975). "Die politische Roll der Frauen um Tiberius." Diss. Innsbruck.

Haupt, M. (1875). *Opuscula*. Vol. 1. Leipzig.

Hawley, R., and B. Levick (eds.). (1995). *Women in Antiquity: New Assessments.* London.

Hellegouarc'h, J. "Les Buts de l'oeuvre de Velleius Paterculus." *Latomus* 33 (1964): 669–84.

Hemelrijk, E. A. (1999). *Matrona Docta: Educated Women in the Roman Elite from Cornelia to Julia Domna.* London.

Hentig, H. von (1924). *Über den Cäsarenwahnsinn, die Krankheit des Kaisers Tiberius.* Munich.

Herbert-Brown, G. (1984). *Ovid and the Fasti: An Historical Study.* Oxford.

Heron de Villefosse, P. "Le Trésor de Boscoreale." *MMAI* 5 (1899): 1–129.

Herrmann, C. (1964). *Le Rôle judiciare et politique des femmes sous la république romaine.* Brussels.

Herrmann, L. (1951). *L'Age d'argent doré.* Paris.

Herrmann, P. "Inschriften aus dem Heraion von Samos." *MDAI(A)* 75 (1960): 68–183.

——. (1968). *Der römische Kaisereid.* Göttingen.

Herz, P. (1975). "Untersuchungen zum Festkalender der römischen Kaiserzeit nach datierten Weih- und Ehreninschriften." Diss. Mainz.

——. "Kaiserfeste der Prinzipatszeit." *ANRW* II.16.2 (1978): 1135–1200.

——. "Die Arvalakten des Jahres 38 n. Chr. Eine Quelle der Geschichte Kaiser Caligulas." *BJ* 181 (1981): 89–110.

Hesberg, H. von, and S. Panciera (1994). *Das Mausoleum des Augustus. Der Bau und seine Inschriften.* Munich.

Heuss, A. (1964). *Römische Geschichte.* Brunswick, 2d ed.

Hill, P. V. "Buildings and Monuments of Rome on Flavian Coins." *NAC* 8 (1979): 207.

Hillard, T. "Republican Politics, Women, and the Evidence." *Helios* 16 (1989): 165–82.

——. "On the Stage, Behind the Curtain: Images of Politically Active Women in the Late Roman Republic." In Garlick, Dixon, and Allen (1992): 37–64.

Hinard, F. (1985). *Les Proscriptions de la Rome républicaine.* Rome.

Hinds, S. "First Among Women: Ovid, *Tristia* 1.6, and the Traditions of the 'Exemplary' Catalogue." In S. M. Braund and R. Mayer (eds.), *Amor: Roma, Love, and Latin Literature* (Cambridge, 1999): 123–42.

Hirschfeld, O. "Der Grundbesitz der römischen Kaiser in den ersten drei Jahrhunderten." *Klio* 2 (1902): 284–315.

——. (1905). *Die kaiserlichen Verwaltungsbeamten bis auf Diocletian.* Berlin.

Hoffsten, R. B. (1939). "Roman Women of Rank of the Early Empire." Diss. Pennsylvania.

Hohl, E. (1931). *Die römische Kaiserzeit.* Berlin.

——. "Primum Facinus Novi Principatus." *Hermes* 70 (1935): 350–55.

——. "Zu den Testamenten des Augustus." *Klio* 12 (1937): 323–42.

——. "Besass Cäsar Tribunengewalt?" *Klio* 14 (1939): 61–75.

Hopkins, M. K. "The Age of Roman Girls at Marriage." *Population Studies* 18 (1965): 309–27.

——. "On the Probable Age Structure of the Roman Population." *Population Studies* 20 (1966): 245–64.

Humbert, M. (1972). *Le Remariage à Rome. Etude d'histoire juridique et sociale.* Milan.

Huntsman, E. (1997). "The Family and Property of Livia Drusilla." Diss. Pennsylvania.

Hurley, D. W. (1993). *An Historical and Historiographical Commentary on Suetonius' Life of C. Caligula.* Atlanta.

Huzar, E. G. "Mark Antony: Marriages vs. Careers." *CJ* 81 (1986): 97–111.

Iacopi, I. (1997). *Palatino: Aula Isiaca. La Decorazione Pittorica dell'Aula Isiaca.* Milan.

Ihm, M. "Suetoniana." *Hermes* 36 (1901): 287–304.

Instinsky, H. U. "Augustus und die Adoption des Tiberius" *Hermes* 94 (1966): 324–43.

Jameson, S. "Augustus and Agrippa Postumus." *Historia* 24 (1975): 287–314.

Jerome, T. S. "The Tacitean Tiberius." *CP* 7 (1912): 265–82.

Johnson, P. J. "Ovid's Livia in Exile." *CW* 90 (1997): 403–20.

Jones, A. H. M. "The Aerarium and the Fiscus." *JRS* 40 (1950): 22–29.

———. (1960). *Studies in Roman Government and Law.* Oxford.

———. (1971). *The Cities of the Eastern Roman Provinces.* Oxford, 2d. ed.

Jones, C. P. "A Leading Family of Roman Thespiae." *HSCP* 74 (1970): 222–55.

Jucker, H. "Der Grosse Pariser Kameo." *JDAI* 91 (1977): 211–50.

———. "Zum Carpentum-Sesterz der Agrippina Major." In *Forschungen und Funde: Festschrift Bernhard Neutsch* (Innsbruck, 1980): 205–17.

Kähler, H. "Triumphbogen (Ehrenbogen)." *RE* 7A1 (1939): 373–493.

———. (1959). *Die Augustusstatue von Primaporta.* Cologne.

Kahrstedt, V. "Frauen auf antiken Münzen." *Klio* 10 (1910): 261–314.

Kampen, N. B. "Between Public and Private: Women as Historical Subjects in Roman Art." In Pomeroy (1991): 218–48.

Kaplan, M. "*Agrippina semper atrox:* A Study in Tacitus' Characterization of Women." *Studies in Latin Literature and Roman History* 1. Collection *Latomus* 164 (1979): 410–17.

Kaser, M. (1965). *Roman Private Law* (trans. R. Dannenbring). Durban.

Kaspar, D. "Neues zum Grand Camée de France." *GNS* 25 (1975): 61–68.

Kehoe, D. "Tacitus and Sallustius Crispus." *CJ* 80 (1985): 247–54.

Kellum, B. A. "The City Adorned: Programmatic Display at the *Aedes Concordiae Augustae.*" In Raaflaub and Toher (1990): 276–96.

———. "The Construction of Landscape in Augustan Rome: The Garden Room at the Villa ad Gallinas." *Art Bulletin* 76 (1994): 211–24.

Kienast, D. (1982). *Augustus: Prinzeps und Monarch.* Darmstadt.

———. "Der heilige Senat. Senatskult und 'kaiserlicher' Senat." *Chiron* 15 (1985): 253–82.

———. (1990). *Römische Kaisertabelle.* Darmstadt.

Kleiner, D. "The Great Friezes of the Ara Pacis Augustae: Greek Sources, Roman Derivatives, and Augustan Social Policy." *MEFRA* 90 (1978): 753–85.

———. "Politics and Gender in the Pictorial Propaganda of Antony and Octavian." *EMC* 36 (1992): 357–67.

———. "Livia Drusilla and the Remarkable Power of Elite Women in Imperial Rome." *IJCT* 6 (2000): 563–69.

Kleiner, D., and S. B. Matheson (1996). *I, Claudia: Women in Ancient Rome.* New Haven.

———. (2000). *I, Claudia II: Women in Roman Art and Society.* Austin.

Kleiner, F. (1985). *The Arch of Nero in Rome.* Rome.

———. "An Extraordinary Posthumous Honor for Livia." *Athenaeum* 78 (1990): 508–14.

Knibbe, D., H. Engelmann, and B. Iplikçioglu, "Neue Inschriften aus Ephesos." *JÖAI* 62 (1993): 113–22.

Koch, C. "Vesta." *RE* 8A2 (1958): 1717–75.

Koeppel, G. "Die 'Ara Pietas Augustae': Ein Geisterbau." *MDAI(R)* 89 (1982): 453–55.

———. "Die historischen Reliefs der römischen Kaiserzeit I: Stadtrömische Denkmäler unbekannter Bauzugenhörigkeit aus augusteischer und julisch-claudischer Zeit." *BJ* 183 (1983): 61–144.

Koestermann, E. "Der Eingang der Annalen des Tacitus." *Historia* 10 (1961): 330–55.

———. (1963–68). *Cornelius Tacitus, Annalen*. Heidelberg.

Kokkinos, Nikos. (1992). *Antonia Augusta: Portrait of a Great Roman Lady*. London.

Kolbe, G. "Noch einmal Vesta auf dem Palatin." *MDAI(R)* 73–74 (1966–67): 94–104.

Königer, H. (1966). *Gestalt und Welt der Frau bei Tacitus*. Erlangen-Nurenberg.

Kornemann, E. (1929). *Neue Dokumente zum lakonischen Kaiserkult. Breslau, Abhandlungen der schlesischen Gesellschaft für vaterländische Cultur*, Heft 1.

———. (1930). *Doppelprinzipat und Reichsteilung im Imperium Romanum*. Leipzig-Berlin.

———. (1952). *Grosse Frauen des Altertums*. Leipzig, 4th ed.

———. (1960). *Tiberius*. Stuttgart.

———. (1963). *Römische Geschichte* (rev. H. Bengston). Stuttgart, 5th ed.

Kraay, C. (1956). *The Aes Coinage of Galba*. New York.

Krause, C., et al. (1985). *Domus Tiberiana: Nuove Richerche, Studi di Restauro*. Zurich.

Krause, K. "Hostia." *RE* suppl. 5 (1931): 236–82.

Kreikenbom, D. (1992). *Griechische und römische Kolossalporträts bis zum späten ersten Jahrhundert n. Chr.* Berlin.

Kromayer, J. "Forschungen zur Geschichte des zweiten Triumvirats." *Hermes* 29 (1894): 561–62.

Kübler, B. "Maiestas." *RE* 14.1 (1928): 542–59.

Kuhoff, W. "Zur Titulatur der römischen Kaiserinnen während der Prinzipatszeit." *Klio* 75 (1993): 244–56.

Kunst, C. "Adoption und Testamentadoption in der Späten Römischen Republik." *Klio* (1996): 87–104.

———. "Zur sozialen Funktion der Domus. Der Haushalt der Kaiserin Livia nach dem Tode des Augustus." In P. Kneissl and P. V. Losemann (eds.), *Imperium Romanum* (Stuttgart, 1998): 450–71.

Kuttner, A. L. (1995). *Dynasty and Empire in the Age of Augustus: The Case of the Boscoreale Cups*. Berkeley.

Labaste, H. "Comme Plutarque, Tacite aurait-il menti?" *Humanités* (Paris): *Cl. de Lettres* 7 (1930): 92–95.

Lacey, W. K. "2 B.C. and Julia's Adultery." *Antichthon* 14 (1980): 127–42.

———. (1996). *Augustus and the Principate*. Leeds.

Lackeit, C. "Iulius (Iulia)." *RE* 10, no. 556 (1918): 909–14.

Lahusen, G. (1983). *Untersuchungen zur Ehrenstatue in Rom*. Rome.

Laistner, M. L. W. (1963). *The Greater Roman Historians*. Berkeley.

Lanciani, R. A. (1893–1901). *Forma Urbis Romae*. Milan.

La Rocca, E. (1983). *Ara Pacis Augustae*. Rome.

Latte K., et al. (1956). *Histoire et historiens dans l'antiquité*. Geneva.

Lear, F. S. (1965). *Treason in Roman and Germanic Law*. Austin.

Le Bas, Ph., and W. H. Waddington. (1870). *Inscriptions Grecques et Latines receuillies en Asie Mineure* (Paris, rpt. New York, 1972).

Lehman, G. "Das Ende der römischen Herrschaft über das 'westelbische' Germanien: Von der Varus-Katastrophe zur Abberufung des Germanicus Caesar 16/17 n. Chr." *ZPE* 86 (1991): 79–96.

Lehner, H. "Zwei Trinkgefässe aus Vetera: II Der Trinkbecher des Chrysippus." *BJ* 122 (1912): 430–35.

Leipoldt, J. (1954). *Die Frau in der antiken Welt und im Urchristentum*. Leipzig.

Leo, F. (1901). *Die griechisch-römische Biographie nach ihrer literarischen Form*. Leipzig.

Leon, E. F. "Scribonia and Her Daughters." *TAPA* 82 (1951): 168–75.

Lesuisse, L. "L'Aspect héréditaire de la succession impériale sous les Julio-Claudiens." *LEC* 30 (1962): 32–50.

Levick, B. "Drusus Caesar and the Adoptions of A.D. 4." *Latomus* 25 (1966): 227–44.

——. "The Beginning of Tiberius' Career." *CQ* 21 (1971): 478–86.

——. "Abdication and Agrippa Postumus." *Historia* 21 (1972): 674–97.

——. "Atrox Fortuna." *CR* 22 (1972): 309–11.

——. "Tiberius' Retirement to Rhodes in 6 B.C." *Latomus* 31 (1972): 779–813.

——. "Julians and Claudians." *GR* 22 (1975): 29–38.

——. "The Fall of Julia the Younger." *Latomus* 35 (1976): 301–39.

——. (1976). *Tiberius the Politician*. London.

——. "Concordia at Rome." In *Scripta Nummaria Romana: Essays Presented to Humphrey Sutherland* (London, 1978): 228.

——. "The SC from Larinum." *JRS* 73 (1983): 97.

——. " 'Caesar omnia habet': Property and Politics Under the Principate." *Entretiens Hardt* 33 (1987): 187–218.

Lewis, J. D. "Primum facinus novi principatus." In B. F. Harris (ed.), *Auckland Classical Essays* (Auckland, 1970): 165–85.

Lewis, M. W. H. (1955). *The Official Priests of Rome Under the Julio-Claudians*. Rome.

Lewis, N. "Notationes Legentis." *BASP* 11 (1972): 44–59.

Lewis, R. G. "Some Mothers." *Athenaeum* 66 (1988): 198–200.

Liebeschutz, W. (1979). *Continuity and Changes in Roman Religion*. Oxford.

Linderski, J. "The Mother of Livia Augusta and the Aufidii Lurcones of the Republic." *Historia* 23 (1974): 463–80.

——. "Julia in Regium." *ZPE* 72 (1988): 181–200.

Ling, R. (1991). *Roman Painting*. Cambridge.

Luce, T. J., and A. J. Woodman (1993). *Tacitus and the Tacitean Tradition*. Princeton.

Lugli, G. "Note topografiche intorno all antiche ville suburbane." *BC* 51 (1923): 3–62.

——. (1938). *I Monumenti Antichi di Roma e Suburbio*. Rome.

——. (1946). *Roma Antica*. Rome.

——. (1947). *Monumenti minori del Foro Romano*. Rome.

——. (1970). *Itinerario di Roma Antica*. Milan.

MacMullen, R. "Women in Public in the Roman Empire." *Historia* 29 (1980): 208–18.

——. "Women's Power in the Principate." *Klio* 68 (1986): 434–43.

Magie, D. (1950). *Roman Rule in Asia Minor*. Princeton.

Manuwald, B. (1979). *Cassius Dio und Augustus: Philologsiche Untersuchungen zu den Büchern 45–6 des dionischen Geschichtswerkes*. Wiesbaden: *Palingenesia* 14.

Marino, P. A. "Woman: Poorly Inferior or Richly Superior?" *CB* 48 (1971): 17–21.

Marsh, F. B. "Roman Parties in the Reign of Tiberius." *AHR* 31 (1926): 65–68.

——. "Tacitus and the Aristocratic Tradition." *CP* 21 (1926): 289–310.

——. (1931). *The Reign of Tiberius*. Oxford.

Marshall, A. J. "Roman Women and the Provinces." *Anc. Soc.* 6 (1975): 109–27.

——. "Tacitus and the Governor's Lady: A Note on Annals iii.33–34." *GR* 22 (1975): 11–18.

Martha, J. "Inscriptions du Vallon des Muses." *BCH* 3 (1879): 441–48.

Martin, R. H. "Tacitus and the Death of Augustus." *CQ* 5 (1955): 123–28.

——. (1981). *Tacitus*. London.

Martin, R. H., and Woodman, A. J. (1989). *Tacitus: Annals Book IV*. Cambridge.

Maslakov, G. "Valerius Maximus and Roman Historiography." *ANRW* II.32 (1984): 437–96.

Matheson, S. B. (1980). *Ancient Glass in the Yale University Art Gallery*. New Haven.

McDaniel, M. J. (1995). "Augustus, the Vestals, and the *Signum Imperii*." Diss. North Carolina.

McDonnell, M. "Divorce Initiated by Women." *AJAH* 8 (1983): 54–80.

Megow, W. R. (1973). *Kameen von Augustus bis Alexander Severus*. Rome.

Meise, E. (1969). *Untersuchungen zur Geschichte der Julisch-Claudischen Dynastie*. Munich.

Mellor, R. (1993). *Tacitus*. London.

Mendell, C. W. (1957). *Tacitus: The Man and His Work*. New Haven.

Messineo, G. "Ollae Perforatae." *Xenia* 8 (1984): 65–82.

Michel, A. (1966). *Tacite et le destin de l'empire*. Paris.

Mikocki, T. (1995). *Sub specie deae: Les Impératrices et princesses romaines assimilés à des déesses. Etude iconologique*. Rome.

Millar, F. (1964). *A Study of Cassius Dio*. Oxford.

——. "Imperial Ideology in the *Tabula Siarensis*." In González and Arce (1988): 11–19.

——. (1992). *The Emperor in the Roman World*. London, 2d ed.

——. "Ovid and the *domus Augusta*: Rome Seen from Tomoi." *JRS* 83 (1993): 1–17.

——. (1993). *The Roman Near East, 31 BC–AD 337*. Cambridge, Mass.

Millar, F., and E. Segal (eds.). (1984). *Caesar Augustus: Seven Aspects*. Oxford.

Miranda, E. (1990). *Iscrizioni greche d'Italia. Napoli I*. Rome.

Mommsen, Th. "Die Familie des Germanicus." *Hermes* (1878): 245–65.

——. (1864–79). *Römische Forschungen*. Berlin.

——. (1883). *Res Gestae Divi Augusti*. Berlin, 2d ed.

——. (1899). *Römisches Strafrecht*. Berlin.

——. "Bruchstücke der Saliarischen Priesterliste." *Hermes* 38 (1903): 125–29.

——. (1904). *Gesammelte Schriften*. Berlin, rpt. Berlin, 1965.

——. (1996). *History of Rome Under the Emperors* (trans. C. Krojz). London.

Montero, S. "Livia y la divinación inductiva." *Polis* 6 (1994): 225–67.

Morford, M. "The Training of Three Roman Emperors." *Phoenix* 22 (1968): 57–72.

Morkholm, O. (1991). *Early Hellenistic Coinage*. Cambridge.

Motzo, B. R. "I commentari di Agrippina madre di Nerone." In *Studi de Storia e Filologia*, vol. 1 (Cagliari, 1927).

Mratschek-Halfmann, S. (1993). *Divites et Praepotentes. Reichtum und soziale Stellung in der Literatur der Prinzipatszeit*. Historia Einzelschriften no. 70, Stuttgart.

Mullens, H. G. "The Women of the Caesars." *GR* 11 (1941–42): 59–67.

Münzer, F. "Claudius." *RE* 3.2 (1899): 2885–86.

———. "Clodia." *RE* 4 (1900): 105–7.

———. "Fulvia." *RE* 7 (1900): 281–84.

———. "Servilia." *RE* 2A (1923): 1817–21.

———. "Livius." *RE* 13.1 (1926): 810.

———. "M. Livius Drusus Claudianus." *RE* 13.1 (1926): 881–84.

Nawotka, K. "The Attitude Towards Rome in the Political Propaganda of the Bosphoran Monarchs." *Latomus* 48 (1989): 326–28.

Nenci, G. "Sei decreti inediti da Entella." *Atti della Scuola Normale Superiore de Pisa* 10 (1980): 1271–75.

Nipperdey, K. (1851–52). *Cornelius Tacitus*. Leipzig.

Norwood, F. "The Riddle of Ovid's *relegatio*." *CP* 58 (1963): 150–63.

Oberleitner, W. (1985). *Geschnittene Steine: Die Prunkkameen der Wiener Antikensammlung*. Vienna, Cologne, and Graz.

Ogilvie, R. M. (1965). *A Commentary on Livy, Books 1–5*. Oxford.

Oliver, J. H. "The Divi of the Hadrianic Period." *HThR* 42 (1949): 35–40.

———. "On the Edict of Germanicus Declining Divine Acclamations." *RSA* 1 (1971): 229–30.

Oliver, J. H., and R. E. A. Palmer. "The Text of the Tabula Hebana." *AJP* 75 (1954): 225–49.

Ollendorff, L. "Livia Drusilla." *RE* 13 (1926): 900–927.

Paladini, M. L. "La Morte di Agrippa Postumo e la Congiurra di Clemente." *Acme* 7 (1954): 313–29.

Palmer, R. E. A. "Roman Shrines of Female Chastity from the Caste Struggle to the Papacy of Innocent I." *RSA* 4 (1974): 113–59.

Paltiel, E. (1991). *Vassals and Rebels in the Roman Empire*. Brussels.

Pannuti, V. (1983). *Museo archeologico nazionale Napoli: Catalogo della collezione glittica*. Vol. 1. Rome.

Pappano, A. E. "Agrippa Postumus." *CP* 36 (1941): 30–45.

Parassoglou, G. (1978). *Imperial Estates in Roman Egypt. American Studies in Papyrology*, vol. 18: Amsterdam.

Paribeni, R. (1876). *Il ritratto nell'era antica*. Milan.

Parker, E. R. "The Education of Heirs in the Julio-Claudian Family." *AJP* 67 (1946): 29–50.

Parsi, B. (1963). *Désignation et investiture de l'empereur romain*. Paris.

Pearce, T. "The Role of the Wife as Custos in Ancient Rome." *Eranos* 72 (1985): 16–33.

Pelham, H. F. (1911). *Essays.* Oxford.

Pelling, C. "Tacitus and Germanicus." In Luce and Woodman (1993): 59–85.

Perkounig, C.-M. (1995). *Livia Drusilla-Iulia Augusta.* Vienna.

Peter, C. (1867). *Geschichte Roms.* Halle.

Pfister, K. (1941). *Der Untergang der antiken Welt.* Leipzig.

———. (1951). *Die Frauen der Cäsaren.* Berlin.

Pflaum, H. G. (1950). *Les Procurateurs équestres sous le Haut-Empire romain.* Paris.

———. (1960–61). *Les Carrières procuratoriennes équestres sous le Haut-Empire romain.* Paris.

Phillips, J. E. "Roman Mothers and the Lives of Their Adult Daughters." *Helios* 6 (1978): 75–76.

Piganiol, A. "Observations sur une loi de l'empereur Claude." *Mélanges Cagnat* (Paris, 1912): 153–67.

Pike, J. B. "Cenat Adulteria in Suetonius." *CJ* 15 (1919): 372–73.

Pippidi, D. M. "Le 'Numen Augusti.'" *REL* 9 (1931): 83–111.

Pistor, H. H. (1965). "Prinzeps und Patriziat in der Zeit von Augustus bis Commodus." Diss. Freiburg.

Platner, S. B., and T. Ashby (1929). *A Topographical Dictionary of Ancient Rome.* Rome, rpt. 1965.

Pollini, J. (1978). "Studies in Augustan 'Historical' Reliefs." Diss. California, Berkeley.

———. "Man or God: Divine Assimilation and Imitation in the Late Republic and Early Principate." In Raaflaub and Toher (1990): 334–57.

Pomeroy, S. (1975). *Goddesses, Whores, Wives, and Slaves: Women in Classical Antiquity.* New York.

———. "The Relationship of the Married Woman to Her Blood Relatives in Rome." *Anc. Soc.* 7 (1976): 215–27.

——— (ed.). (1991). *Women's History and Ancient History.* Chapel Hill.

Pommeray, L. (1937). *Etudes sur l'infamie en droit romain.* Paris.

Poulsen, F. (1928). *Porträtstudien in norditalienischen Provinzmuseen.* Copenhagen.

Poulsen, V. (1973). *Les Portraits Romains.* Vol. 1, *République et dynastie Julienne.* Copenhagen.

Premerstein, A. von (1937). *Von Werden und Wesen des Principats.* Munich.

Prévost, M. H. (1949). *Les Adoptions politiques à Rome sous la république et le principat.* Paris.

Price, S. (1984). *Rituals and Power: The Roman Imperial Cult in Asia Minor.* Cambridge.

Purcell, N. "Livia and the Womanhood of Rome." *PCPhS* 32 (1986): 78–105.

Questa, C. "La morte di Augusto secondo Cassio Dione." *PP* 14 (1959): 41–53.

———. (1960). *Studi sulle fonti degli Annales di Tacito.* Rome.

Raaflaub, K. A., and L. J. Samons II. "Opposition to Augustus." In Raaflaub and Toher (1990): 417–54.

Raaflaub, K. A., and M. Toher (eds.). (1990). *Between Republic and Empire.* Berkeley.

Raditsa, L. F. "Augustus' Legislation Concerning Marriage, Procreation, Love Affairs, and Adultery." *ANRW* 2.13 (1980) 278–339.

Radke, G. "Der Geburtstag des alteren Drusus." *Würz. Jhb.* 4 (1978): 211–13.

———. "Die drei penates und Vesta in Rom." *ANRW* 2.17.1 (1981): 343–73.

Raepsaet-Charlier, M.-Th. "Ordre sénatorial et divorce sous le Haut-Empire: Un chapitre de l'histoire des mentalités." *ACD* 17–18 (1981–82): 161–73.

——. "Epouses et familles de magistrats dans les provinces romaines aux deux premiers siècles de l'empire." *Historia* 31 (1982): 64–69.

Raffay, R. (1884). *Die Memoiren der Kaiserin Agrippina.* Vienna.

Randour, M. J. (1954). *Figures de femmes romaines dans les Annales de Tacite.* Louvain.

Ranke, L. (1883). *Weltgeschichte.* Leipzig.

Rantz, B. "Les Droits de la femme romaine tels qu'on peut les apercevoir dans le pro Caecina de Ciceron." *RIDA* 29 (1982): 56–69.

Rapke, T. T. "Tiberius, Piso, and Germanicus." *AC* 25 (1982): 61–69.

Rawson, B. (1985). *Intellectual Life in the Late Roman Republic.* London.

—— (ed.). (1986). *The Family in Ancient Rome: New Perspectives.* London.

Rawson, E. "The Eastern Clientelae of Clodius and the Claudii." *Historia* 22 (1972): 219–39.

——. "More on the *Clientelae* of the Patrician Claudii." *Historia* 26 (1977): 340–57.

——. "The Life and Death of Asclepiades of Bithynia." *CQ* 32 (1982): 358–70.

Reeder, J. C. "The Statue of Augustus from Prima Porta and the Underground Complex." *Studies in Latin Literature and Roman History,* Collection *Latomus* 8 (1996).

——. "The Statue of Augustus from Prima Porta, the Underground Complex, and the Omen of the Gallina Alba." *AJP* 118 (1997): 89–118.

Rehak, P. "Livia's Dedication in the the Temple of Divus Augustus on the Palatine." *Latomus* 49 (1990): 117–25.

Reinhold, M. (1933). *Marcus Agrippa: A Biography.* New York.

——. (1988). *An Historical Commentary on Cassius Dio's Roman History Books 49–52 (36–29 B.C.).* American Philological Association Monographs, no. 34: Atlanta.

Reinhold, M., and P. M. Swan. "Cassius Dio's Assessment of Augustus." In Raaflaub and Toher (1990): 155–73.

Reynolds, J. M. "The Origins and Beginning of Imperial Cult at Aphrodisias." *PCPhS* 26 (1980): 70–84.

——. "New Evidence for the Imperial Cult in Julio-Claudian Aphrodisias." *ZPE* 43 (1981): 317–27.

——. (1982). *Aphrodisias and Rome.* London.

Reynolds, J. M., and J. B. Ward-Perkins. (1959). *The Inscriptions of Roman Tripolitania.* Rome.

Rich, J. W. (1990). *Cassius Dio: The Augustan Settlement (Roman History 53–55.9).* Warminster.

Richardson, L. "Evolution of the Porticus Octaviae." *AJA* 80 (1976): 57–64.

——. "Concordia and Concordia Augusti." *PP* 33 (1978): 260–72.

——. (1992). *A New Topographical Dictionary of Ancient Rome.* Baltimore.

Richlin, A. "Julia's Jokes, Gallia Placidia, and the Roman Use of Women as Political Icons." In Garlick, Dixon, and Allen (1992): 65–91.

Richmond, J. "Doubtful Works Ascribed to Ovid." *ANRW* 2.31.4 (1981): 2744–83.

Richmond, O. L. "The Temples of Apollo and Divus Augustus on Coins." In *Essays Presented to William Ridgeway* (Cambridge, 1913): 198–212.

Richter, G. (1968). *Engraved Gems of the Greeks, Romans, and Etruscans.* London.

Riposati, B. "Profili di donne nella storia di Tacito." *Aevum* 45 (1971): 25–45.

Ritter. H.-W. "Livia's Erhebung zur Augusta." *Chiron* 2 (1972): 313–38.

Rizzo, G. E. "Base di Augusto." *BC* 60 (1932): 7–109.

Rockwell, K. A. "Vedius and Livia (Tac. *Ann.* 1.10)." *CP* 66 (1971): 110.

Roddaz, J. M. (1984). *Marcus Agrippa.* Rome.

Rodriguez Almeida, E. (1981). *Forma Urbis Marmorea: Aggiornamento generale.* Rome.

Rogers, R. S. "The Conspiracy of Agrippina." *TAPA* 62 (1931): 141–68.

——. (1935). *Criminal Trials and Criminal Legislation Under Tiberius.* Middletown, Conn.

——. (1943). *Studies in the Reign of Tiberius.* Baltimore.

——. "The Roman Emperors as Heirs and Legatees." *TAPA* 78 (1947): 140–58.

Rose, C. B. (1993). *Dynastic Commemoration and Imperial Portraiture in the Julio-Claudian Period.* Cambridge.

Rose, H. J. (1960). *A Handbook of Latin Literature.* New York.

Rostovtsev, M. "Livia und Julia." *Strena Heligania* (Leipzig, 1900): 262–64.

——. (1905). *Römische Bleitesserae. Klio.* Beiheft 3: Lepizig.

——. "Interpretation des tessères en os." *RA* (1905): 110–24.

——. (1922). *A Large Estate in Egypt.* New York, rpt. 1979.

——. (1957). *Social and Economic History of the Roman Empire.* Oxford, 2d ed.

——. "L'Empereur Tibère et le culte impérial." *RH* 163 (1970): 1–26.

Rostovtsev, M., and M. Prou (1900). *Catalogue des Plombs de l'Antiquité, du Moyen Age et des Temps Modernes.* Paris.

Rousselle, A. "Du sanctuaire au thaumaturge: La Guérison en Gaule au IVe siècle." *Annales* 31 (1976): 1085–107.

Rumack, B., and E. Salzman. (1978). *Mushroom Poisoning: Diagnosis and Treatment.* West Palm Beach, Fla.

Rutland, L. W. (1975). "Fortuna Ludens: The Relationship Between Public and Private Imperial Fortune in Tacitus." Diss. Minnesota.

——. "Women as Makers of Kings in Tacitus' *Annals*." *CW* 72 (1978): 15–29.

Ryberg, I. S. "Tacitus' Art of Innuendo." *TAPA* 73 (1942): 383–404.

Sage, M. "Tacitus and the Accession of Tiberius." *Anc. Soc.* 13–14 (1982–83): 292–321.

——. "Tacitus' Historical Works: A Survey and Appraisal." *ANRW* 2.33.2 (1990): 851–1030.

Saletti, C. (1968). *Il ciclo statuario dell Basilica di Velleia.* Milan.

Saller, R. (1982). *Personal Patronage Under the Empire.* Cambridge.

——. "*Familia, domus,* and the Roman Conception of the Family." *Phoenix* 38 (1984): 336–55.

Salomies, O. (1992). *Adoptive and Polyonymous Nomenclature in the Roman Empire.* Helsinki.

Salvatore, A. "L'Immoralité des femmes et la décadence de l'empire selon Tacite." *LEC* 22 (1954): 254–69.

Salway, P. (1981). *Roman Britain.* Oxford.

Salzmann, D. (1990). *Antike Porträts im Römisch-Germanischen Museum Köln.* Cologne.

Sande, S. "Römische Frauenporträts mit Mauerkrone." *AAAH* 5 (1985): 151–245.

Sandels, F. (1912). "Die Stellung der kaiserlichen Frauen aus dem Julisch-Claudischen Hause." Diss. Giessen.

Santoro L'Hoir, F. (1992). *The Rhetoric of Gender Terms*. Leiden.

———. "Tacitus and Women's Usurpation of Power." *CW* 88 (1994): 5–24.

Saria, B. "Pucinum." *RE* 23.2 (1959): 1938.

Sasel, J. "Huldingung norischer Stämme am Magdalensberg in Kärnten. Ein Klärungsversuch." *Historia* 16 (1967): 70–74.

———. "Julia und Tiberius: Beiträge zur römischen Innenpolitik zwischen den Jahren 12 vor und 2 nach Chr." In W. Schmitthenner (ed.), *Augustus* (Darmstadt, 1969): 486–530.

Scaliger, J. (1572). *Publii Virgilii Maronis Appendix*. Leiden.

Scarborough, J. "Roman Medicine to Galen." *ANRW* II.37.1 (1993): 26–29.

——— (ed.). (1984). *Symposium on Byzantine Medicine*. Dumbarton Oaks Papers, no. 38. Washington, D.C.

Scardigli, B. "La sacrosanctitas tribunicia di Ottava e Livia." *Atti della Facoltà di Lettere e Filologia della Università di Siena, Perugia* 3 (1982): 61–64.

Scheid, J. (1975). *Les Frères Arvales. Recruitement et origine sociale sous les empereurs julioclaudiens*. Paris.

———. "Scribonia Caesaris et les Julio-Claudiens. Problèmes de vocabulaire de parenté." *MEFRA* 87 (1975): 349–75.

———. (1990). *Romulus et ses Frères. Le Collège des Frères Arvales, Modèle du Culte Public dans la Rome des Empereurs*. Rome.

Scheid, J., and H. Broise. "Deux nouveaux fragments des Actes des Frères Arvales de l'année 38 ap J.C." *MEFRA* 92 (1980): 215–48.

Scheider, K. Th. (1942). "Zusammensetzung des römischen Senates von Tiberius bis Nero." Diss. Zurich.

Schiller, H. (1872). *Geschichte des römischen Kaiserreichs unter der Regierung des Nero*. Berlin.

Schilling, R. (1977). *Histoire Naturelle* 7. Paris.

Schmidt, J. "Physiognomik." *RE* 20.1 (1941): 1064–74.

Schmidt, W. (1908). *Geburtstag in Altertum*. Giessen.

Schmitthenner, W. (1952). *Oktavian und das Testament Caesars: Eine Untersuchung zu den Politischen Anfängen des Augustus*. Munich.

Scholtz, B. I. (1992). *Untersuchungen zur Tracht der römischen Principats*.

Schoonhoven, H. (1992). *The Pseudo-Ovidian ad Liviam de morte Drusi*. Groningen.

Schove, D. J. (1984). *Chronology of Eclipses and Comets, AD 1–1000*. Woodbridge, Suffolk.

Schrijvers, P. H. "A propos de la datation de la *Consolatio ad Liviam*." *Mnemosyne* 41 (1988): 381–84.

Schrömbges, P. (1986). *Tiberius und die Res Publica Romana. Untersuchungen zur Institutionalisierung des frühen römischen Principats*. Bonn.

Schuller, W. (1987). *Frauen in der römischen Geschichte*. Constance.

Schulz, F. (1951). *Classical Roman Law*. Oxford.

Schürenberg, D. (1975). "Stellung und Bedeutung der Frau in der Geschichtsschreibung des Tacitus." Diss. Marburg.

Schwartz, D. R. (1990). *Agrippa I: The Last King of Judaea*. Tübingen.

———. (1992). *Studies in the Jewish Background of Christianity*. Tübingen.

Scott, K. "Octavian and Antony's *De Sua Ebrietate.*" *CP* 24 (1929): 133–41.
——. "Emperor Worship in Ovid." *TAPA* 61 (1930): 43–69.
——. "Greek and Roman Honorific Months." *YClS* 2 (1931): 199–278.
——. "Tiberius' Refusal of the Title 'Augustus.' " *CP* 27 (1932): 43–50.
——. "The Political Propaganda of 44–30 B.C." *MAAR* 11 (1933): 39–40.
——. "Notes on the Destruction of Two Roman Villas." *AJP* 60 (1939): 459–62.
Seager, R. (1972). *Tiberius.* London.
Sebesta, J., and L. Bonfante (eds.). (1994). *The World of Roman Costume.* Madison, Wis.
Seibt, W. (1969). "Die Majestätsprozesse vor dem Senatsgericht unter Tiberius." Diss. Vienna.
Setälä, P. (1977). *Private Domini in Roman Brickstamps.* Helsinki.
Seyrig, H. "Inscriptions de Gythion." *RA* 29 (1929): 84–106.
Shackleton-Bailey, D. R. "The Roman Nobility in the Second Civil War." *CQ* 10 (1960): 253–70.
——. (1965). *Cicero's Letters to Atticus.* Cambridge.
——. (1991). *Two Studies in Roman Nomenclature.* Atlanta, 2d ed.
Shatzman, I. "Tacitean Rumours." *Latomus* 33 (1974): 547–78.
——. *Senatorial Wealth and Roman Politics.* Collection *Latomus* 142 (1975).
Shaw, B. D. "The Age of Roman Girls at Marriage." *JRS* 77 (1987): 30–46.
Shotter, D. C. A. "Three Problems in Tacitus' *Annals* I." *Mnemosyne* 18 (1965): 361–65.
——. "Tacitus, Tiberius, and Germanicus." *Historia* 17 (1968): 194–214.
——. "Julians, Claudians, and the Accession of Tiberius." *Latomus* 30 (1971): 1120–21.
——. "The Trial of M. Scribonius Libo Drusus." *Historia* 21 (1972): 88–98.
——. "Cn. Cornelius Cinna Magnus and the Adoption of Tiberius." *Latomus* 33 (1974): 306–13.
——. "Cnaeus Calpurnius Piso, Legate of Syria." *Historia* 23 (1974): 229–45.
——. (1989). *Tacitus, Annals IV.* Warminster.
Siber, H. (1952). *Römisches Verfassungsrecht in geschichtlicher Entwicklung.* Lahr.
Sievers, G. R. (1870). *Studien zur Geschichte der Römischen Kaiser.* Berlin.
Simon, E. (1967). *Ara Pacis Augustae.* Greenwich, Conn.
Simpson, C. J. "Livia and the Constitution of the Aedes Concordiae. The Evidence of Ovid, Fasti 637 ff." *Historia* 40 (1991): 449–55.
Sinclair, P. (1995). *Tacitus the Sententious Historian.* University Park, Penn.
Singer, M. W. "Octavia's Mediation at Tarentum." *CJ* 43 (1947): 173–77.
Sirago, V. A. "Livia Drusilla. Una nuova condizione femminile." *Invigilata Lucernis* 1 (1979): 171–207.
Sirks, A. J. B. "A Favour to Rich Freedwomen *(libertinae)* in A.D. 51." *RIDA* 27 (1980): 283–94.
Slater, W. J. "Pueri, Turba Minuta." *BICS* 21 (1974): 133–40.
Small, A. "A New Head of Antonia Minor and Its Significance." *MDAI(R)* 97 (1990): 217–34.
Smallwood, E. M. (1967). *Documents Illustrating the Principates of Gaius, Claudius, and Nero.* Cambridge.
——. (1981). *The Jews Under Roman Rule.* Leiden, 2d ed.
Smilda, H. C. (1896). "Suetonii Tranquilli vita Divi Claudii." Diss. Groningen.

Smith, C. E. (1942). *Tiberius and the Roman Empire*. Baton Rouge.

Smith, H. R. W. "Problems Historical and Numismatic in the Reign of Augustus." *University of California Publications in Classical Archaeology* 2.4 (1951): 133–230.

Smith, R. R. R. "The Imperial Reliefs from the Sebasteion at Aphrodisias." *JRS* 77 (1987): 88–138.

Snyder, W. F. "Public Anniversaries." *YClS* 7 (1940): 223–317.

Southern, P. (1998). *Augustus*. London.

Späth, T. " 'Frauenmacht' in der frühen römischen Kaiserzeit." In Dettenhofer (1994): 159–206.

Spengel, A. "Zur Geschichte des Kaisers Tiberius." *Stizungsberichte der K.B. Akademie des Wissenschaften zu München* (1903): 5–11.

Speyer, W. "Zur Verschwörung des Cn. Cornelius Cinna." *RhM* 99 (1956): 277–84.

Stahr, A. (1865). *Römische Kaiserfrauen*. Berlin.

Starr, C. G. (1960). *The Roman Imperial Navy*. Cambridge, 2d ed.

Steidle, W. (1951). *Sueton und die antike Biographie*. Zetemata 1: Munich.

Stein, A. (1927). *Der römische Ritterstand*. Munich.

———. "Ostorius." *RE* 18, no. 5 (1942): 1671–72.

———. (1950). *Die Präfekten von Ägypten*. Bern.

Steinby, E. M. (ed). (1993). *Lexicon Topographicum Urbis Romae* I. Rome.

Steinwenter, A. "Lex Voconia." *RE* 12 (1925) 2418–30.

Stern, M. E. "A Glass Head Flask Featuring Livia as Hera?" *Kotinos: Festschrift für E. Simon* (Mainz, 1992): 394–99.

Stewart, Z. "Sejanus, Gaetulicus, and Seneca." *AJP* 74 (1953): 70–85.

Strong, E. (1923–26). *La Scultura Romana*. Florence.

Stuart, M. "How Were Imperial Portraits Distributed Throughout the Empire?" *AJA* 43 (1939): 601–17.

Stumpf, G. R. (1991). *Numismatische Studien zur Chrolonolgie der römischen Statthalter in Kleinasien*. Saarbrücken.

Suerbaum, W. "Merkwürdige Geburtstage." *Chiron* 10 (1980): 337–55.

———. "Zweiundvierzig Jahre Tacitus-Forschung: Systematische Gesamtbibliographie zu Tacitus' Annalen 1939–1980." *ANRW* 2.33.2 (1990): 1032–476.

Sulze, H. "Die unteridischen Räume der Villa der Livia in Prima Porta." *MDAI(R)* 47 (1932): 174–92.

Summers, W. C. (1920). *The Silver Age of Latin Literature*. London.

Sumner, G. V. "Germanicus and Drusus Caesar." *Latomus* 26 (1967): 413–35.

———. "The Truth About Velleius Paterculus: Prologomena." *HSCP* 74 (1970): 257–97.

Sutherland, H. C. V. (1951). *Coinage in Roman Imperial Policy, 31 B.C.–A.D. 68*. London.

———. (1976). *The Emperor and the Coinage: Julio-Claudian Studies*. London.

———. (1987). *Roman History and Coinage, 44 BC–AD 69*. Oxford.

Sydenham, E. A. (1952). *The Coinage of the Roman Republic*. London.

Syme, R. (1939). *Roman Revolution*. Oxford.

———. (1958). *Tacitus*. Oxford.

———. (1970). *Ten Studies in Tacitus*. Oxford.

————. (1978). *History in Ovid*. Oxford.

————. (1986). *The Augustan Aristocracy*. Oxford.

Taeger, F. (1960). *Charisma. Studien zur Geschichte des antiken Herrscherkultes* 2. Stuttgart.

Talbert, R. J. A. (1984). *The Senate of Imperial Rome*. Princeton.

Tamm, B. (1963). *Auditorium and Palatium*. Stockholm.

Taubenschlag, R. "Die materna potestas in gräko-ägyptischen Recht." *ZSS* 49 (1929): 115–28.

Taylor, L. R. "Augustales, Seviri Augustales, and Seviri: A Chronological Study." *TAPA* 45 (1914): 231–53.

————. "Tiberius' Refusals of Divine Honours." *TAPA* 60 (1929): 87–101.

————. (1931). *The Divinity of the Roman Emperor*. Middletown, Conn.

————. "Tiberius' *Ovatio* and the *Ara Numinis Augusti*." *AJP* 58 (1937): 185–93.

————. (1949). *Party Politics in the Age of Caesar*. Berkeley.

————. (1960). *Voting Districts of the Roman Republic*. Rome.

Taylor, L. R., and A. B. West. "The Euryclids in Latin Inscriptions from Corinth." *AJA* 30 (1926): 389–400.

Temporini, H. (1978). *Die Frauen am Hofe Trajans. Ein Beitrag zur Stellung der Augustae im Principat*. Berlin and New York.

Thibault, C. J. (1964). *The Mystery of Ovid's Exile*. Berkeley.

Thomas, J. A. C. (1976). *Textbook of Roman Law*. New York.

Thornton, M. K., and R. L. Thornton. "Manpower Needs for the Public Works Programs of the Julio-Claudian Emperors." *Journal of Economic History* 43 (1983): 373–78.

Till, R. "Plinius über Augustus (nat. hist. 7.147–150)." *Würz. Jhb.* 3 (1977): 127–37.

Timpe, D. (1962). *Untersuchungen zur Kontinuität des frühen Prinzipats*. Wiesbaden.

————. (1968). *Der Triumph des Germanicus. Untersuchungen zu den Feldzügen der Jahre 14–16 n. Chr. in Germanien*. Bonn.

Tondriau, J. L. "Romains de la République assimilés à des Divinités." *SO* 27 (1949): 128–40.

Torelli, M. "Trebulla Mutuesca: Iscrizioni corrette ed inedite." *RAL* 18 (1963): 230–84.

————. "La valetudo atrox di Livia del 22 d. C., l'Ara Pietatis Augustae e i calendari." *AFLPer* 15 (1977–78): 179–83.

————. (1982). *Typology and Structure of Roman Historical Reliefs*. Ann Arbor.

Tränkle, H. "Augustus bei Tacitus, Cassius Dio, und dem älteren Plinius." *WS* 82 (1969): 108–30.

Treggiari, S. (1969). *Roman Freedmen During the Late Republic*. Oxford.

————. "Jobs in the Household of Livia." *PBSR* 43 (1975): 48–77.

————. "Jobs for Women." *AJAH* 1 (1976): 76–104.

————. (1991). *Roman Marriage*. Oxford.

Trillmich, W. (1978). *Familienpropaganda der Kaiser Caligula und Claudius. Agrippina Maior und Antonia Augusta auf Münzen*. Berlin.

————. "Julia Agrippina als Schwester des Caligula und Mutter der Nero." *Hefte des Archäologischen Seminars der Universität Bern* 9 (1983): 21–38.

——. "Der Germanicus-Bogen in Rom und das Monument für Germanicus und Drusus in Leptis Magna." In González and Arce (1988): 51–60.

Vallance, J. T. (1990). *The Lost Theory of Asclepiades of Bithynia*. Oxford.

——. "The Medical System of Asclepiades of Bithynia." *ANRW* II.37.1 (1993): 693–727.

Van Berchem, D. (1939). *Les Distributions de blé et d'argent à la plèbe romaine sous l'Empire*. Geneva.

Van Bremen, R. "Women and Wealth." In A. Cameron and A. Kuhrt (eds.), *Images of Women in Antiquity* (London, 1983): 231–33.

Vanggaard, J. H. (1988). *The Flamen: A Study in the History and Sociology of Roman Religion*. Copenhagen.

Veyne, P. "Les Honneurs posthumes de Flavia Domitilla et les dédicaces grecques et latines." *Latomus* 21 (1962): 49–98.

Vidal, H. "Le Dépôt in aede." *RD* 43 (1965): 545–87.

Vidén, G. (1993). *Women in Roman Literature. Studia Graeca et Latina Gotheburgensia* 57: Gotheburg.

Villers, R. "La Dévolution du principat dans la famille d'Auguste." *REL* 28 (1950): 235–51.

Visscher, F. de. "La Politique dynastique sous le règne de Tibère." *Synteleia V. Arangio-Ruiz* (Naples, 1964): 54–65.

Vittoria de la Torre, C. "Los nombres de Livia." *EClás* 34 (1992): 55–61.

Walker, B. (1952). *The Annals of Tacitus: A Study in the Writing of History*. Manchester.

Wallace, K. G., "Women in Tacitus." *ANRW* 2.33.5 (1991): 3556–74.

Wallace-Hadrill, A. (1983). *Suetonius*. London.

——. "Image and Authority in the Coinage of Augustus." *JRS* 76 (1986): 66–87.

——. "Time for Augustus: Ovid, Augustus, and the *Fasti*." In M. Whitby (ed.), *Homo Viator: Classical Essays for John Bramble* (1987): 221–30.

——. "The Social Structure of the Roman House." *PBSR* 56 (1988): 43–98.

——. (1989). *Patronage in Ancient Society*. London.

Wardle, D. "Cluvius Rufus and Suetonius." *Hermes* 120 (1992): 466–82.

Warren, P. M. "Knossos: Stratigraphical Museum Excavation, 1978–82. Part IV." *Archaeological Reports* 34 (1987–88): 86–104.

Watson, A. (1967). *The Law of Persons in the Later Republic*. Oxford.

Watson, P. (1995). *Ancient Stepmothers: Myth, Misogyny, and Reality*. Leiden.

Weaver, P. R. C. "Freedmen Procurators in the Imperial Administration." *Historia* 14 (1965): 460–69.

——. "Social Mobility in the Early Roman Empire: The Evidence of the Imperial Freedmen and Slaves." *Past and Present* 37 (1967): 3–20 = *Studies in Ancient Society*, ed. M. I. Finley (London, 1974): 121–40.

——. (1972). *Familia Caesaris: A Social Study of the Emperors' Freedmen and Slaves*. Cambridge.

——. "Dated Inscriptions of Imperial Freedmen and Slaves." In M. Clauss et al. (eds.), *Epigraphische Studien* (Cologne, 1976): 215–27.

Weber, W. (1936). *Princeps, Studien zur Geschichte des Augustus*. Stuttgart.

Weinribb, E. "The Family Connections of M. Livius Drusus Libo." *HSCP* 72 (1968): 247–78.

Weinrich, O. "Zwölfgötter." In W. H. Roscher (ed.), *Ausführliche Lexikon der Griechischen und römischen Mythologie* (Leipzig and Berlin, 1924–37): 6.764–848.

Weinstock, S. (1971). *Divus Julius.* Oxford.

Wellmann, M. "Asclepiades." *RE* 2.2 (1896): 1632–33.

Wessner, P. (1967). *Scholia in Iuvenalem Vetustiora.* Rpt. Stuttgart.

Wester, M. (1944). *Les Personnages et le monde féminin dans les Annales de Tacite.* Paris.

Westermann, W. L. (1955). *The Slave Systems of Greek and Roman Antiquity.* Philadelphia.

Wilcken, U. "Ehepatrone im römischen Kaiserhaus." *ZSS* 30 (1909): 504–7.

Wilkes, J. "Julio-Claudian Historians." *CW* 65 (1972): 177–203.

Willems, P. (1878). *Le Sénat de la république romaine.* Paris.

Willenbücher, H. (1914). *Der Kaiser Claudius.* Mainz.

Williams, G. "Some Aspects of Roman Marriage Ceremonies and Ideas." *JRS* 48 (1958): 16–29.

Willrich, H. (1911). *Livia.* Leipzig and Berlin.

———. "Augustus bei Tacitus." *Hermes* 62 (1927): 54–78.

Winkes, R. "Der Kameo Marlborough, ein Urbild der Livia." *AA* (1982): 131–38.

———. "Leben und Ehrungen der Livia. Ein Beitrag zur Entwicklung des römischen Herrscherkultes von der Zeit des Triumvirats bis Claudius." *Archeologia* 36 (1985): 55–68.

———. "Bildnistypen der Livia." *Rittrati ufficiale e ritratto privato: Atti della II Conferenza Internazionale sul Ritratto Romano* (Rome: Consiglio Nazionale delle Ricerche, *Quaderni de la Ricerca Scientifica* 116, 1988): 555–61.

———. (1995). *Livia, Octavia, Julia.* Louvain-la-Neuve and Providence.

———. "Livia: Portrait and Propaganda." In Kleiner and Matheson (2000), 29–42.

Winkler, L. (1995). *Salus: Vom Staatskult zur politischen Idee, eine archäologische Untersuchung.* Heidelberg.

Wiseman, T. P. "The Mother of Livia Augusta." *Historia* 14 (1965): 333–34.

———. "Pulcher Claudius." *HSCP* 74 (1970): 207–21.

———. (1971). *New Men in the Roman Senate.* Oxford.

———. "Legendary Genealogies in Late-Republican Rome." *GR* 21 (1974): 153–64.

———. (1979). *Clio's Cosmetics: Three Studies in Greco-Roman Literature.* Leicester.

———. "Calpurnius Siculus and the Claudian Civil War." *JRS* 72 (1982): 57–67.

———. (1991). *Death of an Emperor.* Exeter.

Wissowa, G. "Bona Dea." *RE* 3.1 (1899): 686–94.

———. (1912). *Religion und Kultus der Römer.* Munich, 2d ed.

Wistrand, E. (1976). *The So-Called Laudatio Turiae.* Lund.

Wittrich, H. (1972). "Die Taciteischen Darstellungen vom Sterben historischer Persönlichkeiten." Diss. Vienna.

Wolfe, E. R. "Transportation in Augustan Egypt." *TAPA* 83 (1952): 80–99.

Wood, S. "Agrippina the Elder in Julio-Claudian Art and Propaganda." *AJA* 92 (1988): 409–26.

————. "Diva Drusilla Panthea and the Sisters of Caligula." *AJA* 99 (1995): 457–82.

————. (1999). *Imperial Women: A Study in Public Images, 40 BC–AD 68*. Leiden.

Woodman, A. J. (1977). *Velleius Paterculus: The Tiberian Narrative*. Cambridge.

————. (1998). *Tacitus Reviewed*. Oxford.

Woodman, A. J., and R. H. Martin. (1996). *The Annals of Tacitus: Book 3*. Cambridge.

Wuilleumier, P. (1949). *Tacite, l'homme et l'oeuvre*. Paris.

————. "L'Empoisonnement de Claude." *REL* 53 (1975): 3–4.

Zanker, P. (1988). *The Power of Images in the Age of Augustus*. Ann Arbor.

Zinserling, G. "Der Augustus von Primaporta als offiziöses Denkmal." *AAntHung* 16 (1967): 327–29.

————. "Die Programmatik der Kunstpolitik des Augustus." *Klio* 67 (1985): 74–80.

Zuleta, F. De (1967–69). *The Institutes of Gaius*. Oxford.

Zwierlein-Diel, E. "Der Divus-Augustus-Kameo in Köln." *KölnJb* 17 (1980): 36–37.

INDEX

The lists of inscriptions, papyri and coins found on pages 267–302 are not indexed. Citations in the literary sources are likewise not indexed, unless the author had a direct relationship with Livia. The literary citations are listed on pages 247–58.

Items in the endnotes already indexed through the text are not listed separately.

Emperors and the better-known members of their families are listed in their familiar forms; otherwise Roman names are listed alphabetically by *nomen*, if the *nomen* is known, and by *cognomen* in the absence of a known *nomen*.

Buildings and districts of Rome are listed under "Rome."